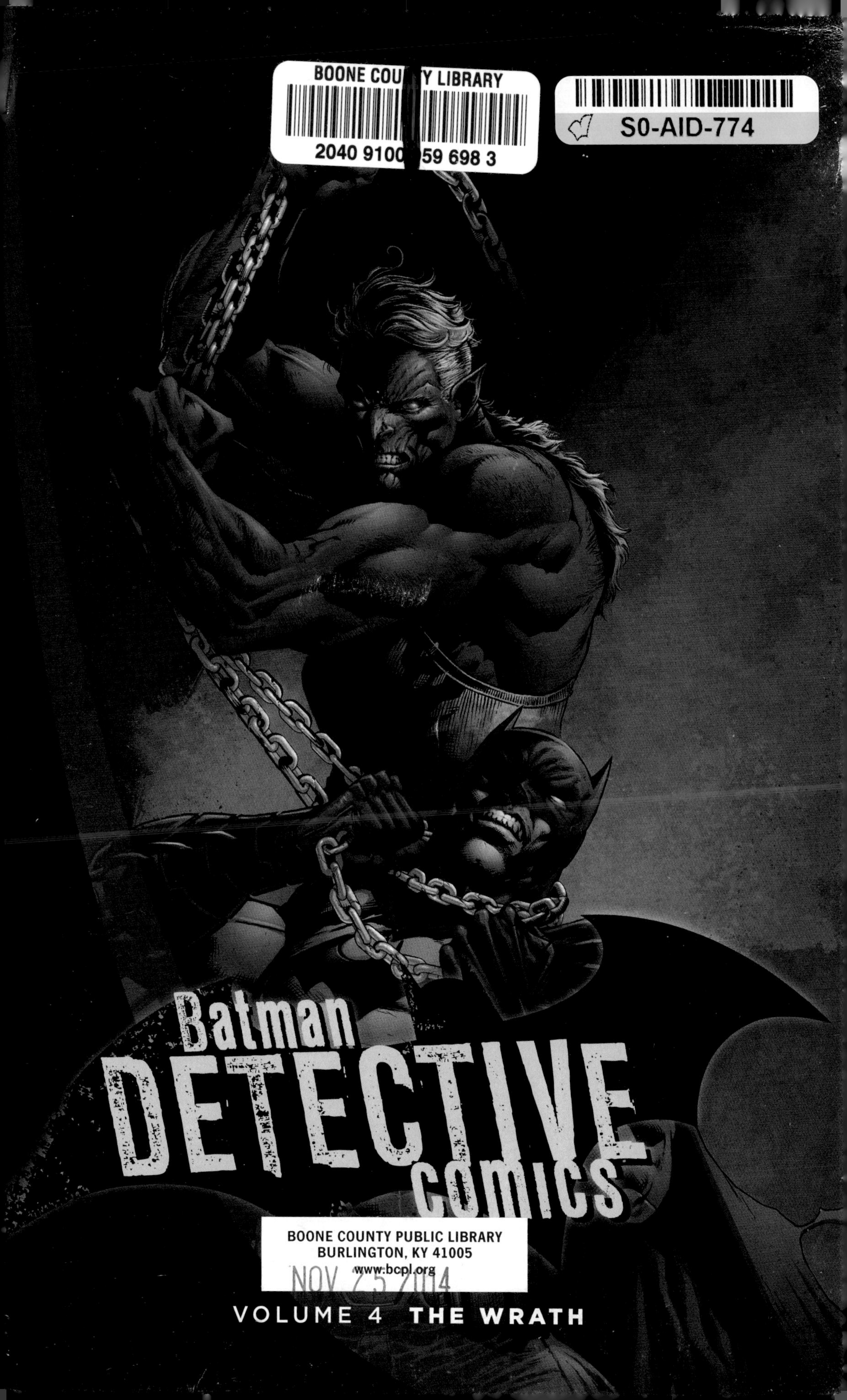

Batman DETECTIVE COMICS

VOLUME 4 THE WRATH

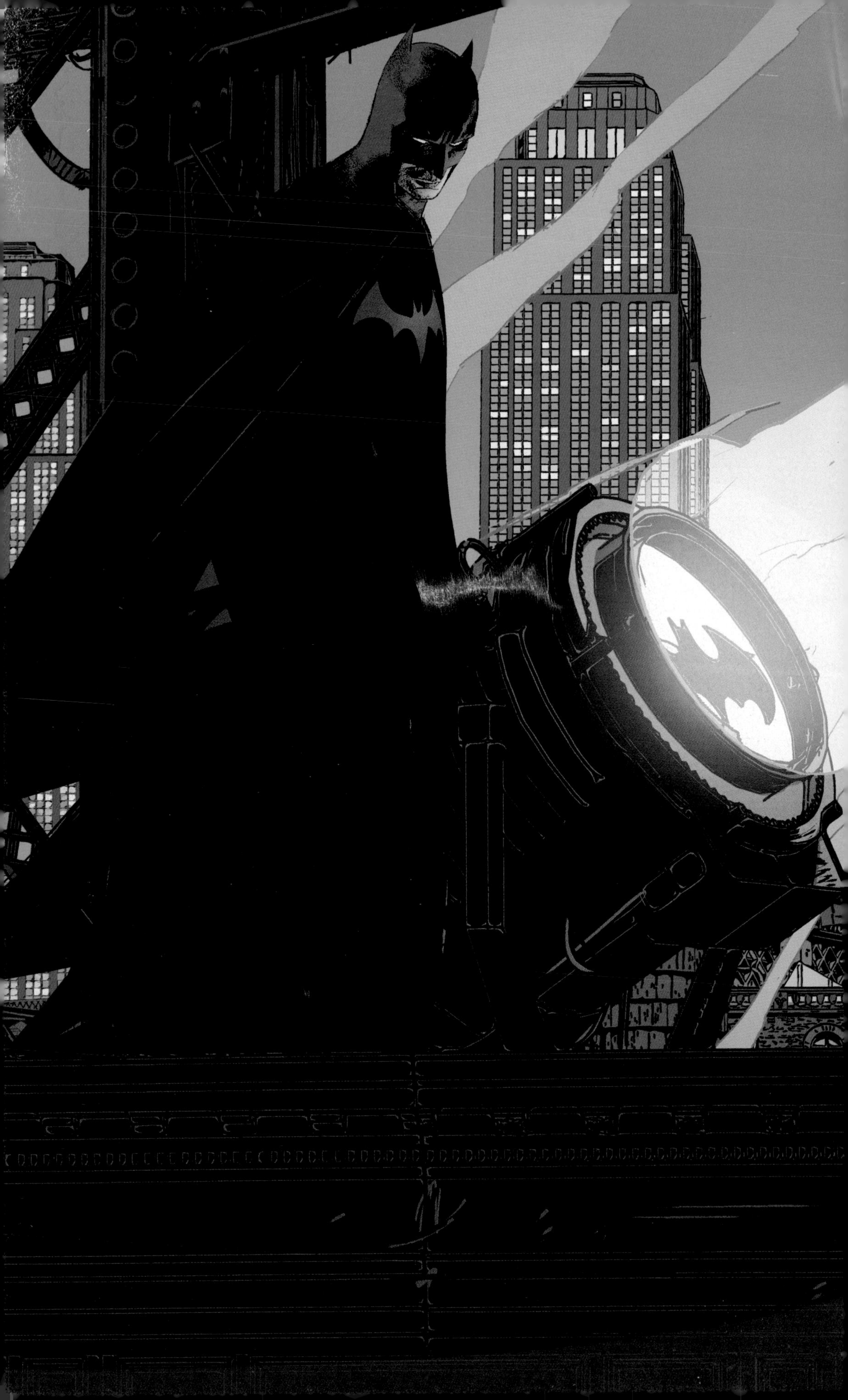

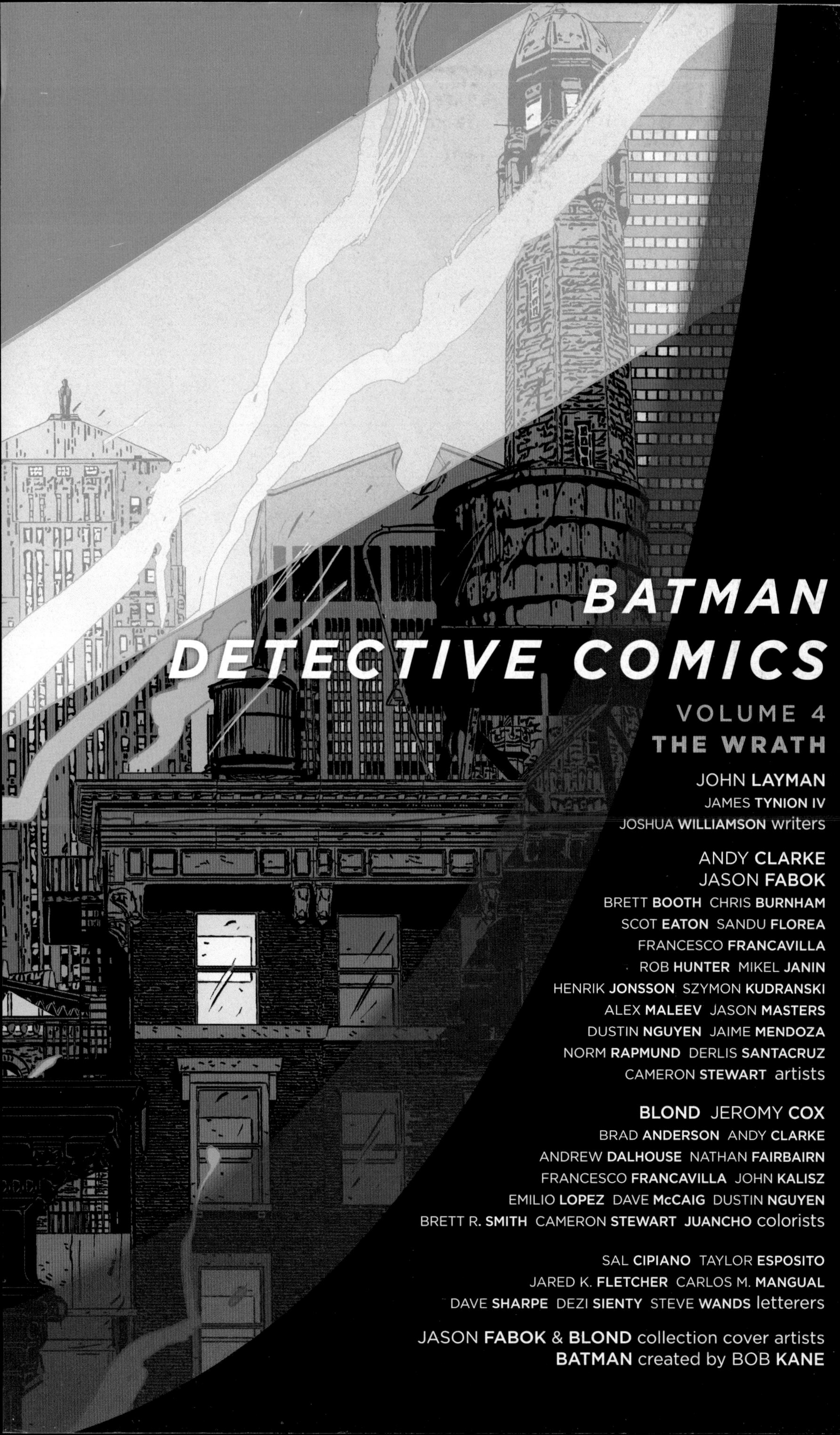

BATMAN DETECTIVE COMICS

VOLUME 4
THE WRATH

JOHN **LAYMAN**
JAMES **TYNION IV**
JOSHUA **WILLIAMSON** writers

ANDY **CLARKE**
JASON **FABOK**
BRETT **BOOTH** CHRIS **BURNHAM**
SCOT **EATON** SANDU **FLOREA**
FRANCESCO **FRANCAVILLA**
ROB **HUNTER** MIKEL **JANIN**
HENRIK **JONSSON** SZYMON **KUDRANSKI**
ALEX **MALEEV** JASON **MASTERS**
DUSTIN **NGUYEN** JAIME **MENDOZA**
NORM **RAPMUND** DERLIS **SANTACRUZ**
CAMERON **STEWART** artists

BLOND JEROMY **COX**
BRAD **ANDERSON** ANDY **CLARKE**
ANDREW **DALHOUSE** NATHAN **FAIRBAIRN**
FRANCESCO **FRANCAVILLA** JOHN **KALISZ**
EMILIO **LOPEZ** DAVE **McCAIG** DUSTIN **NGUYEN**
BRETT R. **SMITH** CAMERON **STEWART** **JUANCHO** colorists

SAL **CIPIANO** TAYLOR **ESPOSITO**
JARED K. **FLETCHER** CARLOS M. **MANGUAL**
DAVE **SHARPE** DEZI **SIENTY** STEVE **WANDS** letterers

JASON **FABOK** & **BLOND** collection cover artists
BATMAN created by BOB **KANE**

MIKE MARTS Editor – Original Series KATIE KUBERT HARVEY RICHARDS Associate Editors – Original Series
RACHEL PINNELAS Editor ROBBIN BROSTERMAN Design Director – Books
ROBBIE BIEDERMAN Publication Design

BOB HARRAS Senior VP – Editor-in-Chief, DC Comics

DIANE NELSON President DAN DIDIO and JIM LEE Co-Publishers GEOFF JOHNS Chief Creative Officer
AMIT DESAI Senior VP – Marketing and Franchise Management
AMY GENKINS Senior VP – Business and Legal Affairs NAIRI GARDINER Senior VP – Finance
JEFF BOISON VP – Publishing Planning MARK CHIARELLO VP – Art Direction and Design
JOHN CUNNINGHAM VP – Marketing TERRI CUNNINGHAM VP – Editorial Administration
LARRY GANEM VP – Talent Relations and Services ALISON GILL Senior VP – Manufacturing and Operations
HANK KANALZ Senior VP – Vertigo and Integrated Publishing JAY KOGAN VP – Business and Legal Affairs, Publishing
JACK MAHAN VP – Business Affairs, Talent NICK NAPOLITANO VP – Manufacturing Administration SUE POHJA VP – Book Sales
FRED RUIZ VP – Manufacturing Operations COURTNEY SIMMONS Senior VP – Publicity BOB WAYNE Senior VP – Sales

BATMAN — DETECTIVE COMICS VOLUME 4: THE WRATH

DC Comics, 1700 Broadway, New York, NY 10019
A Warner Bros. Entertainment Company.
Printed by RR Donnelley, Salem, VA, USA. 10/17/14. First Printing.

ISBN: 978-1-4012-4997-7

SUSTAINABLE FORESTRY INITIATIVE

Certified Chain of Custody
20% Certified Forest Content,
80% Certified Sourcing
www.sfiprogram.org
SFI-01042
APPLIES TO TEXT STOCK ONLY

Library of Congress Cataloging-in-Publication Data

Layman, John, 1967-
Batman/Detective Comics. Volume 4, Wrath / John Layman ; illustrated by Jason Fabok.
pages cm. — (The New 52!)
ISBN 978-1-4012-4997-7
1. Graphic novels. I. Fabok, Jay. II. Title. III. Title: Wrath.
PN6728.B36L393 2014
741.5'973—dc23
2014010795

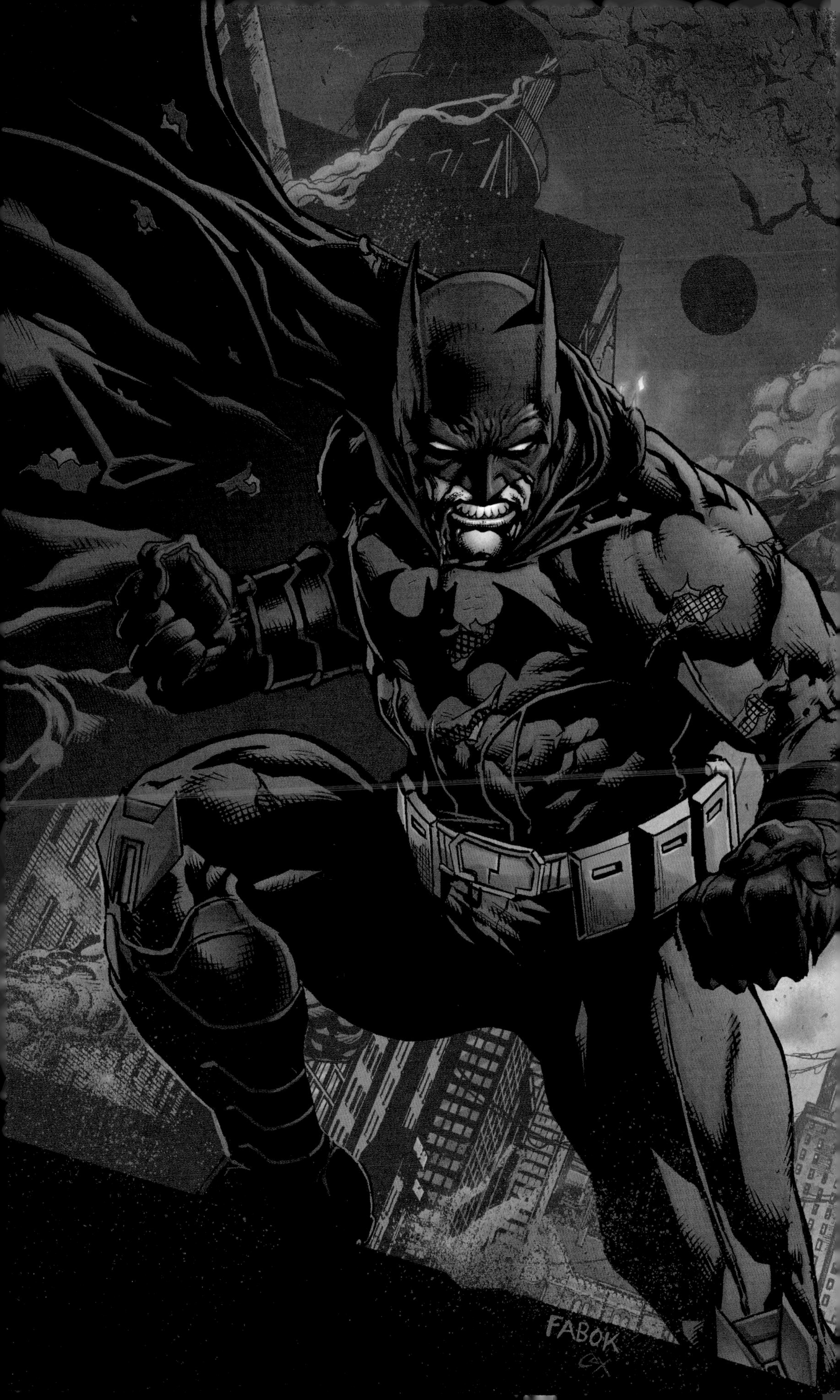
FABOK

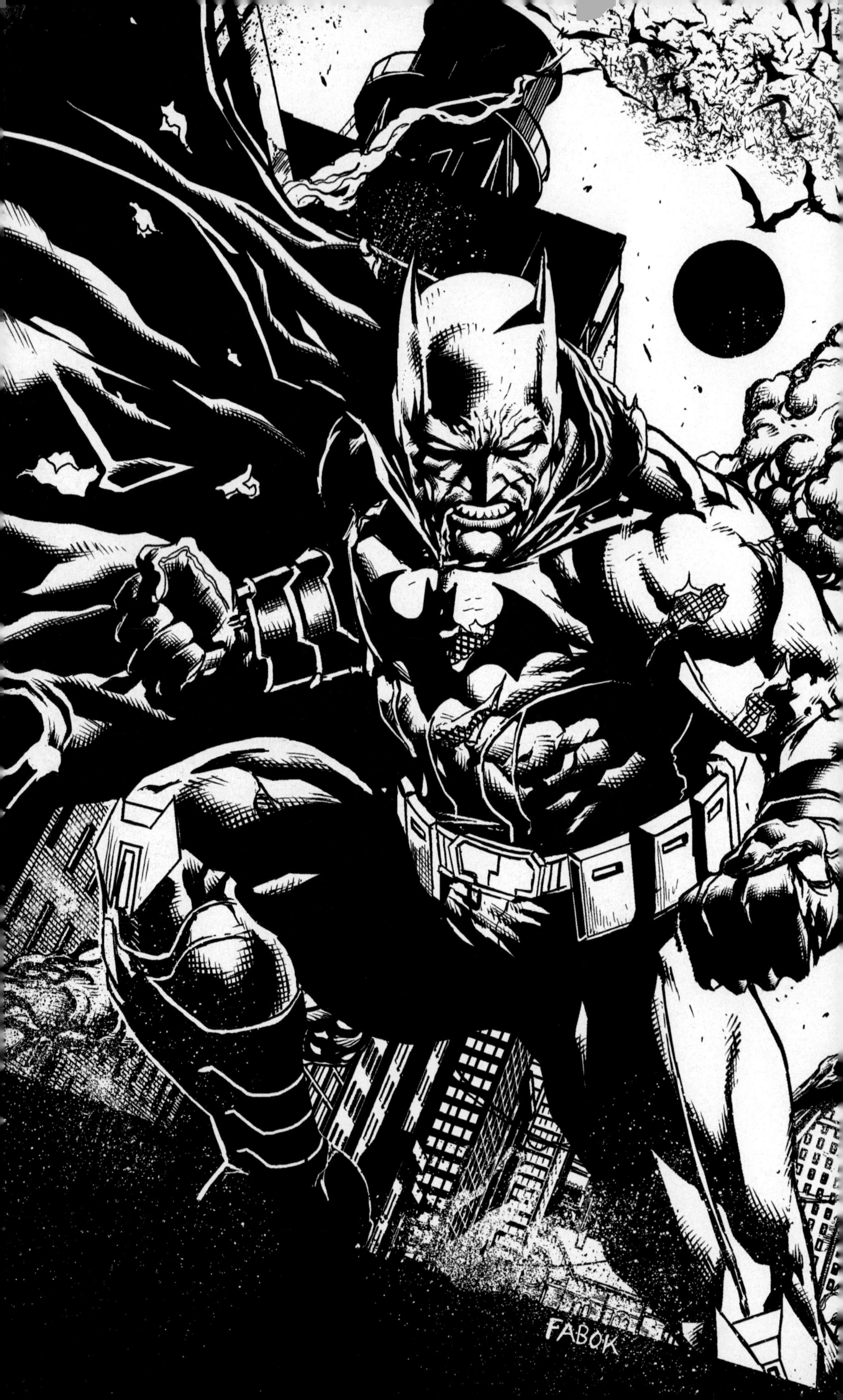
FABOK

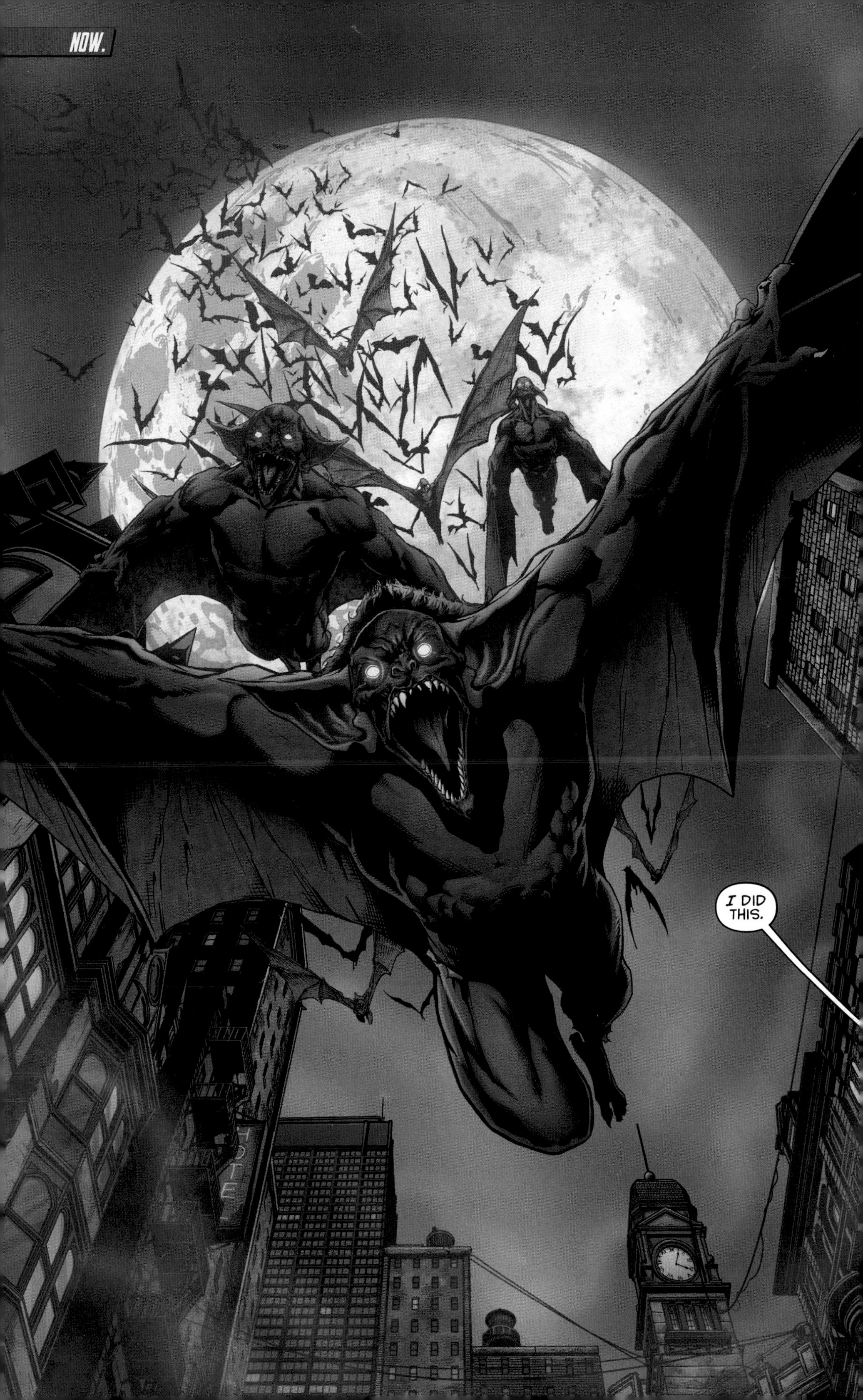
NOW.
I DID THIS.

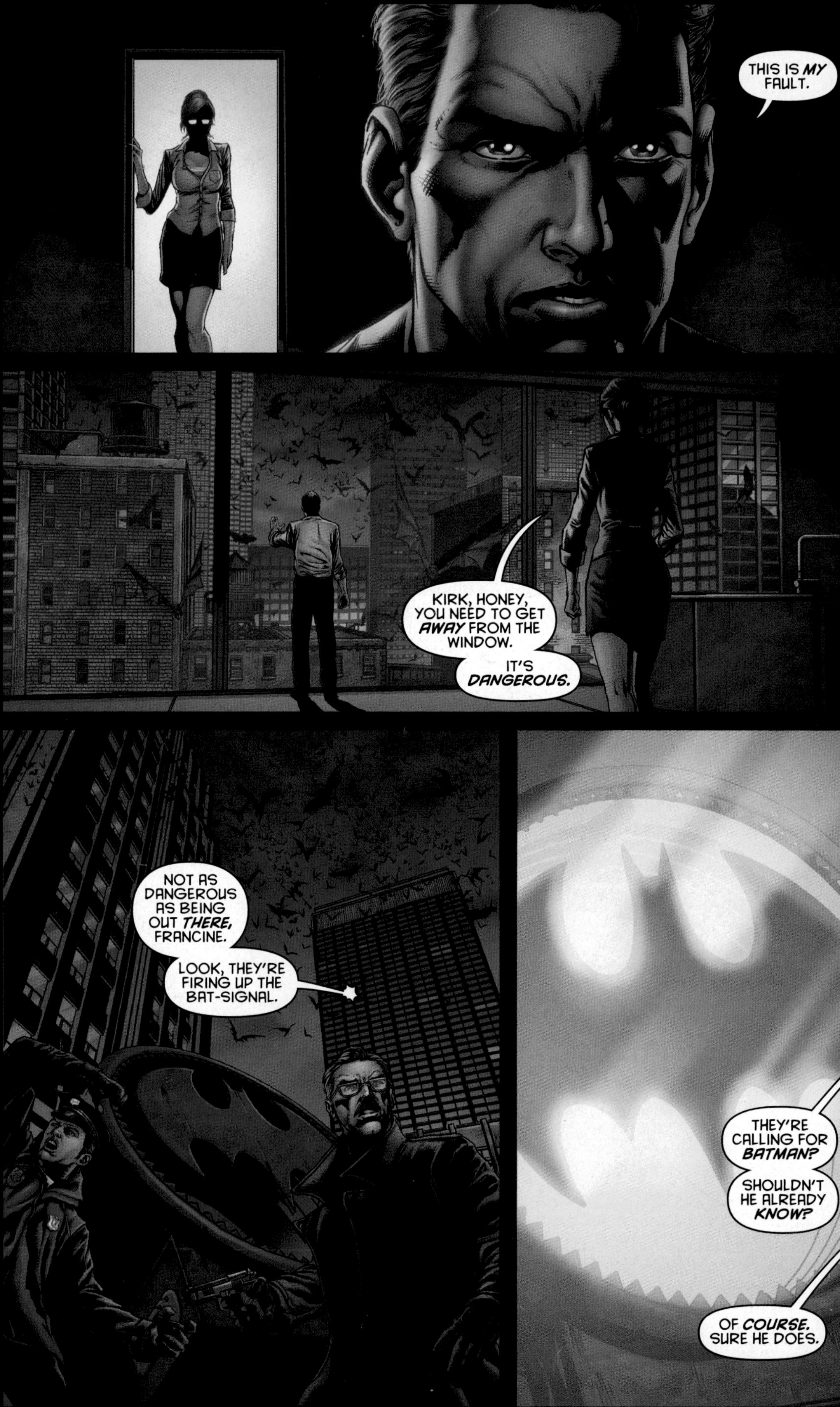
THIS IS MY FAULT.
KIRK, HONEY, YOU NEED TO GET AWAY FROM THE WINDOW.
IT'S DANGEROUS.
NOT AS DANGEROUS AS BEING OUT THERE, FRANCINE.
LOOK, THEY'RE FIRING UP THE BAT-SIGNAL.
THEY'RE CALLING FOR BATMAN?
SHOULDN'T HE ALREADY KNOW?
OF COURSE. SURE HE DOES.

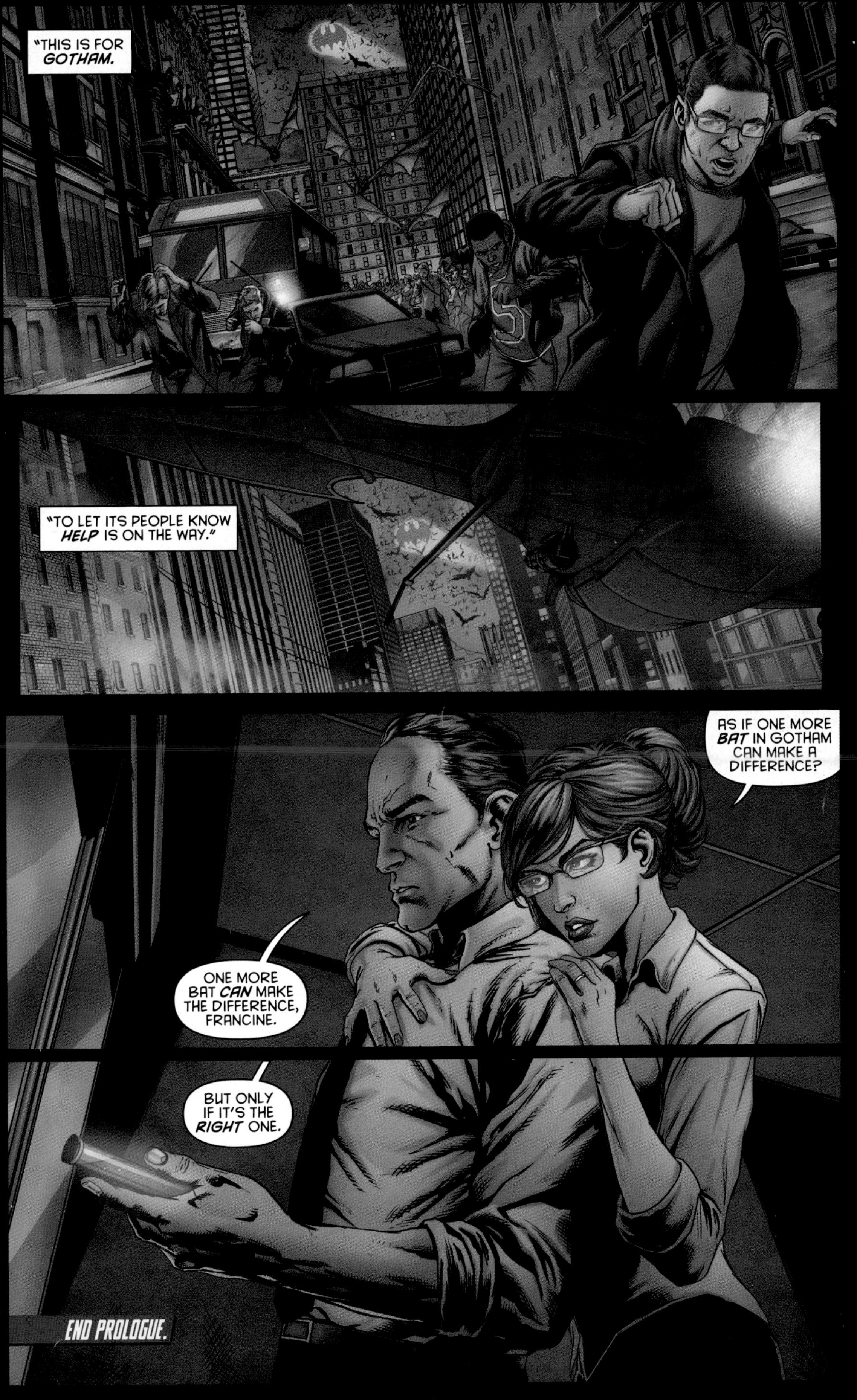
"THIS IS FOR GOTHAM.
"TO LET ITS PEOPLE KNOW HELP IS ON THE WAY."
AS IF ONE MORE BAT IN GOTHAM CAN MAKE A DIFFERENCE?
ONE MORE BAT CAN MAKE THE DIFFERENCE, FRANCINE.
BUT ONLY IF IT'S THE RIGHT ONE.
END PROLOGUE.

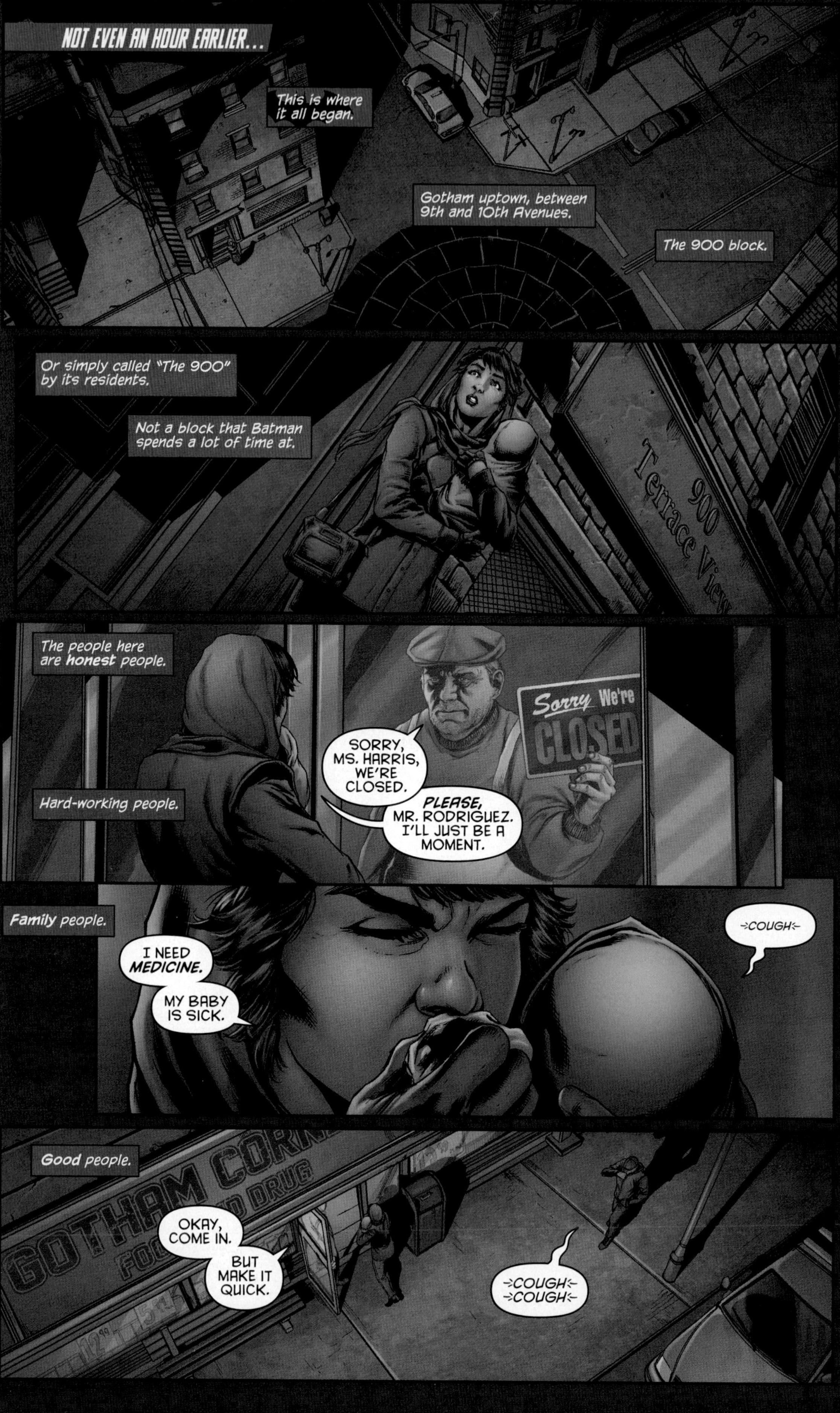

NOT EVEN AN HOUR EARLIER...
This is where it all began.
Gotham uptown, between 9th and 10th Avenues.
The 900 block.
Or simply called "The 900" by its residents.
Not a block that Batman spends a lot of time at.
900 Terrace View
The people here are **honest** people.
Sorry We're CLOSED
SORRY, MS. HARRIS, WE'RE CLOSED.
Hard-working people.
PLEASE, MR. RODRIGUEZ. I'LL JUST BE A MOMENT.
Family people.
I NEED **MEDICINE.**
MY BABY IS SICK.
-COUGH-
Good people.
GOTHAM CORN
FOOD AND DRUG
OKAY, COME IN.
BUT MAKE IT QUICK.
-COUGH- -COUGH-

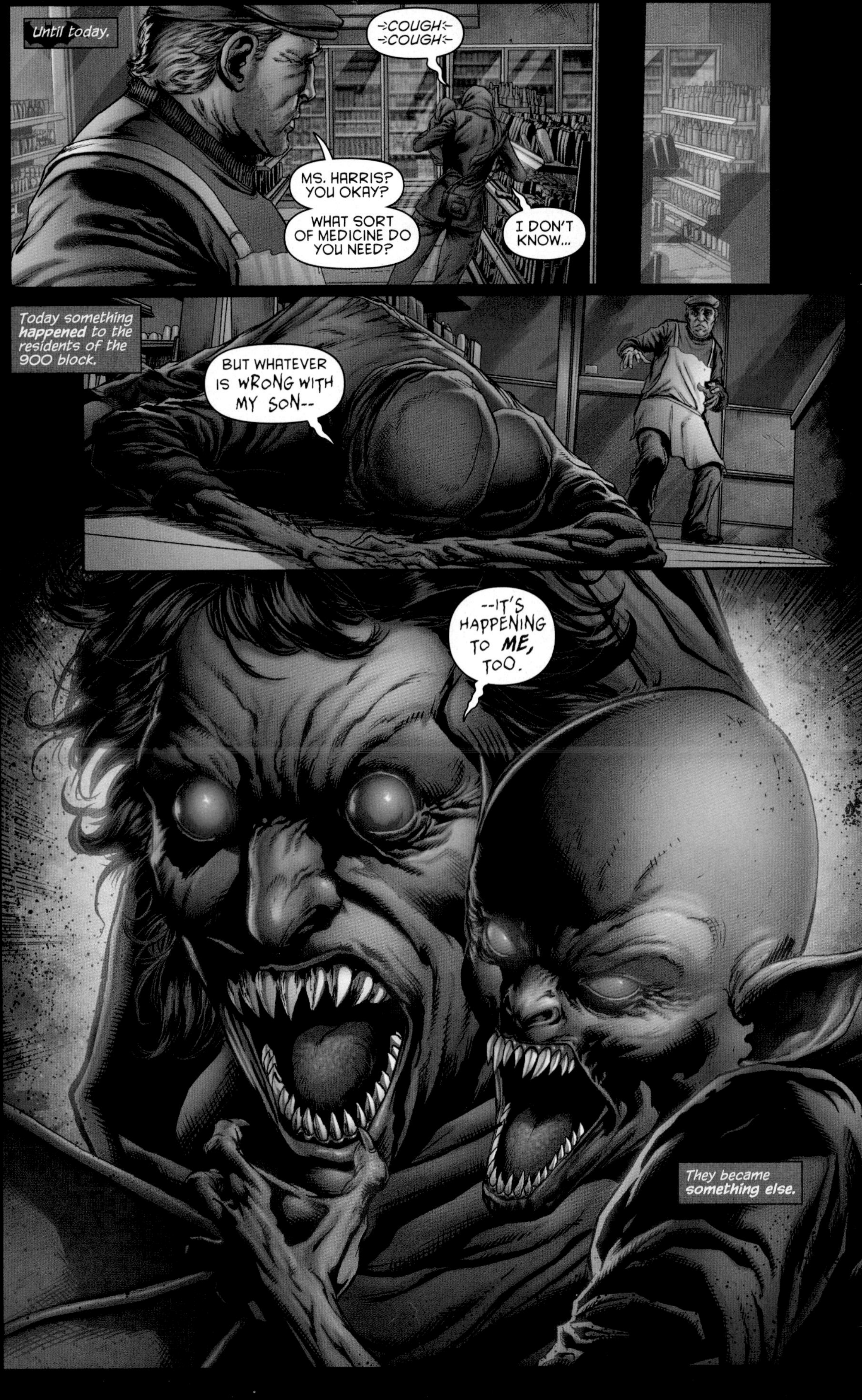
Until today.
-COUGH-
-COUGH-
MS. HARRIS? YOU OKAY?
WHAT SORT OF MEDICINE DO YOU NEED?
I DON'T KNOW...
Today something happened to the residents of the 900 block.
BUT WHATEVER IS WRONG WITH MY SON--
--IT'S HAPPENING TO ME, TOO.
They became something else.

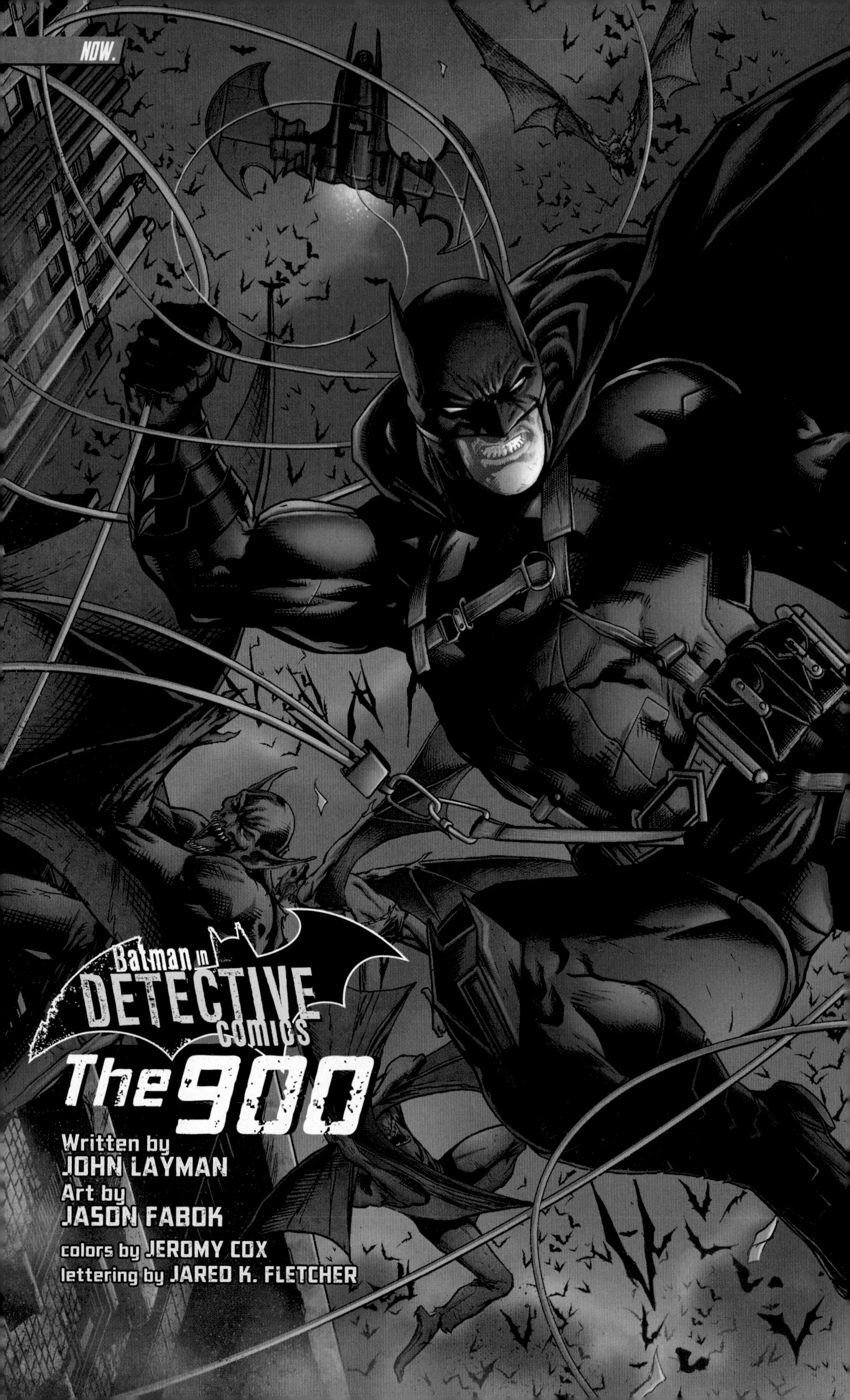
NOW.
Batman in DETECTIVE COMICS
The 900
Written by JOHN LAYMAN
Art by JASON FABOK
colors by JEROMY COX
lettering by JARED K. FLETCHER

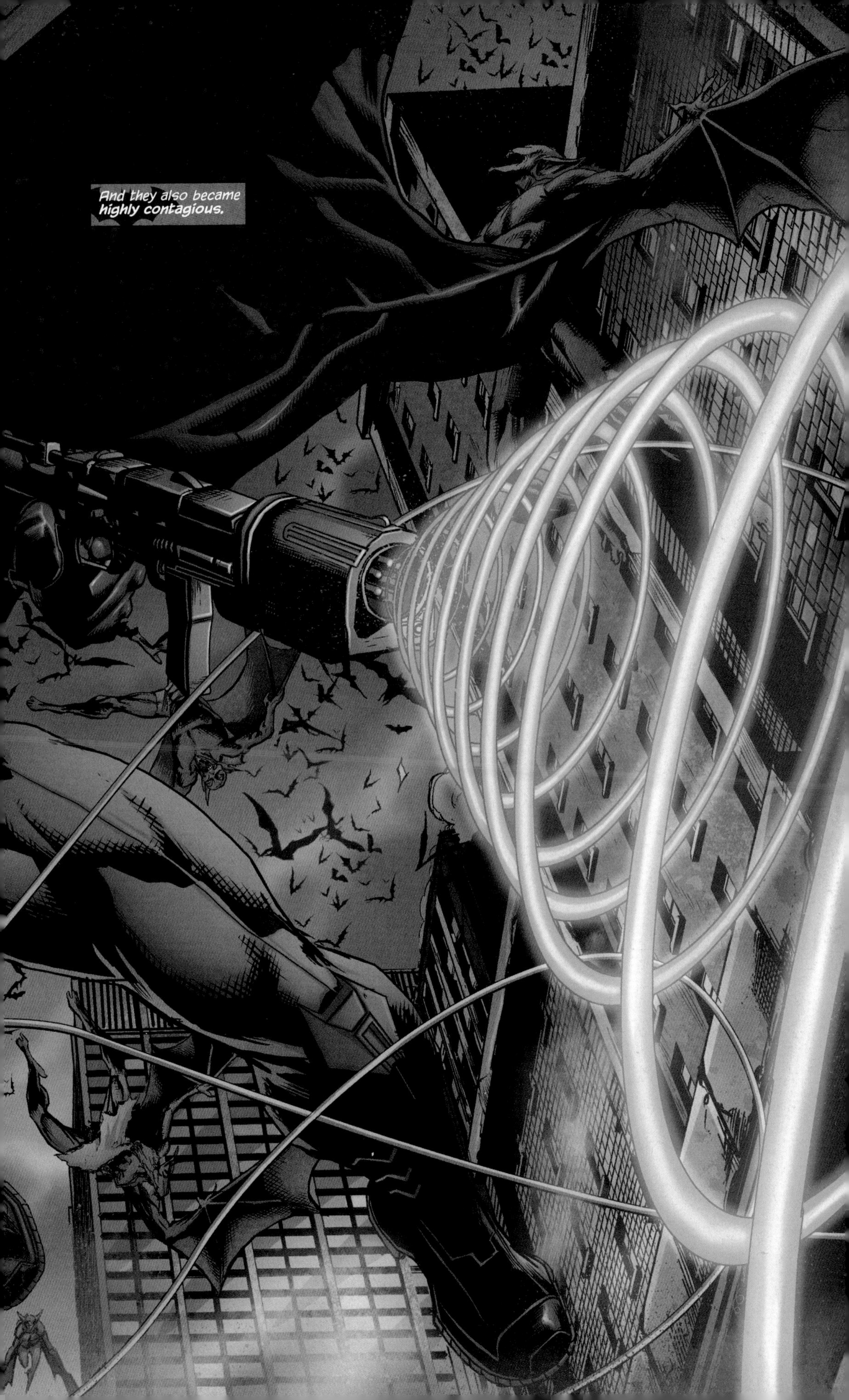
And they also became highly contagious.

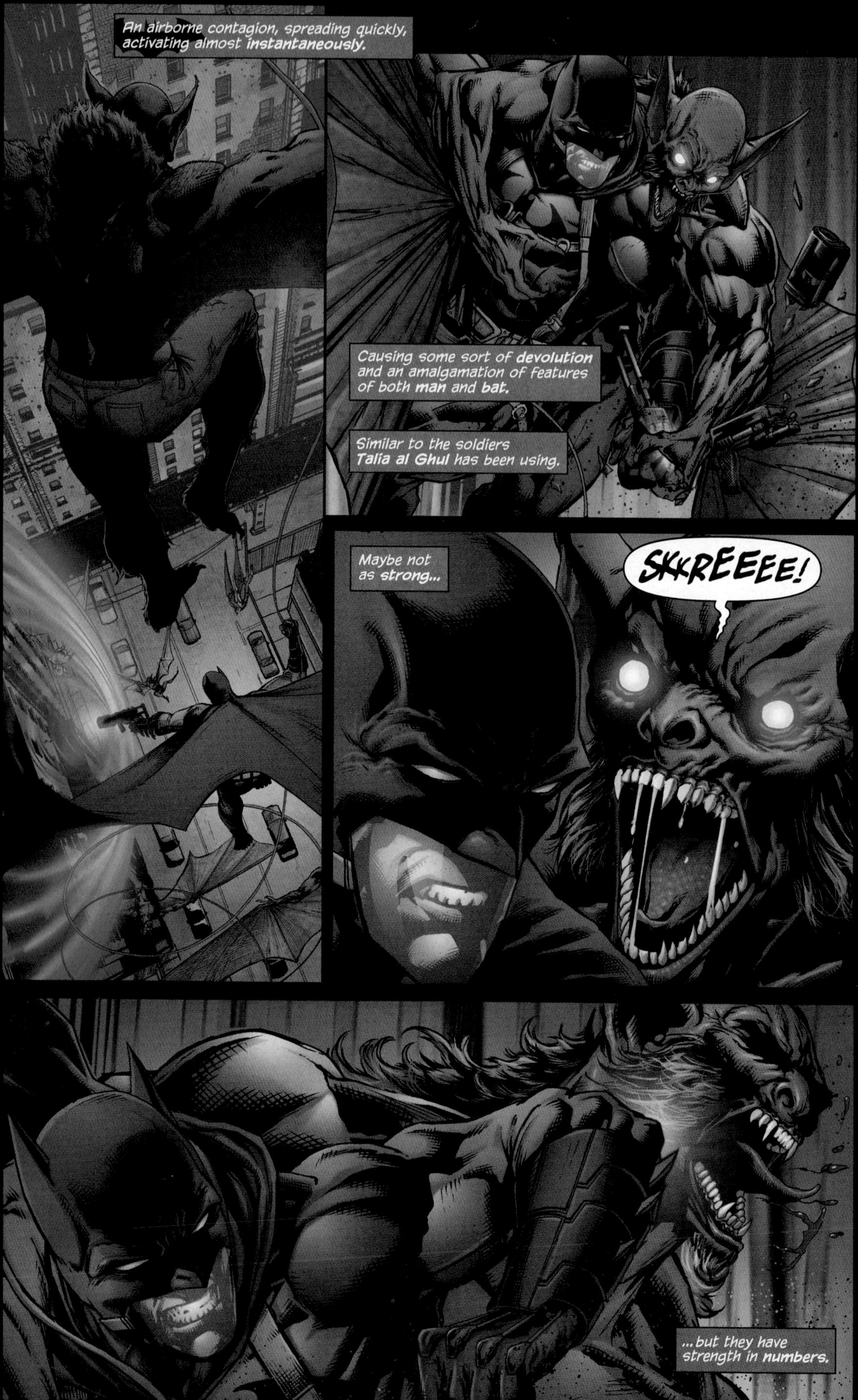
An airborne contagion, spreading quickly, activating almost instantaneously.
Causing some sort of devolution and an amalgamation of features of both man and bat.
Similar to the soldiers Talia al Ghul has been using.
Maybe not as strong...
SKKREEEEE!
...but they have strength in numbers.

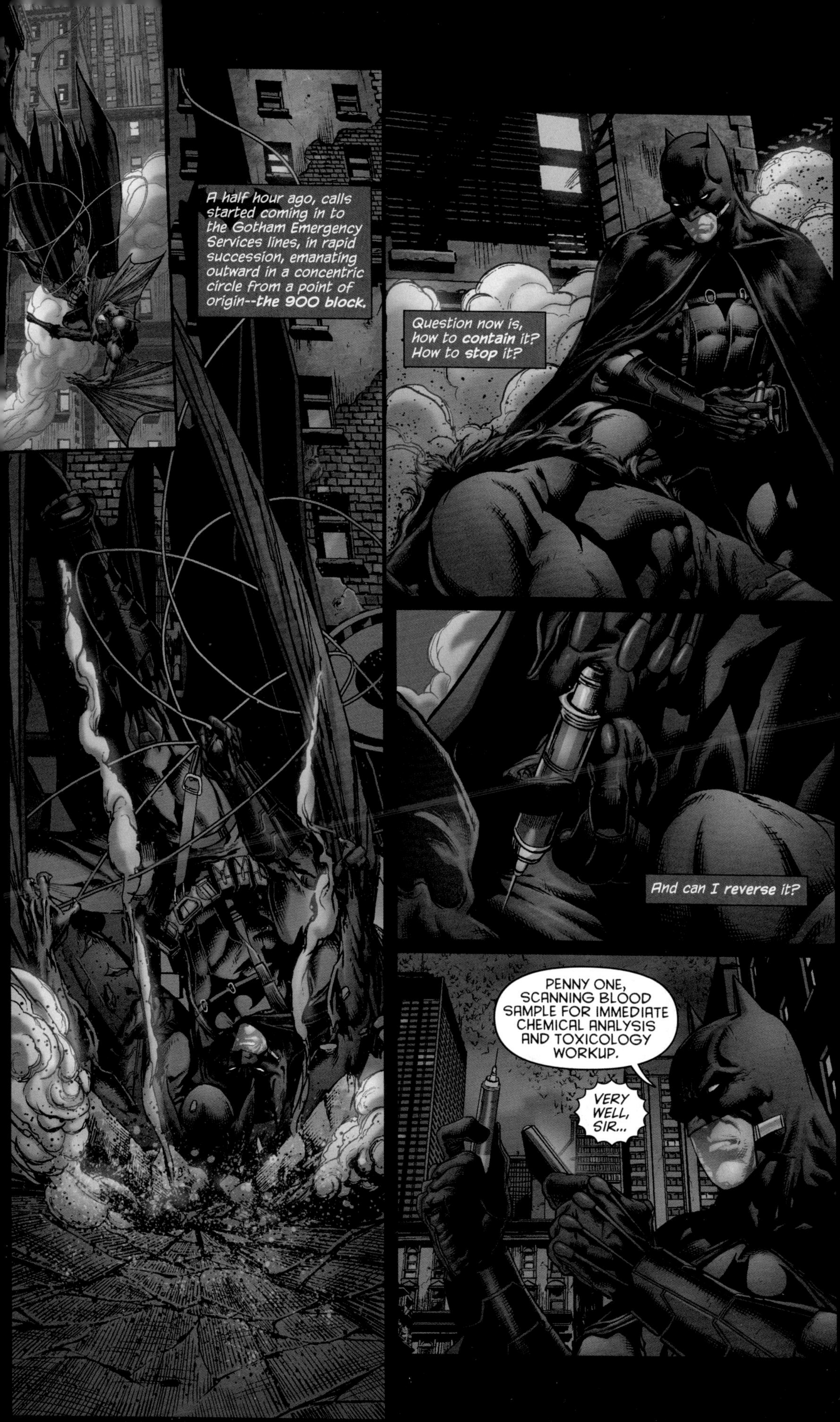
A half hour ago, calls started coming in to the Gotham Emergency Services lines, in rapid succession, emanating outward in a concentric circle from a point of origin--the 900 block.
Question now is, how to contain it? How to stop it?
And can I reverse it?
PENNY ONE, SCANNING BLOOD SAMPLE FOR IMMEDIATE CHEMICAL ANALYSIS AND TOXICOLOGY WORKUP.
VERY WELL, SIR...

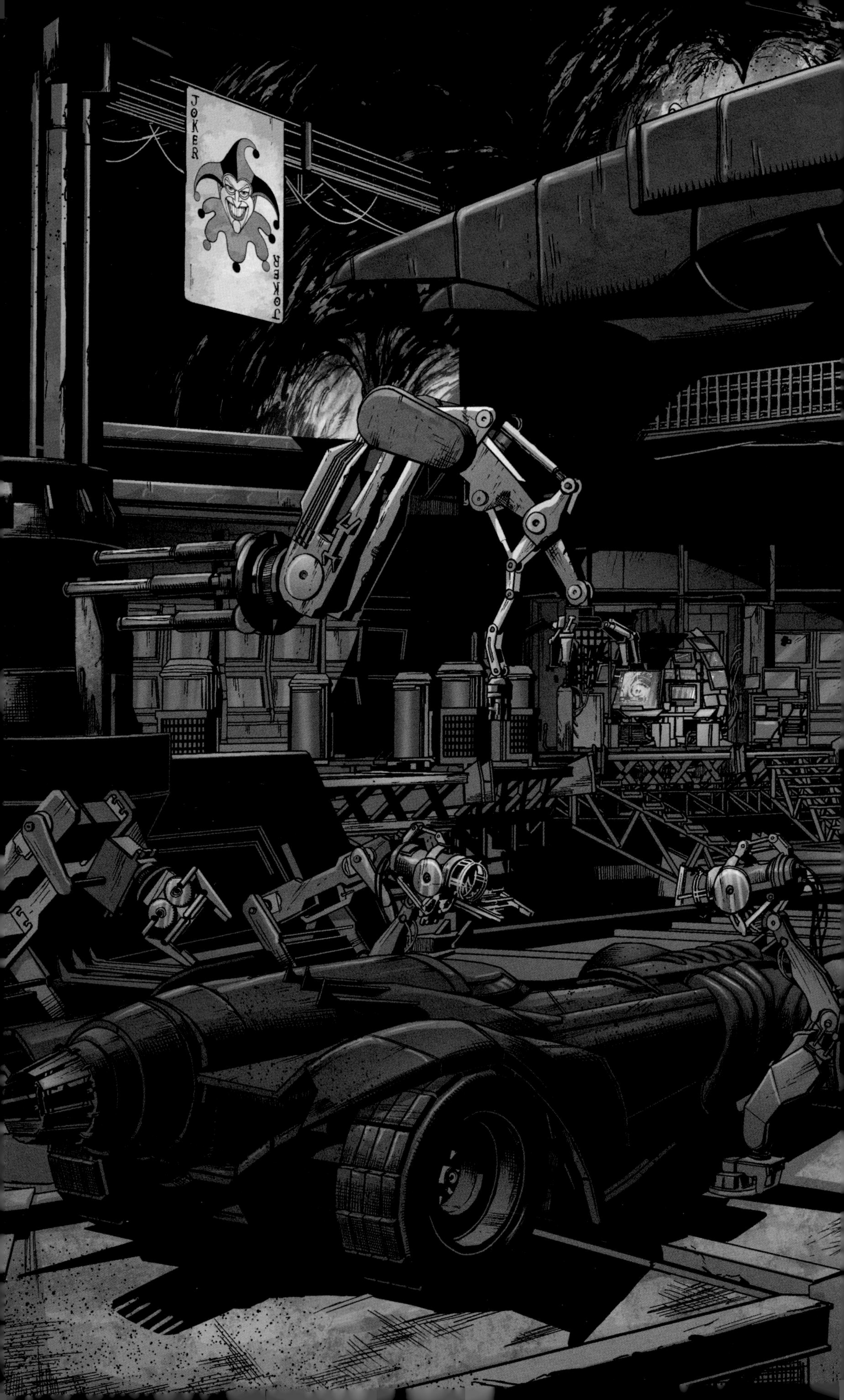
JOKER
JOKER

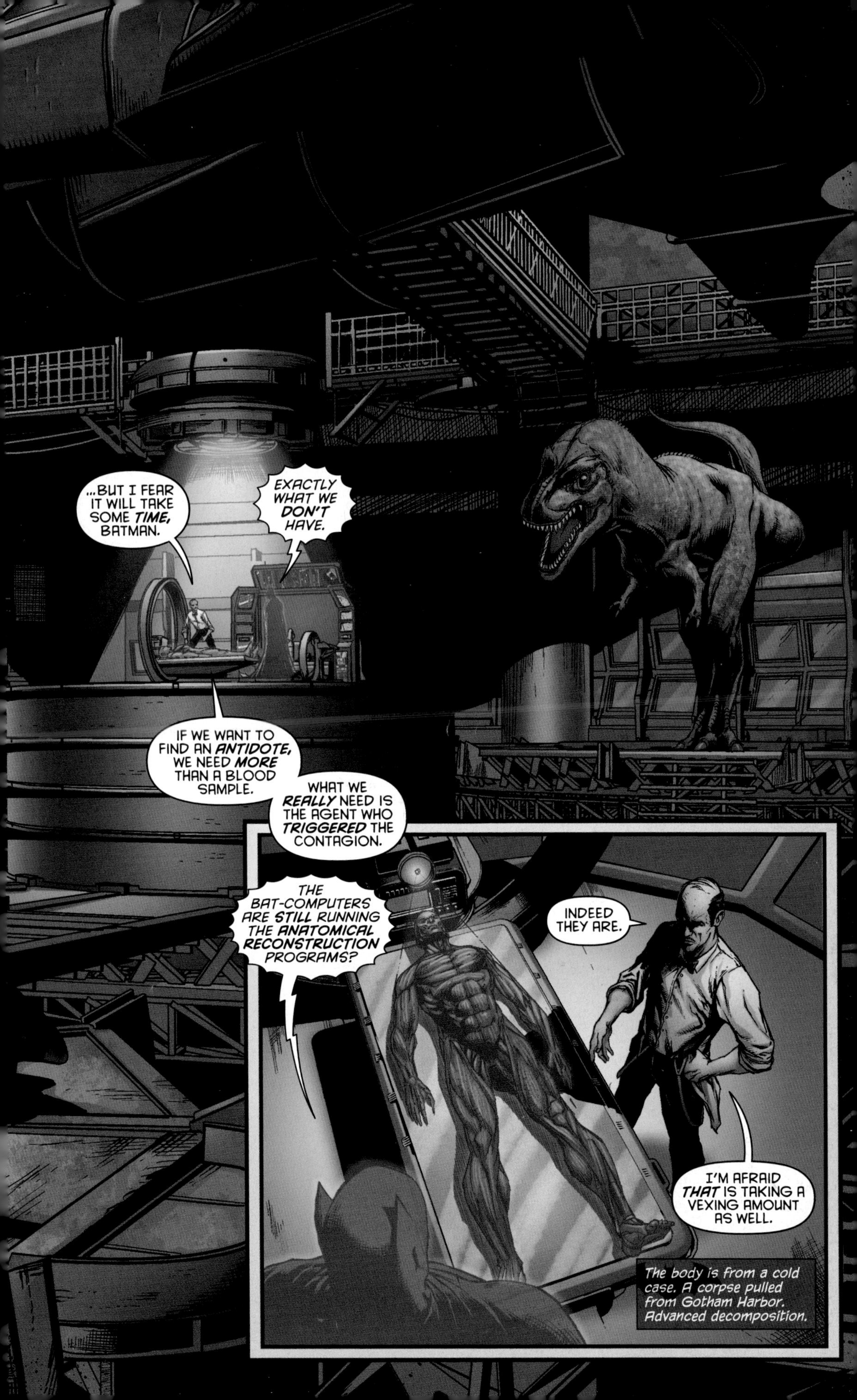

...BUT I FEAR IT WILL TAKE SOME *TIME,* BATMAN.
EXACTLY WHAT WE ***DON'T*** *HAVE.*
IF WE WANT TO FIND AN ***ANTIDOTE,*** WE NEED ***MORE*** THAN A BLOOD SAMPLE.
WHAT WE ***REALLY*** NEED IS THE AGENT WHO ***TRIGGERED*** THE CONTAGION.
THE BAT-COMPUTERS ARE ***STILL*** RUNNING THE ***ANATOMICAL RECONSTRUCTION*** PROGRAMS?
INDEED THEY ARE.
I'M AFRAID ***THAT*** IS TAKING A VEXING AMOUNT AS WELL.
The body is from a cold case. A corpse pulled from Gotham Harbor. Advanced decomposition.

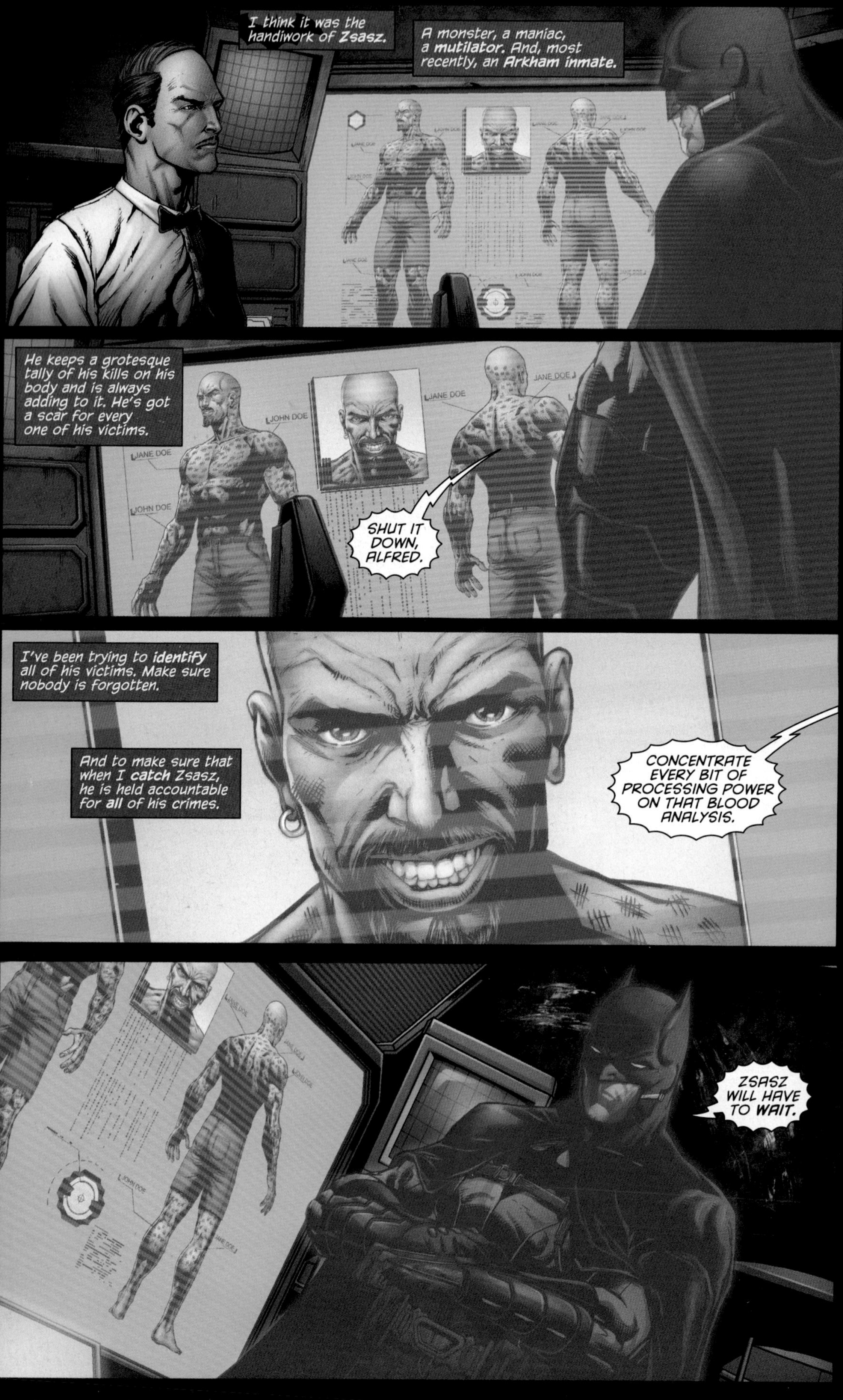
I think it was the handiwork of Zsasz.
A monster, a maniac, a mutilator. And, most recently, an Arkham inmate.
He keeps a grotesque tally of his kills on his body and is always adding to it. He's got a scar for every one of his victims.
JOHN DOE
JANE DOE
JOHN DOE
JANE DOE
SHUT IT DOWN, ALFRED.
I've been trying to identify all of his victims. Make sure nobody is forgotten.
And to make sure that when I catch Zsasz, he is held accountable for all of his crimes.
CONCENTRATE EVERY BIT OF PROCESSING POWER ON THAT BLOOD ANALYSIS.
ZSASZ WILL HAVE TO WAIT.

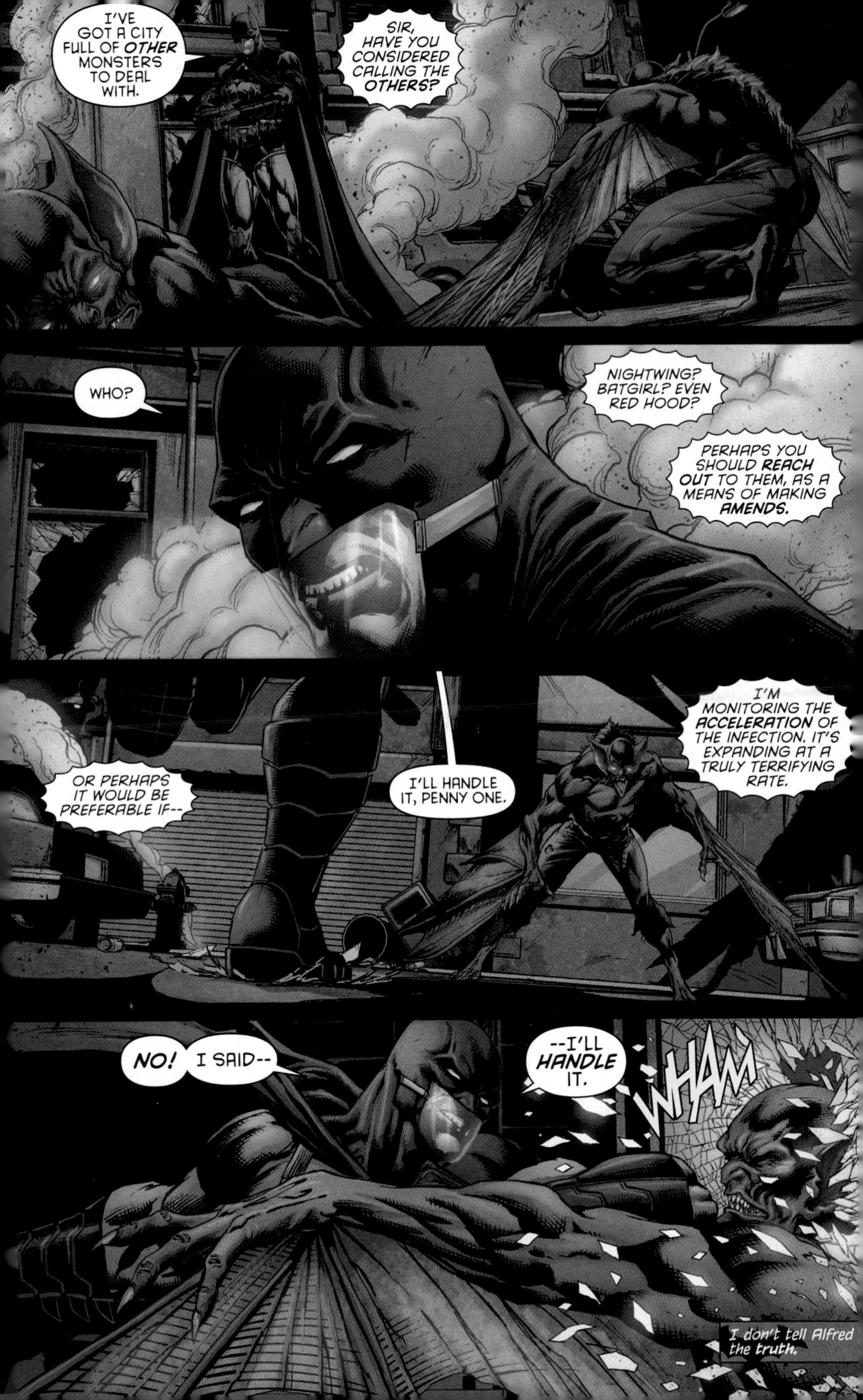
I'VE GOT A CITY FULL OF OTHER MONSTERS TO DEAL WITH.
SIR, HAVE YOU CONSIDERED CALLING THE OTHERS?
WHO?
NIGHTWING? BATGIRL? EVEN RED HOOD?
PERHAPS YOU SHOULD REACH OUT TO THEM, AS A MEANS OF MAKING AMENDS.
OR PERHAPS IT WOULD BE PREFERABLE IF--
I'LL HANDLE IT, PENNY ONE.
I'M MONITORING THE ACCELERATION OF THE INFECTION. IT'S EXPANDING AT A TRULY TERRIFYING RATE.
NO! I SAID--
--I'LL HANDLE IT.
WHAM
I don't tell Alfred the truth.

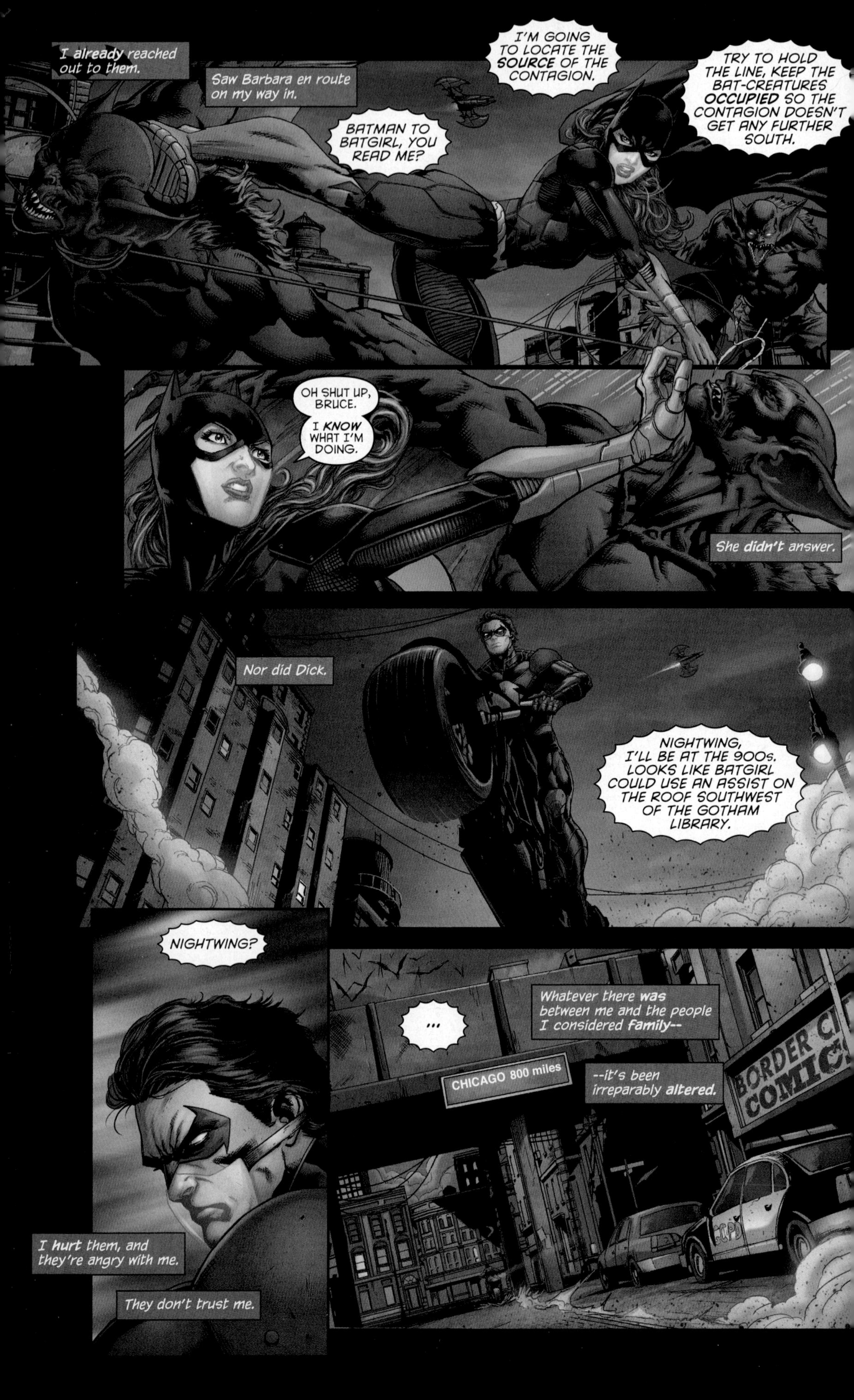

I already reached out to them.
Saw Barbara en route on my way in.
BATMAN TO BATGIRL, YOU READ ME?
I'M GOING TO LOCATE THE SOURCE OF THE CONTAGION.
TRY TO HOLD THE LINE, KEEP THE BAT-CREATURES OCCUPIED SO THE CONTAGION DOESN'T GET ANY FURTHER SOUTH.
OH SHUT UP, BRUCE.
I KNOW WHAT I'M DOING.
She didn't answer.
Nor did Dick.
NIGHTWING, I'LL BE AT THE 900s. LOOKS LIKE BATGIRL COULD USE AN ASSIST ON THE ROOF SOUTHWEST OF THE GOTHAM LIBRARY.
NIGHTWING?
I hurt them, and they're angry with me.
They don't trust me.
...
Whatever there was between me and the people I considered family--
CHICAGO 800 miles
--it's been irreparably altered.
BORDER CI
COMIC

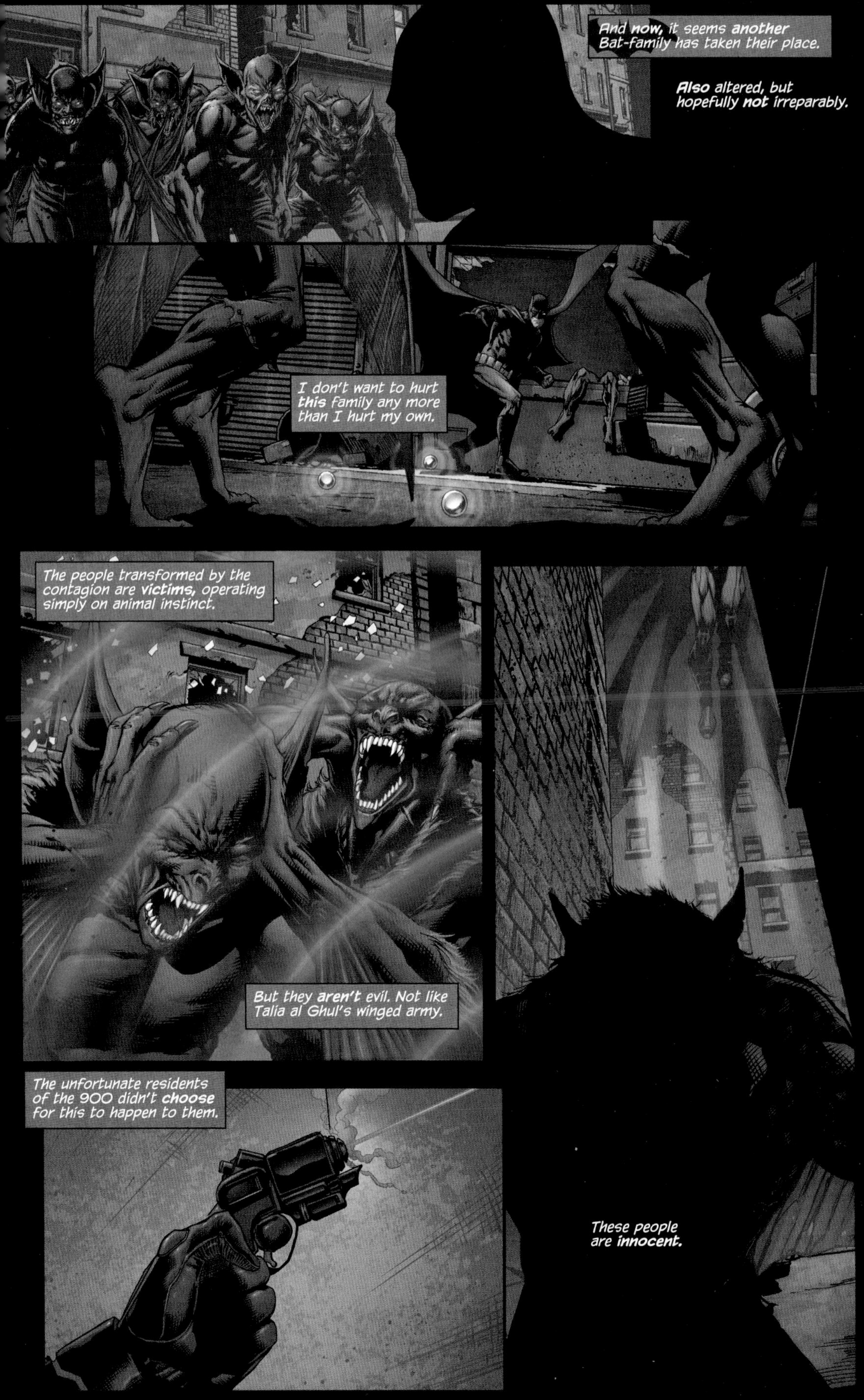
And now, it seems another Bat-family has taken their place.
Also altered, but hopefully not irreparably.
I don't want to hurt this family any more than I hurt my own.
The people transformed by the contagion are victims, operating simply on animal instinct.
But they aren't evil. Not like Talia al Ghul's winged army.
The unfortunate residents of the 900 didn't choose for this to happen to them.
These people are innocent.

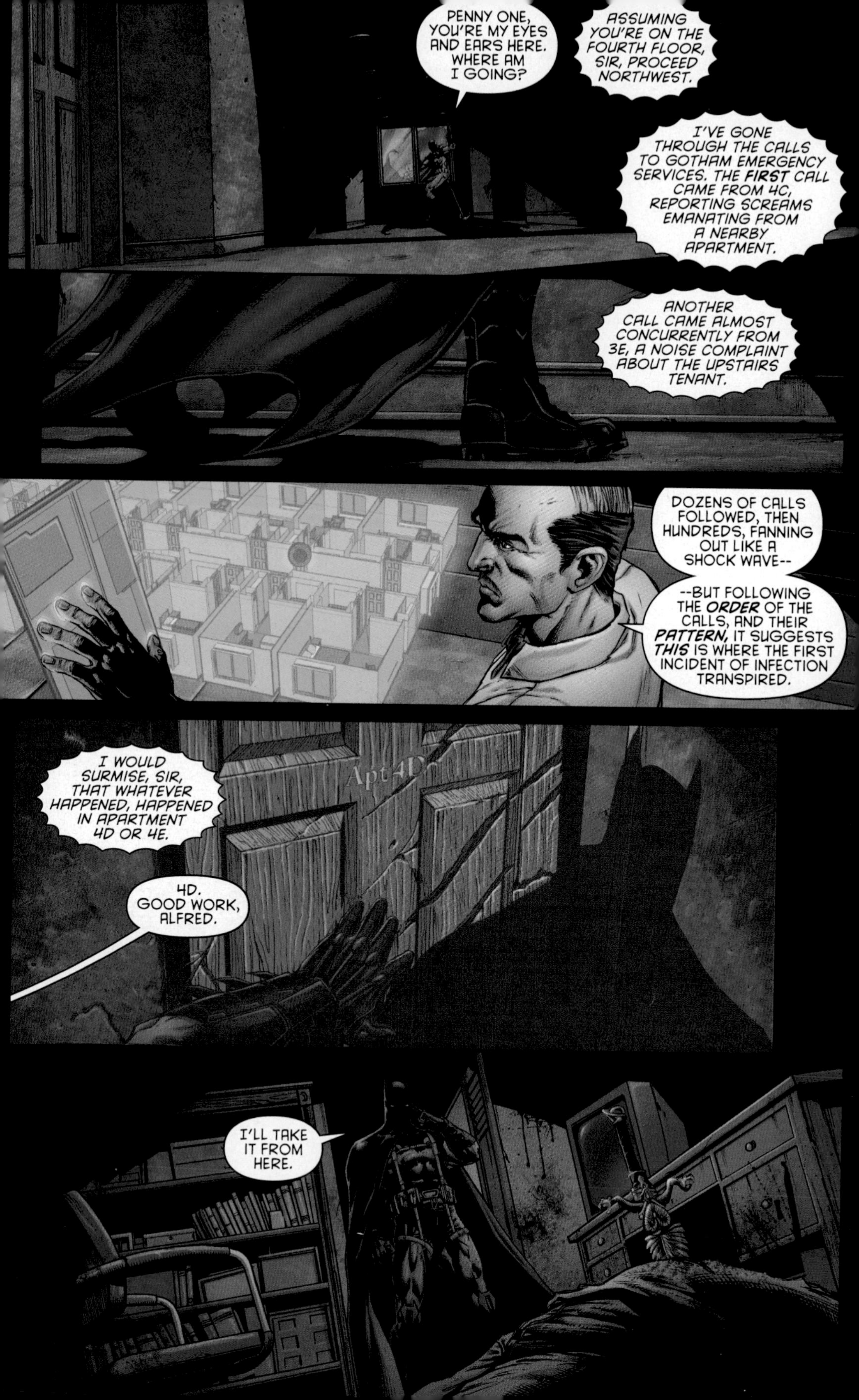
PENNY ONE, YOU'RE MY EYES AND EARS HERE. WHERE AM I GOING?
ASSUMING YOU'RE ON THE FOURTH FLOOR, SIR, PROCEED NORTHWEST.
I'VE GONE THROUGH THE CALLS TO GOTHAM EMERGENCY SERVICES. THE FIRST CALL CAME FROM 4C, REPORTING SCREAMS EMANATING FROM A NEARBY APARTMENT.
ANOTHER CALL CAME ALMOST CONCURRENTLY FROM 3E, A NOISE COMPLAINT ABOUT THE UPSTAIRS TENANT.
DOZENS OF CALLS FOLLOWED, THEN HUNDREDS, FANNING OUT LIKE A SHOCK WAVE--
--BUT FOLLOWING THE ORDER OF THE CALLS, AND THEIR PATTERN, IT SUGGESTS THIS IS WHERE THE FIRST INCIDENT OF INFECTION TRANSPIRED.
Apt 4D
I WOULD SURMISE, SIR, THAT WHATEVER HAPPENED, HAPPENED IN APARTMENT 4D OR 4E.
4D. GOOD WORK, ALFRED.
I'LL TAKE IT FROM HERE.

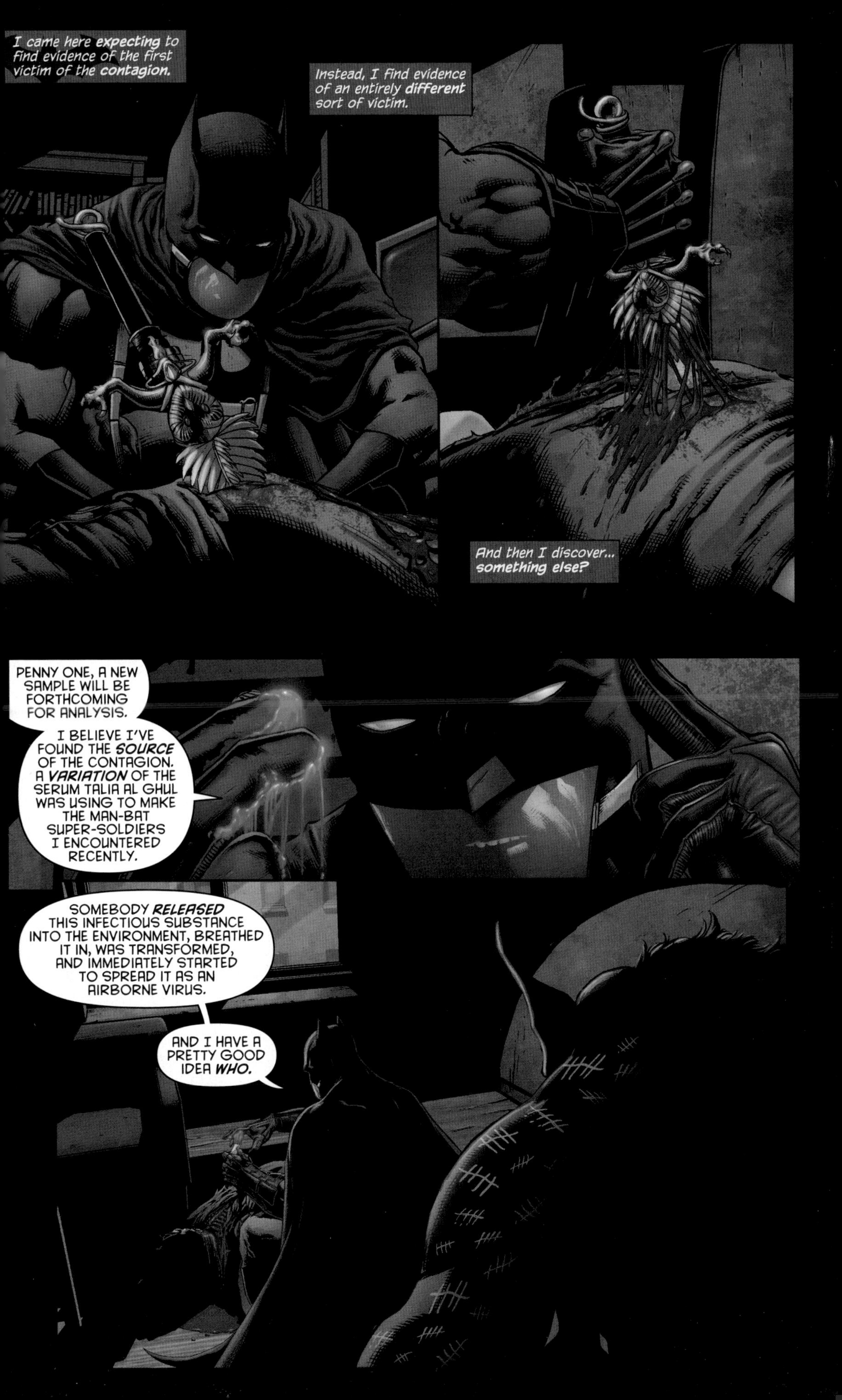

I came here expecting to find evidence of the first victim of the contagion.
Instead, I find evidence of an entirely different sort of victim.
And then I discover... something else?
PENNY ONE, A NEW SAMPLE WILL BE FORTHCOMING FOR ANALYSIS.
I BELIEVE I'VE FOUND THE SOURCE OF THE CONTAGION. A VARIATION OF THE SERUM TALIA AL GHUL WAS USING TO MAKE THE MAN-BAT SUPER-SOLDIERS I ENCOUNTERED RECENTLY.
SOMEBODY RELEASED THIS INFECTIOUS SUBSTANCE INTO THE ENVIRONMENT, BREATHED IT IN, WAS TRANSFORMED, AND IMMEDIATELY STARTED TO SPREAD IT AS AN AIRBORNE VIRUS.
AND I HAVE A PRETTY GOOD IDEA WHO.

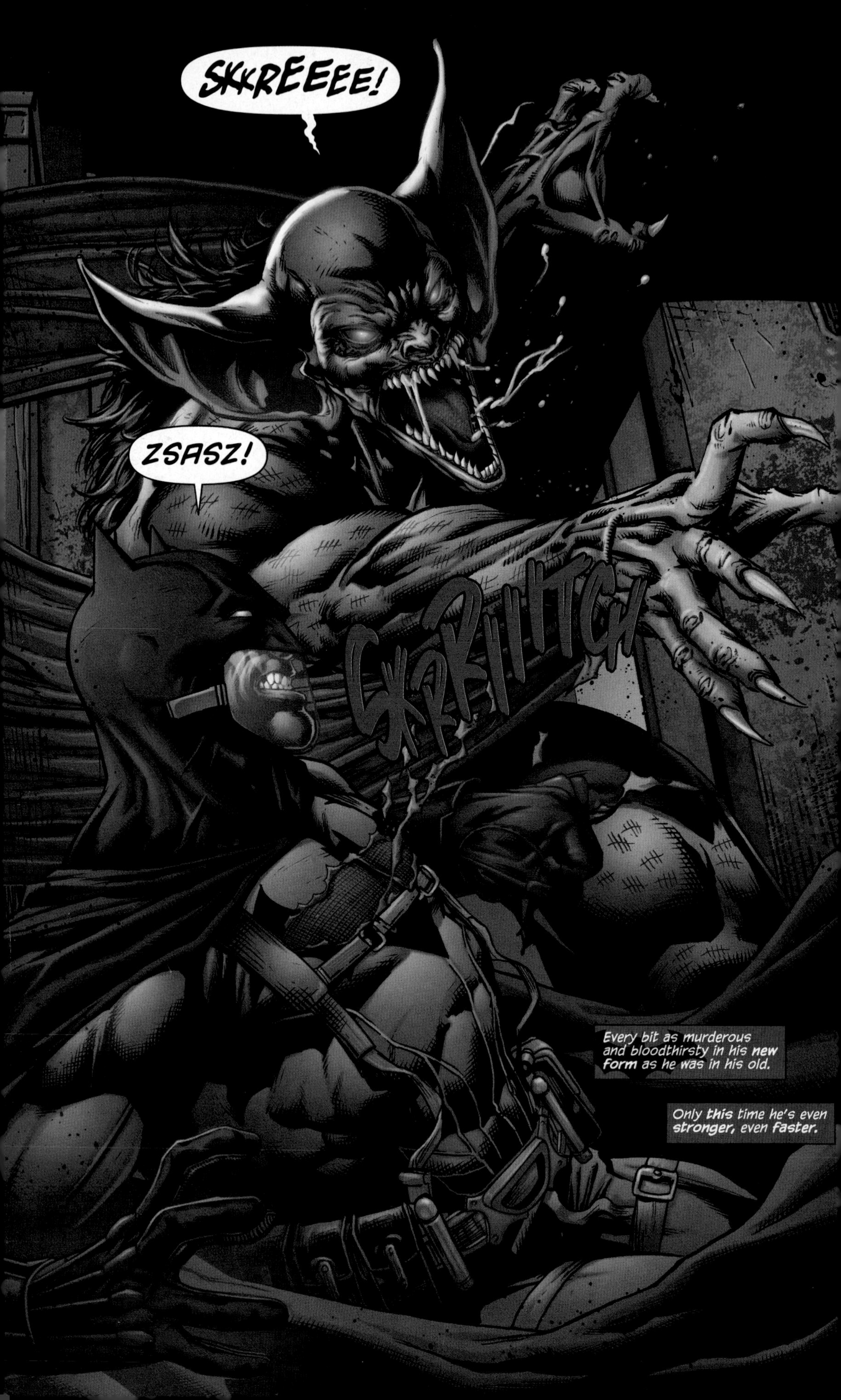
SKKREEEEE!
ZSASZ!
SKRIIITCH
Every bit as murderous and bloodthirsty in his **new form** as he was in his old.
Only **this** time he's even **stronger**, even **faster**.

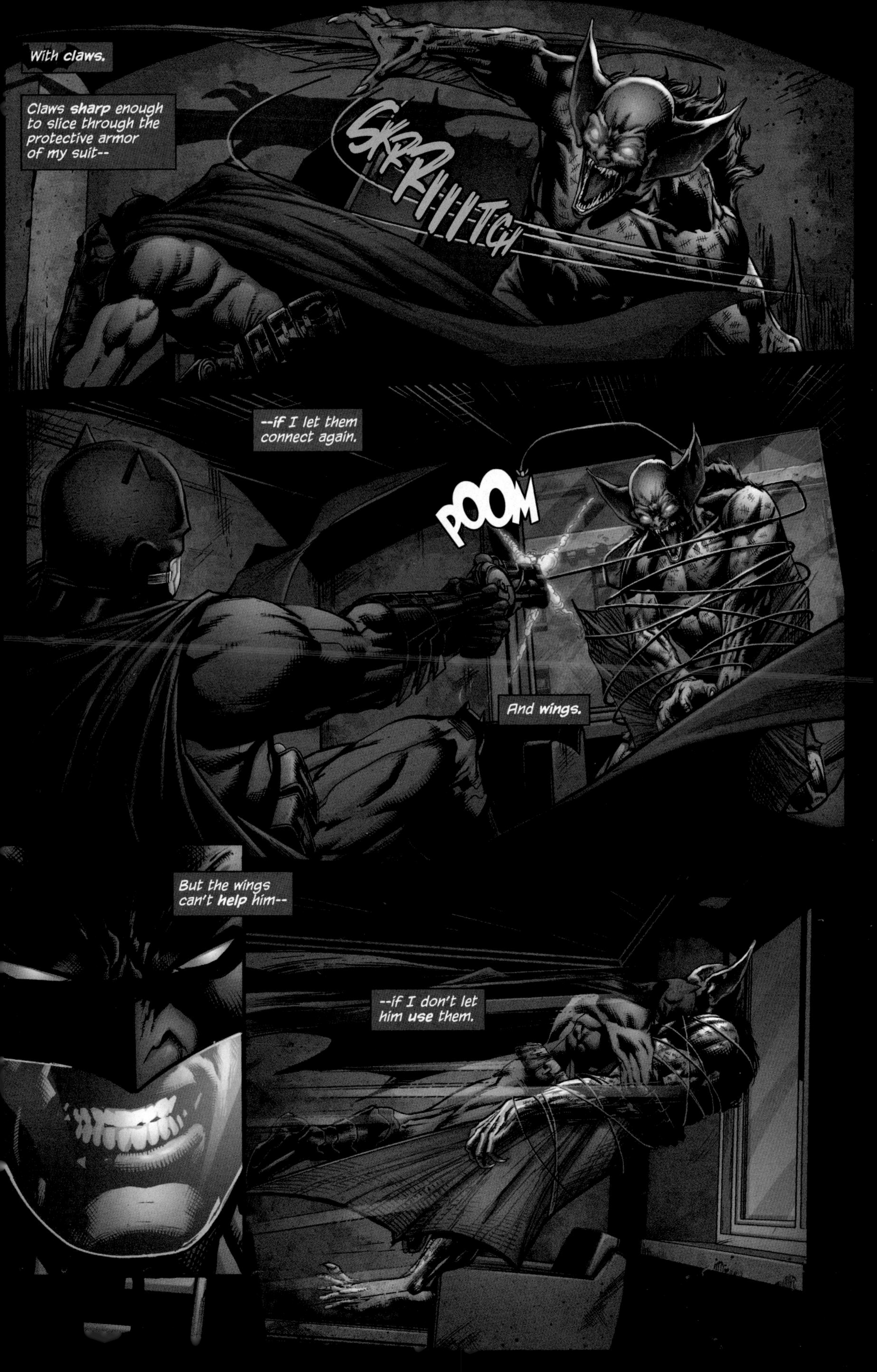
With claws.
Claws sharp enough to slice through the protective armor of my suit--
SKRRIIIITCH
--if I let them connect again.
POOM
And wings.
But the wings can't help him--
--if I don't let him use them.

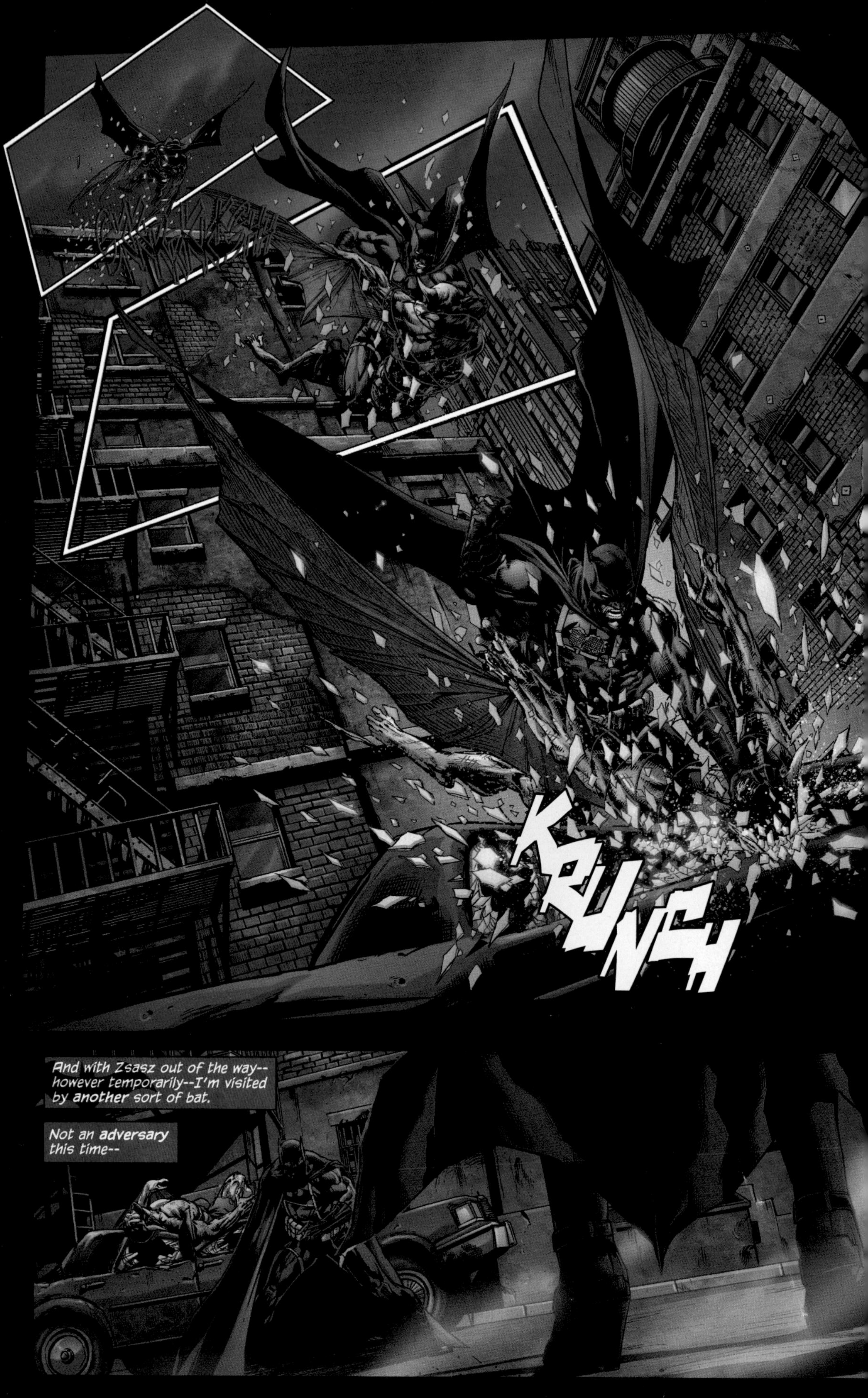
KRUNCH
And with Zsasz out of the way--however temporarily--I'm visited by **another** sort of bat.
Not an **adversary** this time--

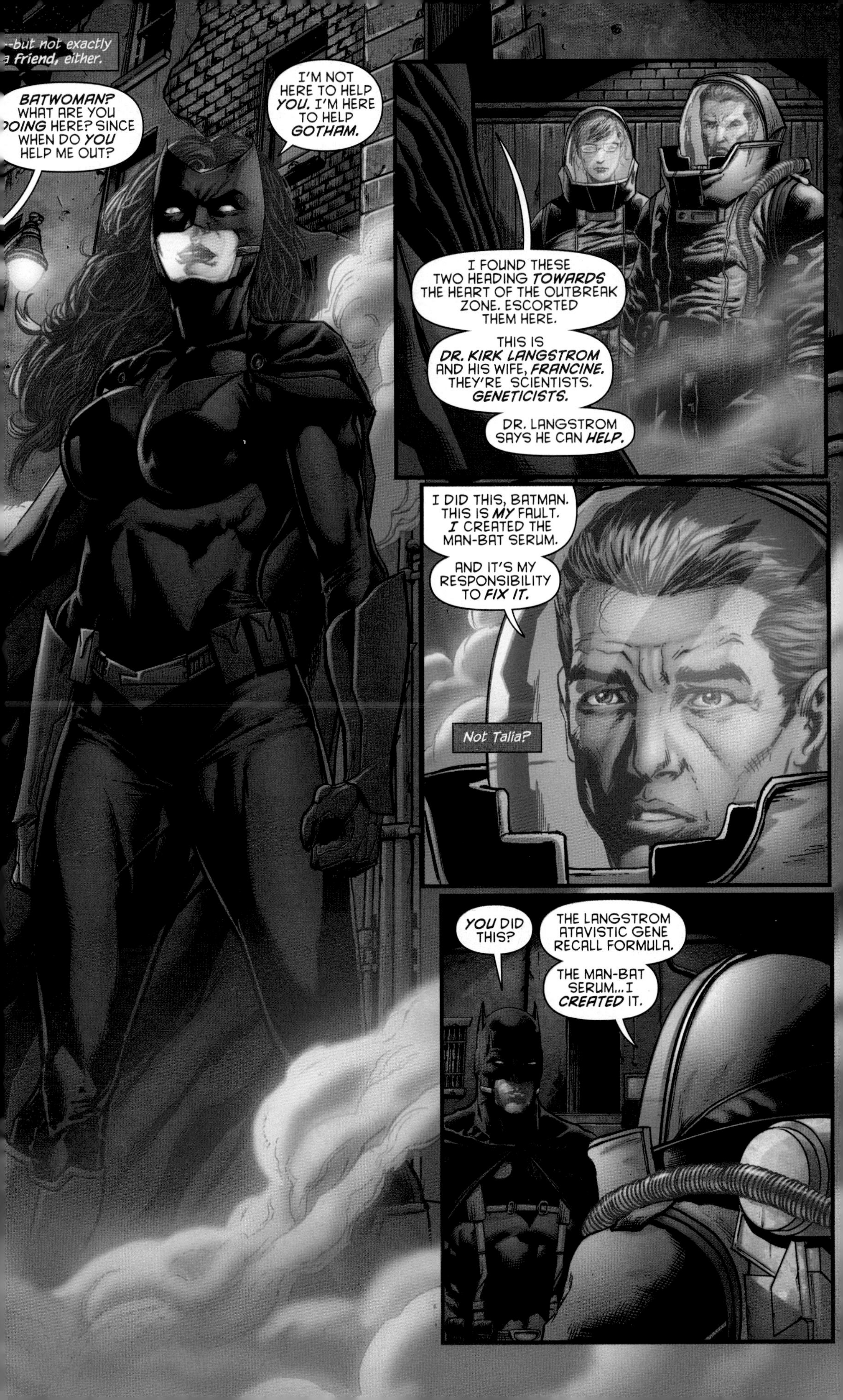
--but not exactly a friend, either.
BATWOMAN? WHAT ARE YOU DOING HERE? SINCE WHEN DO YOU HELP ME OUT?
I'M NOT HERE TO HELP YOU. I'M HERE TO HELP GOTHAM.
I FOUND THESE TWO HEADING TOWARDS THE HEART OF THE OUTBREAK ZONE. ESCORTED THEM HERE.
THIS IS DR. KIRK LANGSTROM AND HIS WIFE, FRANCINE. THEY'RE SCIENTISTS. GENETICISTS.
DR. LANGSTROM SAYS HE CAN HELP.
I DID THIS, BATMAN. THIS IS MY FAULT. I CREATED THE MAN-BAT SERUM.
AND IT'S MY RESPONSIBILITY TO FIX IT.
Not Talia?
YOU DID THIS?
THE LANGSTROM ATAVISTIC GENE RECALL FORMULA.
THE MAN-BAT SERUM... I CREATED IT.

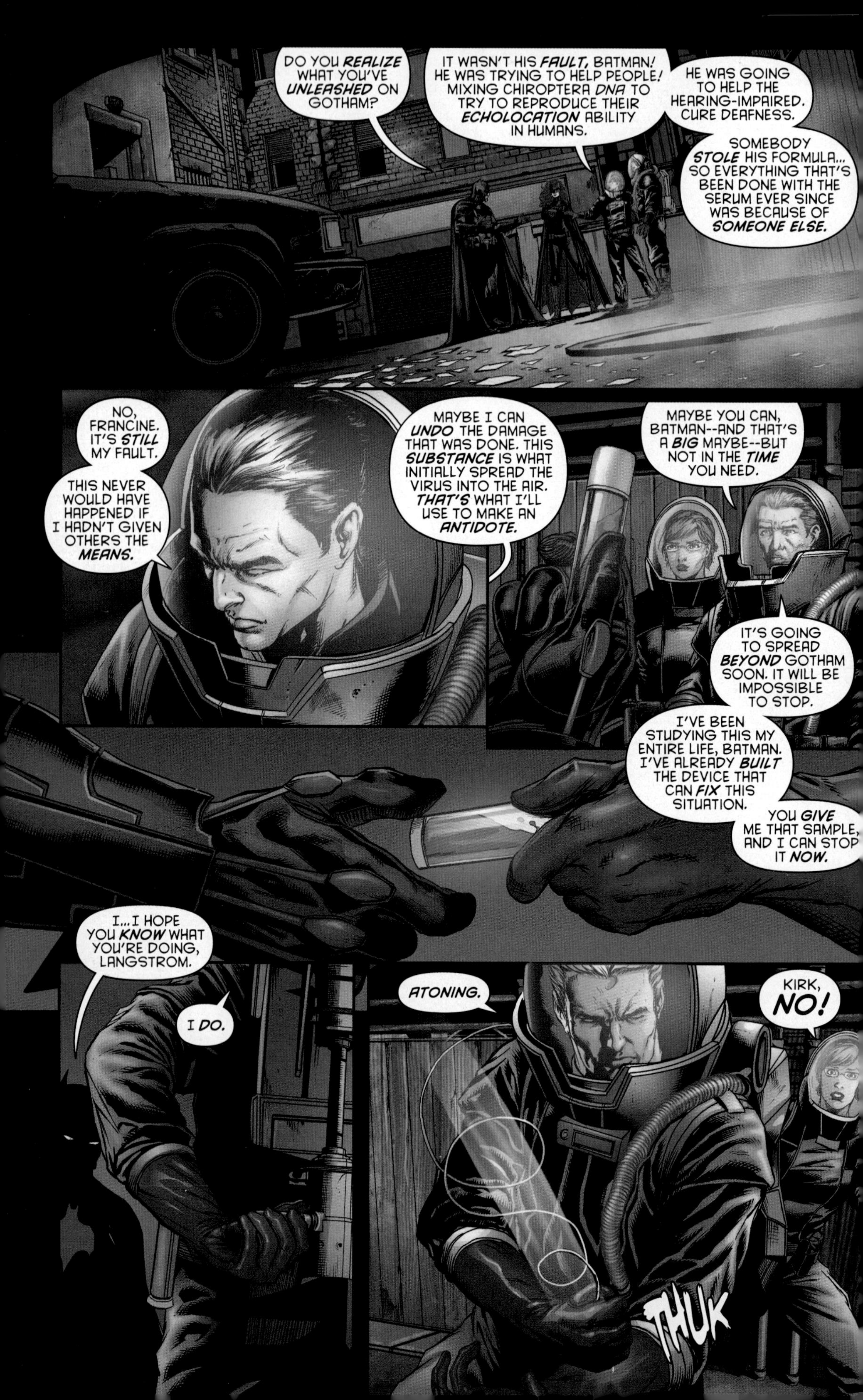
DO YOU REALIZE WHAT YOU'VE UNLEASHED ON GOTHAM?
IT WASN'T HIS FAULT, BATMAN! HE WAS TRYING TO HELP PEOPLE! MIXING CHIROPTERA DNA TO TRY TO REPRODUCE THEIR ECHOLOCATION ABILITY IN HUMANS.
HE WAS GOING TO HELP THE HEARING-IMPAIRED. CURE DEAFNESS.
SOMEBODY STOLE HIS FORMULA... SO EVERYTHING THAT'S BEEN DONE WITH THE SERUM EVER SINCE WAS BECAUSE OF SOMEONE ELSE.
NO, FRANCINE. IT'S STILL MY FAULT.
THIS NEVER WOULD HAVE HAPPENED IF I HADN'T GIVEN OTHERS THE MEANS.
MAYBE I CAN UNDO THE DAMAGE THAT WAS DONE. THIS SUBSTANCE IS WHAT INITIALLY SPREAD THE VIRUS INTO THE AIR. THAT'S WHAT I'LL USE TO MAKE AN ANTIDOTE.
MAYBE YOU CAN, BATMAN--AND THAT'S A BIG MAYBE--BUT NOT IN THE TIME YOU NEED.
IT'S GOING TO SPREAD BEYOND GOTHAM SOON. IT WILL BE IMPOSSIBLE TO STOP.
I'VE BEEN STUDYING THIS MY ENTIRE LIFE, BATMAN. I'VE ALREADY BUILT THE DEVICE THAT CAN FIX THIS SITUATION.
YOU GIVE ME THAT SAMPLE, AND I CAN STOP IT NOW.
I...I HOPE YOU KNOW WHAT YOU'RE DOING, LANGSTROM.
I DO.
ATONING.
KIRK, NO!
THUK

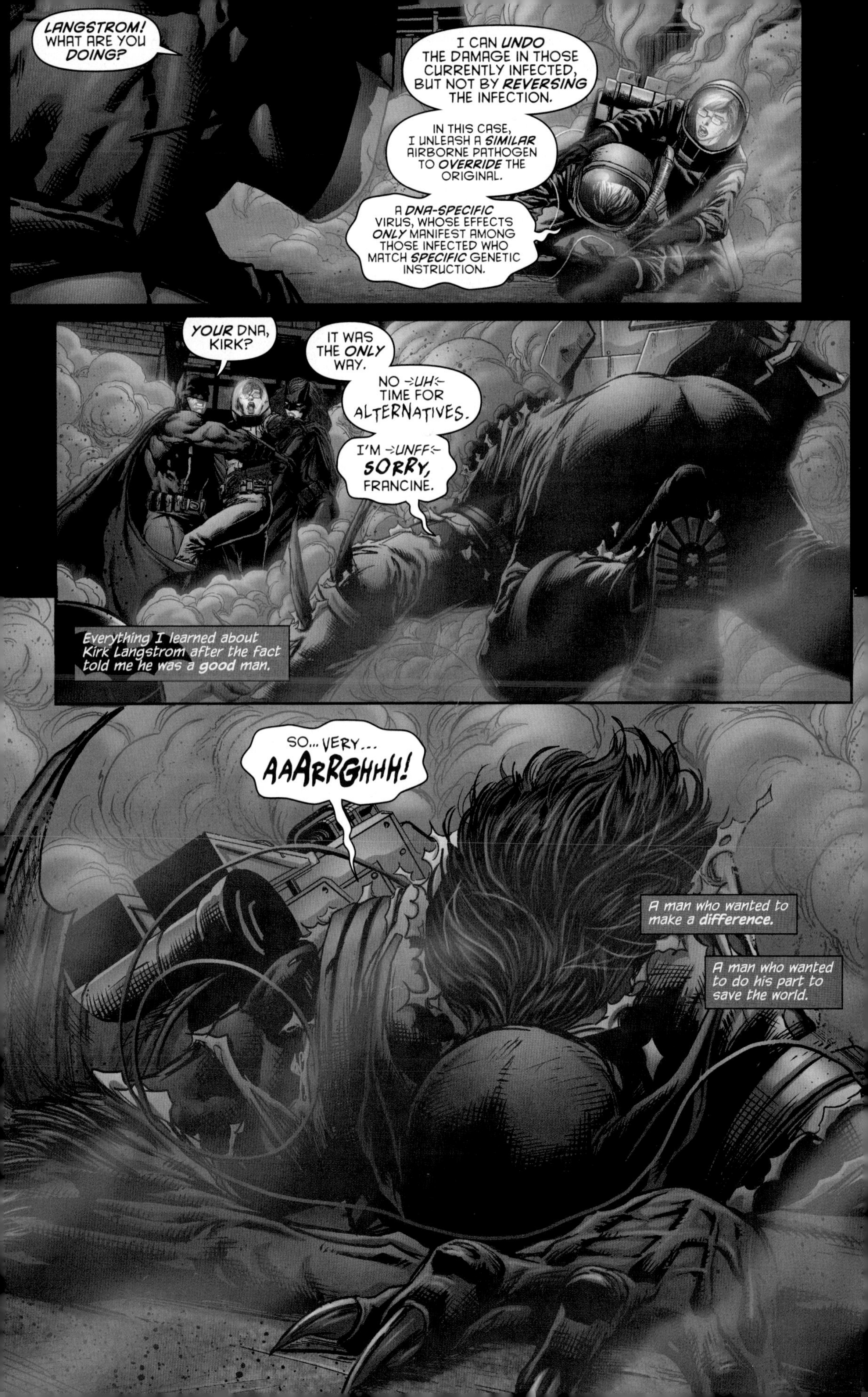

LANGSTROM! WHAT ARE YOU DOING?
I CAN UNDO THE DAMAGE IN THOSE CURRENTLY INFECTED, BUT NOT BY REVERSING THE INFECTION.
IN THIS CASE, I UNLEASH A SIMILAR AIRBORNE PATHOGEN TO OVERRIDE THE ORIGINAL.
A DNA-SPECIFIC VIRUS, WHOSE EFFECTS ONLY MANIFEST AMONG THOSE INFECTED WHO MATCH SPECIFIC GENETIC INSTRUCTION.
YOUR DNA, KIRK?
IT WAS THE ONLY WAY.
NO -UH- TIME FOR ALTERNATIVES.
I'M -UNFF- SORRY, FRANCINE.
Everything I learned about Kirk Langstrom after the fact told me he was a good man.
SO... VERY... AAARRGHHH!
A man who wanted to make a difference.
A man who wanted to do his part to save the world.

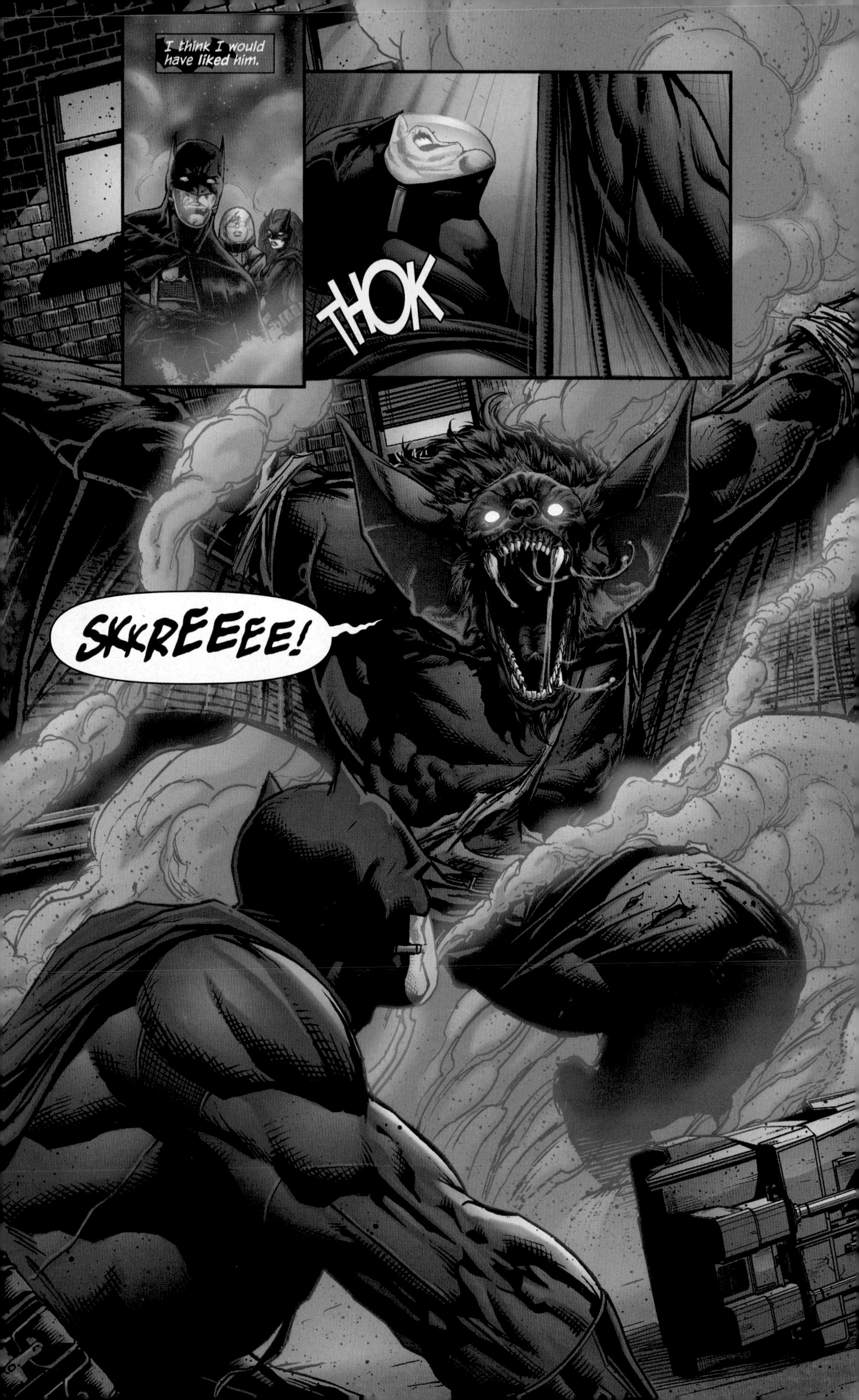
I think I would have liked him.
THOK
SKKREEEEE!

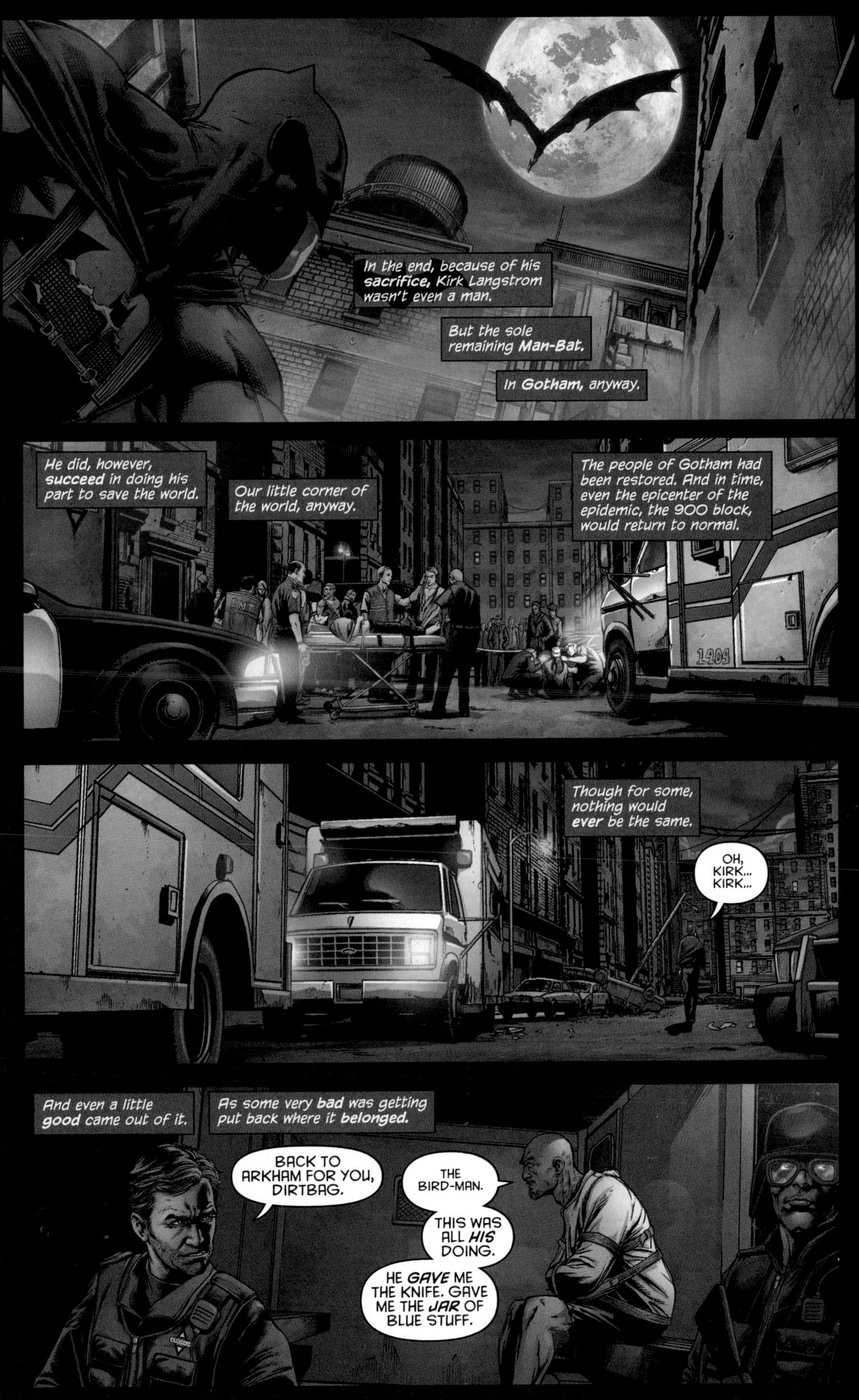
In the end, because of his sacrifice, Kirk Langstrom wasn't even a man.
But the sole remaining Man-Bat.
In Gotham, anyway.
He did, however, succeed in doing his part to save the world.
Our little corner of the world, anyway.
The people of Gotham had been restored. And in time, even the epicenter of the epidemic, the 900 block, would return to normal.
EMT
1404
Though for some, nothing would ever be the same.
OH, KIRK... KIRK...
And even a little good came out of it.
As some very bad was getting put back where it belonged.
BACK TO ARKHAM FOR YOU, DIRTBAG.
THE BIRD-MAN.
THIS WAS ALL HIS DOING.
HE GAVE ME THE KNIFE. GAVE ME THE JAR OF BLUE STUFF.

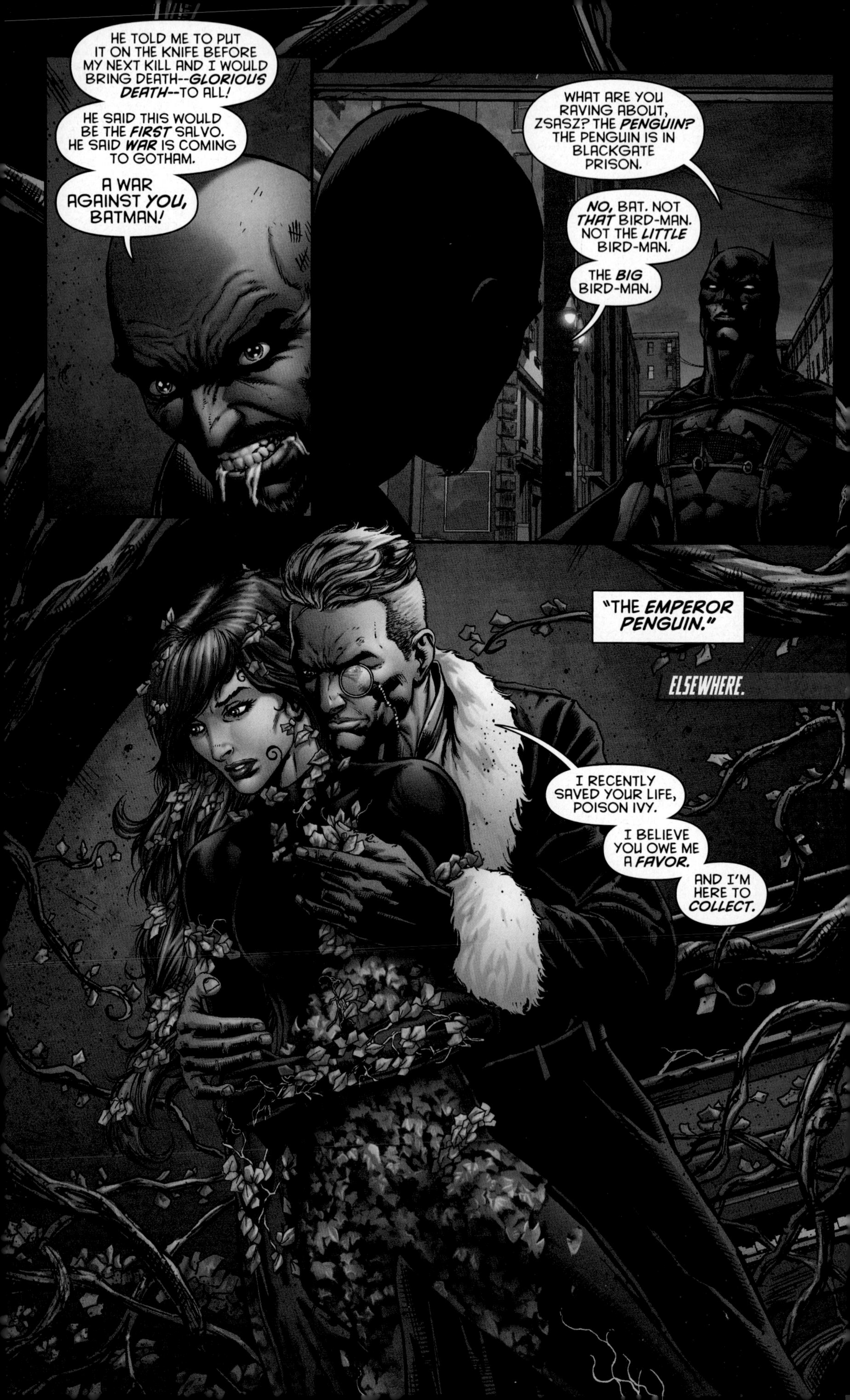
HE TOLD ME TO PUT IT ON THE KNIFE BEFORE MY NEXT KILL AND I WOULD BRING DEATH--GLORIOUS DEATH--TO ALL!
HE SAID THIS WOULD BE THE FIRST SALVO. HE SAID WAR IS COMING TO GOTHAM.
A WAR AGAINST YOU, BATMAN!
WHAT ARE YOU RAVING ABOUT, ZSASZ? THE PENGUIN? THE PENGUIN IS IN BLACKGATE PRISON.
NO, BAT. NOT THAT BIRD-MAN. NOT THE LITTLE BIRD-MAN.
THE BIG BIRD-MAN.
"THE EMPEROR PENGUIN."
ELSEWHERE.
I RECENTLY SAVED YOUR LIFE, POISON IVY.
I BELIEVE YOU OWE ME A FAVOR.
AND I'M HERE TO COLLECT.

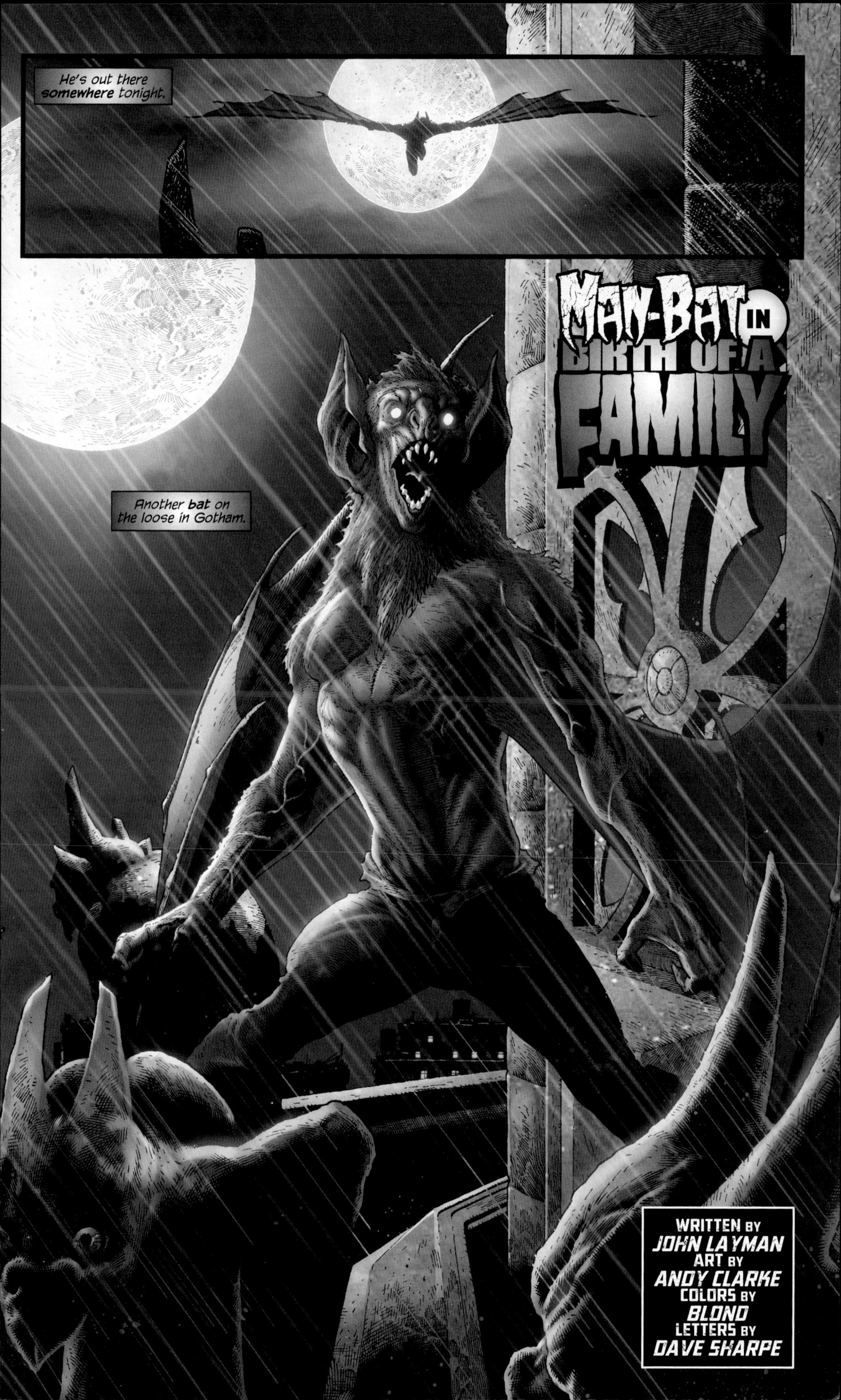

He's out there somewhere tonight.
Another bat on the loose in Gotham.
MAN-BAT IN
BIRTH OF A FAMILY
WRITTEN BY JOHN LAYMAN
ART BY ANDY CLARKE
COLORS BY BLOND
LETTERS BY DAVE SHARPE

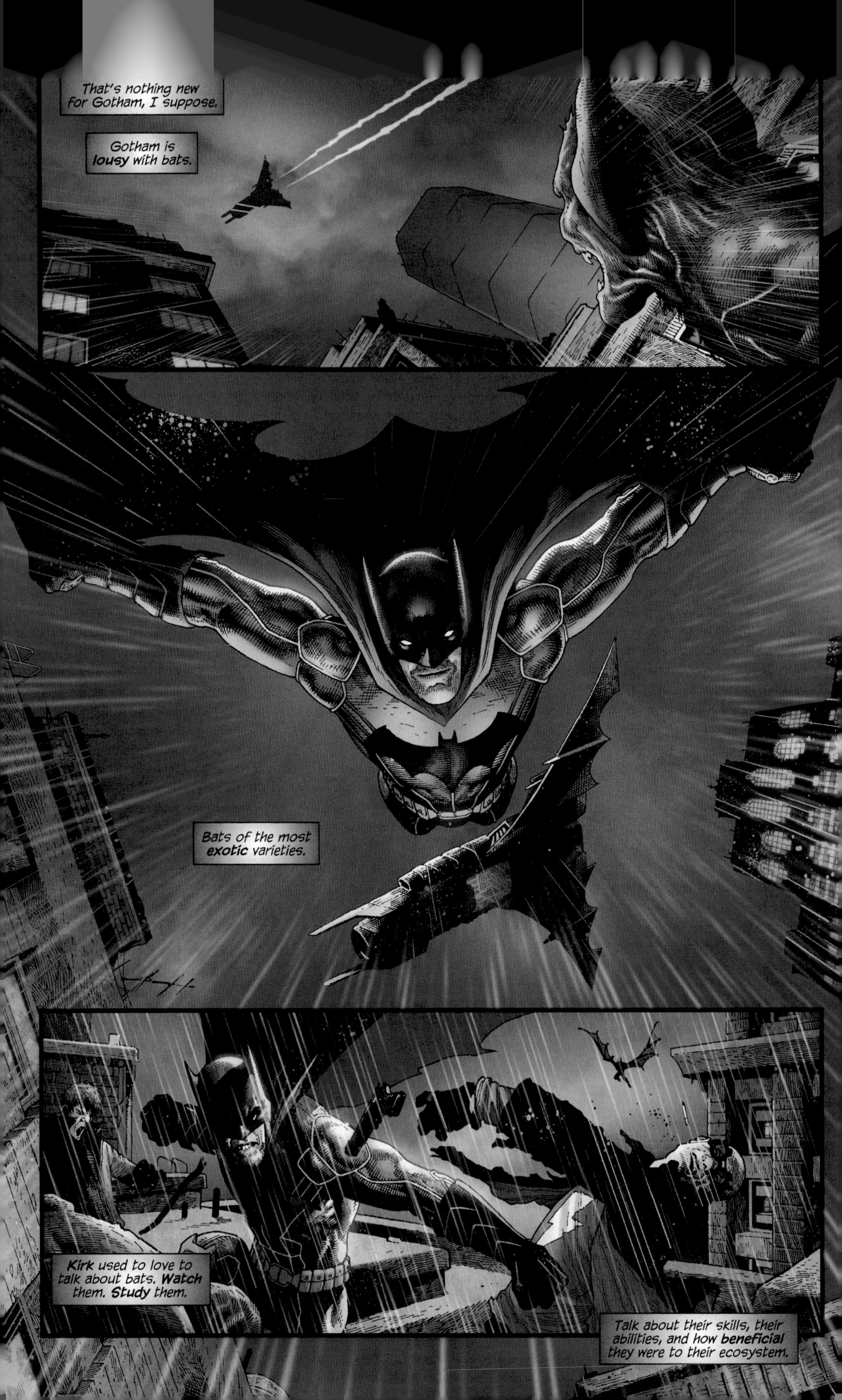

That's nothing new for Gotham, I suppose.
Gotham is **lousy** with bats.
Bats of the most **exotic** varieties.
Kirk used to love to talk about bats. **Watch** them. **Study** them.
Talk about their skills, their abilities, and how **beneficial** they were to their ecosystem.

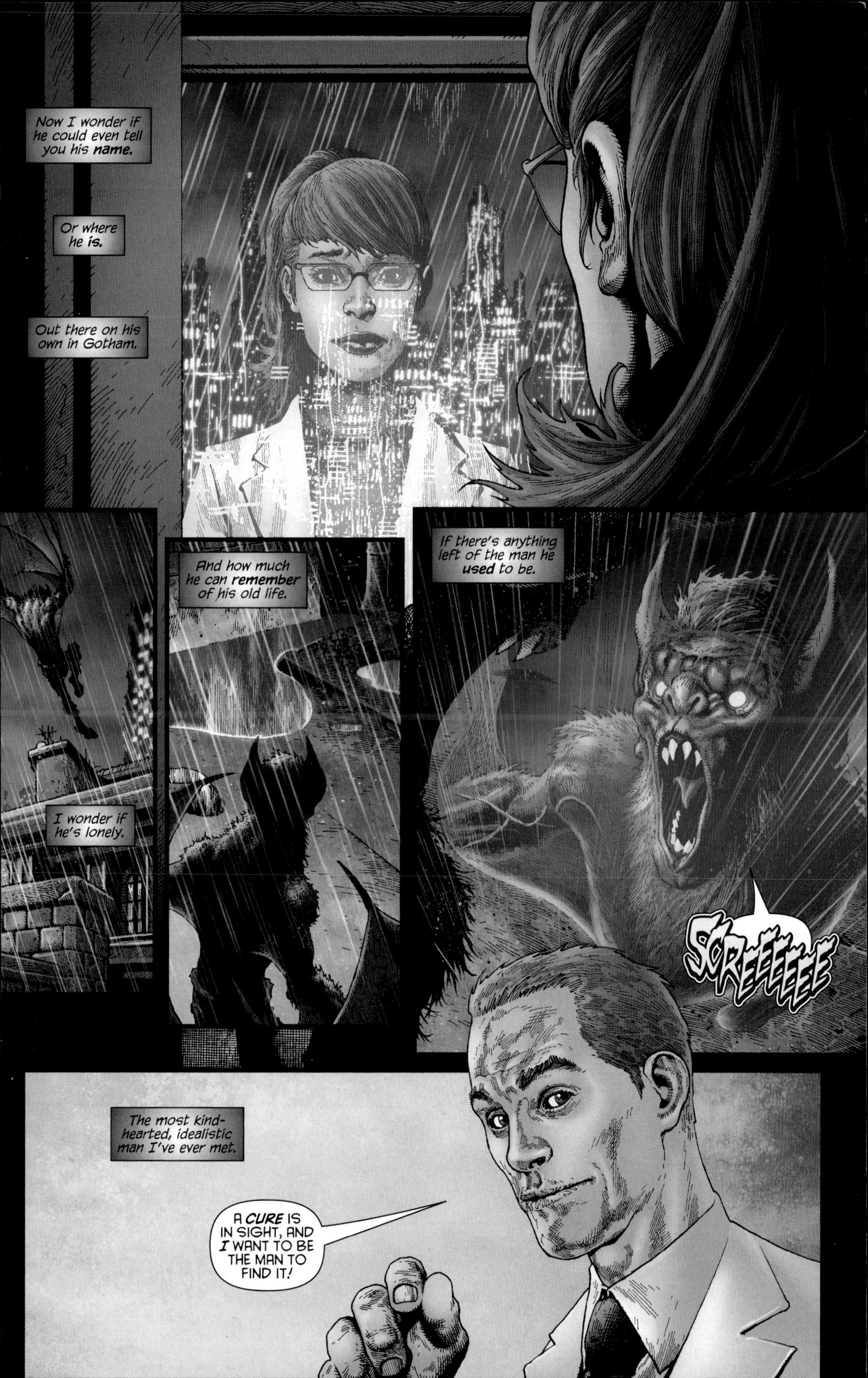
Now I wonder if he could even tell you his name.
Or where he is.
Out there on his own in Gotham.
I wonder if he's lonely.
And how much he can remember of his old life.
If there's anything left of the man he used to be.
SCREEEEEE
The most kind-hearted, idealistic man I've ever met.
A CURE IS IN SIGHT, AND I WANT TO BE THE MAN TO FIND IT!

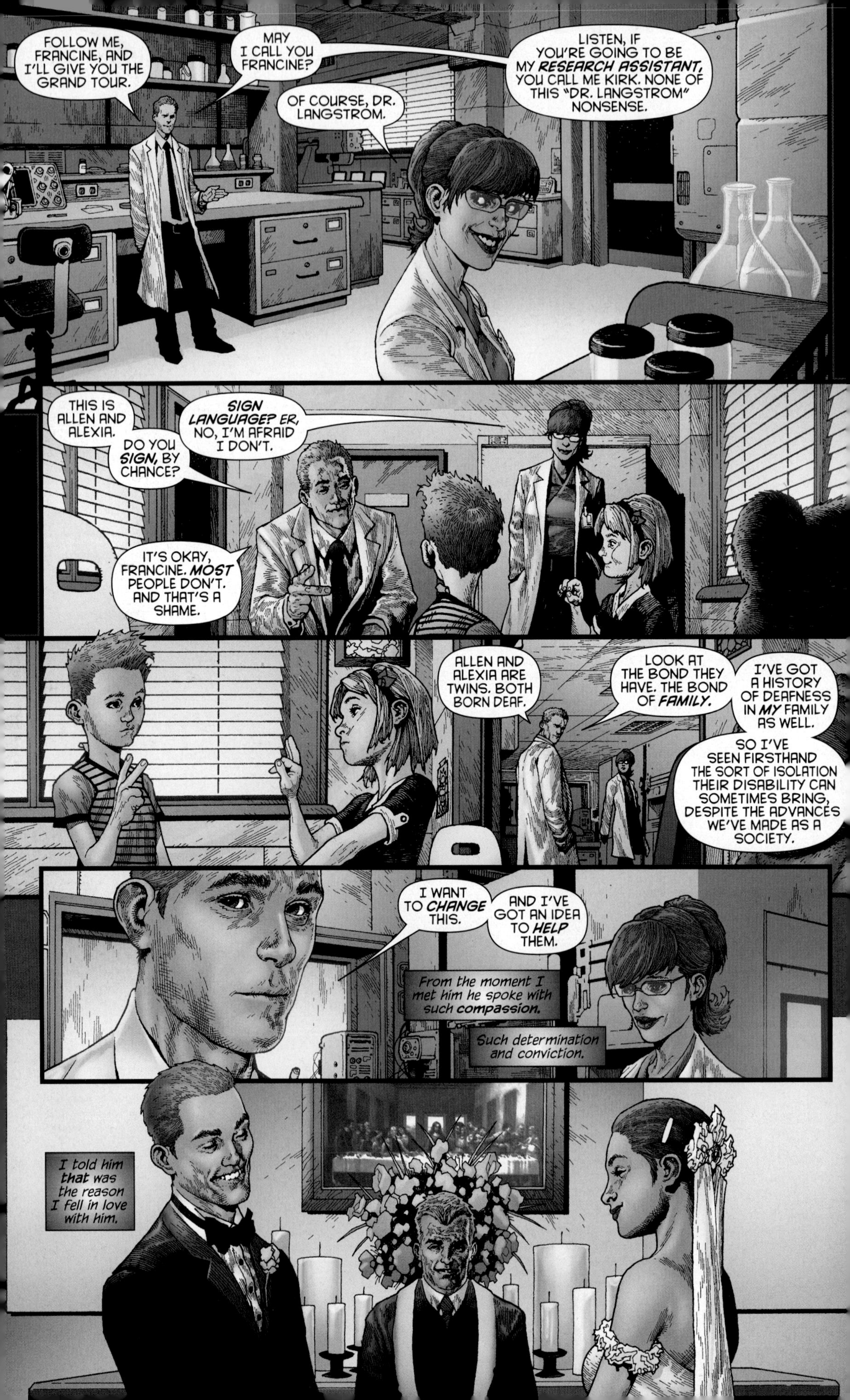
FOLLOW ME, FRANCINE, AND I'LL GIVE YOU THE GRAND TOUR.
MAY I CALL YOU FRANCINE?
OF COURSE, DR. LANGSTROM.
LISTEN, IF YOU'RE GOING TO BE MY RESEARCH ASSISTANT, YOU CALL ME KIRK. NONE OF THIS "DR. LANGSTROM" NONSENSE.
THIS IS ALLEN AND ALEXIA.
DO YOU SIGN, BY CHANCE?
SIGN LANGUAGE? ER, NO, I'M AFRAID I DON'T.
IT'S OKAY, FRANCINE. MOST PEOPLE DON'T. AND THAT'S A SHAME.
ALLEN AND ALEXIA ARE TWINS. BOTH BORN DEAF.
LOOK AT THE BOND THEY HAVE. THE BOND OF FAMILY.
I'VE GOT A HISTORY OF DEAFNESS IN MY FAMILY AS WELL.
SO I'VE SEEN FIRSTHAND THE SORT OF ISOLATION THEIR DISABILITY CAN SOMETIMES BRING, DESPITE THE ADVANCES WE'VE MADE AS A SOCIETY.
I WANT TO CHANGE THIS.
AND I'VE GOT AN IDEA TO HELP THEM.
From the moment I met him he spoke with such compassion.
Such determination and conviction.
I told him that was the reason I fell in love with him.

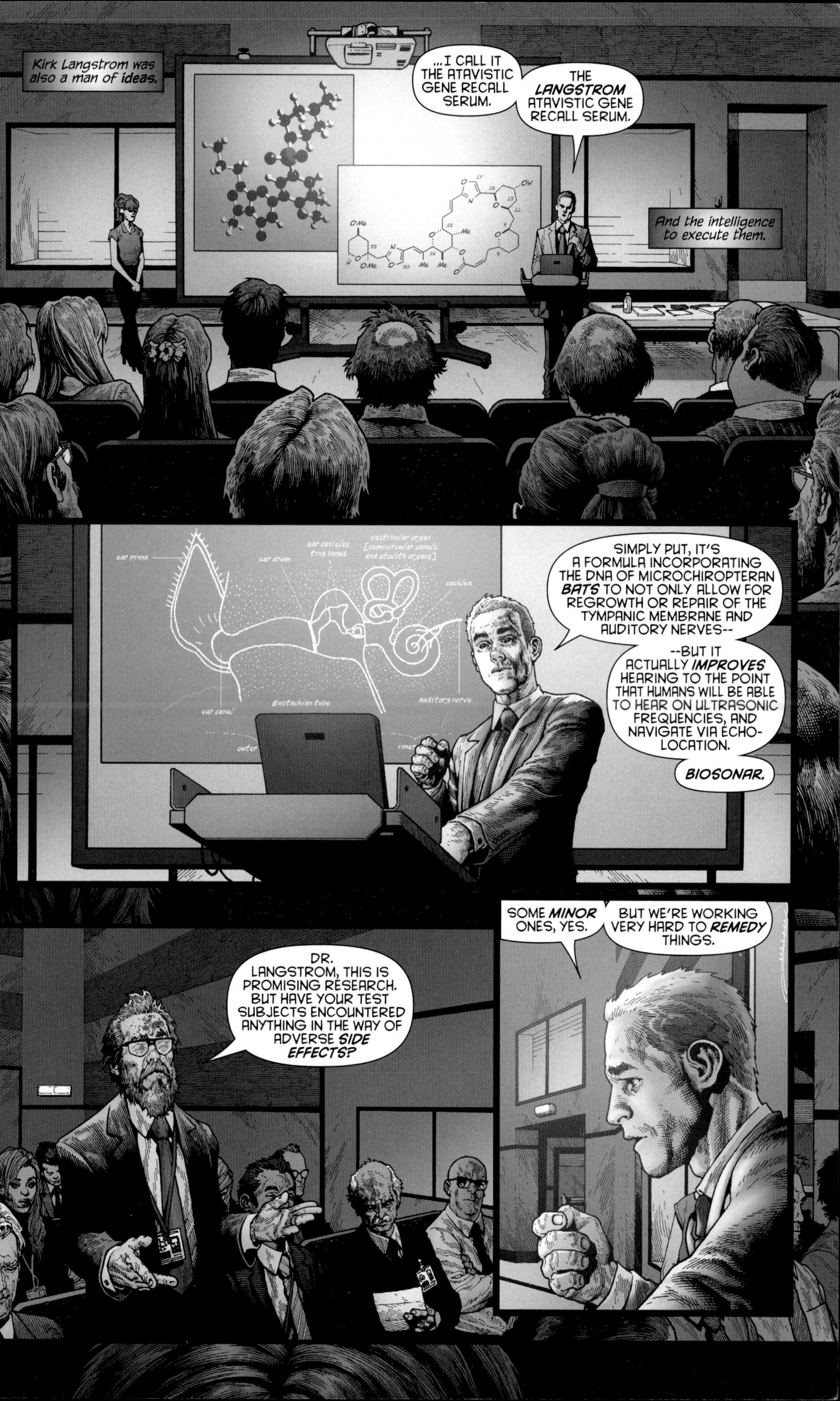
Kirk Langstrom was also a man of ideas.
...I CALL IT THE ATAVISTIC GENE RECALL SERUM.
THE LANGSTROM ATAVISTIC GENE RECALL SERUM.
And the intelligence to execute them.
ear pinna
ear drum
ear ossicles tiny bones
vestibular organ [semicircular canals and otolith organs]
cochlea
ear canal
Eustachian tube
auditory nerve
outer
inner
SIMPLY PUT, IT'S A FORMULA INCORPORATING THE DNA OF MICROCHIROPTERAN BATS TO NOT ONLY ALLOW FOR REGROWTH OR REPAIR OF THE TYMPANIC MEMBRANE AND AUDITORY NERVES--
--BUT IT ACTUALLY IMPROVES HEARING TO THE POINT THAT HUMANS WILL BE ABLE TO HEAR ON ULTRASONIC FREQUENCIES, AND NAVIGATE VIA ECHO-LOCATION.
BIOSONAR.
DR. LANGSTROM, THIS IS PROMISING RESEARCH. BUT HAVE YOUR TEST SUBJECTS ENCOUNTERED ANYTHING IN THE WAY OF ADVERSE SIDE EFFECTS?
SOME MINOR ONES, YES.
BUT WE'RE WORKING VERY HARD TO REMEDY THINGS.

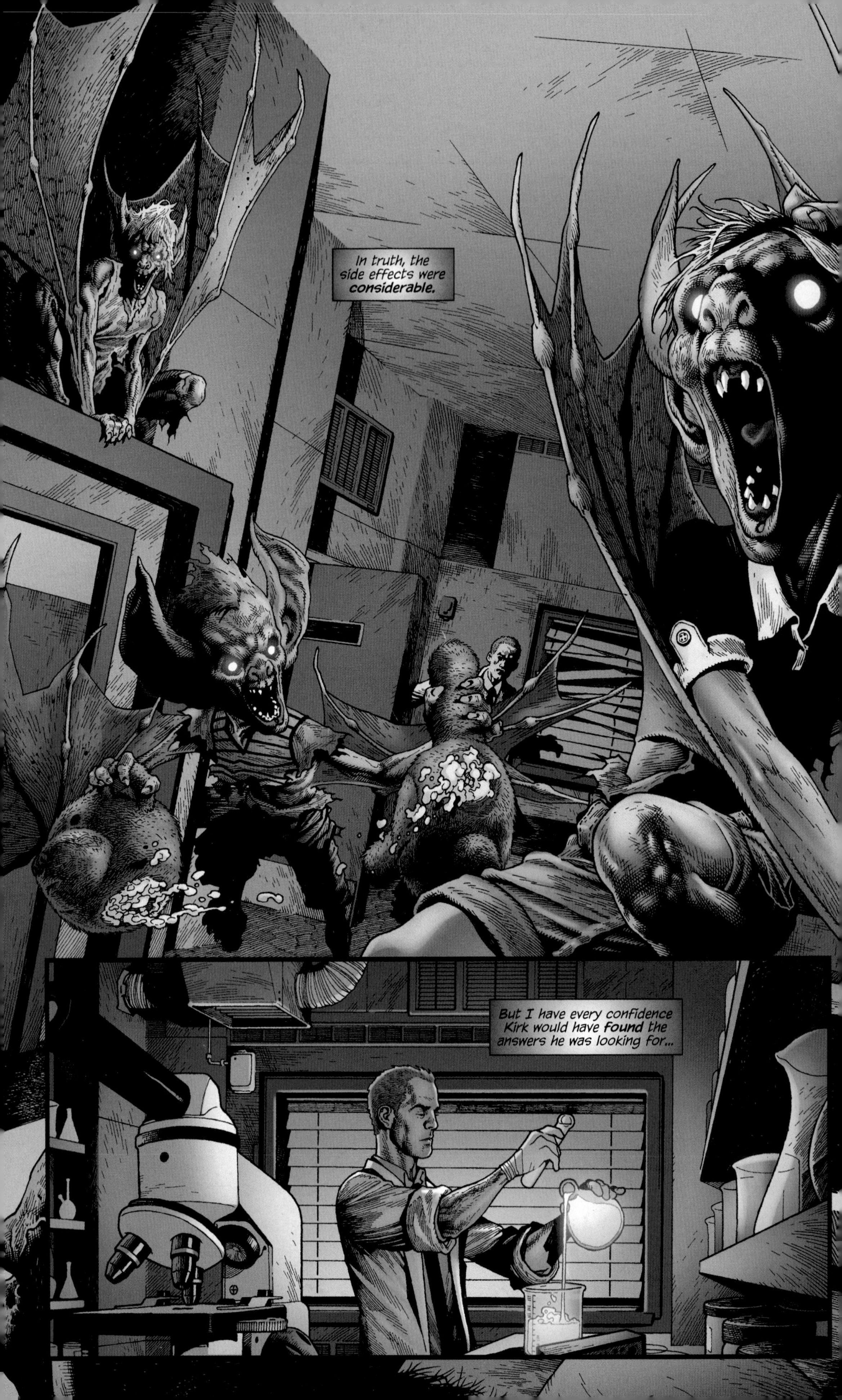
In truth, the side effects were considerable.
But I have every confidence Kirk would have found the answers he was looking for...

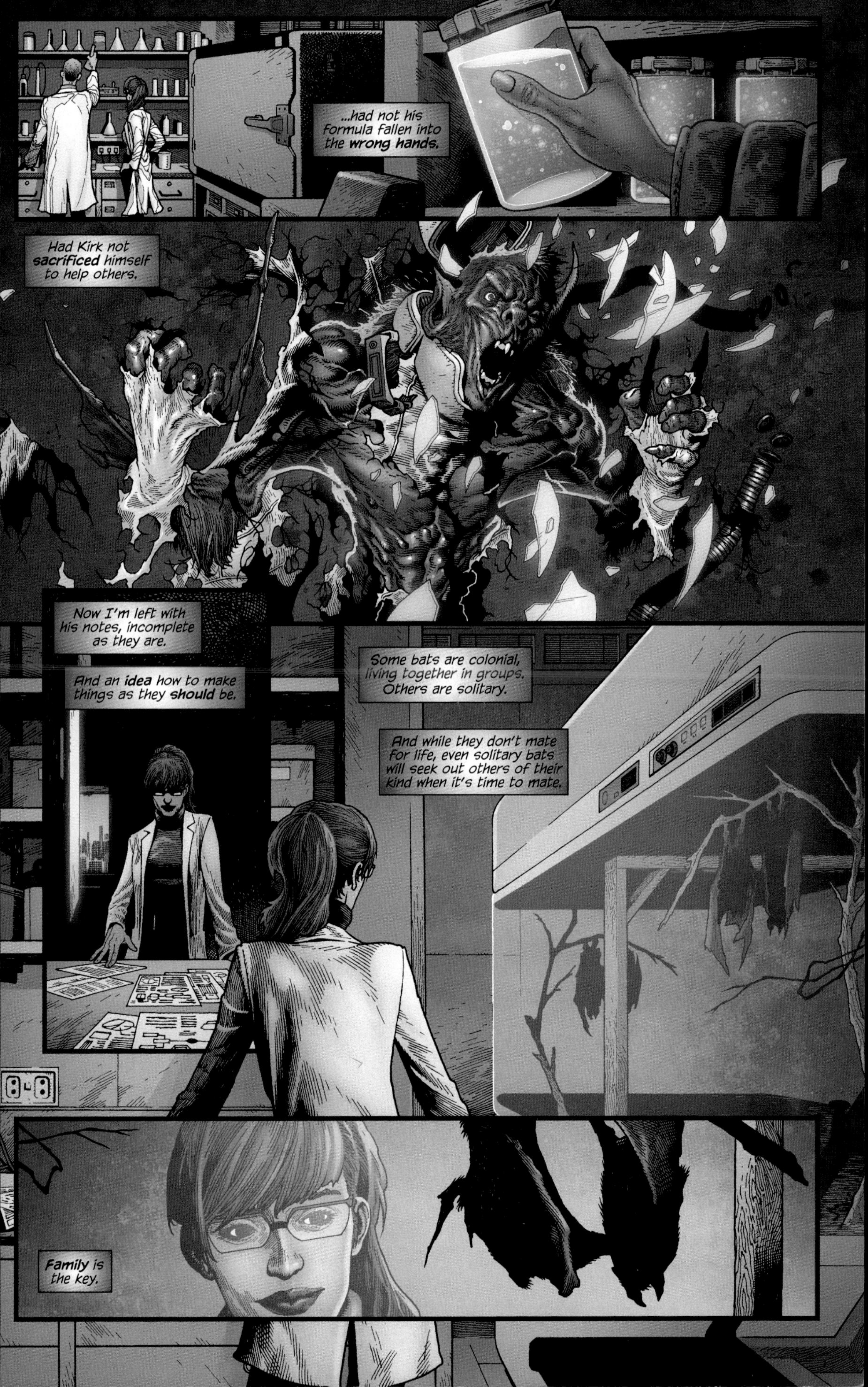
...had not his formula fallen into the wrong hands.
Had Kirk not sacrificed himself to help others.
Now I'm left with his notes, incomplete as they are.
And an idea how to make things as they should be.
Some bats are colonial, living together in groups. Others are solitary.
And while they don't mate for life, even solitary bats will seek out others of their kind when it's time to mate.
Family is the key.

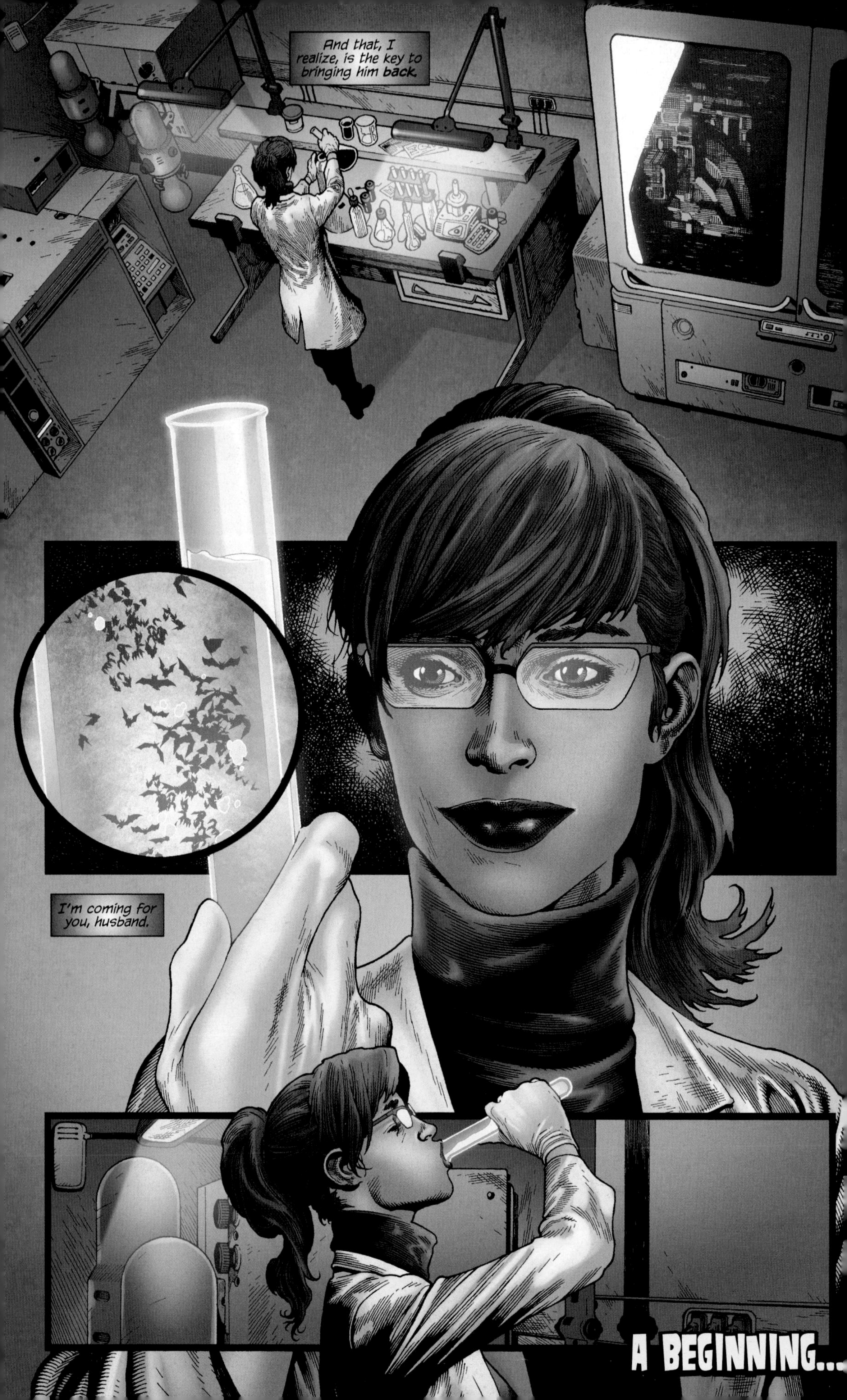
And that, I realize, is the key to bringing him back.
I'm coming for you, husband.
A BEGINNING...

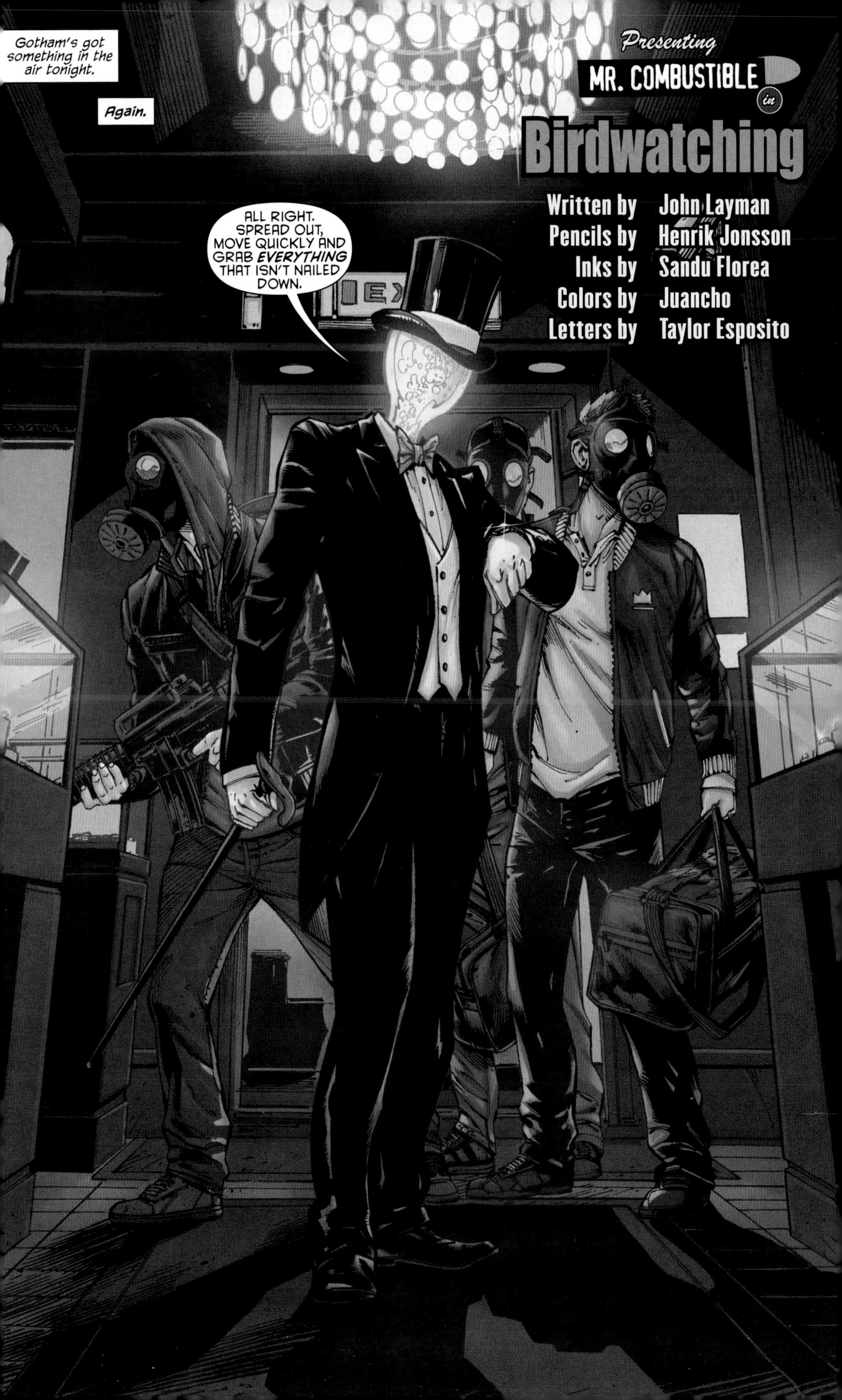

Gotham's got something in the air tonight.
Again.
Presenting
MR. COMBUSTIBLE
in
Birdwatching
Written by John Layman
Pencils by Henrik Jonsson
Inks by Sandu Florea
Colors by Juancho
Letters by Taylor Esposito
ALL RIGHT. SPREAD OUT, MOVE QUICKLY AND GRAB *EVERYTHING* THAT ISN'T NAILED DOWN.

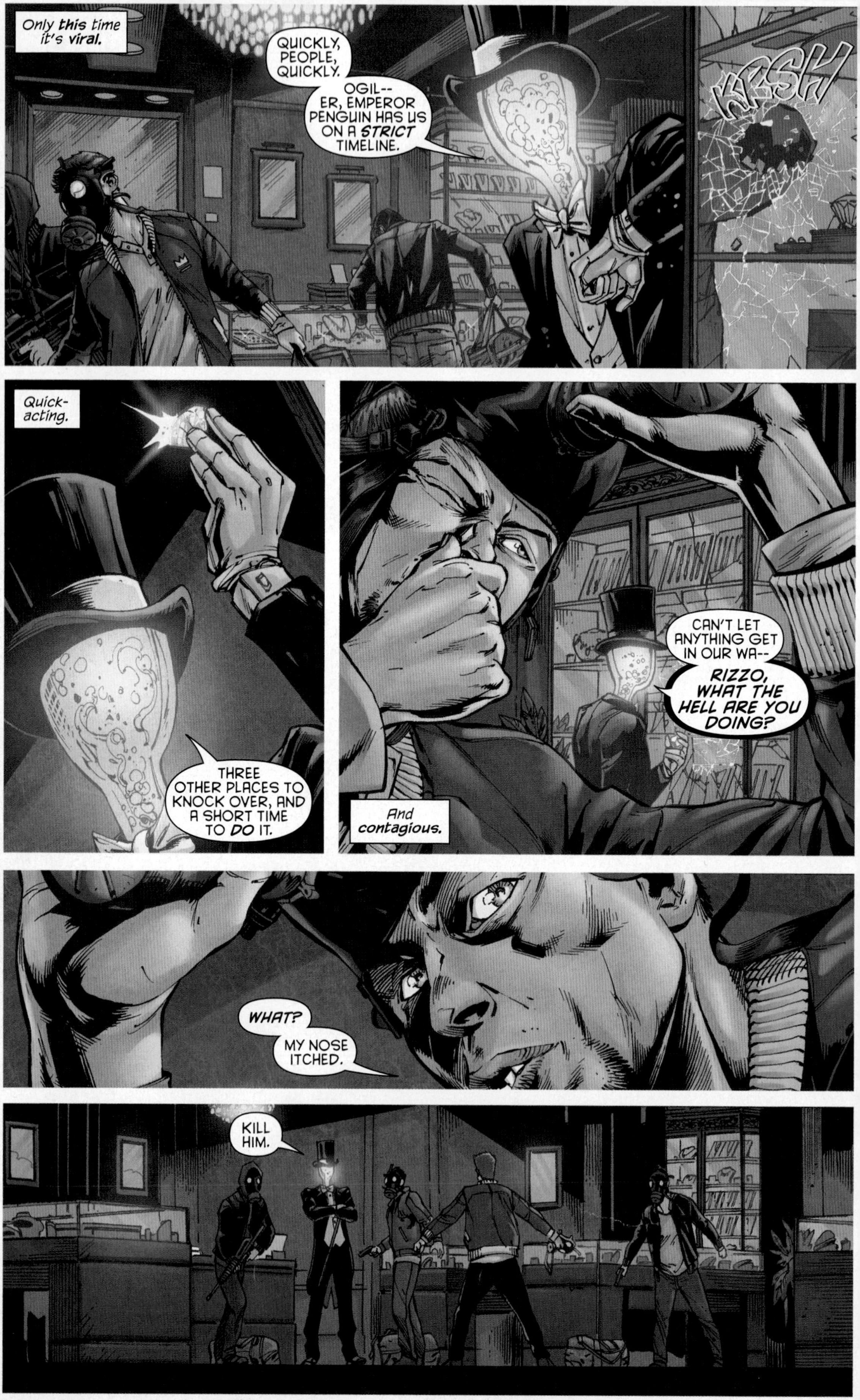
Only this time it's viral.
QUICKLY, PEOPLE, QUICKLY.
OGIL-- ER, EMPEROR PENGUIN HAS US ON A STRICT TIMELINE.
KRSH
Quick-acting.
THREE OTHER PLACES TO KNOCK OVER, AND A SHORT TIME TO DO IT.
CAN'T LET ANYTHING GET IN OUR WA--
RIZZO, WHAT THE HELL ARE YOU DOING?
And contagious.
WHAT?
MY NOSE ITCHED.
KILL HIM.

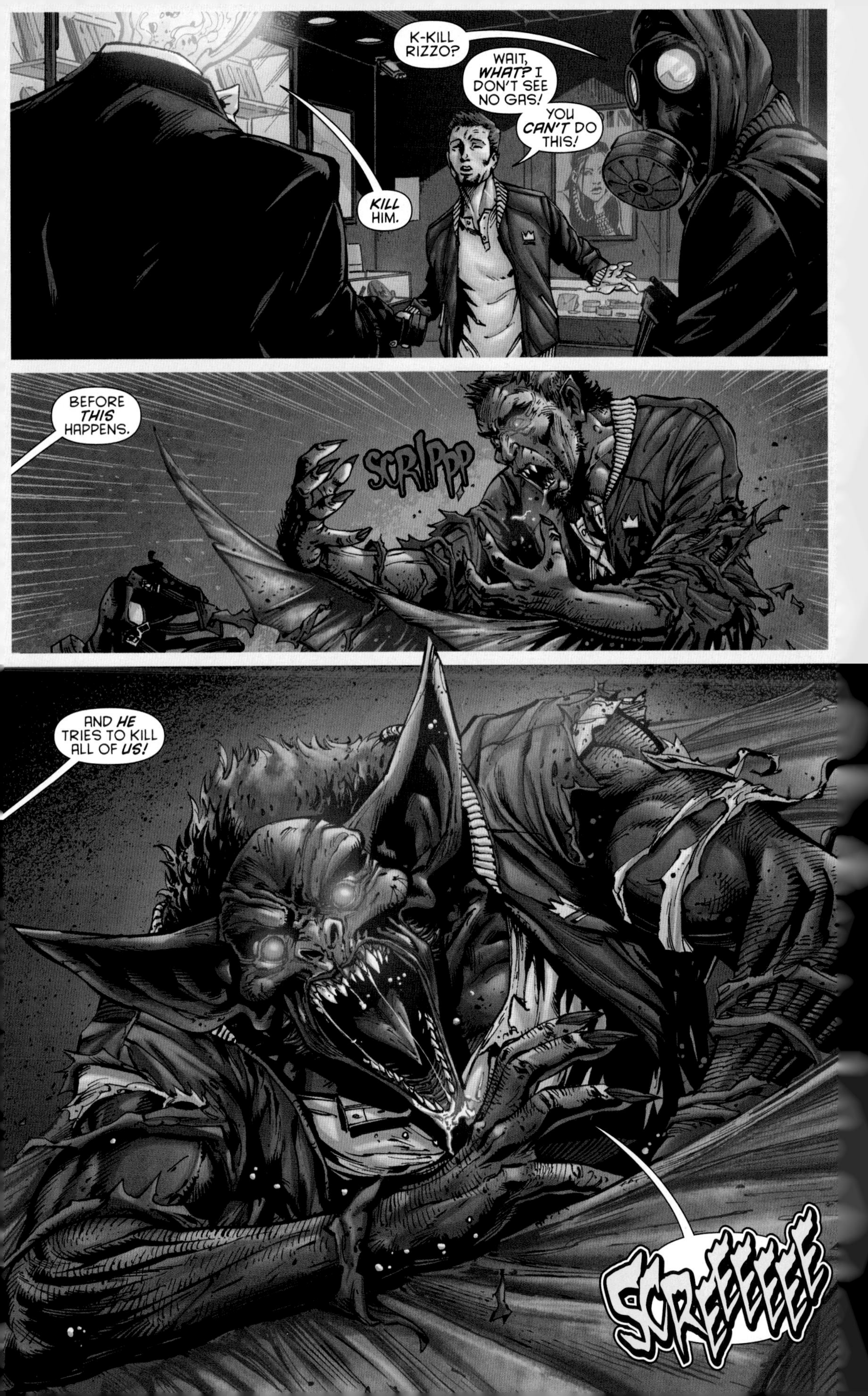
K-KILL RIZZO?
WAIT, WHAT? I DON'T SEE NO GAS!
YOU CAN'T DO THIS!
KILL HIM.
BEFORE THIS HAPPENS.
SCRIPPP
AND HE TRIES TO KILL ALL OF US!
SCREEEEEE

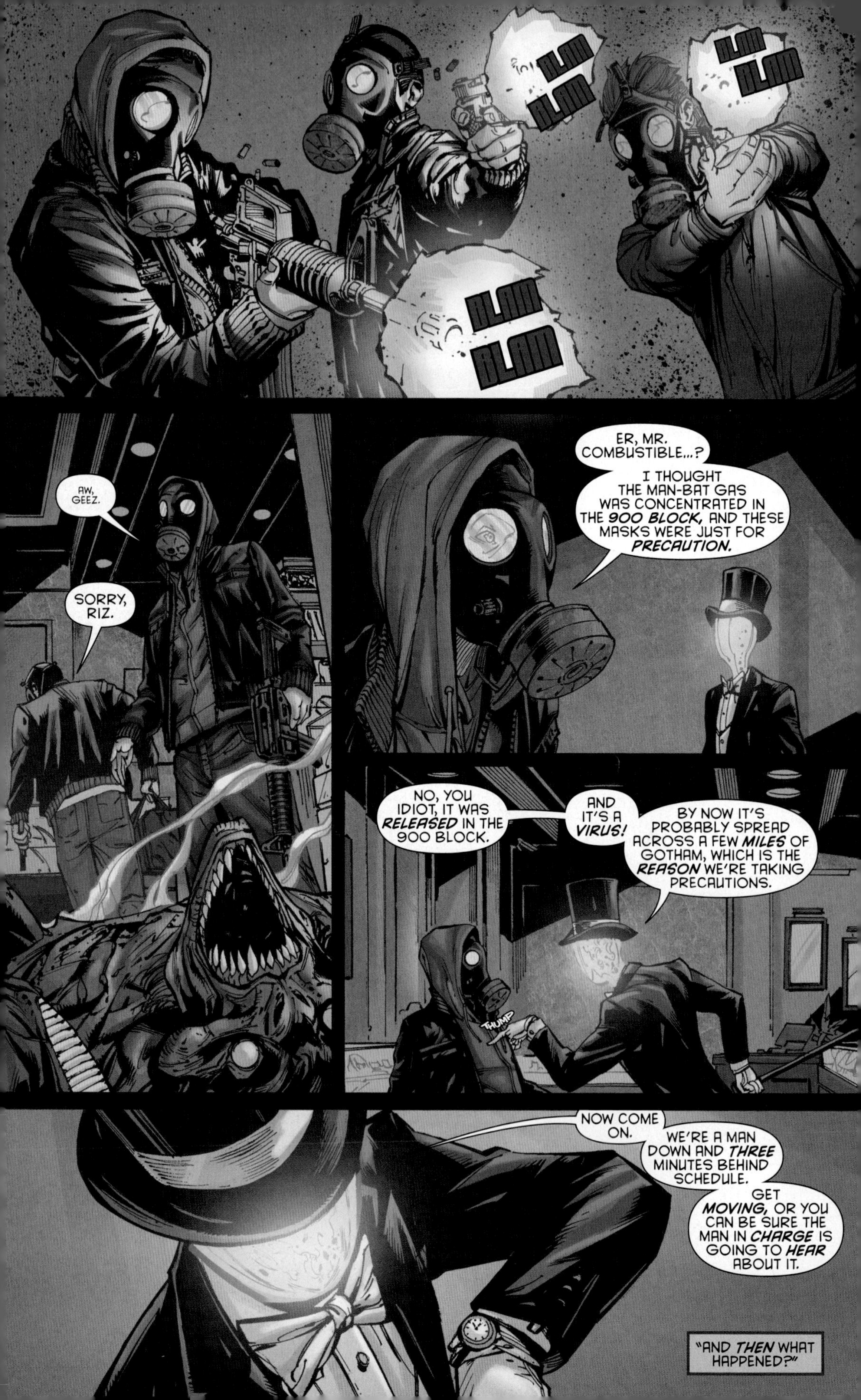
BLAM BLAM
BLAM BLAM
BLAM BLAM
AW, GEEZ.
SORRY, RIZ.
ER, MR. COMBUSTIBLE...?
I THOUGHT THE MAN-BAT GAS WAS CONCENTRATED IN THE 900 BLOCK, AND THESE MASKS WERE JUST FOR PRECAUTION.
NO, YOU IDIOT, IT WAS RELEASED IN THE 900 BLOCK.
AND IT'S A VIRUS!
BY NOW IT'S PROBABLY SPREAD ACROSS A FEW MILES OF GOTHAM, WHICH IS THE REASON WE'RE TAKING PRECAUTIONS.
THUMP
NOW COME ON.
WE'RE A MAN DOWN AND THREE MINUTES BEHIND SCHEDULE.
GET MOVING, OR YOU CAN BE SURE THE MAN IN CHARGE IS GOING TO HEAR ABOUT IT.
"AND THEN WHAT HAPPENED?"

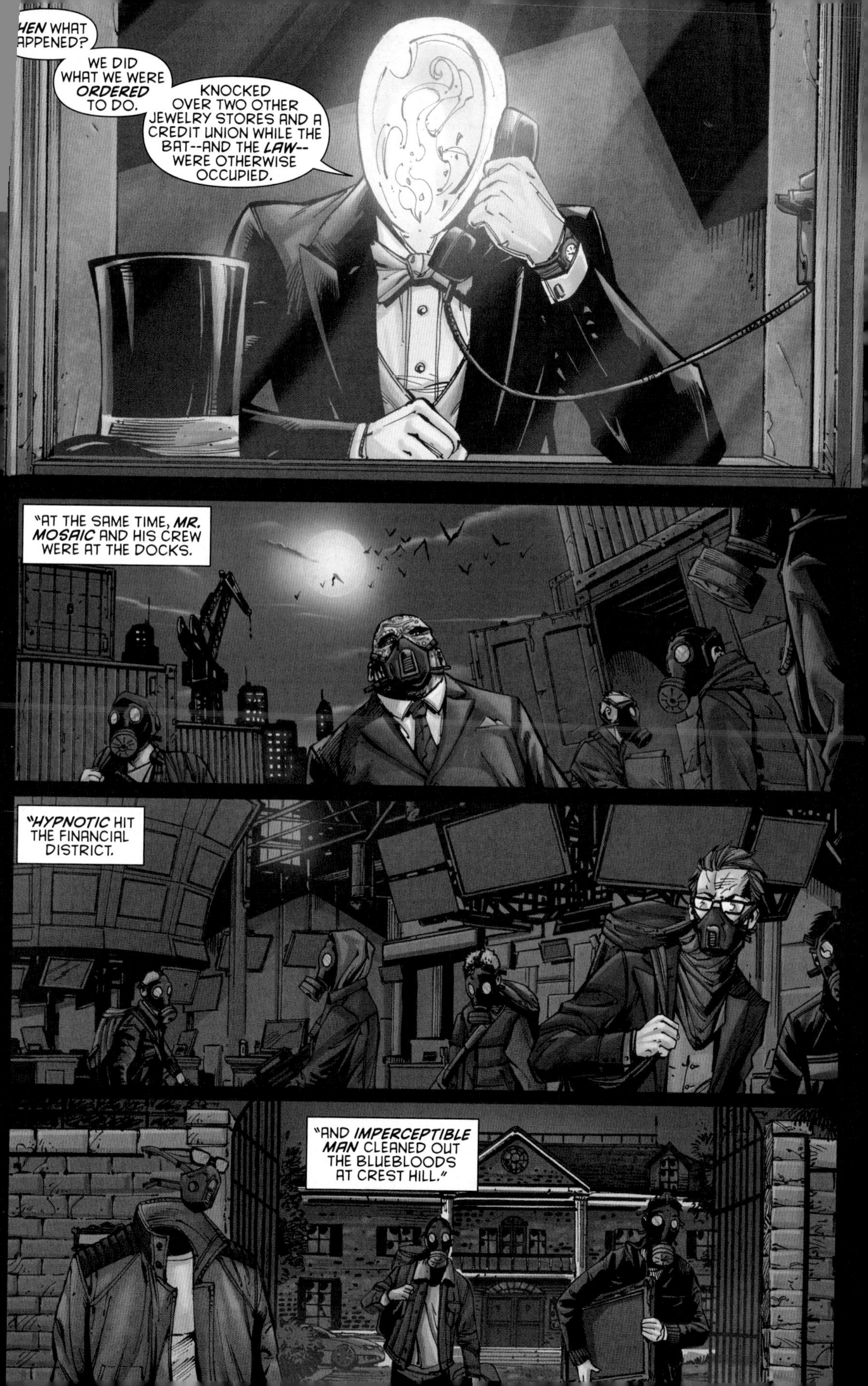
HEN WHAT APPENED?
WE DID WHAT WE WERE ORDERED TO DO.
KNOCKED OVER TWO OTHER JEWELRY STORES AND A CREDIT UNION WHILE THE BAT--AND THE LAW--WERE OTHERWISE OCCUPIED.
"AT THE SAME TIME, MR. MOSAIC AND HIS CREW WERE AT THE DOCKS.
"HYPNOTIC HIT THE FINANCIAL DISTRICT.
"AND IMPERCEPTIBLE MAN CLEANED OUT THE BLUEBLOODS AT CREST HILL."

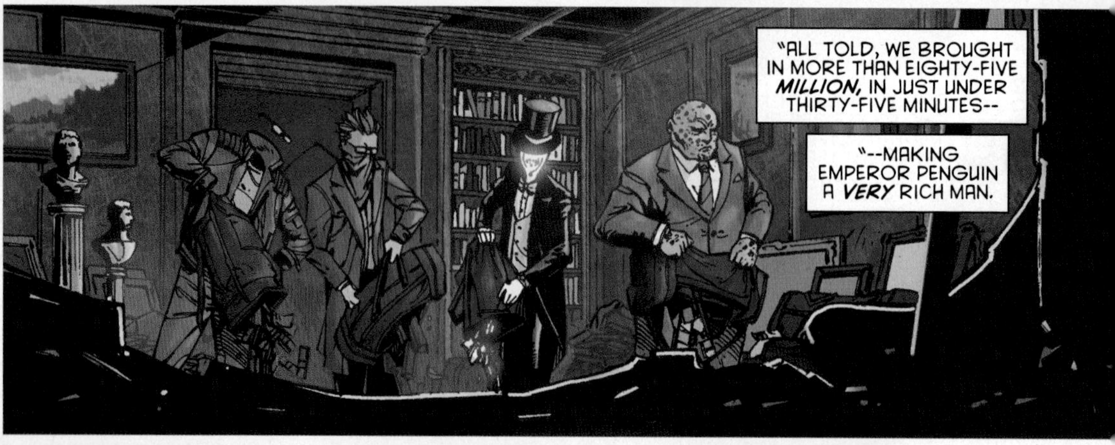
"ALL TOLD, WE BROUGHT IN MORE THAN EIGHTY-FIVE *MILLION,* IN JUST UNDER THIRTY-FIVE MINUTES--
"--MAKING EMPEROR PENGUIN A *VERY* RICH MAN.

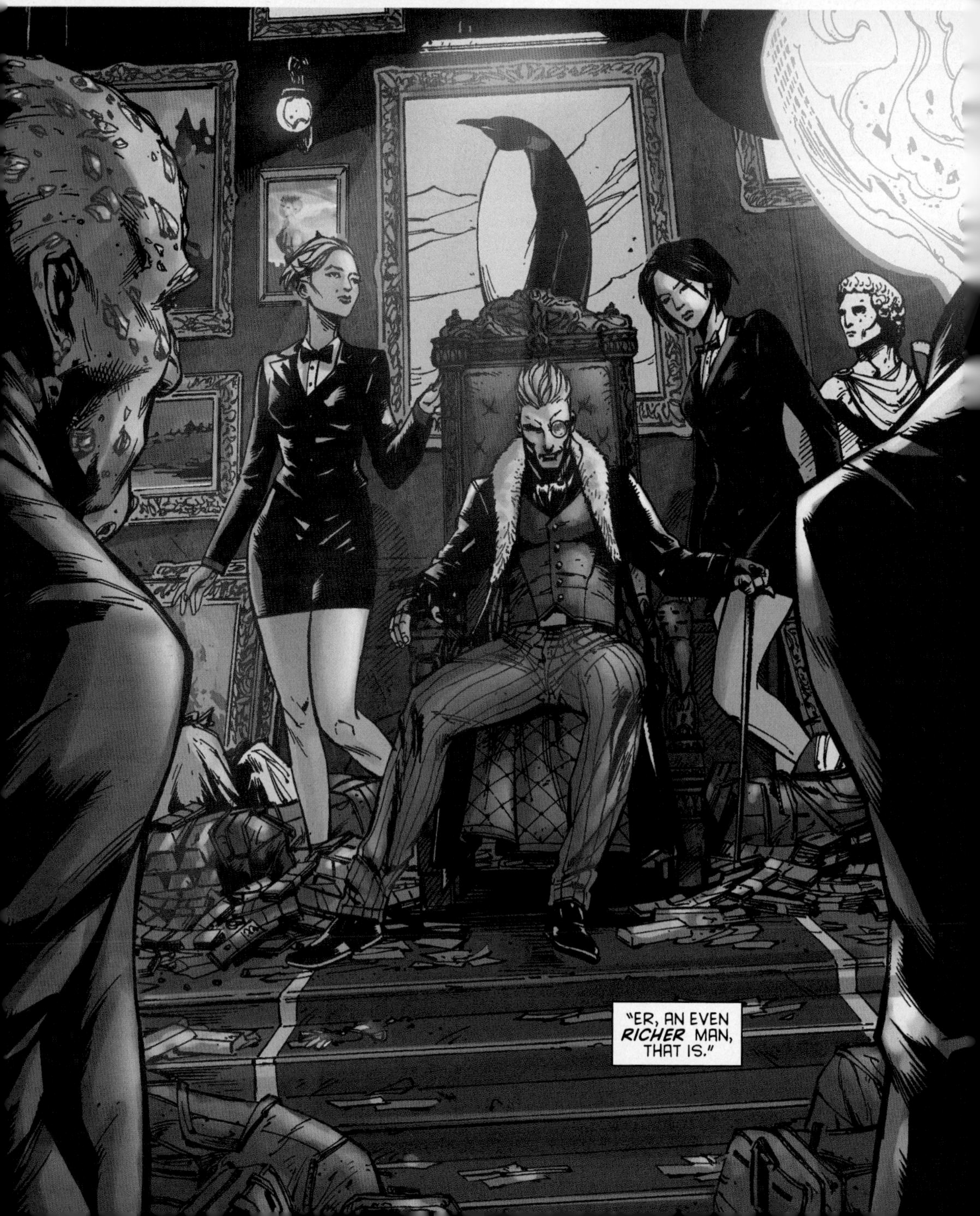
"ER, AN EVEN *RICHER* MAN, THAT IS."

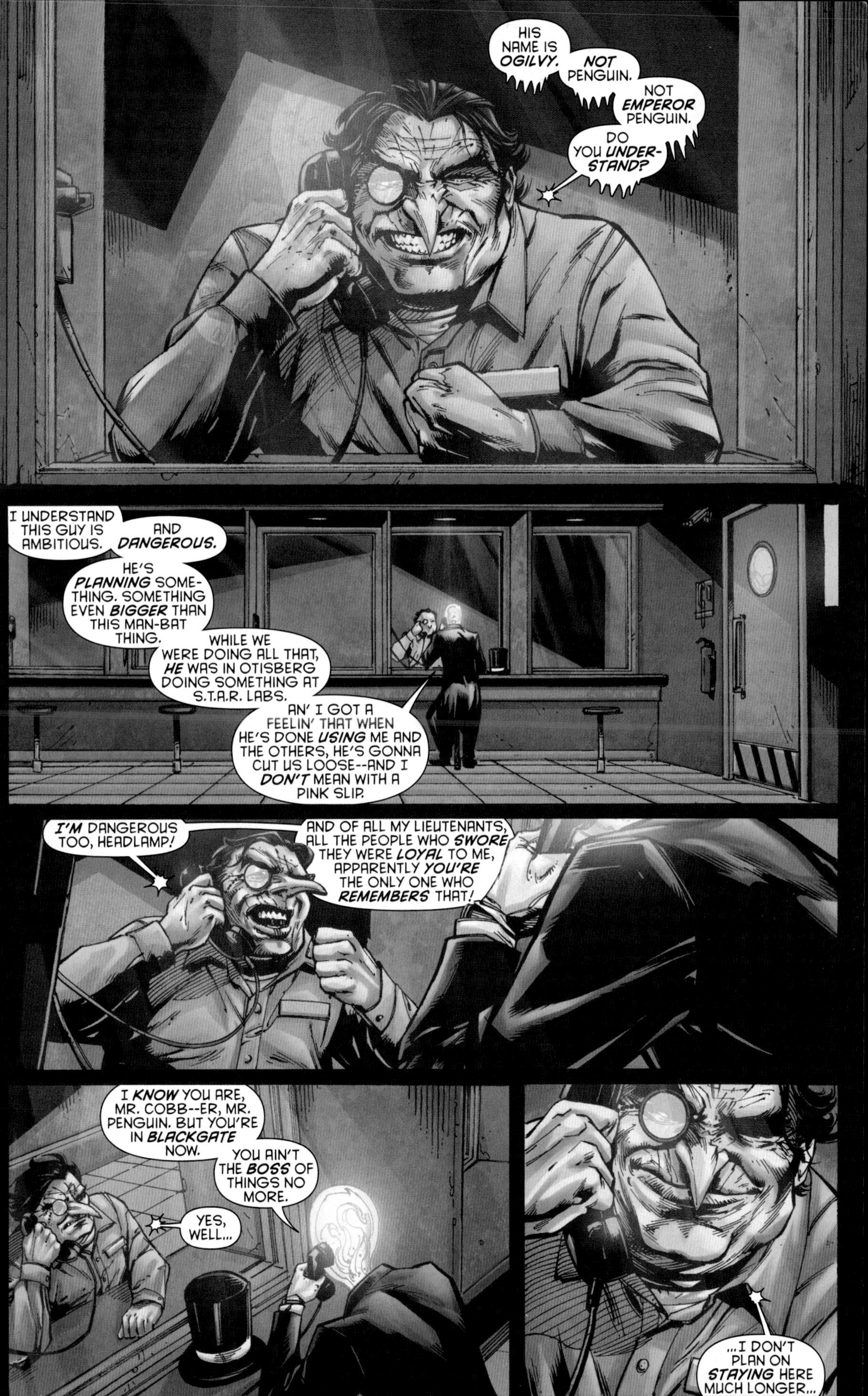
HIS NAME IS OGILVY.
NOT PENGUIN.
NOT EMPEROR PENGUIN.
DO YOU UNDER-STAND?
I UNDERSTAND THIS GUY IS AMBITIOUS.
AND DANGEROUS.
HE'S PLANNING SOME-THING. SOMETHING EVEN BIGGER THAN THIS MAN-BAT THING.
WHILE WE WERE DOING ALL THAT, HE WAS IN OTISBERG DOING SOMETHING AT S.T.A.R. LABS.
AN' I GOT A FEELIN' THAT WHEN HE'S DONE USING ME AND THE OTHERS, HE'S GONNA CUT US LOOSE--AND I DON'T MEAN WITH A PINK SLIP.
I'M DANGEROUS TOO, HEADLAMP!
AND OF ALL MY LIEUTENANTS, ALL THE PEOPLE WHO SWORE THEY WERE LOYAL TO ME, APPARENTLY YOU'RE THE ONLY ONE WHO REMEMBERS THAT!
I KNOW YOU ARE, MR. COBB--ER, MR. PENGUIN. BUT YOU'RE IN BLACKGATE NOW.
YOU AIN'T THE BOSS OF THINGS NO MORE.
YES, WELL...
...I DON'T PLAN ON STAYING HERE MUCH LONGER...

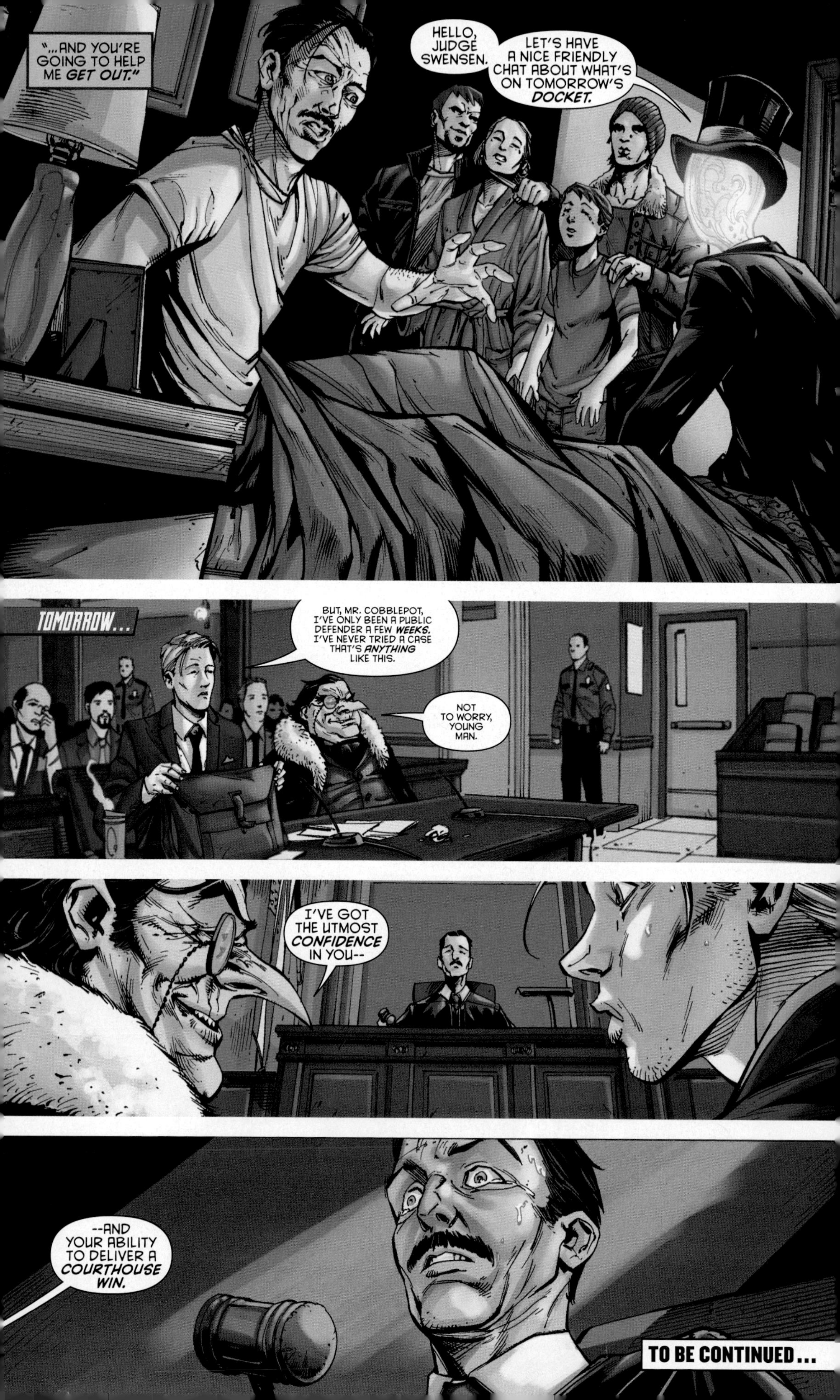
"...AND YOU'RE GOING TO HELP ME GET OUT."
HELLO, JUDGE SWENSEN.
LET'S HAVE A NICE FRIENDLY CHAT ABOUT WHAT'S ON TOMORROW'S DOCKET.
TOMORROW...
BUT, MR. COBBLEPOT, I'VE ONLY BEEN A PUBLIC DEFENDER A FEW WEEKS. I'VE NEVER TRIED A CASE THAT'S ANYTHING LIKE THIS.
NOT TO WORRY, YOUNG MAN.
I'VE GOT THE UTMOST CONFIDENCE IN YOU--
--AND YOUR ABILITY TO DELIVER A COURTHOUSE WIN.
TO BE CONTINUED...

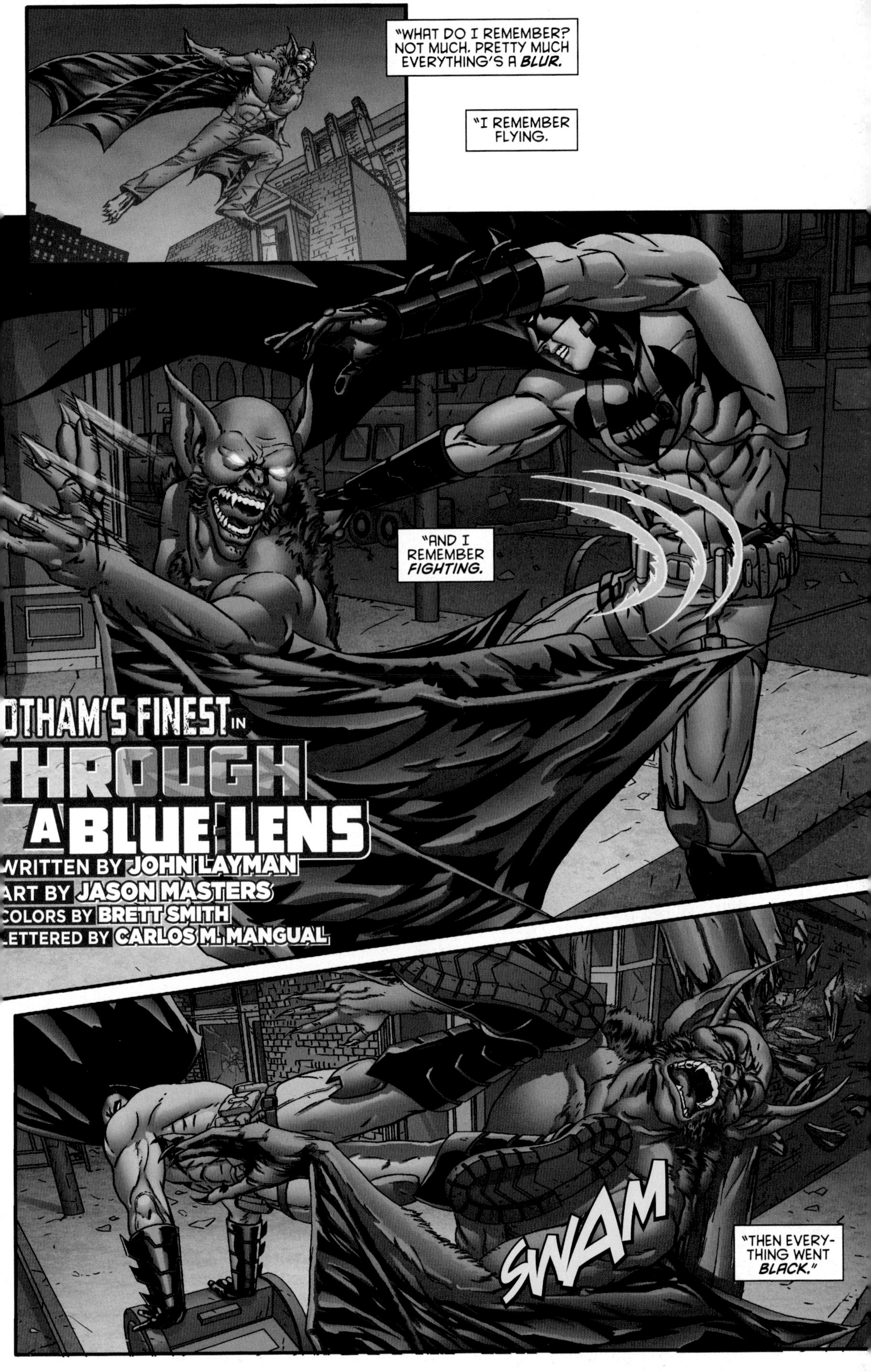
"WHAT DO I REMEMBER? NOT MUCH. PRETTY MUCH EVERYTHING'S A BLUR.
"I REMEMBER FLYING.
"AND I REMEMBER FIGHTING.
OTHAM'S FINEST IN
THROUGH A BLUE LENS
WRITTEN BY JOHN LAYMAN
ART BY JASON MASTERS
COLORS BY BRETT SMITH
LETTERED BY CARLOS M. MANGUAL
SWAM
"THEN EVERY-THING WENT BLACK."

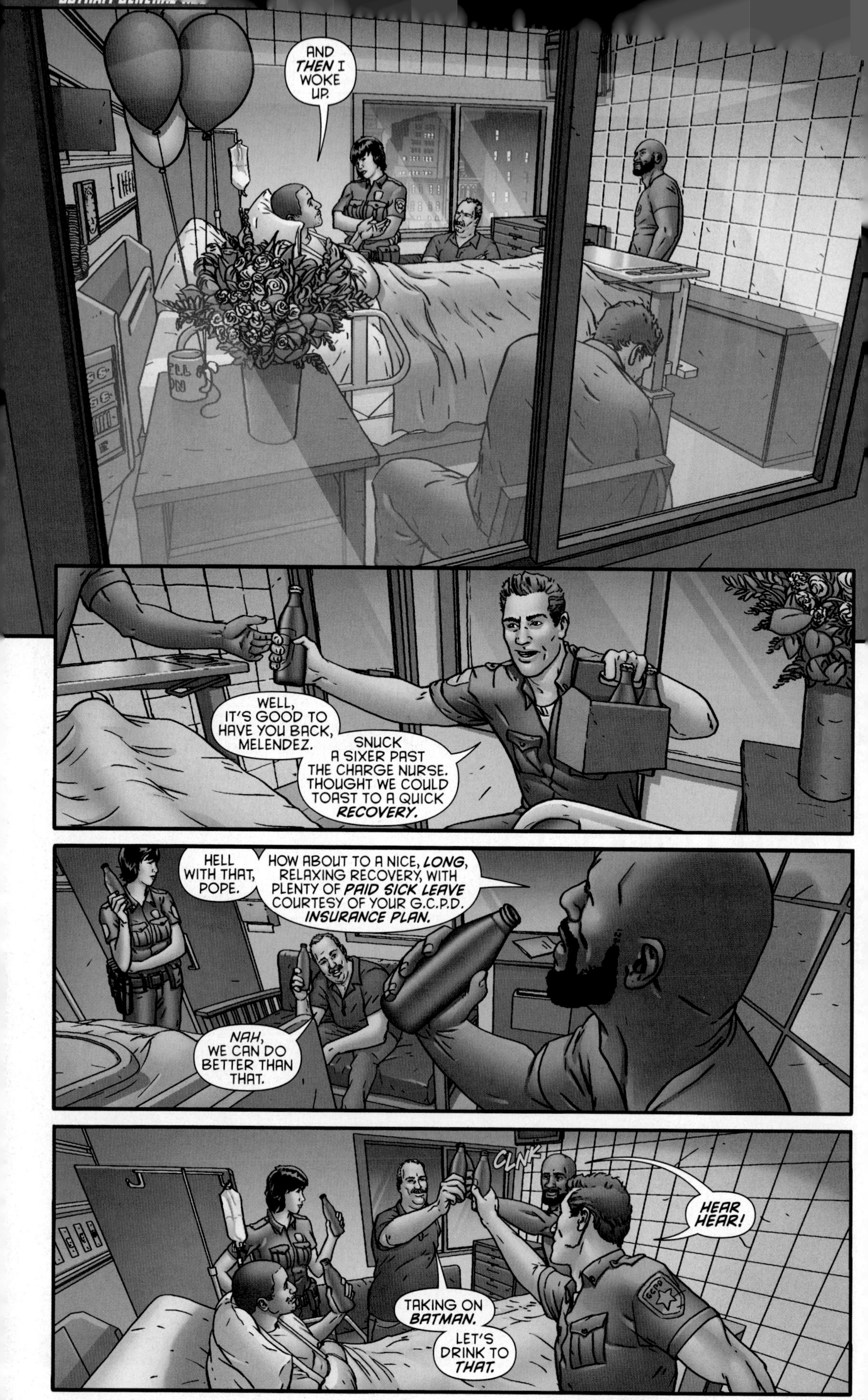
AND THEN I WOKE UP.
WELL, IT'S GOOD TO HAVE YOU BACK, MELENDEZ.
SNUCK A SIXER PAST THE CHARGE NURSE. THOUGHT WE COULD TOAST TO A QUICK RECOVERY.
HELL WITH THAT, POPE.
HOW ABOUT TO A NICE, LONG, RELAXING RECOVERY, WITH PLENTY OF PAID SICK LEAVE COURTESY OF YOUR G.C.P.D. INSURANCE PLAN.
NAH, WE CAN DO BETTER THAN THAT.
CLNK
HEAR HEAR!
TAKING ON BATMAN.
LET'S DRINK TO THAT.

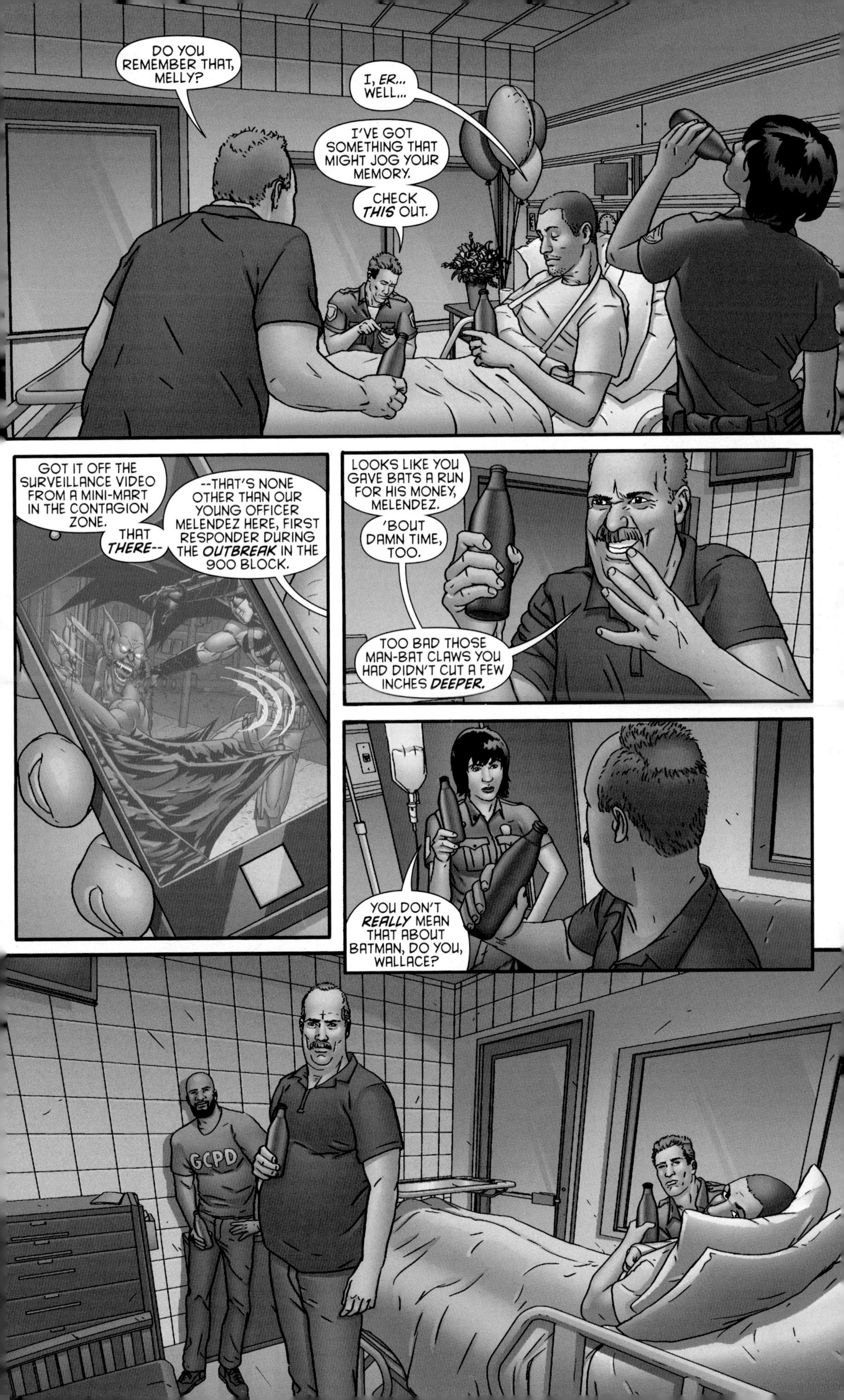
DO YOU REMEMBER THAT, MELLY?
I, ER... WELL...
I'VE GOT SOMETHING THAT MIGHT JOG YOUR MEMORY.
CHECK THIS OUT.
GOT IT OFF THE SURVEILLANCE VIDEO FROM A MINI-MART IN THE CONTAGION ZONE.
THAT THERE--
--THAT'S NONE OTHER THAN OUR YOUNG OFFICER MELENDEZ HERE, FIRST RESPONDER DURING THE OUTBREAK IN THE 900 BLOCK.
LOOKS LIKE YOU GAVE BATS A RUN FOR HIS MONEY, MELENDEZ.
'BOUT DAMN TIME, TOO.
TOO BAD THOSE MAN-BAT CLAWS YOU HAD DIDN'T CUT A FEW INCHES DEEPER.
YOU DON'T REALLY MEAN THAT ABOUT BATMAN, DO YOU, WALLACE?
GCPD

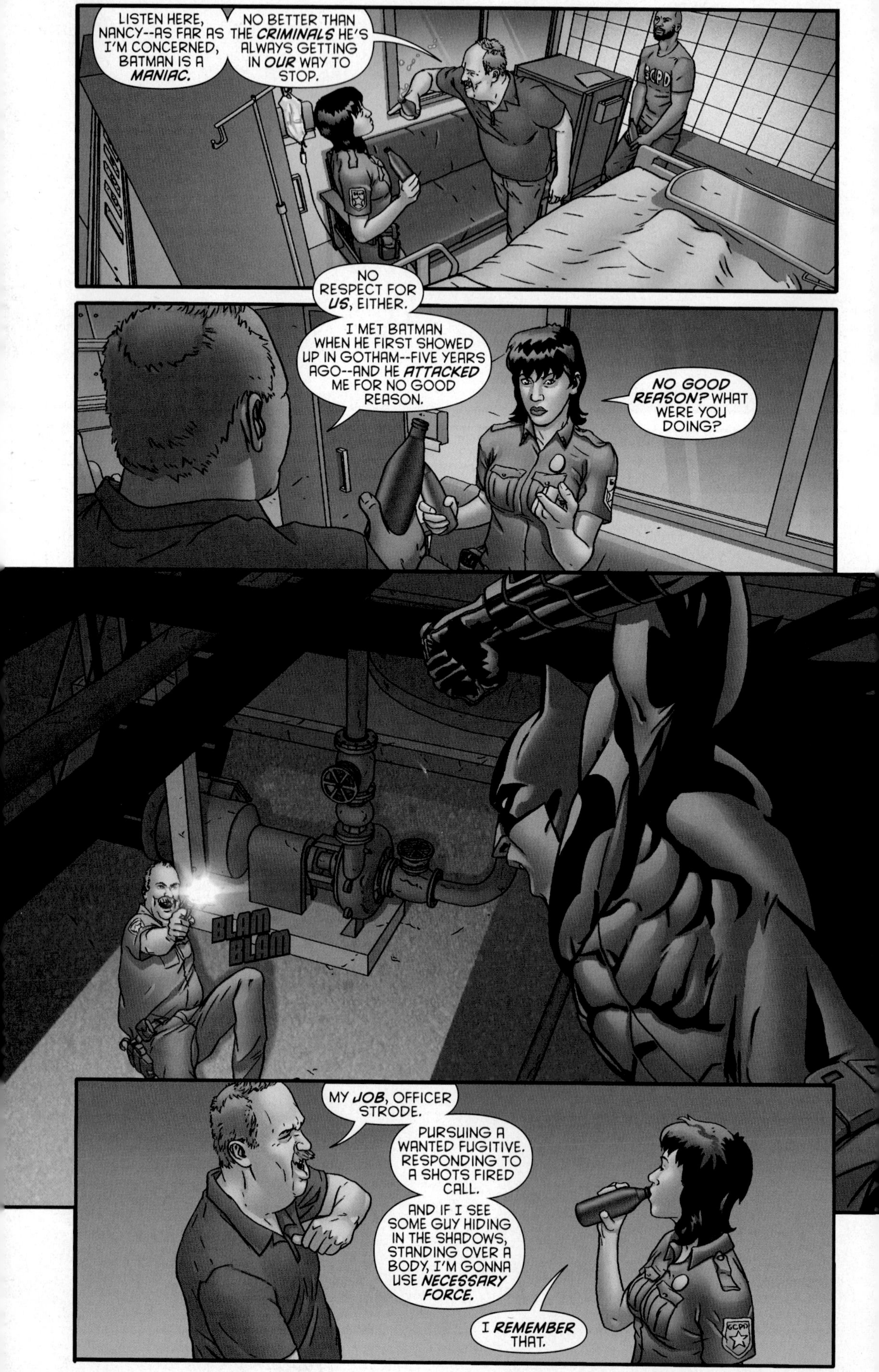
LISTEN HERE, NANCY--AS FAR AS I'M CONCERNED, BATMAN IS A *MANIAC.*
NO BETTER THAN THE *CRIMINALS* HE'S ALWAYS GETTING IN *OUR* WAY TO STOP.
GCPD
NO RESPECT FOR *US*, EITHER.
I MET BATMAN WHEN HE FIRST SHOWED UP IN GOTHAM--FIVE YEARS AGO--AND HE *ATTACKED* ME FOR NO GOOD REASON.
NO GOOD REASON? WHAT WERE YOU DOING?
BLAM
BLAM
MY *JOB*, OFFICER STRODE.
PURSUING A WANTED FUGITIVE. RESPONDING TO A SHOTS FIRED CALL.
AND IF I SEE SOME GUY HIDING IN THE SHADOWS, STANDING OVER A BODY, I'M GONNA USE *NECESSARY FORCE.*
I *REMEMBER* THAT.
GCPD

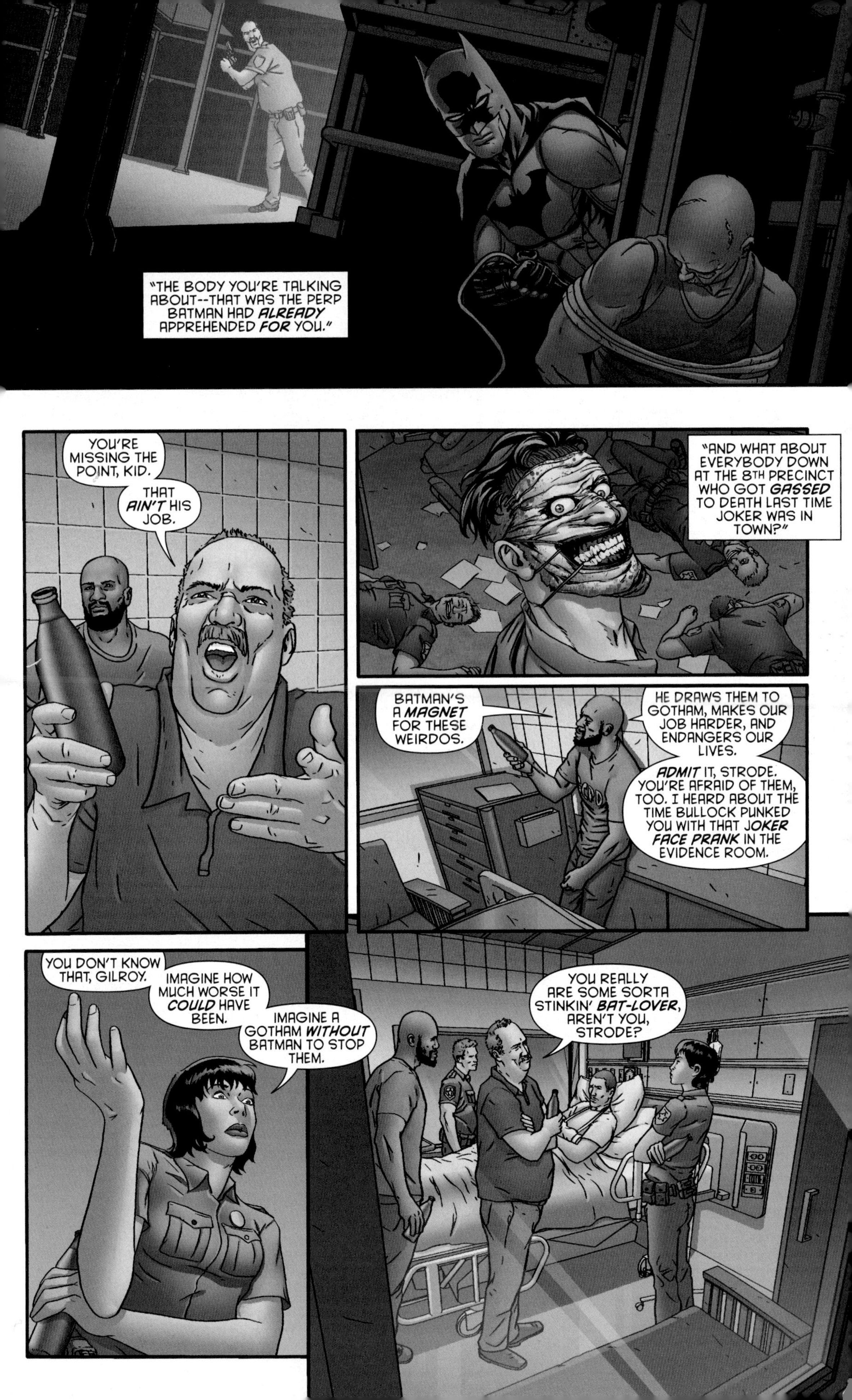
"THE BODY YOU'RE TALKING ABOUT--THAT WAS THE PERP BATMAN HAD ALREADY APPREHENDED FOR YOU."
YOU'RE MISSING THE POINT, KID.
THAT AIN'T HIS JOB.
"AND WHAT ABOUT EVERYBODY DOWN AT THE 8TH PRECINCT WHO GOT GASSED TO DEATH LAST TIME JOKER WAS IN TOWN?"
BATMAN'S A MAGNET FOR THESE WEIRDOS.
HE DRAWS THEM TO GOTHAM, MAKES OUR JOB HARDER, AND ENDANGERS OUR LIVES.
ADMIT IT, STRODE. YOU'RE AFRAID OF THEM, TOO. I HEARD ABOUT THE TIME BULLOCK PUNKED YOU WITH THAT JOKER FACE PRANK IN THE EVIDENCE ROOM.
YOU DON'T KNOW THAT, GILROY.
IMAGINE HOW MUCH WORSE IT COULD HAVE BEEN.
IMAGINE A GOTHAM WITHOUT BATMAN TO STOP THEM.
YOU REALLY ARE SOME SORTA STINKIN' BAT-LOVER, AREN'T YOU, STRODE?

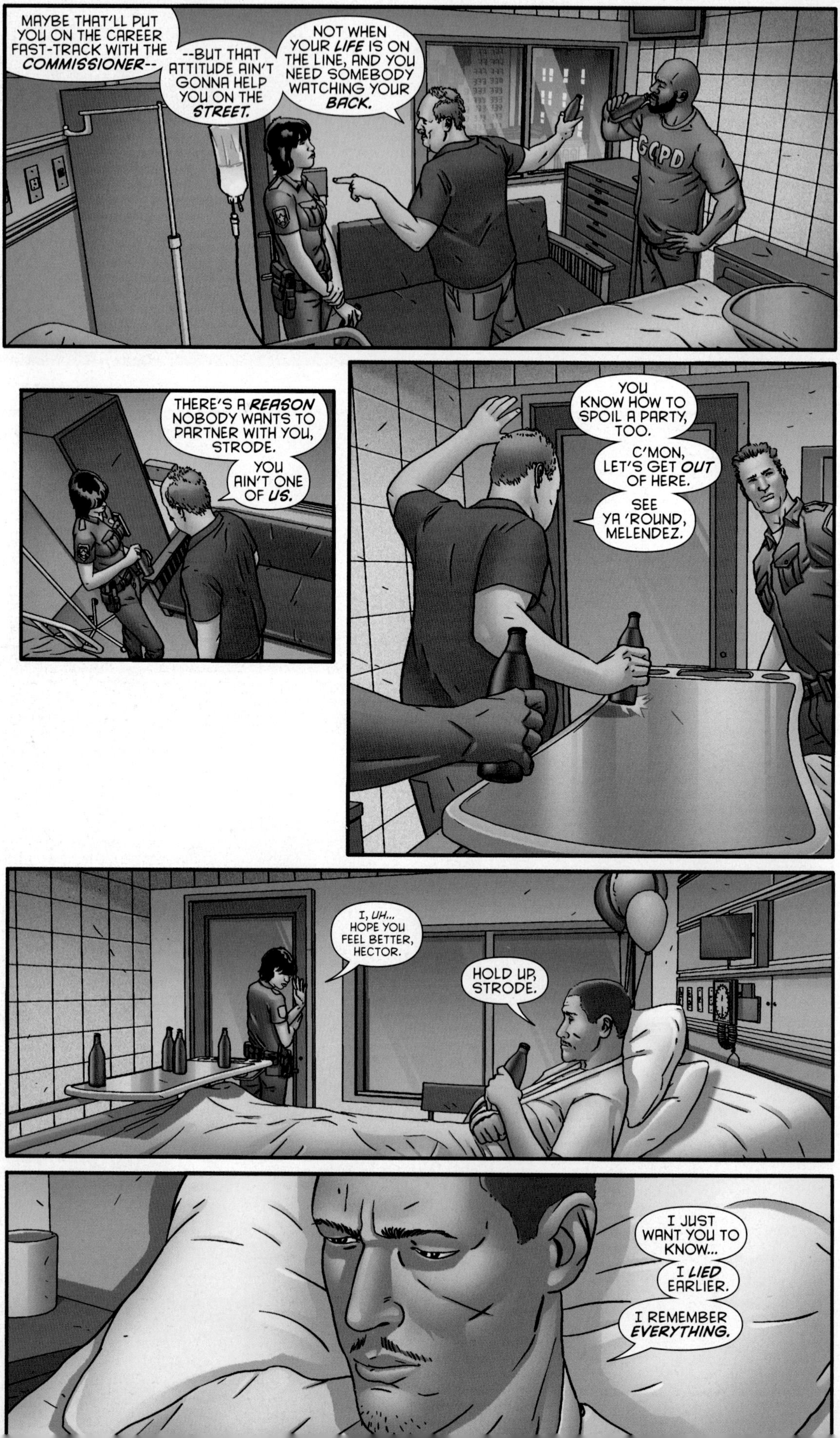
MAYBE THAT'LL PUT YOU ON THE CAREER FAST-TRACK WITH THE COMMISSIONER--
--BUT THAT ATTITUDE AIN'T GONNA HELP YOU ON THE STREET.
NOT WHEN YOUR LIFE IS ON THE LINE, AND YOU NEED SOMEBODY WATCHING YOUR BACK.
GCPD
THERE'S A REASON NOBODY WANTS TO PARTNER WITH YOU, STRODE.
YOU AIN'T ONE OF US.
YOU KNOW HOW TO SPOIL A PARTY, TOO.
C'MON, LET'S GET OUT OF HERE.
SEE YA 'ROUND, MELENDEZ.
I, UH... HOPE YOU FEEL BETTER, HECTOR.
HOLD UP, STRODE.
I JUST WANT YOU TO KNOW...
I LIED EARLIER.
I REMEMBER EVERYTHING.

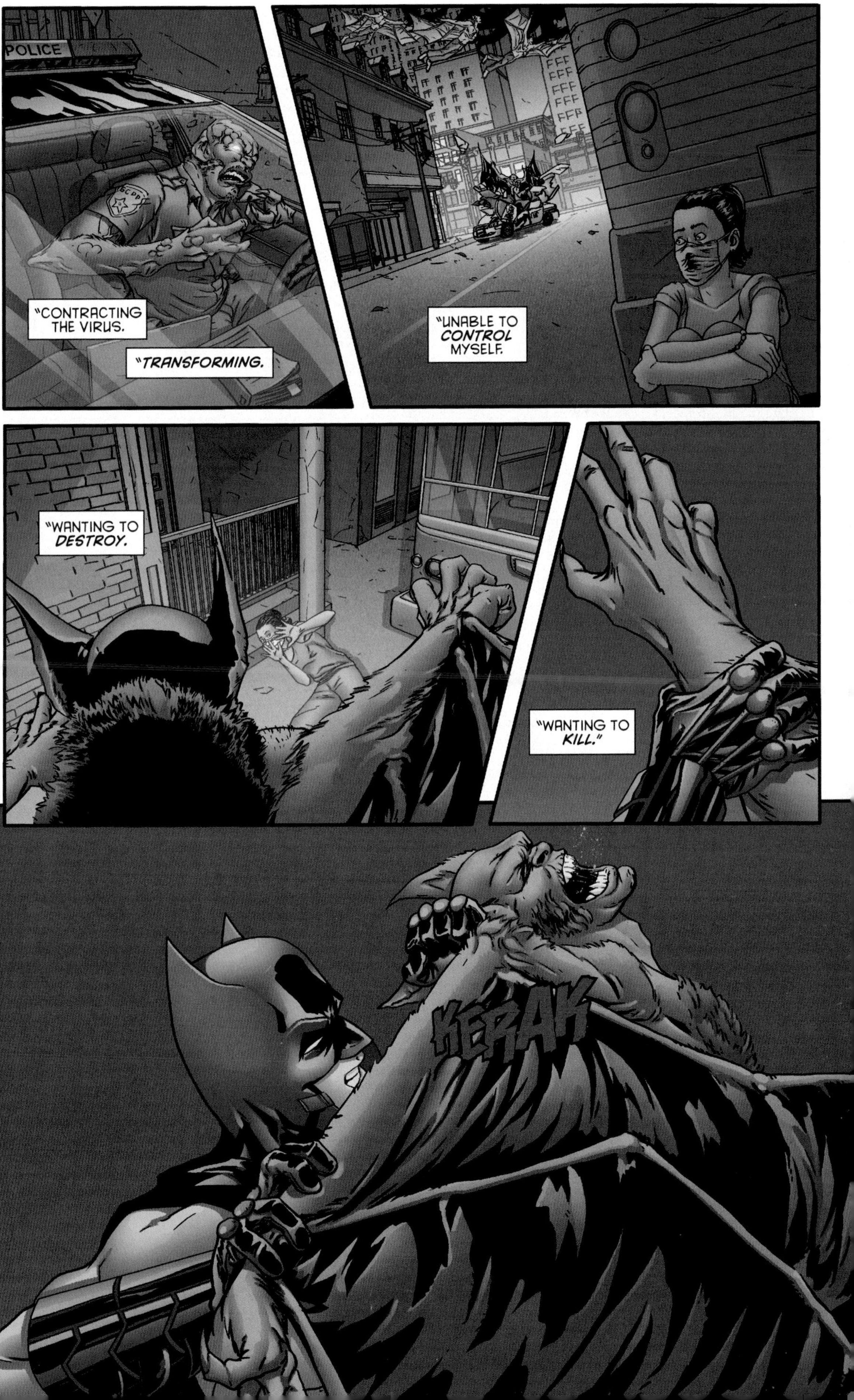
POLICE
"CONTRACTING THE VIRUS.
"TRANSFORMING.
"UNABLE TO CONTROL MYSELF.
"WANTING TO DESTROY.
"WANTING TO KILL."
KERAK

THERE WAS ONE LADY... SHE HADN'T *CHANGED* YET, HADN'T CONTRACTED THE VIRUS--

--AND IF *BATMAN* HADN'T BEEN THERE TO *STOP* ME--

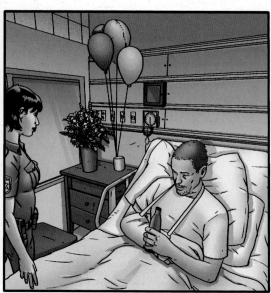

SOME OF THE *OTHERS*, THEY DON'T UNDERSTAND. AND MAYBE THEY NEVER WILL.

BUT WHEN I GET *OUT* OF HERE, STRODE, *I'D* BE WILLING TO PARTNER UP WITH YOU.

YOU MIGHT WANT TO RETHINK THAT. YOU HEARD WALLACE.

YOU PARTNER UP WITH *ME*, WHO'S GONNA WATCH *OUR* BACKS?

THAT ONE'S EASY, STRODE.

BATMAN.

END

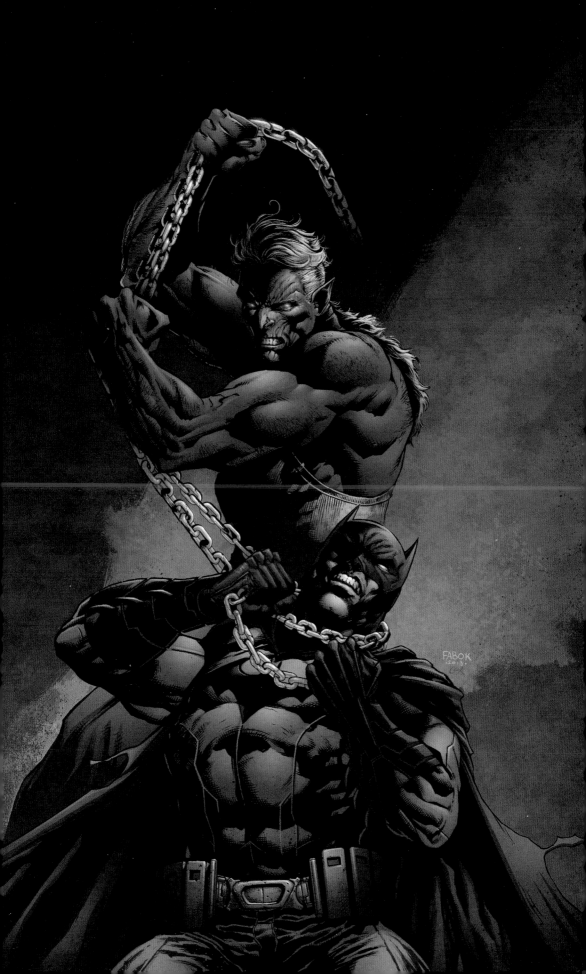

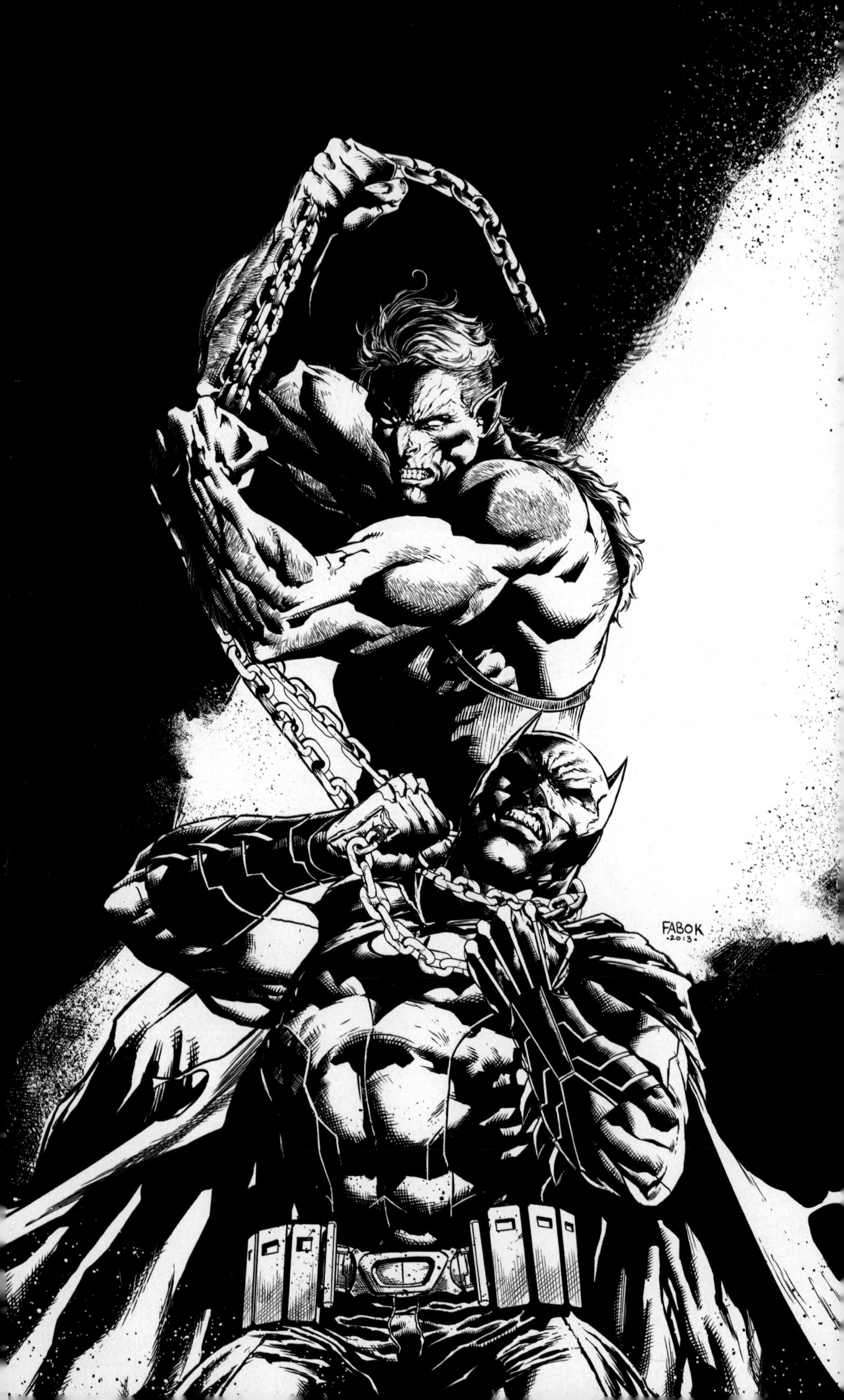
FABOK
·2013·

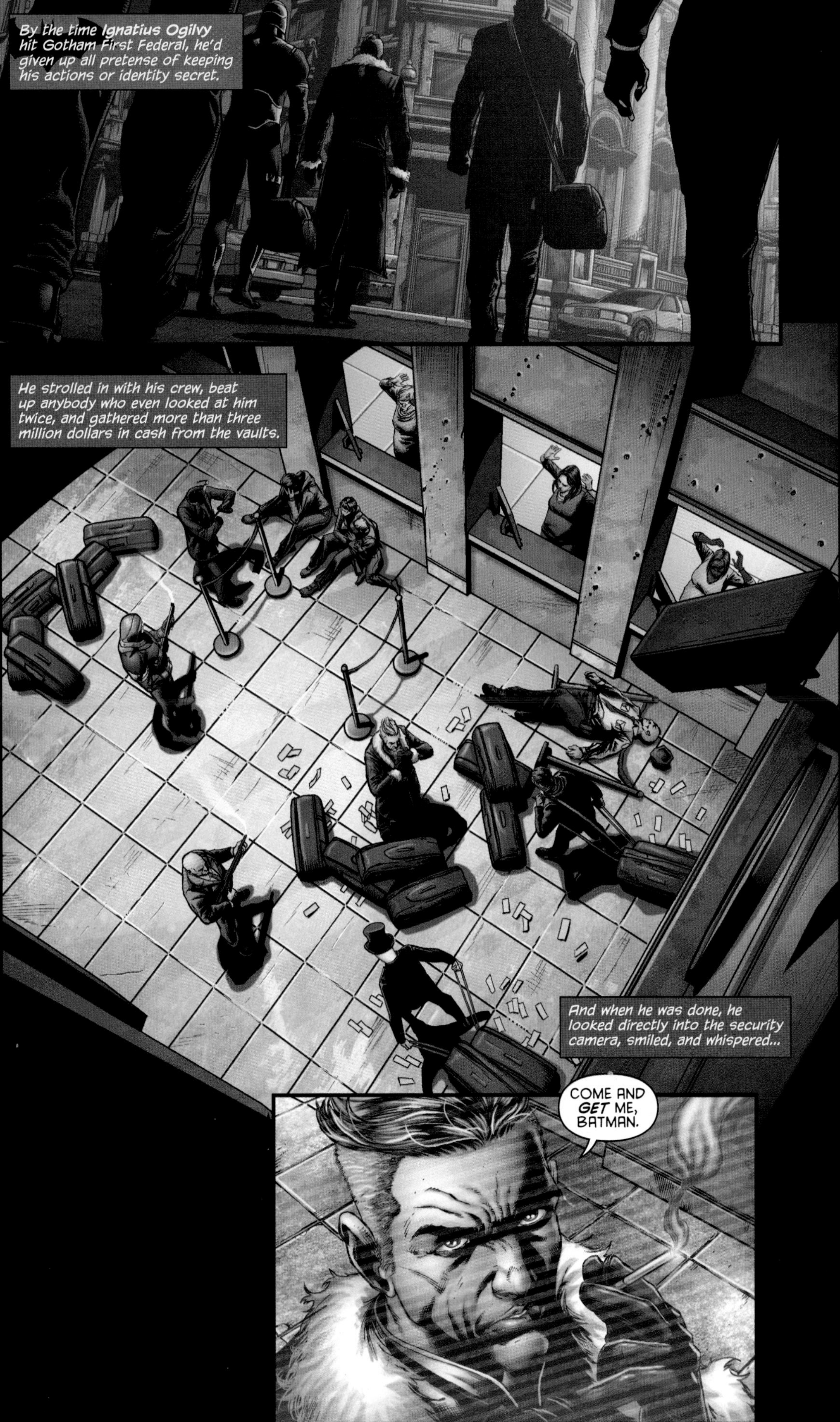

By the time Ignatius Ogilvy hit Gotham First Federal, he'd given up all pretense of keeping his actions or identity secret.
He strolled in with his crew, beat up anybody who even looked at him twice, and gathered more than three million dollars in cash from the vaults.
And when he was done, he looked directly into the security camera, smiled, and whispered...
COME AND GET ME, BATMAN.

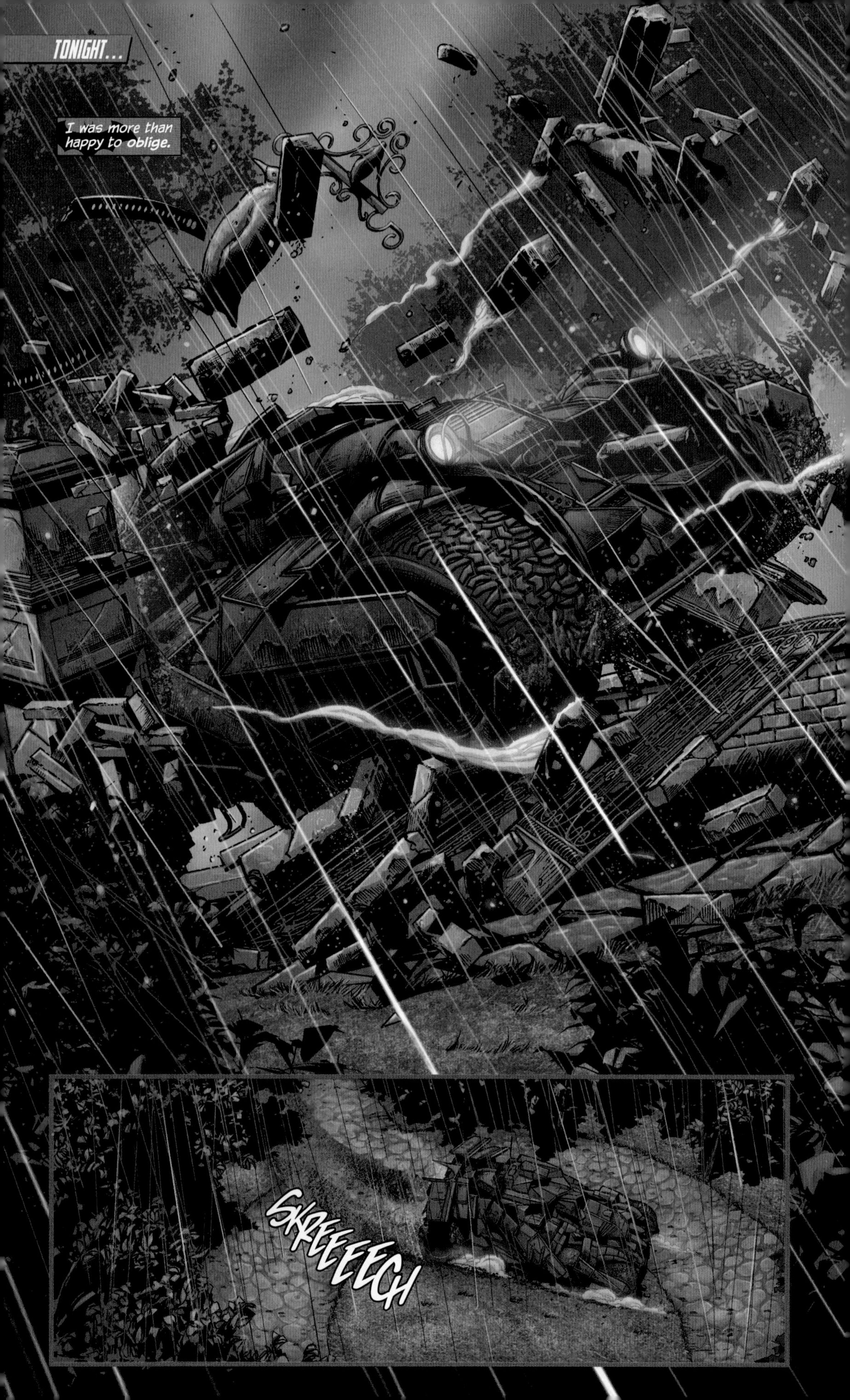
TONIGHT...
I was more than happy to oblige.
SKREEEECH

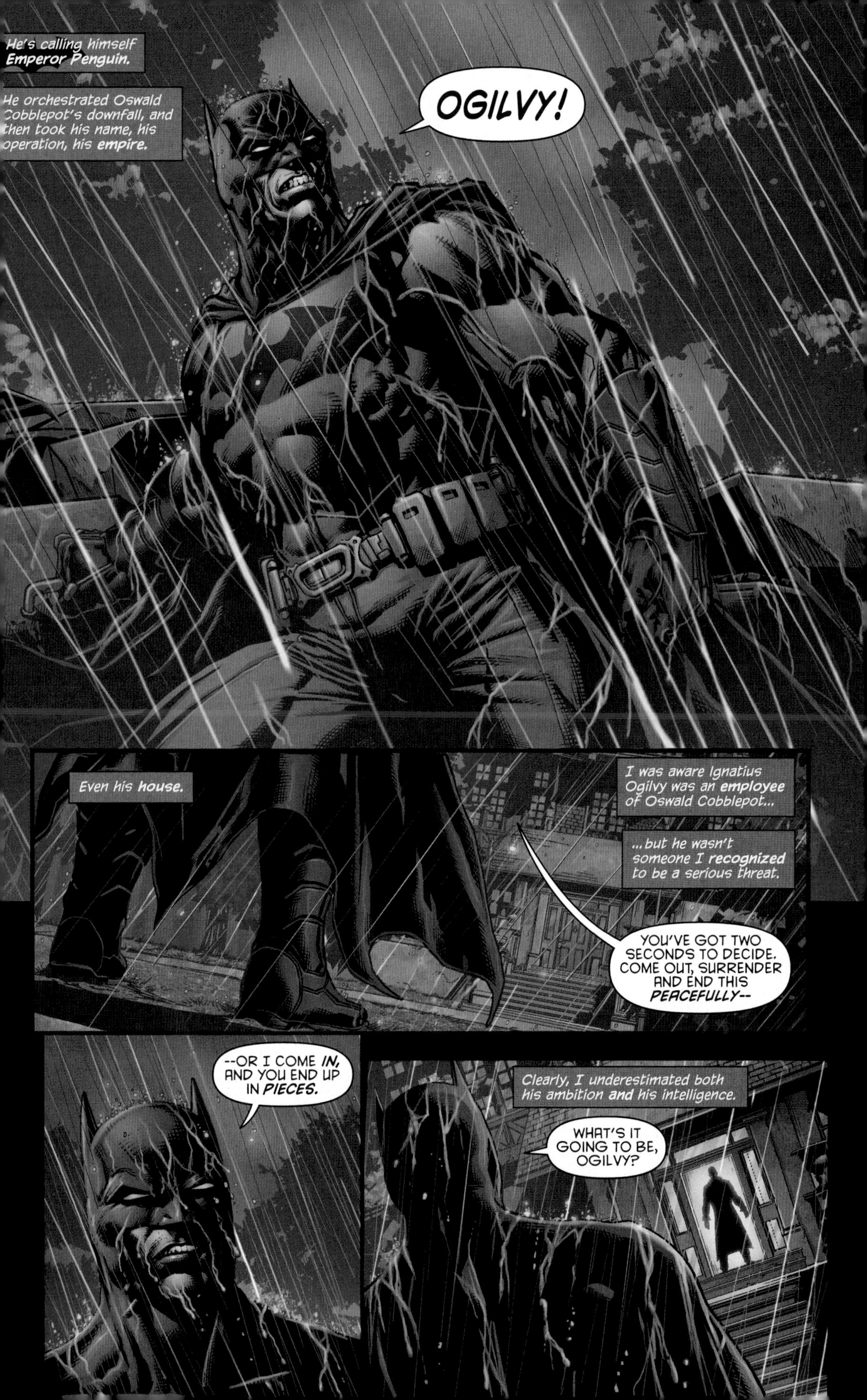
He's calling himself Emperor Penguin.
He orchestrated Oswald Cobblepot's downfall, and then took his name, his operation, his empire.
OGILVY!
Even his house.
I was aware Ignatius Ogilvy was an employee of Oswald Cobblepot...
...but he wasn't someone I recognized to be a serious threat.
YOU'VE GOT TWO SECONDS TO DECIDE. COME OUT, SURRENDER AND END THIS PEACEFULLY--
--OR I COME IN, AND YOU END UP IN PIECES.
Clearly, I underestimated both his ambition and his intelligence.
WHAT'S IT GOING TO BE, OGILVY?

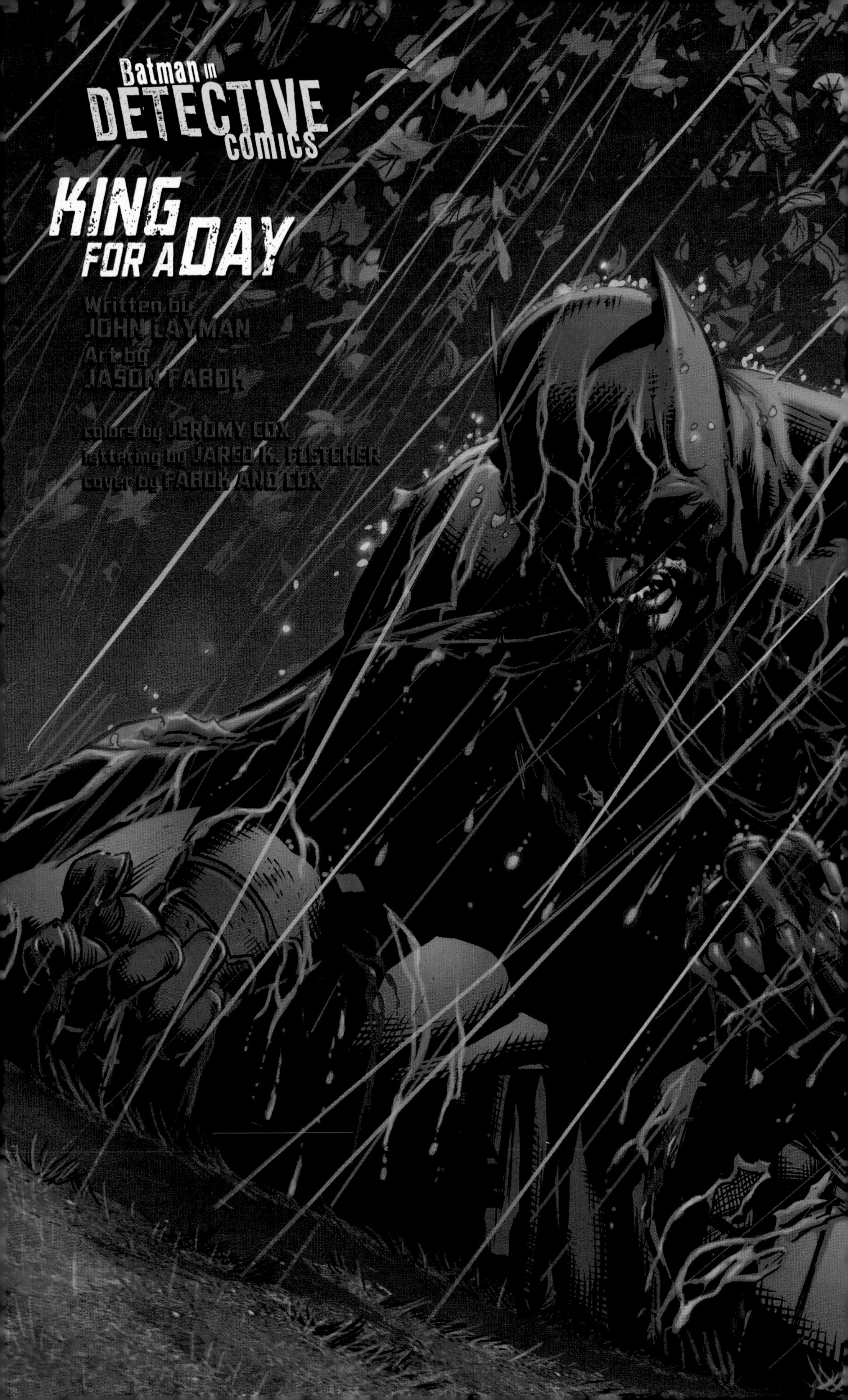
Batman in
DETECTIVE
COMICS
KING FOR A DAY
Written by
JOHN LAYMAN
Art by
JASON FABOK
colors by JEROMY COX
lettering by JARED K. FLETCHER
cover by FABOK AND COX

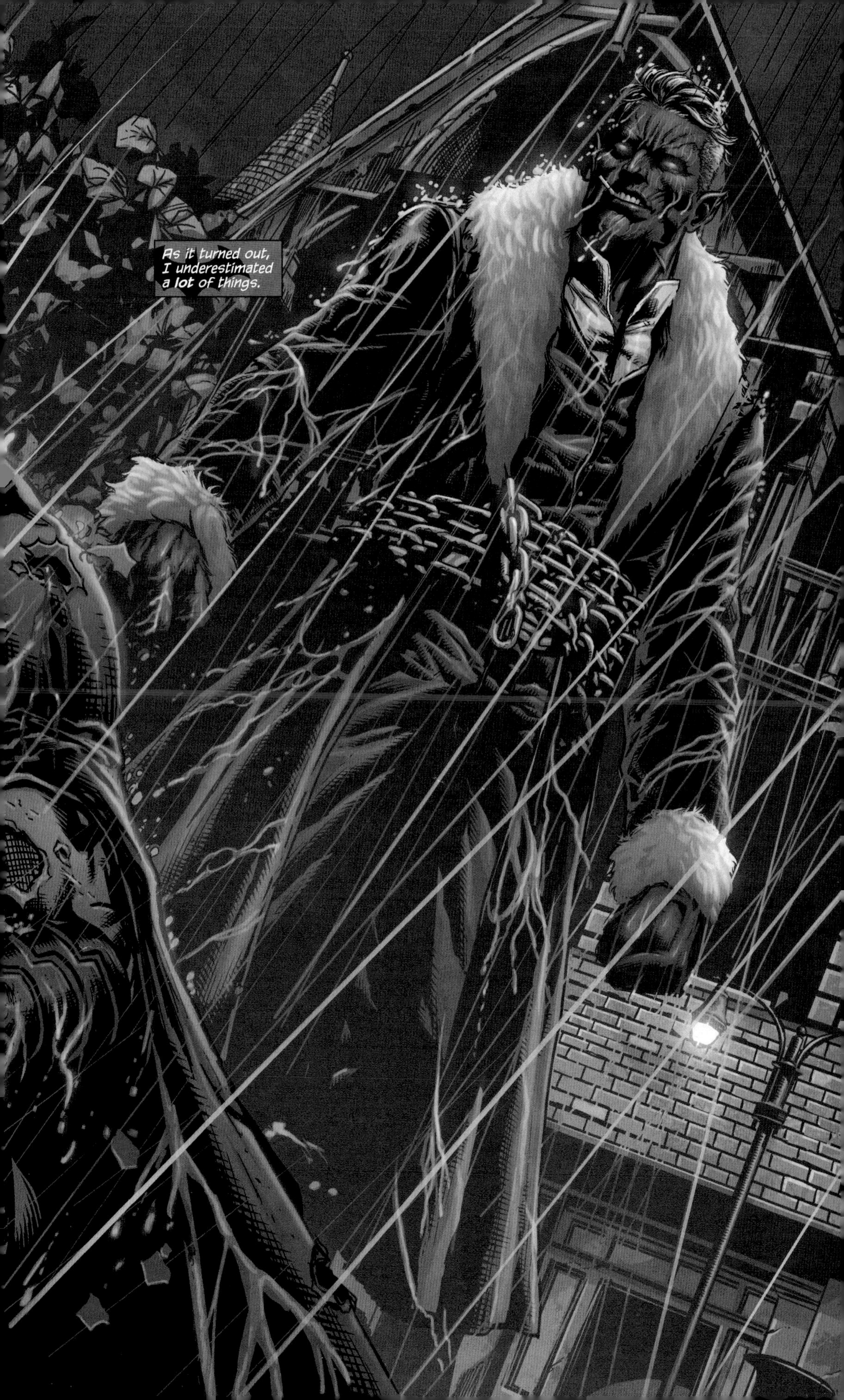
As it turned out, I underestimated a lot of things.

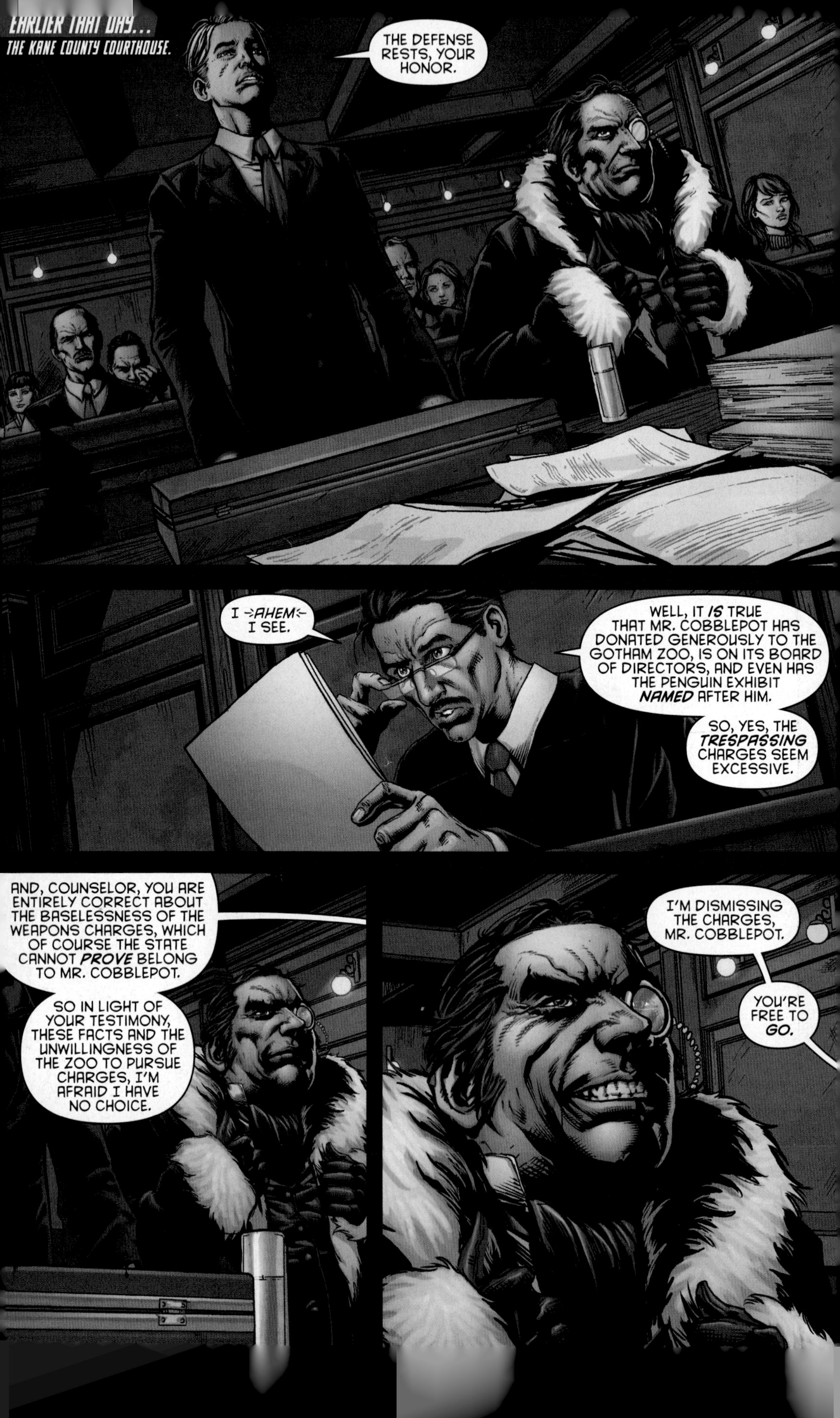
EARLIER THAT DAY...
THE KANE COUNTY COURTHOUSE.
THE DEFENSE RESTS, YOUR HONOR.
I ~AHEM~ I SEE.
WELL, IT IS TRUE THAT MR. COBBLEPOT HAS DONATED GENEROUSLY TO THE GOTHAM ZOO, IS ON ITS BOARD OF DIRECTORS, AND EVEN HAS THE PENGUIN EXHIBIT NAMED AFTER HIM.
SO, YES, THE TRESPASSING CHARGES SEEM EXCESSIVE.
AND, COUNSELOR, YOU ARE ENTIRELY CORRECT ABOUT THE BASELESSNESS OF THE WEAPONS CHARGES, WHICH OF COURSE THE STATE CANNOT PROVE BELONG TO MR. COBBLEPOT.
SO IN LIGHT OF YOUR TESTIMONY, THESE FACTS AND THE UNWILLINGNESS OF THE ZOO TO PURSUE CHARGES, I'M AFRAID I HAVE NO CHOICE.
I'M DISMISSING THE CHARGES, MR. COBBLEPOT.
YOU'RE FREE TO GO.

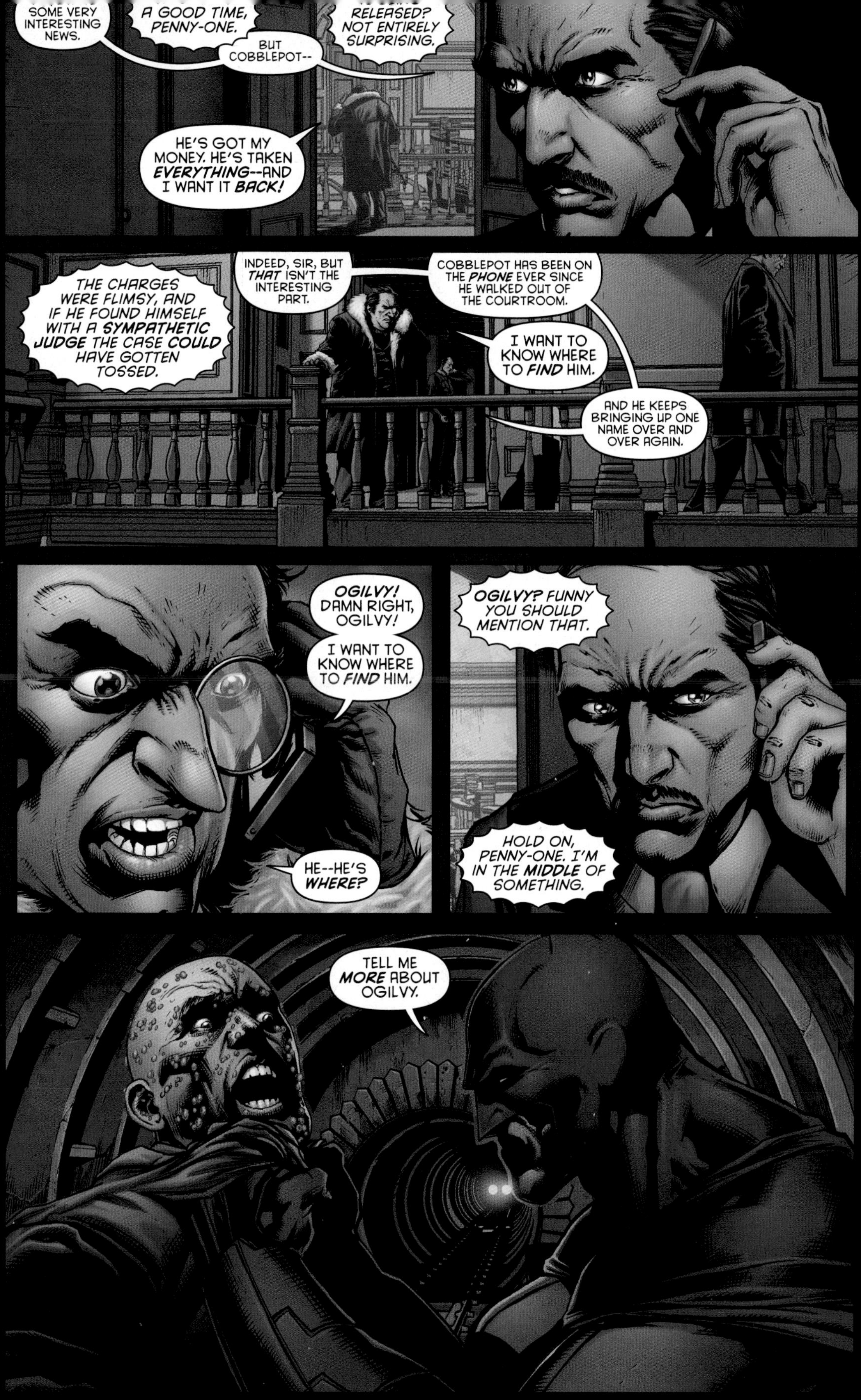
SOME VERY INTERESTING NEWS.
A GOOD TIME, PENNY-ONE.
BUT COBBLEPOT--
RELEASED? NOT ENTIRELY SURPRISING.
HE'S GOT MY MONEY. HE'S TAKEN EVERYTHING--AND I WANT IT BACK!
THE CHARGES WERE FLIMSY, AND IF HE FOUND HIMSELF WITH A SYMPATHETIC JUDGE THE CASE COULD HAVE GOTTEN TOSSED.
INDEED, SIR, BUT THAT ISN'T THE INTERESTING PART.
COBBLEPOT HAS BEEN ON THE PHONE EVER SINCE HE WALKED OUT OF THE COURTROOM.
I WANT TO KNOW WHERE TO FIND HIM.
AND HE KEEPS BRINGING UP ONE NAME OVER AND OVER AGAIN.
OGILVY! DAMN RIGHT, OGILVY!
I WANT TO KNOW WHERE TO FIND HIM.
HE--HE'S WHERE?
OGILVY? FUNNY YOU SHOULD MENTION THAT.
HOLD ON, PENNY-ONE. I'M IN THE MIDDLE OF SOMETHING.
TELL ME MORE ABOUT OGILVY.

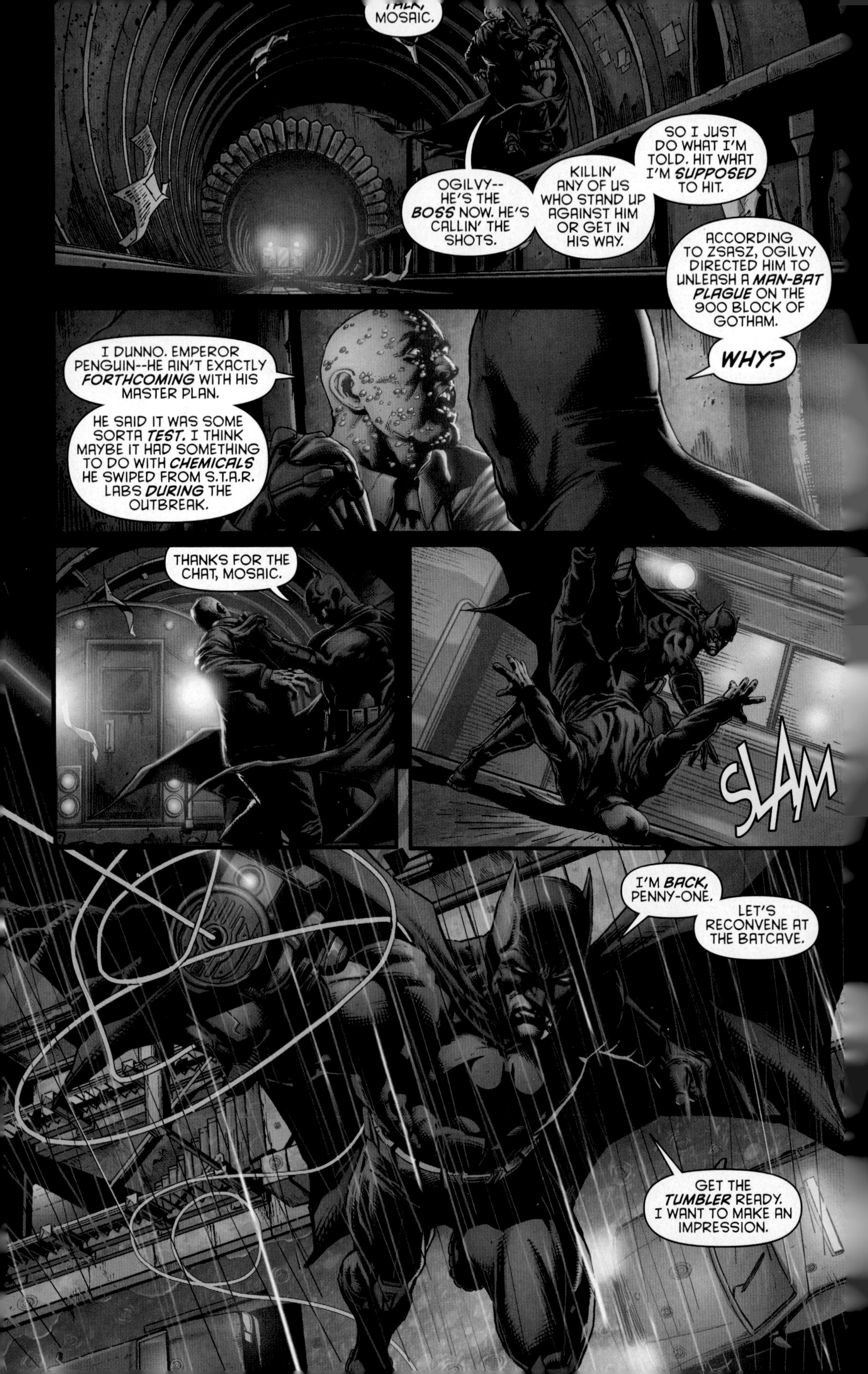

MOSAIC.
OGILVY-- HE'S THE BOSS NOW. HE'S CALLIN' THE SHOTS.
KILLIN' ANY OF US WHO STAND UP AGAINST HIM OR GET IN HIS WAY.
SO I JUST DO WHAT I'M TOLD. HIT WHAT I'M SUPPOSED TO HIT.
ACCORDING TO ZSASZ, OGILVY DIRECTED HIM TO UNLEASH A MAN-BAT PLAGUE ON THE 900 BLOCK OF GOTHAM.
WHY?
I DUNNO. EMPEROR PENGUIN--HE AIN'T EXACTLY FORTHCOMING WITH HIS MASTER PLAN.
HE SAID IT WAS SOME SORTA TEST. I THINK MAYBE IT HAD SOMETHING TO DO WITH CHEMICALS HE SWIPED FROM S.T.A.R. LABS DURING THE OUTBREAK.
THANKS FOR THE CHAT, MOSAIC.
SLAM
I'M BACK, PENNY-ONE.
LET'S RECONVENE AT THE BATCAVE.
GET THE TUMBLER READY. I WANT TO MAKE AN IMPRESSION.

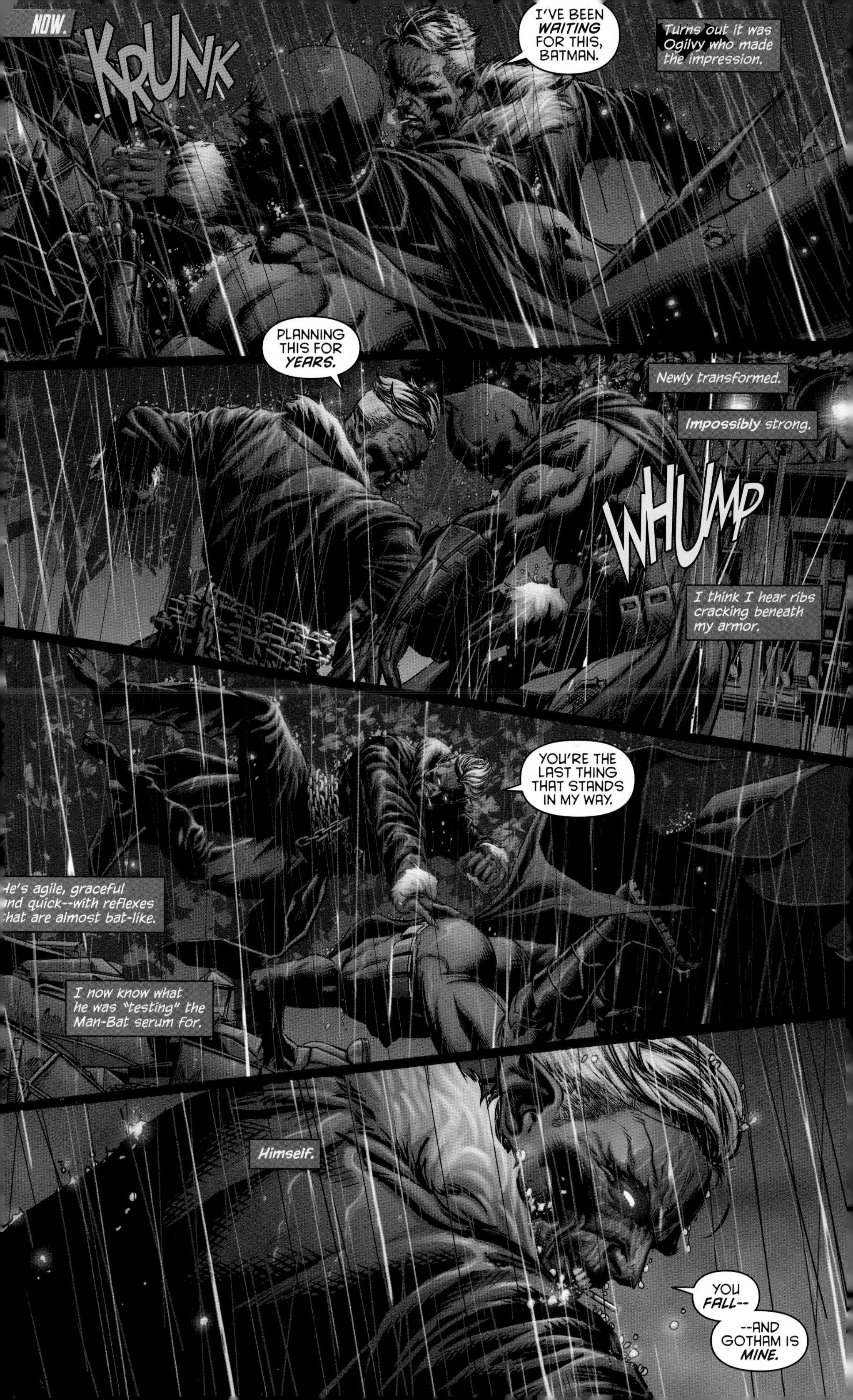
NOW.
KRUNK
I'VE BEEN WAITING FOR THIS, BATMAN.
Turns out it was Ogilvy who made the impression.
PLANNING THIS FOR YEARS.
Newly transformed.
Impossibly strong.
WHUMP
I think I hear ribs cracking beneath my armor.
YOU'RE THE LAST THING THAT STANDS IN MY WAY.
He's agile, graceful and quick--with reflexes that are almost bat-like.
I now know what he was "testing" the Man-Bat serum for.
Himself.
YOU FALL--
--AND GOTHAM IS MINE.

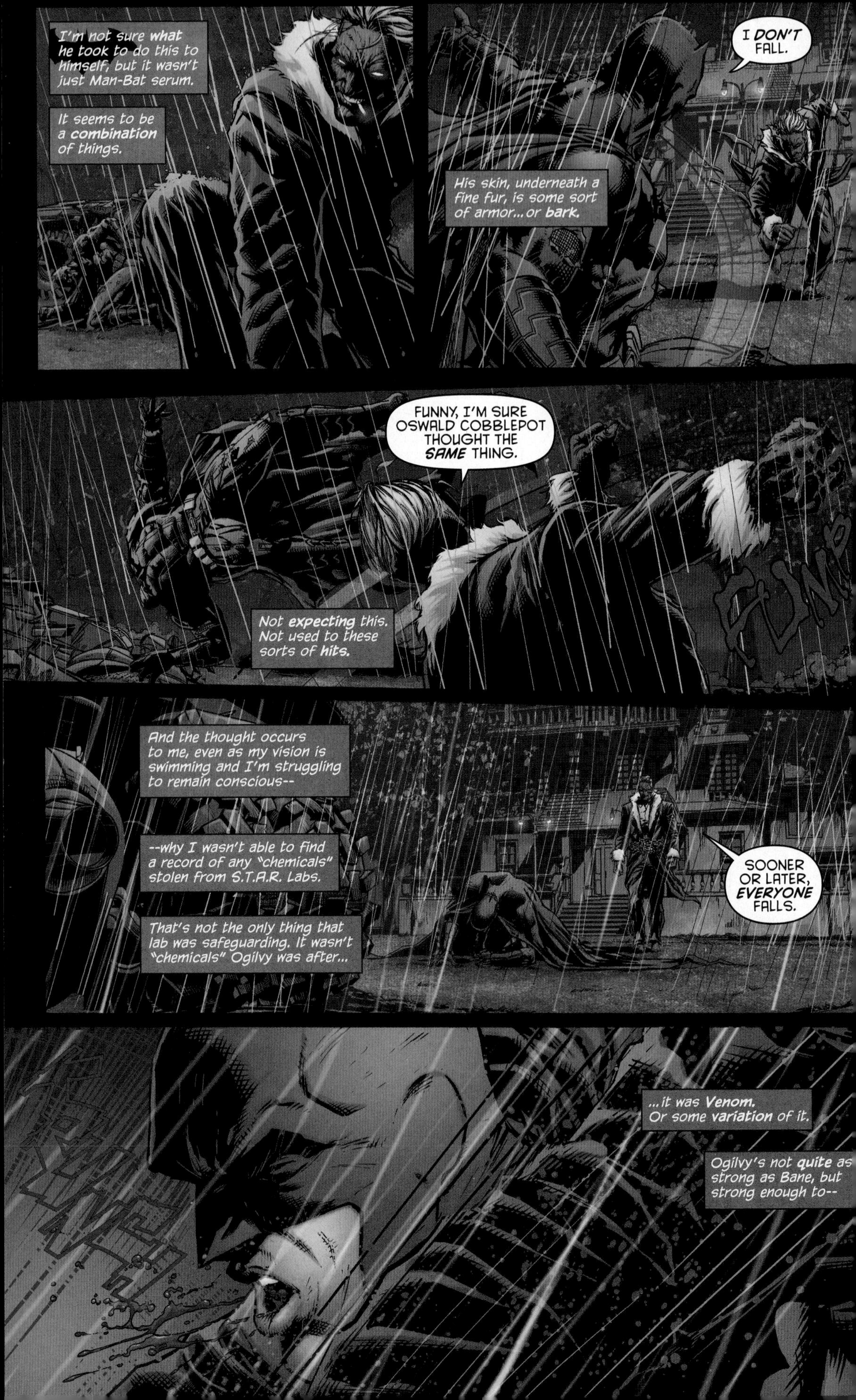
I'm not sure what he took to do this to himself, but it wasn't just Man-Bat serum.
It seems to be a combination of things.
I DON'T FALL.
His skin, underneath a fine fur, is some sort of armor...or bark.
FUNNY, I'M SURE OSWALD COBBLEPOT THOUGHT THE SAME THING.
Not expecting this. Not used to these sorts of hits.
And the thought occurs to me, even as my vision is swimming and I'm struggling to remain conscious--
--why I wasn't able to find a record of any "chemicals" stolen from S.T.A.R. Labs.
That's not the only thing that lab was safeguarding. It wasn't "chemicals" Ogilvy was after...
SOONER OR LATER, EVERYONE FALLS.
...it was Venom. Or some variation of it.
Ogilvy's not quite as strong as Bane, but strong enough to--

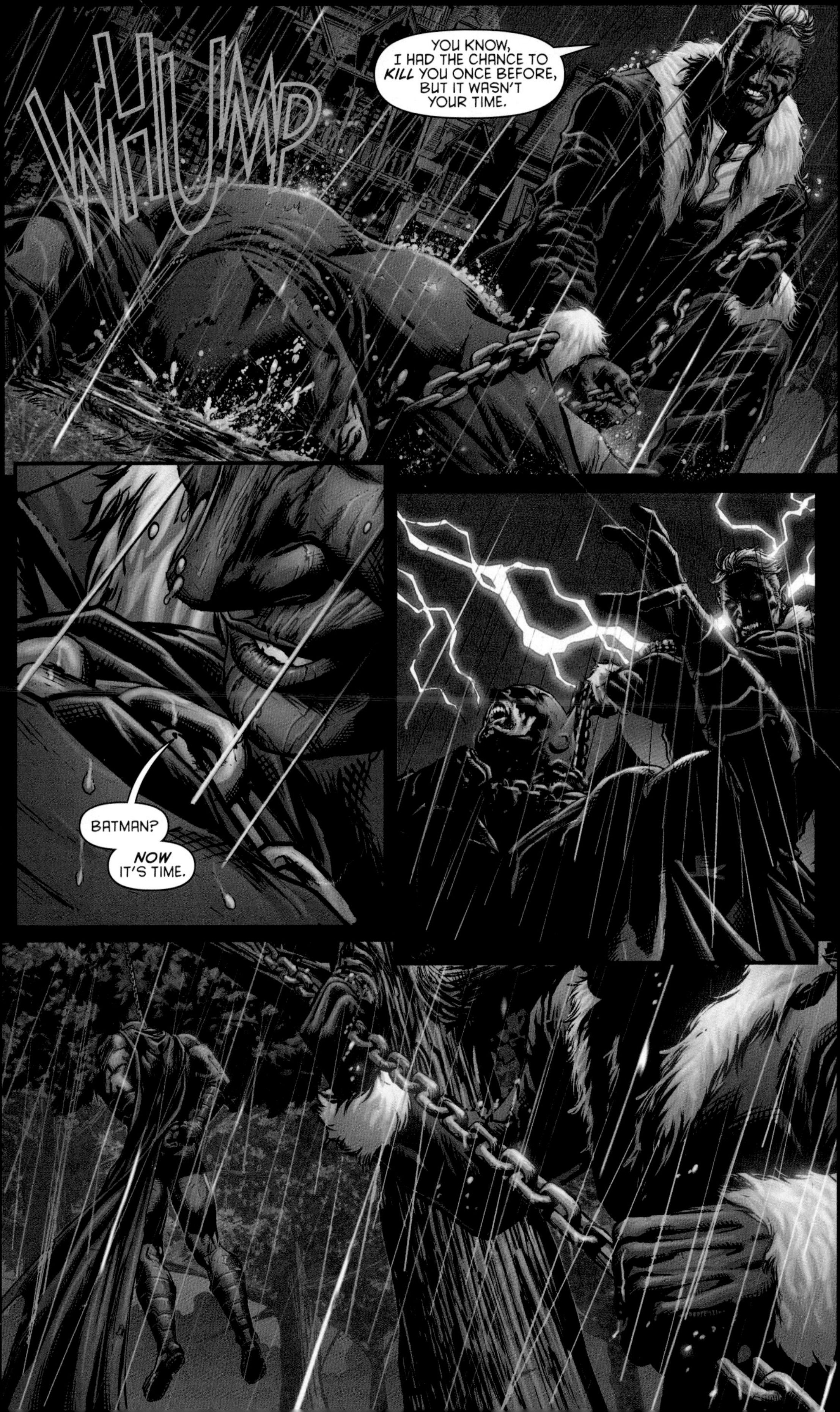
WHUMP
YOU KNOW, I HAD THE CHANCE TO KILL YOU ONCE BEFORE, BUT IT WASN'T YOUR TIME.
BATMAN?
NOW IT'S TIME.

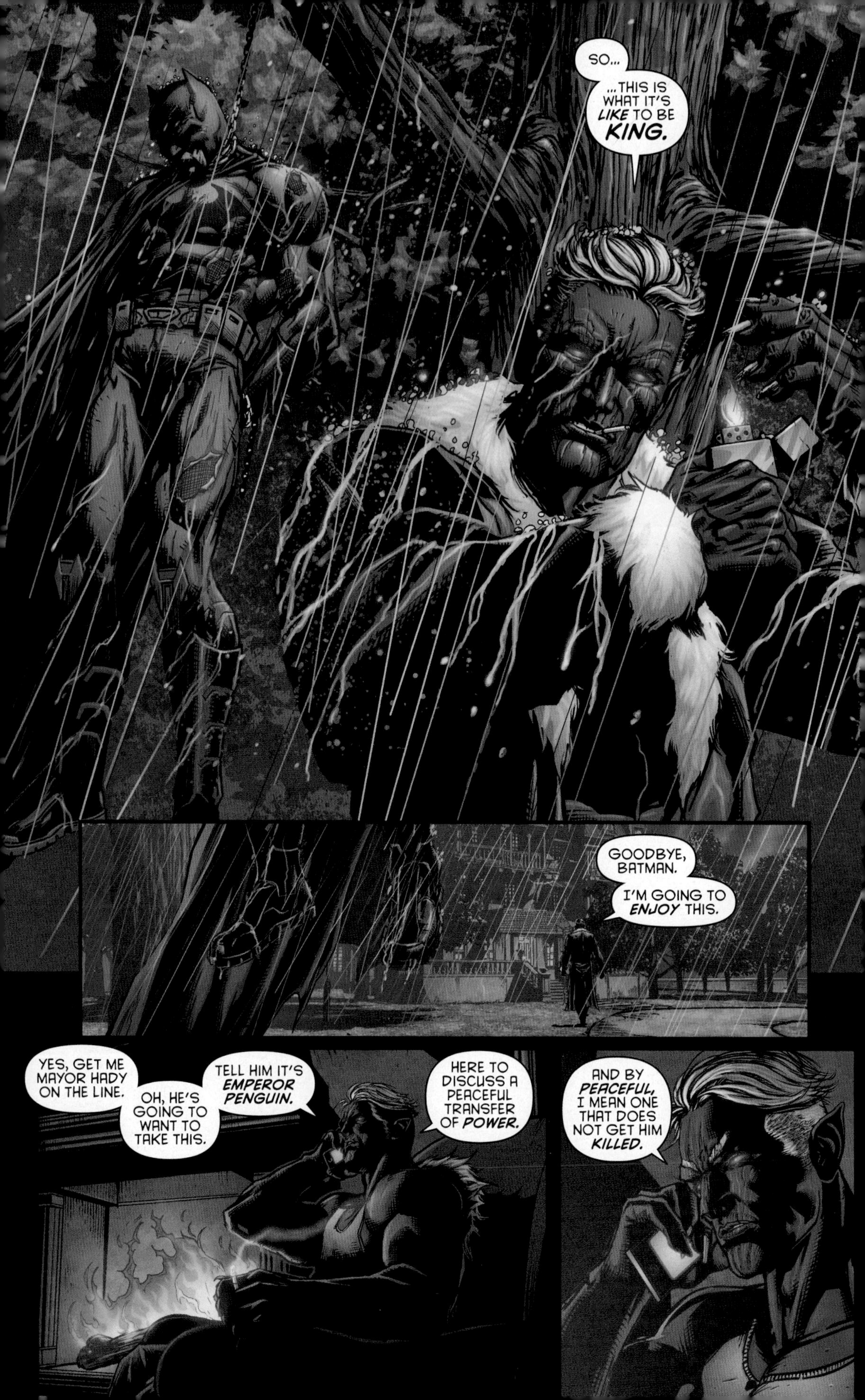
SO...
...THIS IS WHAT IT'S LIKE TO BE KING.
GOODBYE, BATMAN.
I'M GOING TO ENJOY THIS.
YES, GET ME MAYOR HADY ON THE LINE.
OH, HE'S GOING TO WANT TO TAKE THIS.
TELL HIM IT'S EMPEROR PENGUIN.
HERE TO DISCUSS A PEACEFUL TRANSFER OF POWER.
AND BY PEACEFUL, I MEAN ONE THAT DOES NOT GET HIM KILLED.

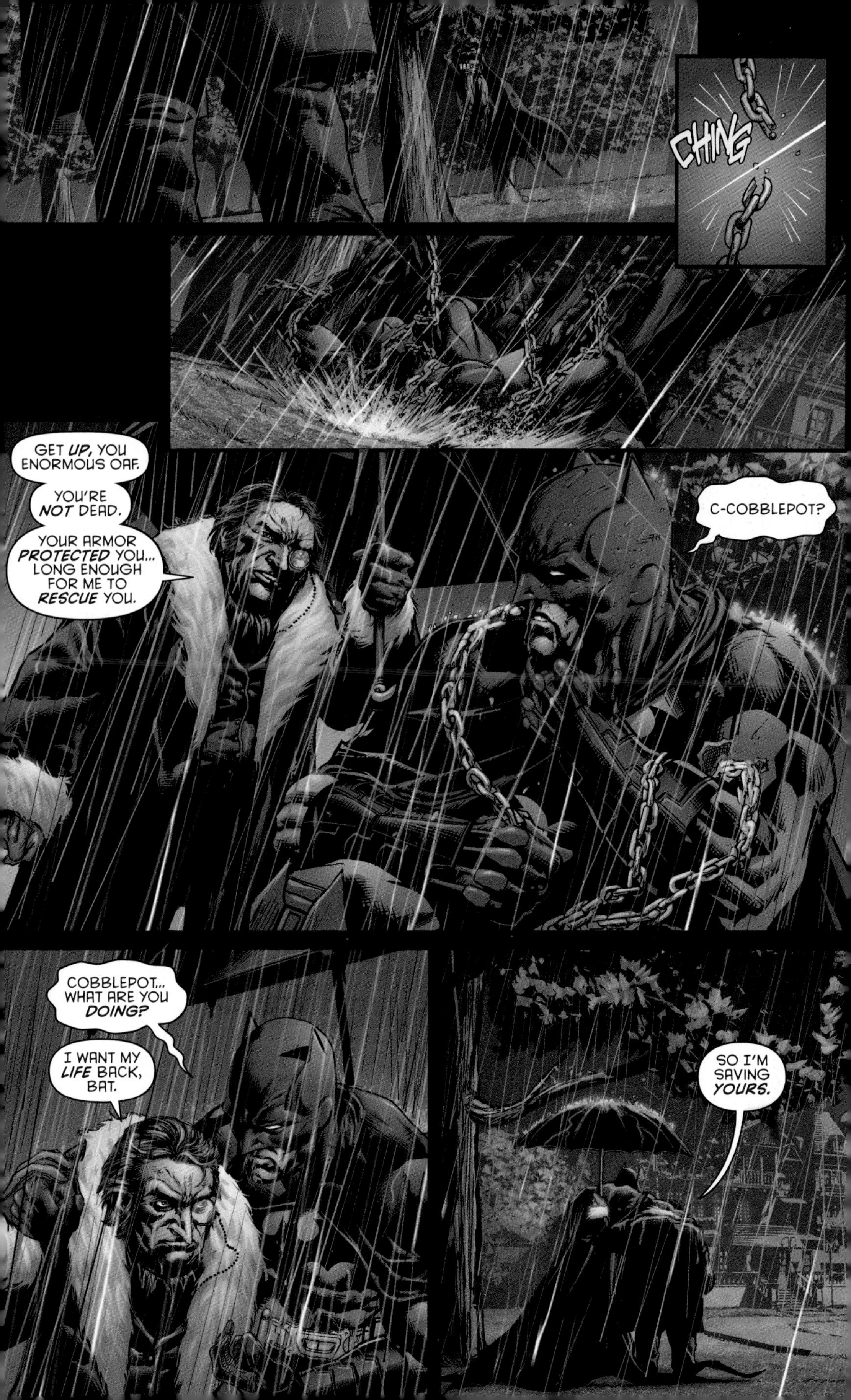
CHING
GET UP, YOU ENORMOUS OAF.
YOU'RE NOT DEAD.
YOUR ARMOR PROTECTED YOU... LONG ENOUGH FOR ME TO RESCUE YOU.
C-COBBLEPOT?
COBBLEPOT... WHAT ARE YOU DOING?
I WANT MY LIFE BACK, BAT.
SO I'M SAVING YOURS.

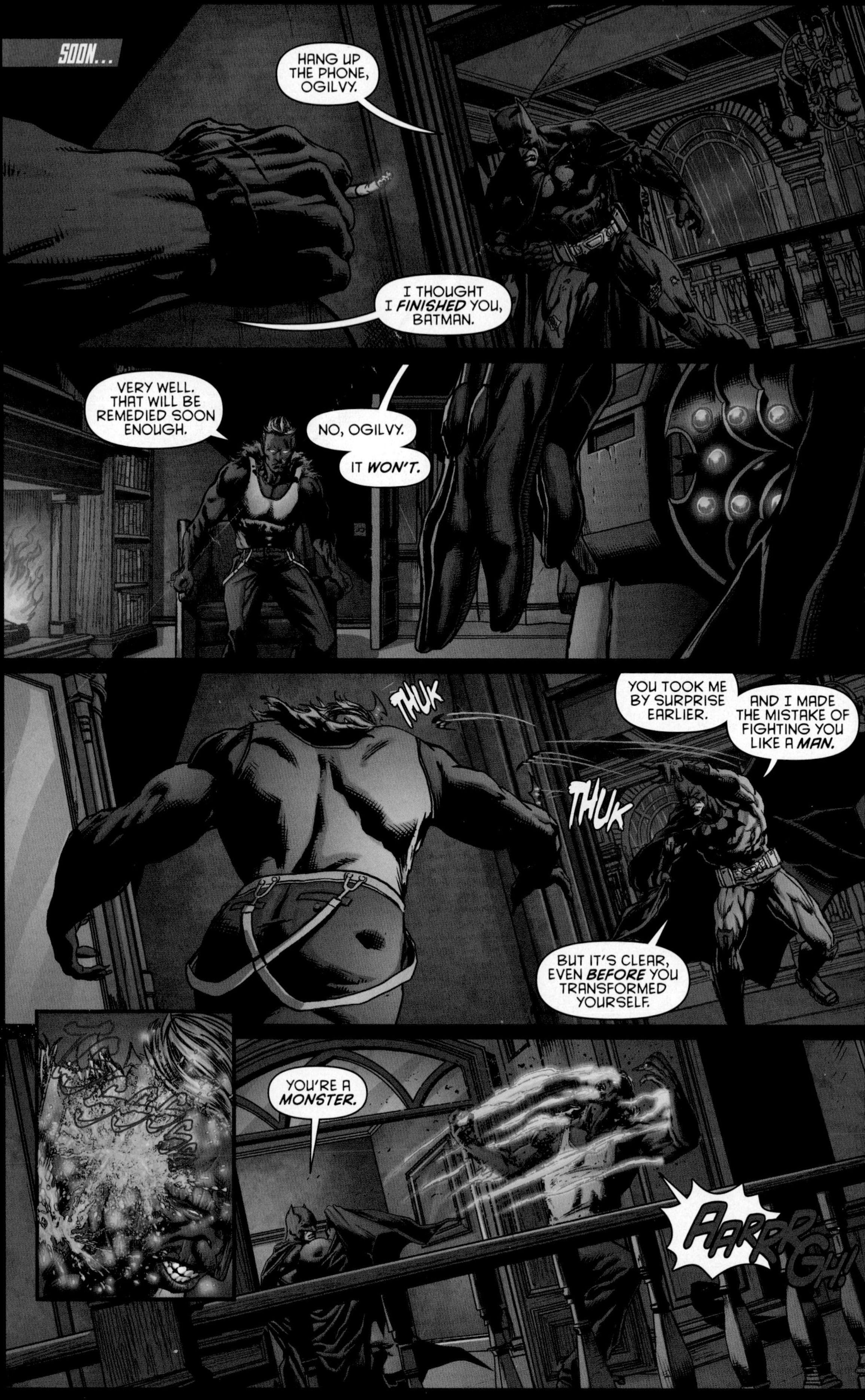
SOON...
HANG UP THE PHONE, OGILVY.
I THOUGHT I FINISHED YOU, BATMAN.
VERY WELL. THAT WILL BE REMEDIED SOON ENOUGH.
NO, OGILVY.
IT WON'T.
THUK
YOU TOOK ME BY SURPRISE EARLIER.
AND I MADE THE MISTAKE OF FIGHTING YOU LIKE A MAN.
THUK
BUT IT'S CLEAR, EVEN BEFORE YOU TRANSFORMED YOURSELF.
YOU'RE A MONSTER.
AARRRGH!

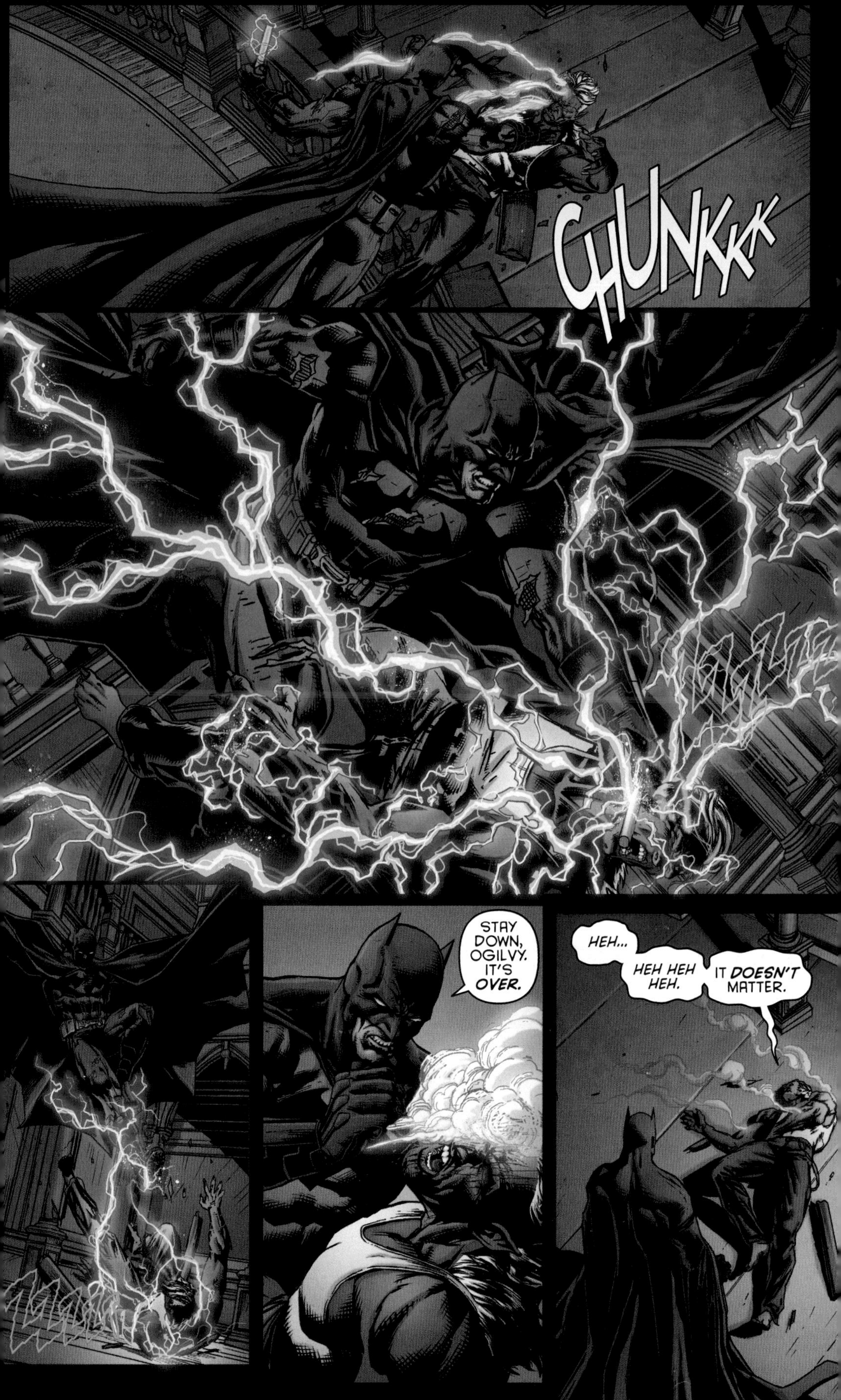
CHUNKKK
STAY DOWN, OGILVY. IT'S *OVER.*
HEH...
HEH HEH HEH.
IT *DOESN'T* MATTER.

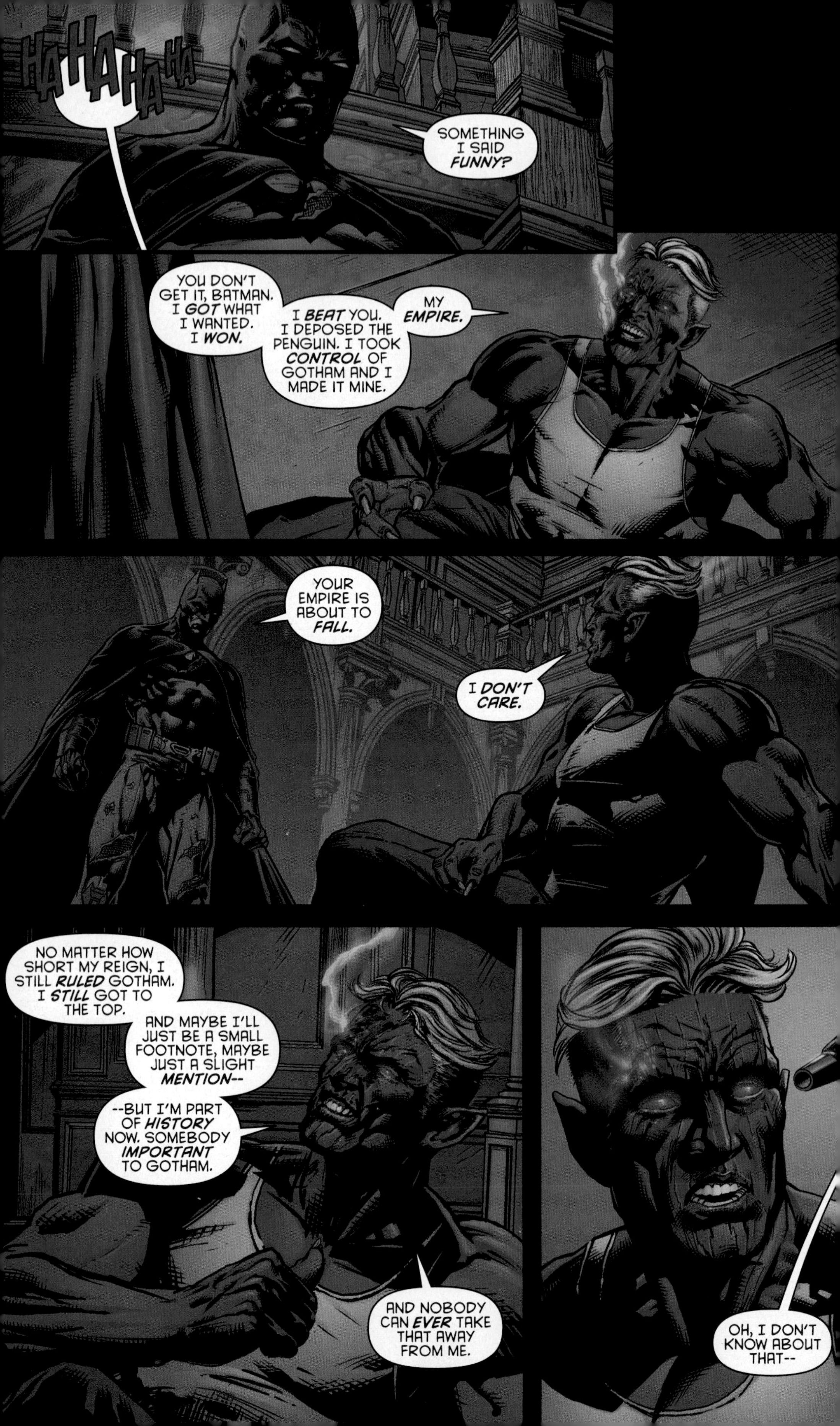
HA HA HA HA HA
SOMETHING I SAID FUNNY?
YOU DON'T GET IT, BATMAN. I GOT WHAT I WANTED. I WON.
I BEAT YOU. I DEPOSED THE PENGUIN. I TOOK CONTROL OF GOTHAM AND I MADE IT MINE.
MY EMPIRE.
YOUR EMPIRE IS ABOUT TO FALL.
I DON'T CARE.
NO MATTER HOW SHORT MY REIGN, I STILL RULED GOTHAM. I STILL GOT TO THE TOP.
AND MAYBE I'LL JUST BE A SMALL FOOTNOTE, MAYBE JUST A SLIGHT MENTION--
--BUT I'M PART OF HISTORY NOW. SOMEBODY IMPORTANT TO GOTHAM.
AND NOBODY CAN EVER TAKE THAT AWAY FROM ME.
OH, I DON'T KNOW ABOUT THAT--

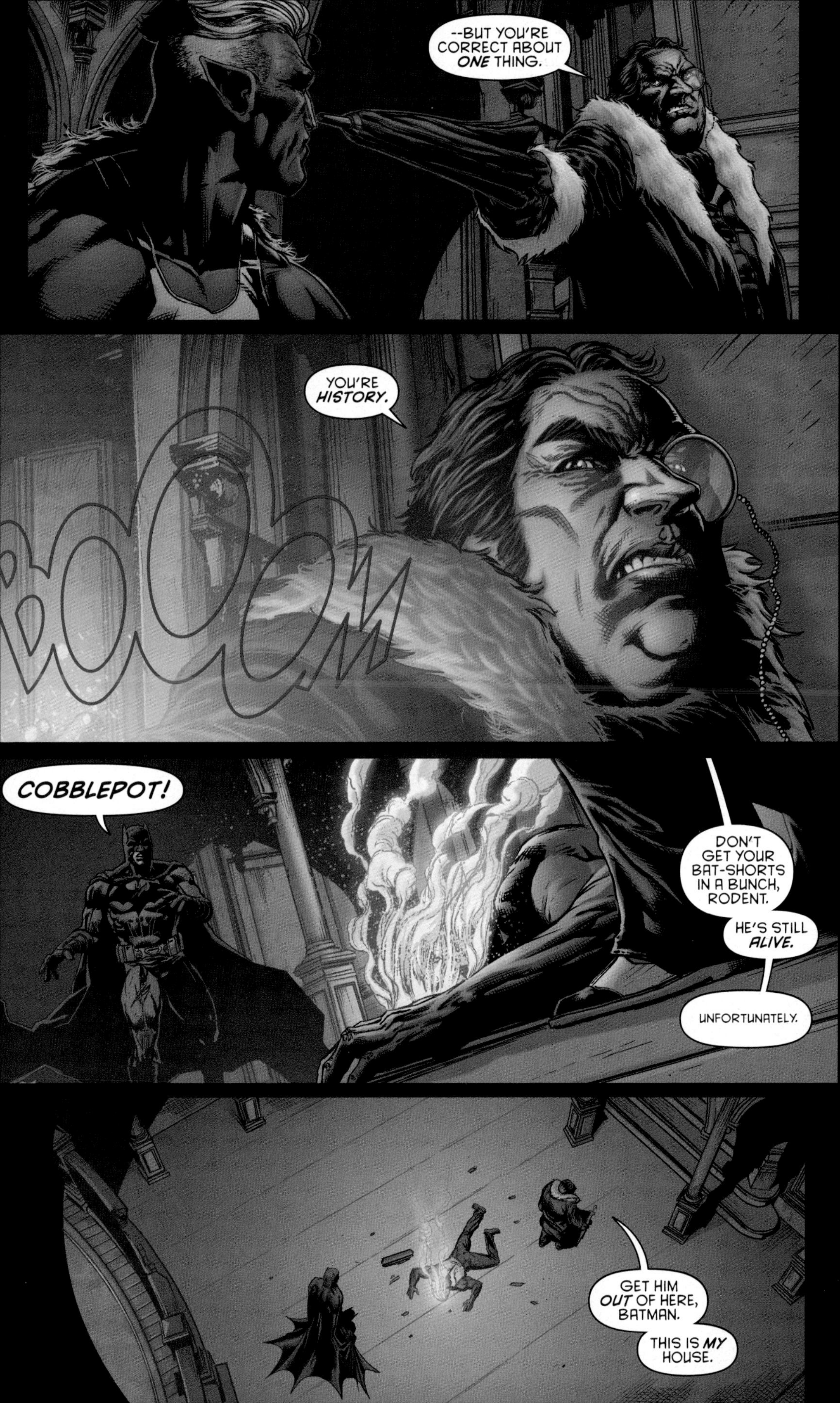
--BUT YOU'RE CORRECT ABOUT ONE THING.
YOU'RE HISTORY.
BOOOM
COBBLEPOT!
DON'T GET YOUR BAT-SHORTS IN A BUNCH, RODENT.
HE'S STILL ALIVE.
UNFORTUNATELY.
GET HIM OUT OF HERE, BATMAN.
THIS IS MY HOUSE.

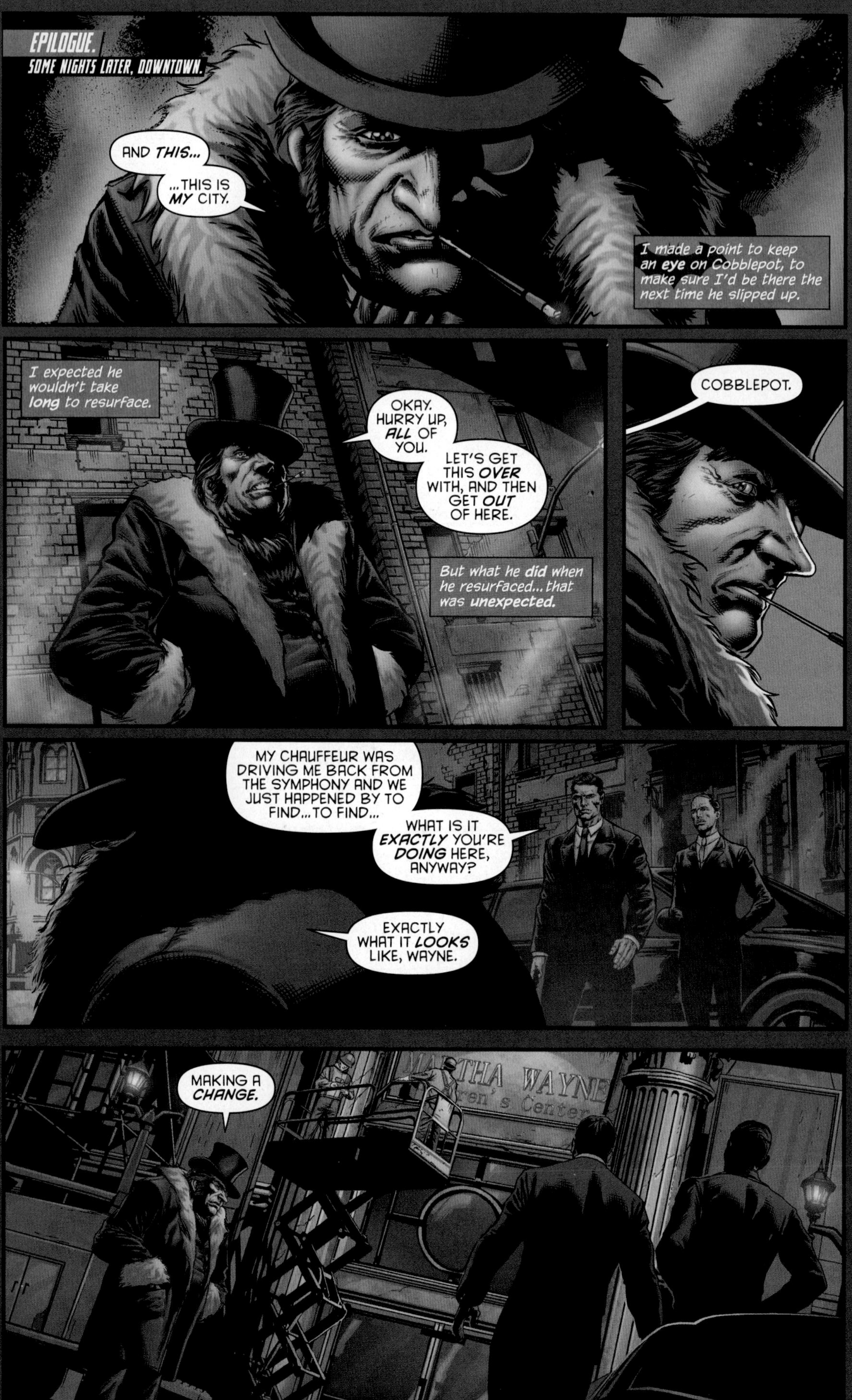
EPILOGUE.
SOME NIGHTS LATER, DOWNTOWN.
AND THIS...
...THIS IS MY CITY.
I made a point to keep an eye on Cobblepot, to make sure I'd be there the next time he slipped up.
I expected he wouldn't take long to resurface.
OKAY. HURRY UP, ALL OF YOU.
LET'S GET THIS OVER WITH, AND THEN GET OUT OF HERE.
But what he did when he resurfaced... that was unexpected.
COBBLEPOT.
MY CHAUFFEUR WAS DRIVING ME BACK FROM THE SYMPHONY AND WE JUST HAPPENED BY TO FIND... TO FIND...
WHAT IS IT EXACTLY YOU'RE DOING HERE, ANYWAY?
EXACTLY WHAT IT LOOKS LIKE, WAYNE.
MAKING A CHANGE.
MARTHA WAYNE
ren's Center

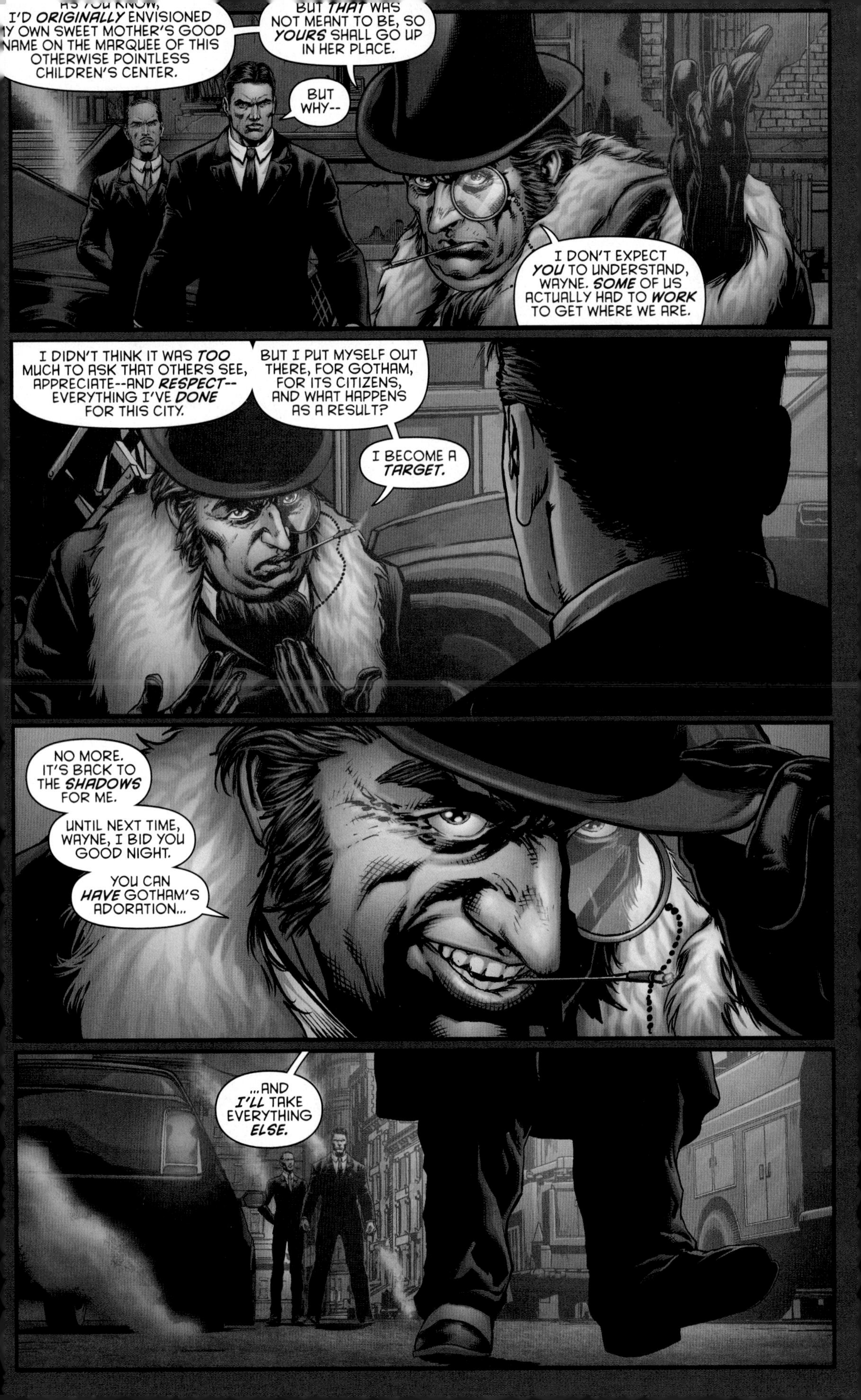

I'D ORIGINALLY ENVISIONED Y OWN SWEET MOTHER'S GOOD NAME ON THE MARQUEE OF THIS OTHERWISE POINTLESS CHILDREN'S CENTER.
BUT THAT WAS NOT MEANT TO BE, SO YOURS SHALL GO UP IN HER PLACE.
BUT WHY--
I DON'T EXPECT YOU TO UNDERSTAND, WAYNE. SOME OF US ACTUALLY HAD TO WORK TO GET WHERE WE ARE.
I DIDN'T THINK IT WAS TOO MUCH TO ASK THAT OTHERS SEE, APPRECIATE--AND RESPECT--EVERYTHING I'VE DONE FOR THIS CITY.
BUT I PUT MYSELF OUT THERE, FOR GOTHAM, FOR ITS CITIZENS, AND WHAT HAPPENS AS A RESULT?
I BECOME A TARGET.
NO MORE. IT'S BACK TO THE SHADOWS FOR ME.
UNTIL NEXT TIME, WAYNE, I BID YOU GOOD NIGHT.
YOU CAN HAVE GOTHAM'S ADORATION...
...AND I'LL TAKE EVERYTHING ELSE.

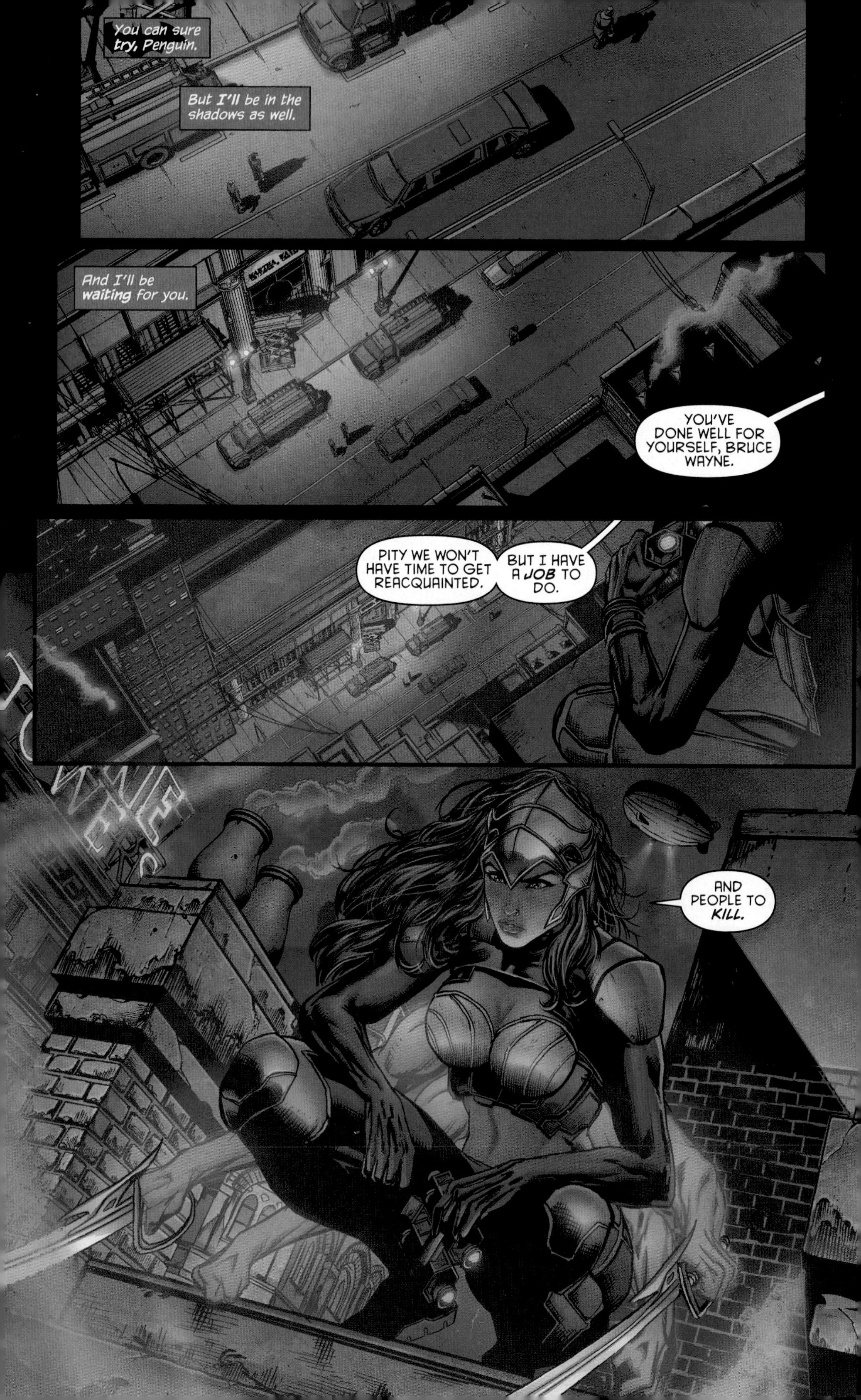
You can sure try, Penguin.
But I'll be in the shadows as well.
And I'll be waiting for you.
YOU'VE DONE WELL FOR YOURSELF, BRUCE WAYNE.
PITY WE WON'T HAVE TIME TO GET REACQUAINTED.
BUT I HAVE A JOB TO DO.
AND PEOPLE TO KILL.

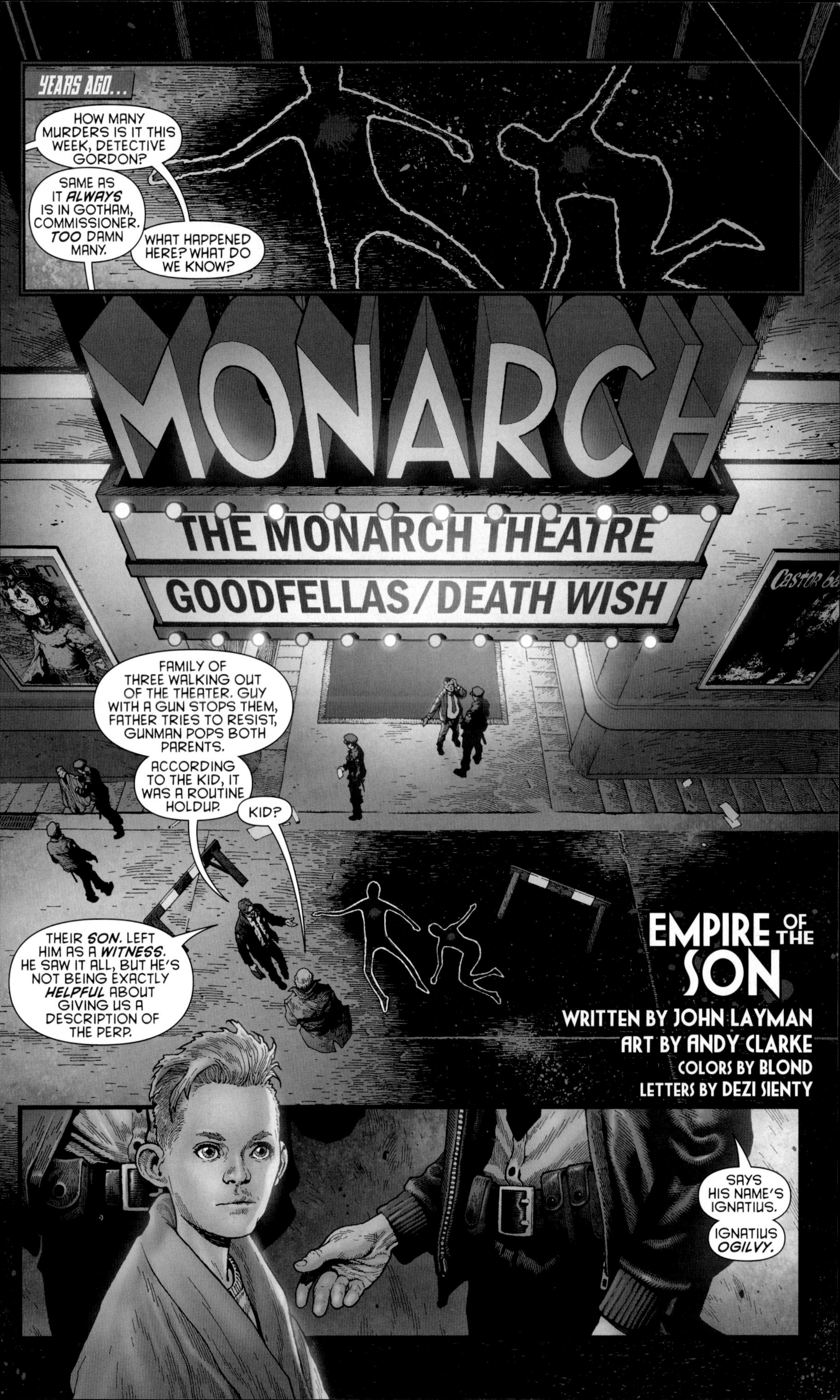

YEARS AGO...
HOW MANY MURDERS IS IT THIS WEEK, DETECTIVE GORDON?
SAME AS IT ALWAYS IS IN GOTHAM, COMMISSIONER. TOO DAMN MANY.
WHAT HAPPENED HERE? WHAT DO WE KNOW?
MONARCH
THE MONARCH THEATRE
GOODFELLAS/DEATH WISH
FAMILY OF THREE WALKING OUT OF THE THEATER. GUY WITH A GUN STOPS THEM, FATHER TRIES TO RESIST, GUNMAN POPS BOTH PARENTS.
ACCORDING TO THE KID, IT WAS A ROUTINE HOLDUP.
KID?
THEIR SON. LEFT HIM AS A WITNESS. HE SAW IT ALL, BUT HE'S NOT BEING EXACTLY HELPFUL ABOUT GIVING US A DESCRIPTION OF THE PERP.
EMPIRE OF THE SON
WRITTEN BY JOHN LAYMAN
ART BY ANDY CLARKE
COLORS BY BLOND
LETTERS BY DEZI SIENTY
SAYS HIS NAME'S IGNATIUS.
IGNATIUS OGILVY.

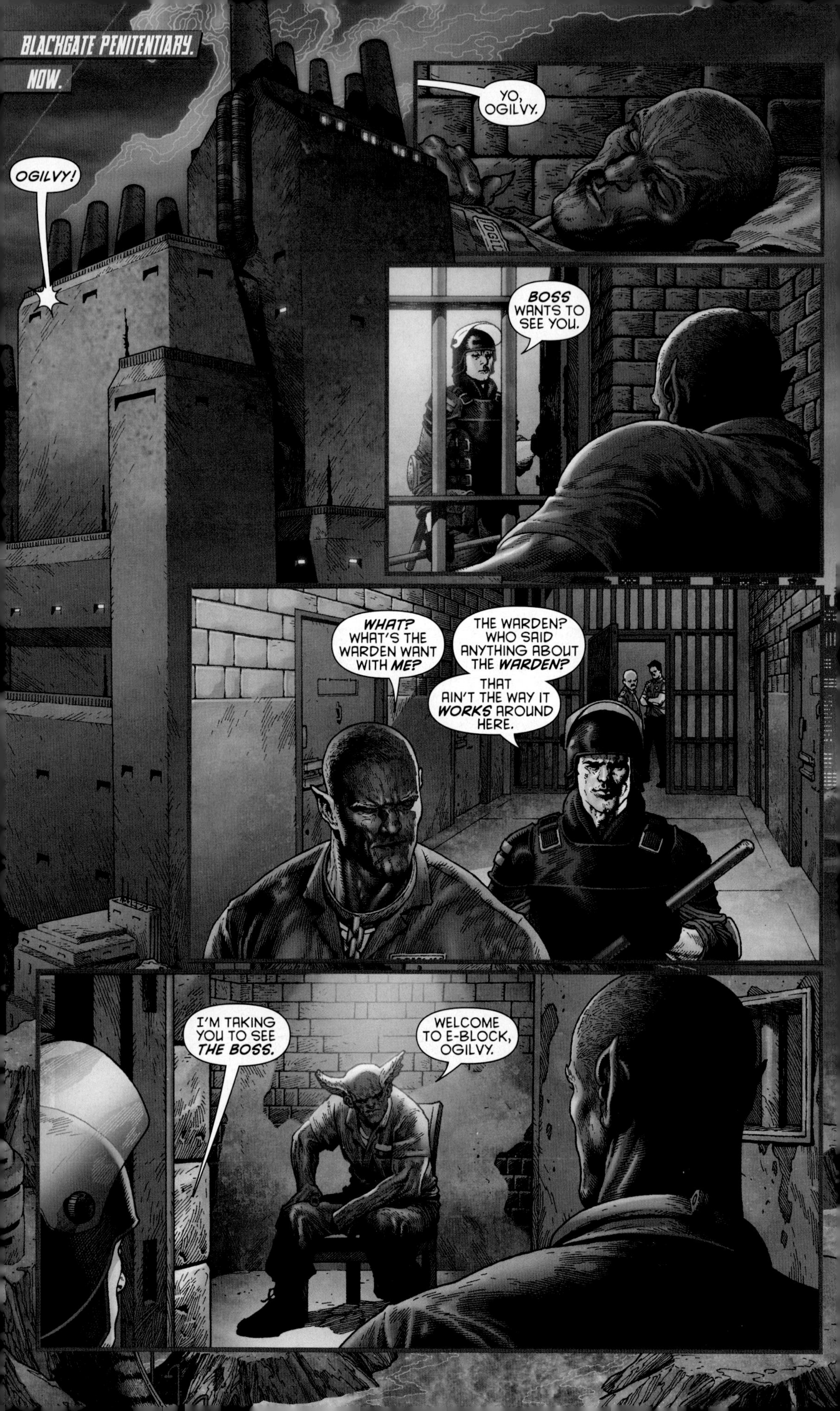

BLACKGATE PENITENTIARY.
NOW.
OGILVY!
YO, OGILVY.
BOSS WANTS TO SEE YOU.
WHAT? WHAT'S THE WARDEN WANT WITH ME?
THE WARDEN? WHO SAID ANYTHING ABOUT THE WARDEN?
THAT AIN'T THE WAY IT WORKS AROUND HERE.
I'M TAKING YOU TO SEE THE BOSS.
WELCOME TO E-BLOCK, OGILVY.

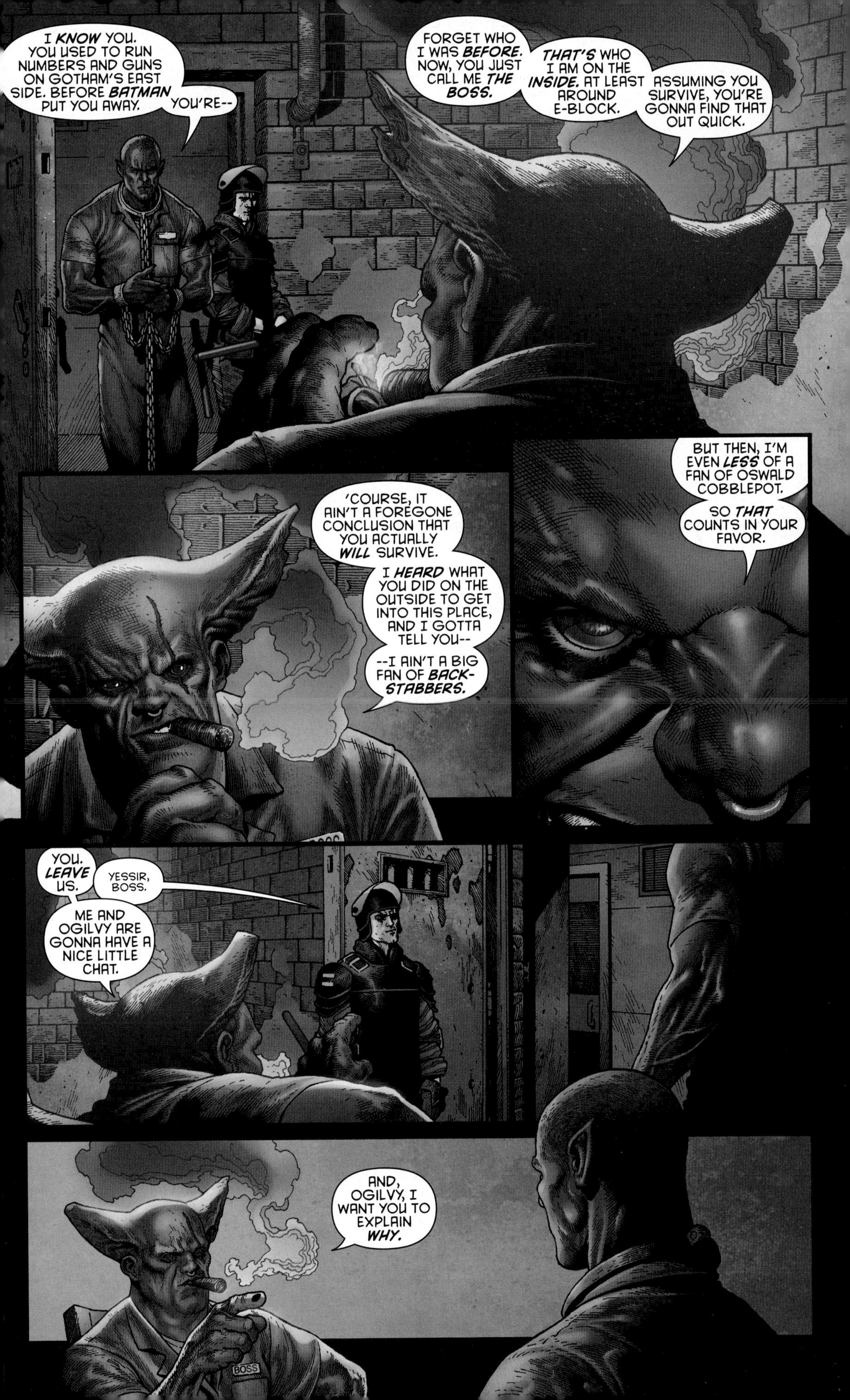
I KNOW YOU. YOU USED TO RUN NUMBERS AND GUNS ON GOTHAM'S EAST SIDE. BEFORE BATMAN PUT YOU AWAY.
YOU'RE--
FORGET WHO I WAS BEFORE. NOW, YOU JUST CALL ME THE BOSS.
THAT'S WHO I AM ON THE INSIDE. AT LEAST AROUND E-BLOCK.
ASSUMING YOU SURVIVE, YOU'RE GONNA FIND THAT OUT QUICK.
'COURSE, IT AIN'T A FOREGONE CONCLUSION THAT YOU ACTUALLY WILL SURVIVE.
I HEARD WHAT YOU DID ON THE OUTSIDE TO GET INTO THIS PLACE, AND I GOTTA TELL YOU--
--I AIN'T A BIG FAN OF BACK-STABBERS.
BUT THEN, I'M EVEN LESS OF A FAN OF OSWALD COBBLEPOT.
SO THAT COUNTS IN YOUR FAVOR.
YOU. LEAVE US.
YESSIR, BOSS.
ME AND OGILVY ARE GONNA HAVE A NICE LITTLE CHAT.
AND, OGILVY, I WANT YOU TO EXPLAIN WHY.
BOSS

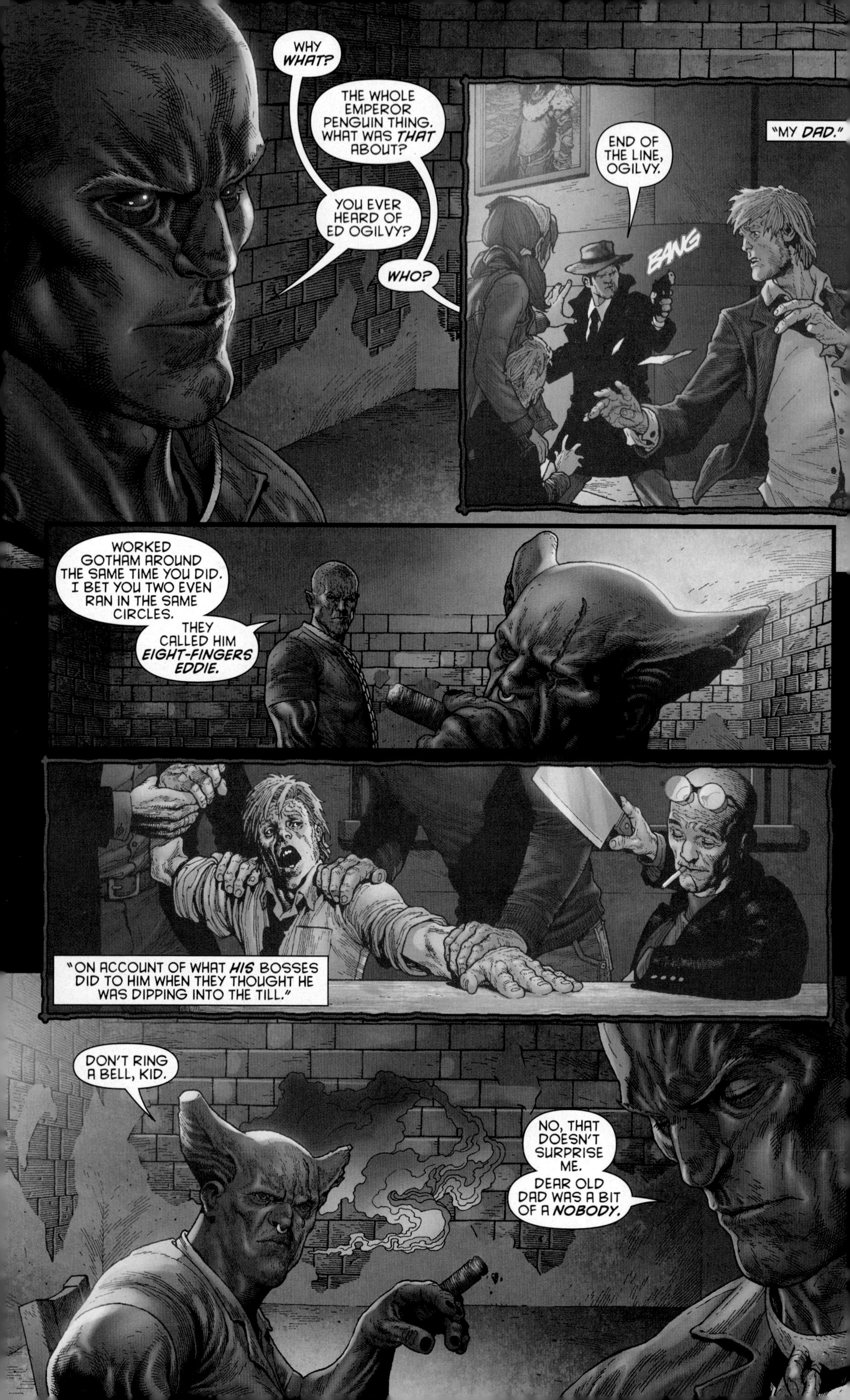
WHY WHAT?
THE WHOLE EMPEROR PENGUIN THING. WHAT WAS THAT ABOUT?
YOU EVER HEARD OF ED OGILVY?
WHO?
END OF THE LINE, OGILVY.
BANG
"MY DAD."
WORKED GOTHAM AROUND THE SAME TIME YOU DID. I BET YOU TWO EVEN RAN IN THE SAME CIRCLES.
THEY CALLED HIM EIGHT-FINGERS EDDIE.
"ON ACCOUNT OF WHAT HIS BOSSES DID TO HIM WHEN THEY THOUGHT HE WAS DIPPING INTO THE TILL."
DON'T RING A BELL, KID.
NO, THAT DOESN'T SURPRISE ME.
DEAR OLD DAD WAS A BIT OF A NOBODY.

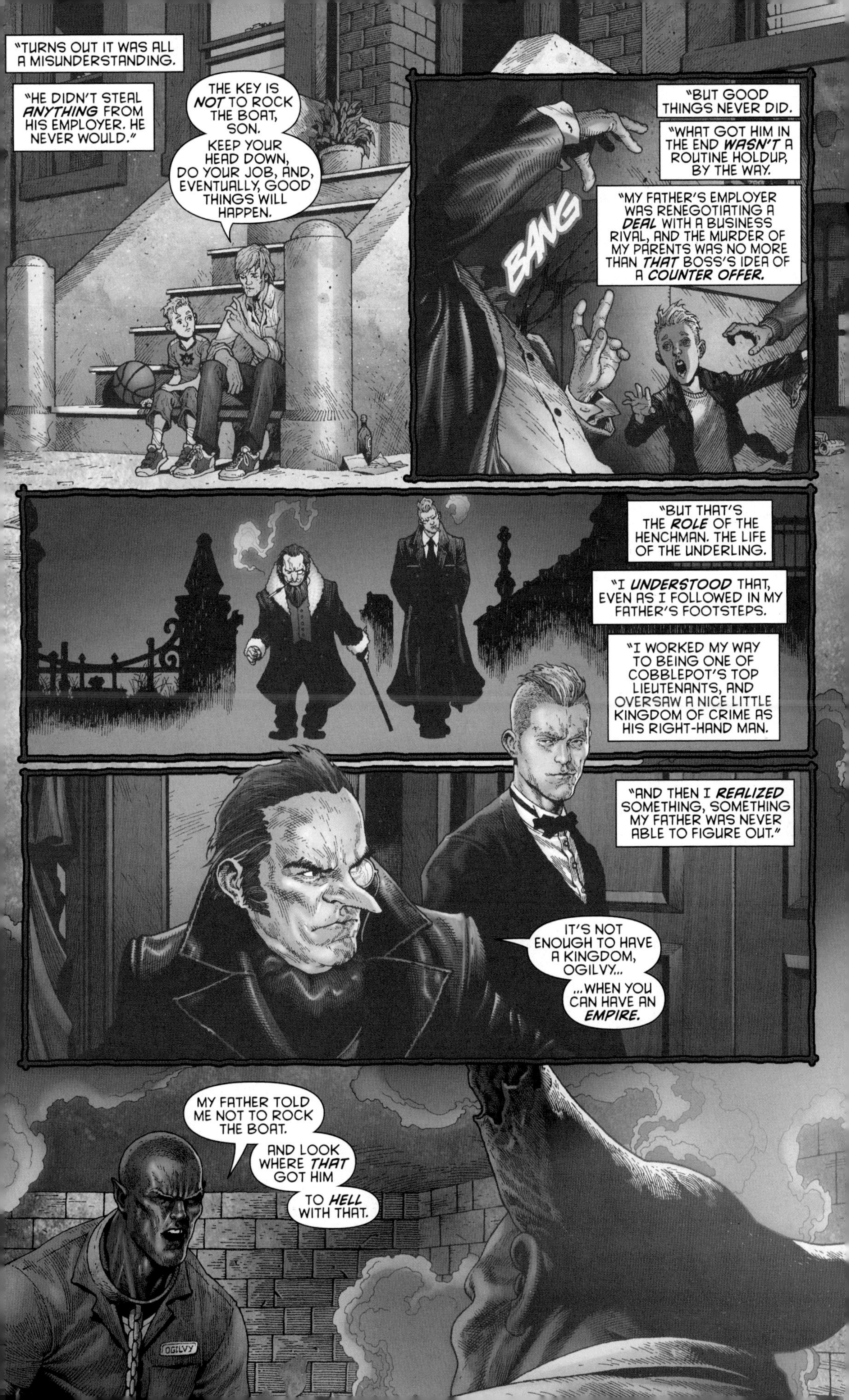

"TURNS OUT IT WAS ALL A MISUNDERSTANDING.
"HE DIDN'T STEAL ***ANYTHING*** FROM HIS EMPLOYER. HE NEVER WOULD."
THE KEY IS ***NOT*** TO ROCK THE BOAT, SON.
KEEP YOUR HEAD DOWN, DO YOUR JOB, AND, EVENTUALLY, GOOD THINGS WILL HAPPEN.
"BUT GOOD THINGS NEVER DID.
"WHAT GOT HIM IN THE END ***WASN'T*** A ROUTINE HOLDUP, BY THE WAY.
BANG
"MY FATHER'S EMPLOYER WAS RENEGOTIATING A ***DEAL*** WITH A BUSINESS RIVAL, AND THE MURDER OF MY PARENTS WAS NO MORE THAN ***THAT*** BOSS'S IDEA OF A ***COUNTER OFFER.***
"BUT THAT'S THE ***ROLE*** OF THE HENCHMAN. THE LIFE OF THE UNDERLING.
"I ***UNDERSTOOD*** THAT, EVEN AS I FOLLOWED IN MY FATHER'S FOOTSTEPS.
"I WORKED MY WAY TO BEING ONE OF COBBLEPOT'S TOP LIEUTENANTS, AND OVERSAW A NICE LITTLE KINGDOM OF CRIME AS HIS RIGHT-HAND MAN.
"AND THEN I ***REALIZED*** SOMETHING, SOMETHING MY FATHER WAS NEVER ABLE TO FIGURE OUT."
IT'S NOT ENOUGH TO HAVE A KINGDOM, OGILVY...
...WHEN YOU CAN HAVE AN ***EMPIRE.***
MY FATHER TOLD ME NOT TO ROCK THE BOAT.
AND LOOK WHERE ***THAT*** GOT HIM
TO ***HELL*** WITH THAT.
OGILVY

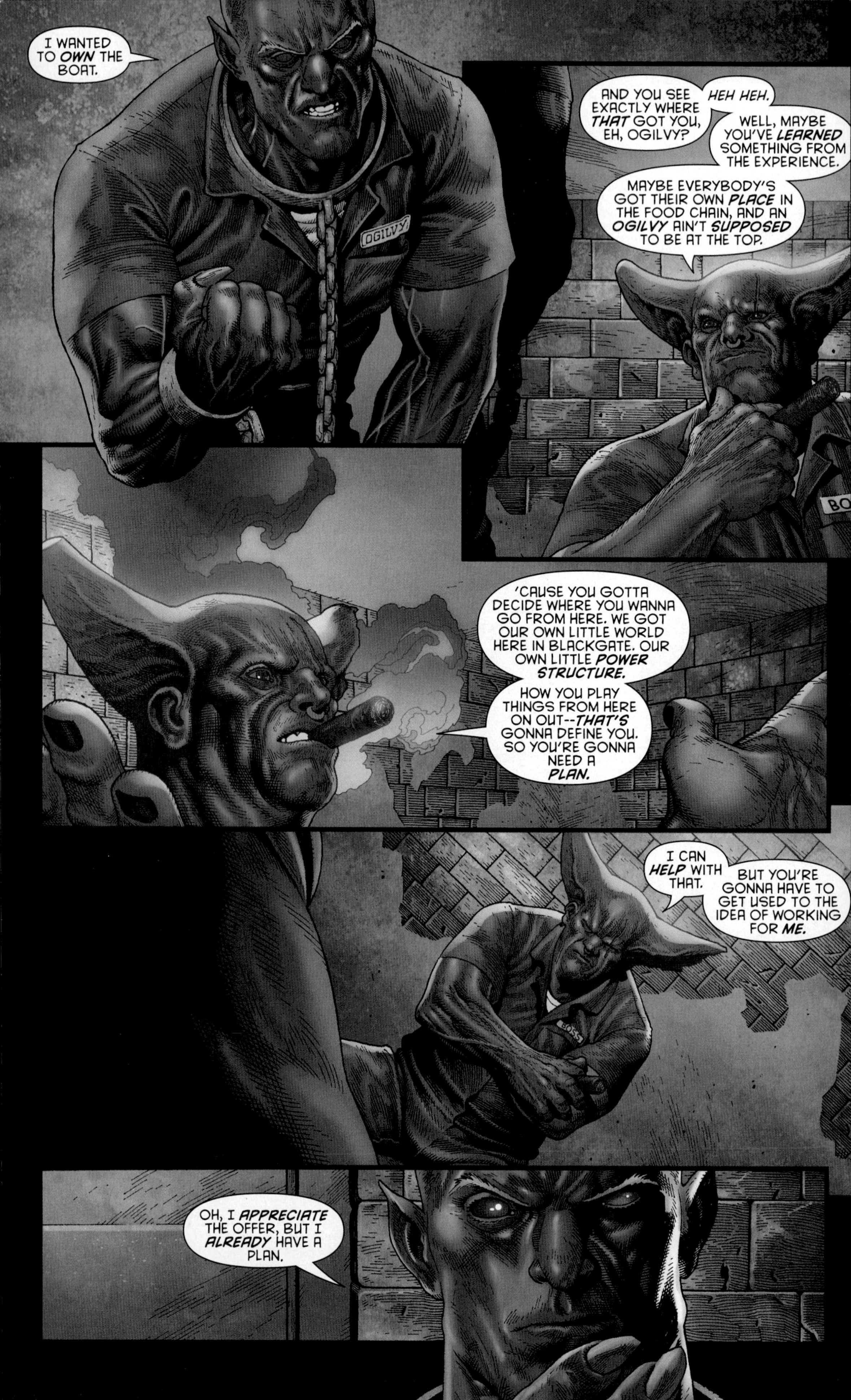
I WANTED TO OWN THE BOAT.
AND YOU SEE EXACTLY WHERE THAT GOT YOU, EH, OGILVY?
HEH HEH.
WELL, MAYBE YOU'VE LEARNED SOMETHING FROM THE EXPERIENCE.
MAYBE EVERYBODY'S GOT THEIR OWN PLACE IN THE FOOD CHAIN, AND AN OGILVY AIN'T SUPPOSED TO BE AT THE TOP.
'CAUSE YOU GOTTA DECIDE WHERE YOU WANNA GO FROM HERE. WE GOT OUR OWN LITTLE WORLD HERE IN BLACKGATE. OUR OWN LITTLE POWER STRUCTURE.
HOW YOU PLAY THINGS FROM HERE ON OUT--THAT'S GONNA DEFINE YOU. SO YOU'RE GONNA NEED A PLAN.
I CAN HELP WITH THAT.
BUT YOU'RE GONNA HAVE TO GET USED TO THE IDEA OF WORKING FOR ME.
OH, I APPRECIATE THE OFFER, BUT I ALREADY HAVE A PLAN.

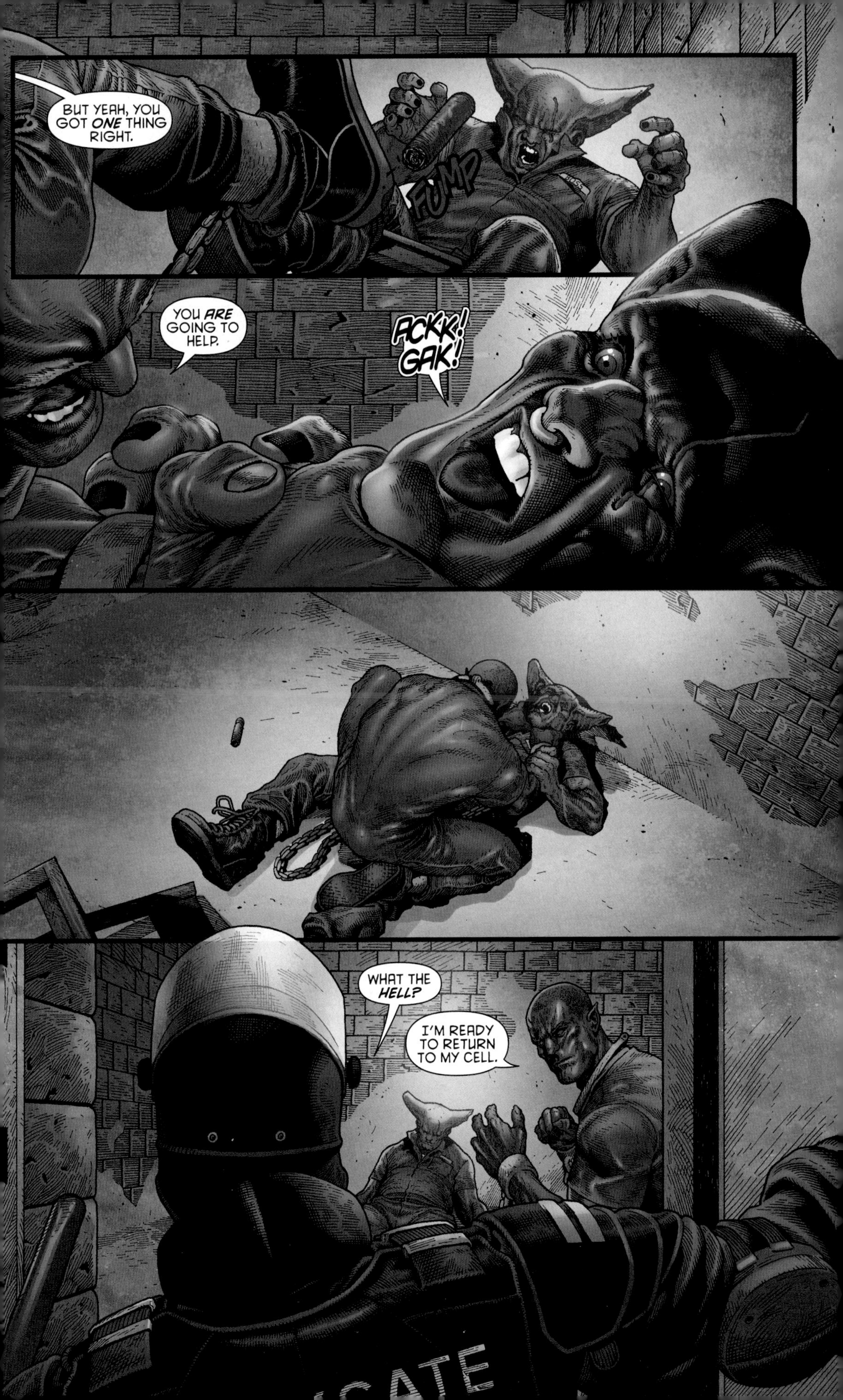

BUT YEAH, YOU GOT ONE THING RIGHT.
FUMP
YOU ARE GOING TO HELP.
ACKK! GAK!
WHAT THE HELL?
I'M READY TO RETURN TO MY CELL.

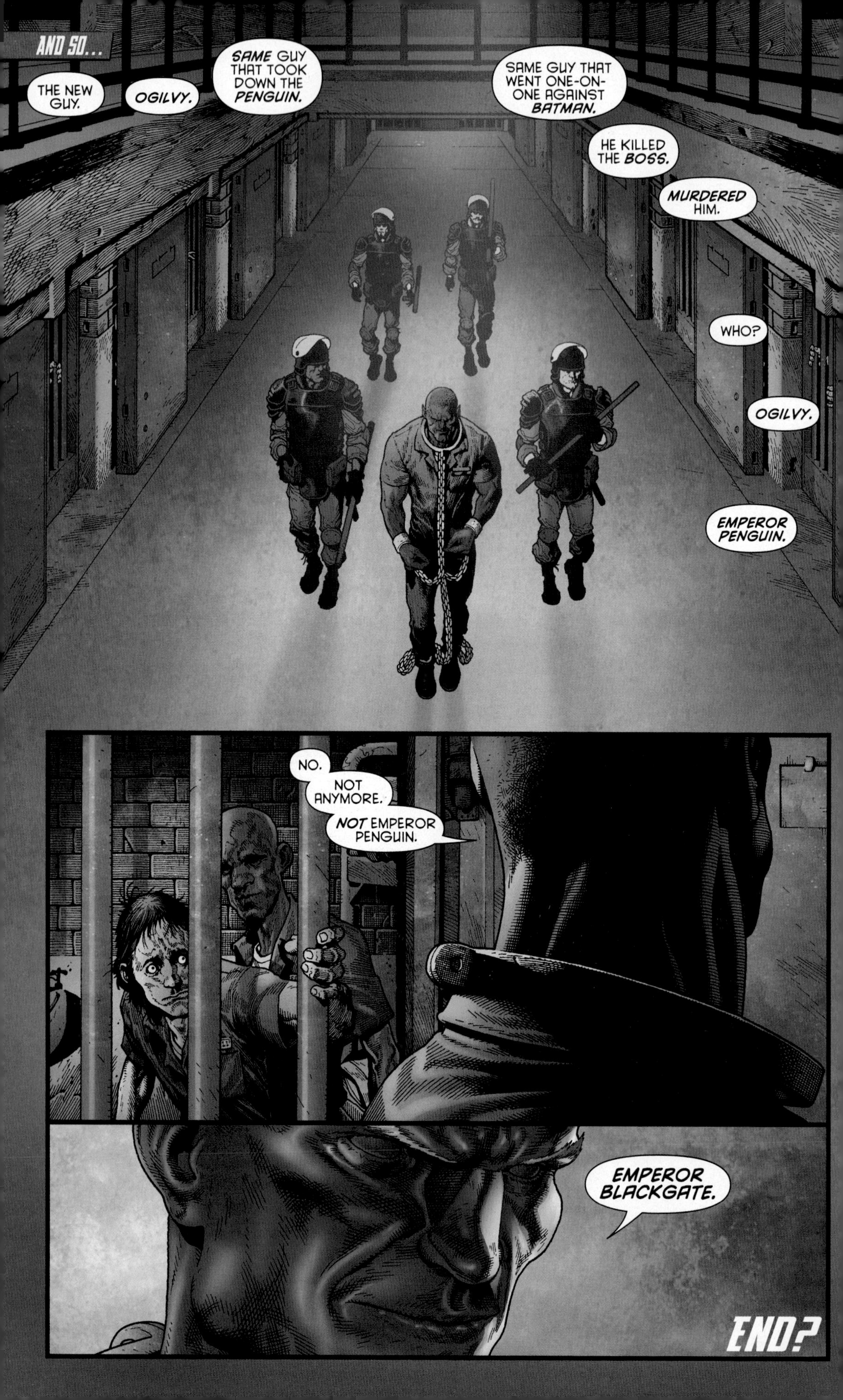

AND SO...
THE NEW GUY.
OGILVY.
SAME GUY THAT TOOK DOWN THE PENGUIN.
SAME GUY THAT WENT ONE-ON-ONE AGAINST BATMAN.
HE KILLED THE BOSS.
MURDERED HIM.
WHO?
OGILVY.
EMPEROR PENGUIN.
NO.
NOT ANYMORE.
NOT EMPEROR PENGUIN.
EMPEROR BLACKGATE.
END?

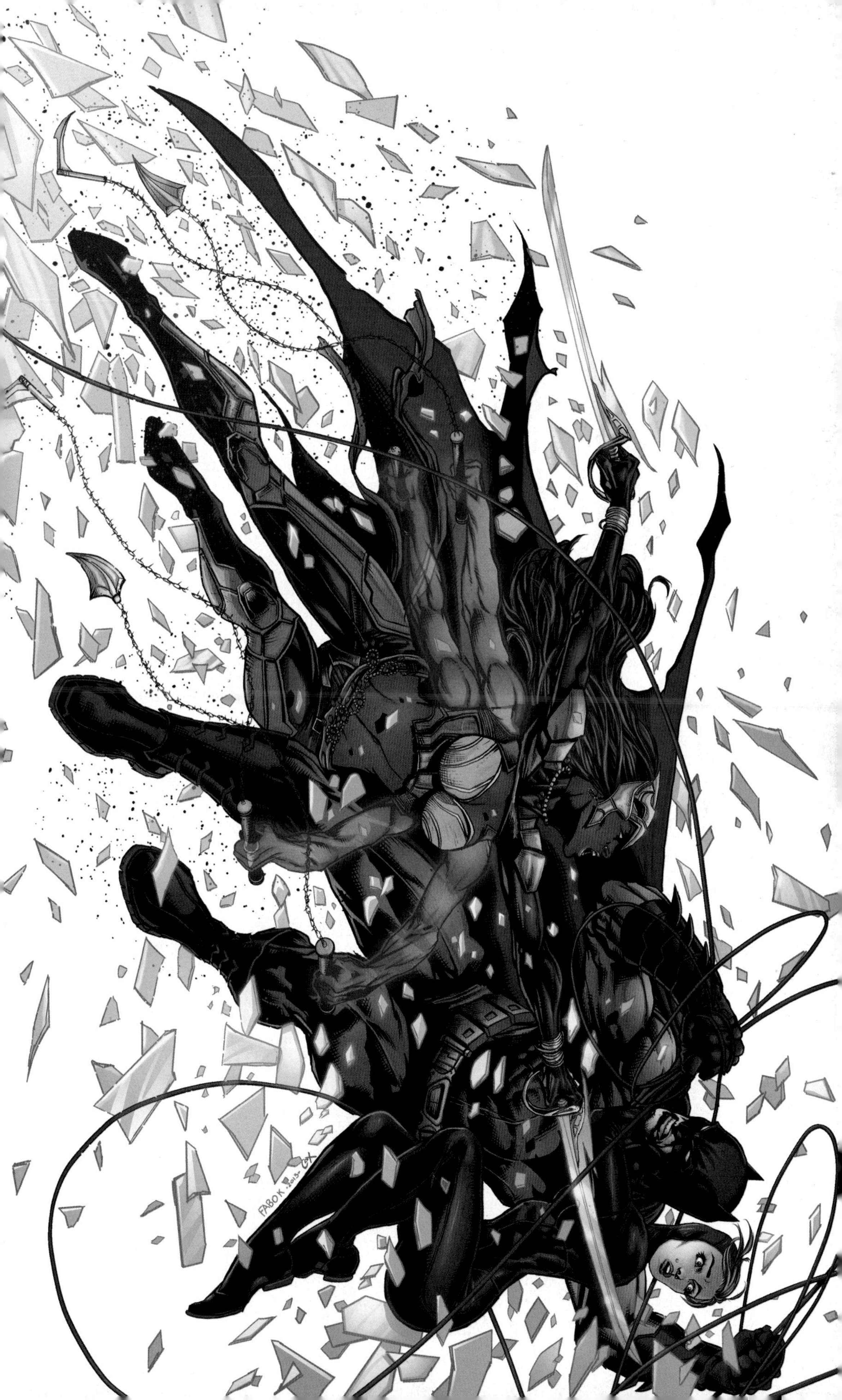
FABOK 2013

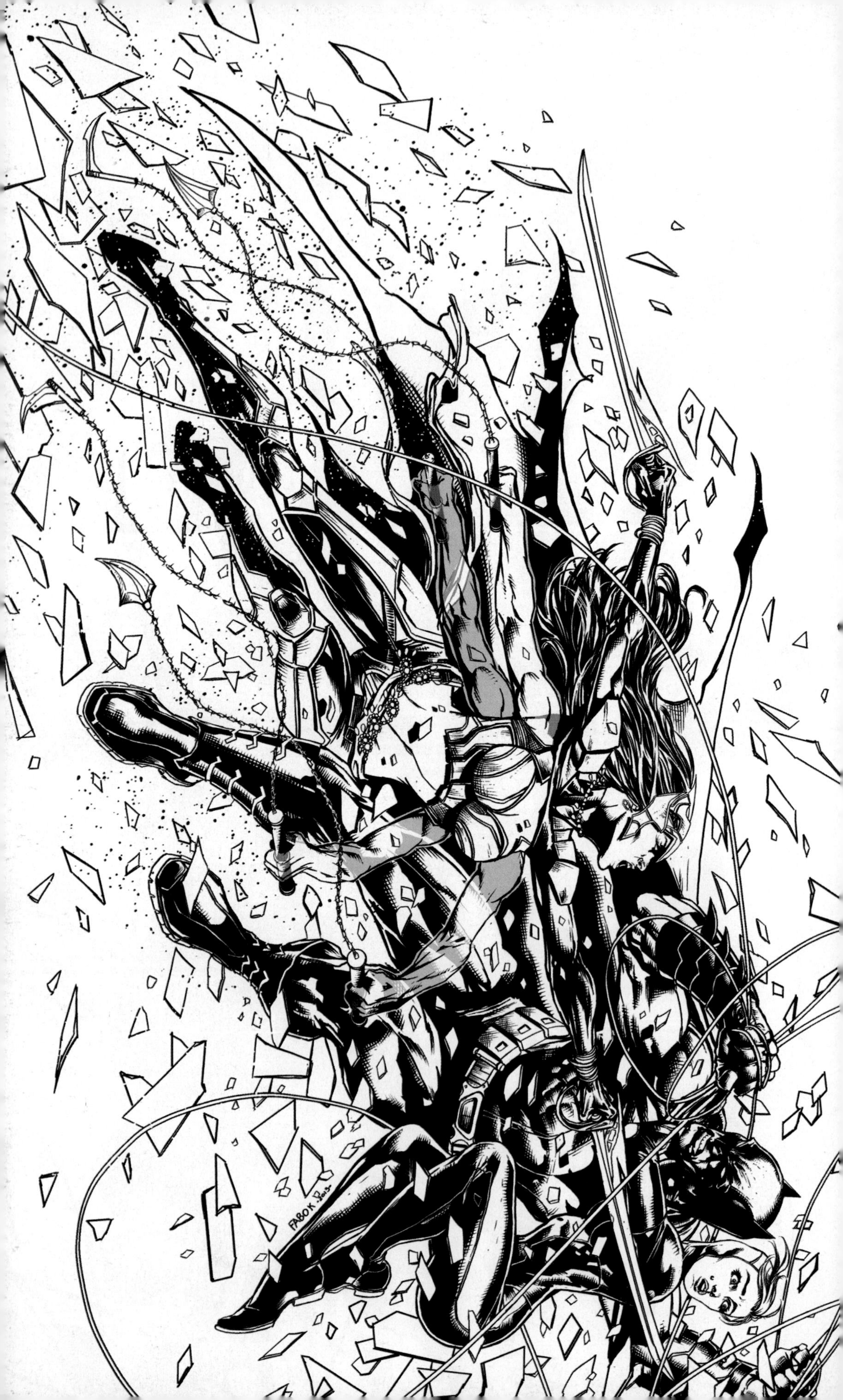
FABOK

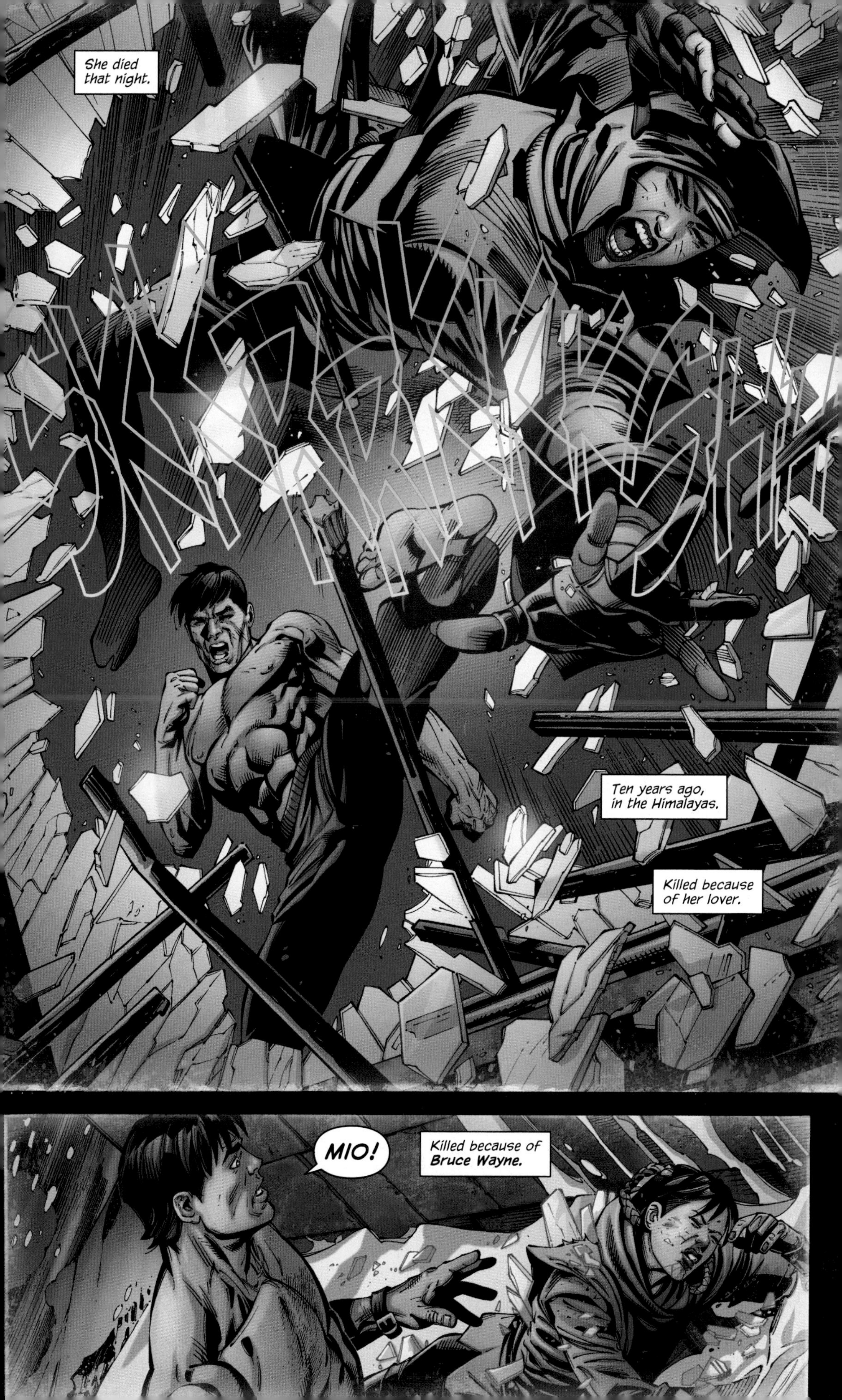
She died
that night.
Ten years ago,
in the Himalayas.
Killed because
of her lover.
MIO!
Killed because of
Bruce Wayne.

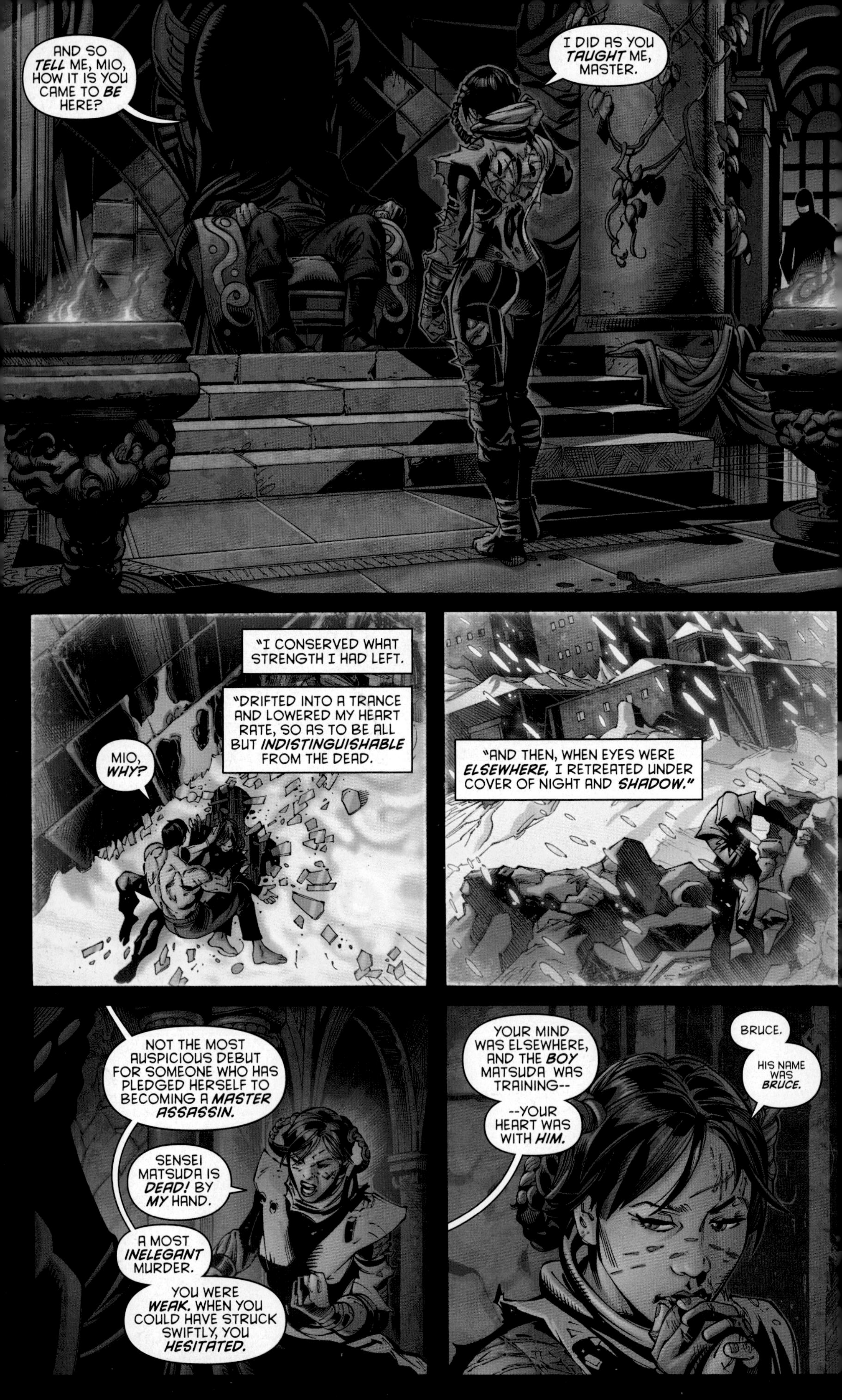
AND SO TELL ME, MIO, HOW IT IS YOU CAME TO BE HERE?
I DID AS YOU TAUGHT ME, MASTER.
"I CONSERVED WHAT STRENGTH I HAD LEFT.
"DRIFTED INTO A TRANCE AND LOWERED MY HEART RATE, SO AS TO BE ALL BUT INDISTINGUISHABLE FROM THE DEAD.
MIO, WHY?
"AND THEN, WHEN EYES WERE ELSEWHERE, I RETREATED UNDER COVER OF NIGHT AND SHADOW."
NOT THE MOST AUSPICIOUS DEBUT FOR SOMEONE WHO HAS PLEDGED HERSELF TO BECOMING A MASTER ASSASSIN.
SENSEI MATSUDA IS DEAD! BY MY HAND.
A MOST INELEGANT MURDER.
YOU WERE WEAK. WHEN YOU COULD HAVE STRUCK SWIFTLY, YOU HESITATED.
YOUR MIND WAS ELSEWHERE, AND THE BOY MATSUDA WAS TRAINING--
--YOUR HEART WAS WITH HIM.
BRUCE.
HIS NAME WAS BRUCE.

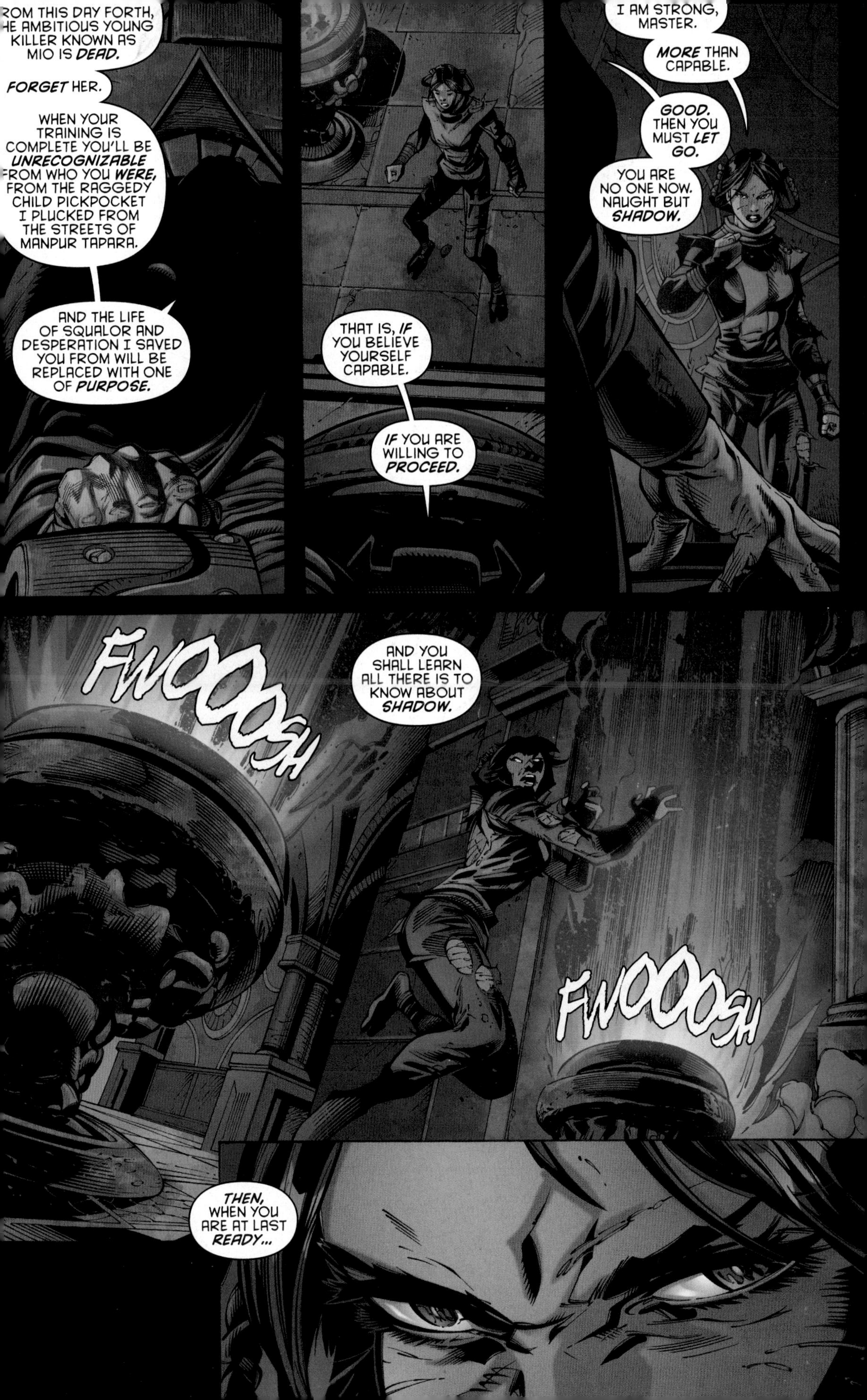
ROM THIS DAY FORTH, HE AMBITIOUS YOUNG KILLER KNOWN AS MIO IS DEAD.
FORGET HER.
WHEN YOUR TRAINING IS COMPLETE YOU'LL BE UNRECOGNIZABLE FROM WHO YOU WERE, FROM THE RAGGEDY CHILD PICKPOCKET I PLUCKED FROM THE STREETS OF MANPUR TAPARA.
AND THE LIFE OF SQUALOR AND DESPERATION I SAVED YOU FROM WILL BE REPLACED WITH ONE OF PURPOSE.
THAT IS, IF YOU BELIEVE YOURSELF CAPABLE.
IF YOU ARE WILLING TO PROCEED.
I AM STRONG, MASTER.
MORE THAN CAPABLE.
GOOD. THEN YOU MUST LET GO.
YOU ARE NO ONE NOW. NAUGHT BUT SHADOW.
FWOOOSH
AND YOU SHALL LEARN ALL THERE IS TO KNOW ABOUT SHADOW.
FWOOOSH
THEN, WHEN YOU ARE AT LAST READY...

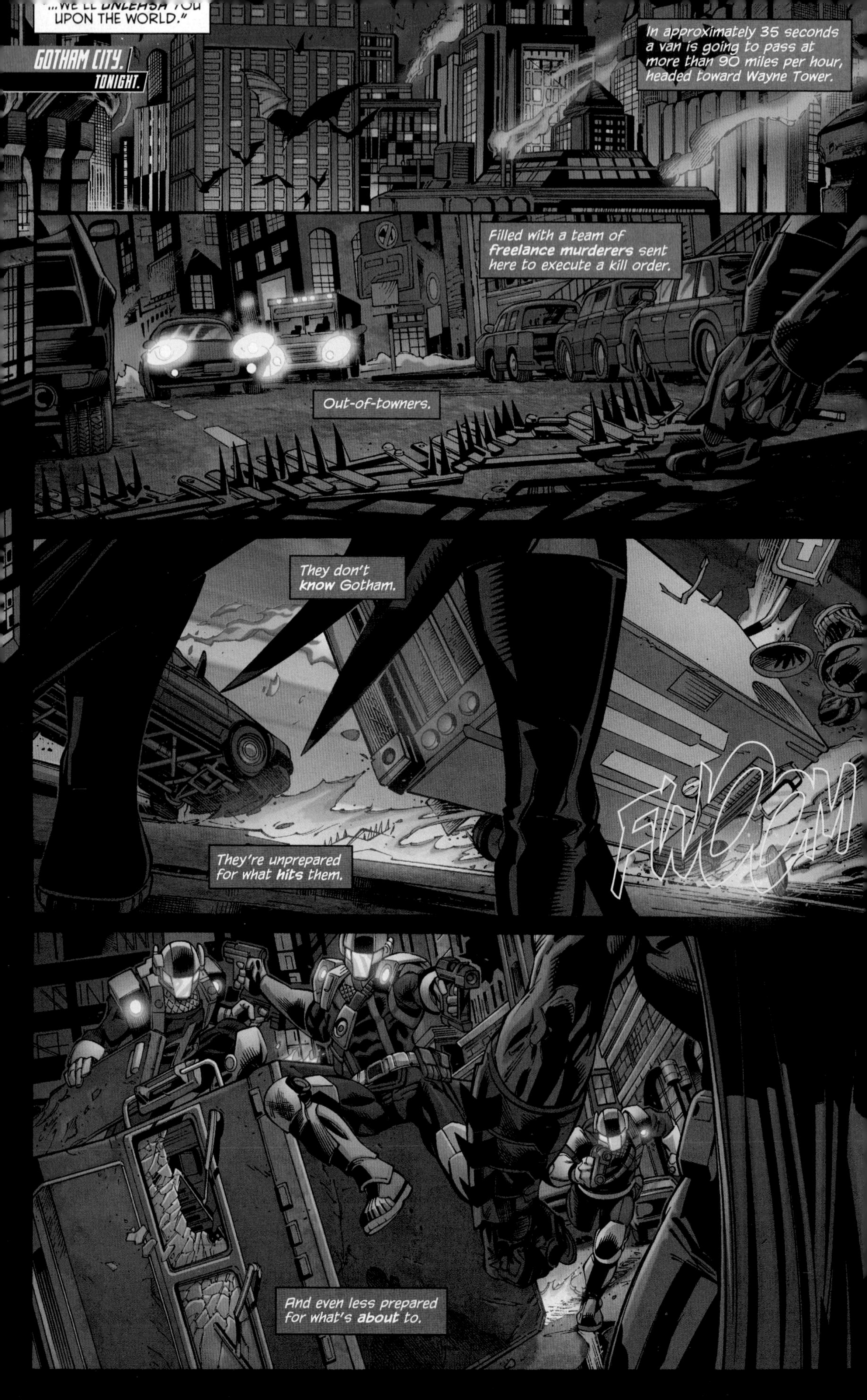
UPON THE WORLD."
GOTHAM CITY.
TONIGHT.
In approximately 35 seconds a van is going to pass at more than 90 miles per hour, headed toward Wayne Tower.
Filled with a team of freelance murderers sent here to execute a kill order.
Out-of-towners.
They don't know Gotham.
They're unprepared for what hits them.
FWOOM
And even less prepared for what's about to.

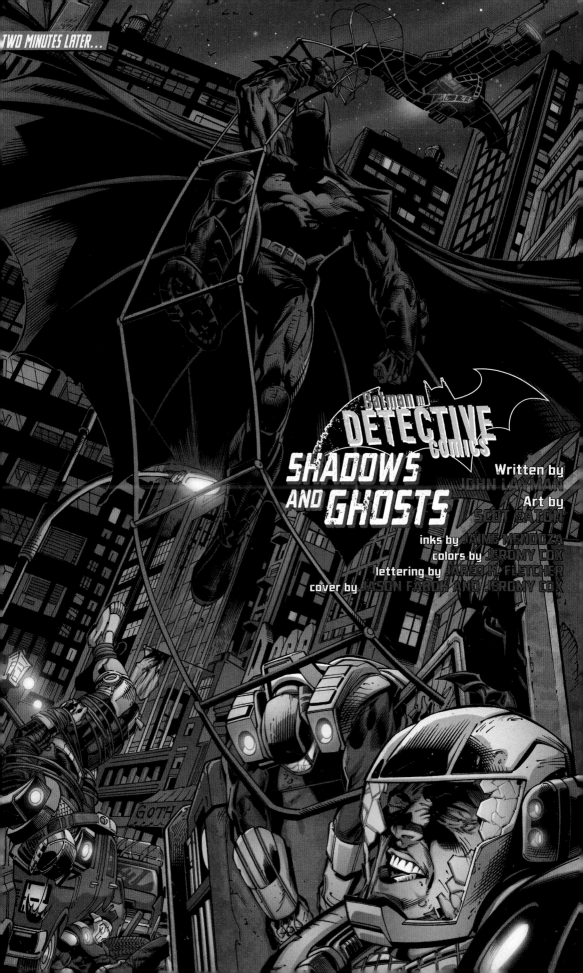

TWO MINUTES LATER...

Batman in
DETECTIVE Comics
SHADOWS AND GHOSTS

Written by
JOHN LAYMAN

Art by
SCOT EATON

inks by JAIME MENDOZA
colors by JEROMY COX
lettering by JARED K. FLETCHER
cover by JASON FABOK AND JEROMY COX

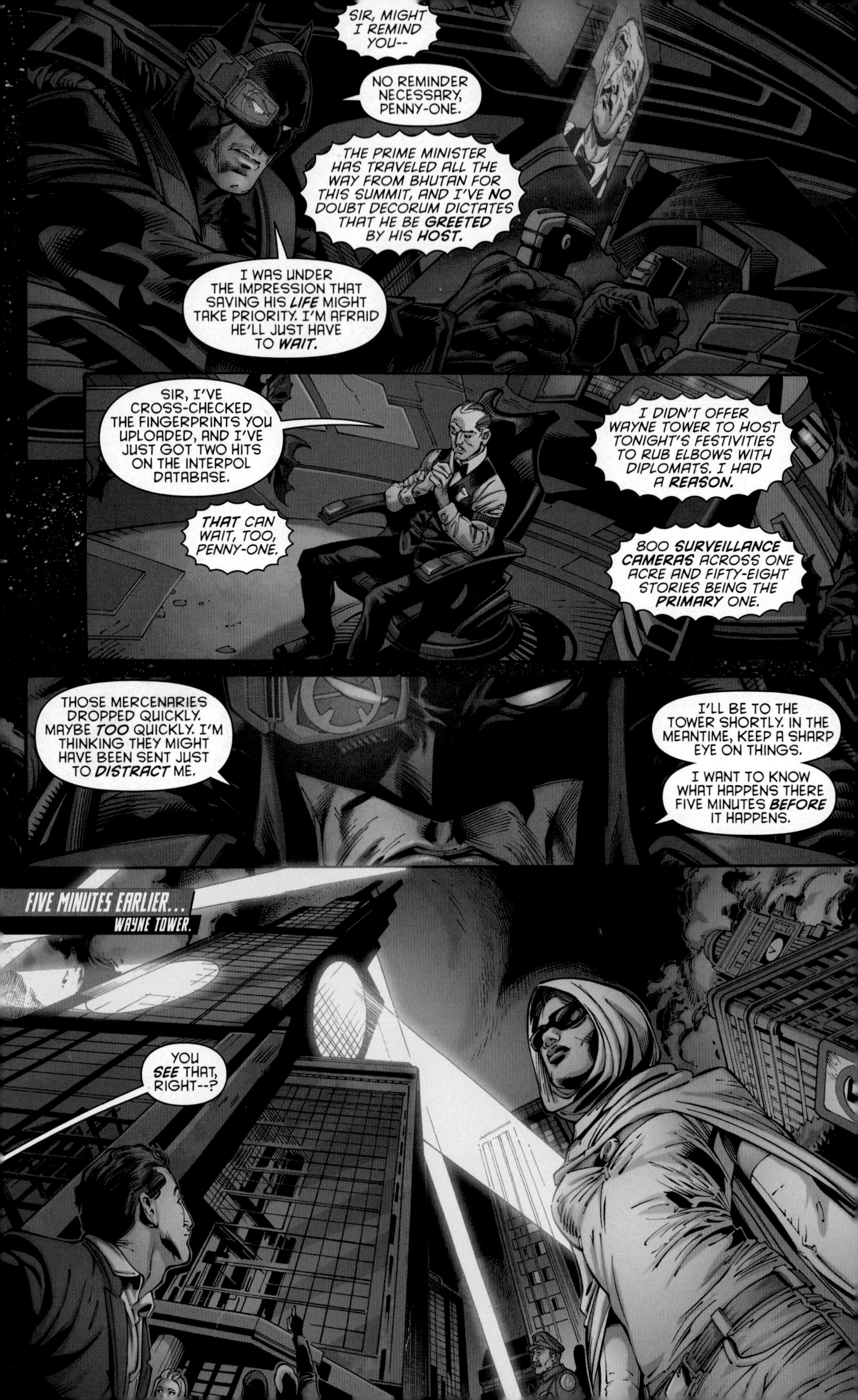
SIR, MIGHT I REMIND YOU--
NO REMINDER NECESSARY, PENNY-ONE.
THE PRIME MINISTER HAS TRAVELED ALL THE WAY FROM BHUTAN FOR THIS SUMMIT, AND I'VE NO DOUBT DECORUM DICTATES THAT HE BE GREETED BY HIS HOST.
I WAS UNDER THE IMPRESSION THAT SAVING HIS LIFE MIGHT TAKE PRIORITY. I'M AFRAID HE'LL JUST HAVE TO WAIT.
SIR, I'VE CROSS-CHECKED THE FINGERPRINTS YOU UPLOADED, AND I'VE JUST GOT TWO HITS ON THE INTERPOL DATABASE.
THAT CAN WAIT, TOO, PENNY-ONE.
I DIDN'T OFFER WAYNE TOWER TO HOST TONIGHT'S FESTIVITIES TO RUB ELBOWS WITH DIPLOMATS. I HAD A REASON.
800 SURVEILLANCE CAMERAS ACROSS ONE ACRE AND FIFTY-EIGHT STORIES BEING THE PRIMARY ONE.
THOSE MERCENARIES DROPPED QUICKLY. MAYBE TOO QUICKLY. I'M THINKING THEY MIGHT HAVE BEEN SENT JUST TO DISTRACT ME.
I'LL BE TO THE TOWER SHORTLY. IN THE MEANTIME, KEEP A SHARP EYE ON THINGS.
I WANT TO KNOW WHAT HAPPENS THERE FIVE MINUTES BEFORE IT HAPPENS.
FIVE MINUTES EARLIER...
WAYNE TOWER.
YOU SEE THAT, RIGHT--?

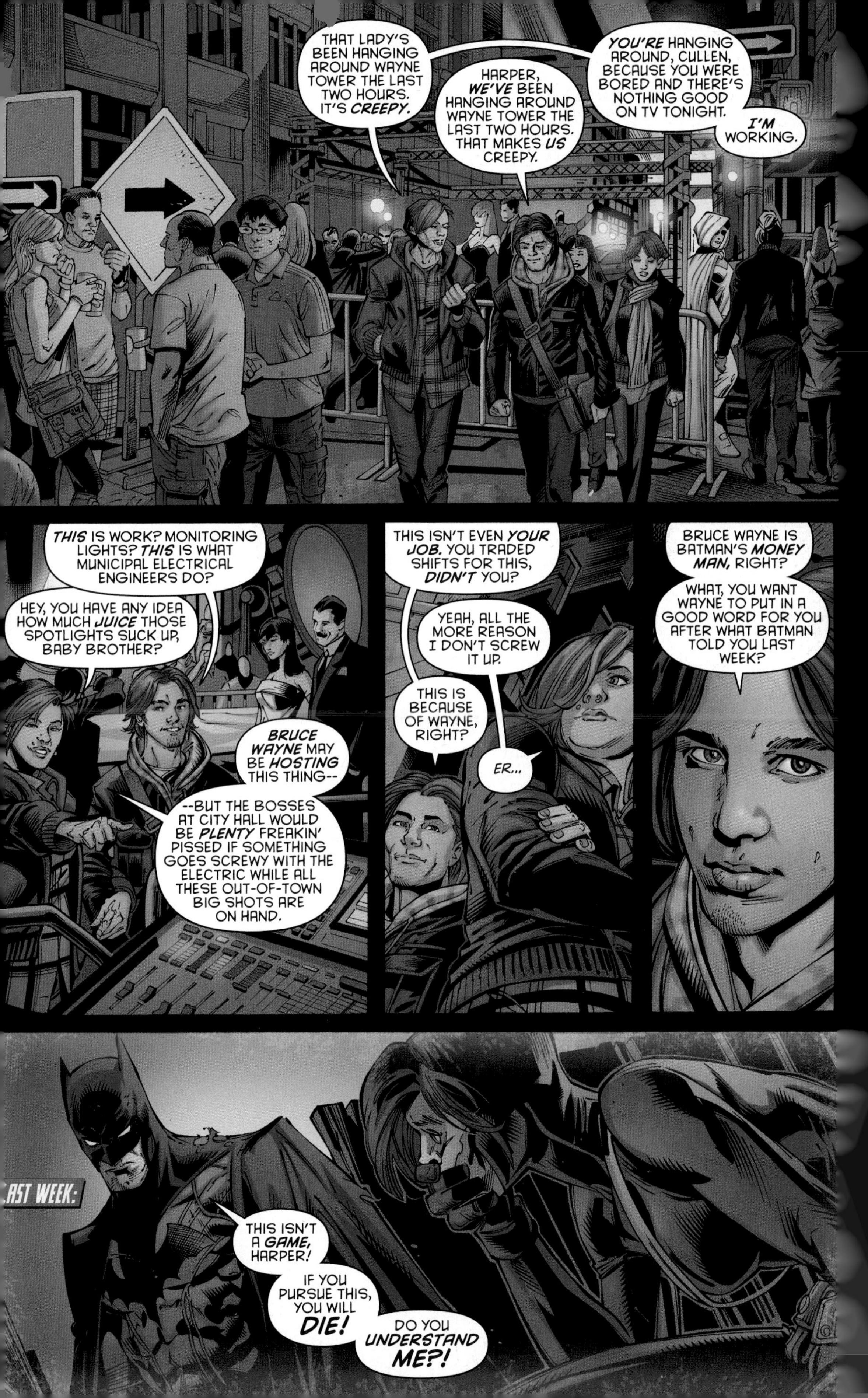
THAT LADY'S BEEN HANGING AROUND WAYNE TOWER THE LAST TWO HOURS. IT'S CREEPY.
HARPER, WE'VE BEEN HANGING AROUND WAYNE TOWER THE LAST TWO HOURS. THAT MAKES US CREEPY.
YOU'RE HANGING AROUND, CULLEN, BECAUSE YOU WERE BORED AND THERE'S NOTHING GOOD ON TV TONIGHT.
I'M WORKING.
THIS IS WORK? MONITORING LIGHTS? THIS IS WHAT MUNICIPAL ELECTRICAL ENGINEERS DO?
HEY, YOU HAVE ANY IDEA HOW MUCH JUICE THOSE SPOTLIGHTS SUCK UP, BABY BROTHER?
BRUCE WAYNE MAY BE HOSTING THIS THING--
--BUT THE BOSSES AT CITY HALL WOULD BE PLENTY FREAKIN' PISSED IF SOMETHING GOES SCREWY WITH THE ELECTRIC WHILE ALL THESE OUT-OF-TOWN BIG SHOTS ARE ON HAND.
THIS ISN'T EVEN YOUR JOB. YOU TRADED SHIFTS FOR THIS, DIDN'T YOU?
YEAH, ALL THE MORE REASON I DON'T SCREW IT UP.
THIS IS BECAUSE OF WAYNE, RIGHT?
ER...
BRUCE WAYNE IS BATMAN'S MONEY MAN, RIGHT?
WHAT, YOU WANT WAYNE TO PUT IN A GOOD WORD FOR YOU AFTER WHAT BATMAN TOLD YOU LAST WEEK?
LAST WEEK:
THIS ISN'T A GAME, HARPER!
IF YOU PURSUE THIS, YOU WILL DIE!
DO YOU UNDERSTAND ME?!

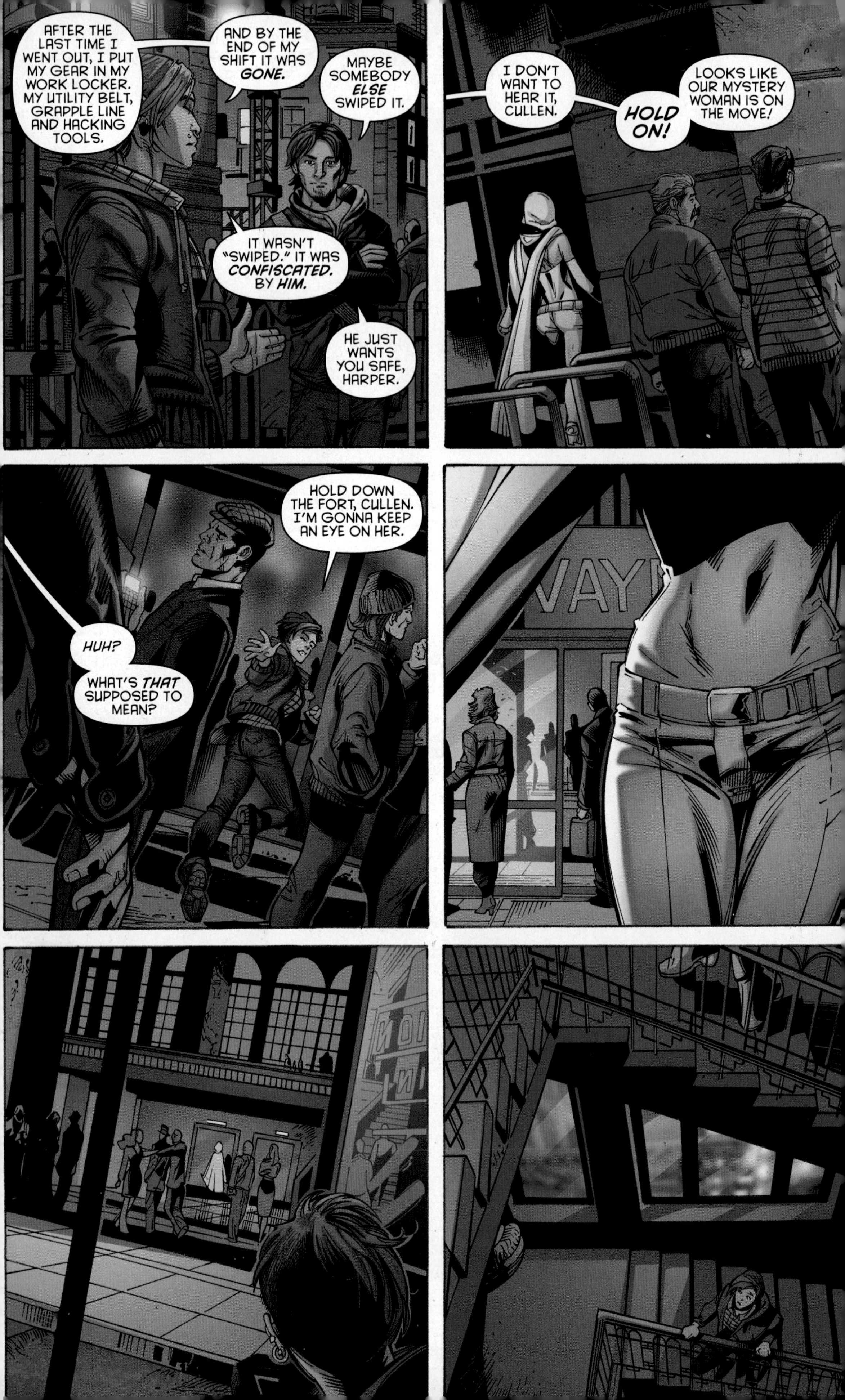
AFTER THE LAST TIME I WENT OUT, I PUT MY GEAR IN MY WORK LOCKER. MY UTILITY BELT, GRAPPLE LINE AND HACKING TOOLS.
AND BY THE END OF MY SHIFT IT WAS GONE.
MAYBE SOMEBODY ELSE SWIPED IT.
IT WASN'T "SWIPED." IT WAS CONFISCATED. BY HIM.
HE JUST WANTS YOU SAFE, HARPER.
I DON'T WANT TO HEAR IT, CULLEN.
HOLD ON!
LOOKS LIKE OUR MYSTERY WOMAN IS ON THE MOVE!
HOLD DOWN THE FORT, CULLEN. I'M GONNA KEEP AN EYE ON HER.
HUH?
WHAT'S THAT SUPPOSED TO MEAN?
WAYN

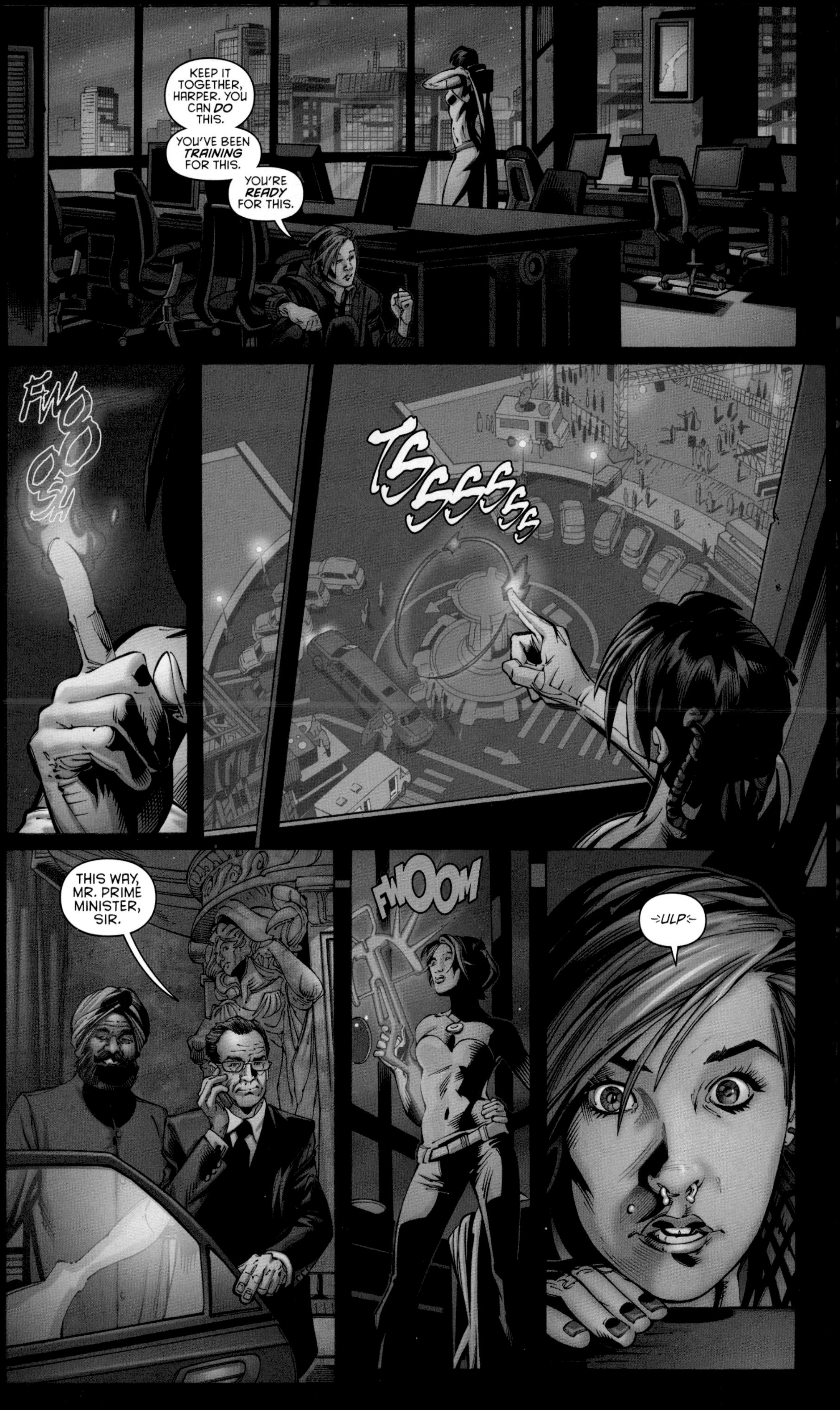
KEEP IT TOGETHER, HARPER. YOU CAN DO THIS.
YOU'VE BEEN TRAINING FOR THIS.
YOU'RE READY FOR THIS.
FWOOOSH
TSSSSSSS
THIS WAY, MR. PRIME MINISTER, SIR.
FWOOM
ULP

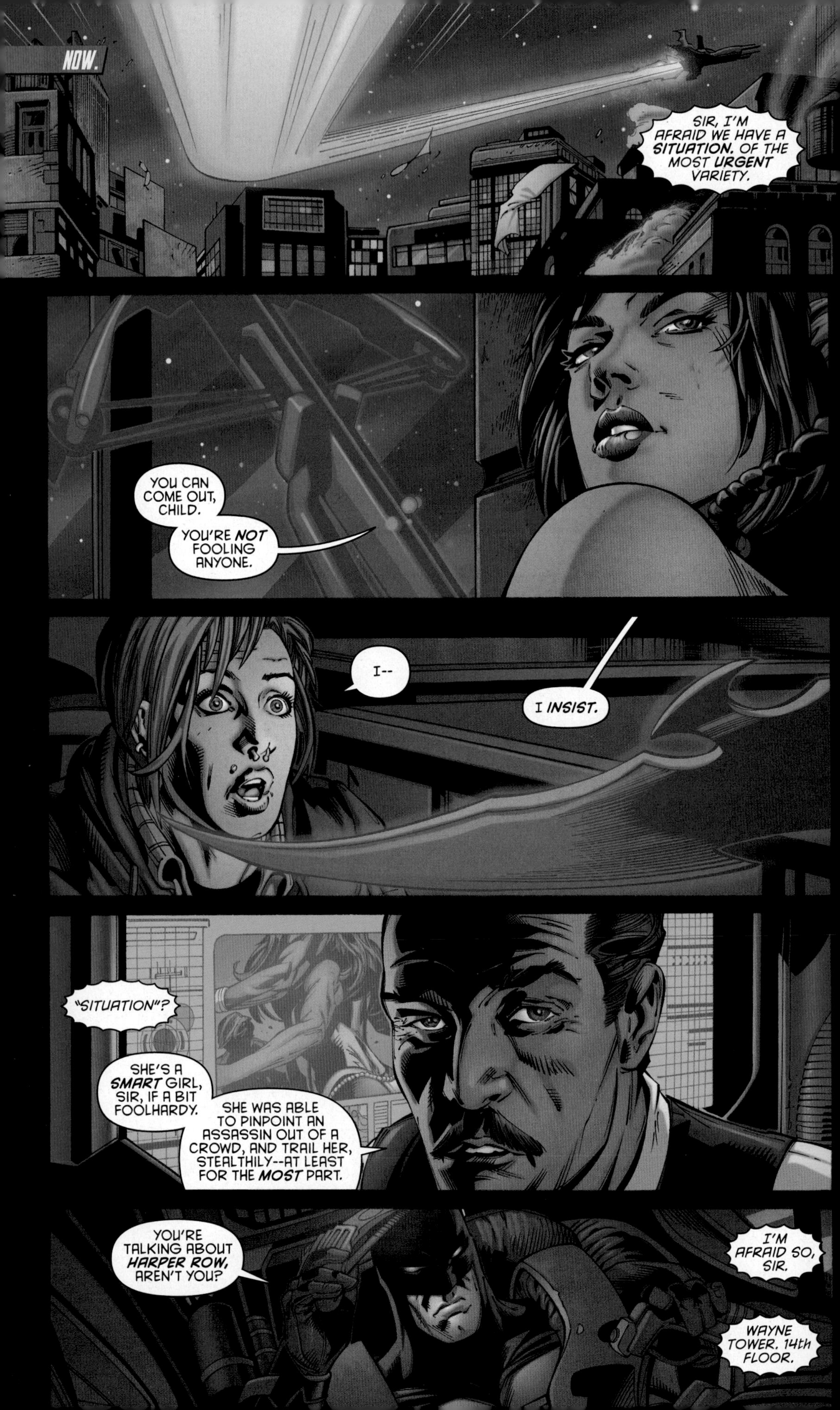

NOW.
SIR, I'M AFRAID WE HAVE A SITUATION. OF THE MOST URGENT VARIETY.
YOU CAN COME OUT, CHILD.
YOU'RE NOT FOOLING ANYONE.
I--
I INSIST.
"SITUATION"?
SHE'S A SMART GIRL, SIR, IF A BIT FOOLHARDY.
SHE WAS ABLE TO PINPOINT AN ASSASSIN OUT OF A CROWD, AND TRAIL HER, STEALTHILY--AT LEAST FOR THE MOST PART.
YOU'RE TALKING ABOUT HARPER ROW, AREN'T YOU?
I'M AFRAID SO, SIR.
WAYNE TOWER. 14th FLOOR.

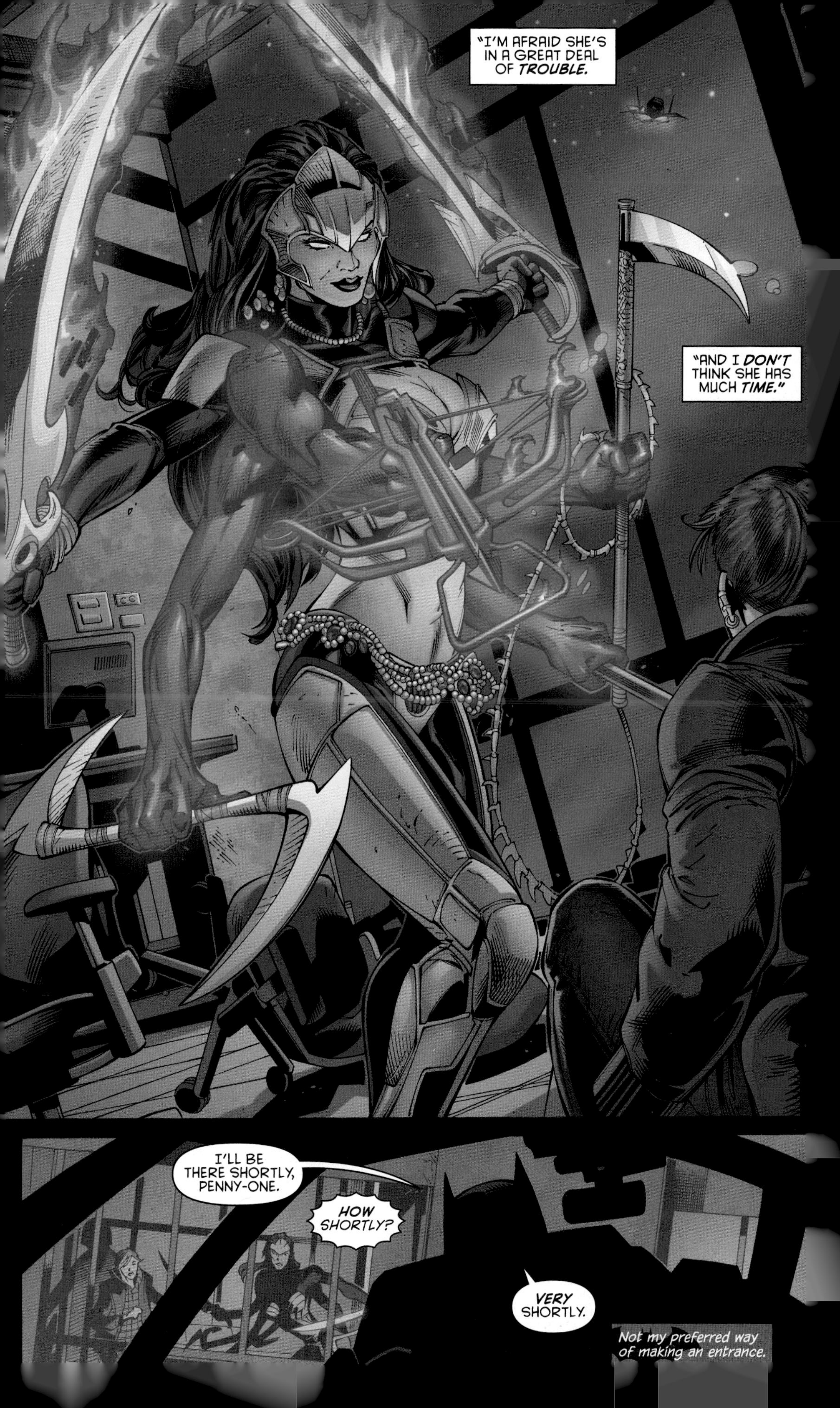
"I'M AFRAID SHE'S IN A GREAT DEAL OF *TROUBLE.*
"AND I *DON'T* THINK SHE HAS MUCH *TIME.*"
I'LL BE THERE SHORTLY, PENNY-ONE.
HOW SHORTLY?
VERY SHORTLY.
Not my preferred way of making an entrance.

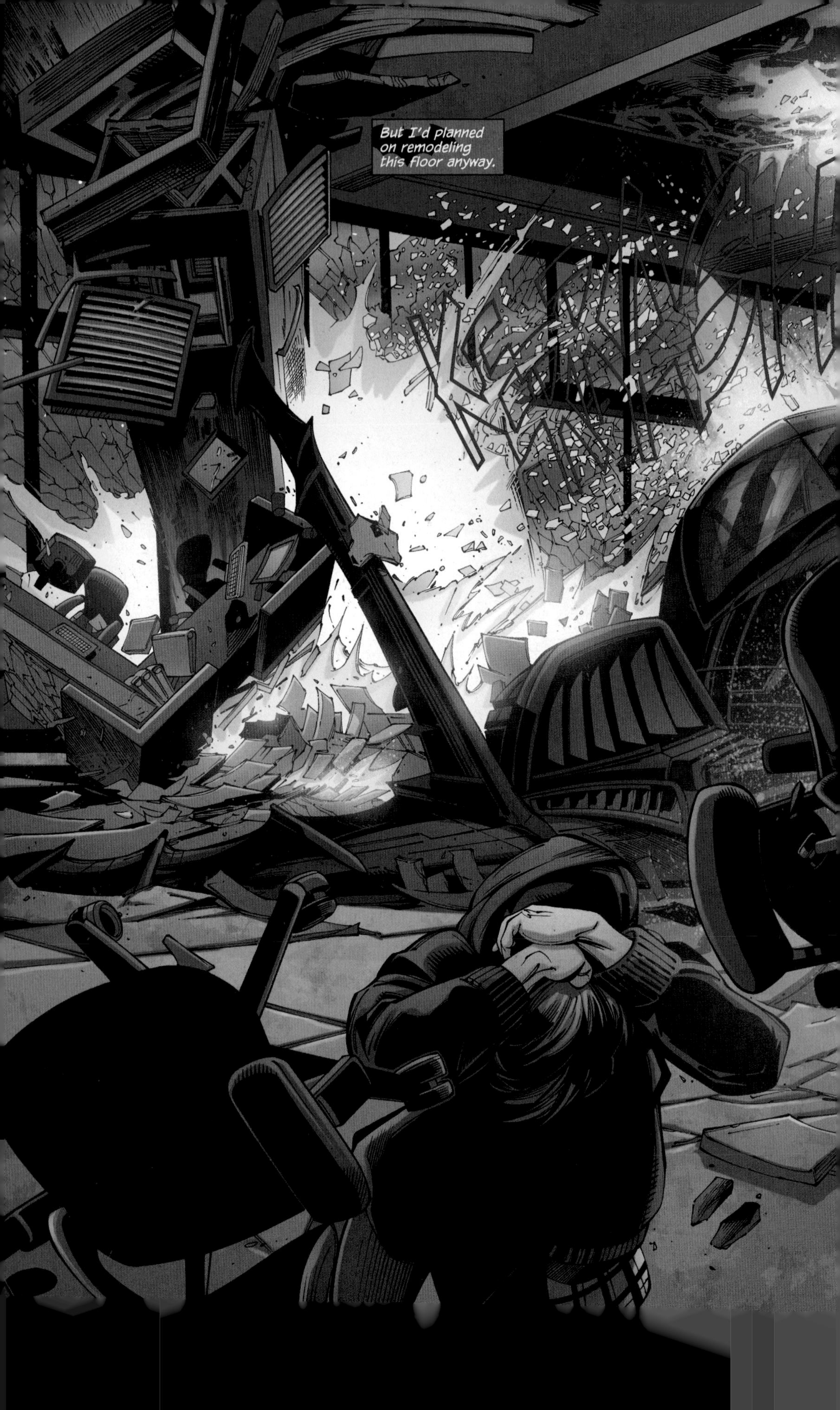
But I'd planned on remodeling this floor anyway.

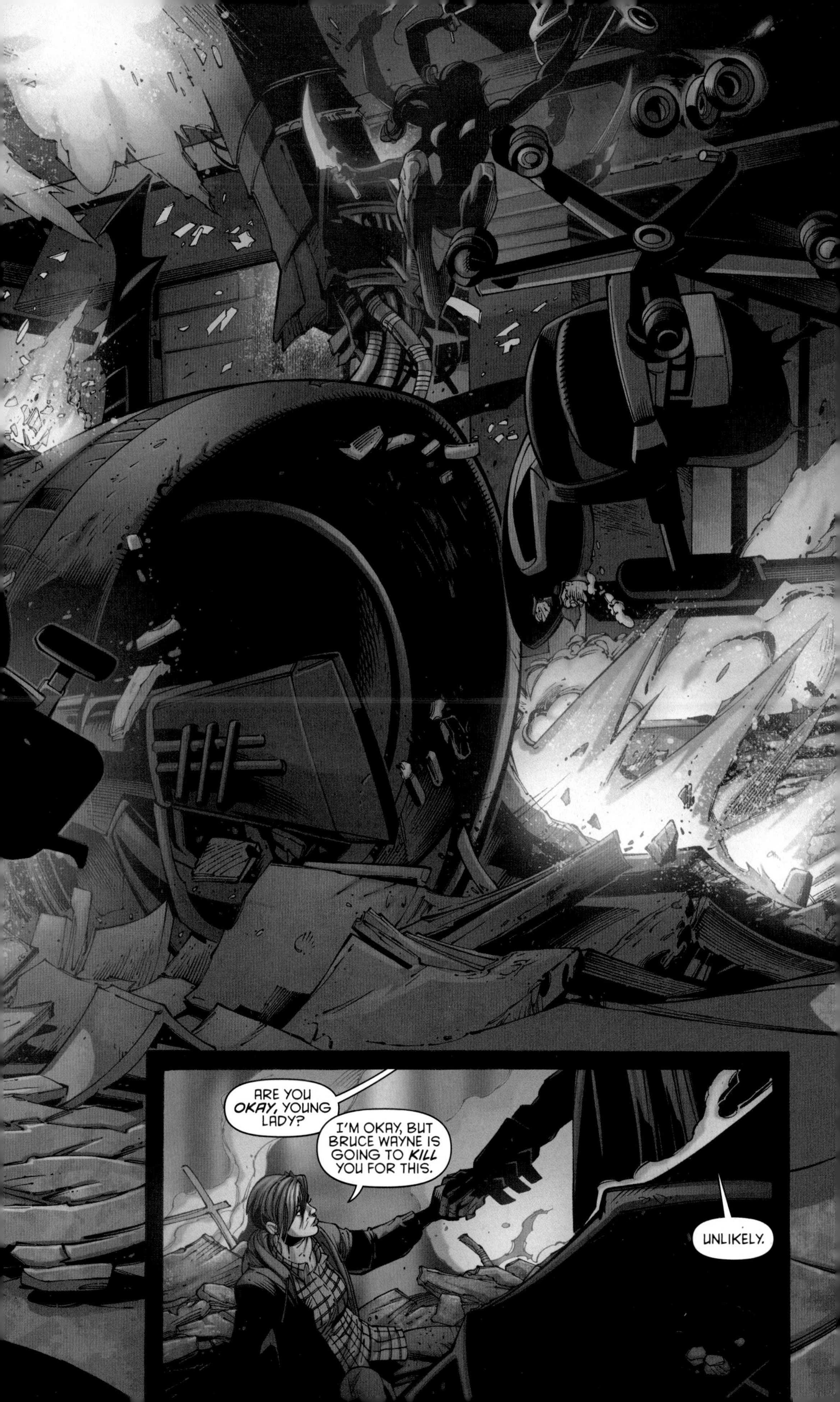

ARE YOU OKAY, YOUNG LADY?
I'M OKAY, BUT BRUCE WAYNE IS GOING TO KILL YOU FOR THIS.
UNLIKELY.

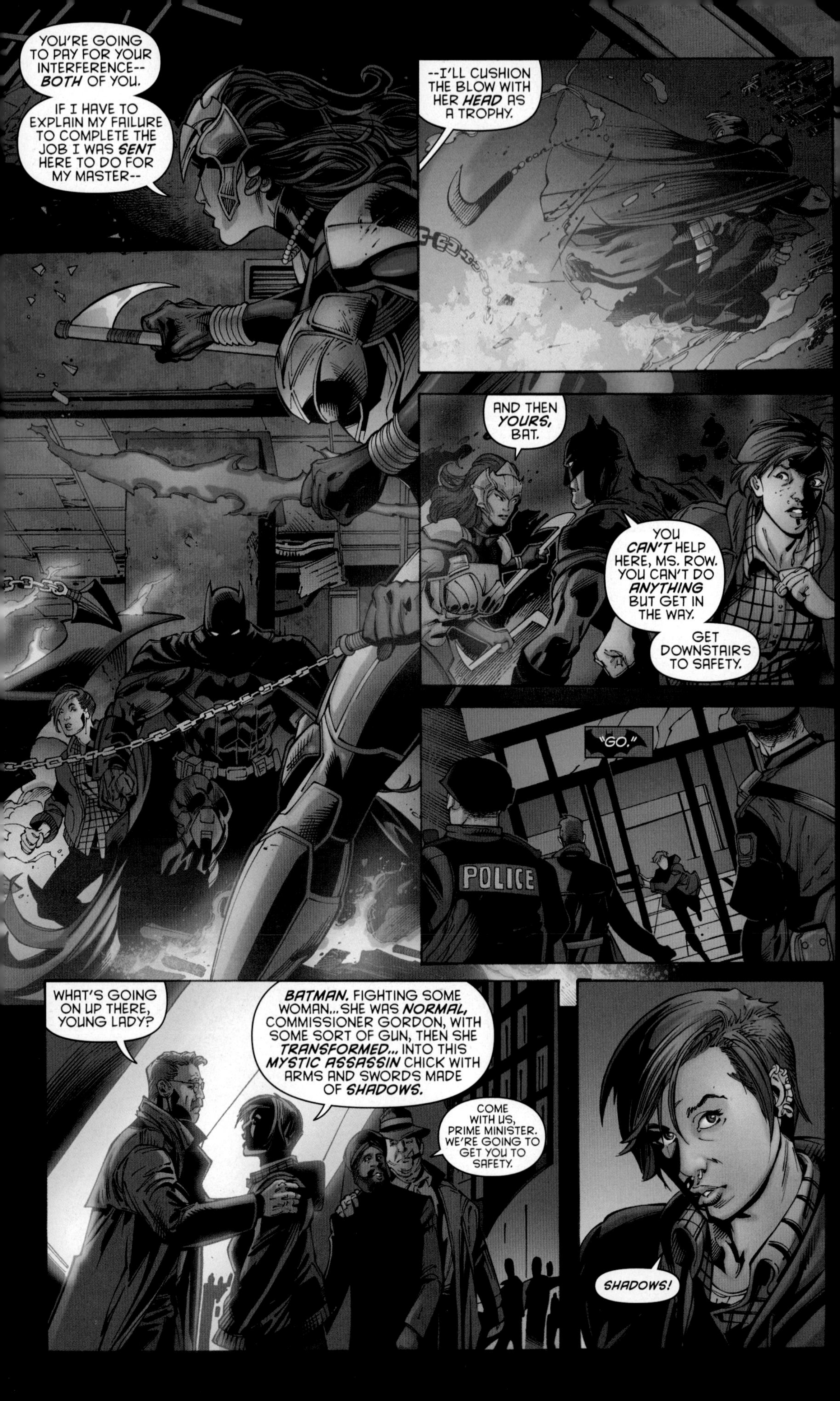
YOU'RE GOING TO PAY FOR YOUR INTERFERENCE-- BOTH OF YOU.
IF I HAVE TO EXPLAIN MY FAILURE TO COMPLETE THE JOB I WAS SENT HERE TO DO FOR MY MASTER--
--I'LL CUSHION THE BLOW WITH HER HEAD AS A TROPHY.
AND THEN YOURS, BAT.
YOU CAN'T HELP HERE, MS. ROW. YOU CAN'T DO ANYTHING BUT GET IN THE WAY.
GET DOWNSTAIRS TO SAFETY.
"GO."
POLICE
WHAT'S GOING ON UP THERE, YOUNG LADY?
BATMAN. FIGHTING SOME WOMAN... SHE WAS NORMAL, COMMISSIONER GORDON, WITH SOME SORT OF GUN, THEN SHE TRANSFORMED... INTO THIS MYSTIC ASSASSIN CHICK WITH ARMS AND SWORDS MADE OF SHADOWS.
COME WITH US, PRIME MINISTER. WE'RE GOING TO GET YOU TO SAFETY.
SHADOWS!

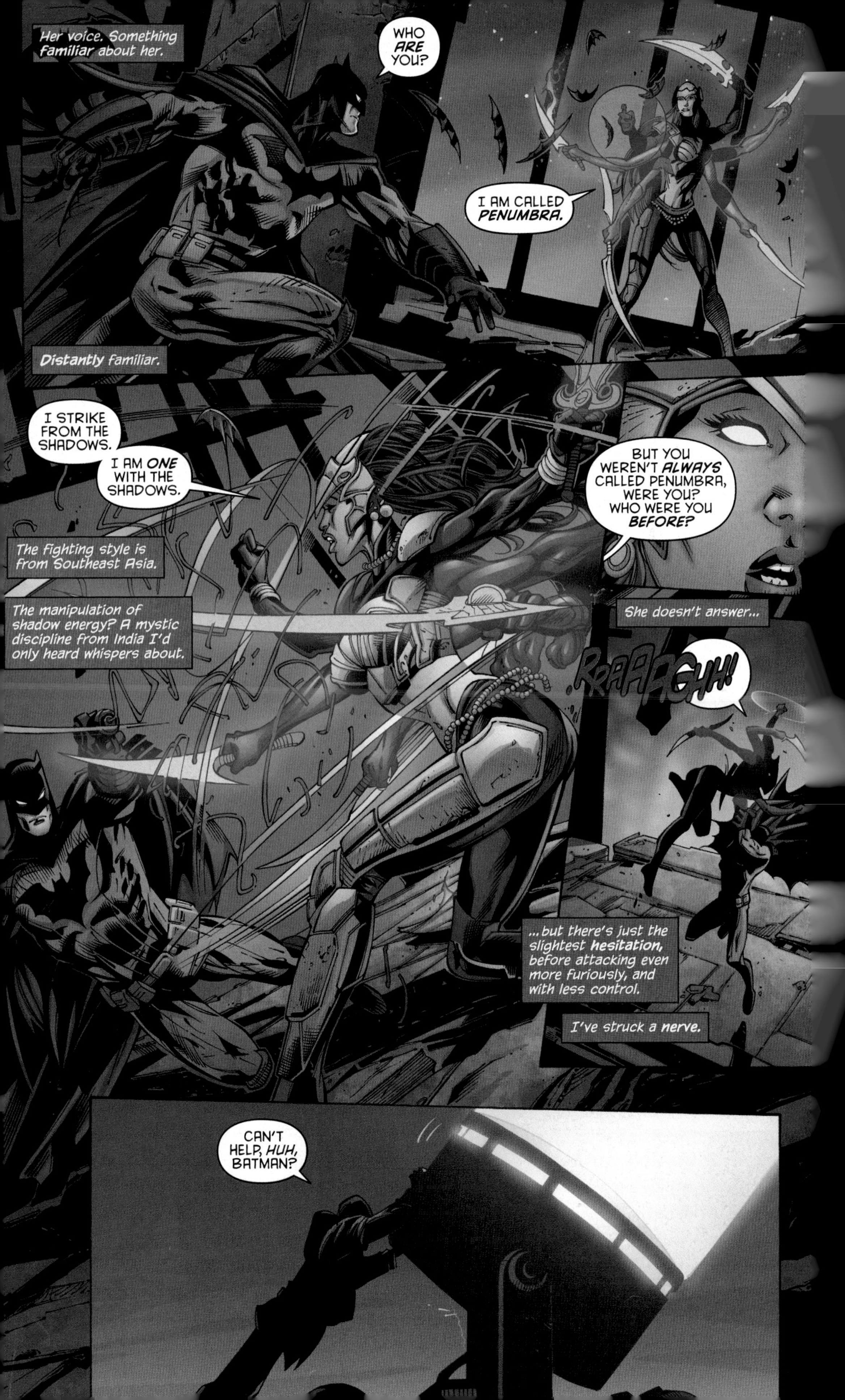
Her voice. Something familiar about her.
WHO ARE YOU?
I AM CALLED PENUMBRA.
Distantly familiar.
I STRIKE FROM THE SHADOWS.
I AM ONE WITH THE SHADOWS.
The fighting style is from Southeast Asia.
The manipulation of shadow energy? A mystic discipline from India I'd only heard whispers about.
BUT YOU WEREN'T ALWAYS CALLED PENUMBRA, WERE YOU? WHO WERE YOU BEFORE?
She doesn't answer...
RRAAAAGHH!
...but there's just the slightest hesitation, before attacking even more furiously, and with less control.
I've struck a nerve.
CAN'T HELP, HUH, BATMAN?

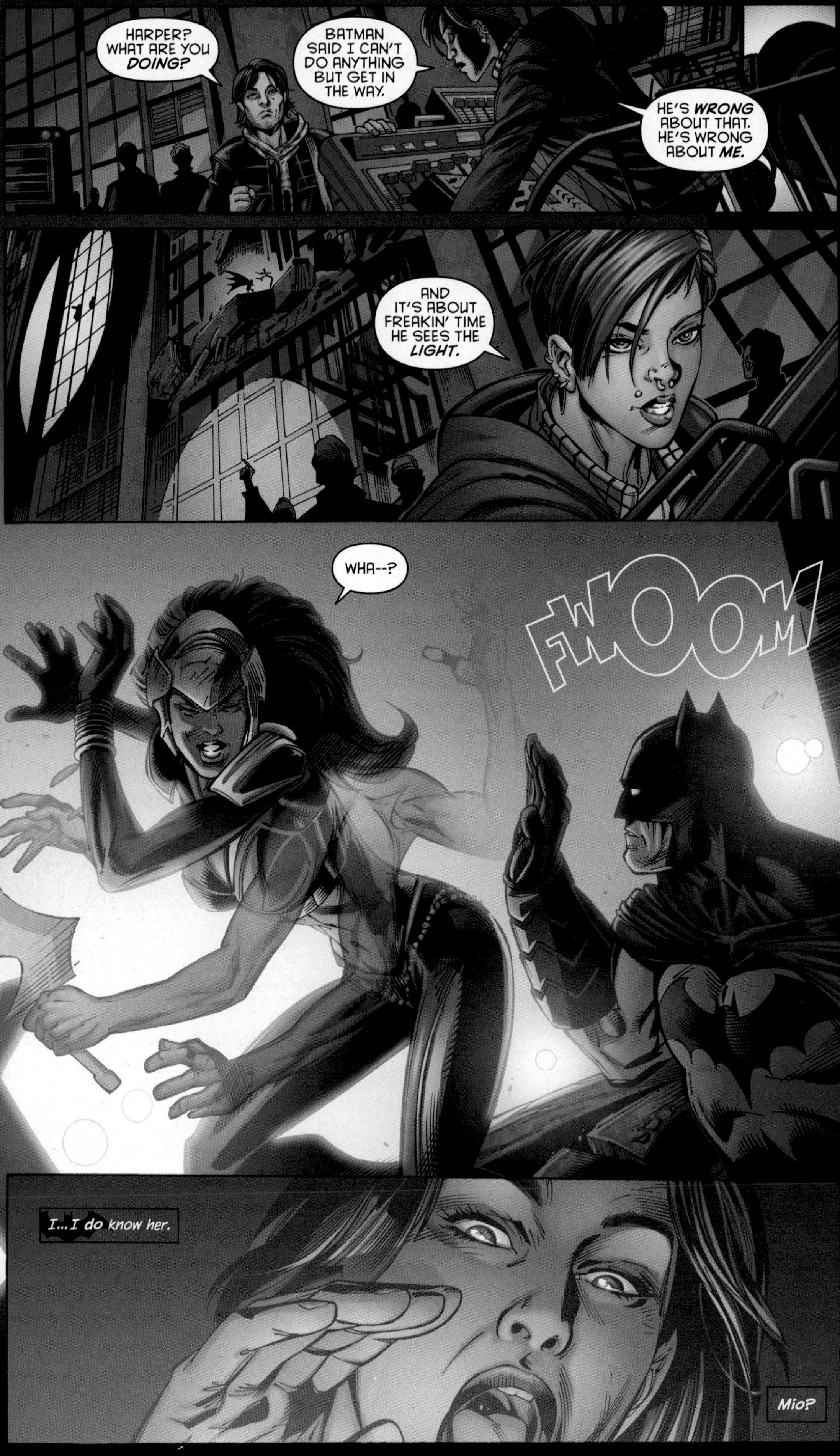
HARPER? WHAT ARE YOU DOING?
BATMAN SAID I CAN'T DO ANYTHING BUT GET IN THE WAY.
HE'S WRONG ABOUT THAT. HE'S WRONG ABOUT ME.
AND IT'S ABOUT FREAKIN' TIME HE SEES THE LIGHT.
WHA--?
FWOOOM
I...I do know her.
Mio?

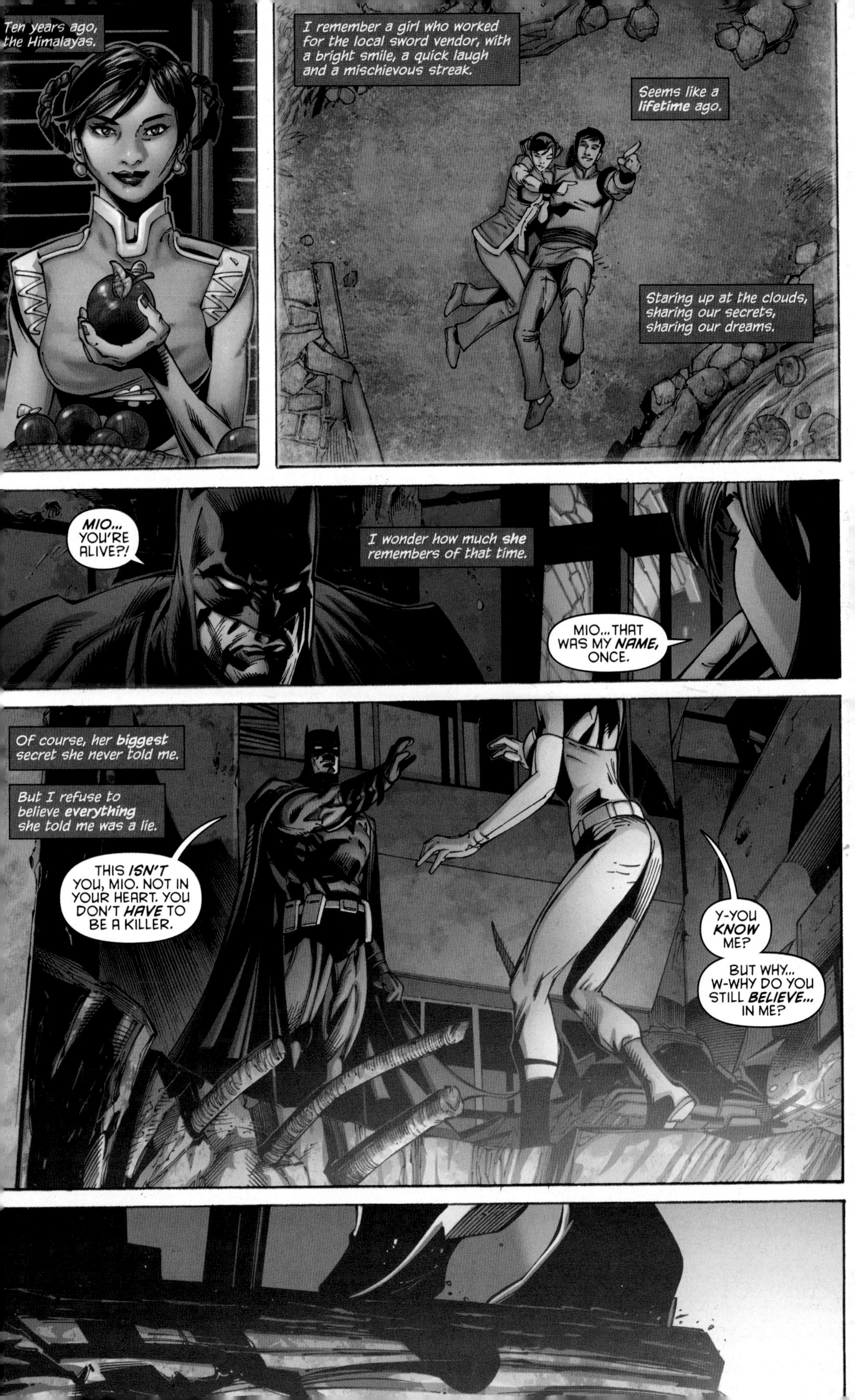

Ten years ago, the Himalayas.
I remember a girl who worked for the local sword vendor, with a bright smile, a quick laugh and a mischievous streak.
Seems like a lifetime ago.
Staring up at the clouds, sharing our secrets, sharing our dreams.
MIO... YOU'RE ALIVE?!
I wonder how much she remembers of that time.
MIO... THAT WAS MY NAME, ONCE.
Of course, her biggest secret she never told me.
But I refuse to believe everything she told me was a lie.
THIS ISN'T YOU, MIO. NOT IN YOUR HEART. YOU DON'T HAVE TO BE A KILLER.
Y-YOU KNOW ME?
BUT WHY... W-WHY DO YOU STILL BELIEVE... IN ME?

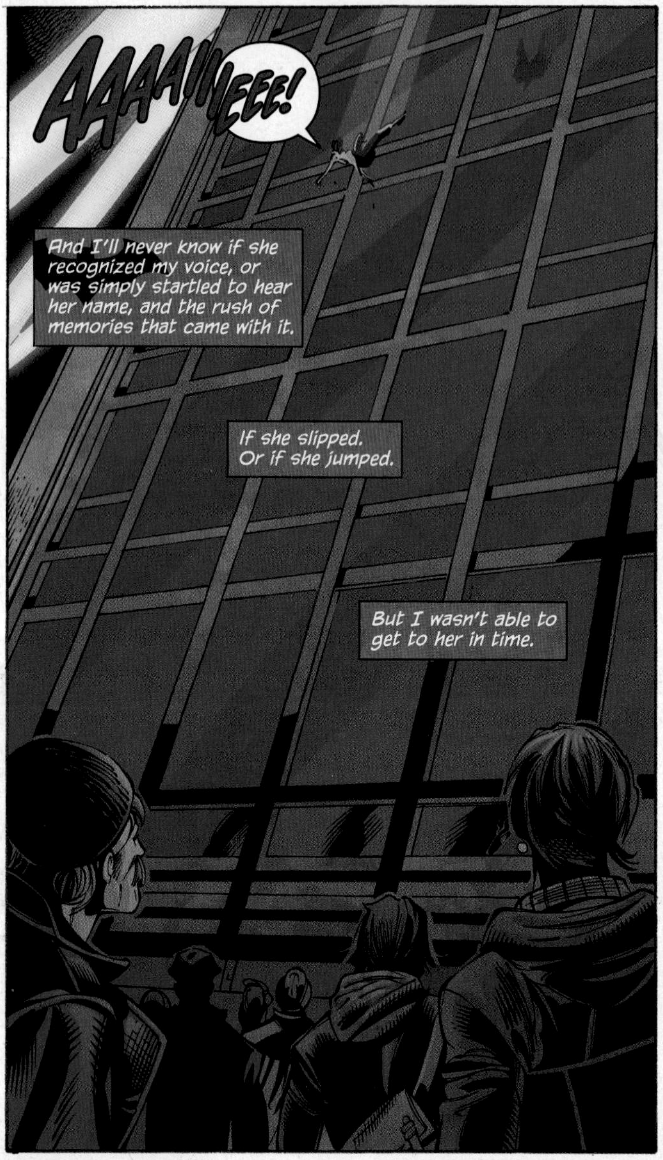
AAAAIIIEEE!
And I'll never know if she recognized my voice, or was simply startled to hear her name, and the rush of memories that came with it.
If she slipped. Or if she jumped.
But I wasn't able to get to her in time.

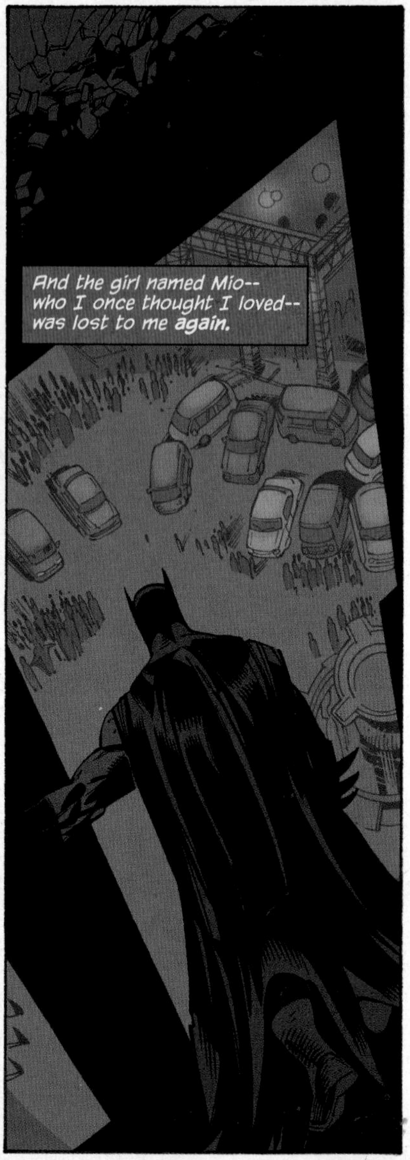
And the girl named Mio-- who I once thought I loved-- was lost to me again.

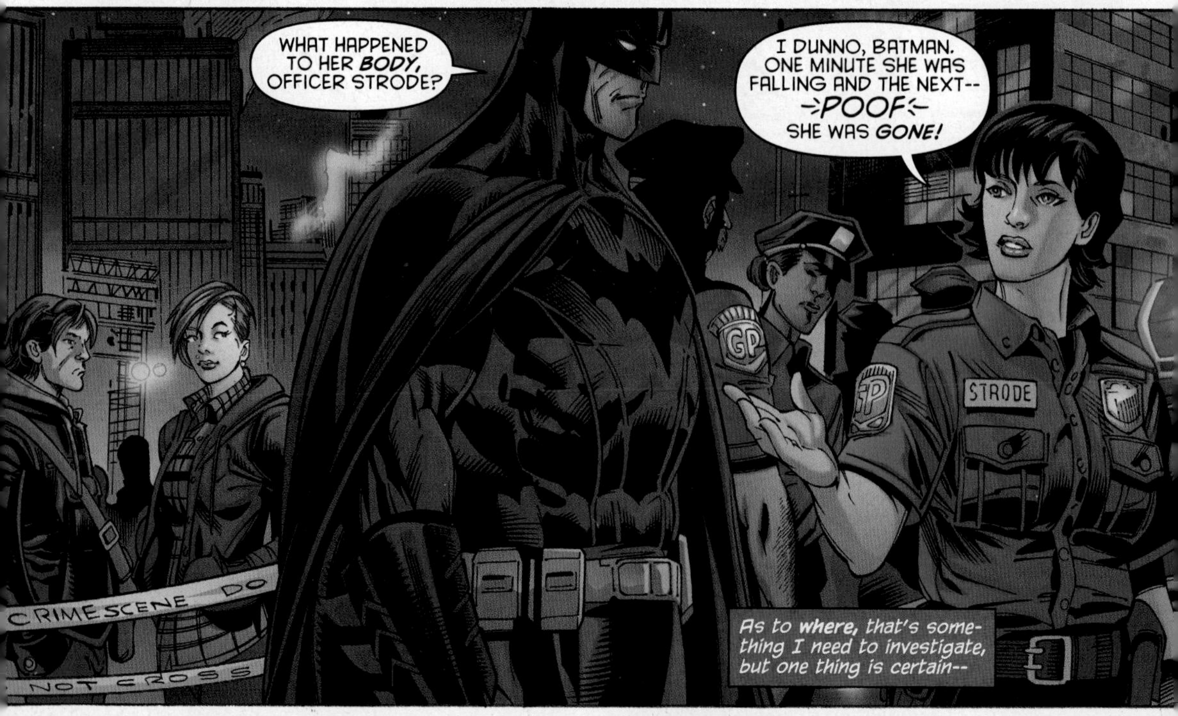
WHAT HAPPENED TO HER BODY, OFFICER STRODE?
I DUNNO, BATMAN. ONE MINUTE SHE WAS FALLING AND THE NEXT-- POOF SHE WAS GONE!
STRODE
GP
CRIME SCENE DO NOT CROSS
As to where, that's something I need to investigate, but one thing is certain--

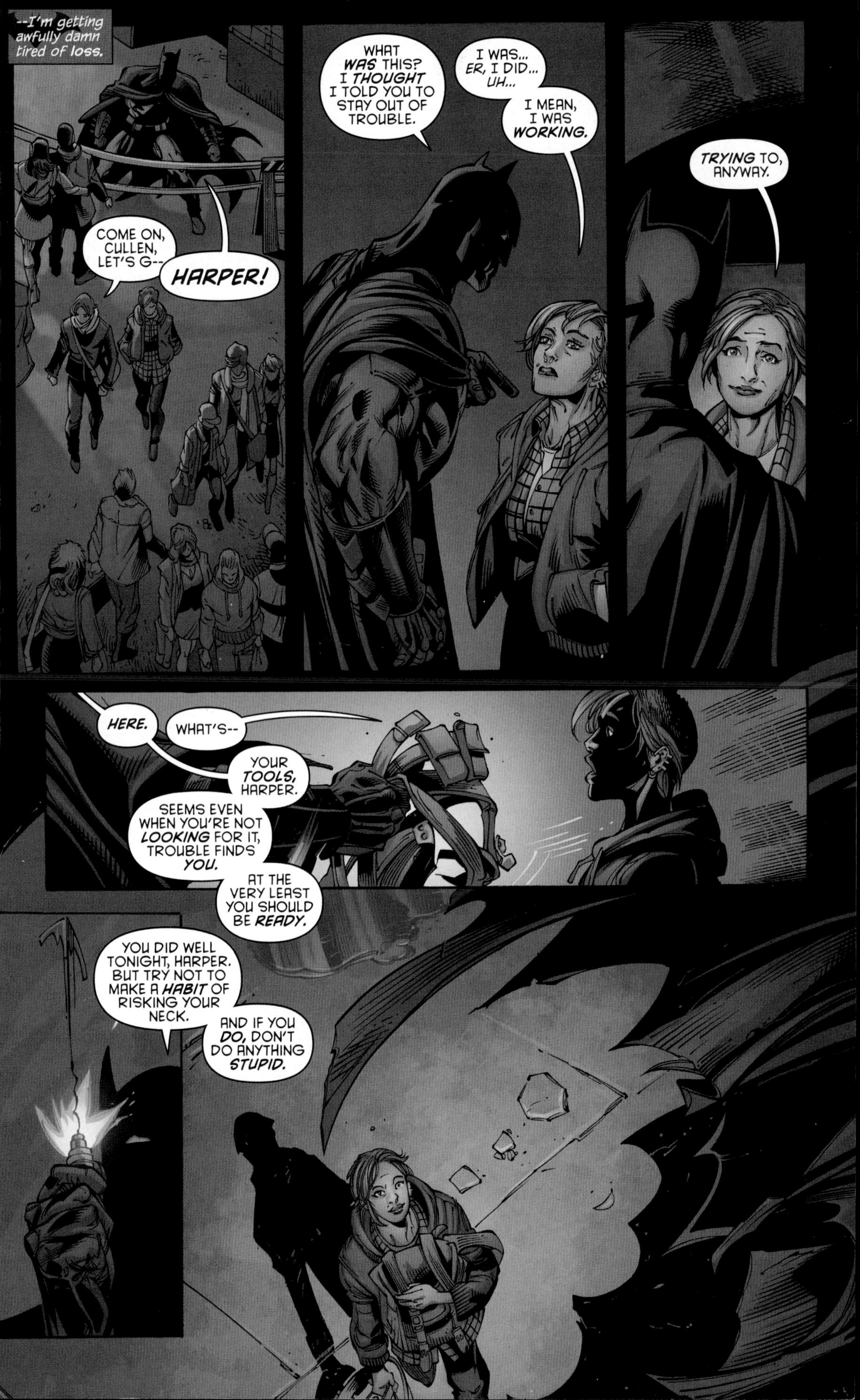
--I'm getting awfully damn tired of loss.
COME ON, CULLEN, LET'S G--
HARPER!
WHAT WAS THIS? I THOUGHT I TOLD YOU TO STAY OUT OF TROUBLE.
I WAS... ER, I DID... UH...
I MEAN, I WAS WORKING.
TRYING TO, ANYWAY.
HERE.
WHAT'S--
YOUR TOOLS, HARPER.
SEEMS EVEN WHEN YOU'RE NOT LOOKING FOR IT, TROUBLE FINDS YOU.
AT THE VERY LEAST YOU SHOULD BE READY.
YOU DID WELL TONIGHT, HARPER. BUT TRY NOT TO MAKE A HABIT OF RISKING YOUR NECK.
AND IF YOU DO, DON'T DO ANYTHING STUPID.

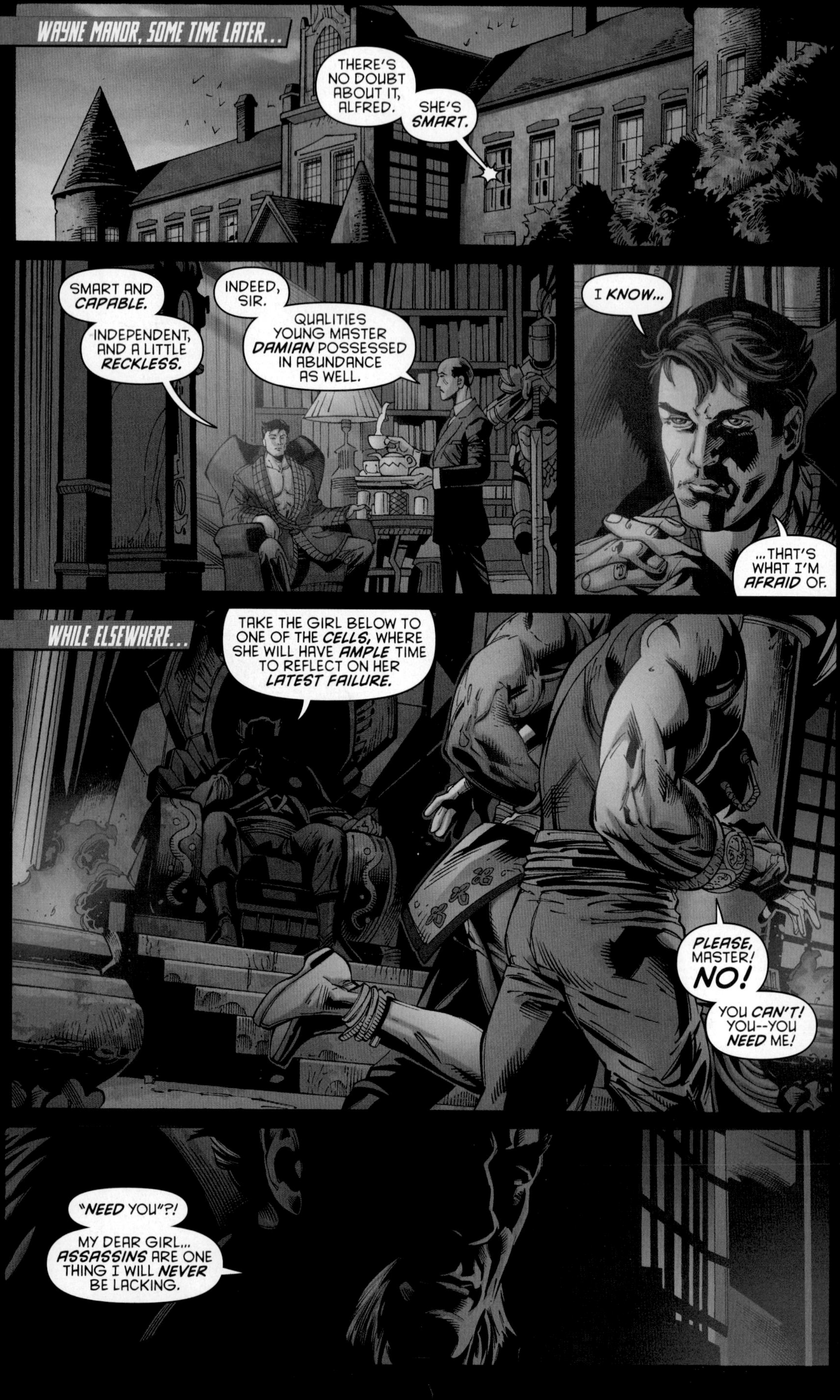
WAYNE MANOR, SOME TIME LATER...
THERE'S NO DOUBT ABOUT IT, ALFRED.
SHE'S SMART.
SMART AND CAPABLE.
INDEPENDENT, AND A LITTLE RECKLESS.
INDEED, SIR.
QUALITIES YOUNG MASTER DAMIAN POSSESSED IN ABUNDANCE AS WELL.
I KNOW...
...THAT'S WHAT I'M AFRAID OF.
WHILE ELSEWHERE...
TAKE THE GIRL BELOW TO ONE OF THE CELLS, WHERE SHE WILL HAVE AMPLE TIME TO REFLECT ON HER LATEST FAILURE.
PLEASE, MASTER! NO!
YOU CAN'T! YOU--YOU NEED ME!
"NEED YOU"?!
MY DEAR GIRL... ASSASSINS ARE ONE THING I WILL NEVER BE LACKING.

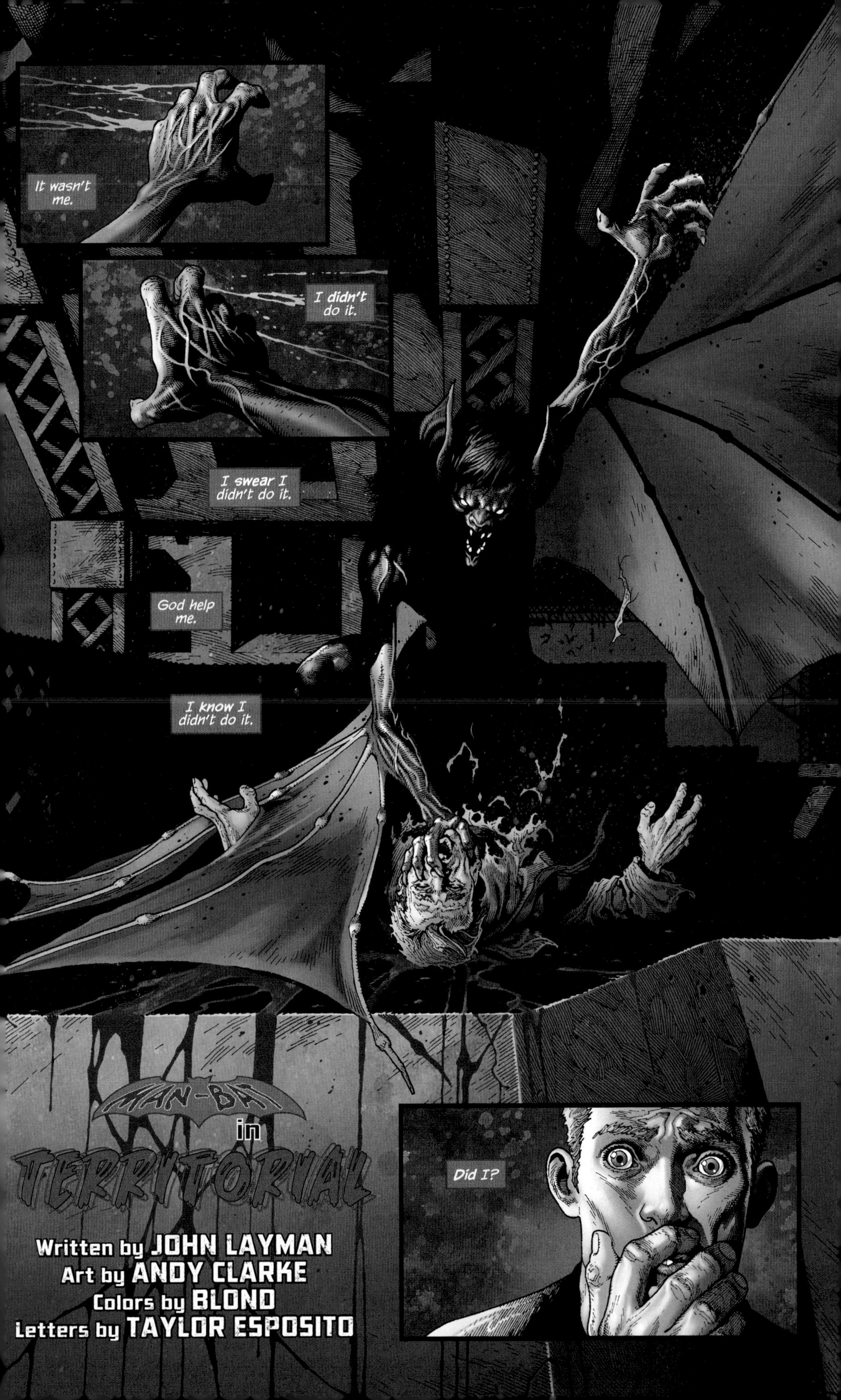
It wasn't me.
I didn't do it.
I swear I didn't do it.
God help me.
I know I didn't do it.
MAN-BAT
in
TERRITORIAL
Written by JOHN LAYMAN
Art by ANDY CLARKE
Colors by BLOND
Letters by TAYLOR ESPOSITO
Did I?

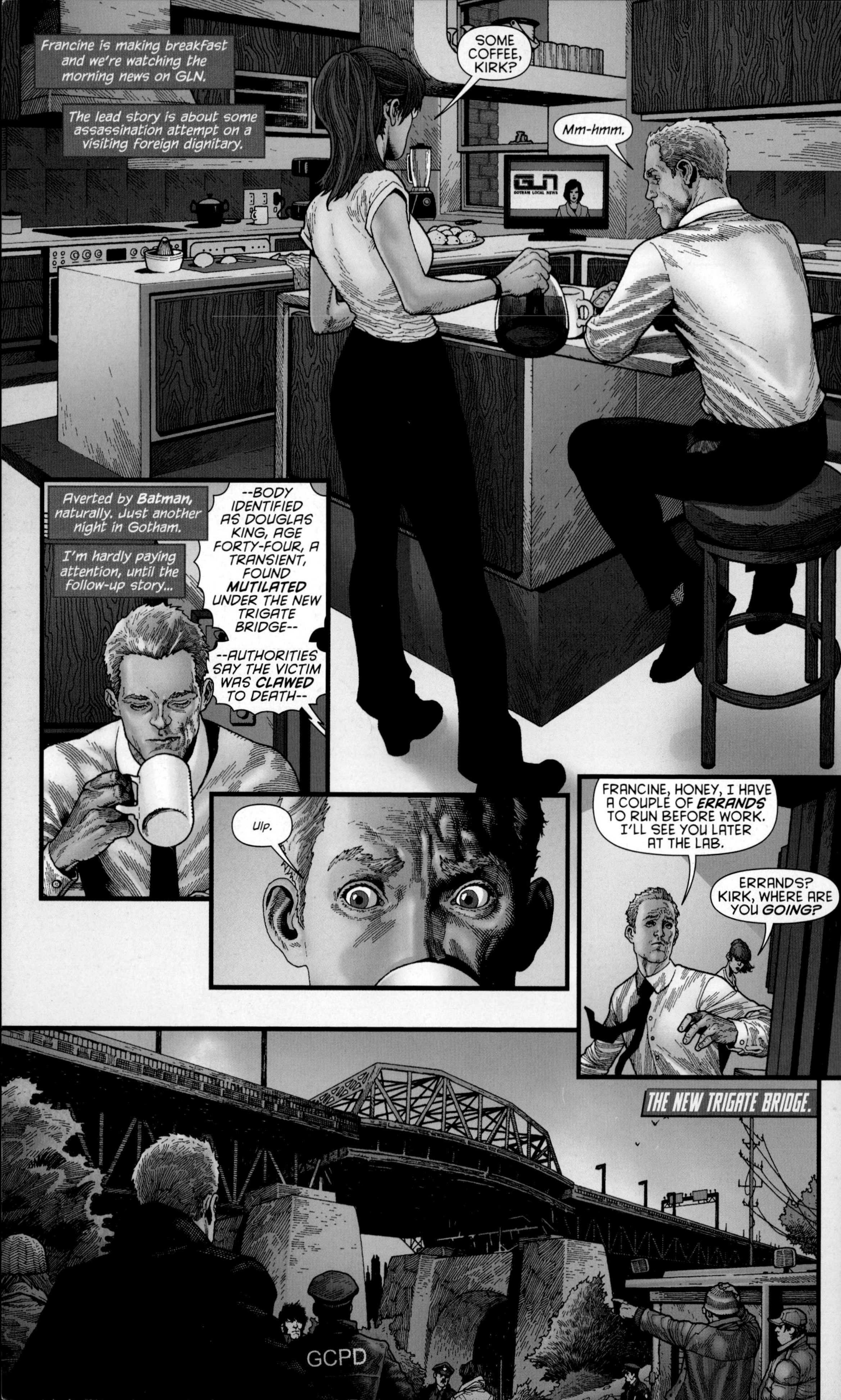

Francine is making breakfast and we're watching the morning news on GLN.
The lead story is about some assassination attempt on a visiting foreign dignitary.
SOME COFFEE, KIRK?
Mm-hmm.
GLN
GOTHAM LOCAL NEWS
Averted by Batman, naturally. Just another night in Gotham.
I'm hardly paying attention, until the follow-up story...
--BODY IDENTIFIED AS DOUGLAS KING, AGE FORTY-FOUR, A TRANSIENT, FOUND MUTILATED UNDER THE NEW TRIGATE BRIDGE--
--AUTHORITIES SAY THE VICTIM WAS CLAWED TO DEATH--
Ulp.
FRANCINE, HONEY, I HAVE A COUPLE OF ERRANDS TO RUN BEFORE WORK. I'LL SEE YOU LATER AT THE LAB.
ERRANDS? KIRK, WHERE ARE YOU GOING?
THE NEW TRIGATE BRIDGE.
GCPD

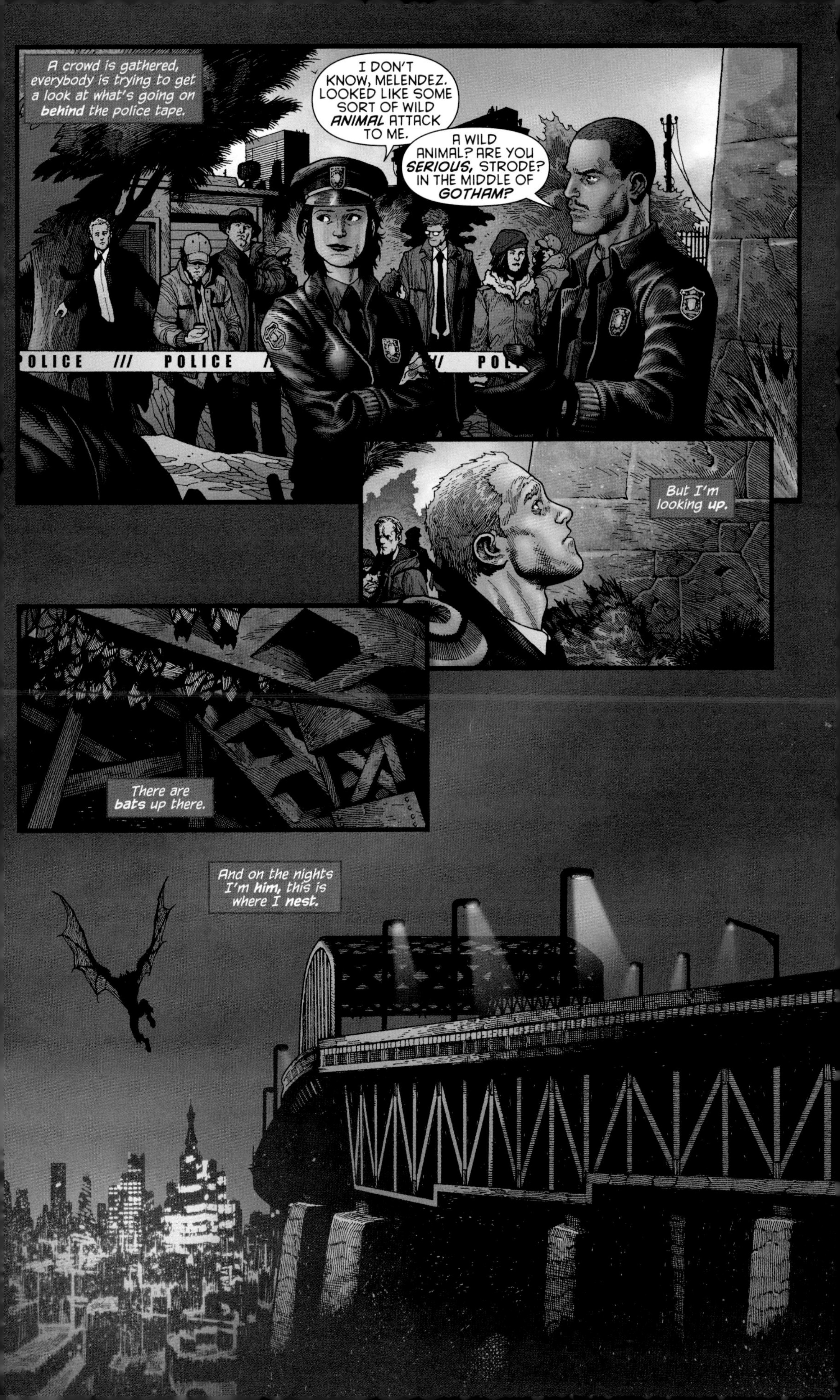

A crowd is gathered, everybody is trying to get a look at what's going on behind the police tape.
I DON'T KNOW, MELENDEZ. LOOKED LIKE SOME SORT OF WILD ANIMAL ATTACK TO ME.
A WILD ANIMAL? ARE YOU SERIOUS, STRODE? IN THE MIDDLE OF GOTHAM?
POLICE /// POLICE /// POL
But I'm looking up.
There are bats up there.
And on the nights I'm him, this is where I nest.

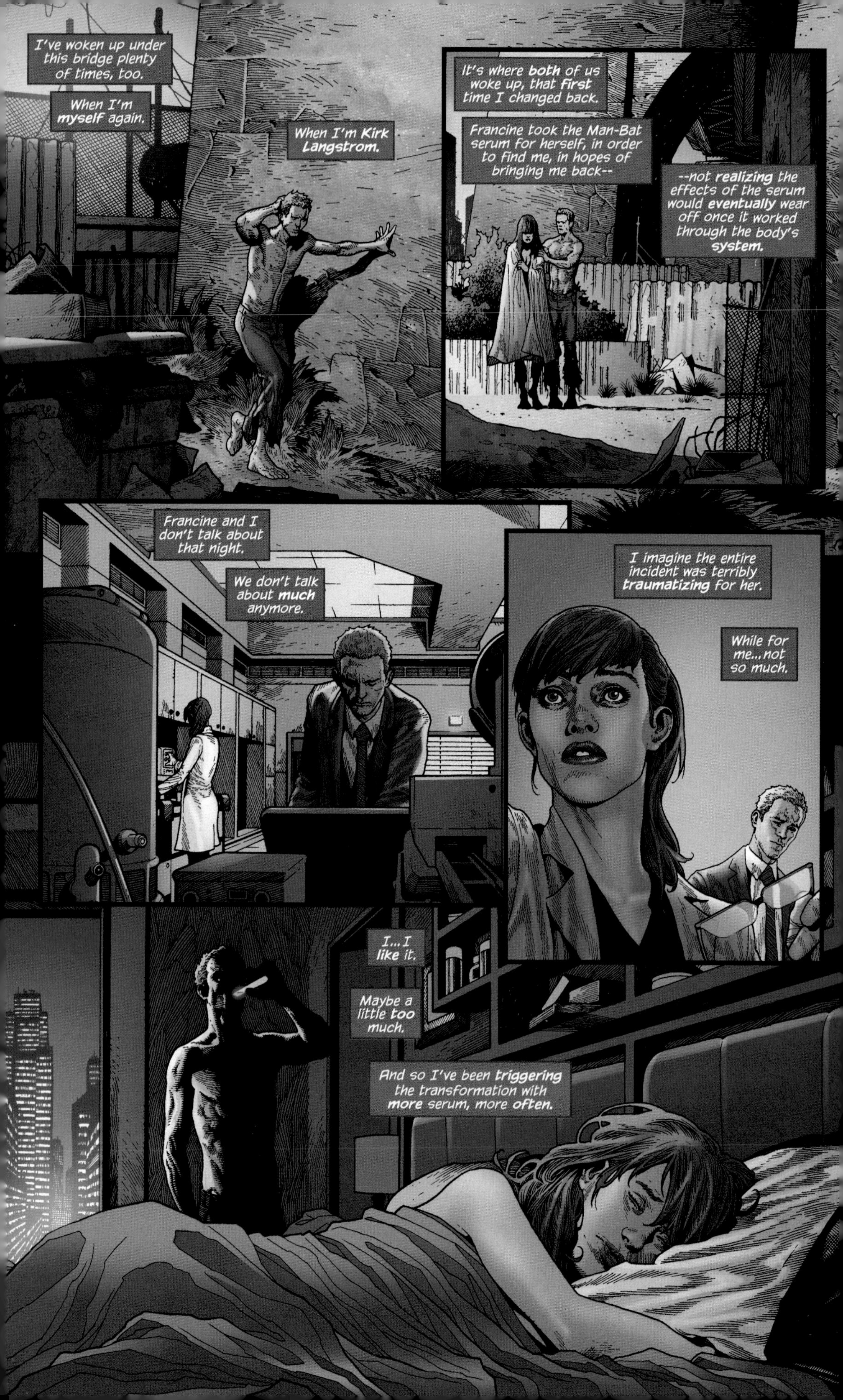
I've woken up under this bridge plenty of times, too.
When I'm myself again.
When I'm Kirk Langstrom.
It's where both of us woke up, that first time I changed back.
Francine took the Man-Bat serum for herself, in order to find me, in hopes of bringing me back--
--not realizing the effects of the serum would eventually wear off once it worked through the body's system.
Francine and I don't talk about that night.
We don't talk about much anymore.
I imagine the entire incident was terribly traumatizing for her.
While for me...not so much.
I...I like it.
Maybe a little too much.
And so I've been triggering the transformation with more serum, more often.

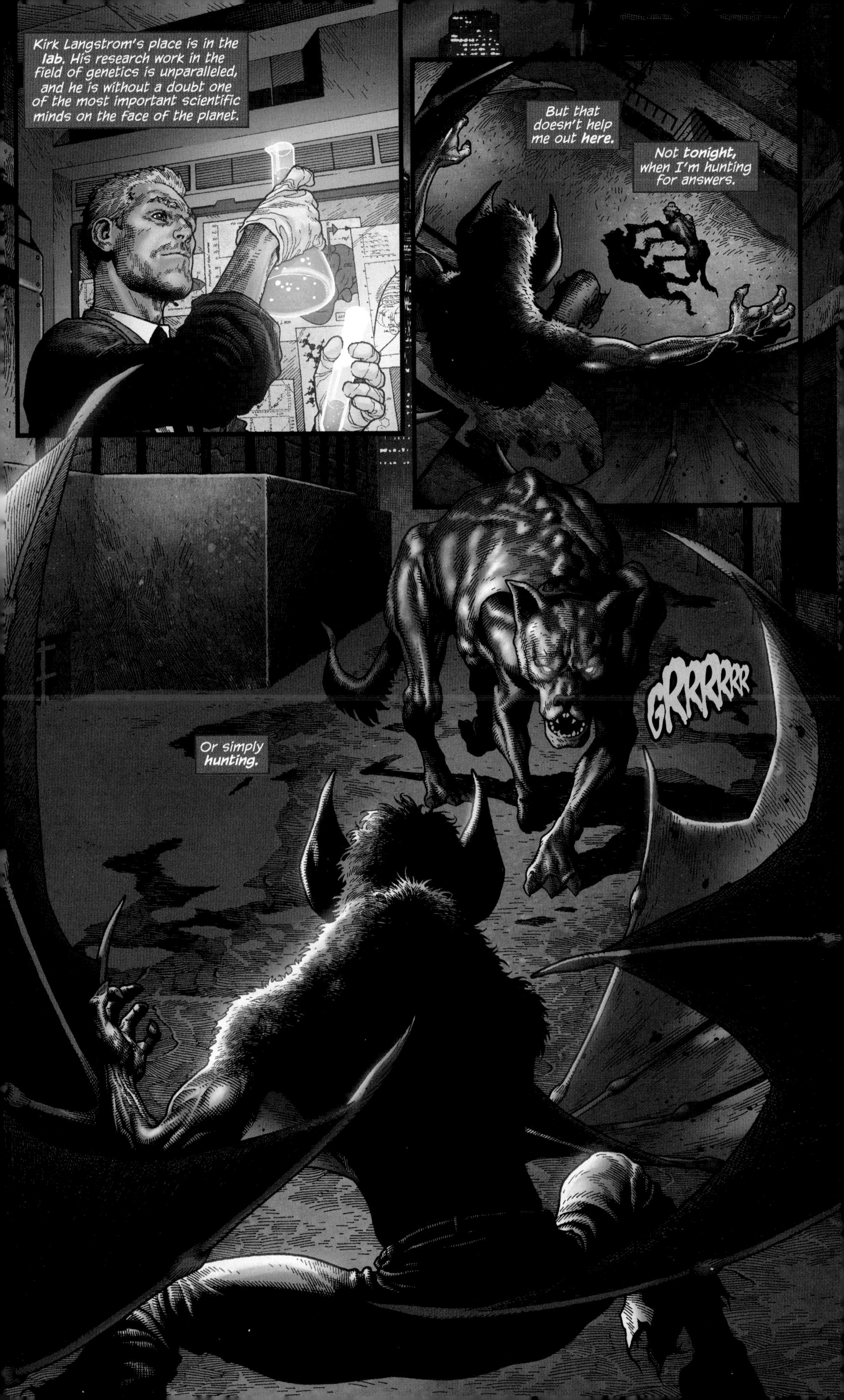
Kirk Langstrom's place is in the **lab.** His research work in the field of genetics is unparalleled, and he is without a doubt one of the most important scientific minds on the face of the planet.
But that doesn't help me out **here.**
Not **tonight,** when I'm hunting for answers.
Or simply **hunting.**
GRRRRRR

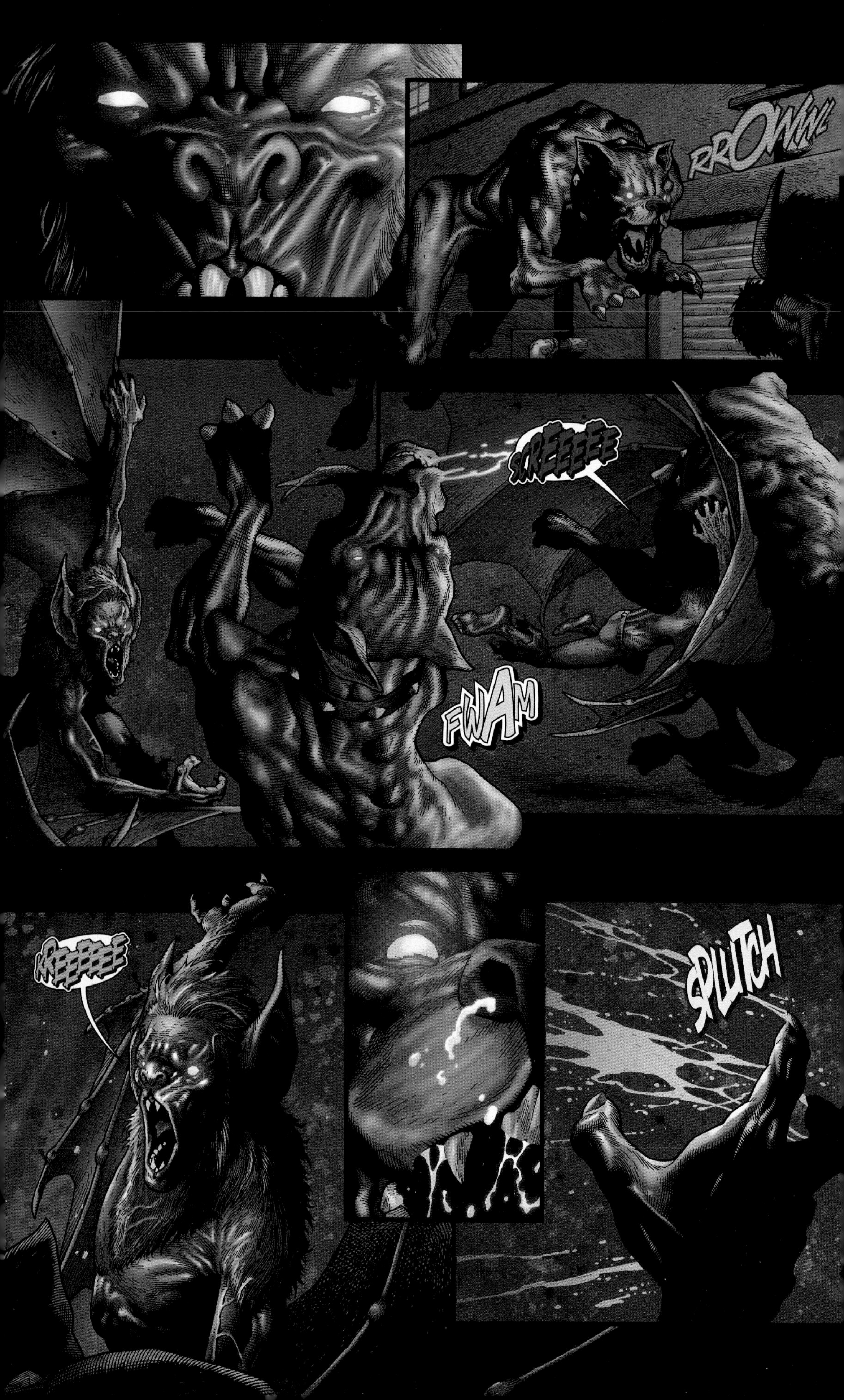
RROWWL
SCREEEEEE
FWAM
KREEEEEE
SPLUTCH

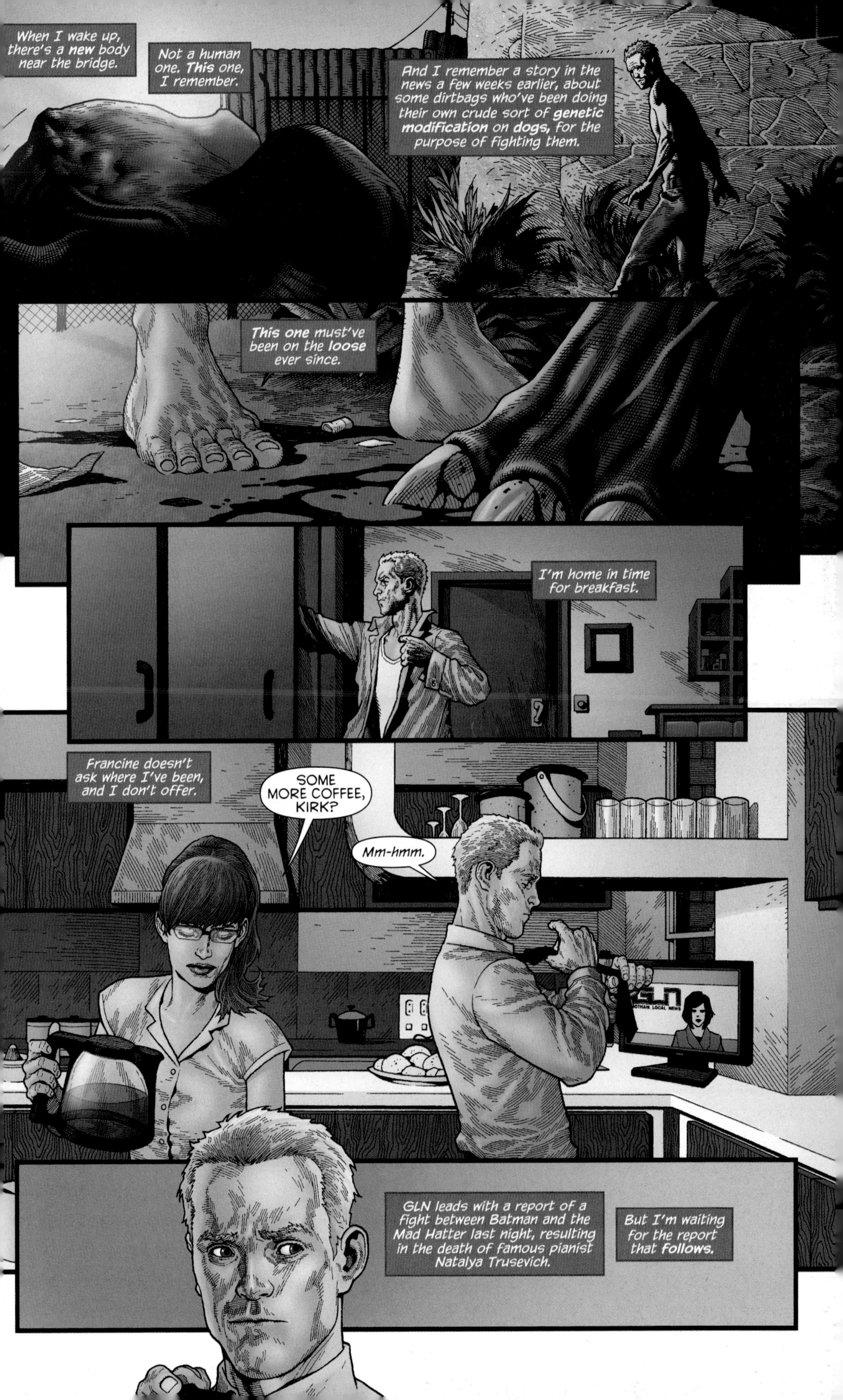

When I wake up, there's a **new** body near the bridge.
Not a human one. **This** one, I remember.
And I remember a story in the news a few weeks earlier, about some dirtbags who've been doing their own crude sort of **genetic modification** on **dogs,** for the purpose of fighting them.
This one must've been on the **loose** ever since.
I'm home in time for breakfast.
Francine doesn't ask where I've been, and I don't offer.
SOME MORE COFFEE, KIRK?
Mm-hmm.
GLN leads with a report of a fight between Batman and the Mad Hatter last night, resulting in the death of famous pianist Natalya Trusevich.
But I'm waiting for the report that **follows.**

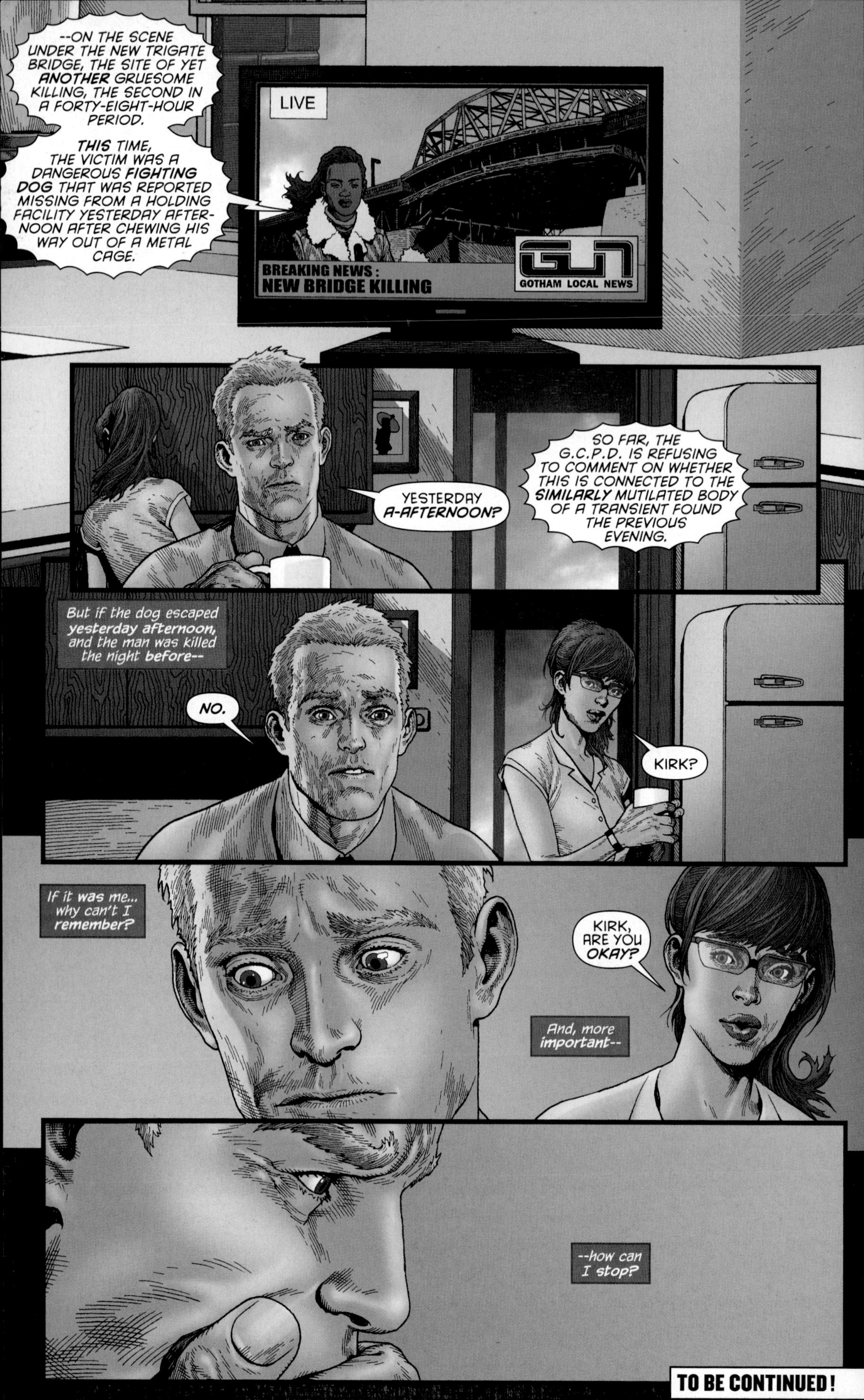
--ON THE SCENE UNDER THE NEW TRIGATE BRIDGE, THE SITE OF YET ANOTHER GRUESOME KILLING, THE SECOND IN A FORTY-EIGHT-HOUR PERIOD.
THIS TIME, THE VICTIM WAS A DANGEROUS FIGHTING DOG THAT WAS REPORTED MISSING FROM A HOLDING FACILITY YESTERDAY AFTER-NOON AFTER CHEWING HIS WAY OUT OF A METAL CAGE.
LIVE
BREAKING NEWS : NEW BRIDGE KILLING
GLN
GOTHAM LOCAL NEWS
YESTERDAY A-AFTERNOON?
SO FAR, THE G.C.P.D. IS REFUSING TO COMMENT ON WHETHER THIS IS CONNECTED TO THE SIMILARLY MUTILATED BODY OF A TRANSIENT FOUND THE PREVIOUS EVENING.
But if the dog escaped yesterday afternoon, and the man was killed the night before--
NO.
KIRK?
If it was me... why can't I remember?
KIRK, ARE YOU OKAY?
And, more important--
--how can I stop?
TO BE CONTINUED!

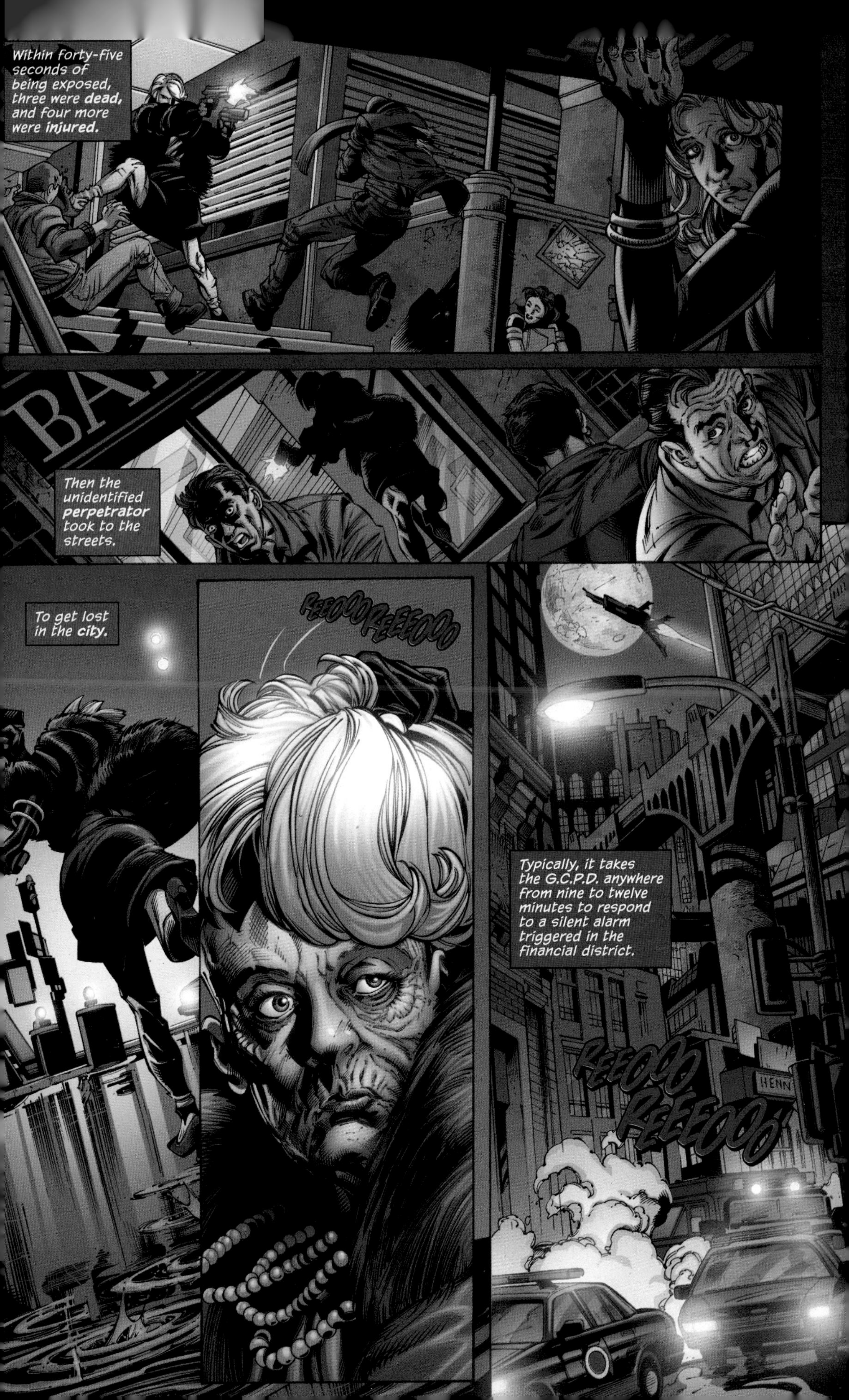

Within forty-five seconds of being exposed, three were dead, and four more were injured.
BA
Then the unidentified perpetrator took to the streets.
To get lost in the city.
REEOOOREEEOOO
Typically, it takes the G.C.P.D. anywhere from nine to twelve minutes to respond to a silent alarm triggered in the financial district.
HENN
REEOOO REEEOOO

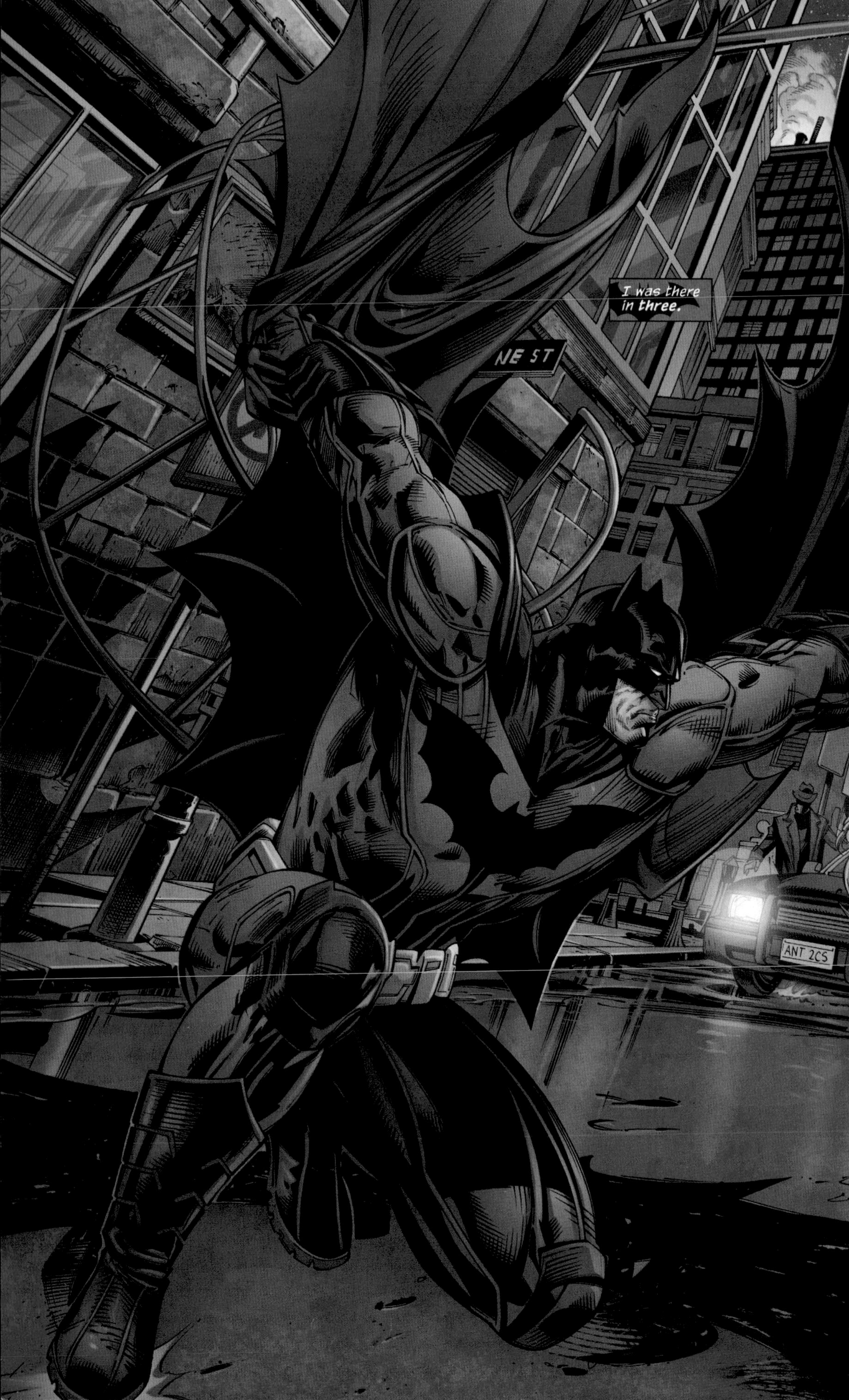
I was there in three.
NE ST
ANT 2CS

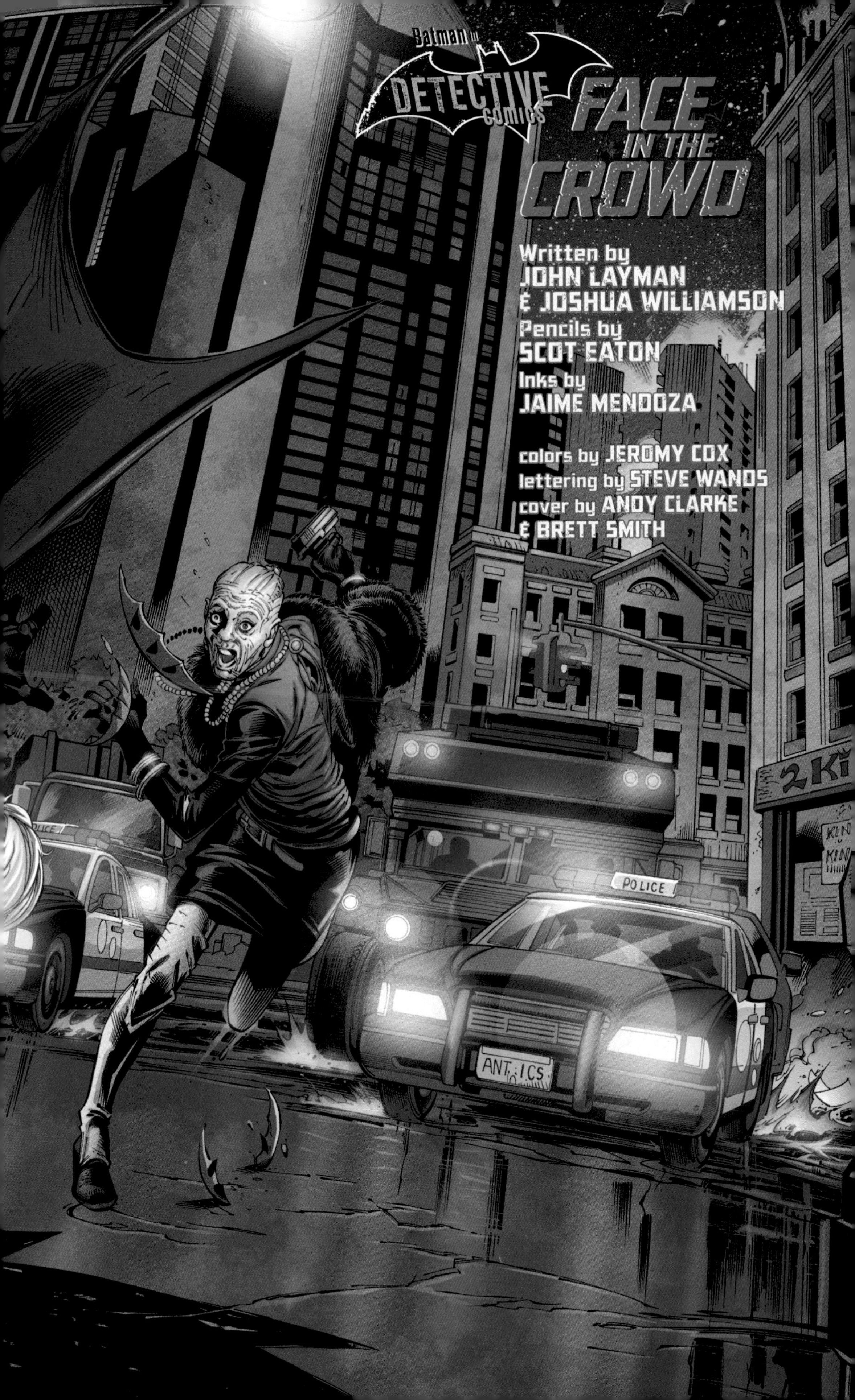
Batman in
DETECTIVE COMICS
FACE IN THE CROWD
Written by
JOHN LAYMAN
& JOSHUA WILLIAMSON
Pencils by
SCOT EATON
Inks by
JAIME MENDOZA
colors by JEROMY COX
lettering by STEVE WANDS
cover by ANDY CLARKE
& BRETT SMITH
POLICE
ANT.ICS

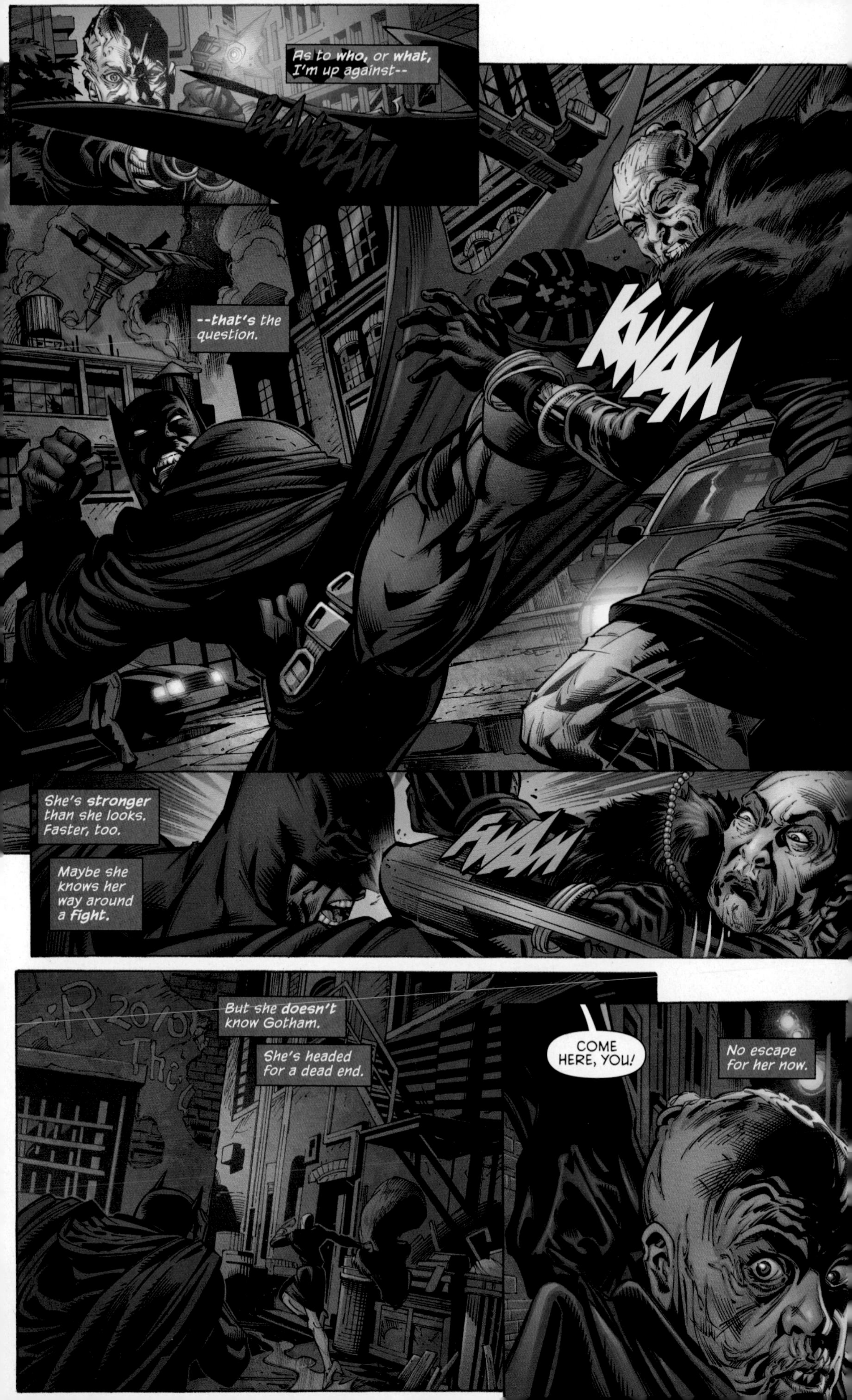
As to who, or what, I'm up against--
BLAMBLAM
--that's the question.
KWAM
She's stronger than she looks. Faster, too.
Maybe she knows her way around a fight.
FWAM
But she doesn't know Gotham.
She's headed for a dead end.
COME HERE, YOU!
No escape for her now.

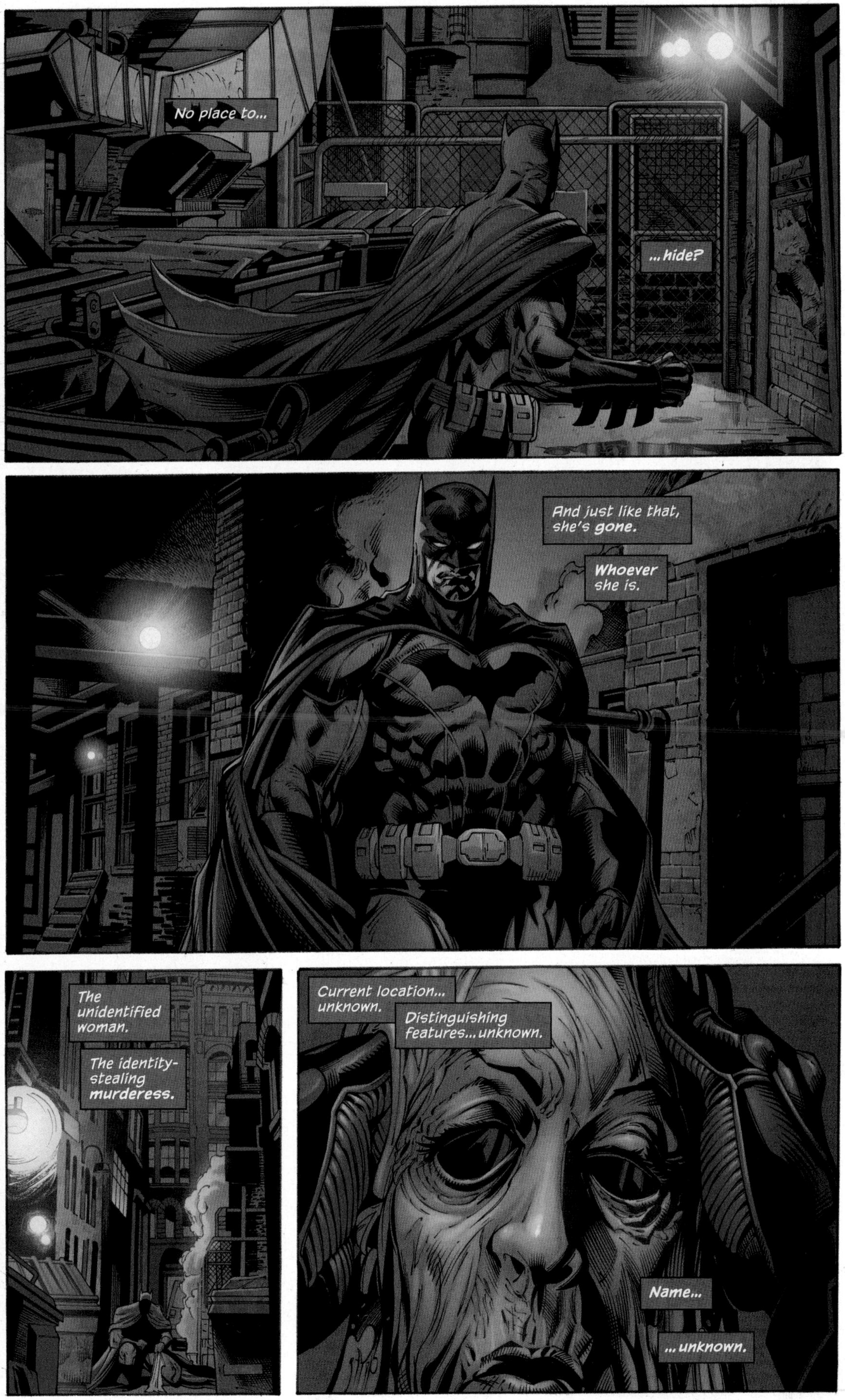

No place to...
...hide?
And just like that, she's gone.
Whoever she is.
The unidentified woman.
The identity-stealing murderess.
Current location... unknown.
Distinguishing features... unknown.
Name...
...unknown.

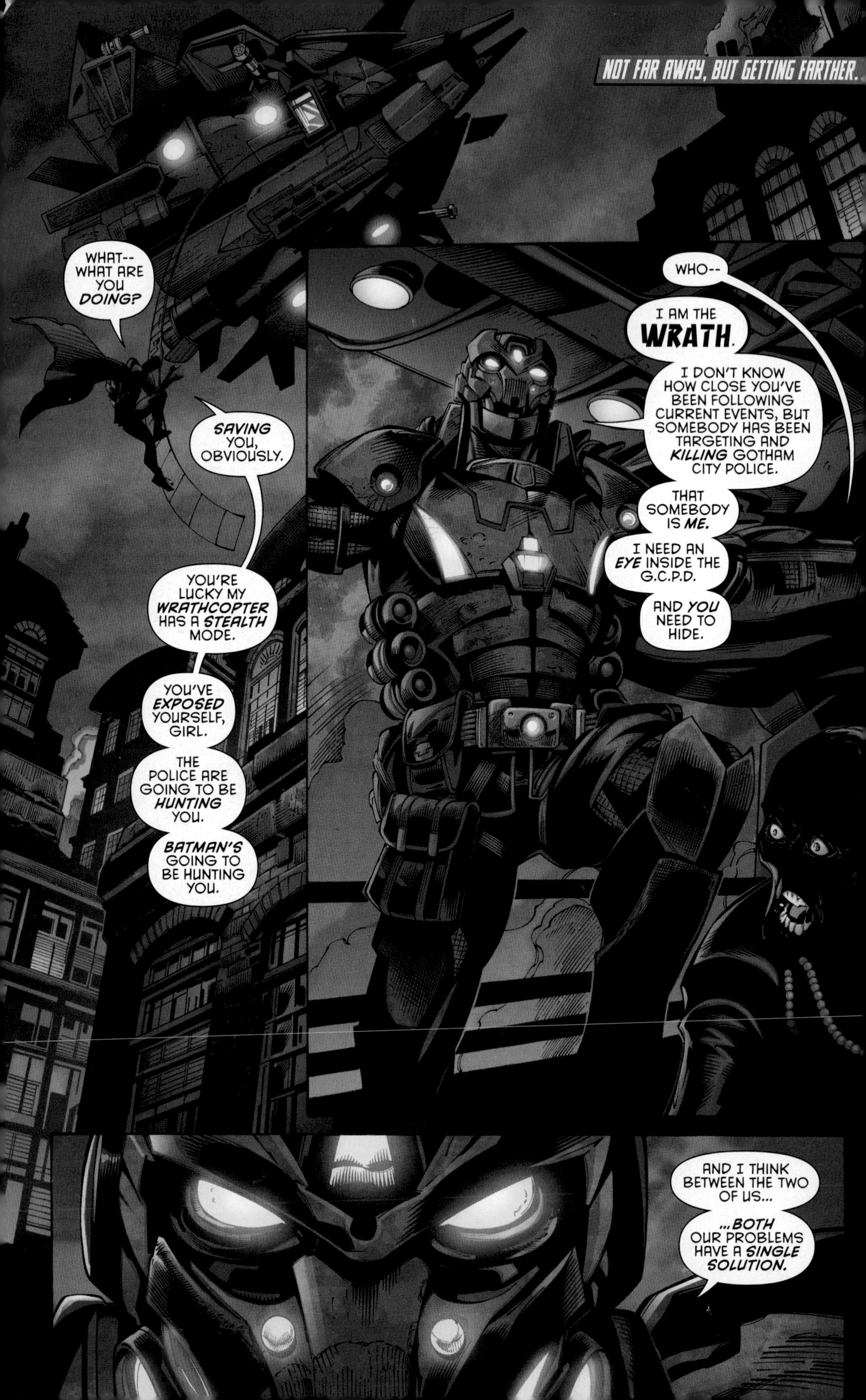
NOT FAR AWAY, BUT GETTING FARTHER.
WHAT-- WHAT ARE YOU DOING?
SAVING YOU, OBVIOUSLY.
YOU'RE LUCKY MY WRATHCOPTER HAS A STEALTH MODE.
YOU'VE EXPOSED YOURSELF, GIRL.
THE POLICE ARE GOING TO BE HUNTING YOU.
BATMAN'S GOING TO BE HUNTING YOU.
WHO--
I AM THE WRATH.
I DON'T KNOW HOW CLOSE YOU'VE BEEN FOLLOWING CURRENT EVENTS, BUT SOMEBODY HAS BEEN TARGETING AND KILLING GOTHAM CITY POLICE.
THAT SOMEBODY IS ME.
I NEED AN EYE INSIDE THE G.C.P.D.
AND YOU NEED TO HIDE.
AND I THINK BETWEEN THE TWO OF US...
...BOTH OUR PROBLEMS HAVE A SINGLE SOLUTION.

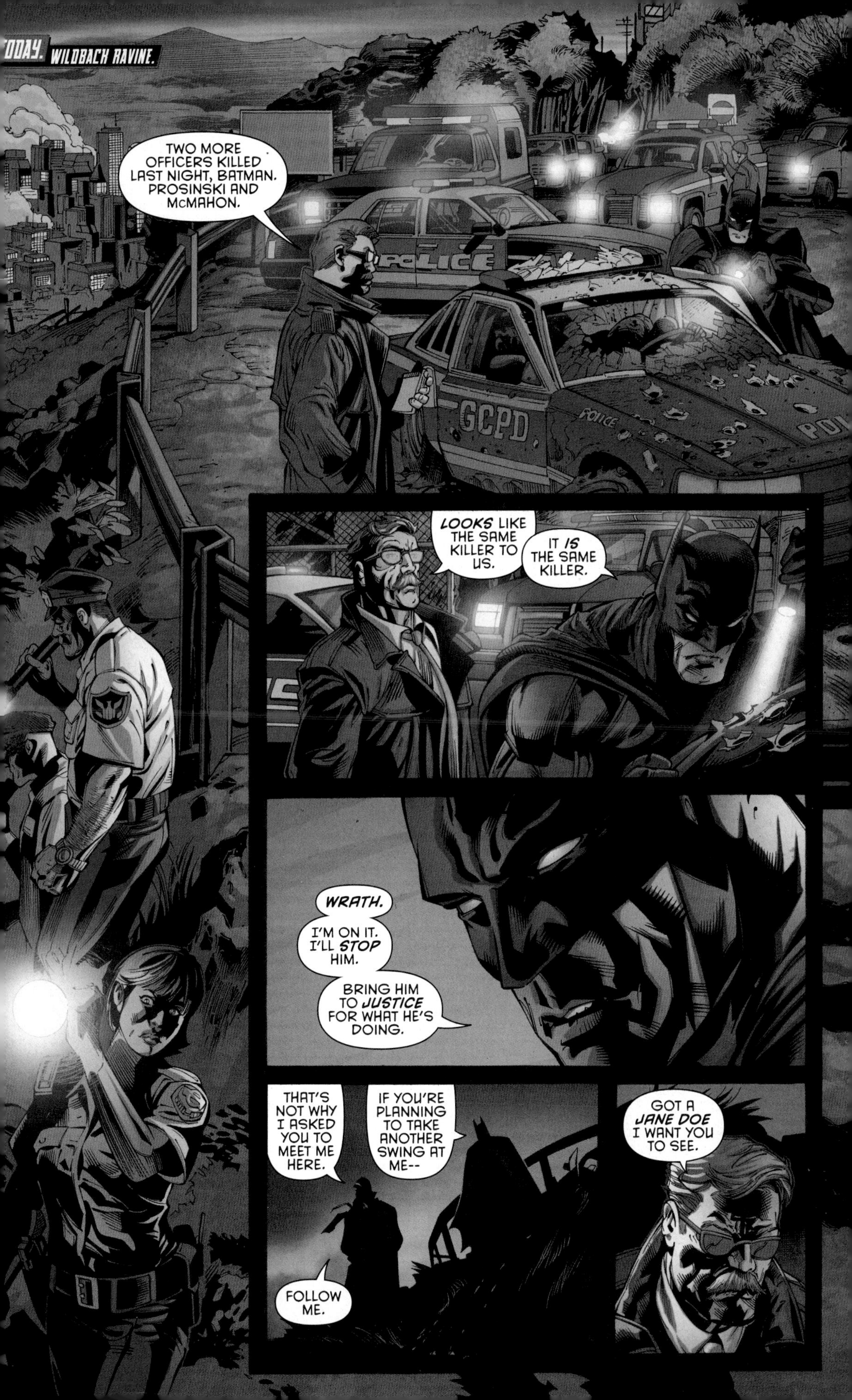
TODAY. WILDBACH RAVINE.
TWO MORE OFFICERS KILLED LAST NIGHT, BATMAN. PROSINSKI AND McMAHON.
GCPD
POLICE
LOOKS LIKE THE SAME KILLER TO US.
IT IS THE SAME KILLER.
WRATH.
I'M ON IT. I'LL STOP HIM.
BRING HIM TO JUSTICE FOR WHAT HE'S DOING.
THAT'S NOT WHY I ASKED YOU TO MEET ME HERE.
IF YOU'RE PLANNING TO TAKE ANOTHER SWING AT ME--
GOT A JANE DOE I WANT YOU TO SEE.
FOLLOW ME.

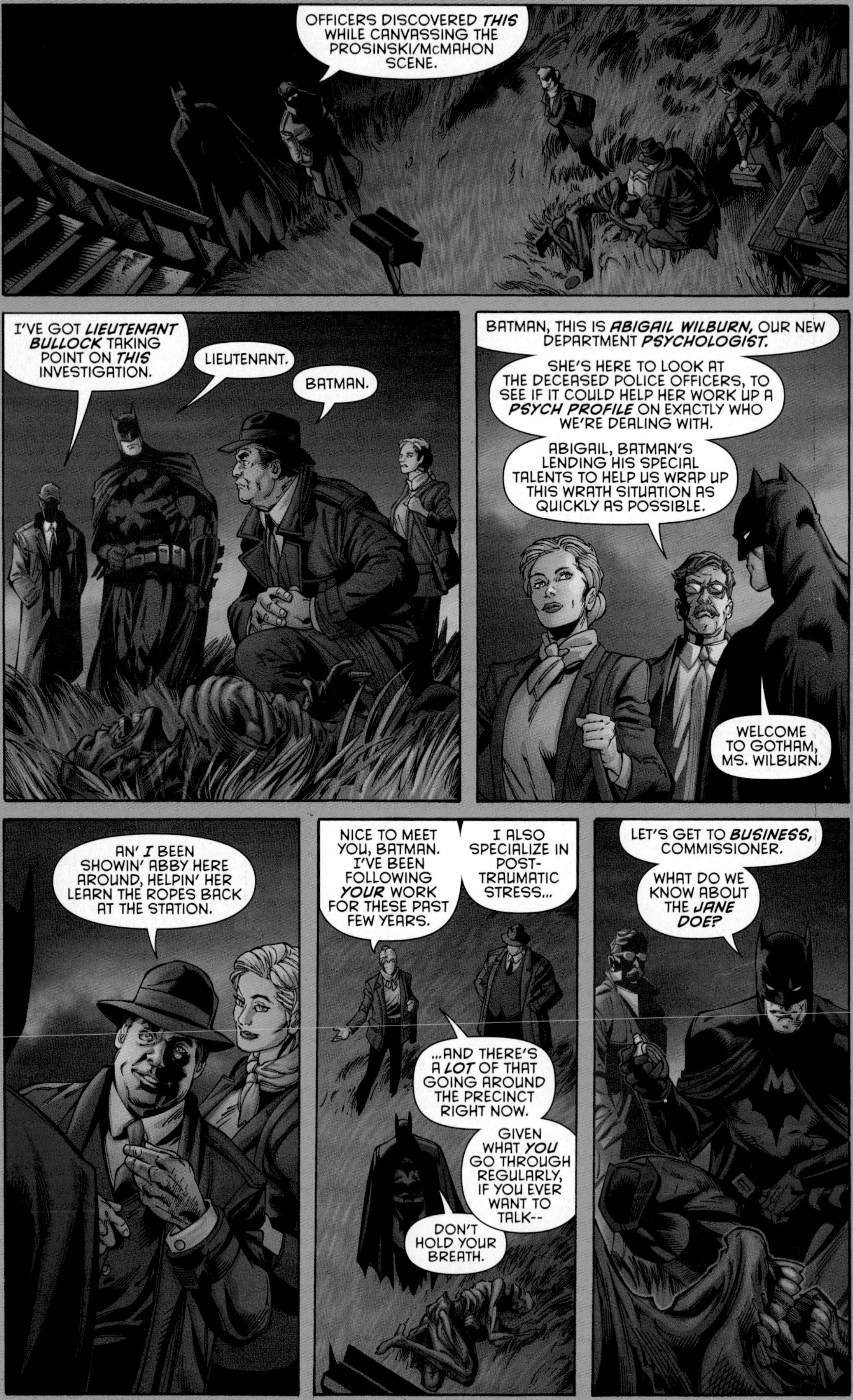
OFFICERS DISCOVERED THIS WHILE CANVASSING THE PROSINSKI/McMAHON SCENE.
I'VE GOT LIEUTENANT BULLOCK TAKING POINT ON THIS INVESTIGATION.
LIEUTENANT.
BATMAN.
BATMAN, THIS IS ABIGAIL WILBURN, OUR NEW DEPARTMENT PSYCHOLOGIST.
SHE'S HERE TO LOOK AT THE DECEASED POLICE OFFICERS, TO SEE IF IT COULD HELP HER WORK UP A PSYCH PROFILE ON EXACTLY WHO WE'RE DEALING WITH.
ABIGAIL, BATMAN'S LENDING HIS SPECIAL TALENTS TO HELP US WRAP UP THIS WRATH SITUATION AS QUICKLY AS POSSIBLE.
WELCOME TO GOTHAM, MS. WILBURN.
AN' I BEEN SHOWIN' ABBY HERE AROUND, HELPIN' HER LEARN THE ROPES BACK AT THE STATION.
NICE TO MEET YOU, BATMAN. I'VE BEEN FOLLOWING YOUR WORK FOR THESE PAST FEW YEARS.
I ALSO SPECIALIZE IN POST-TRAUMATIC STRESS...
...AND THERE'S A LOT OF THAT GOING AROUND THE PRECINCT RIGHT NOW.
GIVEN WHAT YOU GO THROUGH REGULARLY, IF YOU EVER WANT TO TALK--
DON'T HOLD YOUR BREATH.
LET'S GET TO BUSINESS, COMMISSIONER.
WHAT DO WE KNOW ABOUT THE JANE DOE?

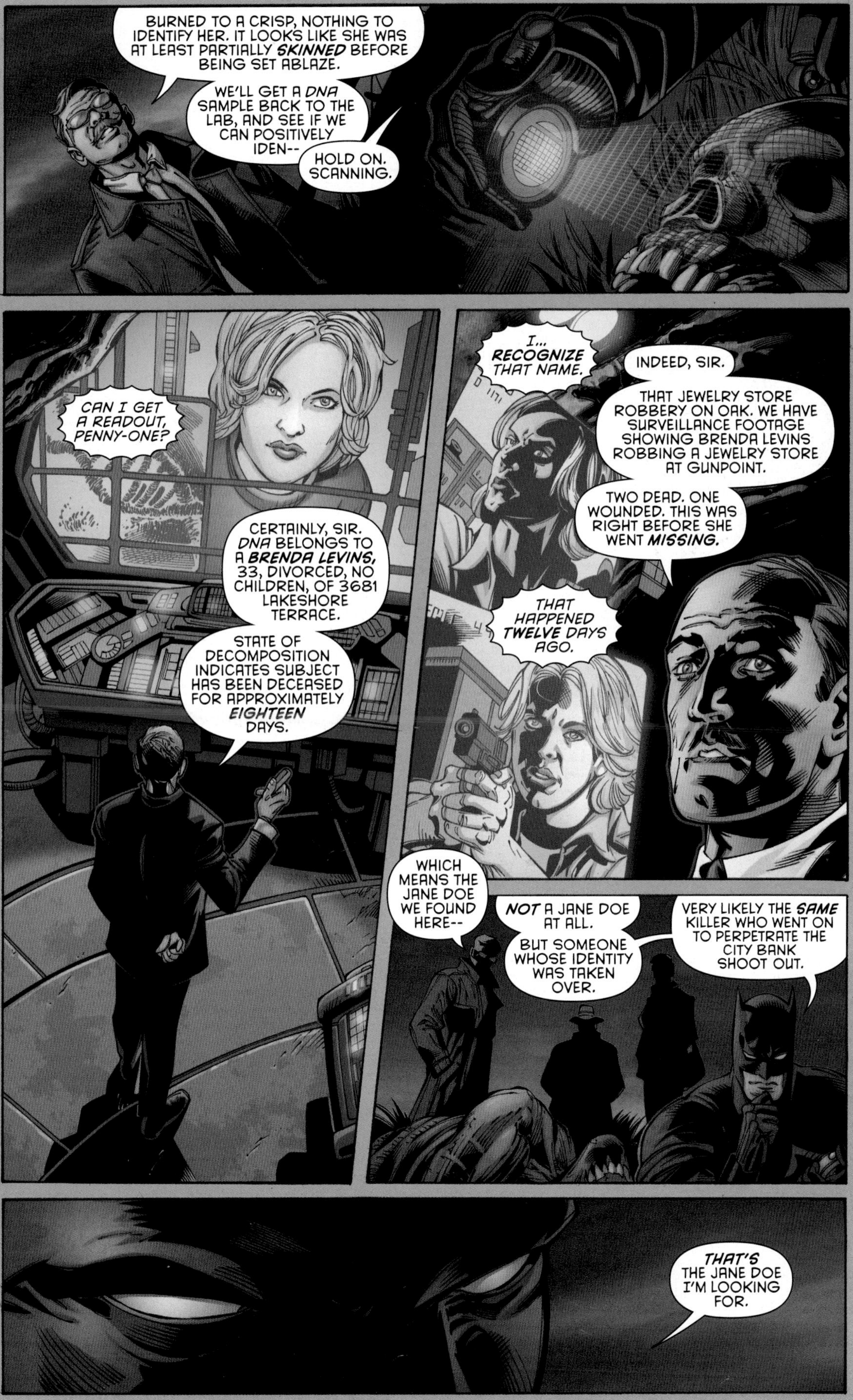

BURNED TO A CRISP, NOTHING TO IDENTIFY HER. IT LOOKS LIKE SHE WAS AT LEAST PARTIALLY SKINNED BEFORE BEING SET ABLAZE.
WE'LL GET A DNA SAMPLE BACK TO THE LAB, AND SEE IF WE CAN POSITIVELY IDEN--
HOLD ON. SCANNING.
CAN I GET A READOUT, PENNY-ONE?
CERTAINLY, SIR. DNA BELONGS TO A BRENDA LEVINS, 33, DIVORCED, NO CHILDREN, OF 3681 LAKESHORE TERRACE.
STATE OF DECOMPOSITION INDICATES SUBJECT HAS BEEN DECEASED FOR APPROXIMATELY EIGHTEEN DAYS.
I... RECOGNIZE THAT NAME.
INDEED, SIR.
THAT JEWELRY STORE ROBBERY ON OAK. WE HAVE SURVEILLANCE FOOTAGE SHOWING BRENDA LEVINS ROBBING A JEWELRY STORE AT GUNPOINT.
TWO DEAD. ONE WOUNDED. THIS WAS RIGHT BEFORE SHE WENT MISSING.
THAT HAPPENED TWELVE DAYS AGO.
WHICH MEANS THE JANE DOE WE FOUND HERE--
NOT A JANE DOE AT ALL.
BUT SOMEONE WHOSE IDENTITY WAS TAKEN OVER.
VERY LIKELY THE SAME KILLER WHO WENT ON TO PERPETRATE THE CITY BANK SHOOT OUT.
THAT'S THE JANE DOE I'M LOOKING FOR.

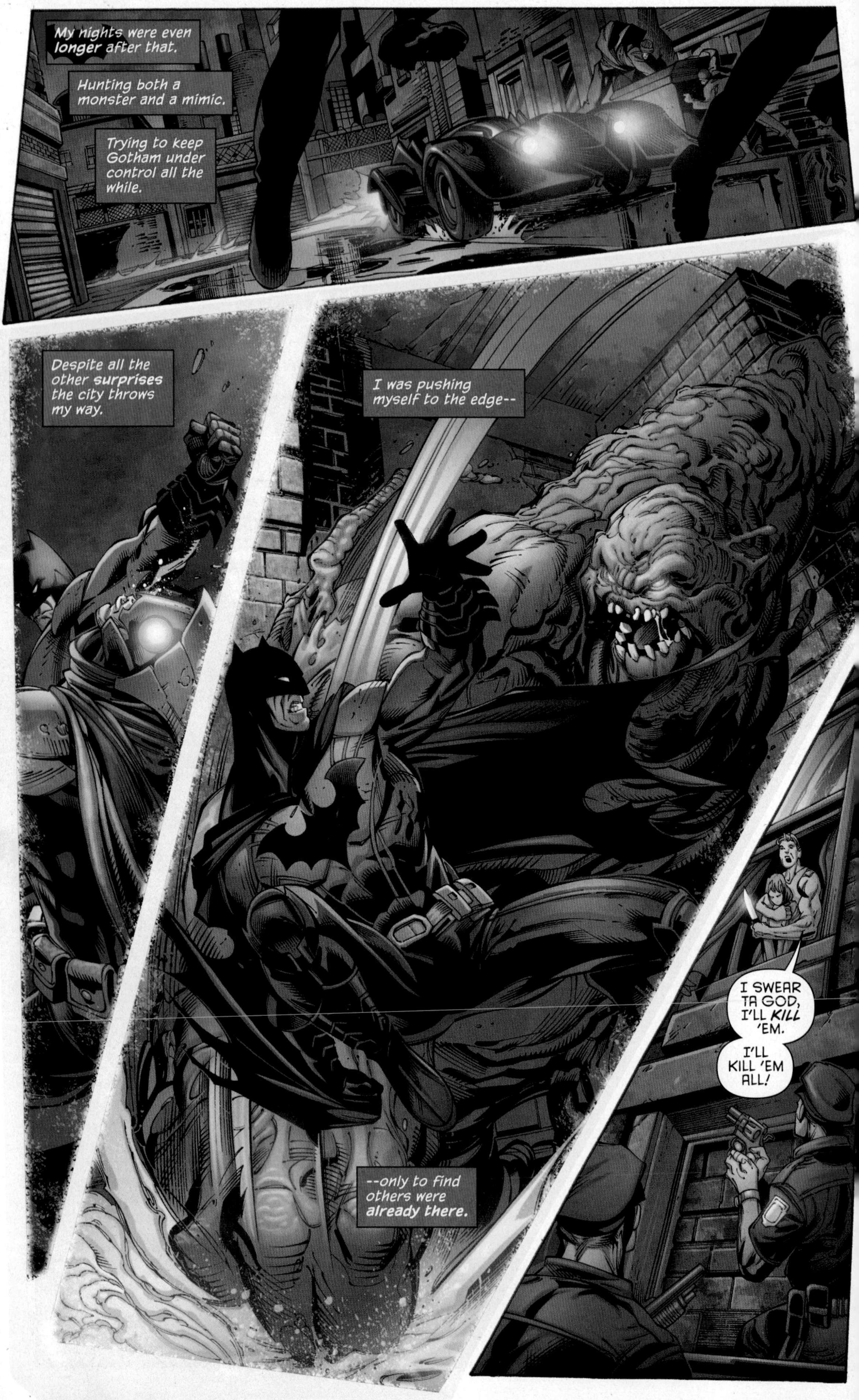
My nights were even **longer** after that.
Hunting both a monster and a mimic.
Trying to keep Gotham under control all the while.
Despite all the other **surprises** the city throws my way.
I was pushing myself to the edge--
I SWEAR TA GOD, I'LL ***KILL*** 'EM.
I'LL KILL 'EM ALL!
--only to find others were **already there.**

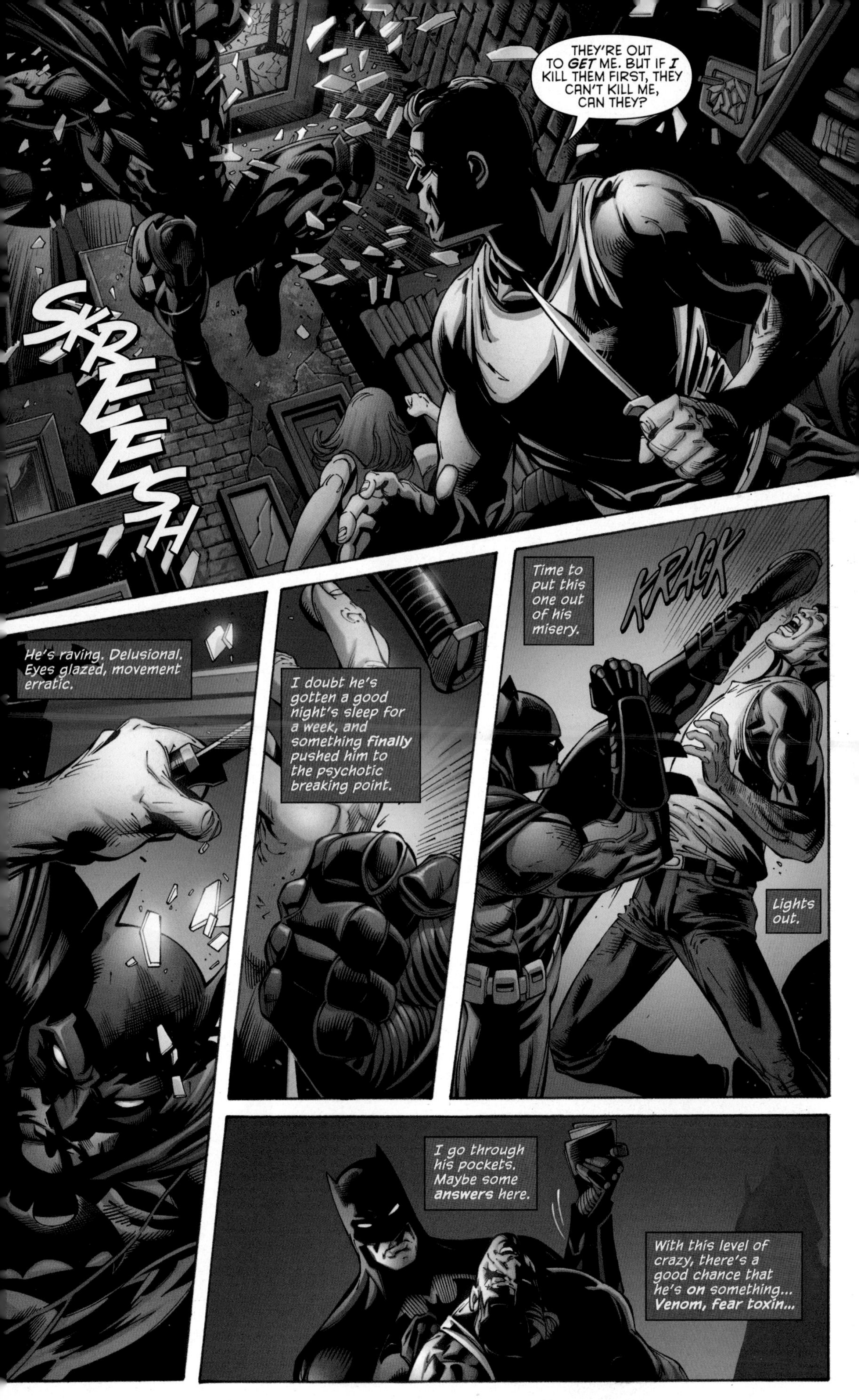

THEY'RE OUT TO GET ME. BUT IF I KILL THEM FIRST, THEY CAN'T KILL ME, CAN THEY?
SKREESH
He's raving. Delusional. Eyes glazed, movement erratic.
I doubt he's gotten a good night's sleep for a week, and something finally pushed him to the psychotic breaking point.
Time to put this one out of his misery.
KRACK
Lights out.
I go through his pockets. Maybe some answers here.
With this level of crazy, there's a good chance that he's on something... Venom, fear toxin...

...what I find is far worse.

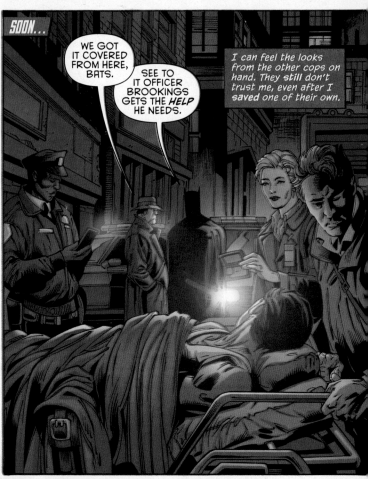

WE GOT IT COVERED FROM HERE, BATS.

SEE TO IT OFFICER BROOKINGS GETS THE *HELP* HE NEEDS.

I can feel the looks from the other cops on hand. They *still* don't trust me, even after I *saved* one of their own.

CITY OF GOTHAM POLICE

18 BROOKINGS

TRUST IS IN SHORT SUPPLY AMONG THE G.C.P.D.--IT'S BEEN REPLACED BY *FEAR.*

YOU *KNOW* HIM?

NOT WELL.

LOST HIS PARTNER TO *THE WRATH* A FEW DAYS AGO. HIS PARTNER *BEFORE* THAT DIED THE LAST TIME *JOKER* WENT ALL NUTS ON THE CITY.

Harvey Bullock looks *different* from the last time I've seen him.

Paying a little more attention to his *hygiene* than I'm used to.

YOU MIGHT WANT TO TALK TO ABBY.

DR. WILBURN, I MEAN.

He's actually wearing...*cologne?*

And I think I know *why.*

SHE SPENT SOME TIME *COUNSELING* BROOKINGS.

I'VE BEEN TALKING TO AS MANY G.C.P.D. OFFICERS AFFECTED BY THESE TRAGEDIES AS I CAN, BATMAN.

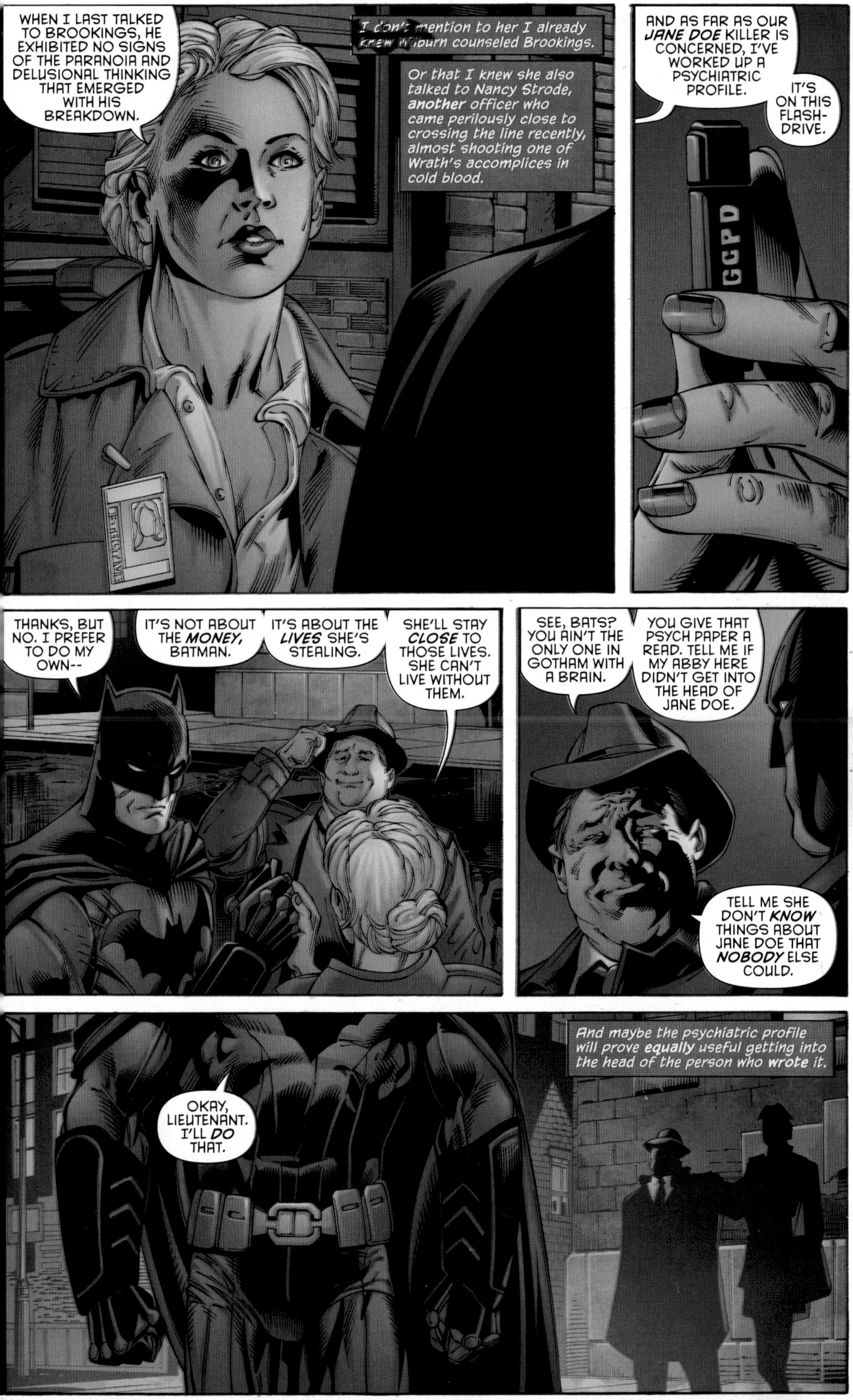

WHEN I LAST TALKED TO BROOKINGS, HE EXHIBITED NO SIGNS OF THE PARANOIA AND DELUSIONAL THINKING THAT EMERGED WITH HIS BREAKDOWN.
I don't mention to her I already knew Wilburn counseled Brookings.
Or that I knew she also talked to Nancy Strode, **another** officer who came perilously close to crossing the line recently, almost shooting one of Wrath's accomplices in cold blood.
AND AS FAR AS OUR ***JANE DOE*** KILLER IS CONCERNED, I'VE WORKED UP A PSYCHIATRIC PROFILE.
IT'S ON THIS FLASH-DRIVE.
GCPD
THANKS, BUT NO. I PREFER TO DO MY OWN--
IT'S NOT ABOUT THE ***MONEY,*** BATMAN.
IT'S ABOUT THE ***LIVES*** SHE'S STEALING.
SHE'LL STAY ***CLOSE*** TO THOSE LIVES. SHE CAN'T LIVE WITHOUT THEM.
SEE, BATS? YOU AIN'T THE ONLY ONE IN GOTHAM WITH A BRAIN.
YOU GIVE THAT PSYCH PAPER A READ. TELL ME IF MY ABBY HERE DIDN'T GET INTO THE HEAD OF JANE DOE.
TELL ME SHE DON'T ***KNOW*** THINGS ABOUT JANE DOE THAT ***NOBODY*** ELSE COULD.
OKAY, LIEUTENANT. I'LL ***DO*** THAT.
And maybe the psychiatric profile will prove **equally** useful getting into the head of the person who **wrote** it.

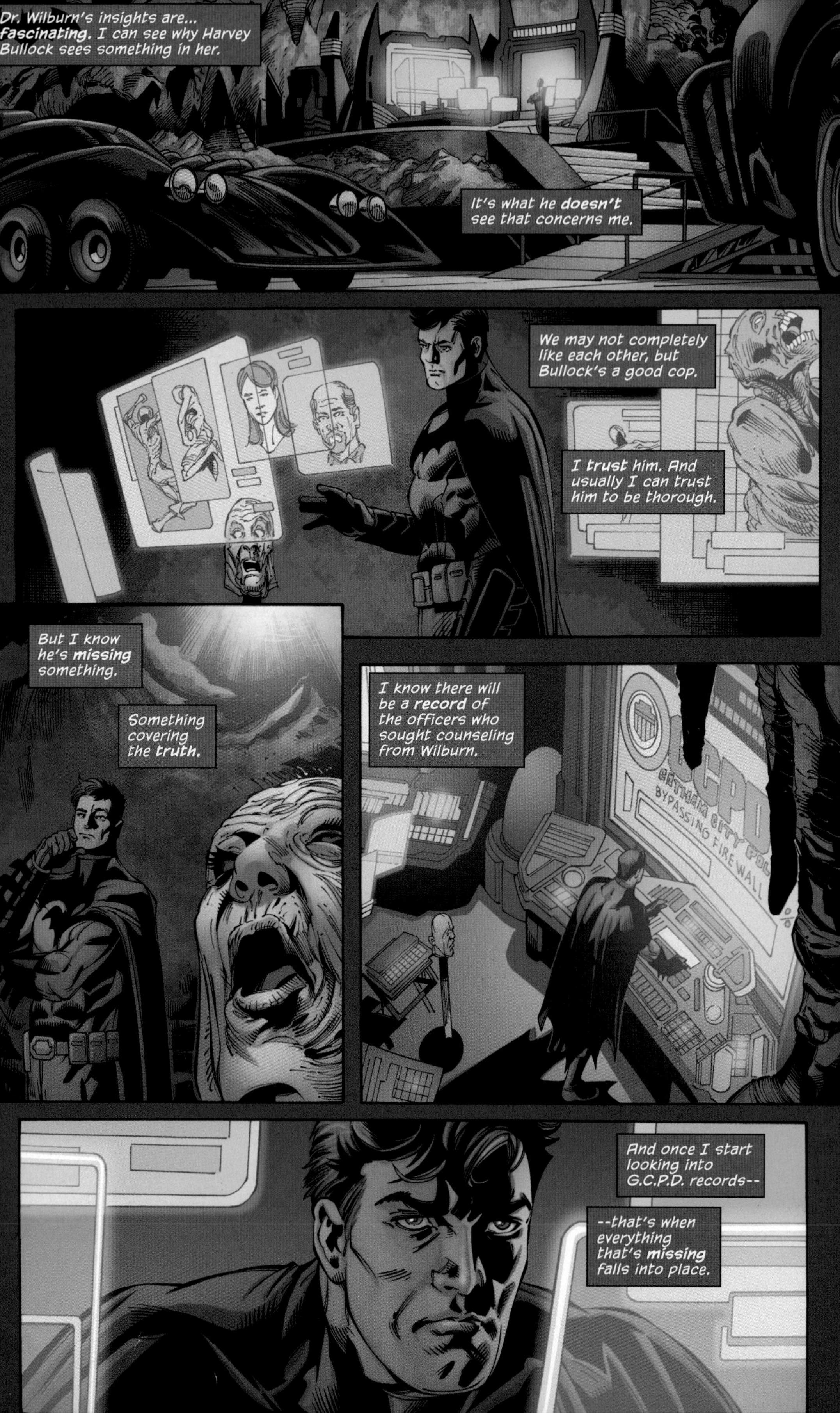
Dr. Wilburn's insights are... **fascinating.** I can see why Harvey Bullock sees something in her.
It's what he **doesn't** see that concerns me.
We may not completely like each other, but Bullock's a good cop.
I **trust** him. And usually I can trust him to be thorough.
But I know he's **missing** something.
Something covering the **truth.**
I know there will be a **record** of the officers who sought counseling from Wilburn.
GCPD
GOTHAM CITY POL
BYPASSING FIREWALL
And once I start looking into G.C.P.D. records--
--that's when everything that's **missing** falls into place.

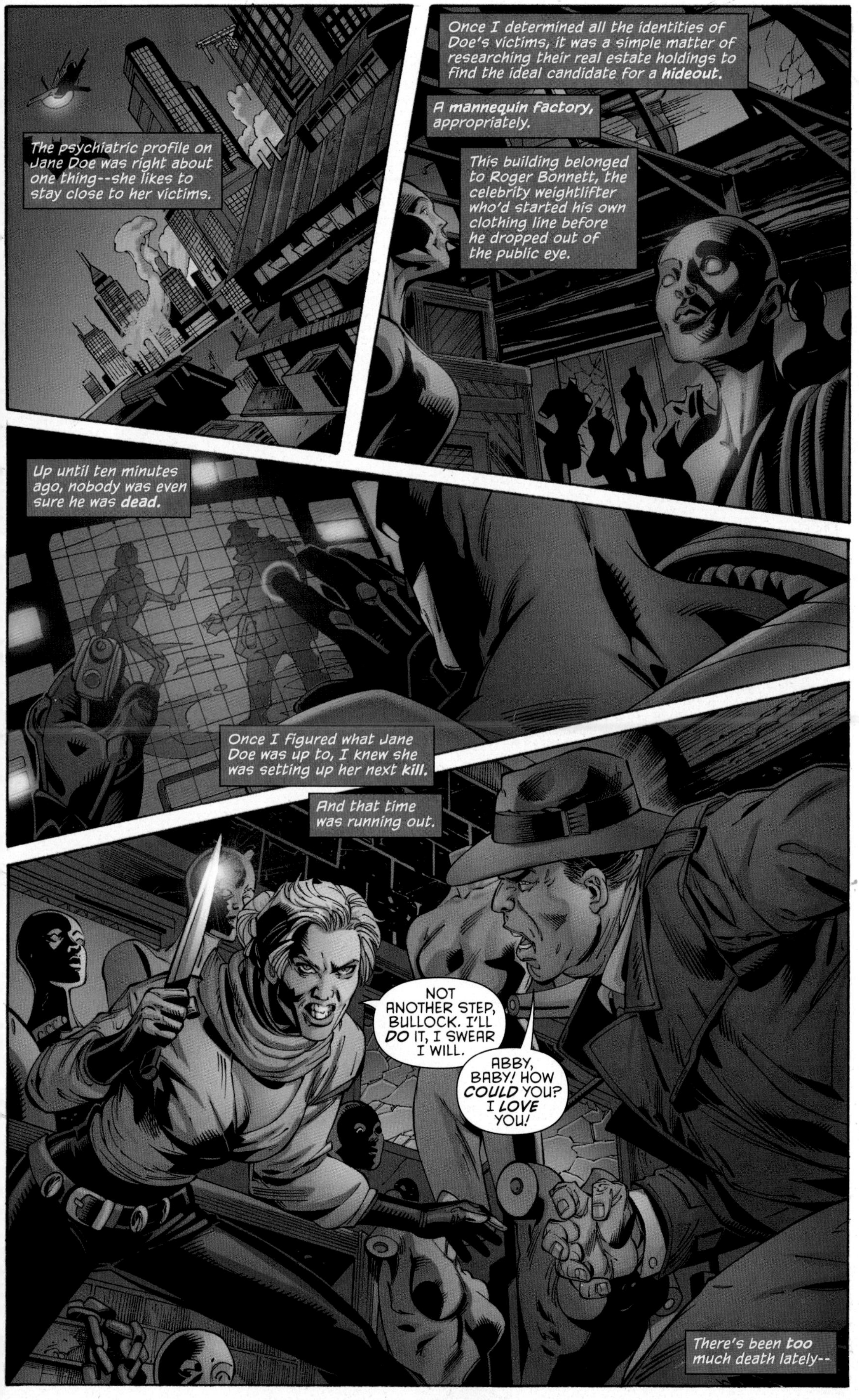
The psychiatric profile on Jane Doe was right about one thing--she likes to stay close to her victims.
Once I determined all the identities of Doe's victims, it was a simple matter of researching their real estate holdings to find the ideal candidate for a hideout.
A mannequin factory, appropriately.
This building belonged to Roger Bonnett, the celebrity weightlifter who'd started his own clothing line before he dropped out of the public eye.
Up until ten minutes ago, nobody was even sure he was dead.
Once I figured what Jane Doe was up to, I knew she was setting up her next kill.
And that time was running out.
NOT ANOTHER STEP, BULLOCK. I'LL DO IT, I SWEAR I WILL.
ABBY, BABY! HOW COULD YOU? I LOVE YOU!
There's been too much death lately--

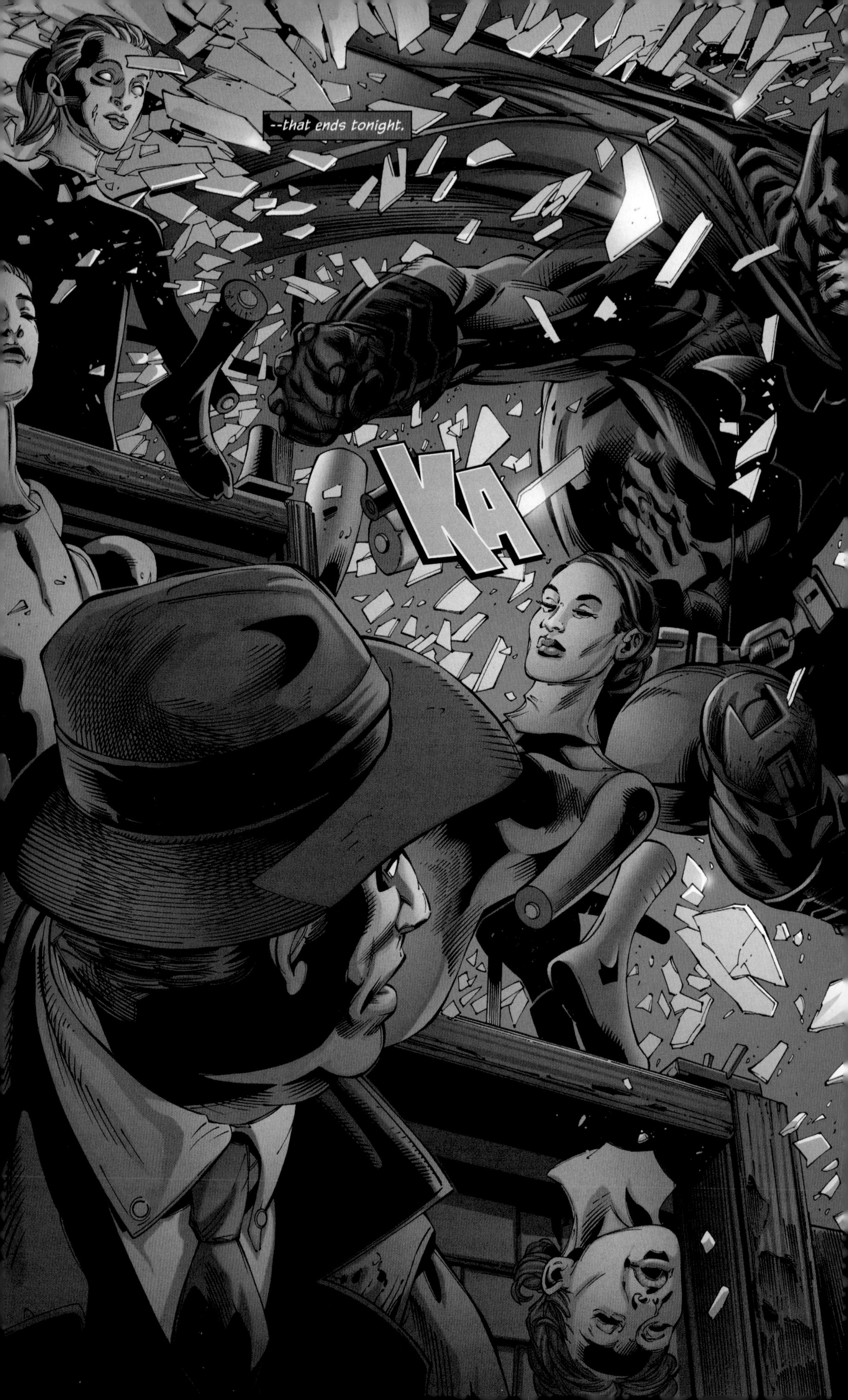
--that ends tonight.
KA

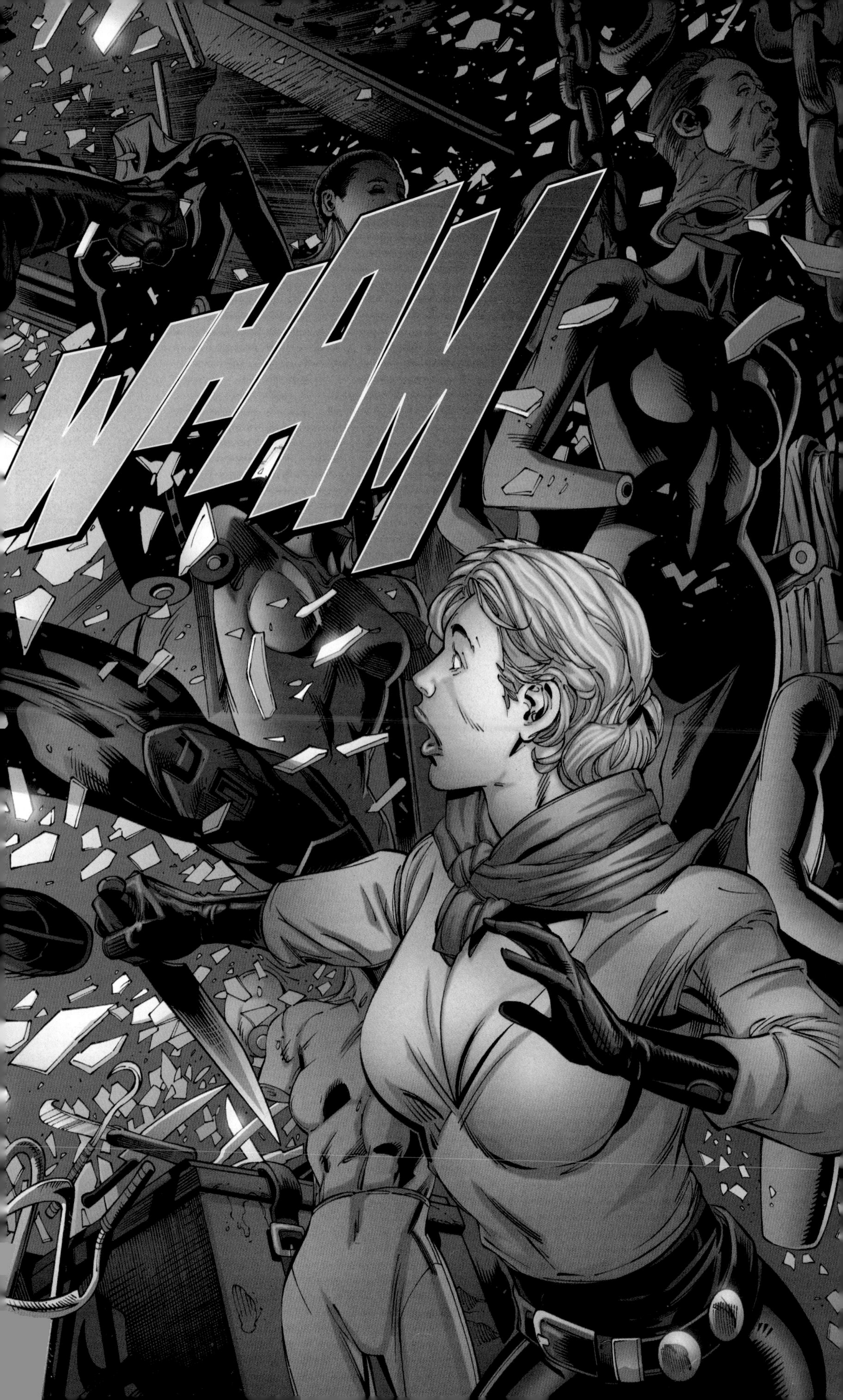
WHAM

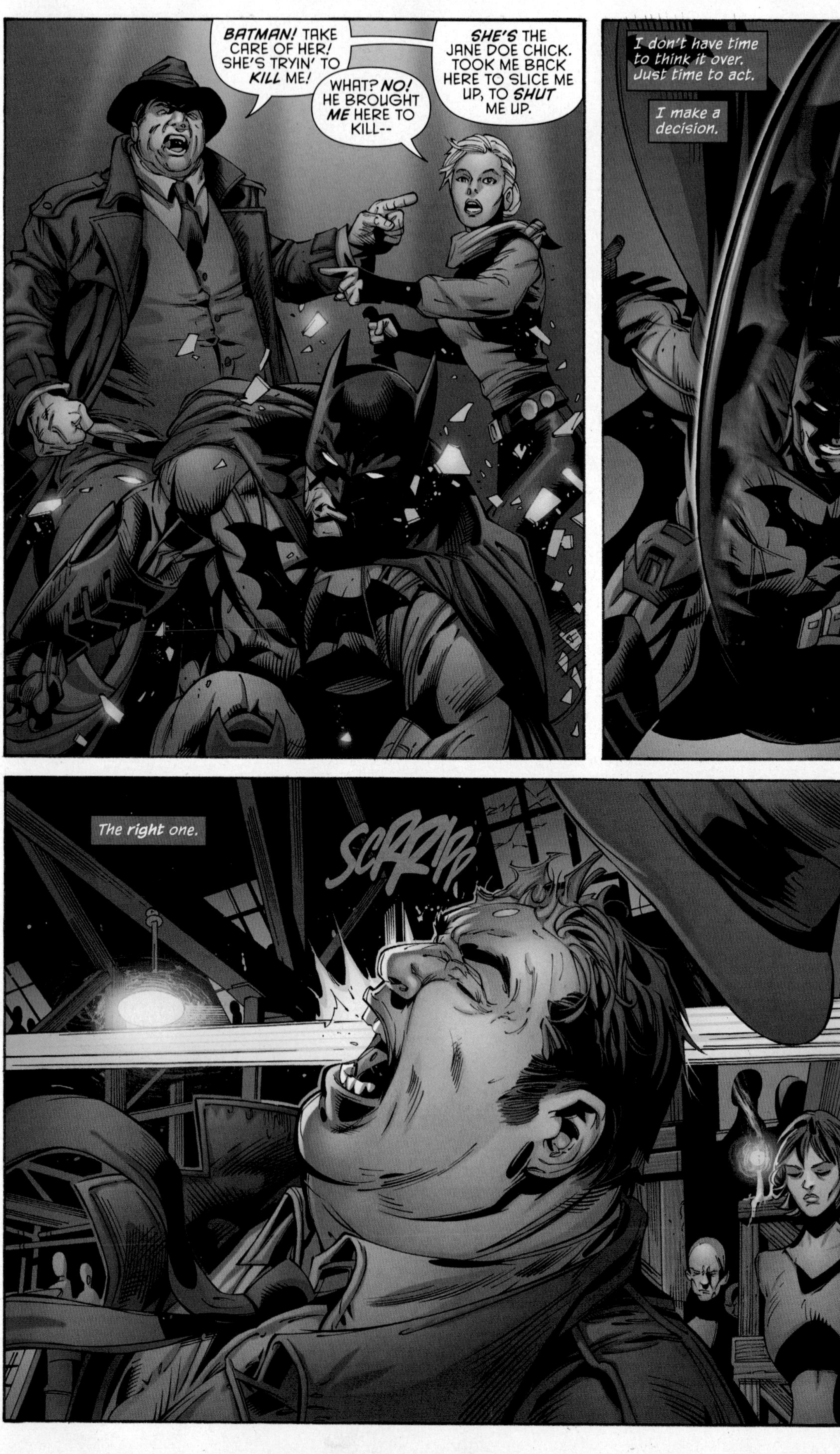
BATMAN! TAKE CARE OF HER! SHE'S TRYIN' TO KILL ME!
WHAT? NO! HE BROUGHT ME HERE TO KILL--
SHE'S THE JANE DOE CHICK. TOOK ME BACK HERE TO SLICE ME UP, TO SHUT ME UP.
I don't have time to think it over. Just time to act.
I make a decision.
The right one.
SCRRRR

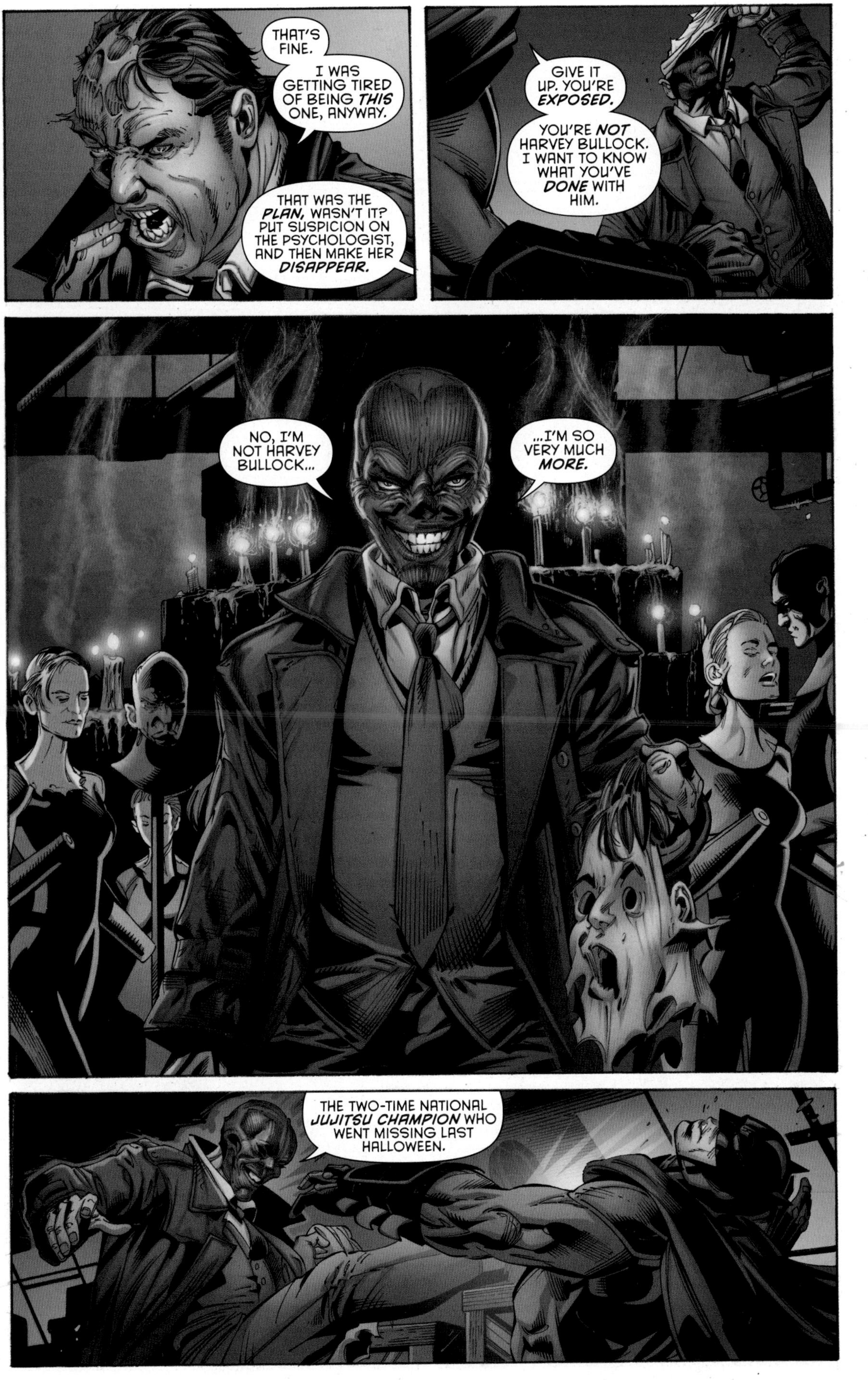
THAT'S FINE.
I WAS GETTING TIRED OF BEING *THIS* ONE, ANYWAY.
THAT WAS THE *PLAN,* WASN'T IT? PUT SUSPICION ON THE PSYCHOLOGIST, AND THEN MAKE HER *DISAPPEAR.*
GIVE IT UP. YOU'RE *EXPOSED.*
YOU'RE *NOT* HARVEY BULLOCK. I WANT TO KNOW WHAT YOU'VE *DONE* WITH HIM.
NO, I'M NOT HARVEY BULLOCK...
...I'M SO VERY MUCH *MORE.*
THE TWO-TIME NATIONAL *JUJITSU CHAMPION* WHO WENT MISSING LAST HALLOWEEN.

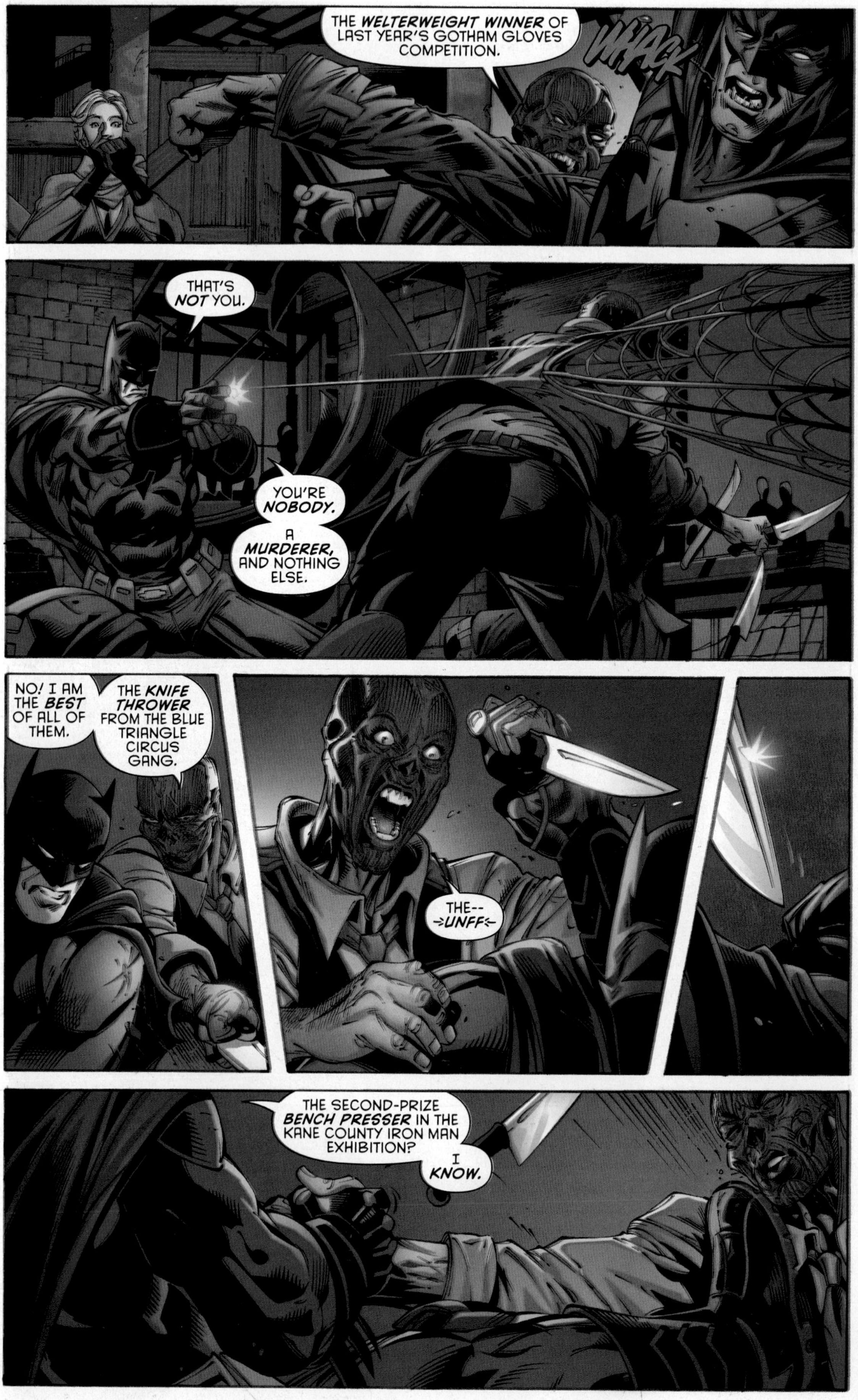
THE WELTERWEIGHT WINNER OF LAST YEAR'S GOTHAM GLOVES COMPETITION.
WHACK
THAT'S NOT YOU.
YOU'RE NOBODY.
A MURDERER, AND NOTHING ELSE.
NO! I AM THE BEST OF ALL OF THEM.
THE KNIFE THROWER FROM THE BLUE TRIANGLE CIRCUS GANG.
THE--
UNFF
THE SECOND-PRIZE BENCH PRESSER IN THE KANE COUNTY IRON MAN EXHIBITION?
I KNOW.

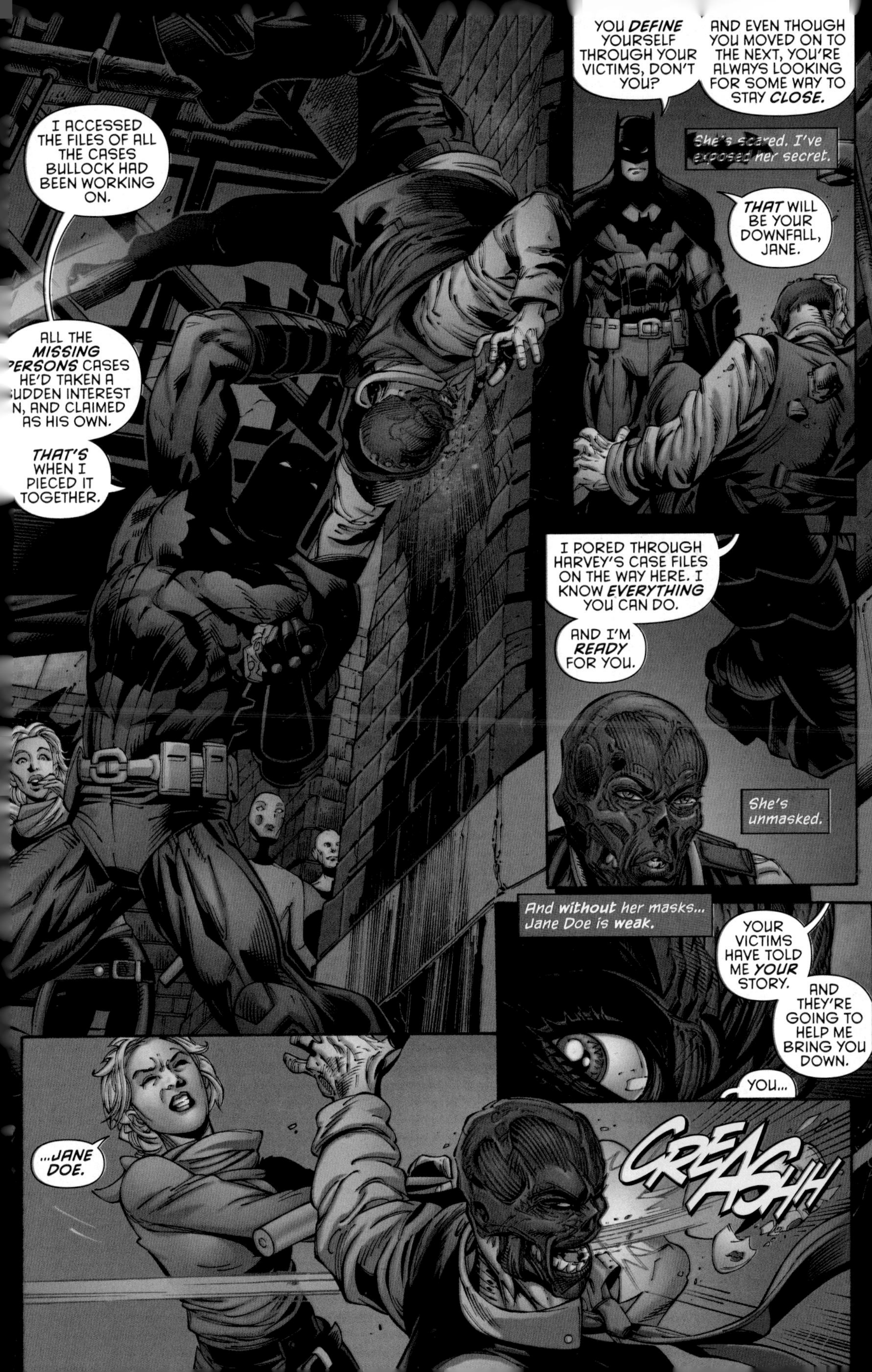
I ACCESSED THE FILES OF ALL THE CASES BULLOCK HAD BEEN WORKING ON.
ALL THE *MISSING PERSONS* CASES HE'D TAKEN A SUDDEN INTEREST IN, AND CLAIMED AS HIS OWN.
THAT'S WHEN I PIECED IT TOGETHER.
YOU *DEFINE* YOURSELF THROUGH YOUR VICTIMS, DON'T YOU?
AND EVEN THOUGH YOU MOVED ON TO THE NEXT, YOU'RE ALWAYS LOOKING FOR SOME WAY TO STAY *CLOSE.*
She's scared. I've exposed her secret.
THAT WILL BE YOUR DOWNFALL, JANE.
I PORED THROUGH HARVEY'S CASE FILES ON THE WAY HERE. I KNOW *EVERYTHING* YOU CAN DO.
AND I'M *READY* FOR YOU.
She's unmasked.
And **without** her masks... Jane Doe is **weak.**
YOUR VICTIMS HAVE TOLD ME *YOUR* STORY.
AND THEY'RE GOING TO HELP ME BRING YOU DOWN.
YOU...
...JANE DOE.
CREASHHH

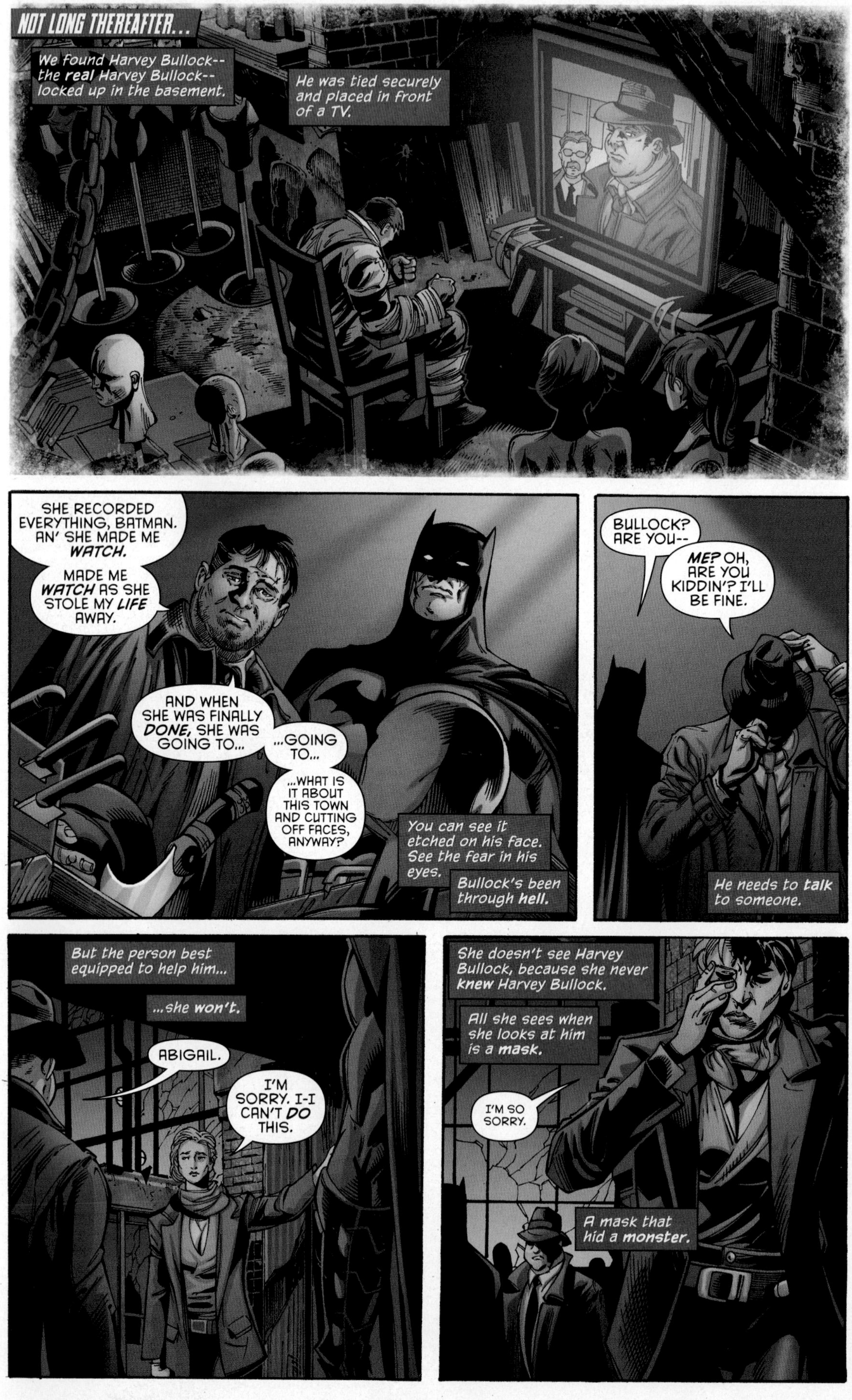
NOT LONG THEREAFTER...
We found Harvey Bullock--the real Harvey Bullock--locked up in the basement.
He was tied securely and placed in front of a TV.
SHE RECORDED EVERYTHING, BATMAN. AN' SHE MADE ME WATCH.
MADE ME WATCH AS SHE STOLE MY LIFE AWAY.
AND WHEN SHE WAS FINALLY DONE, SHE WAS GOING TO...
...GOING TO...
...WHAT IS IT ABOUT THIS TOWN AND CUTTING OFF FACES, ANYWAY?
You can see it etched on his face. See the fear in his eyes.
Bullock's been through hell.
BULLOCK? ARE YOU--
ME? OH, ARE YOU KIDDIN'? I'LL BE FINE.
He needs to talk to someone.
But the person best equipped to help him...
...she won't.
ABIGAIL.
I'M SORRY. I-I CAN'T DO THIS.
She doesn't see Harvey Bullock, because she never knew Harvey Bullock.
All she sees when she looks at him is a mask.
I'M SO SORRY.
A mask that hid a monster.

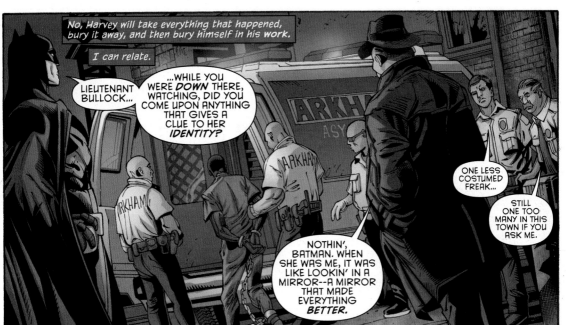

No, Harvey will take everything that happened, bury it away, and then bury himself in his work.

I can relate.

LIEUTENANT BULLOCK...

...WHILE YOU WERE *DOWN* THERE, WATCHING, DID YOU COME UPON ANYTHING THAT GIVES A CLUE TO HER *IDENTITY?*

ONE LESS COSTUMED FREAK...

STILL ONE TOO MANY IN THIS TOWN IF YOU ASK ME.

NOTHIN', BATMAN. WHEN SHE WAS ME, IT WAS LIKE LOOKIN' IN A MIRROR--A MIRROR THAT MADE EVERYTHING *BETTER.*

"BUT THOSE RARE TIMES SHE TOOK *OFF* HER MASK...

"...IT WAS LIKE SHE WASN'T EVEN THERE.

"LIKE SHE *DOESN'T EXIST* UNLESS SHE INSERTED HERSELF INTO THE LIFE OF SOMEONE ELSE."

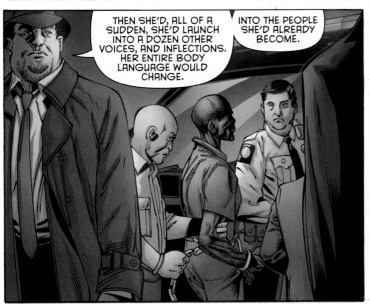

THEN SHE'D, ALL OF A SUDDEN, SHE'D LAUNCH INTO A DOZEN OTHER VOICES, AND INFLECTIONS. HER ENTIRE BODY LANGUAGE WOULD CHANGE.

INTO THE PEOPLE SHE'D ALREADY BECOME.

OR WHOEVER SHE'D SET HER SIGHTS ON *NEXT.*

IT DOESN'T MATTER.

ALL THAT MATTERS IS ANOTHER *LUNATIC* IS OFF THE STREETS OF GOTHAM, AND LOCKED AWAY INTO ARKHAM WHERE SHE CAN NO LONGER DO ANY HARM.

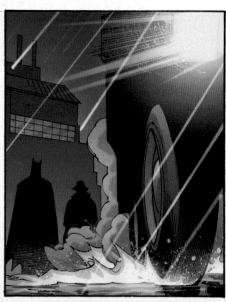

IT DOESN'T MATTER.

ALL THAT MATTERS IS ANOTHER *LUNATIC* IS OFF THE STREETS OF GOTHAM, AND LOCKED AWAY INTO ARKHAM WHERE SHE CAN NO LONGER DO ANY HARM.

THE END?

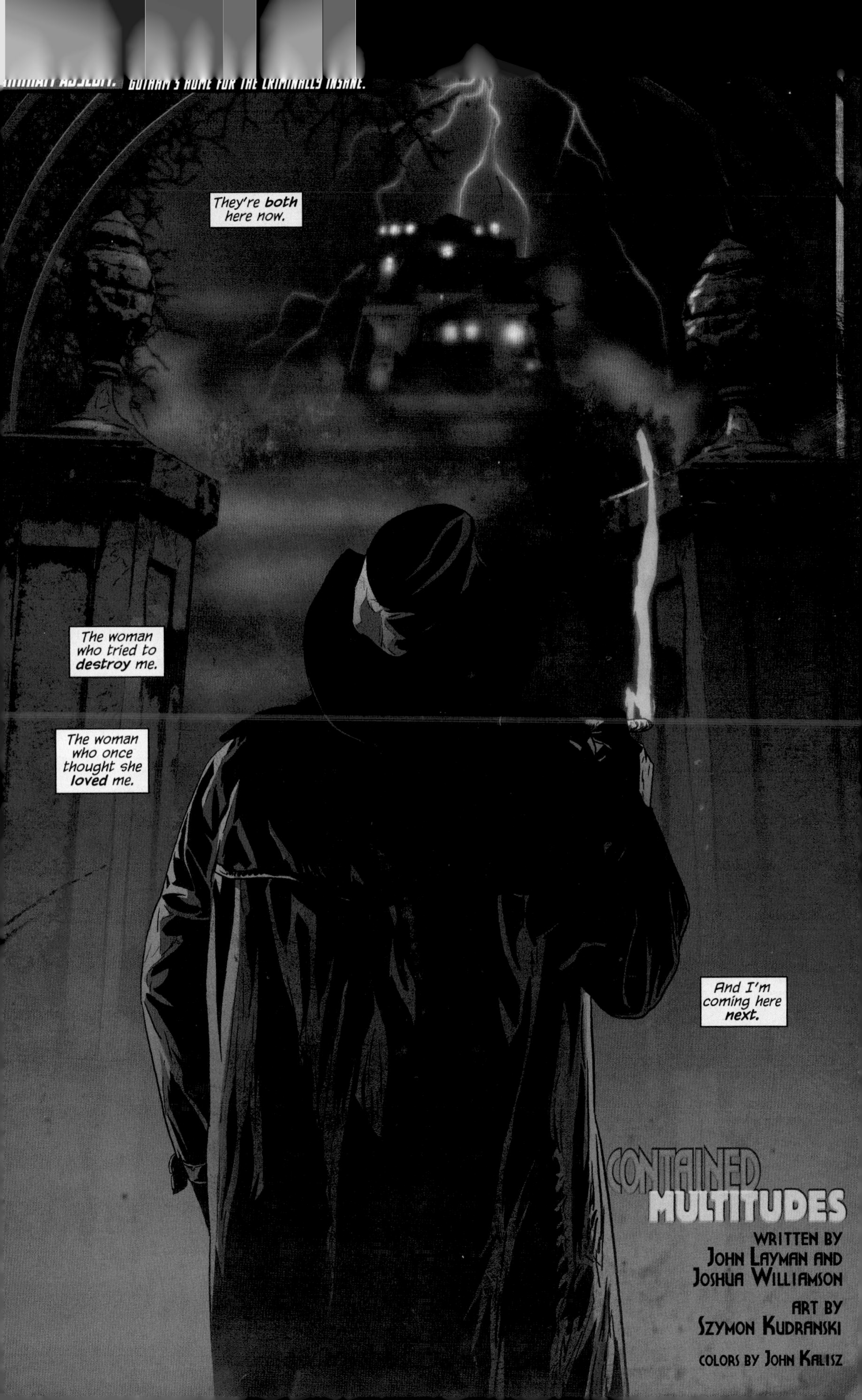
They're **both** here now.
The woman who tried to **destroy** me.
The woman who once thought she **loved** me.
And I'm coming here **next.**
CONTAINED
MULTITUDES
WRITTEN BY
JOHN LAYMAN AND
JOSHUA WILLIAMSON
ART BY
SZYMON KUDRANSKI
COLORS BY JOHN KALISZ

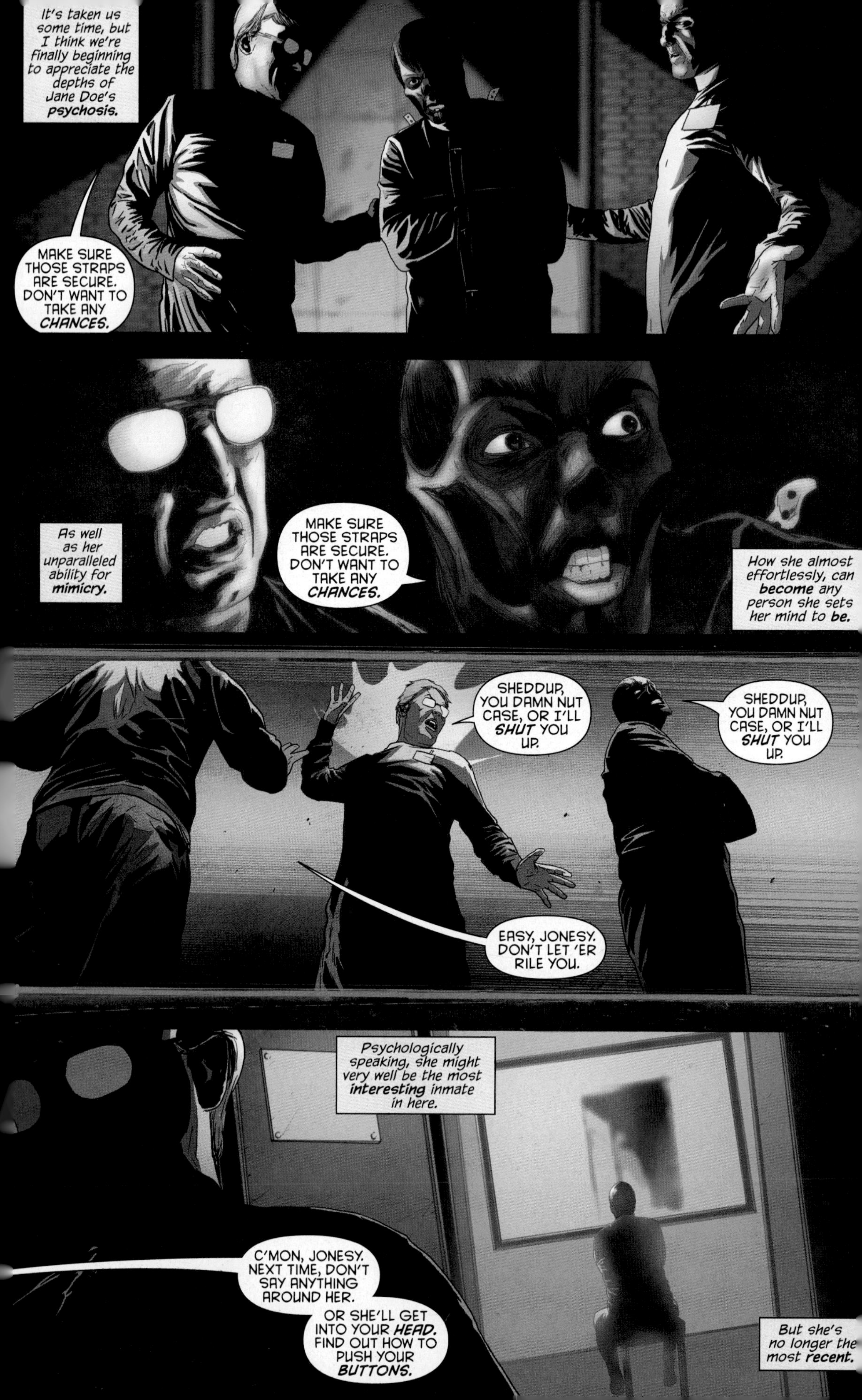
It's taken us some time, but I think we're finally beginning to appreciate the depths of Jane Doe's **psychosis.**
MAKE SURE THOSE STRAPS ARE SECURE. DON'T WANT TO TAKE ANY *CHANCES.*
As well as her unparalleled ability for **mimicry.**
MAKE SURE THOSE STRAPS ARE SECURE. DON'T WANT TO TAKE ANY *CHANCES.*
How she almost effortlessly, can **become** any person she sets her mind to **be.**
SHEDDUP, YOU DAMN NUT CASE, OR I'LL *SHUT* YOU UP.
SHEDDUP, YOU DAMN NUT CASE, OR I'LL *SHUT* YOU UP.
EASY, JONESY. DON'T LET 'ER RILE YOU.
Psychologically speaking, she might very well be the most **interesting** inmate in here.
C'MON, JONESY. NEXT TIME, DON'T SAY ANYTHING AROUND HER.
OR SHE'LL GET INTO YOUR *HEAD.* FIND OUT HOW TO PUSH YOUR *BUTTONS.*
But she's no longer the most **recent.**

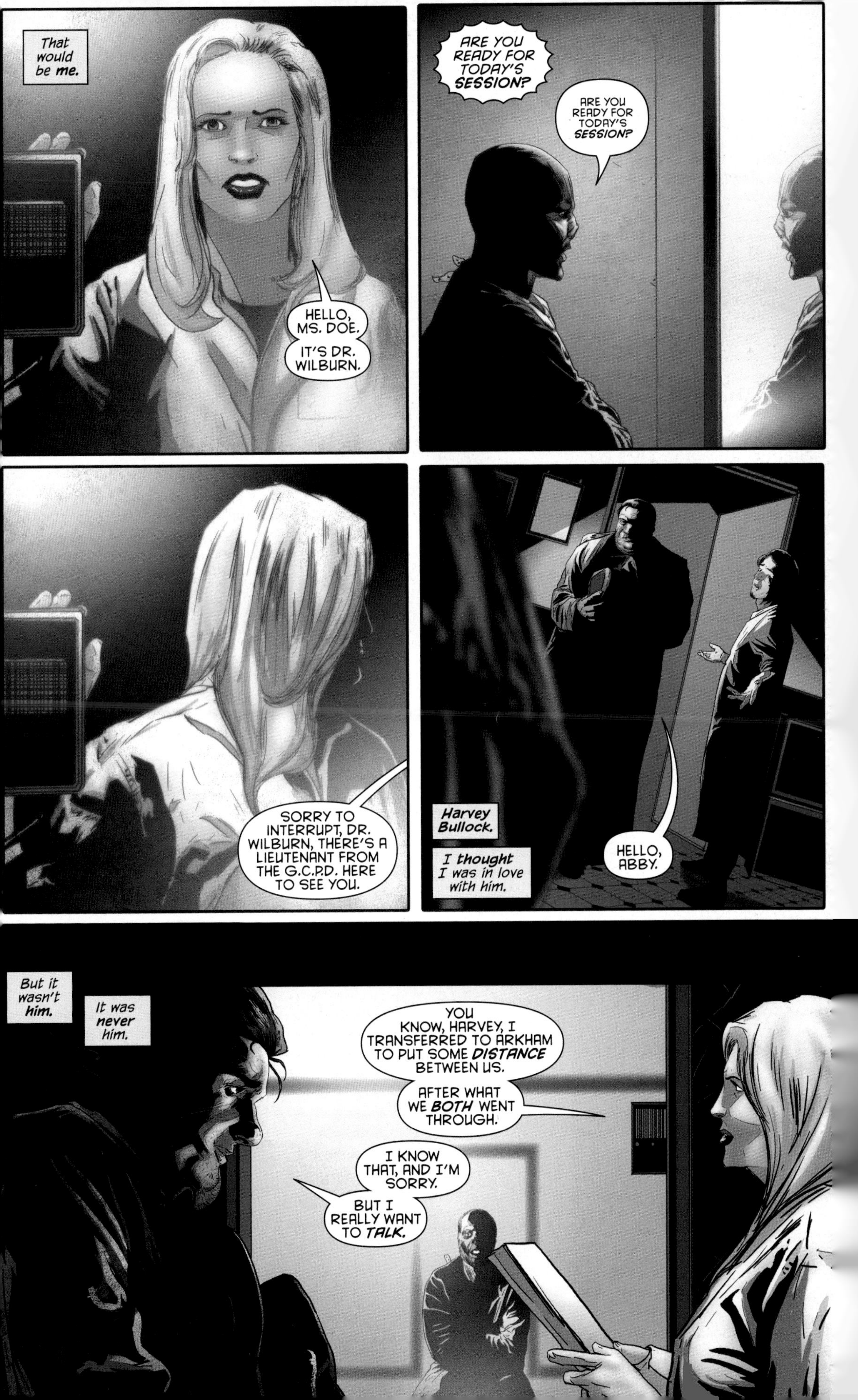
That would be *me.*
HELLO, MS. DOE.
IT'S DR. WILBURN.
ARE YOU READY FOR TODAY'S *SESSION?*
ARE YOU READY FOR TODAY'S *SESSION?*
SORRY TO INTERRUPT, DR. WILBURN, THERE'S A LIEUTENANT FROM THE G.C.P.D. HERE TO SEE YOU.
Harvey Bullock.
I thought I was in love with him.
HELLO, ABBY.
But it wasn't *him.*
It was *never* him.
YOU KNOW, HARVEY, I TRANSFERRED TO ARKHAM TO PUT SOME *DISTANCE* BETWEEN US.
AFTER WHAT WE *BOTH* WENT THROUGH.
I KNOW THAT, AND I'M SORRY.
BUT I REALLY WANT TO *TALK.*

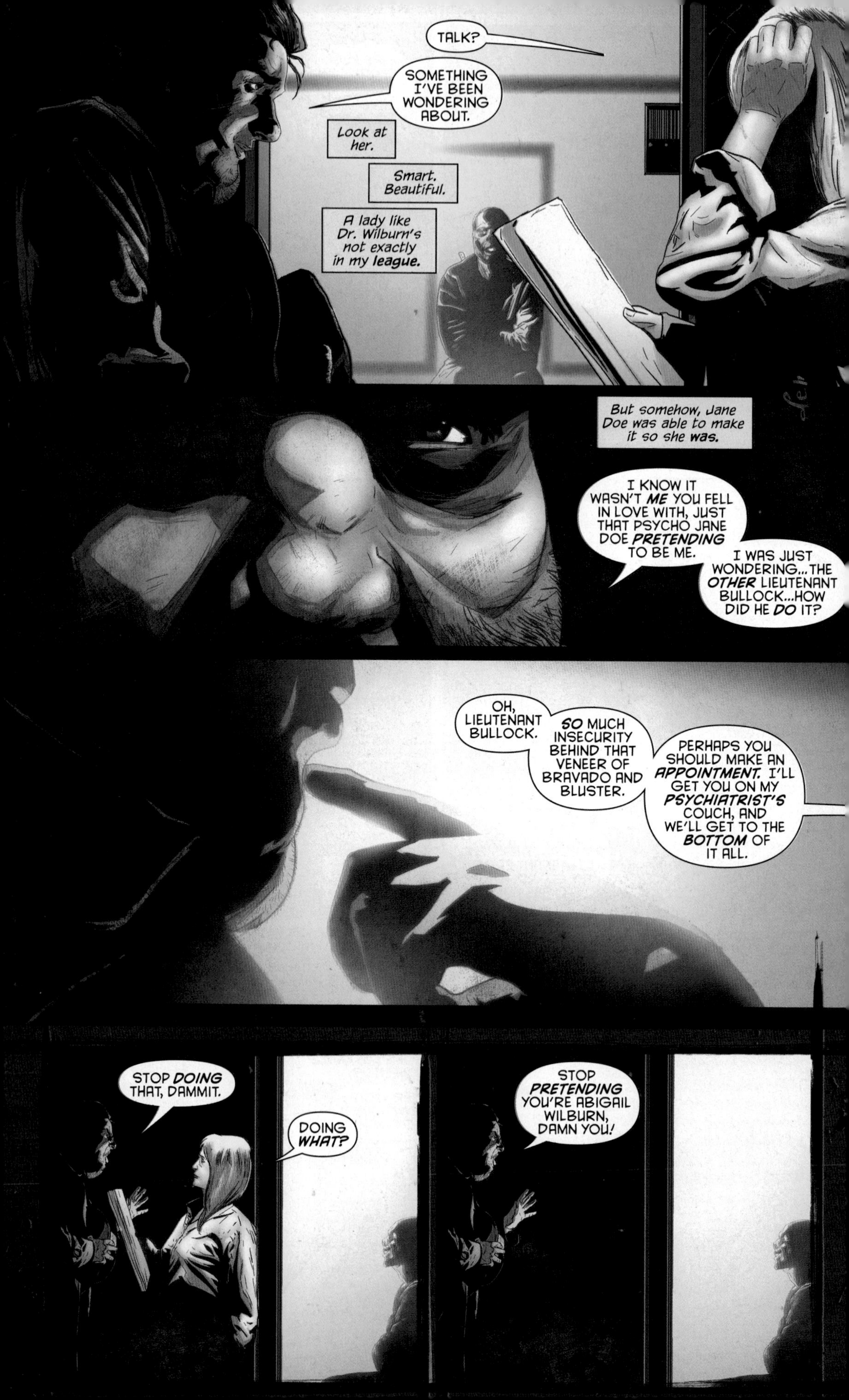
TALK?
SOMETHING I'VE BEEN WONDERING ABOUT.
Look at her.
Smart. Beautiful.
A lady like Dr. Wilburn's not exactly in my league.
But somehow, Jane Doe was able to make it so she was.
I KNOW IT WASN'T ME YOU FELL IN LOVE WITH, JUST THAT PSYCHO JANE DOE PRETENDING TO BE ME.
I WAS JUST WONDERING...THE OTHER LIEUTENANT BULLOCK...HOW DID HE DO IT?
OH, LIEUTENANT BULLOCK.
SO MUCH INSECURITY BEHIND THAT VENEER OF BRAVADO AND BLUSTER.
PERHAPS YOU SHOULD MAKE AN APPOINTMENT. I'LL GET YOU ON MY PSYCHIATRIST'S COUCH, AND WE'LL GET TO THE BOTTOM OF IT ALL.
STOP DOING THAT, DAMMIT.
DOING WHAT?
STOP PRETENDING YOU'RE ABIGAIL WILBURN, DAMN YOU!

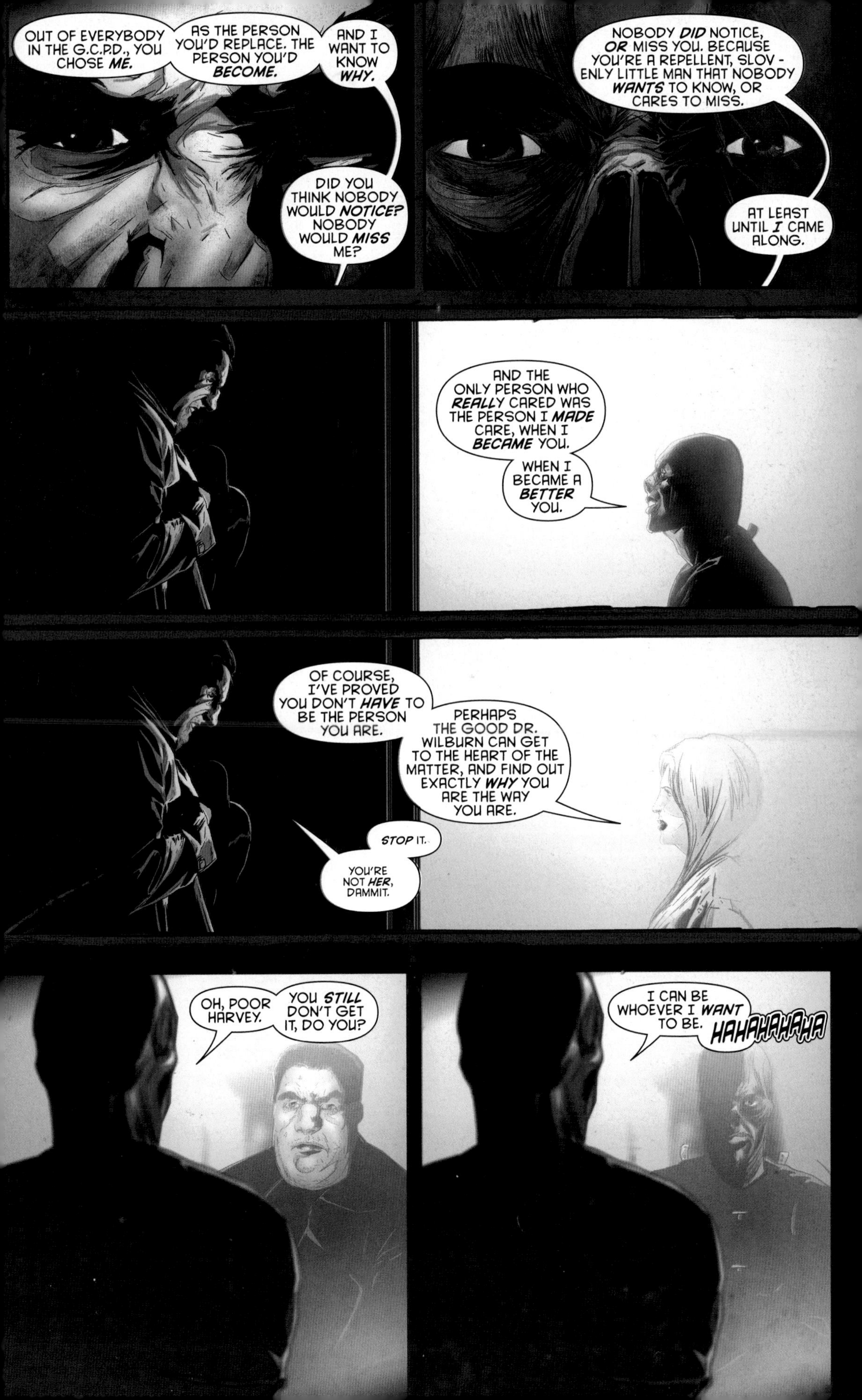

OUT OF EVERYBODY IN THE G.C.P.D., YOU CHOSE ME.
AS THE PERSON YOU'D REPLACE. THE PERSON YOU'D BECOME.
AND I WANT TO KNOW WHY.
DID YOU THINK NOBODY WOULD NOTICE? NOBODY WOULD MISS ME?
NOBODY DID NOTICE, OR MISS YOU. BECAUSE YOU'RE A REPELLENT, SLOV - ENLY LITTLE MAN THAT NOBODY WANTS TO KNOW, OR CARES TO MISS.
AT LEAST UNTIL I CAME ALONG.
AND THE ONLY PERSON WHO REALLY CARED WAS THE PERSON I MADE CARE, WHEN I BECAME YOU.
WHEN I BECAME A BETTER YOU.
OF COURSE, I'VE PROVED YOU DON'T HAVE TO BE THE PERSON YOU ARE.
PERHAPS THE GOOD DR. WILBURN CAN GET TO THE HEART OF THE MATTER, AND FIND OUT EXACTLY WHY YOU ARE THE WAY YOU ARE.
STOP IT.
YOU'RE NOT HER, DAMMIT.
OH, POOR HARVEY.
YOU STILL DON'T GET IT, DO YOU?
I CAN BE WHOEVER I WANT TO BE.
HAHAHAHAHA

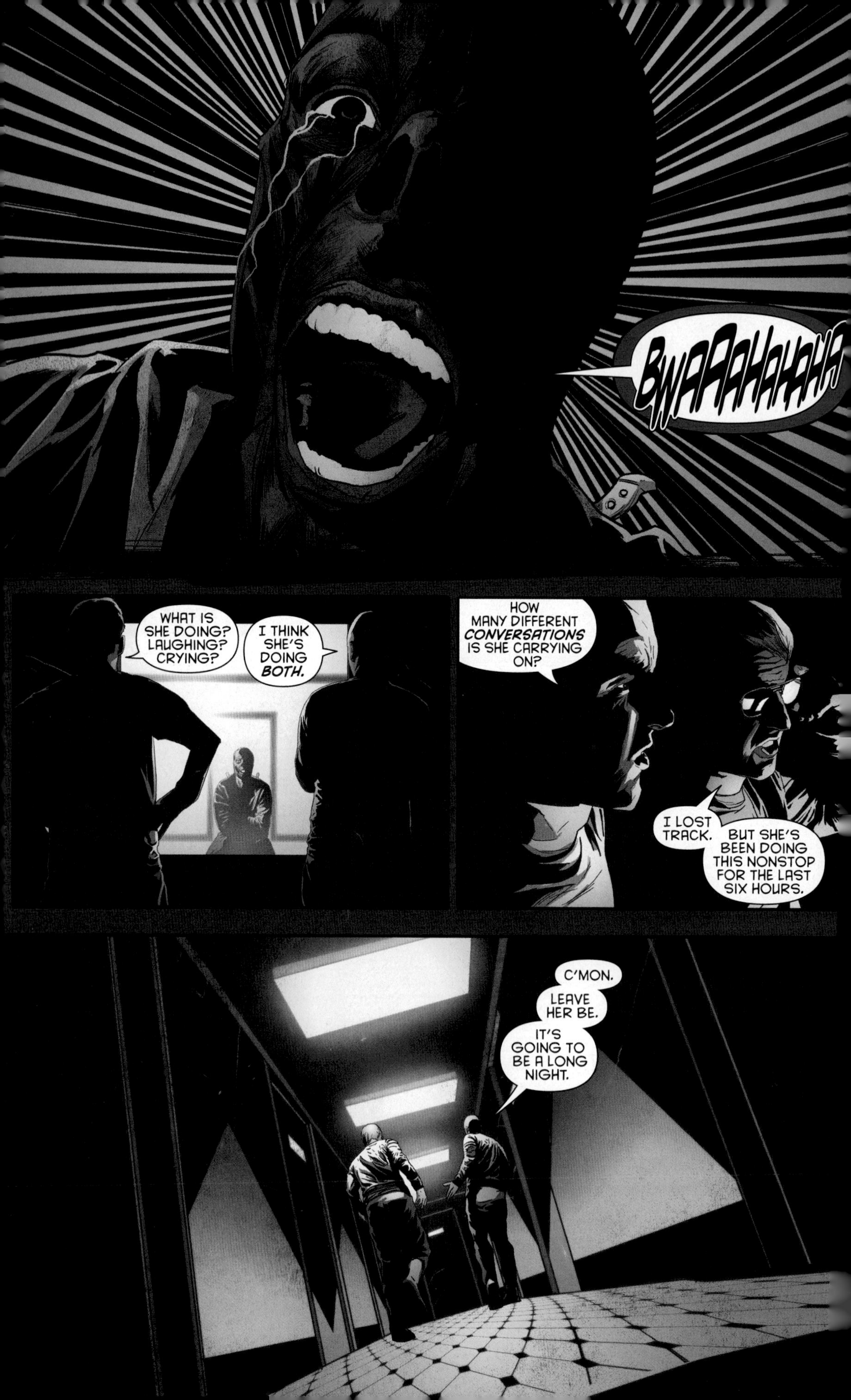
BWAAAAHAHAHA
WHAT IS SHE DOING? LAUGHING? CRYING?
I THINK SHE'S DOING *BOTH.*
HOW MANY DIFFERENT *CONVERSATIONS* IS SHE CARRYING ON?
I LOST TRACK.
BUT SHE'S BEEN DOING THIS NONSTOP FOR THE LAST SIX HOURS.
C'MON.
LEAVE HER BE.
IT'S GOING TO BE A LONG NIGHT.

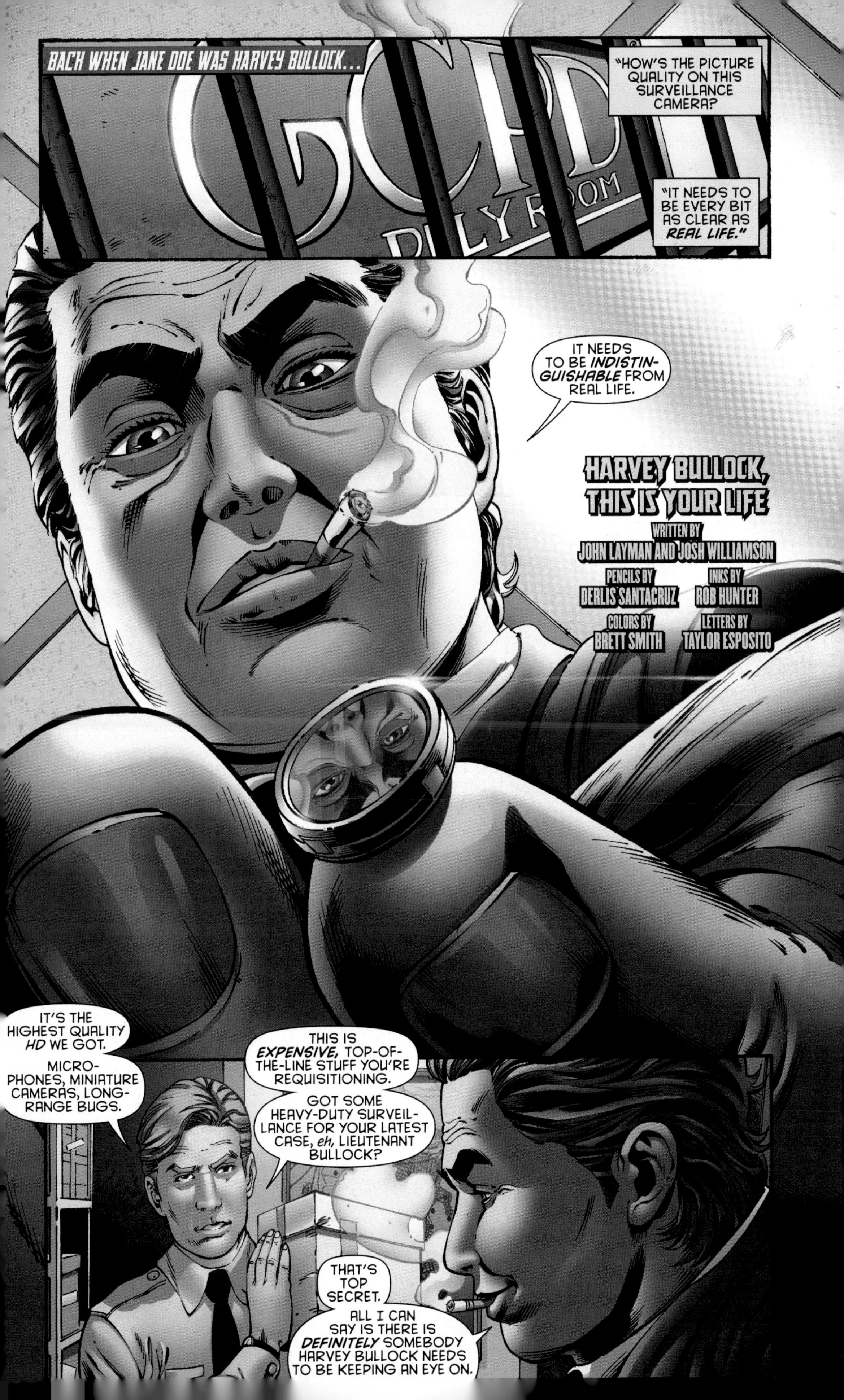
BACK WHEN JANE DOE WAS HARVEY BULLOCK...
"HOW'S THE PICTURE QUALITY ON THIS SURVEILLANCE CAMERA?
"IT NEEDS TO BE EVERY BIT AS CLEAR AS REAL LIFE."
IT NEEDS TO BE INDISTIN-GUISHABLE FROM REAL LIFE.
HARVEY BULLOCK, THIS IS YOUR LIFE
WRITTEN BY JOHN LAYMAN AND JOSH WILLIAMSON
PENCILS BY DERLIS SANTACRUZ
INKS BY ROB HUNTER
COLORS BY BRETT SMITH
LETTERS BY TAYLOR ESPOSITO
IT'S THE HIGHEST QUALITY HD WE GOT.
MICRO-PHONES, MINIATURE CAMERAS, LONG-RANGE BUGS.
THIS IS EXPENSIVE, TOP-OF-THE-LINE STUFF YOU'RE REQUISITIONING.
GOT SOME HEAVY-DUTY SURVEIL-LANCE FOR YOUR LATEST CASE, eh, LIEUTENANT BULLOCK?
THAT'S TOP SECRET.
ALL I CAN SAY IS THERE IS DEFINITELY SOMEBODY HARVEY BULLOCK NEEDS TO BE KEEPING AN EYE ON.

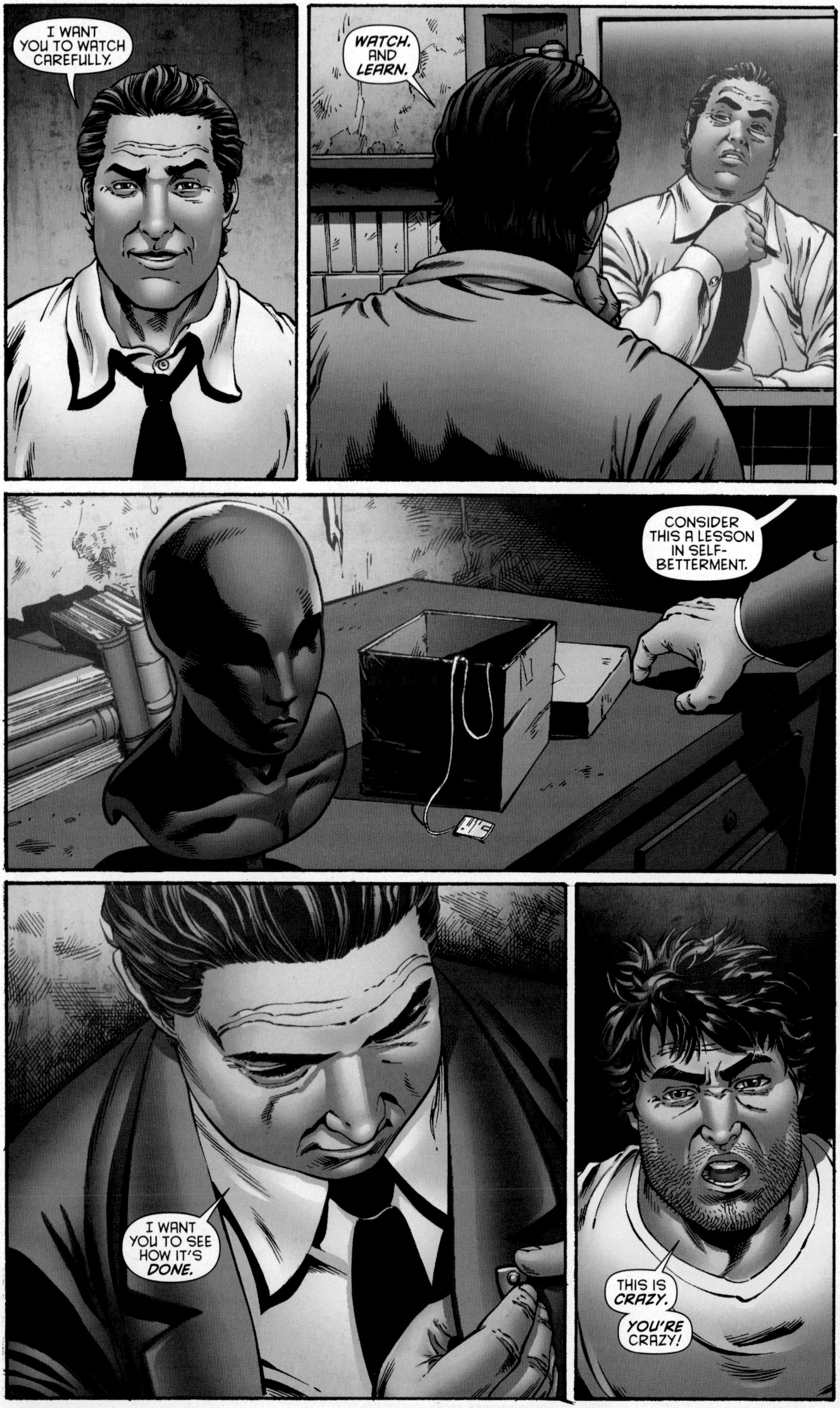

I WANT YOU TO WATCH CAREFULLY.
WATCH. AND LEARN.
CONSIDER THIS A LESSON IN SELF-BETTERMENT.
I WANT YOU TO SEE HOW IT'S DONE.
THIS IS CRAZY.
YOU'RE CRAZY!

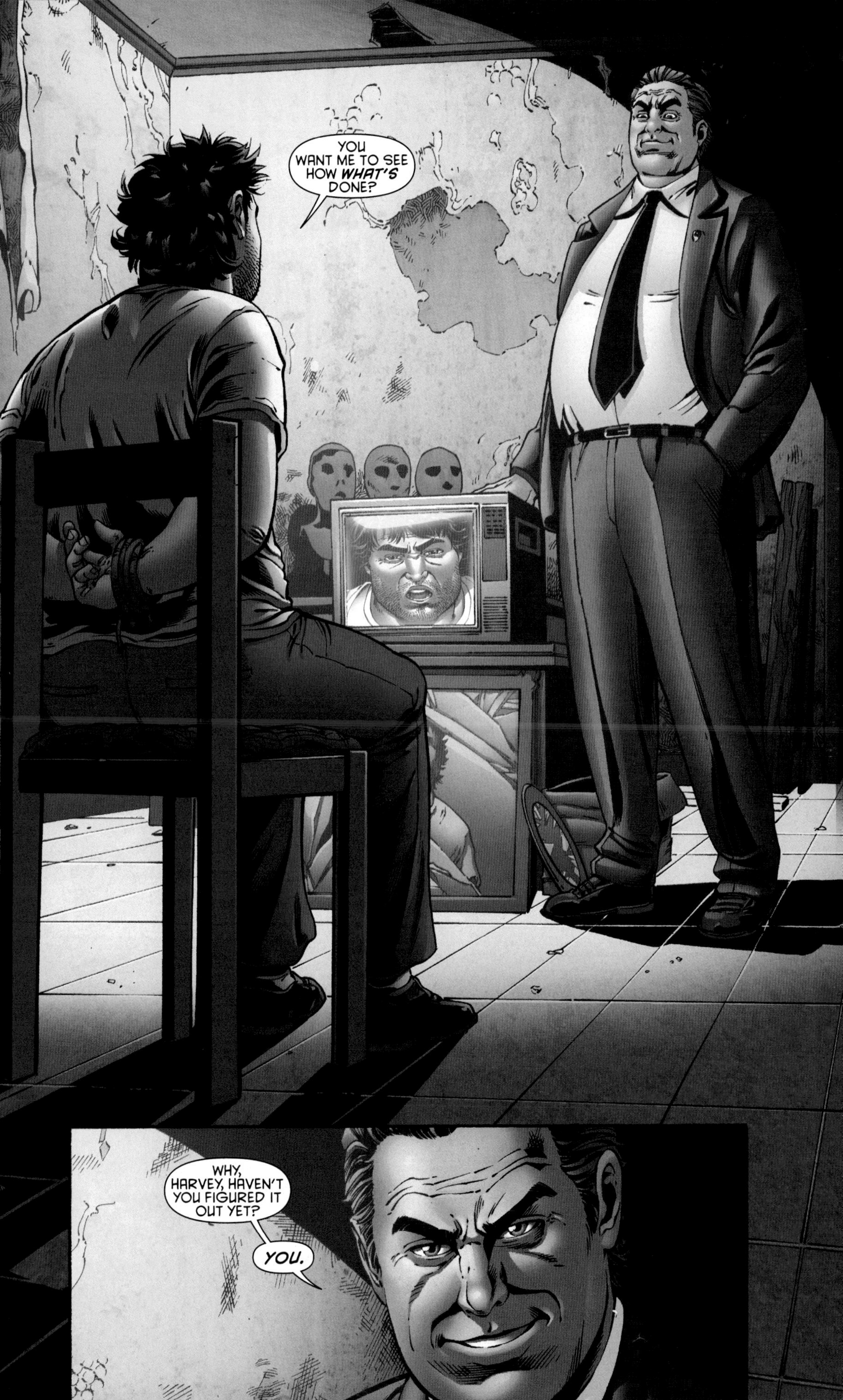
YOU WANT ME TO SEE HOW *WHAT'S* DONE?
WHY, HARVEY, HAVEN'T YOU FIGURED IT OUT YET?
YOU.

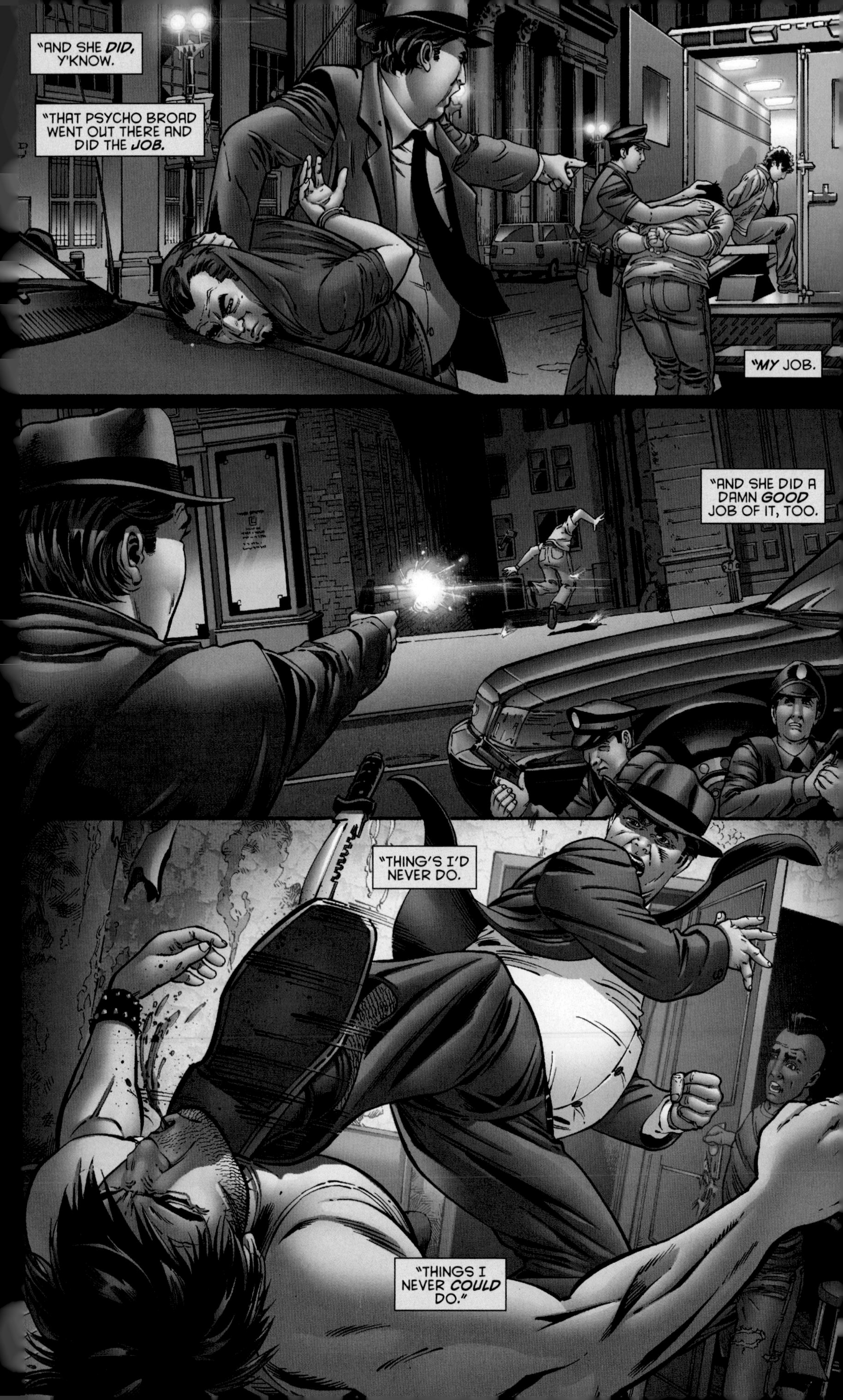
"AND SHE DID, Y'KNOW.
"THAT PSYCHO BROAD WENT OUT THERE AND DID THE JOB.
"MY JOB.
"AND SHE DID A DAMN GOOD JOB OF IT, TOO.
"THING'S I'D NEVER DO.
"THINGS I NEVER COULD DO."

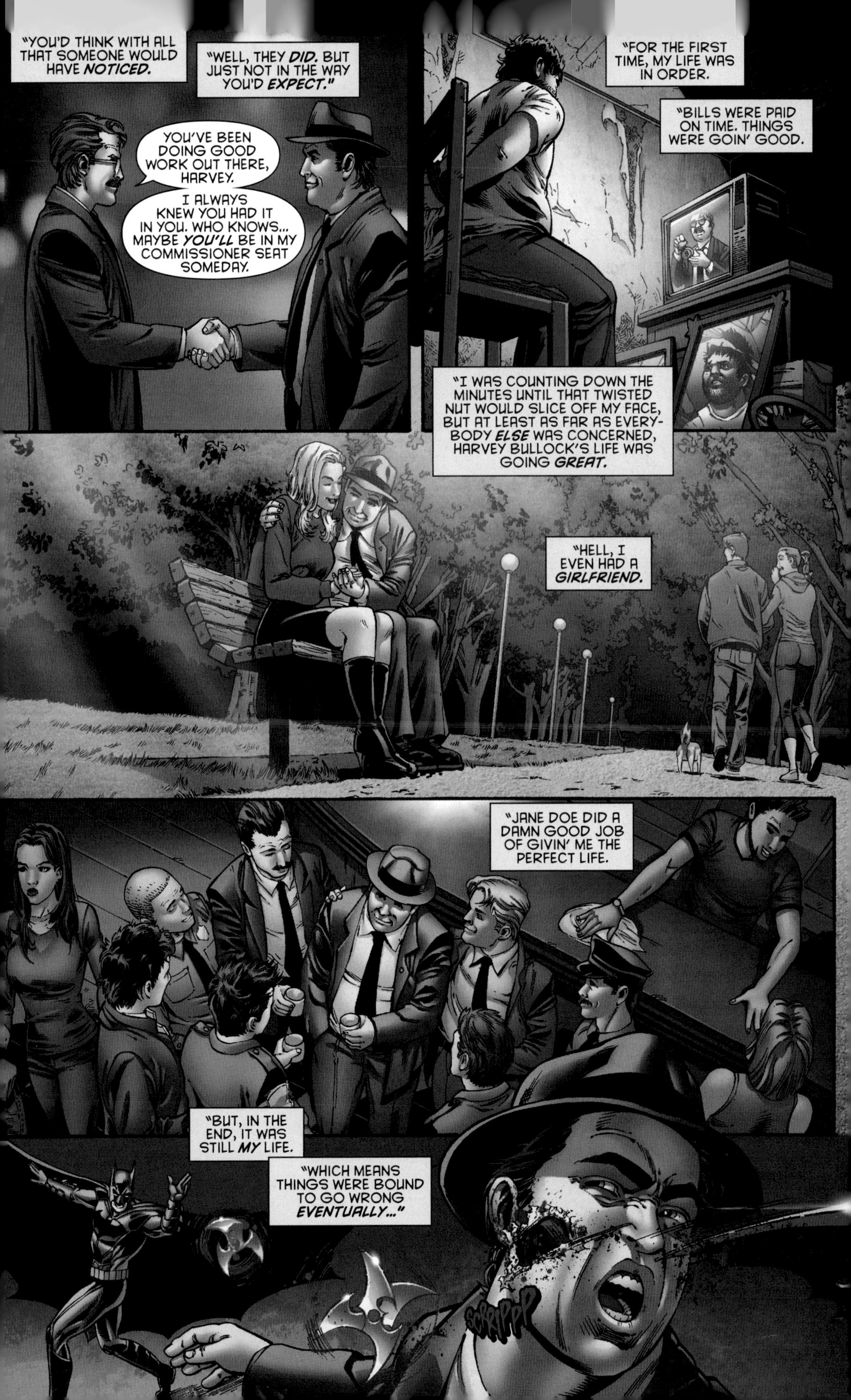
"YOU'D THINK WITH ALL THAT SOMEONE WOULD HAVE NOTICED.
"WELL, THEY DID. BUT JUST NOT IN THE WAY YOU'D EXPECT."
YOU'VE BEEN DOING GOOD WORK OUT THERE, HARVEY.
I ALWAYS KNEW YOU HAD IT IN YOU. WHO KNOWS... MAYBE YOU'LL BE IN MY COMMISSIONER SEAT SOMEDAY.
"FOR THE FIRST TIME, MY LIFE WAS IN ORDER.
"BILLS WERE PAID ON TIME. THINGS WERE GOIN' GOOD.
"I WAS COUNTING DOWN THE MINUTES UNTIL THAT TWISTED NUT WOULD SLICE OFF MY FACE, BUT AT LEAST AS FAR AS EVERYBODY ELSE WAS CONCERNED, HARVEY BULLOCK'S LIFE WAS GOING GREAT.
"HELL, I EVEN HAD A GIRLFRIEND.
"JANE DOE DID A DAMN GOOD JOB OF GIVIN' ME THE PERFECT LIFE.
"BUT, IN THE END, IT WAS STILL MY LIFE.
"WHICH MEANS THINGS WERE BOUND TO GO WRONG EVENTUALLY..."
SCRRPPP

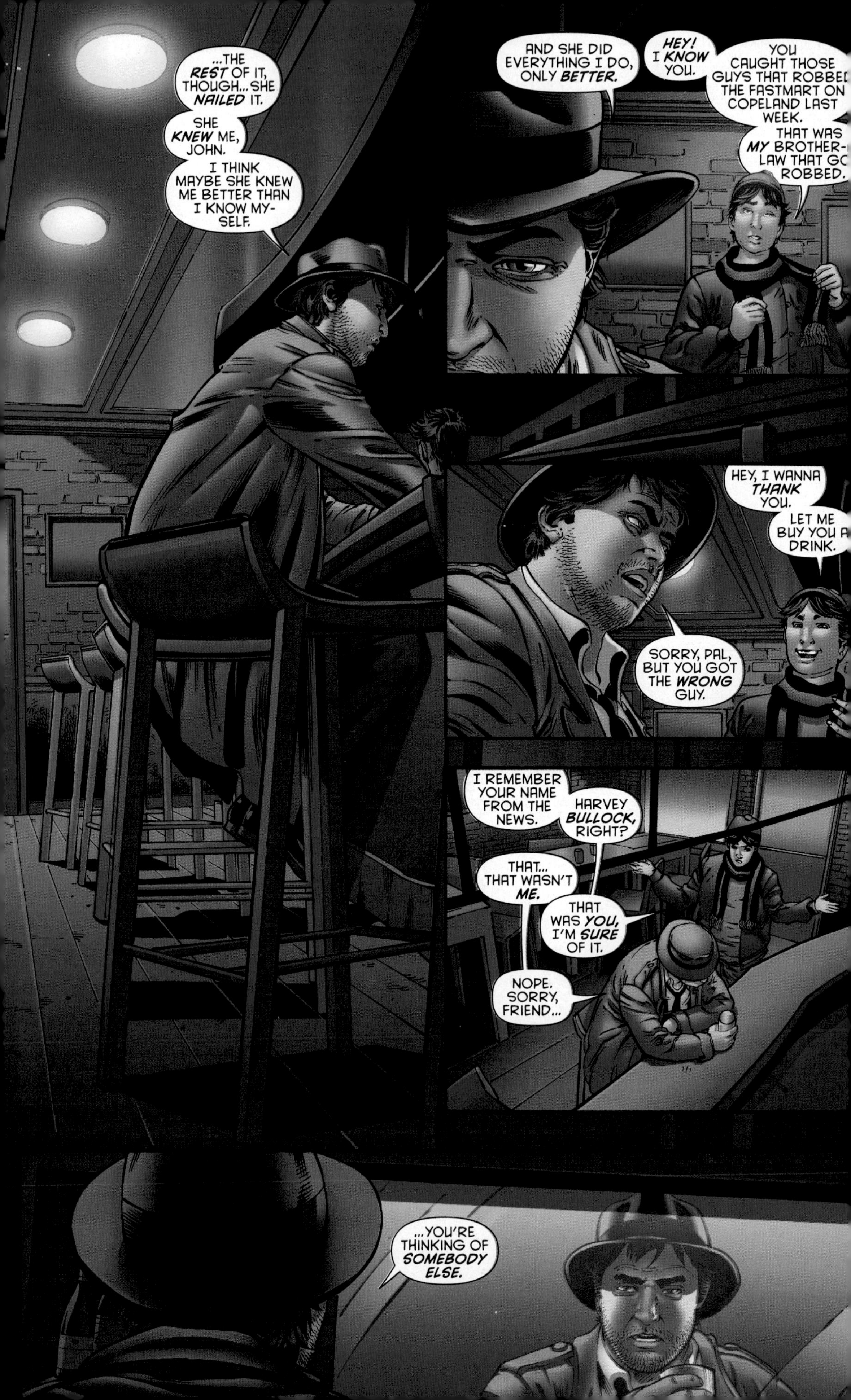
...THE REST OF IT, THOUGH... SHE NAILED IT.
SHE KNEW ME, JOHN.
I THINK MAYBE SHE KNEW ME BETTER THAN I KNOW MY-SELF.
AND SHE DID EVERYTHING I DO, ONLY BETTER.
HEY! I KNOW YOU.
YOU CAUGHT THOSE GUYS THAT ROBBED THE FASTMART ON COPELAND LAST WEEK.
THAT WAS MY BROTHER-LAW THAT GO ROBBED.
HEY, I WANNA THANK YOU.
LET ME BUY YOU A DRINK.
SORRY, PAL, BUT YOU GOT THE WRONG GUY.
I REMEMBER YOUR NAME FROM THE NEWS.
HARVEY BULLOCK, RIGHT?
THAT... THAT WASN'T ME.
THAT WAS YOU, I'M SURE OF IT.
NOPE. SORRY, FRIEND...
...YOU'RE THINKING OF SOMEBODY ELSE.

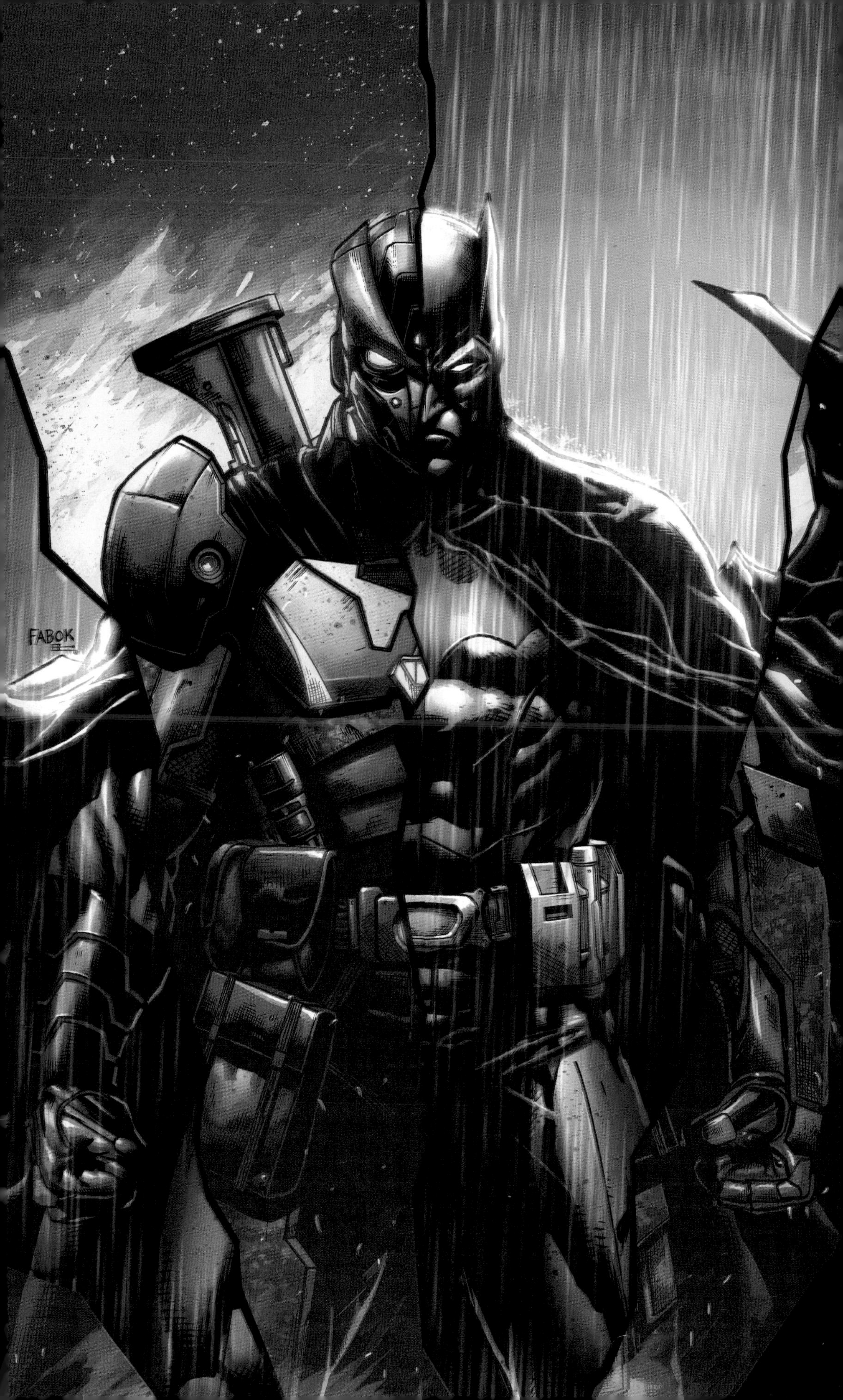
FABOK

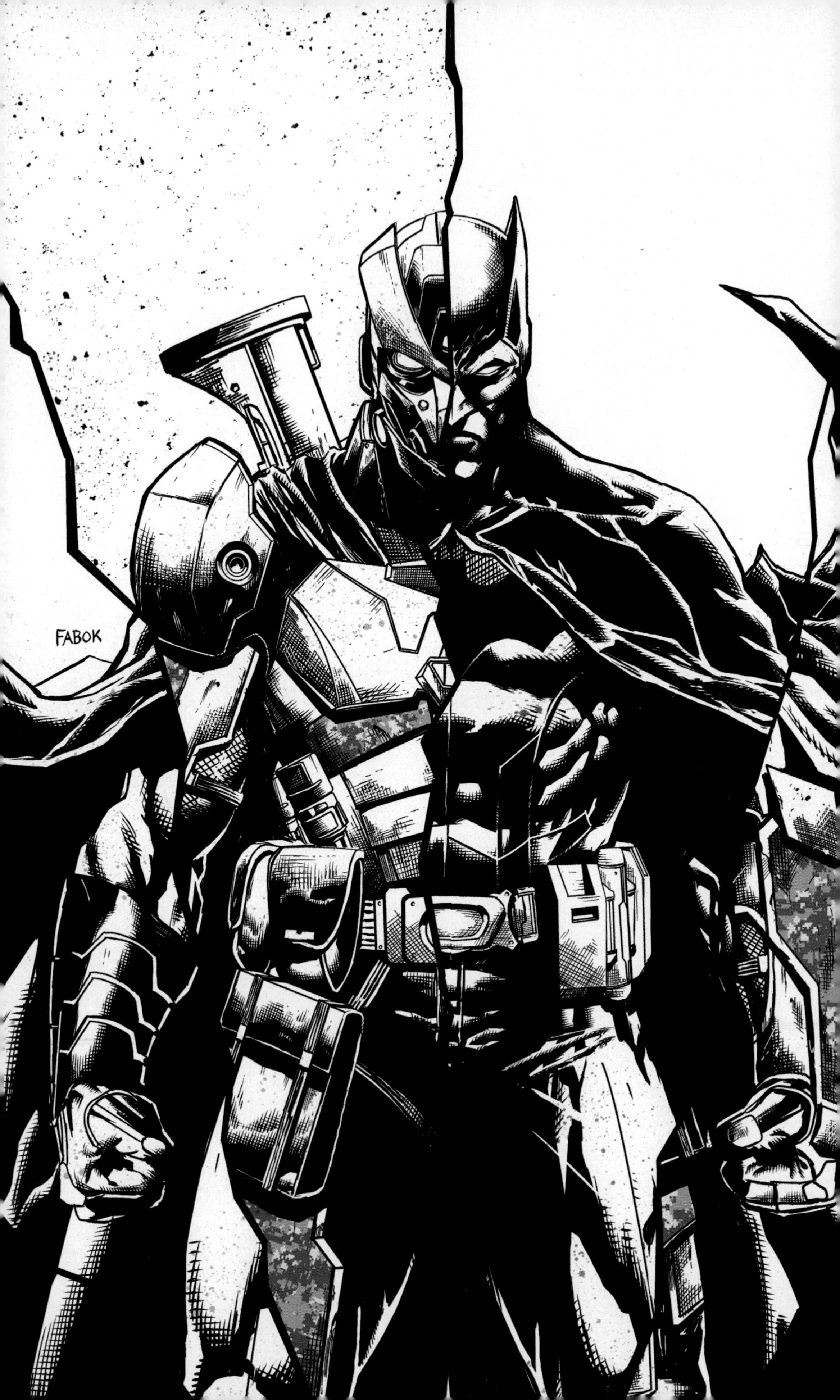
FABOK

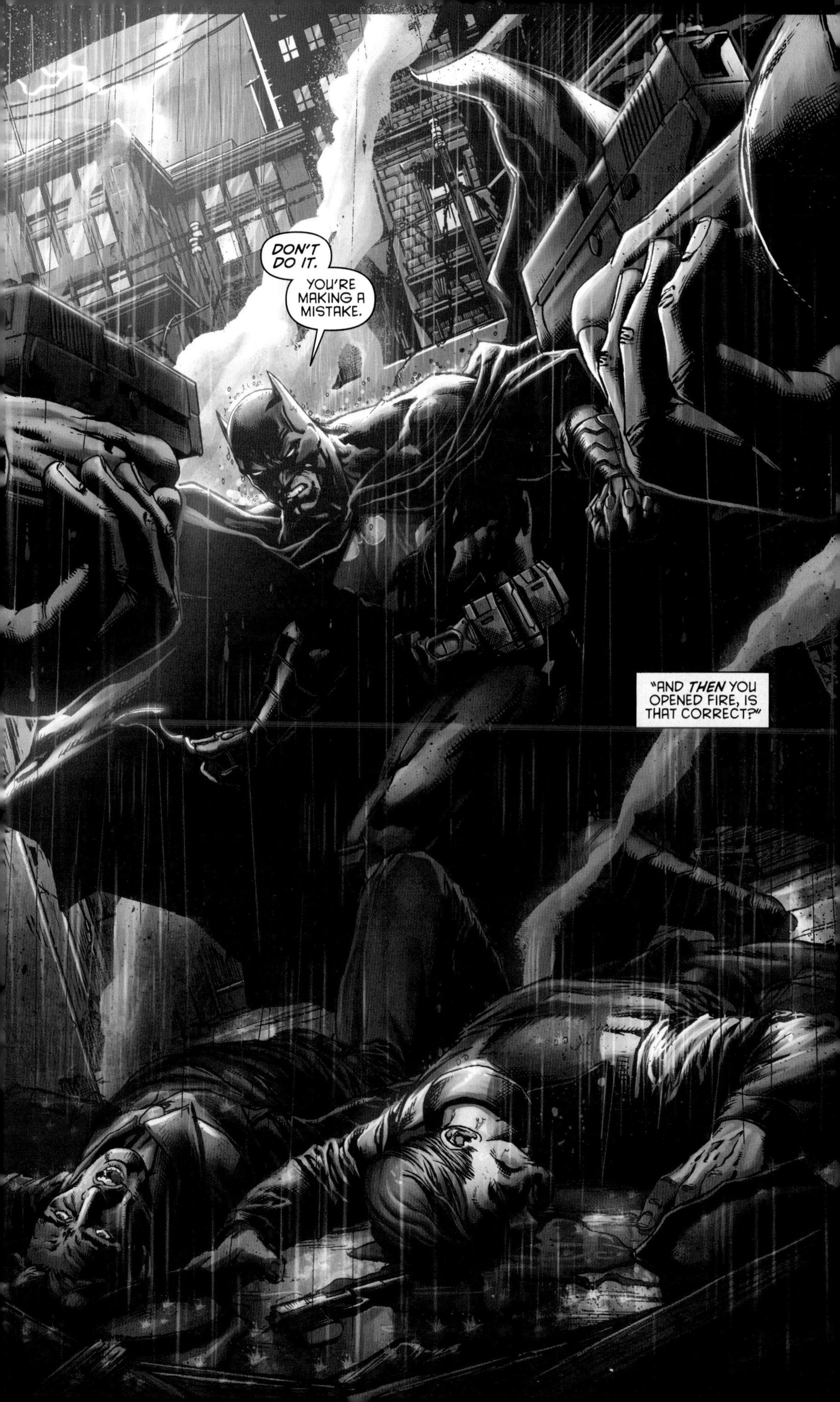
DON'T DO IT.
YOU'RE MAKING A MISTAKE.
"AND THEN YOU OPENED FIRE, IS THAT CORRECT?"

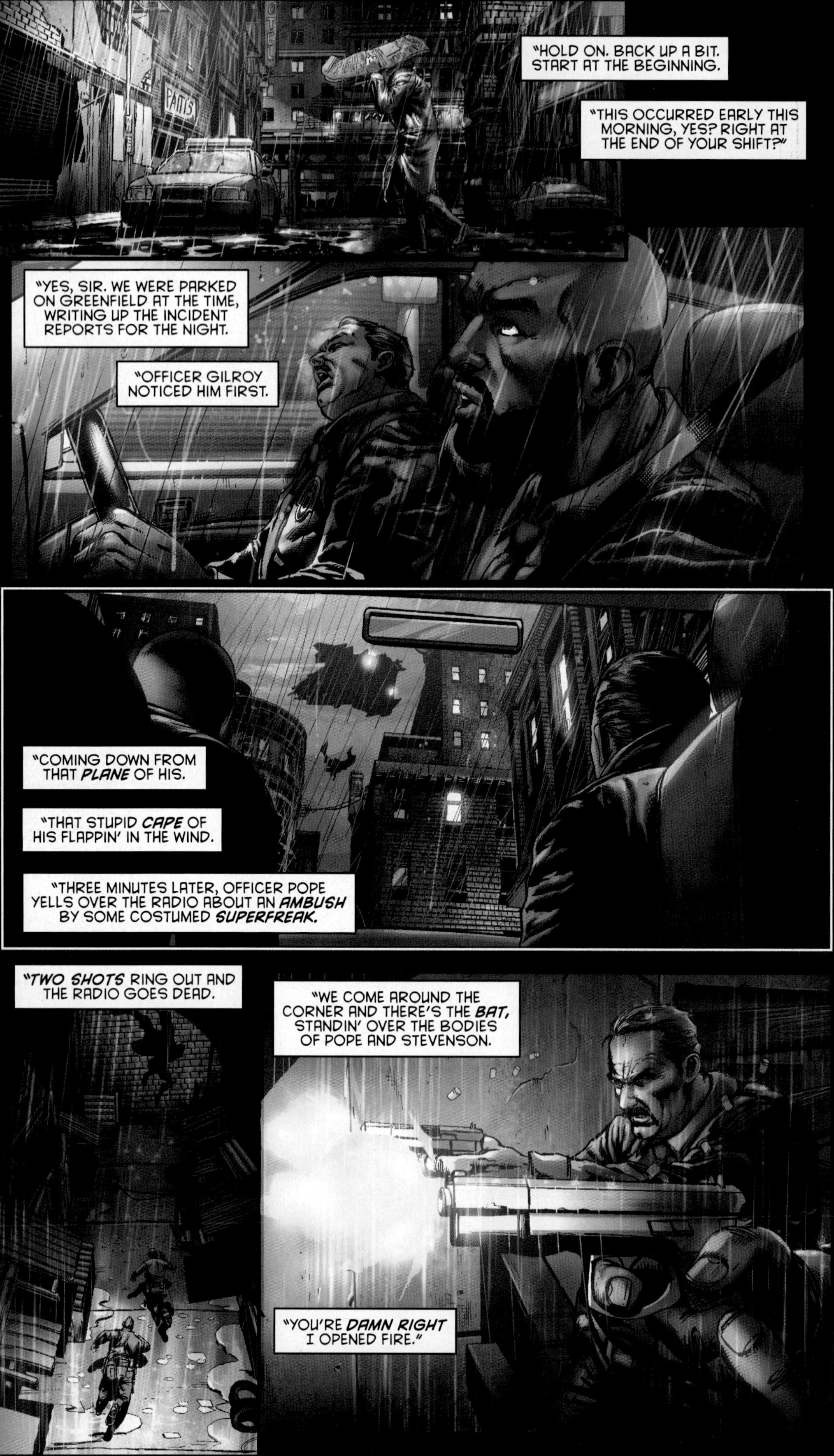

"HOLD ON. BACK UP A BIT. START AT THE BEGINNING.
"THIS OCCURRED EARLY THIS MORNING, YES? RIGHT AT THE END OF YOUR SHIFT?"
"YES, SIR. WE WERE PARKED ON GREENFIELD AT THE TIME, WRITING UP THE INCIDENT REPORTS FOR THE NIGHT.
"OFFICER GILROY NOTICED HIM FIRST.
"COMING DOWN FROM THAT *PLANE* OF HIS.
"THAT STUPID *CAPE* OF HIS FLAPPIN' IN THE WIND.
"THREE MINUTES LATER, OFFICER POPE YELLS OVER THE RADIO ABOUT AN ***AMBUSH*** BY SOME COSTUMED ***SUPERFREAK.***
"***TWO SHOTS*** RING OUT AND THE RADIO GOES DEAD.
"WE COME AROUND THE CORNER AND THERE'S THE *BAT,* STANDIN' OVER THE BODIES OF POPE AND STEVENSON.
"YOU'RE ***DAMN RIGHT*** I OPENED FIRE."

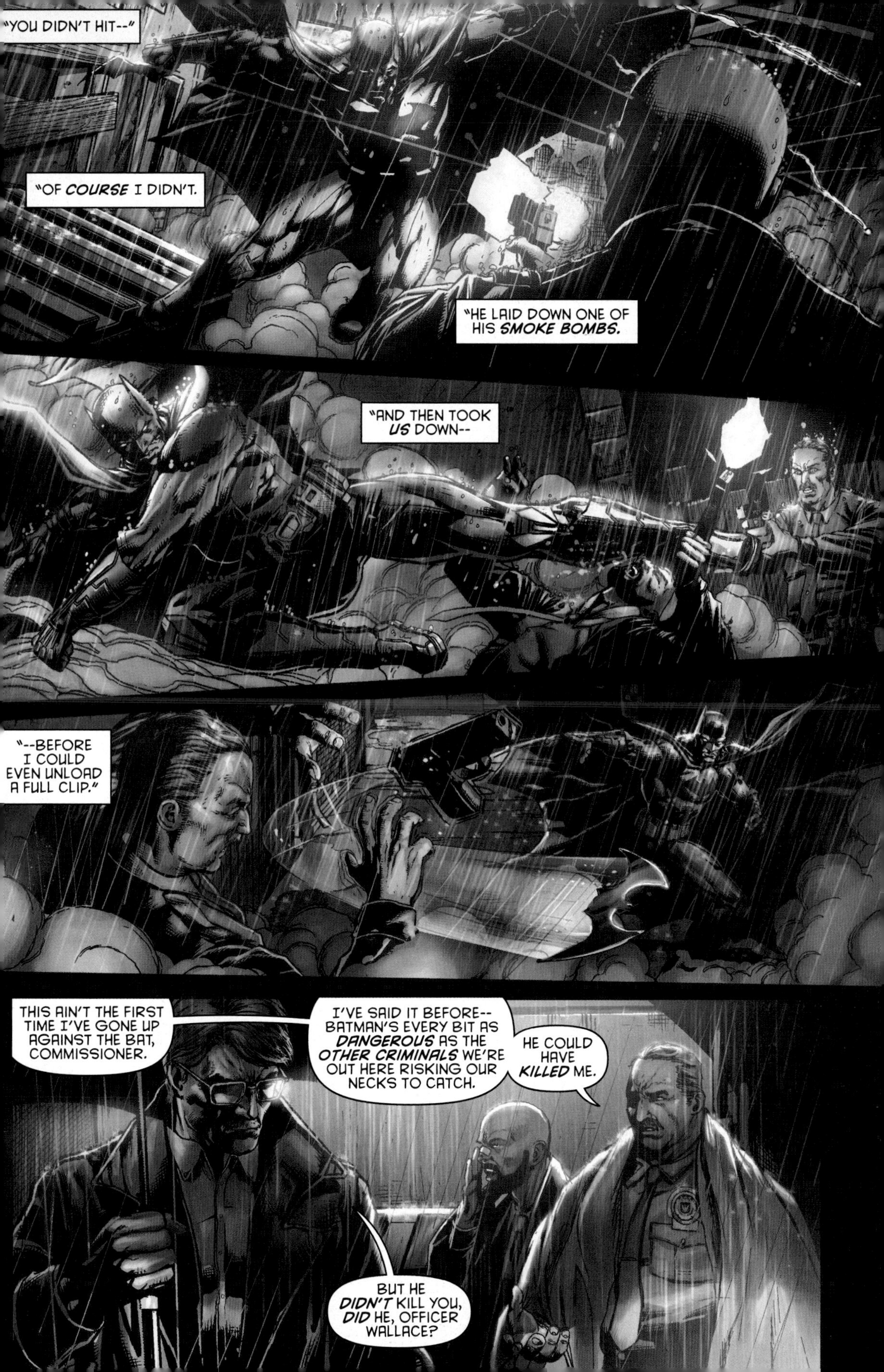
"YOU DIDN'T HIT--"
"OF COURSE I DIDN'T.
"HE LAID DOWN ONE OF HIS SMOKE BOMBS.
"AND THEN TOOK US DOWN--
"--BEFORE I COULD EVEN UNLOAD A FULL CLIP."
THIS AIN'T THE FIRST TIME I'VE GONE UP AGAINST THE BAT, COMMISSIONER.
I'VE SAID IT BEFORE-- BATMAN'S EVERY BIT AS DANGEROUS AS THE OTHER CRIMINALS WE'RE OUT HERE RISKING OUR NECKS TO CATCH.
HE COULD HAVE KILLED ME.
BUT HE DIDN'T KILL YOU, DID HE, OFFICER WALLACE?

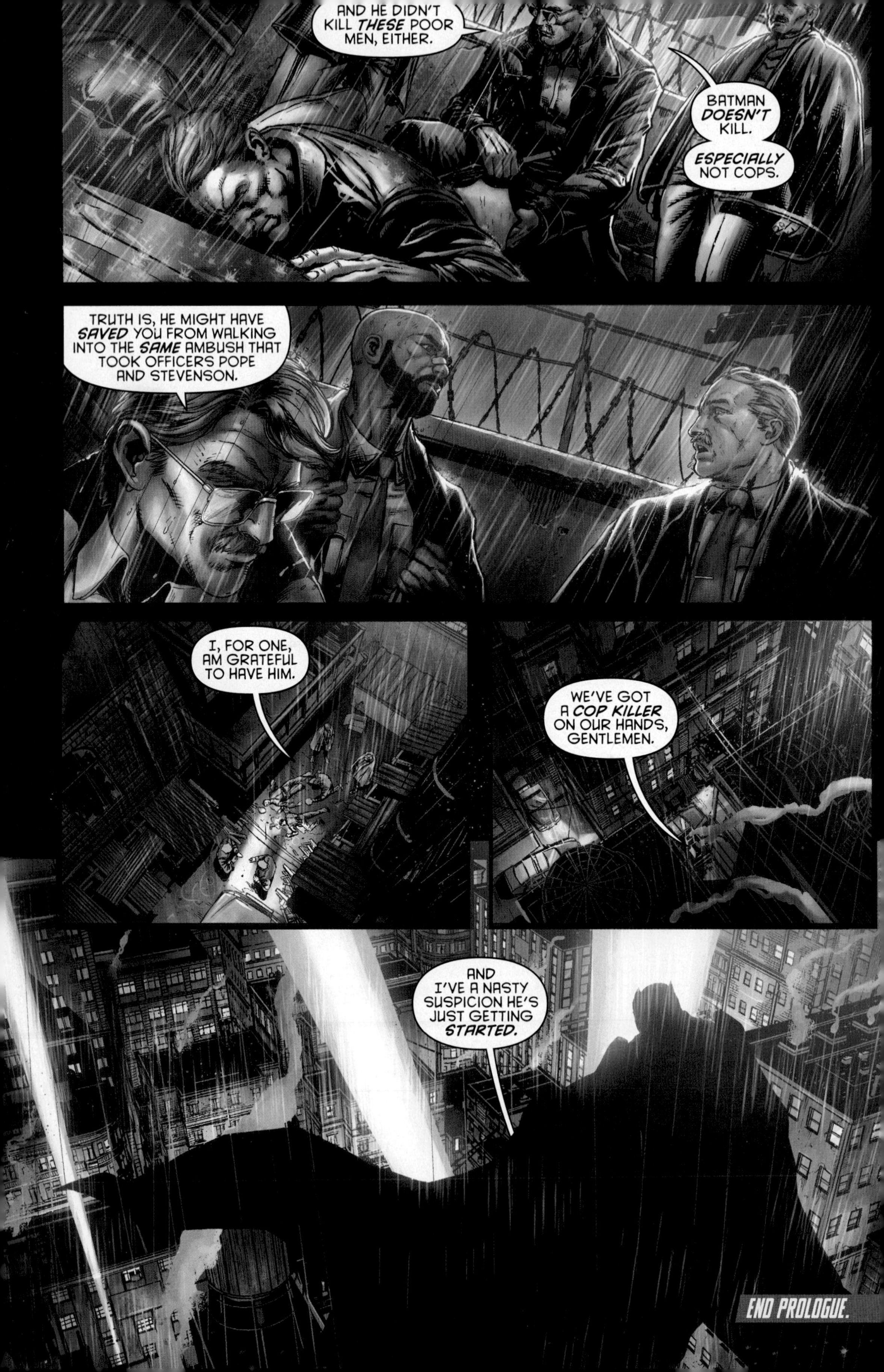
AND HE DIDN'T KILL *THESE* POOR MEN, EITHER.
BATMAN *DOESN'T* KILL.
ESPECIALLY NOT COPS.
TRUTH IS, HE MIGHT HAVE *SAVED* YOU FROM WALKING INTO THE *SAME* AMBUSH THAT TOOK OFFICERS POPE AND STEVENSON.
I, FOR ONE, AM GRATEFUL TO HAVE HIM.
WE'VE GOT A *COP KILLER* ON OUR HANDS, GENTLEMEN.
AND I'VE A NASTY SUSPICION HE'S JUST GETTING *STARTED.*
END PROLOGUE.

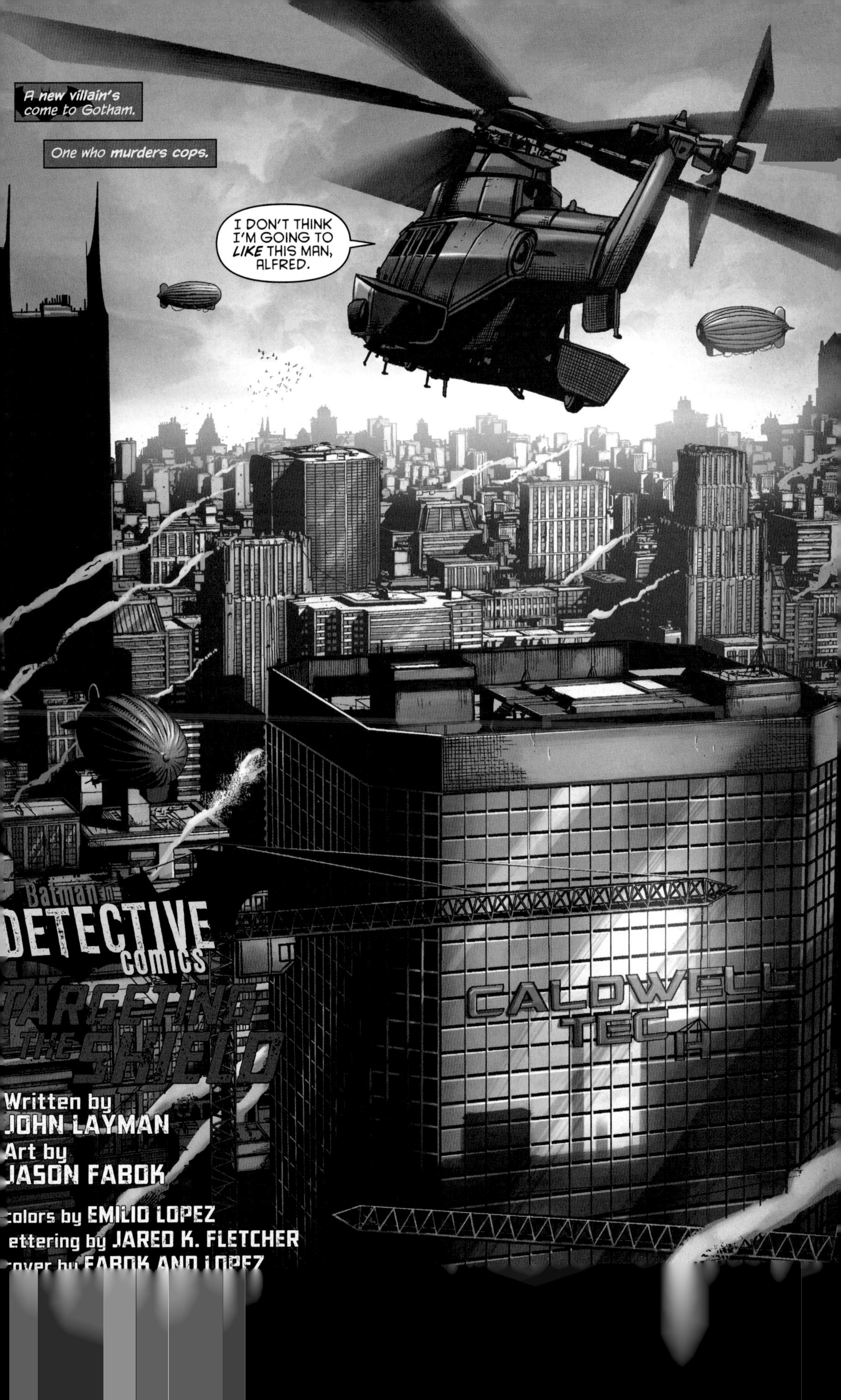

A new villain's come to Gotham.
One who murders cops.
I DON'T THINK I'M GOING TO LIKE THIS MAN, ALFRED.
CALDWELL TEC
Batman in
DETECTIVE COMICS
TARGETING THE SHIELD
Written by JOHN LAYMAN
Art by JASON FABOK
colors by EMILIO LOPEZ
lettering by JARED K. FLETCHER

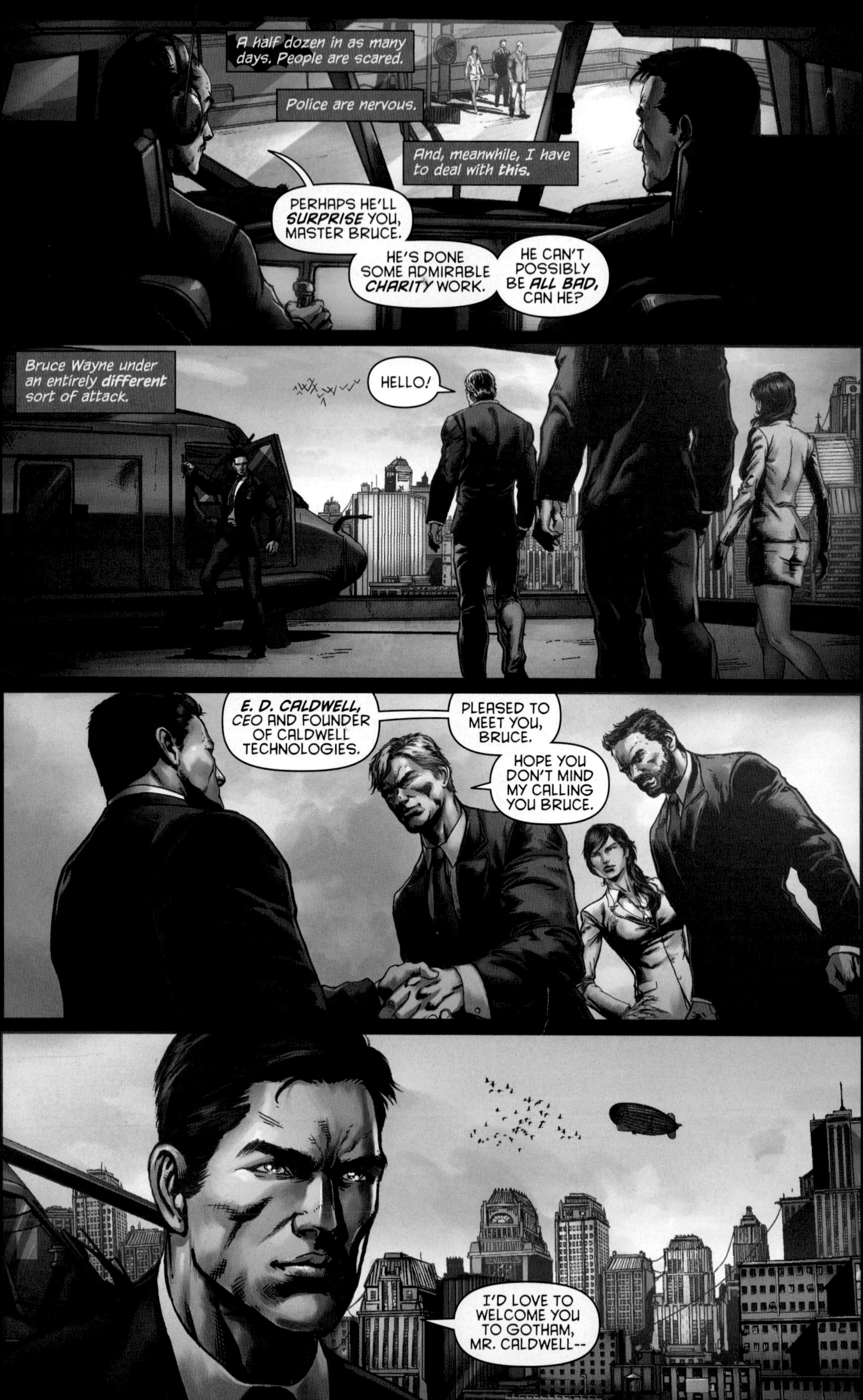

A half dozen in as many days. People are scared.
Police are nervous.
And, meanwhile, I have to deal with this.
PERHAPS HE'LL SURPRISE YOU, MASTER BRUCE.
HE'S DONE SOME ADMIRABLE CHARITY WORK.
HE CAN'T POSSIBLY BE ALL BAD, CAN HE?
Bruce Wayne under an entirely different sort of attack.
HELLO!
E. D. CALDWELL, CEO AND FOUNDER OF CALDWELL TECHNOLOGIES.
PLEASED TO MEET YOU, BRUCE.
HOPE YOU DON'T MIND MY CALLING YOU BRUCE.
I'D LOVE TO WELCOME YOU TO GOTHAM, MR. CALDWELL--

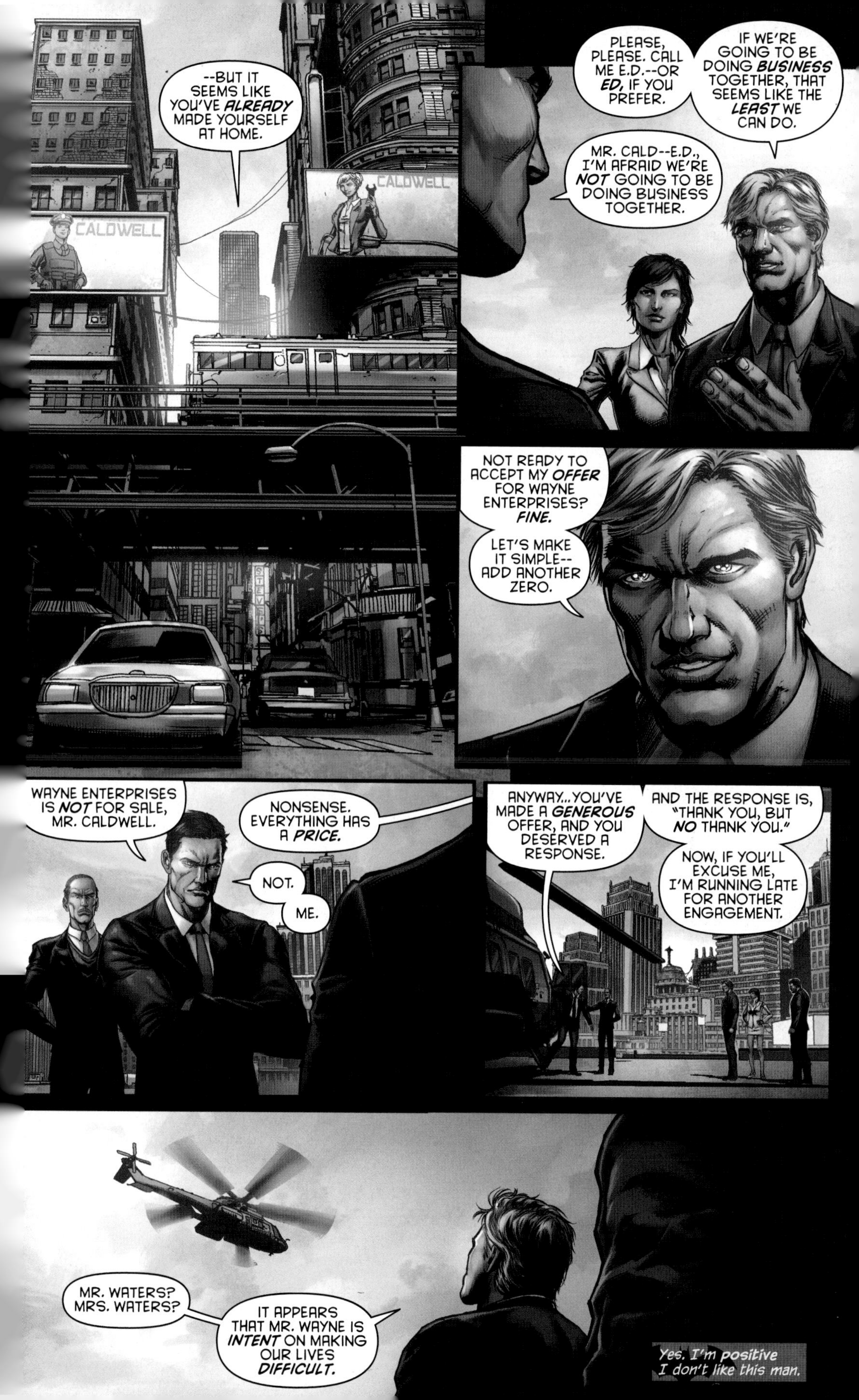

--BUT IT SEEMS LIKE YOU'VE *ALREADY* MADE YOURSELF AT HOME.
CALDWELL
CALDWELL
PLEASE, PLEASE. CALL ME E.D.--OR *ED,* IF YOU PREFER.
IF WE'RE GOING TO BE DOING *BUSINESS* TOGETHER, THAT SEEMS LIKE THE *LEAST* WE CAN DO.
MR. CALD--E.D., I'M AFRAID WE'RE *NOT* GOING TO BE DOING BUSINESS TOGETHER.
NOT READY TO ACCEPT MY *OFFER* FOR WAYNE ENTERPRISES? *FINE.*
LET'S MAKE IT SIMPLE--ADD ANOTHER ZERO.
WAYNE ENTERPRISES IS *NOT* FOR SALE, MR. CALDWELL.
NONSENSE. EVERYTHING HAS A *PRICE.*
NOT.
ME.
ANYWAY...YOU'VE MADE A *GENEROUS* OFFER, AND YOU DESERVED A RESPONSE.
AND THE RESPONSE IS, "THANK YOU, BUT *NO* THANK YOU."
NOW, IF YOU'LL EXCUSE ME, I'M RUNNING LATE FOR ANOTHER ENGAGEMENT.
MR. WATERS? MRS. WATERS?
IT APPEARS THAT MR. WAYNE IS *INTENT* ON MAKING OUR LIVES *DIFFICULT.*
Yes. I'm positive I don't like this man.

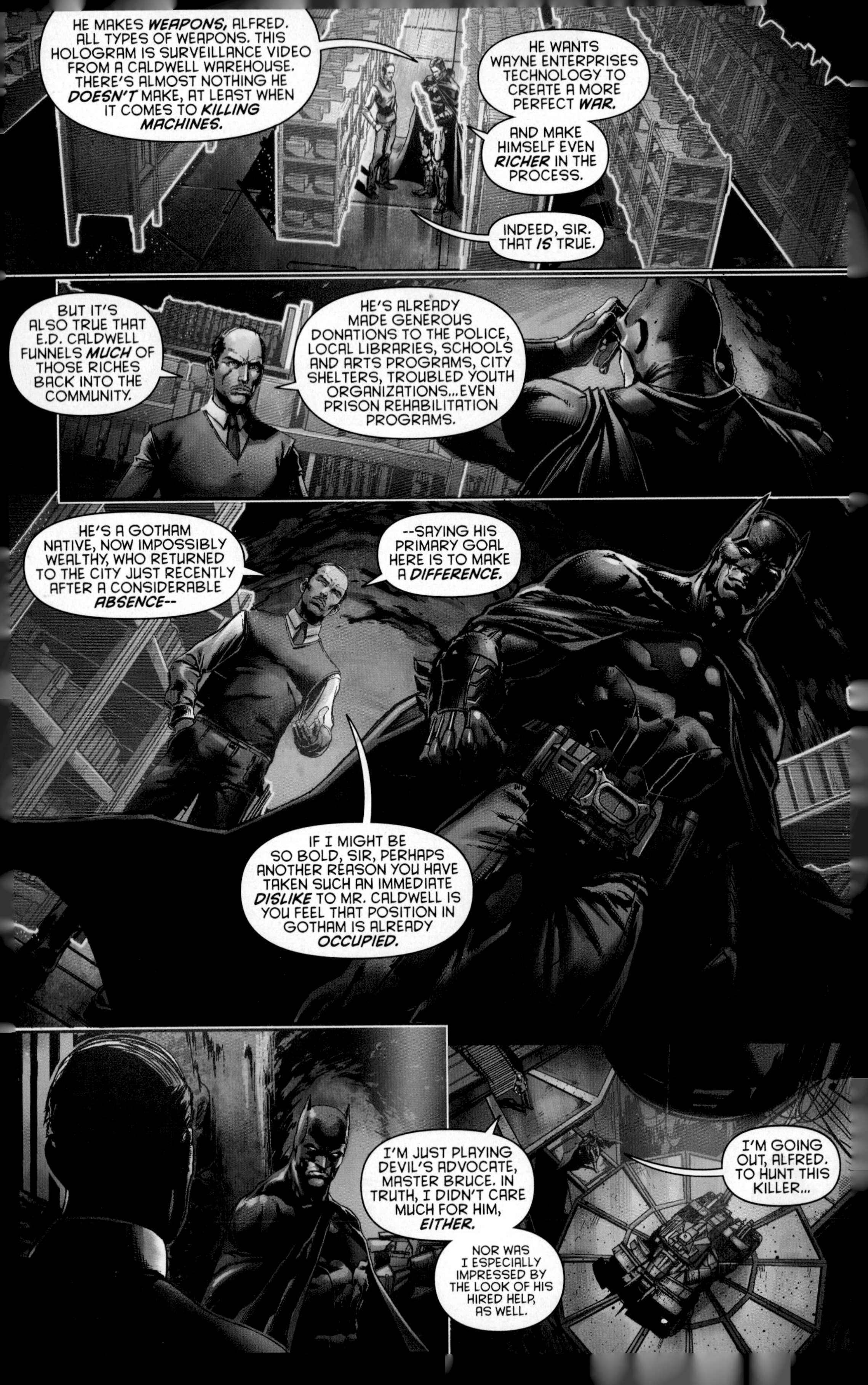
HE MAKES WEAPONS, ALFRED. ALL TYPES OF WEAPONS. THIS HOLOGRAM IS SURVEILLANCE VIDEO FROM A CALDWELL WAREHOUSE. THERE'S ALMOST NOTHING HE DOESN'T MAKE, AT LEAST WHEN IT COMES TO KILLING MACHINES.
HE WANTS WAYNE ENTERPRISES TECHNOLOGY TO CREATE A MORE PERFECT WAR.
AND MAKE HIMSELF EVEN RICHER IN THE PROCESS.
INDEED, SIR. THAT IS TRUE.
BUT IT'S ALSO TRUE THAT E.D. CALDWELL FUNNELS MUCH OF THOSE RICHES BACK INTO THE COMMUNITY.
HE'S ALREADY MADE GENEROUS DONATIONS TO THE POLICE, LOCAL LIBRARIES, SCHOOLS AND ARTS PROGRAMS, CITY SHELTERS, TROUBLED YOUTH ORGANIZATIONS...EVEN PRISON REHABILITATION PROGRAMS.
HE'S A GOTHAM NATIVE, NOW IMPOSSIBLY WEALTHY, WHO RETURNED TO THE CITY JUST RECENTLY AFTER A CONSIDERABLE ABSENCE--
--SAYING HIS PRIMARY GOAL HERE IS TO MAKE A DIFFERENCE.
IF I MIGHT BE SO BOLD, SIR, PERHAPS ANOTHER REASON YOU HAVE TAKEN SUCH AN IMMEDIATE DISLIKE TO MR. CALDWELL IS YOU FEEL THAT POSITION IN GOTHAM IS ALREADY OCCUPIED.
I'M JUST PLAYING DEVIL'S ADVOCATE, MASTER BRUCE. IN TRUTH, I DIDN'T CARE MUCH FOR HIM, EITHER.
NOR WAS I ESPECIALLY IMPRESSED BY THE LOOK OF HIS HIRED HELP, AS WELL.
I'M GOING OUT, ALFRED. TO HUNT THIS KILLER...

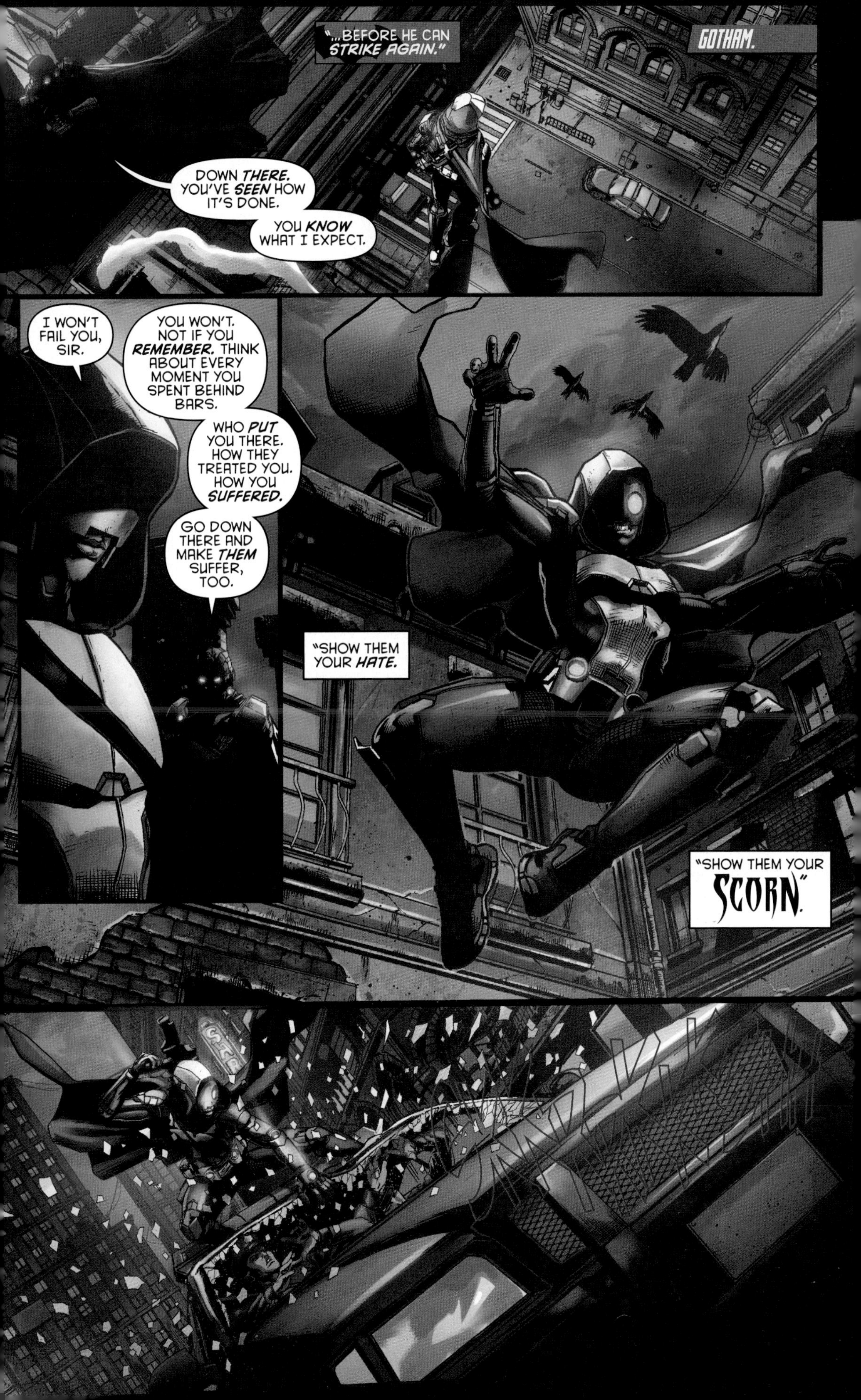

"...BEFORE HE CAN STRIKE AGAIN."
GOTHAM.
DOWN THERE. YOU'VE SEEN HOW IT'S DONE.
YOU KNOW WHAT I EXPECT.
I WON'T FAIL YOU, SIR.
YOU WON'T. NOT IF YOU REMEMBER. THINK ABOUT EVERY MOMENT YOU SPENT BEHIND BARS.
WHO PUT YOU THERE. HOW THEY TREATED YOU. HOW YOU SUFFERED.
GO DOWN THERE AND MAKE THEM SUFFER, TOO.
"SHOW THEM YOUR HATE.
"SHOW THEM YOUR SCORN."

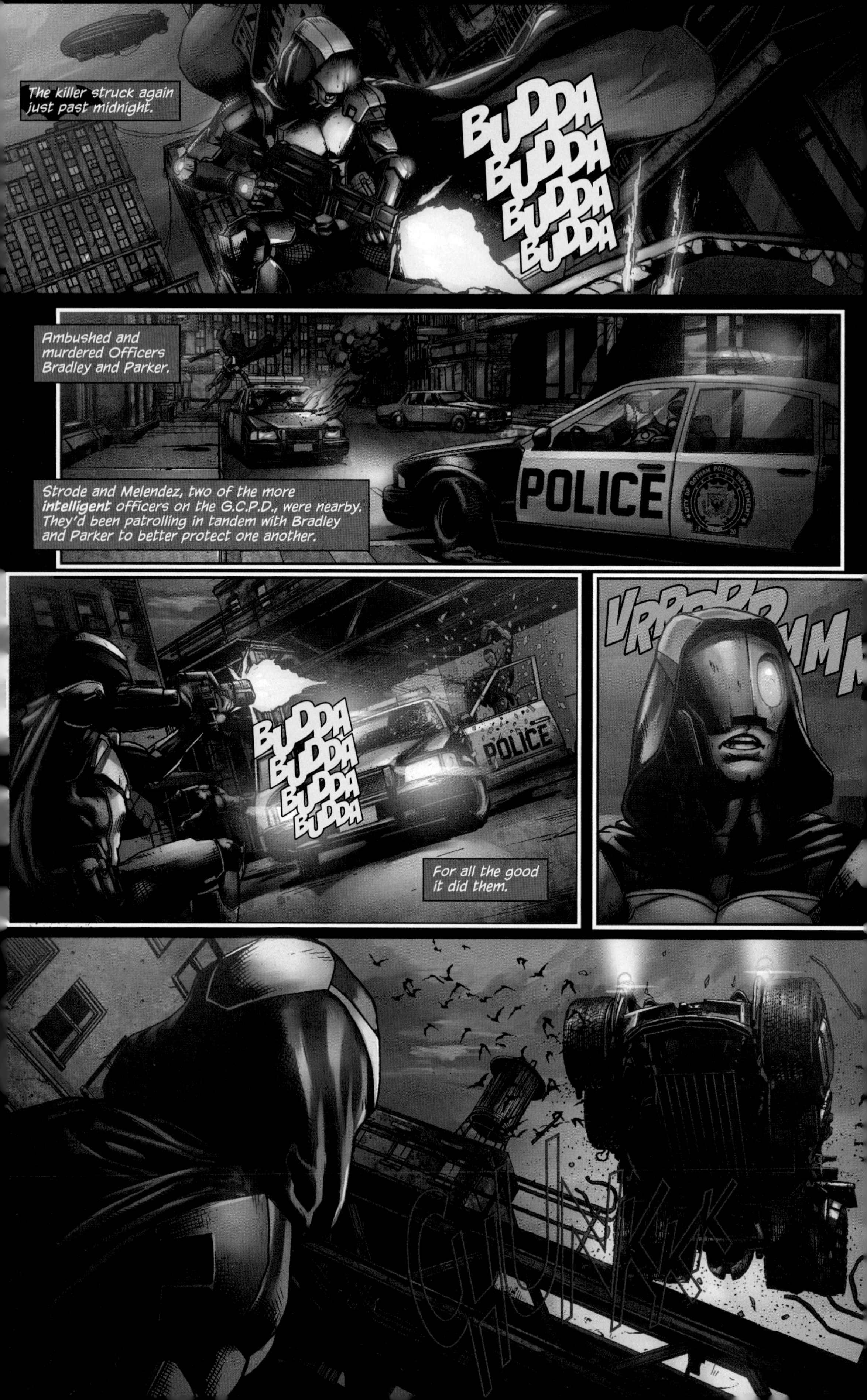
The killer struck again just past midnight.
BUDDA BUDDA BUDDA BUDDA
Ambushed and murdered Officers Bradley and Parker.
Strode and Melendez, two of the more **intelligent** officers on the G.C.P.D., were nearby. They'd been patrolling in tandem with Bradley and Parker to better protect one another.
POLICE
BUDDA BUDDA BUDDA BUDDA
POLICE
For all the good it did them.
GLUNKK

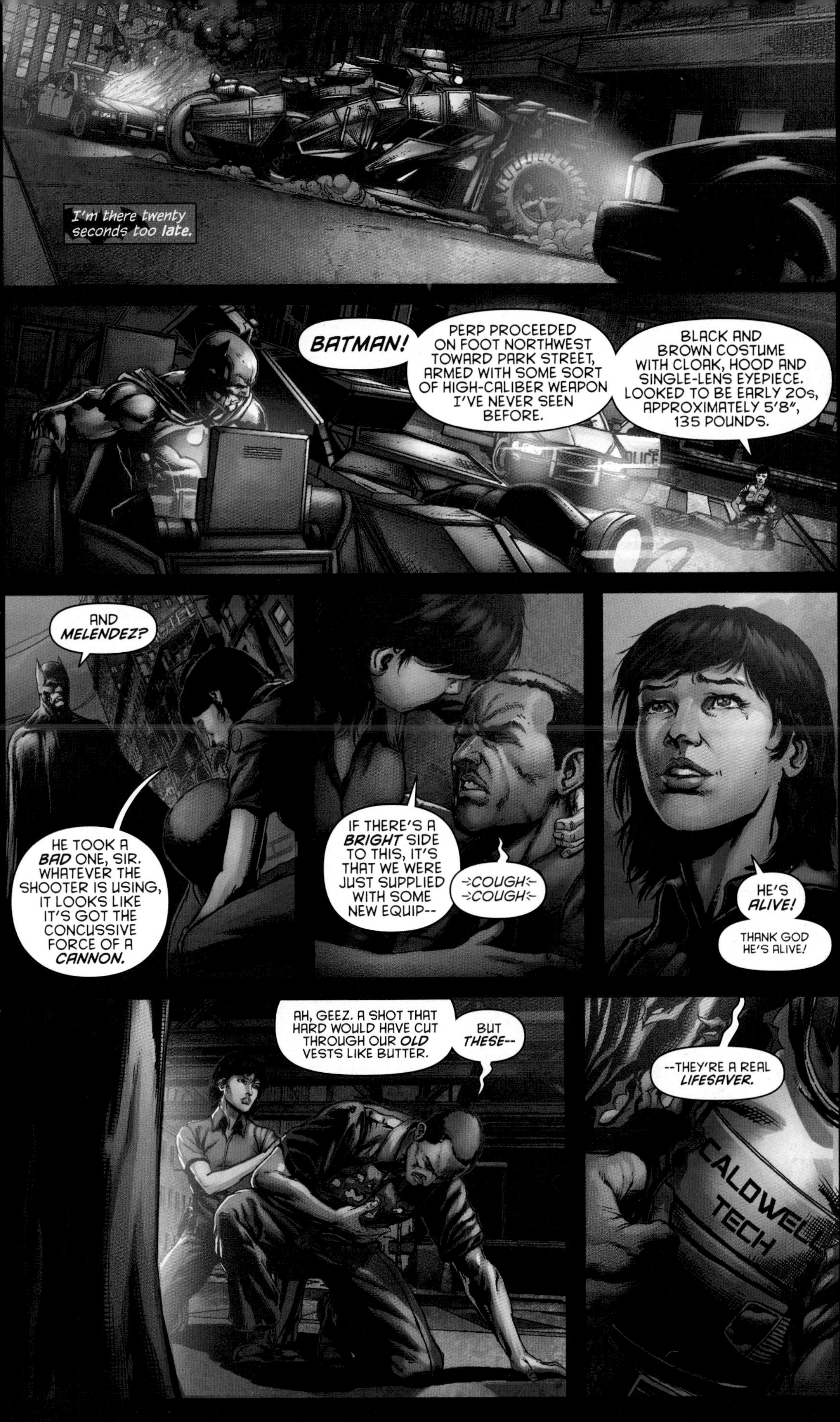
I'm there twenty seconds too late.
BATMAN!
PERP PROCEEDED ON FOOT NORTHWEST TOWARD PARK STREET, ARMED WITH SOME SORT OF HIGH-CALIBER WEAPON I'VE NEVER SEEN BEFORE.
BLACK AND BROWN COSTUME WITH CLOAK, HOOD AND SINGLE-LENS EYEPIECE. LOOKED TO BE EARLY 20s, APPROXIMATELY 5'8", 135 POUNDS.
AND MELENDEZ?
HE TOOK A BAD ONE, SIR. WHATEVER THE SHOOTER IS USING, IT LOOKS LIKE IT'S GOT THE CONCUSSIVE FORCE OF A CANNON.
IF THERE'S A BRIGHT SIDE TO THIS, IT'S THAT WE WERE JUST SUPPLIED WITH SOME NEW EQUIP--
COUGH
COUGH
HE'S ALIVE!
THANK GOD HE'S ALIVE!
AH, GEEZ. A SHOT THAT HARD WOULD HAVE CUT THROUGH OUR OLD VESTS LIKE BUTTER.
BUT THESE--
--THEY'RE A REAL LIFESAVER.
CALDWELL TECH

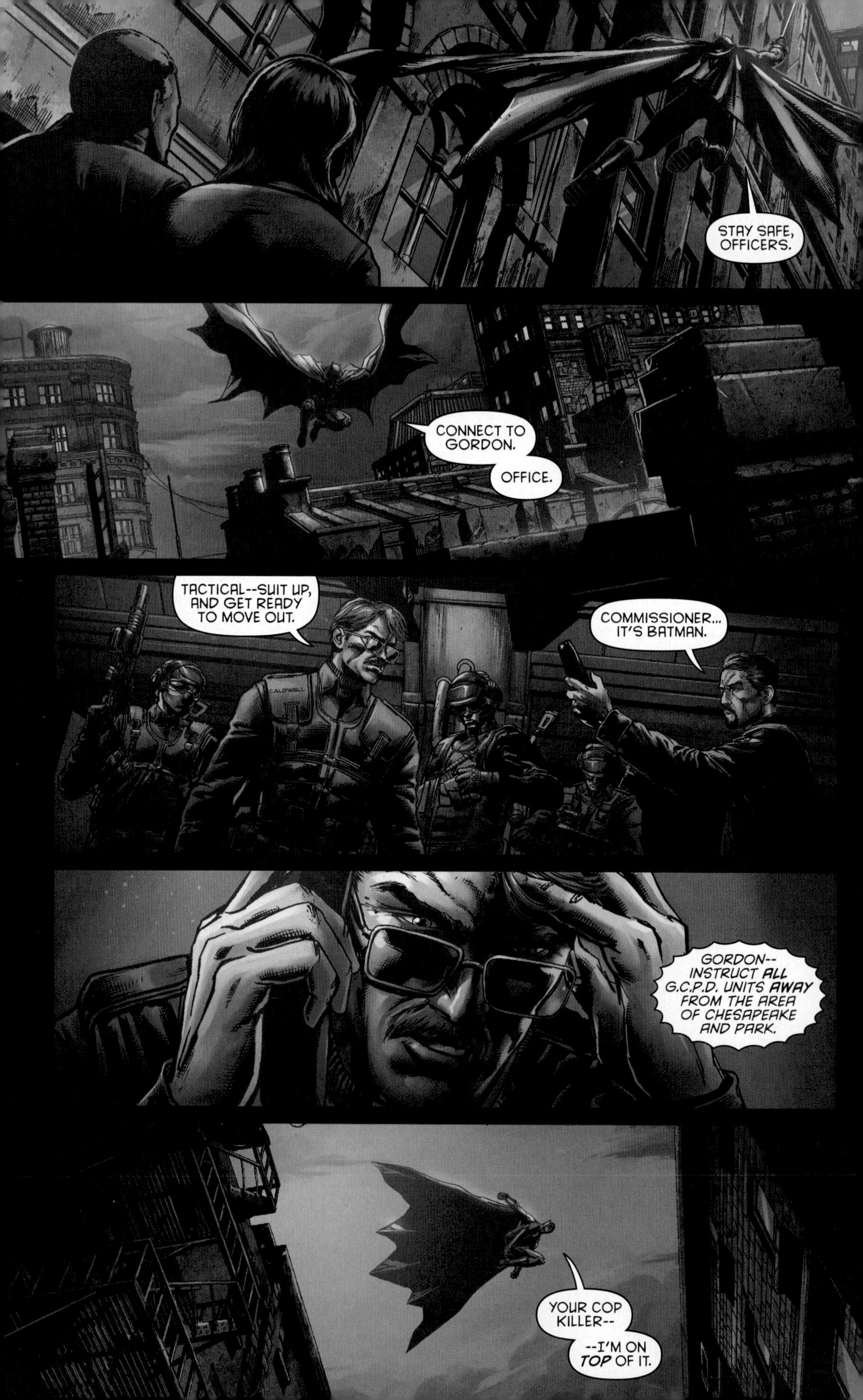
STAY SAFE, OFFICERS.
CONNECT TO GORDON.
OFFICE.
TACTICAL--SUIT UP, AND GET READY TO MOVE OUT.
COMMISSIONER... IT'S BATMAN.
GORDON-- INSTRUCT ALL G.C.P.D. UNITS AWAY FROM THE AREA OF CHESAPEAKE AND PARK.
YOUR COP KILLER--
--I'M ON TOP OF IT.

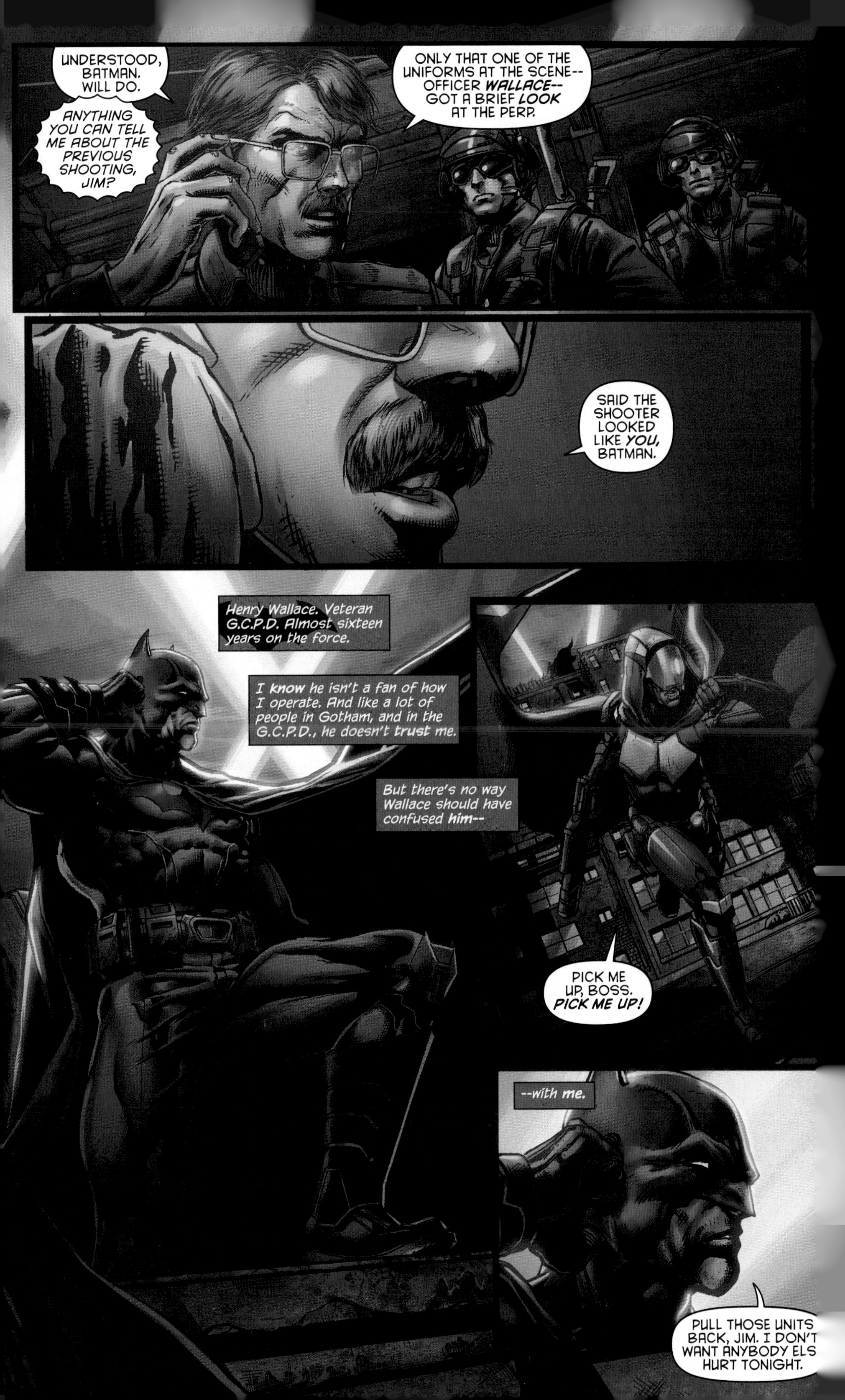
UNDERSTOOD, BATMAN. WILL DO.
ANYTHING YOU CAN TELL ME ABOUT THE PREVIOUS SHOOTING, JIM?
ONLY THAT ONE OF THE UNIFORMS AT THE SCENE-- OFFICER WALLACE-- GOT A BRIEF LOOK AT THE PERP.
SAID THE SHOOTER LOOKED LIKE YOU, BATMAN.
Henry Wallace. Veteran G.C.P.D. Almost sixteen years on the force.
I know he isn't a fan of how I operate. And like a lot of people in Gotham, and in the G.C.P.D., he doesn't trust me.
But there's no way Wallace should have confused him--
PICK ME UP, BOSS. PICK ME UP!
--with me.
PULL THOSE UNITS BACK, JIM. I DON'T WANT ANYBODY ELS HURT TONIGHT.

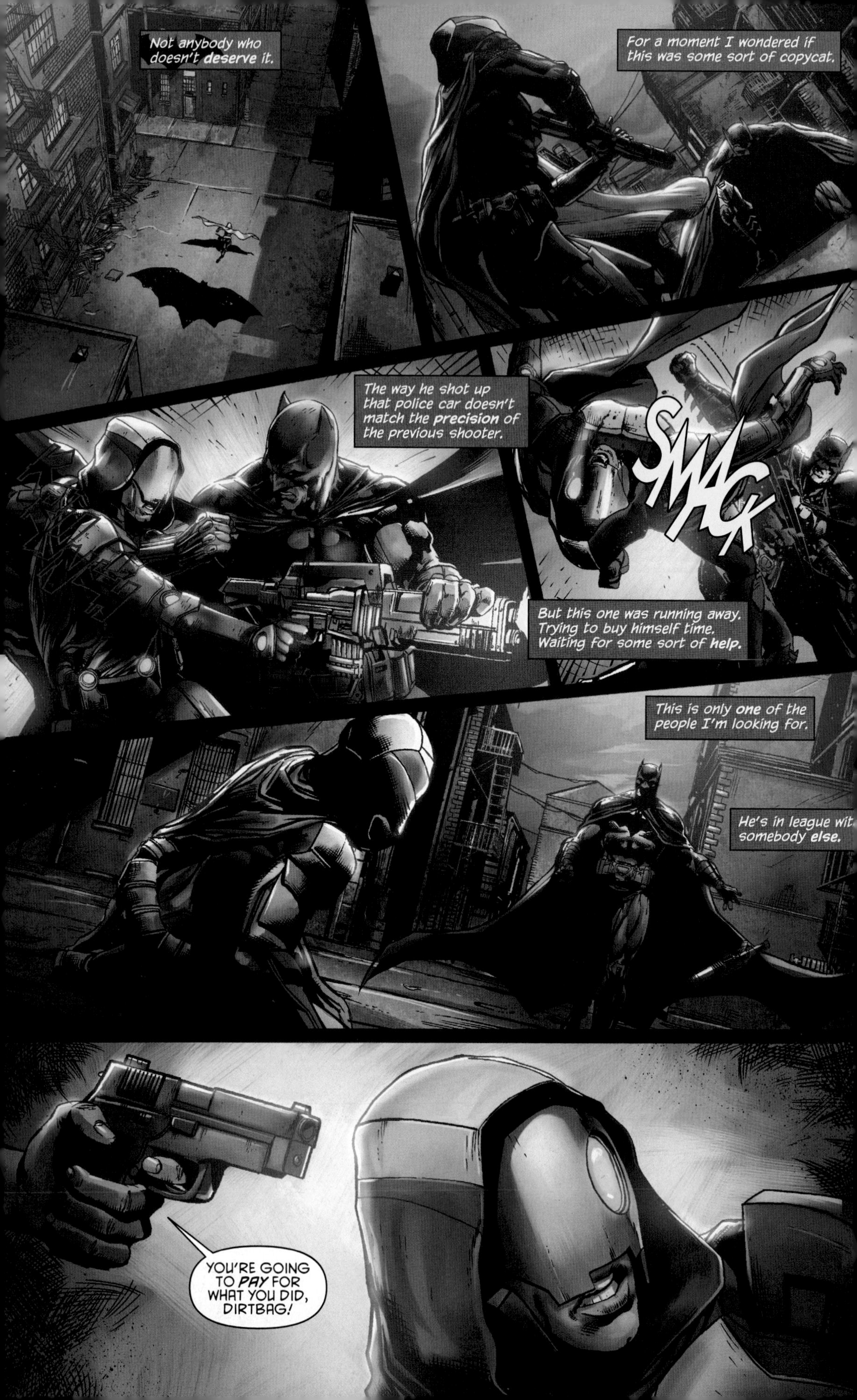
Not anybody who doesn't deserve it.
For a moment I wondered if this was some sort of copycat.
The way he shot up that police car doesn't match the precision of the previous shooter.
SMACK
But this one was running away. Trying to buy himself time. Waiting for some sort of help.
This is only one of the people I'm looking for.
He's in league wit somebody else.
YOU'RE GOING TO PAY FOR WHAT YOU DID, DIRTBAG!

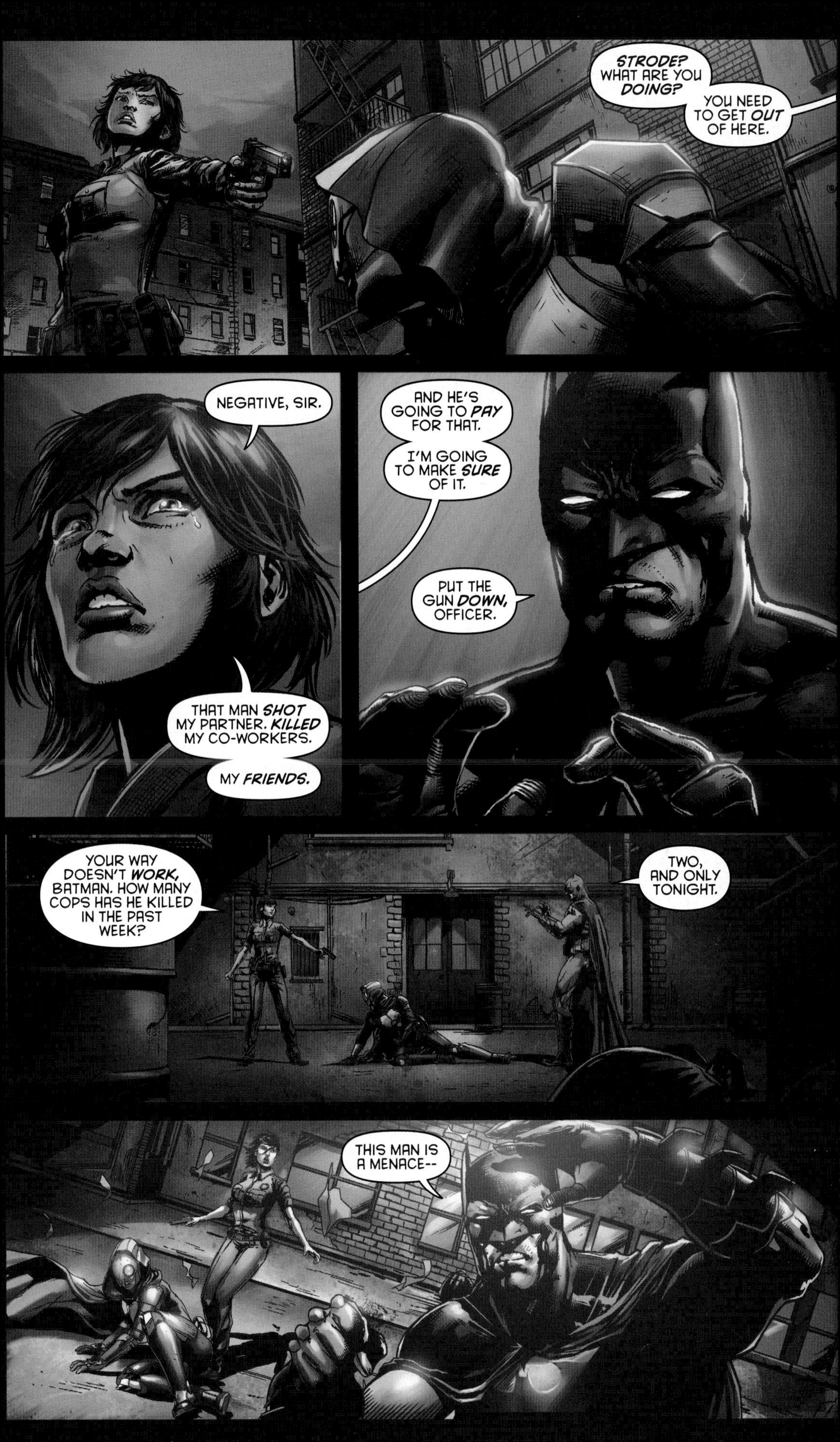
STRODE? WHAT ARE YOU DOING?
YOU NEED TO GET OUT OF HERE.
NEGATIVE, SIR.
AND HE'S GOING TO PAY FOR THAT.
I'M GOING TO MAKE SURE OF IT.
PUT THE GUN DOWN, OFFICER.
THAT MAN SHOT MY PARTNER. KILLED MY CO-WORKERS.
MY FRIENDS.
YOUR WAY DOESN'T WORK, BATMAN. HOW MANY COPS HAS HE KILLED IN THE PAST WEEK?
TWO, AND ONLY TONIGHT.
THIS MAN IS A MENACE--

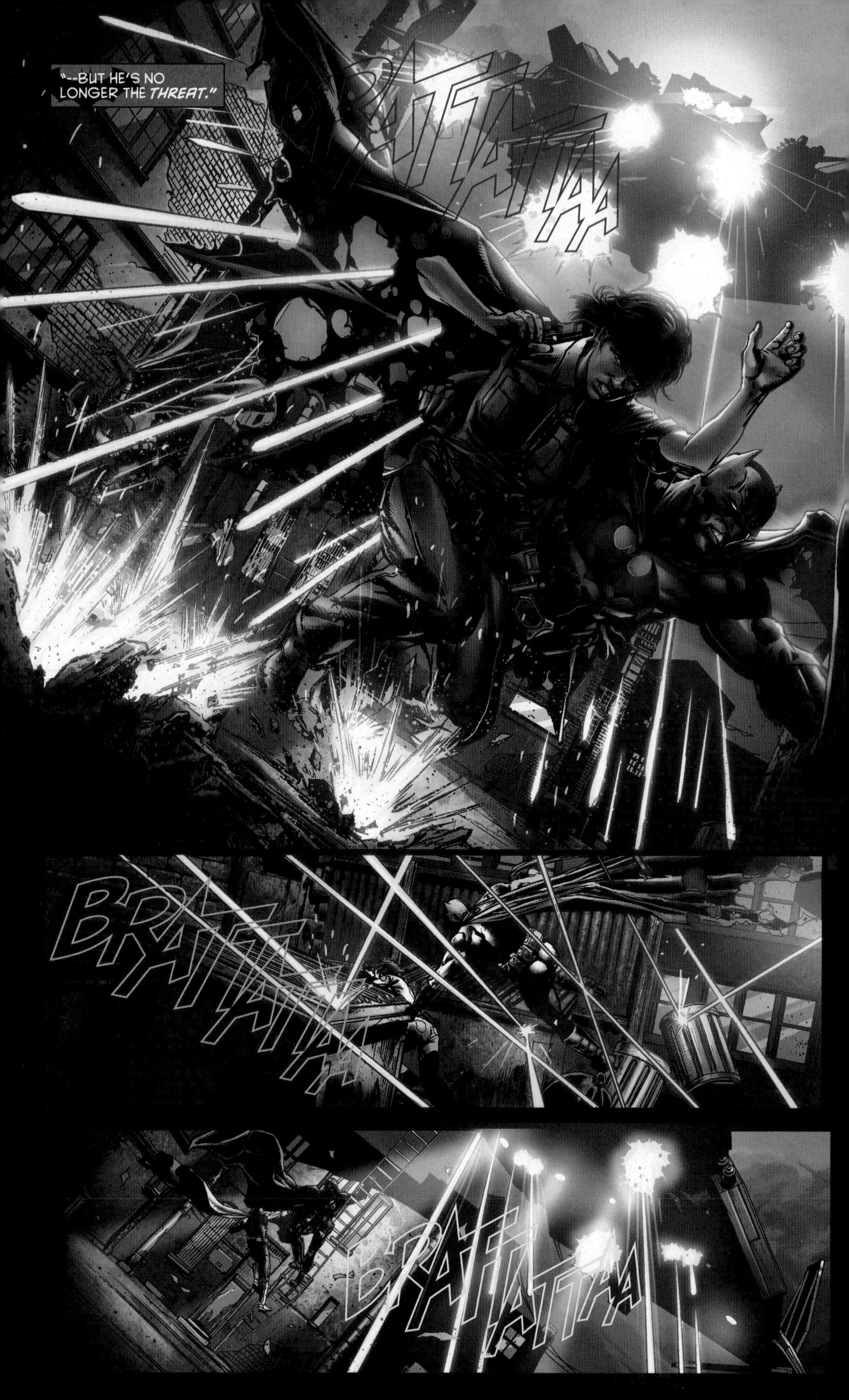
"--BUT HE'S NO LONGER THE *THREAT.*"

I've lost him.

But maybe--

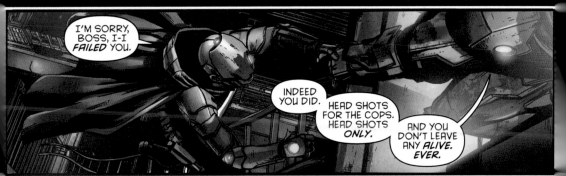

I'M SORRY, BOSS, I-I FAILED YOU.

INDEED YOU DID. HEAD SHOTS FOR THE COPS. HEAD SHOTS ONLY.

AND YOU DON'T LEAVE ANY ALIVE. EVER.

Maybe I know where to start looking in order to find him.

I WOULD HAVE FINISHED THEM-- AND O-OTHERS.

B-BUT B-B-BATMAN--

BATMAN SHOULD NOT HAVE GOTTEN IN THE WAY.

AND TRUST ME, JUST LIKE THE REST OF THE GOTHAM CITY LAW ENFORCEMENT--

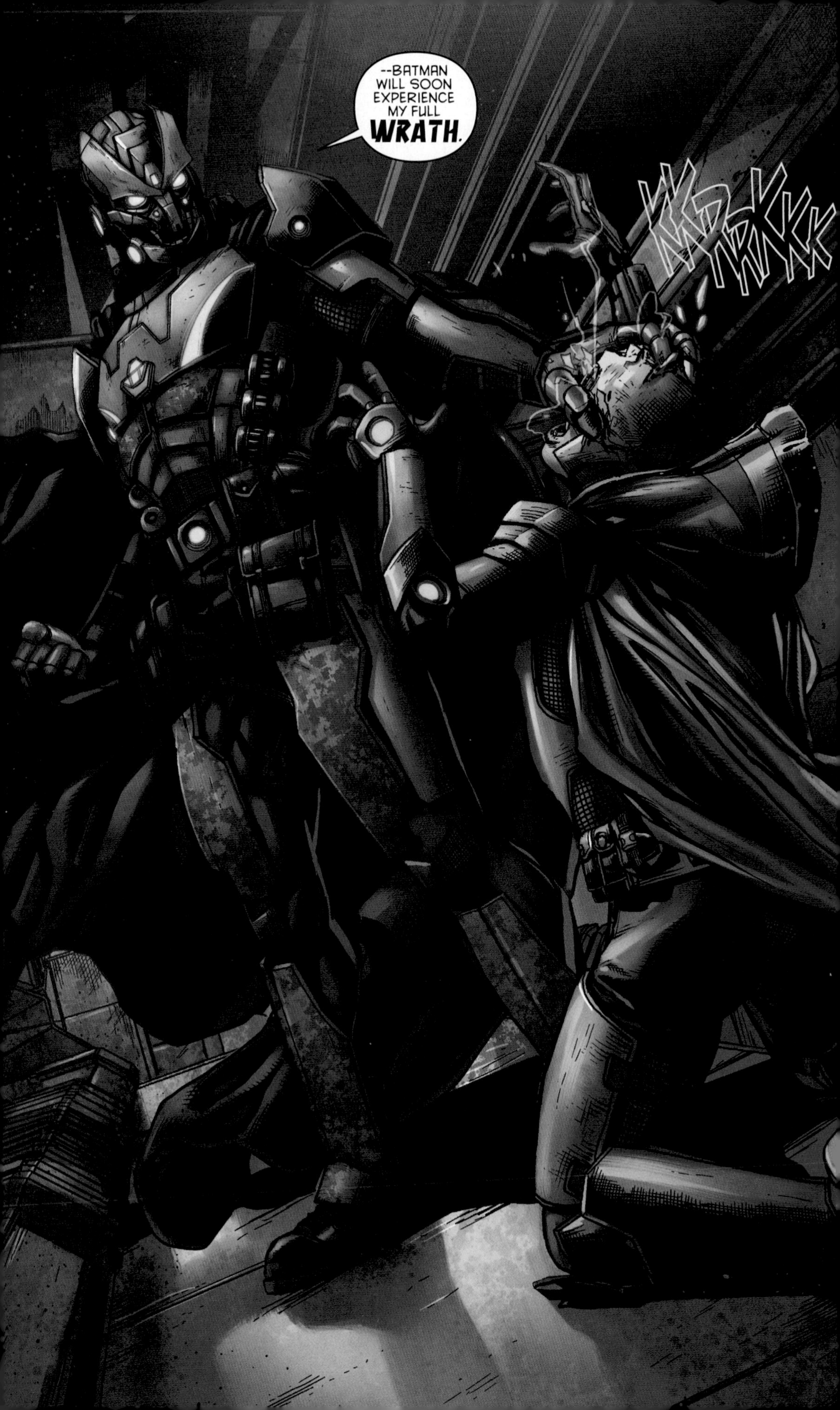
--BATMAN WILL SOON EXPERIENCE MY FULL WRATH.

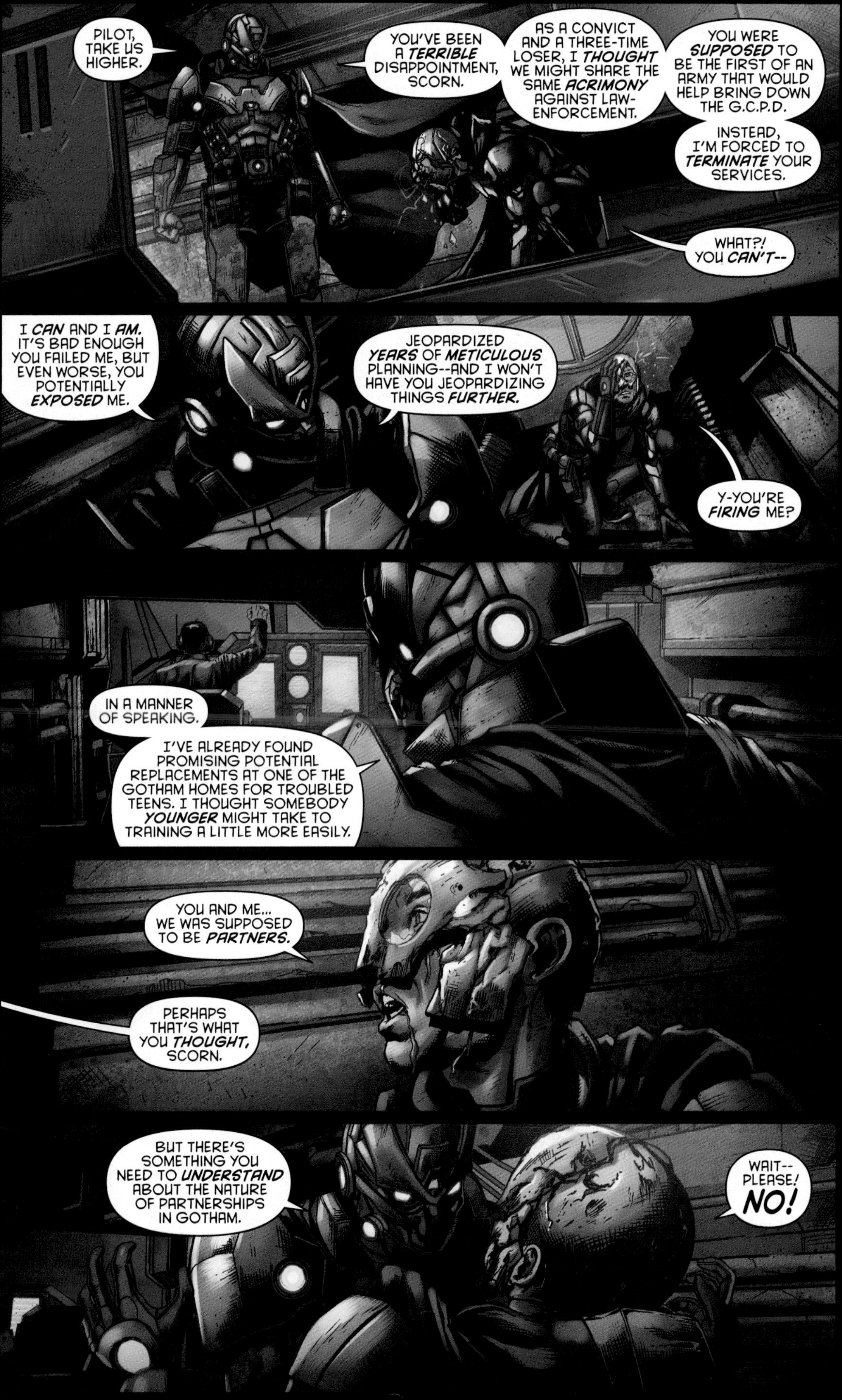
PILOT, TAKE US HIGHER.
YOU'VE BEEN A TERRIBLE DISAPPOINTMENT, SCORN.
AS A CONVICT AND A THREE-TIME LOSER, I THOUGHT WE MIGHT SHARE THE SAME ACRIMONY AGAINST LAW-ENFORCEMENT.
YOU WERE SUPPOSED TO BE THE FIRST OF AN ARMY THAT WOULD HELP BRING DOWN THE G.C.P.D.
INSTEAD, I'M FORCED TO TERMINATE YOUR SERVICES.
WHAT?! YOU CAN'T--
I CAN AND I AM. IT'S BAD ENOUGH YOU FAILED ME, BUT EVEN WORSE, YOU POTENTIALLY EXPOSED ME.
JEOPARDIZED YEARS OF METICULOUS PLANNING--AND I WON'T HAVE YOU JEOPARDIZING THINGS FURTHER.
Y-YOU'RE FIRING ME?
IN A MANNER OF SPEAKING.
I'VE ALREADY FOUND PROMISING POTENTIAL REPLACEMENTS AT ONE OF THE GOTHAM HOMES FOR TROUBLED TEENS. I THOUGHT SOMEBODY YOUNGER MIGHT TAKE TO TRAINING A LITTLE MORE EASILY.
YOU AND ME... WE WAS SUPPOSED TO BE PARTNERS.
PERHAPS THAT'S WHAT YOU THOUGHT, SCORN.
BUT THERE'S SOMETHING YOU NEED TO UNDERSTAND ABOUT THE NATURE OF PARTNERSHIPS IN GOTHAM.
WAIT-- PLEASE! NO!

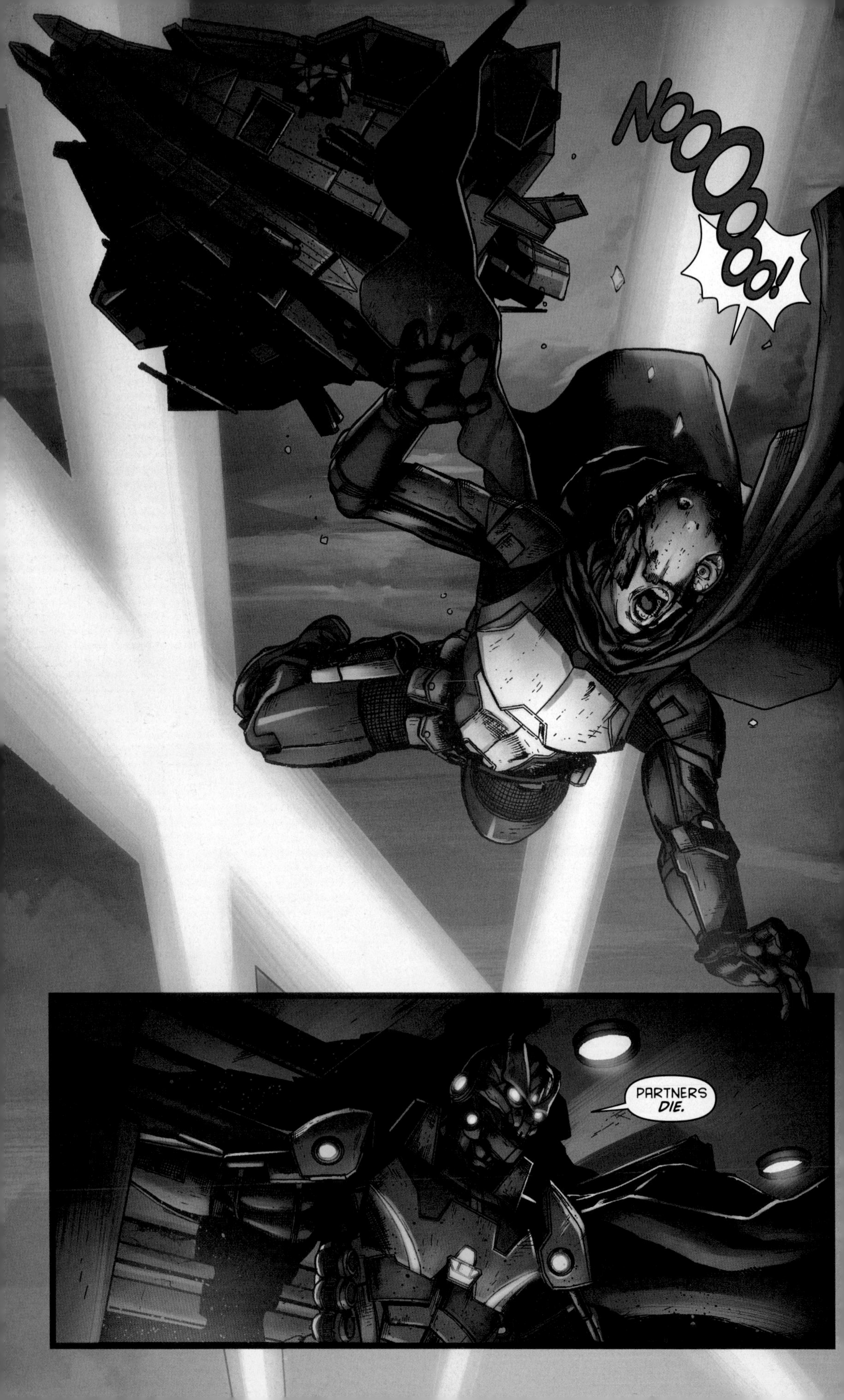
NOOOOOOOO!
PARTNERS DIE.

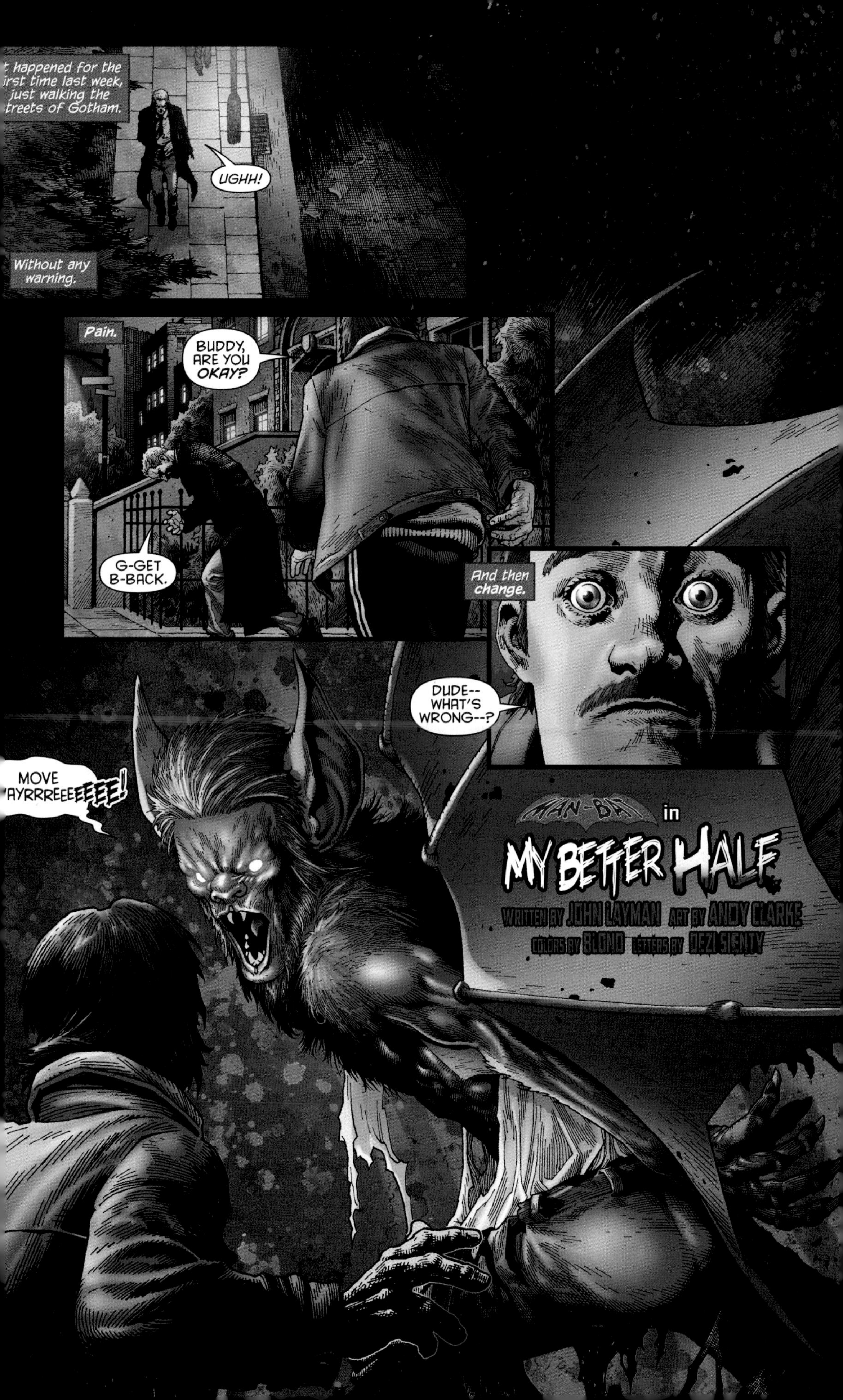

t happened for the irst time last week, just walking the treets of Gotham.
UGHH!
Without any warning.
Pain.
BUDDY, ARE YOU OKAY?
G-GET B-BACK.
And then change.
DUDE-- WHAT'S WRONG--?
MOVE AYRRREEEEEEE!
MAN-BAT in
MY BETTER HALF
WRITTEN BY JOHN LAYMAN ART BY ANDY CLARKE
COLORS BY BLOND LETTERS BY DEZI SIENTY

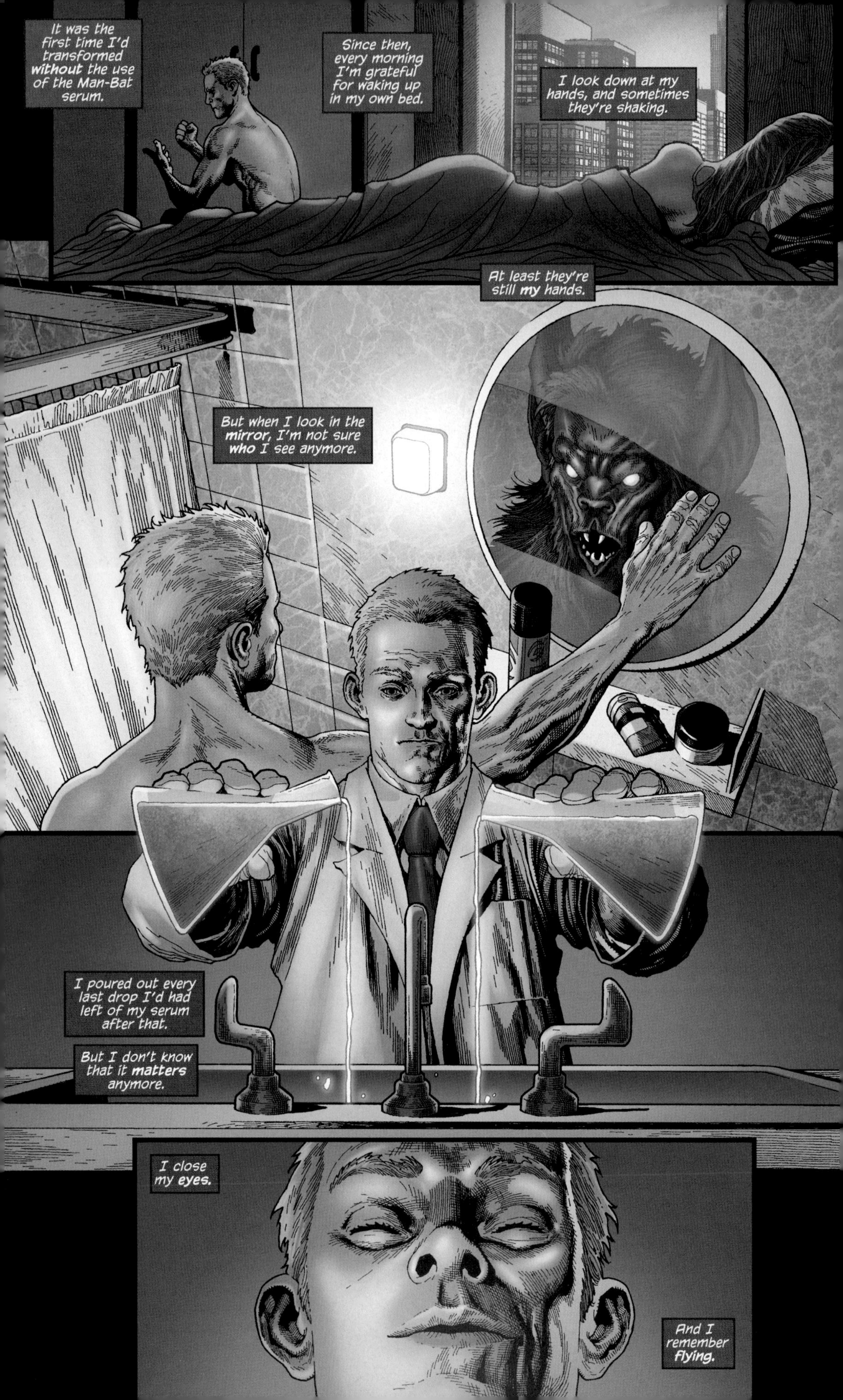

It was the first time I'd transformed **without** the use of the Man-Bat serum.
Since then, every morning I'm grateful for waking up in my own bed.
I look down at my hands, and sometimes they're shaking.
At least they're still **my** hands.
But when I look in the **mirror**, I'm not sure **who** I see anymore.
I poured out every last drop I'd had left of my serum after that.
But I don't know that it **matters** anymore.
I close my **eyes**.
And I remember **flying**.

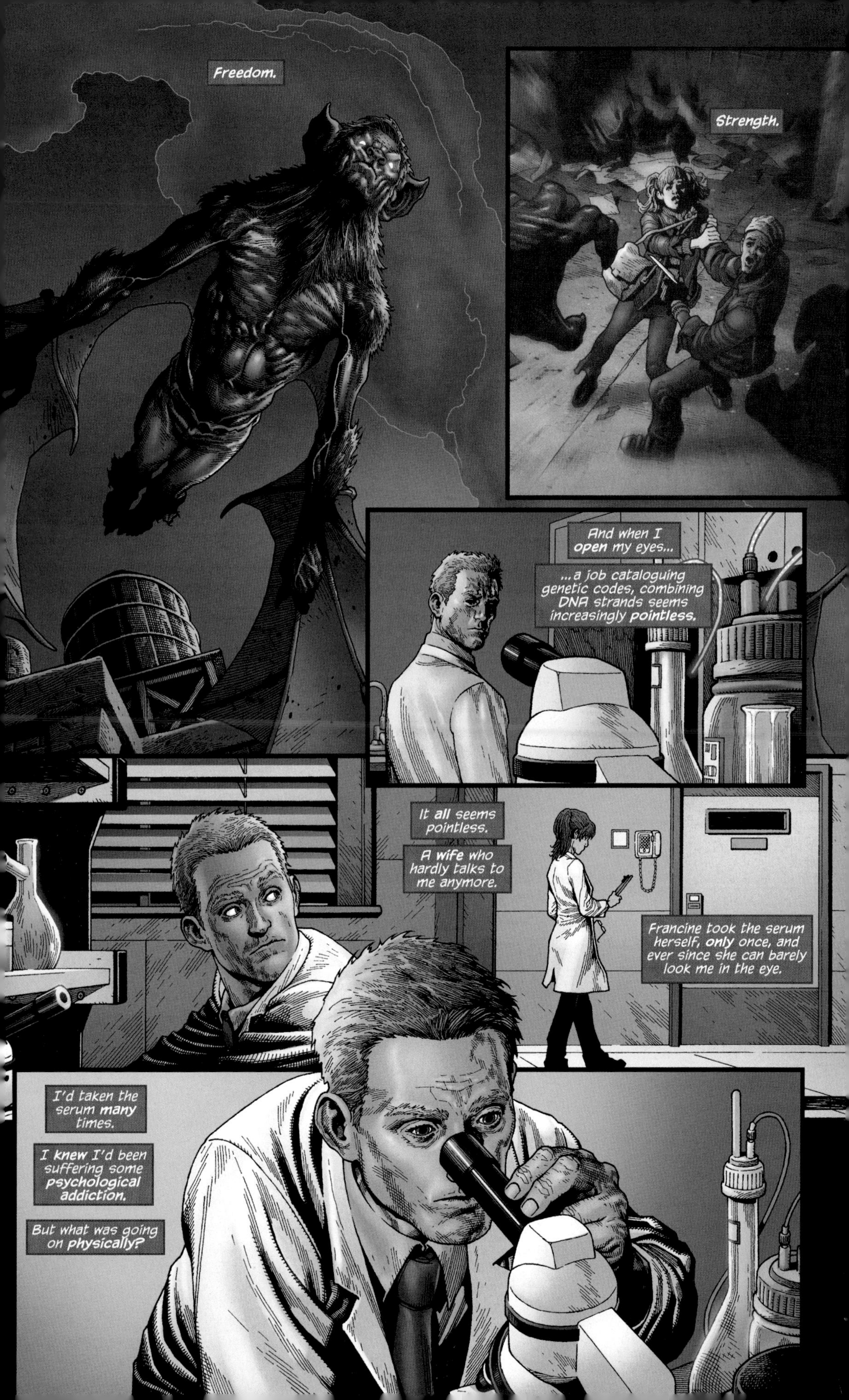
Freedom.
Strength.
And when I open my eyes...
...a job cataloguing genetic codes, combining DNA strands seems increasingly pointless.
It all seems pointless.
A wife who hardly talks to me anymore.
Francine took the serum herself, only once, and ever since she can barely look me in the eye.
I'd taken the serum many times.
I knew I'd been suffering some psychological addiction.
But what was going on physically?

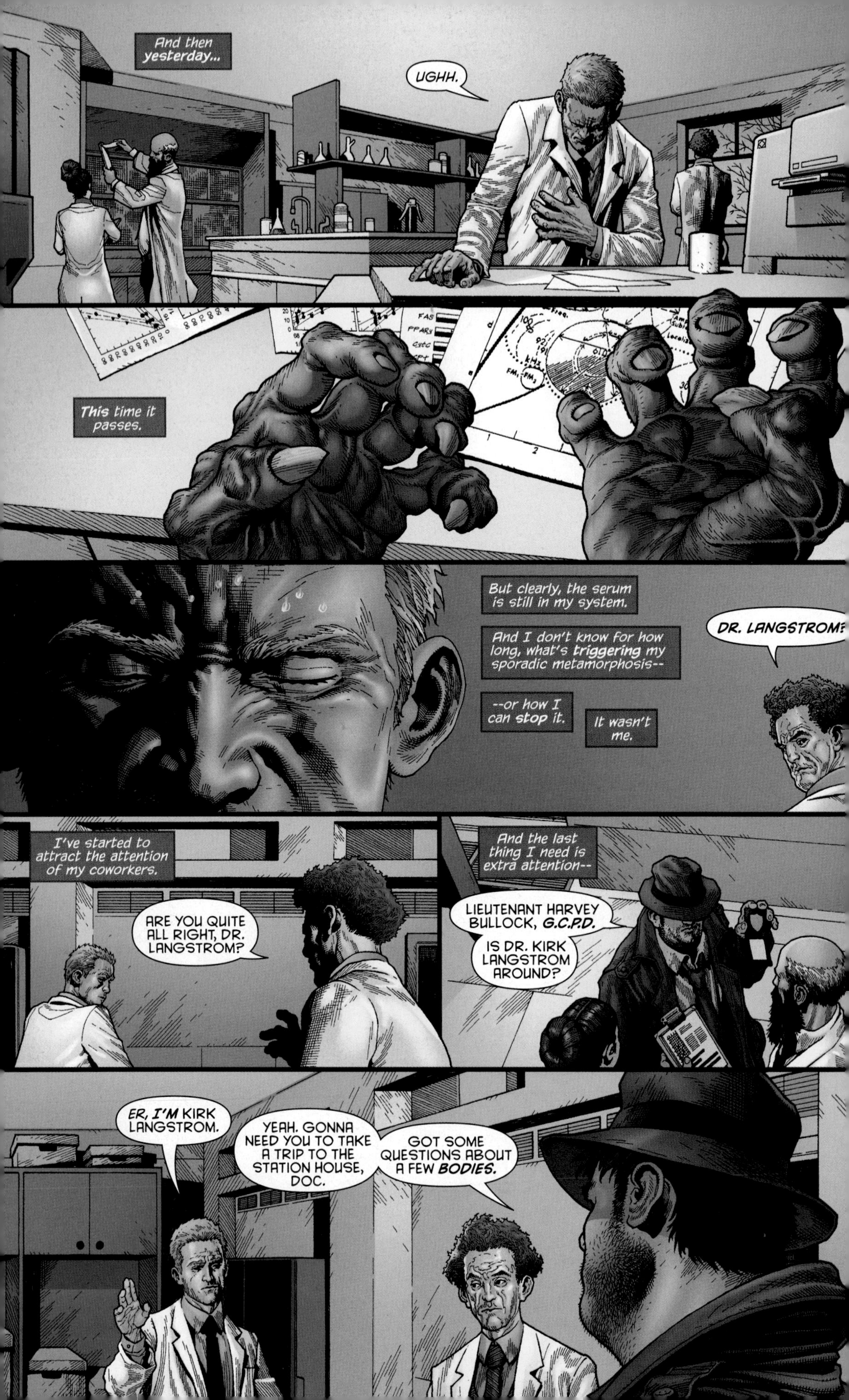

And then yesterday...
UGHH.
This time it passes.
But clearly, the serum is still in my system.
And I don't know for how long, what's triggering my sporadic metamorphosis--
--or how I can stop it.
It wasn't me.
DR. LANGSTROM?
I've started to attract the attention of my coworkers.
ARE YOU QUITE ALL RIGHT, DR. LANGSTROM?
And the last thing I need is extra attention--
LIEUTENANT HARVEY BULLOCK, G.C.P.D.
IS DR. KIRK LANGSTROM AROUND?
ER, I'M KIRK LANGSTROM.
YEAH. GONNA NEED YOU TO TAKE A TRIP TO THE STATION HOUSE, DOC.
GOT SOME QUESTIONS ABOUT A FEW BODIES.

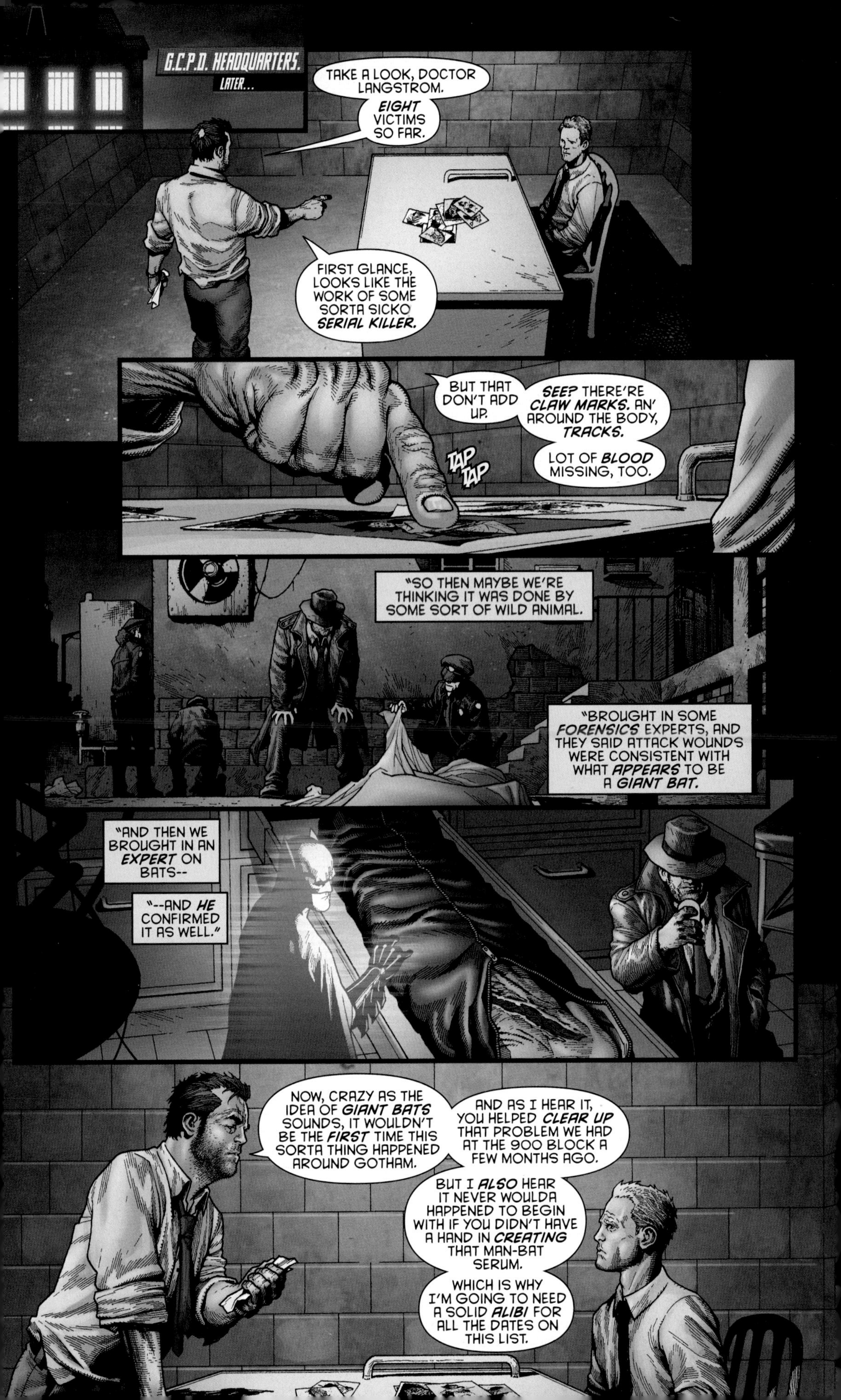
G.C.P.D. HEADQUARTERS.
LATER...
TAKE A LOOK, DOCTOR LANGSTROM.
EIGHT VICTIMS SO FAR.
FIRST GLANCE, LOOKS LIKE THE WORK OF SOME SORTA SICKO SERIAL KILLER.
BUT THAT DON'T ADD UP.
SEE? THERE'RE CLAW MARKS. AN' AROUND THE BODY, TRACKS.
LOT OF BLOOD MISSING, TOO.
TAP TAP
"SO THEN MAYBE WE'RE THINKING IT WAS DONE BY SOME SORT OF WILD ANIMAL.
"BROUGHT IN SOME FORENSICS EXPERTS, AND THEY SAID ATTACK WOUNDS WERE CONSISTENT WITH WHAT APPEARS TO BE A GIANT BAT.
"AND THEN WE BROUGHT IN AN EXPERT ON BATS--
"--AND HE CONFIRMED IT AS WELL."
NOW, CRAZY AS THE IDEA OF GIANT BATS SOUNDS, IT WOULDN'T BE THE FIRST TIME THIS SORTA THING HAPPENED AROUND GOTHAM.
AND AS I HEAR IT, YOU HELPED CLEAR UP THAT PROBLEM WE HAD AT THE 900 BLOCK A FEW MONTHS AGO.
BUT I ALSO HEAR IT NEVER WOULDA HAPPENED TO BEGIN WITH IF YOU DIDN'T HAVE A HAND IN CREATING THAT MAN-BAT SERUM.
WHICH IS WHY I'M GOING TO NEED A SOLID ALIBI FOR ALL THE DATES ON THIS LIST.

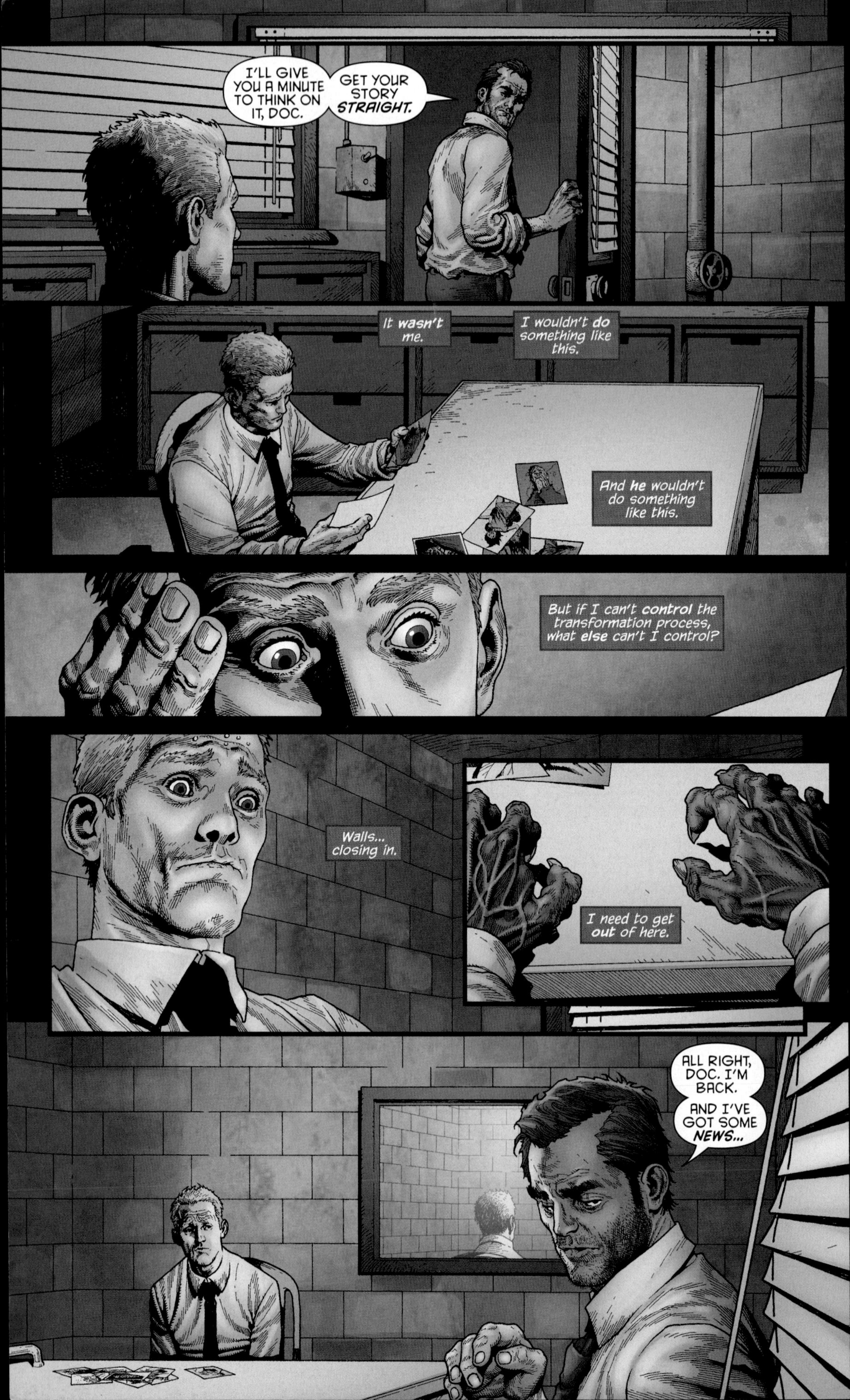

I'LL GIVE YOU A MINUTE TO THINK ON IT, DOC.
GET YOUR STORY STRAIGHT.
It wasn't me.
I wouldn't do something like this.
And he wouldn't do something like this.
But if I can't control the transformation process, what else can't I control?
Walls... closing in.
I need to get out of here.
ALL RIGHT, DOC. I'M BACK.
AND I'VE GOT SOME NEWS...

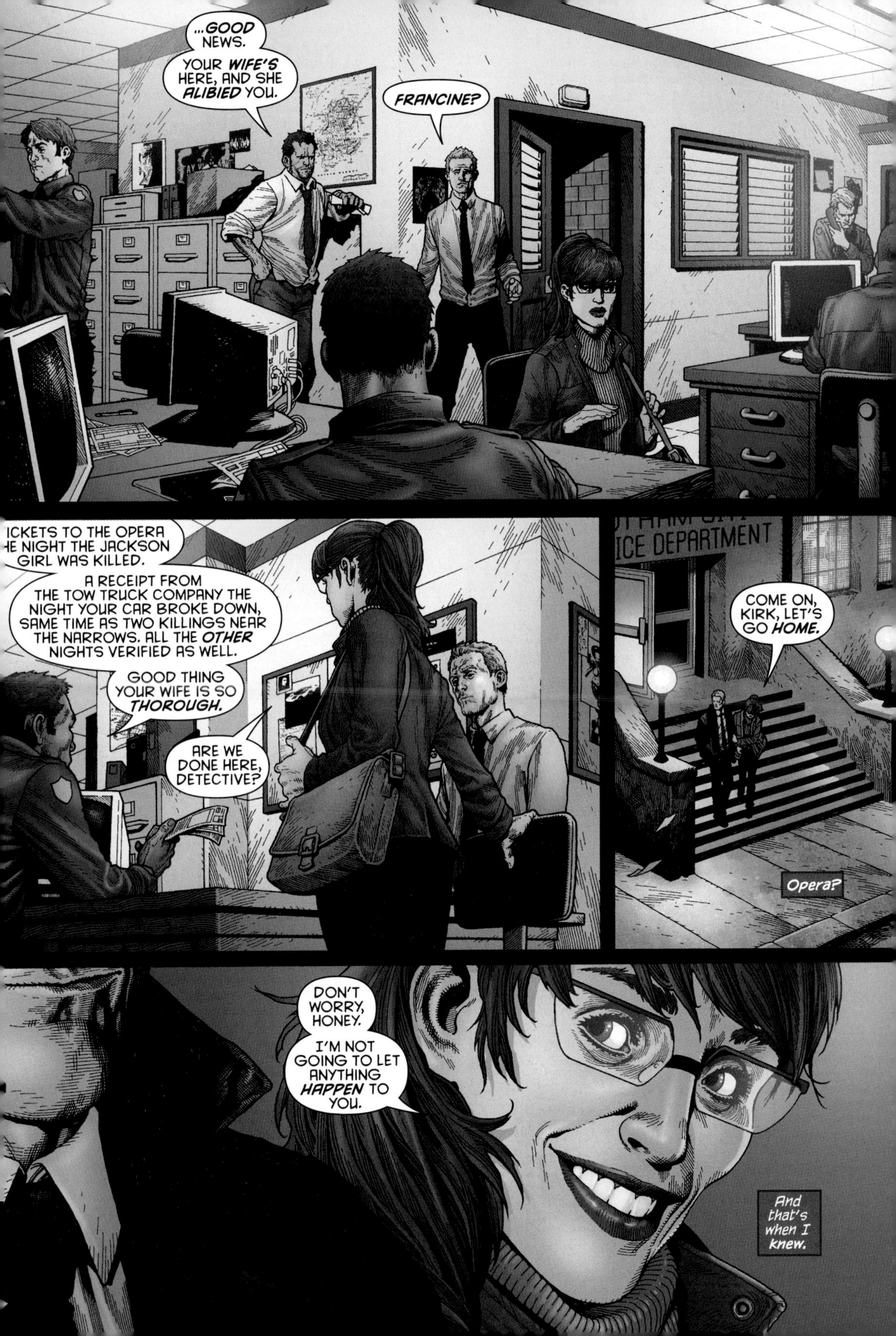

...GOOD NEWS.
YOUR WIFE'S HERE, AND SHE ALIBIED YOU.
FRANCINE?
ICKETS TO THE OPERA HE NIGHT THE JACKSON GIRL WAS KILLED.
A RECEIPT FROM THE TOW TRUCK COMPANY THE NIGHT YOUR CAR BROKE DOWN, SAME TIME AS TWO KILLINGS NEAR THE NARROWS. ALL THE OTHER NIGHTS VERIFIED AS WELL.
GOOD THING YOUR WIFE IS SO THOROUGH.
ARE WE DONE HERE, DETECTIVE?
ICE DEPARTMENT
COME ON, KIRK, LET'S GO HOME.
Opera?
DON'T WORRY, HONEY.
I'M NOT GOING TO LET ANYTHING HAPPEN TO YOU.
And that's when I knew.

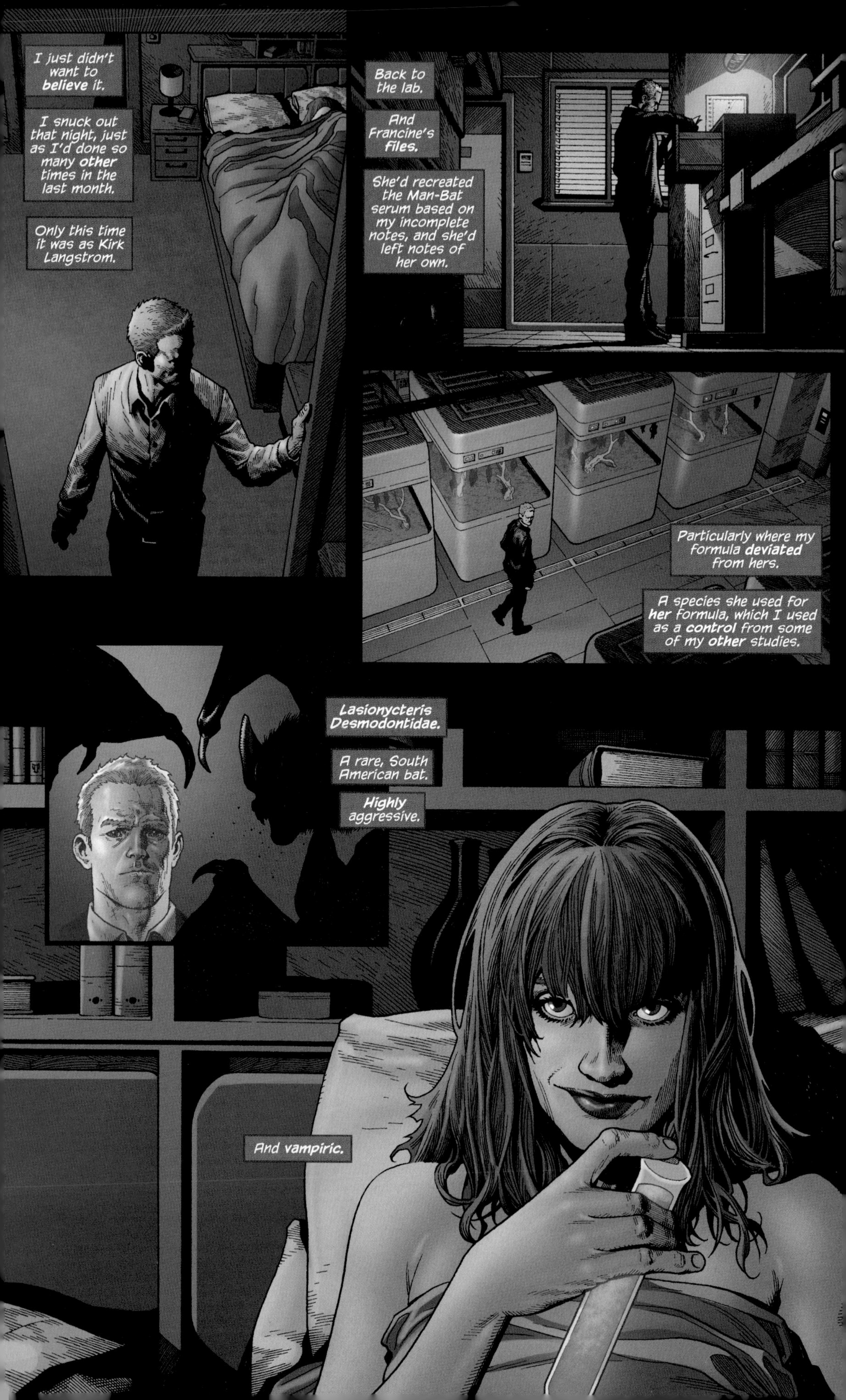
I just didn't want to believe it.
I snuck out that night, just as I'd done so many other times in the last month.
Only this time it was as Kirk Langstrom.
Back to the lab.
And Francine's files.
She'd recreated the Man-Bat serum based on my incomplete notes, and she'd left notes of her own.
Particularly where my formula deviated from hers.
A species she used for her formula, which I used as a control from some of my other studies.
Lasionycteris Desmodontidae.
A rare, South American bat.
Highly aggressive.
And vampiric.

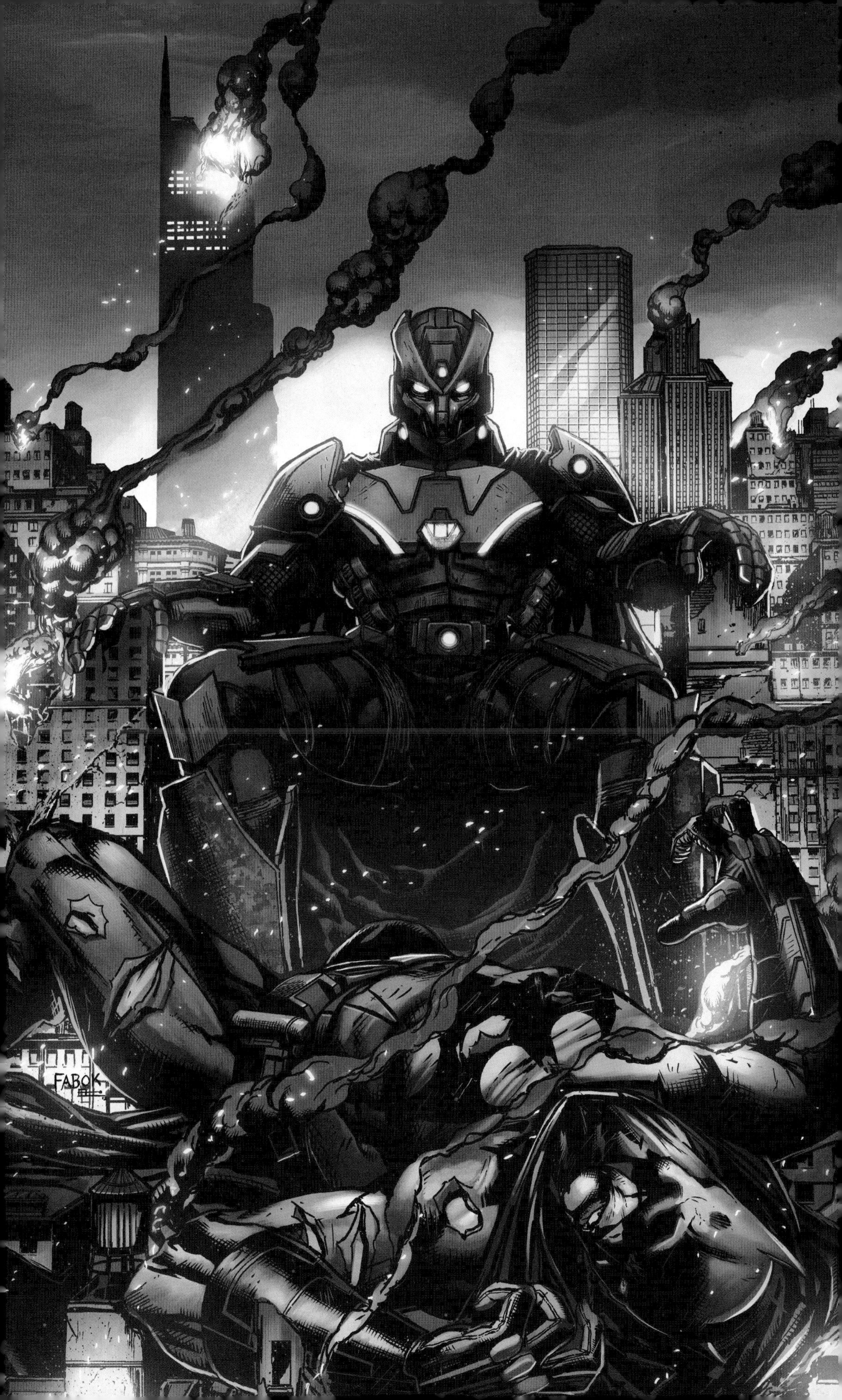
FABOK

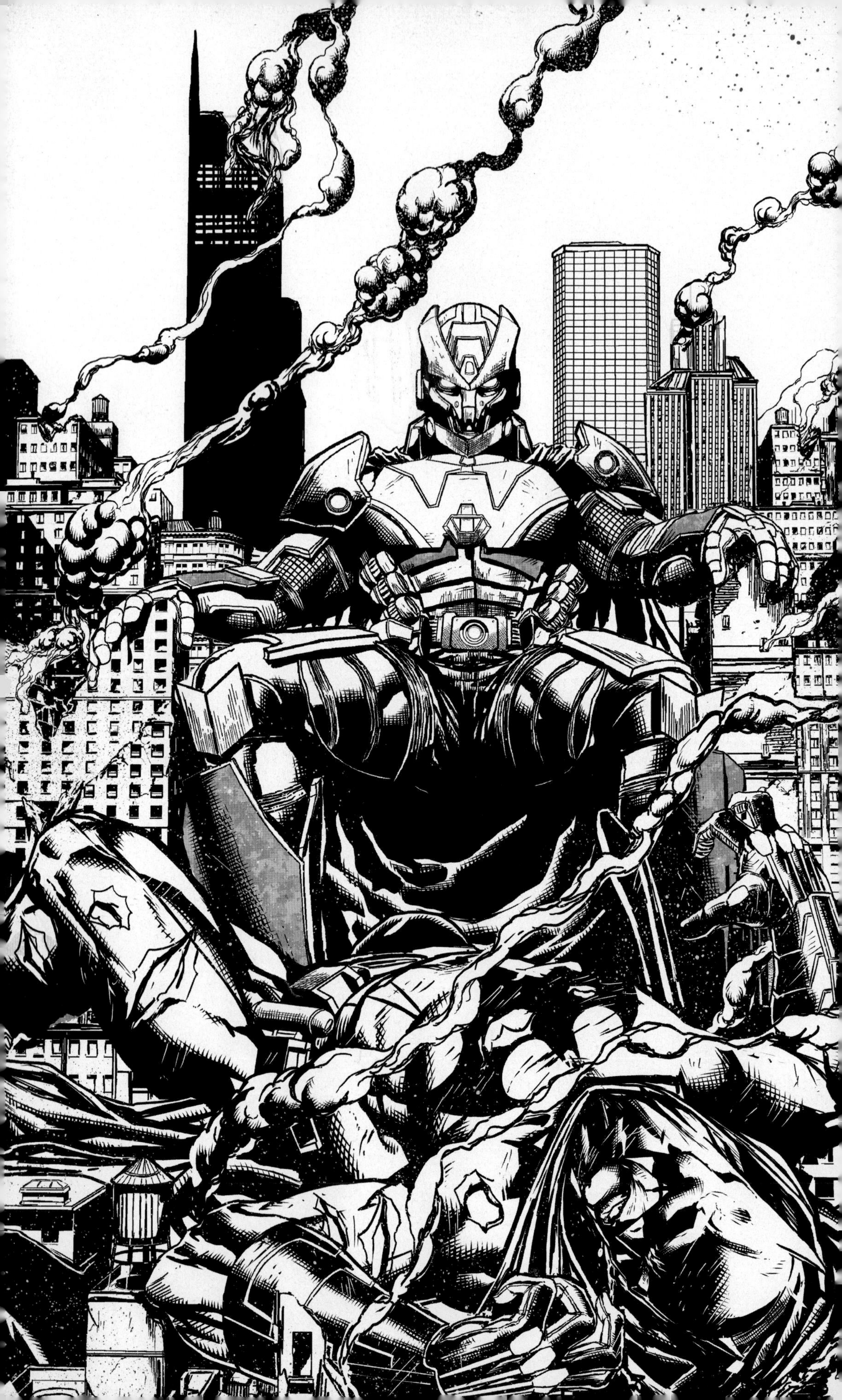

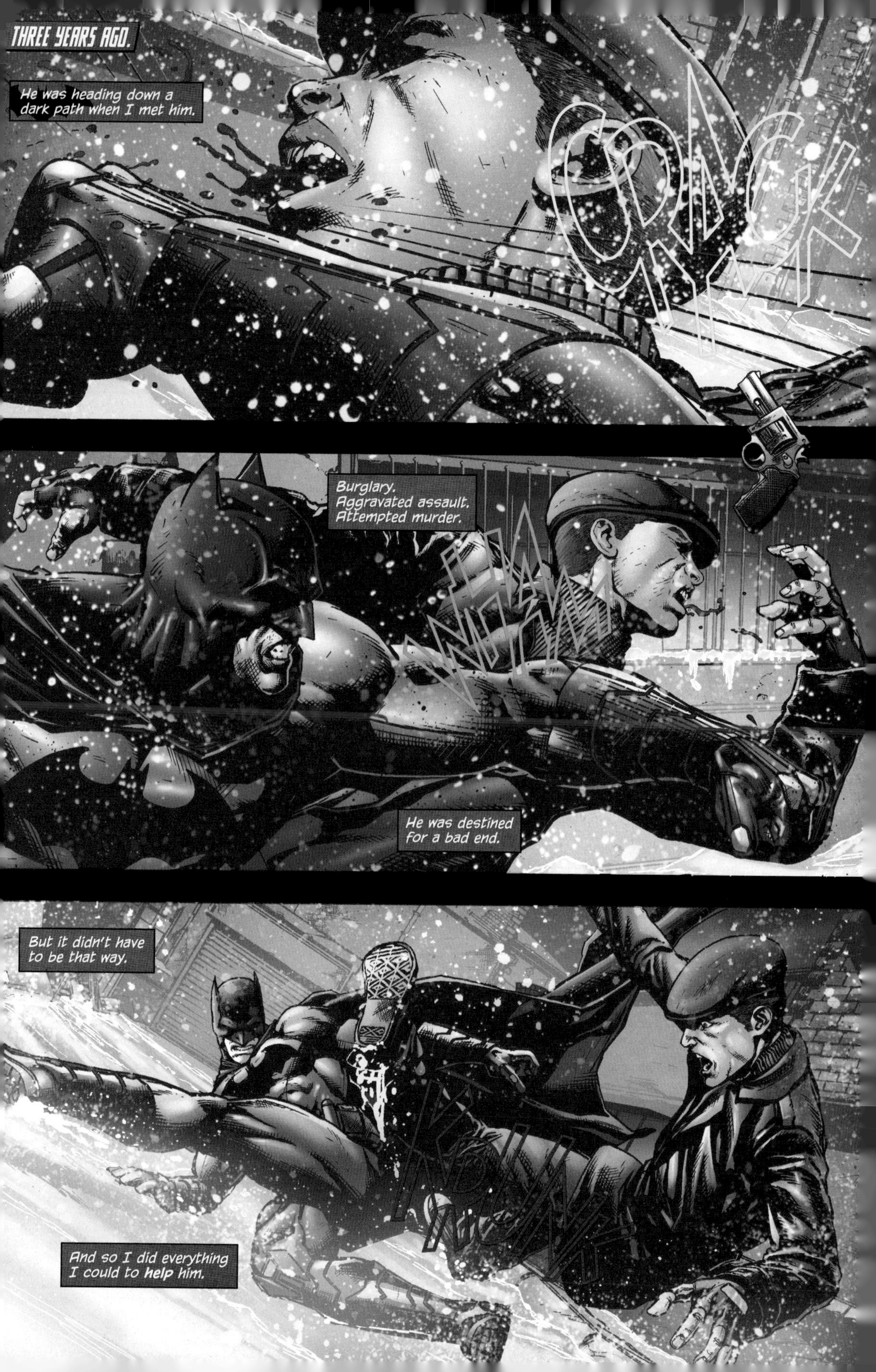
THREE YEARS AGO.
He was heading down a dark path when I met him.
CRACK
Burglary. Aggravated assault. Attempted murder.
He was destined for a bad end.
But it didn't have to be that way.
And so I did everything I could to **help** him.

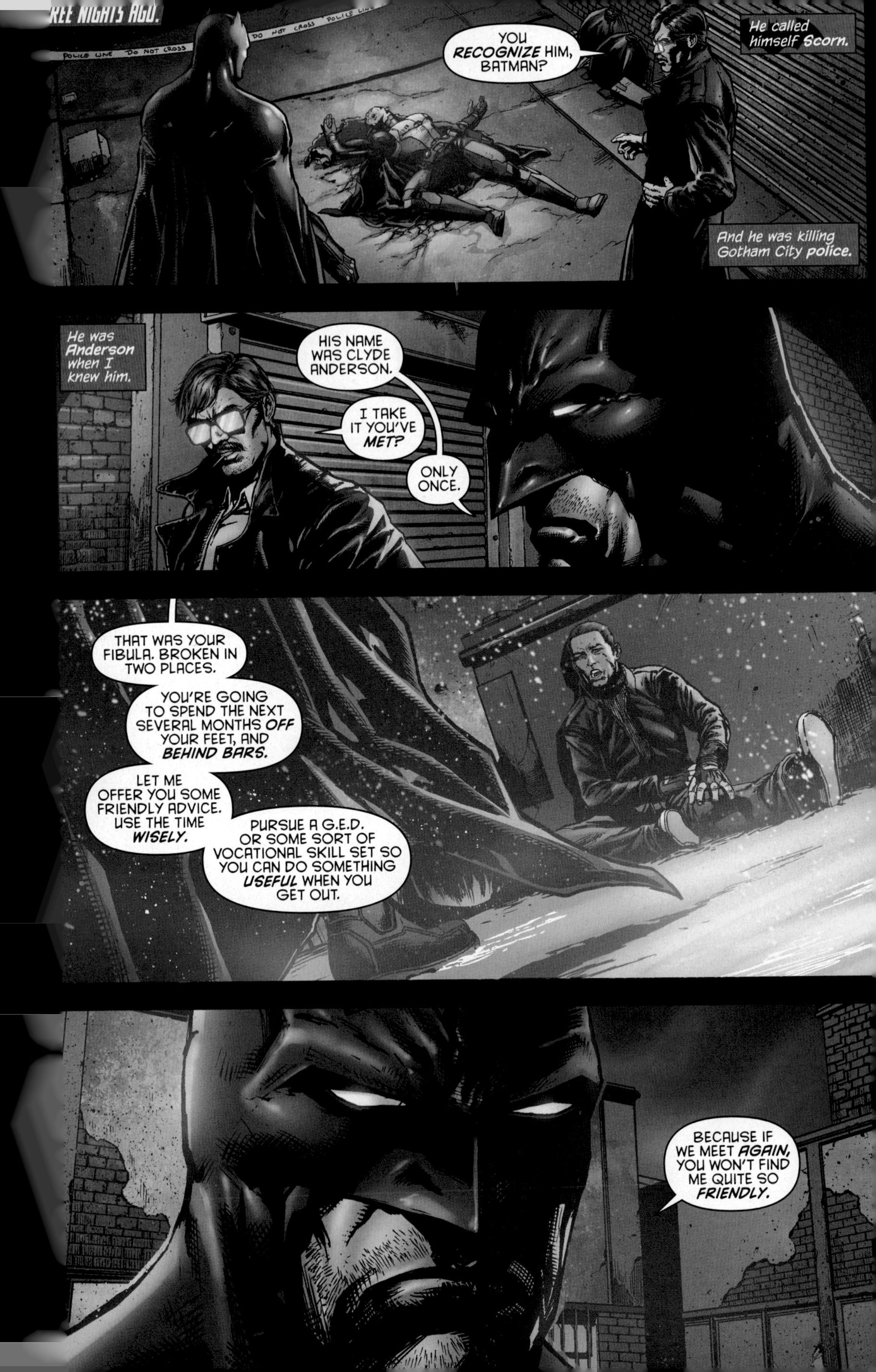
REE NIGHTS AGO.
POLICE LINE DO NOT CROSS
YOU RECOGNIZE HIM, BATMAN?
He called himself Scorn.
And he was killing Gotham City police.
He was Anderson when I knew him.
HIS NAME WAS CLYDE ANDERSON.
I TAKE IT YOU'VE MET?
ONLY ONCE.
THAT WAS YOUR FIBULA. BROKEN IN TWO PLACES.
YOU'RE GOING TO SPEND THE NEXT SEVERAL MONTHS OFF YOUR FEET, AND BEHIND BARS.
LET ME OFFER YOU SOME FRIENDLY ADVICE. USE THE TIME WISELY.
PURSUE A G.E.D. OR SOME SORT OF VOCATIONAL SKILL SET SO YOU CAN DO SOMETHING USEFUL WHEN YOU GET OUT.
BECAUSE IF WE MEET AGAIN, YOU WON'T FIND ME QUITE SO FRIENDLY.

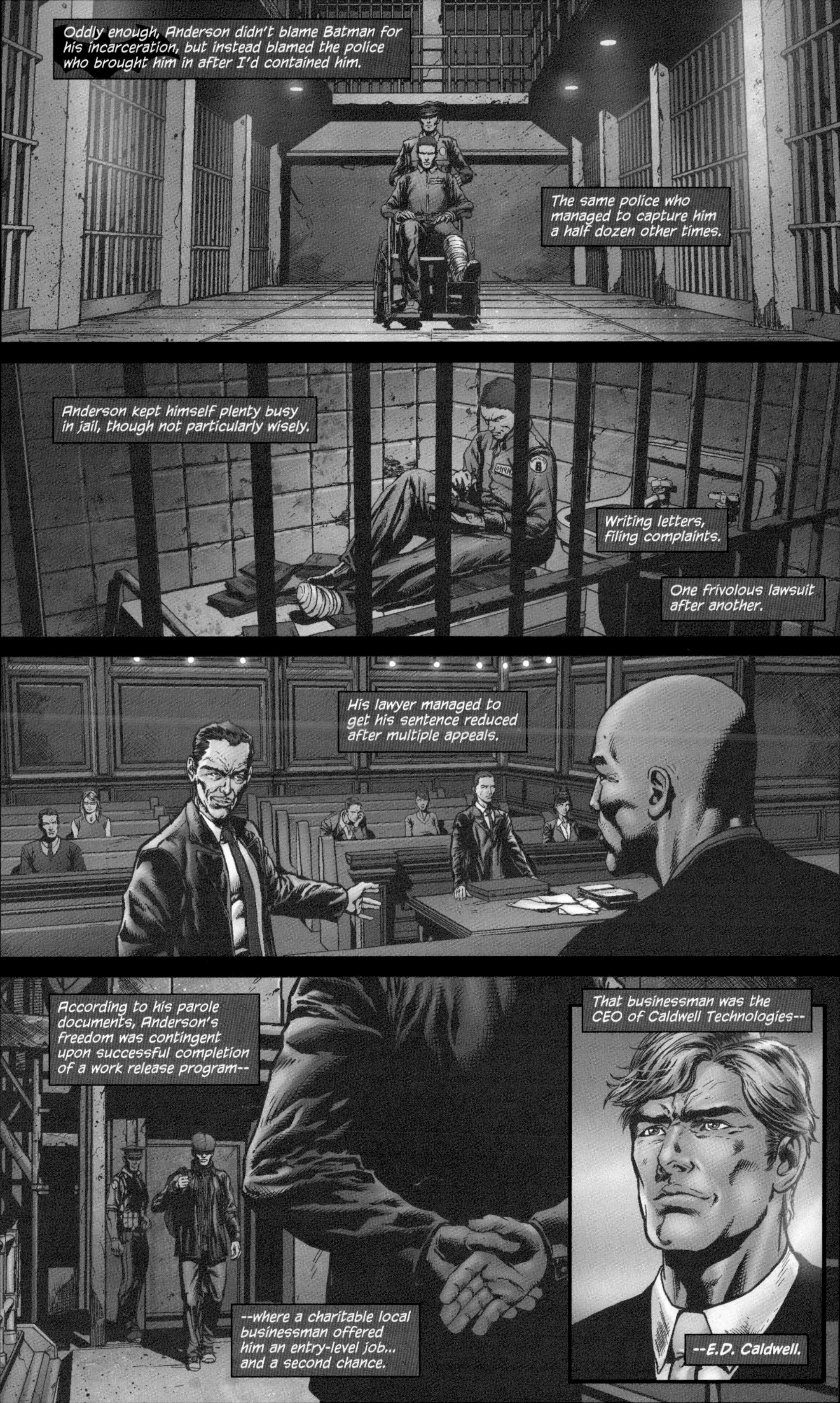

Oddly enough, Anderson didn't blame Batman for his incarceration, but instead blamed the police who brought him in after I'd contained him.
The same police who managed to capture him a half dozen other times.
Anderson kept himself plenty busy in jail, though not particularly wisely.
Writing letters, filing complaints.
One frivolous lawsuit after another.
His lawyer managed to get his sentence reduced after multiple appeals.
According to his parole documents, Anderson's freedom was contingent upon successful completion of a work release program--
--where a charitable local businessman offered him an entry-level job... and a second chance.
That businessman was the CEO of Caldwell Technologies--
--E.D. Caldwell.

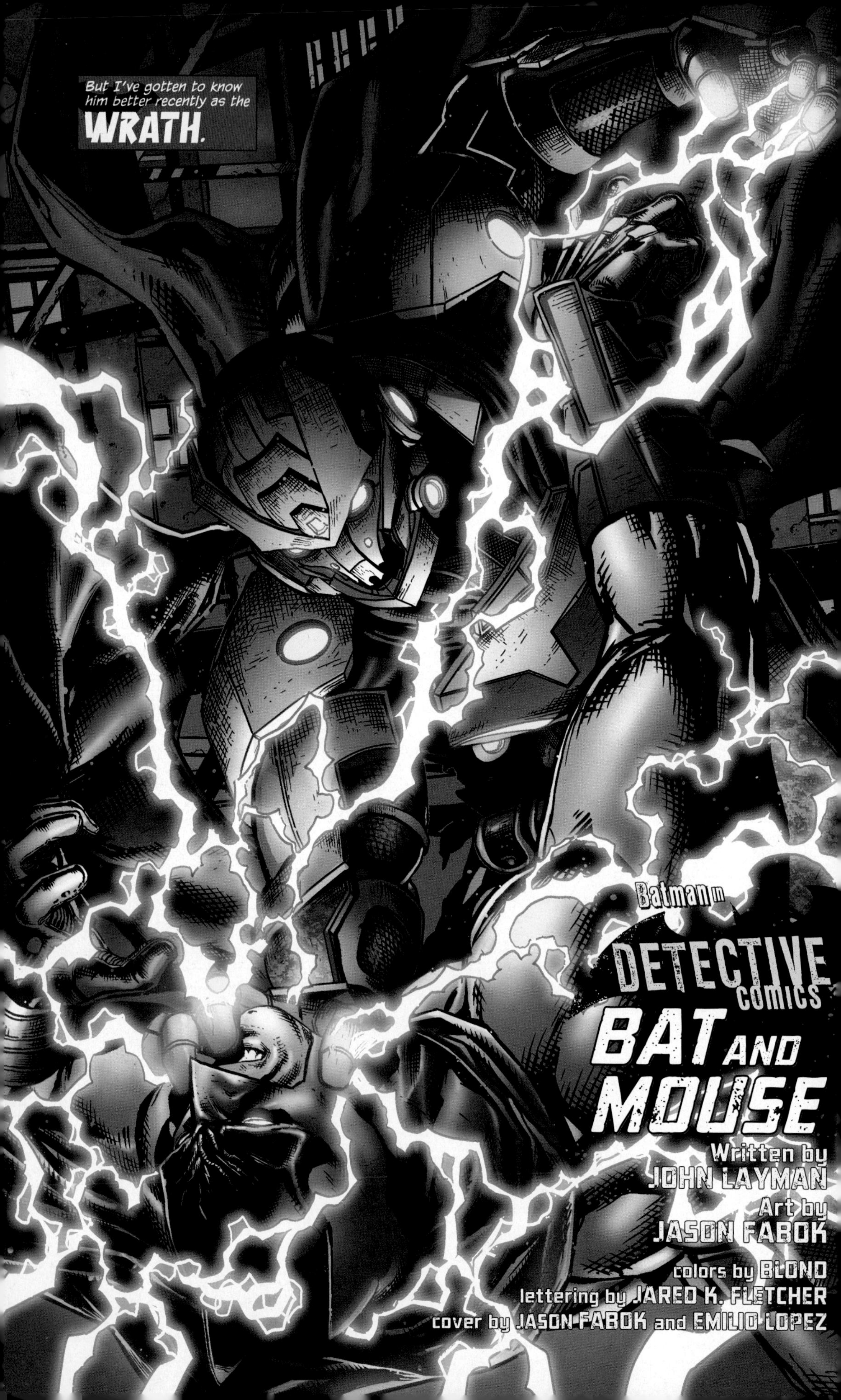

But I've gotten to know him better recently as the WRATH.
Batman in
DETECTIVE comics
BAT AND MOUSE
Written by JOHN LAYMAN
Art by JASON FABOK
colors by BLOND
lettering by JARED K. FLETCHER
cover by JASON FABOK and EMILIO LOPEZ

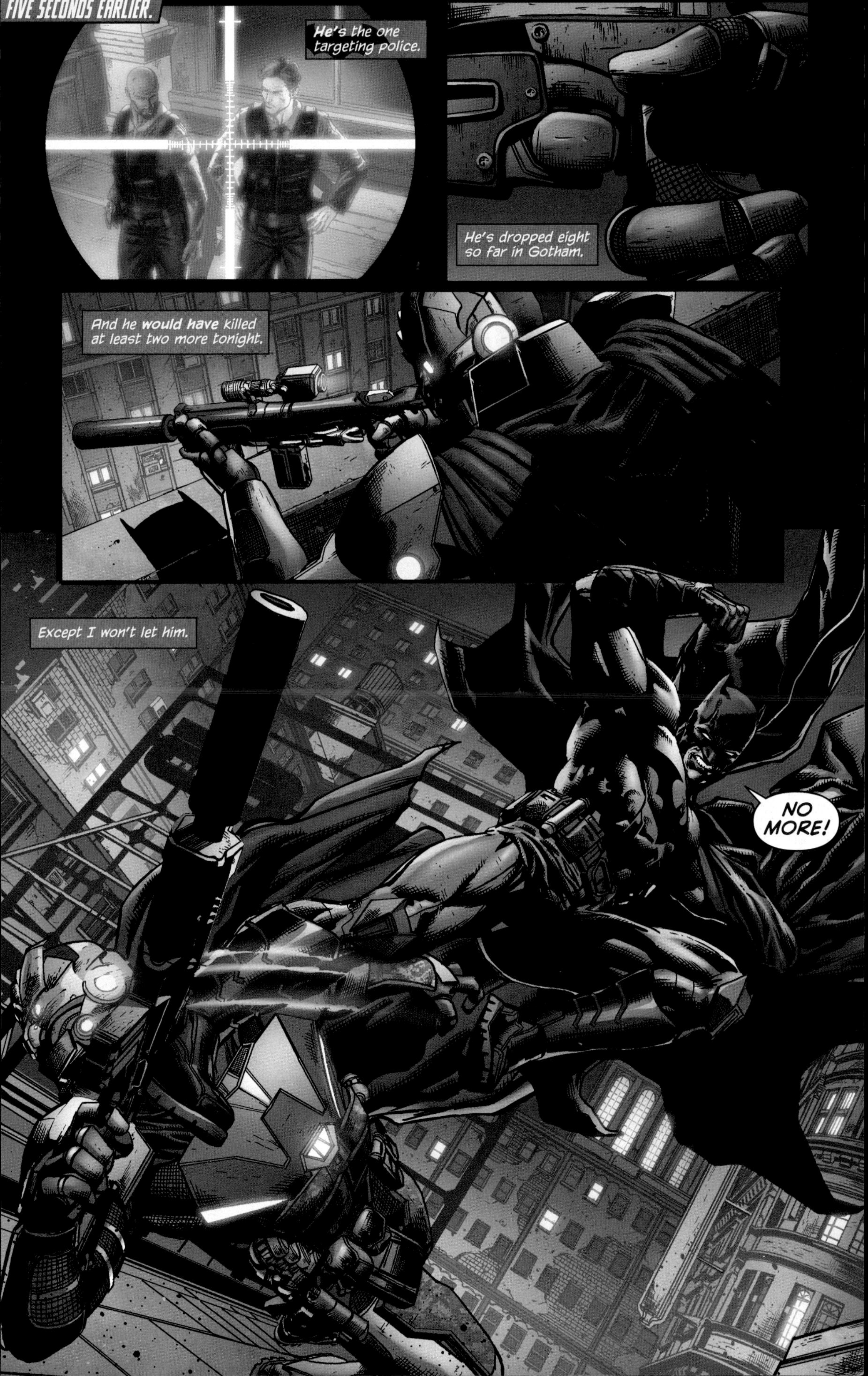
FIVE SECONDS EARLIER.
He's the one targeting police.
He's dropped eight so far in Gotham.
And he would have killed at least two more tonight.
Except I won't let him.
NO MORE!

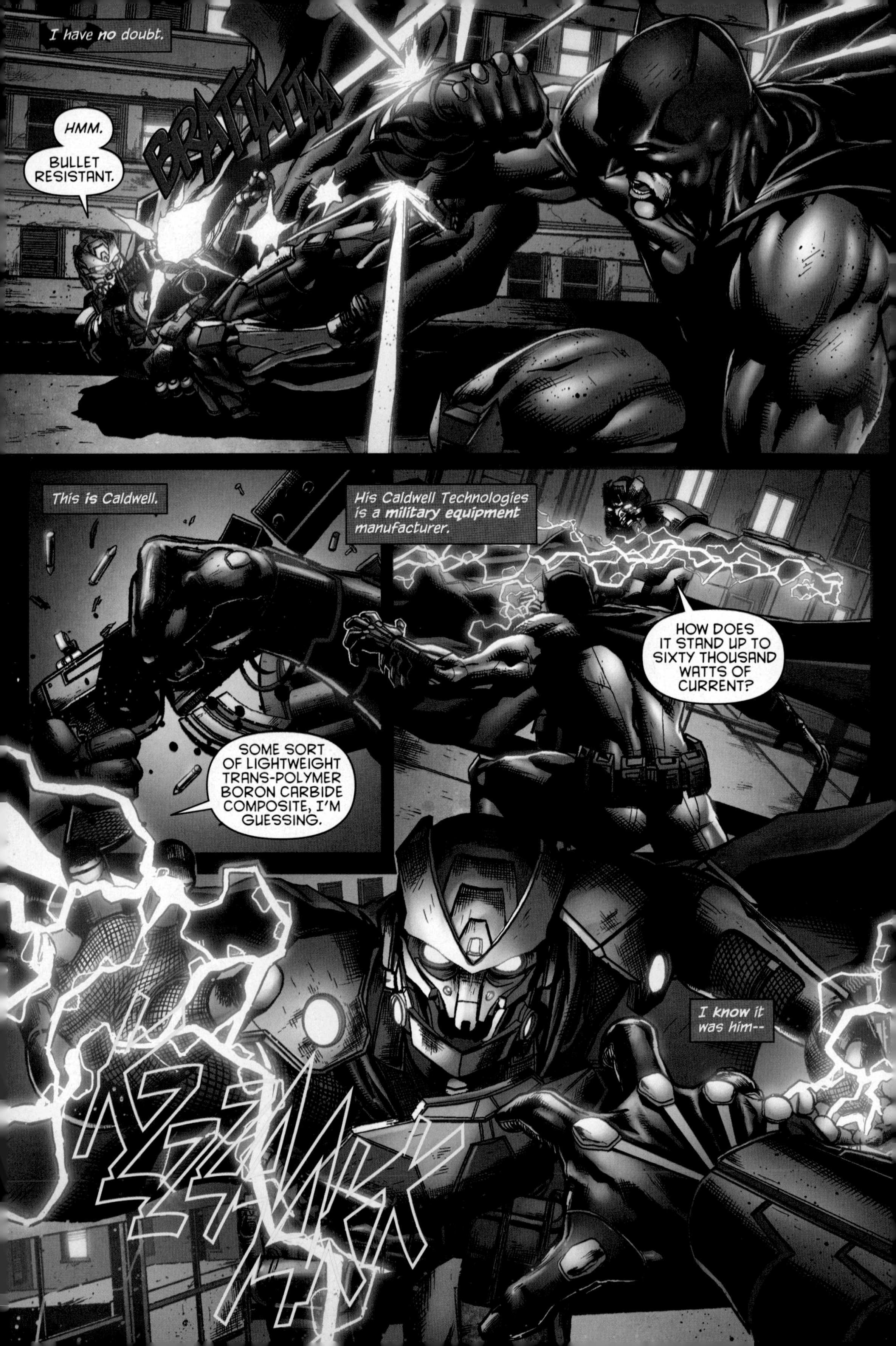
I have no doubt.
HMM.
BULLET RESISTANT.
This is Caldwell.
His Caldwell Technologies is a military equipment manufacturer.
HOW DOES IT STAND UP TO SIXTY THOUSAND WATTS OF CURRENT?
SOME SORT OF LIGHTWEIGHT TRANS-POLYMER BORON CARBIDE COMPOSITE, I'M GUESSING.
I know it was him--

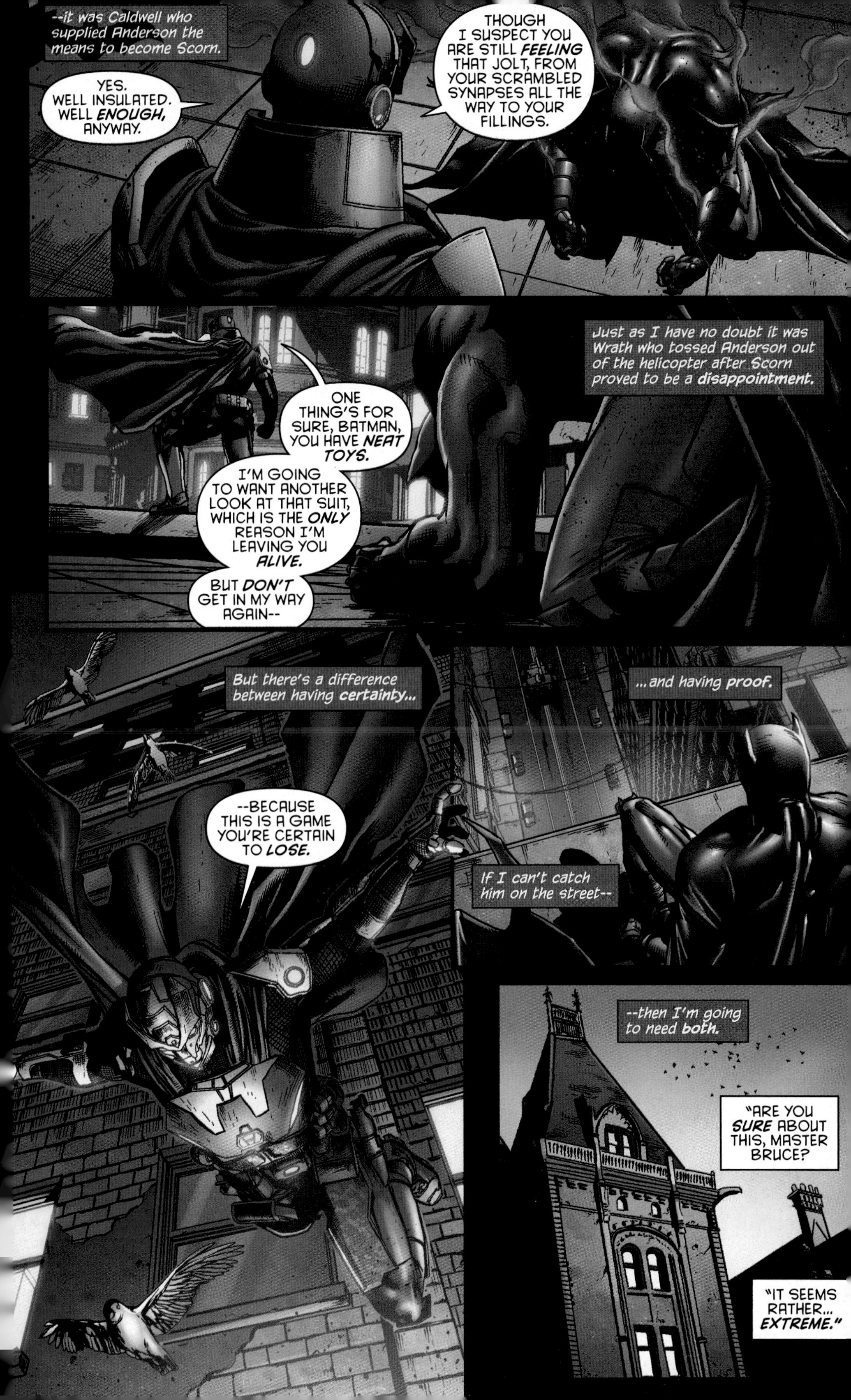
--it was Caldwell who supplied Anderson the means to become Scorn.
YES. WELL INSULATED. WELL ENOUGH, ANYWAY.
THOUGH I SUSPECT YOU ARE STILL FEELING THAT JOLT, FROM YOUR SCRAMBLED SYNAPSES ALL THE WAY TO YOUR FILLINGS.
Just as I have no doubt it was Wrath who tossed Anderson out of the helicopter after Scorn proved to be a disappointment.
ONE THING'S FOR SURE, BATMAN, YOU HAVE NEAT TOYS.
I'M GOING TO WANT ANOTHER LOOK AT THAT SUIT, WHICH IS THE ONLY REASON I'M LEAVING YOU ALIVE.
BUT DON'T GET IN MY WAY AGAIN--
But there's a difference between having certainty...
--BECAUSE THIS IS A GAME YOU'RE CERTAIN TO LOSE.
...and having proof.
If I can't catch him on the street--
--then I'm going to need both.
"ARE YOU SURE ABOUT THIS, MASTER BRUCE?
"IT SEEMS RATHER... EXTREME."

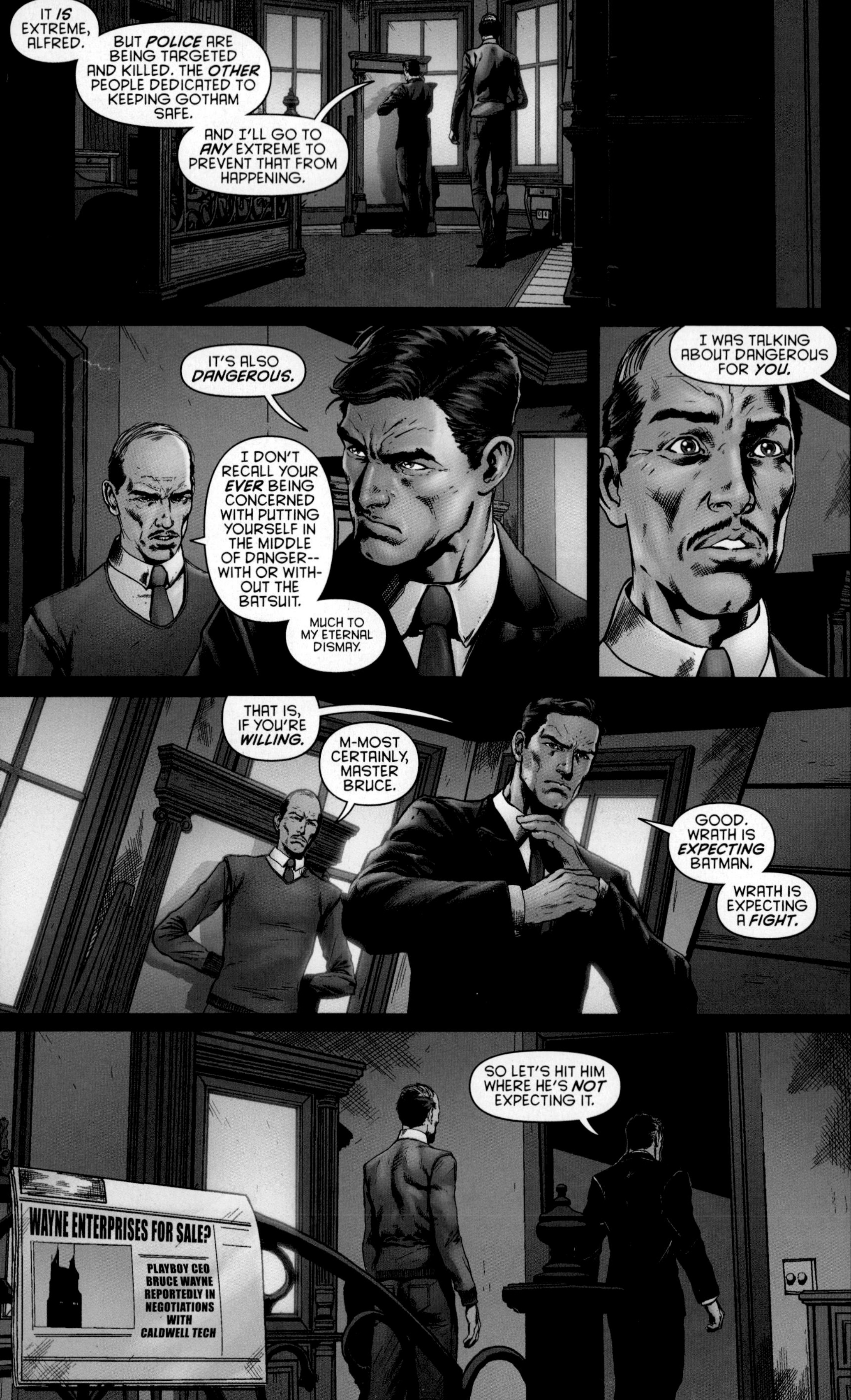
IT IS EXTREME, ALFRED.
BUT POLICE ARE BEING TARGETED AND KILLED. THE OTHER PEOPLE DEDICATED TO KEEPING GOTHAM SAFE.
AND I'LL GO TO ANY EXTREME TO PREVENT THAT FROM HAPPENING.
IT'S ALSO DANGEROUS.
I DON'T RECALL YOUR EVER BEING CONCERNED WITH PUTTING YOURSELF IN THE MIDDLE OF DANGER-- WITH OR WITH-OUT THE BATSUIT.
MUCH TO MY ETERNAL DISMAY.
I WAS TALKING ABOUT DANGEROUS FOR YOU.
THAT IS, IF YOU'RE WILLING.
M-MOST CERTAINLY, MASTER BRUCE.
GOOD. WRATH IS EXPECTING BATMAN.
WRATH IS EXPECTING A FIGHT.
SO LET'S HIT HIM WHERE HE'S NOT EXPECTING IT.
WAYNE ENTERPRISES FOR SALE?
PLAYBOY CEO BRUCE WAYNE REPORTEDLY IN NEGOTIATIONS WITH CALDWELL TECH

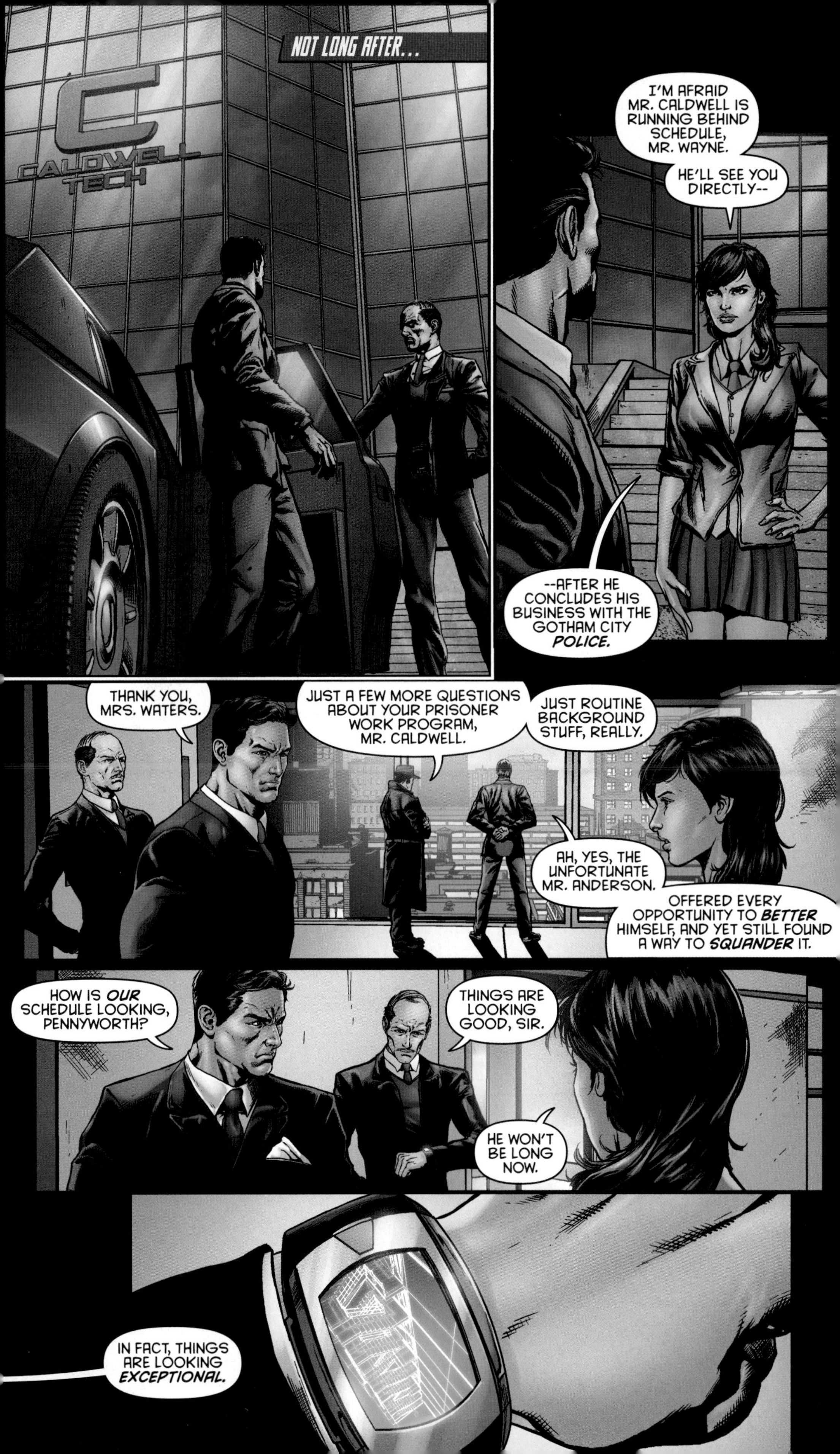
NOT LONG AFTER...
CALDWELL TECH
I'M AFRAID MR. CALDWELL IS RUNNING BEHIND SCHEDULE, MR. WAYNE.
HE'LL SEE YOU DIRECTLY--
--AFTER HE CONCLUDES HIS BUSINESS WITH THE GOTHAM CITY *POLICE.*
THANK YOU, MRS. WATERS.
JUST A FEW MORE QUESTIONS ABOUT YOUR PRISONER WORK PROGRAM, MR. CALDWELL.
JUST ROUTINE BACKGROUND STUFF, REALLY.
AH, YES, THE UNFORTUNATE MR. ANDERSON.
OFFERED EVERY OPPORTUNITY TO *BETTER* HIMSELF, AND YET STILL FOUND A WAY TO *SQUANDER* IT.
HOW IS *OUR* SCHEDULE LOOKING, PENNYWORTH?
THINGS ARE LOOKING GOOD, SIR.
HE WON'T BE LONG NOW.
IN FACT, THINGS ARE LOOKING *EXCEPTIONAL.*

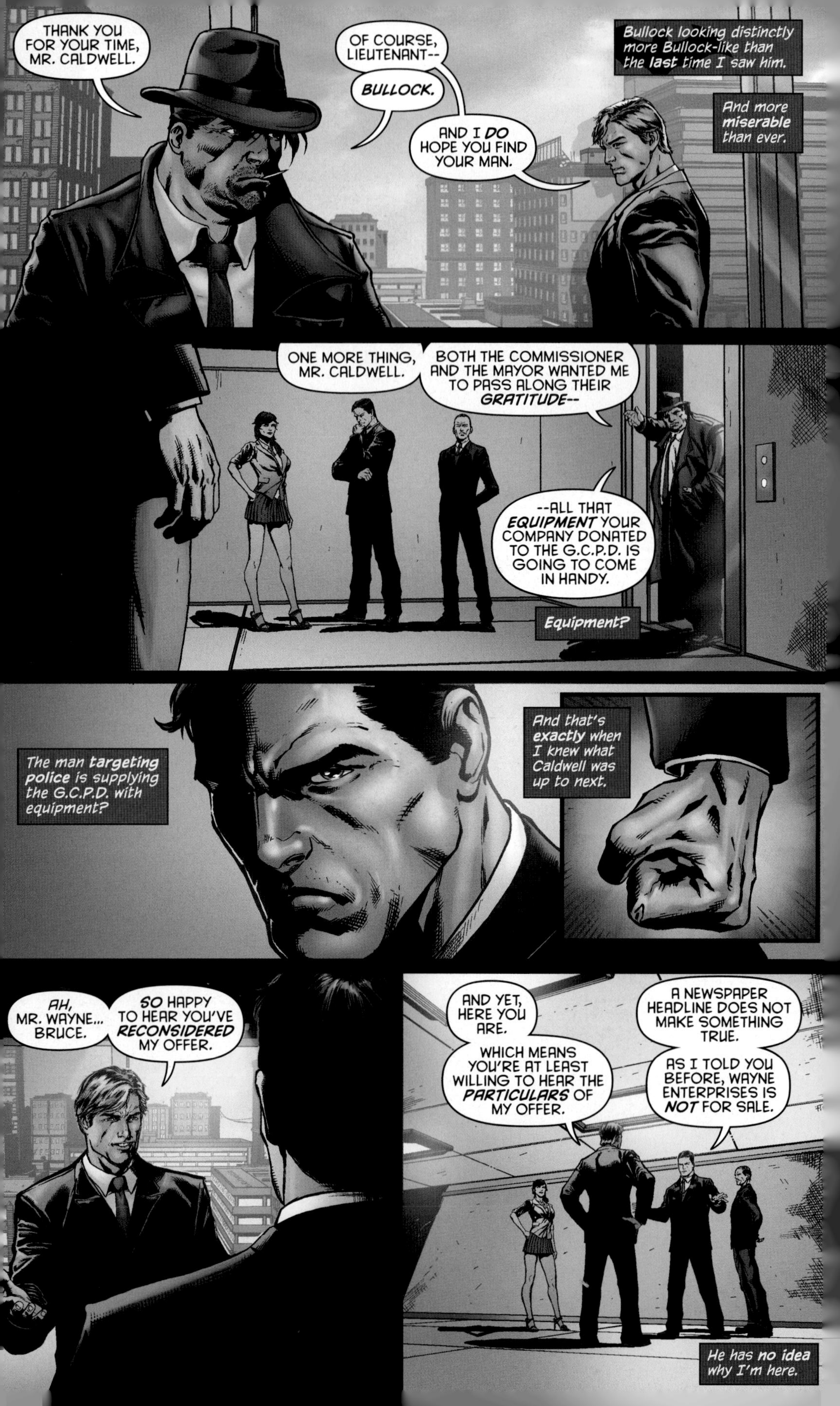
THANK YOU FOR YOUR TIME, MR. CALDWELL.
OF COURSE, LIEUTENANT--
BULLOCK.
AND I DO HOPE YOU FIND YOUR MAN.
Bullock looking distinctly more Bullock-like than the last time I saw him.
And more miserable than ever.
ONE MORE THING, MR. CALDWELL.
BOTH THE COMMISSIONER AND THE MAYOR WANTED ME TO PASS ALONG THEIR GRATITUDE--
--ALL THAT EQUIPMENT YOUR COMPANY DONATED TO THE G.C.P.D. IS GOING TO COME IN HANDY.
Equipment?
The man targeting police is supplying the G.C.P.D. with equipment?
And that's exactly when I knew what Caldwell was up to next.
AH, MR. WAYNE... BRUCE.
SO HAPPY TO HEAR YOU'VE RECONSIDERED MY OFFER.
AND YET, HERE YOU ARE.
WHICH MEANS YOU'RE AT LEAST WILLING TO HEAR THE PARTICULARS OF MY OFFER.
A NEWSPAPER HEADLINE DOES NOT MAKE SOMETHING TRUE.
AS I TOLD YOU BEFORE, WAYNE ENTERPRISES IS NOT FOR SALE.
He has no idea why I'm here.

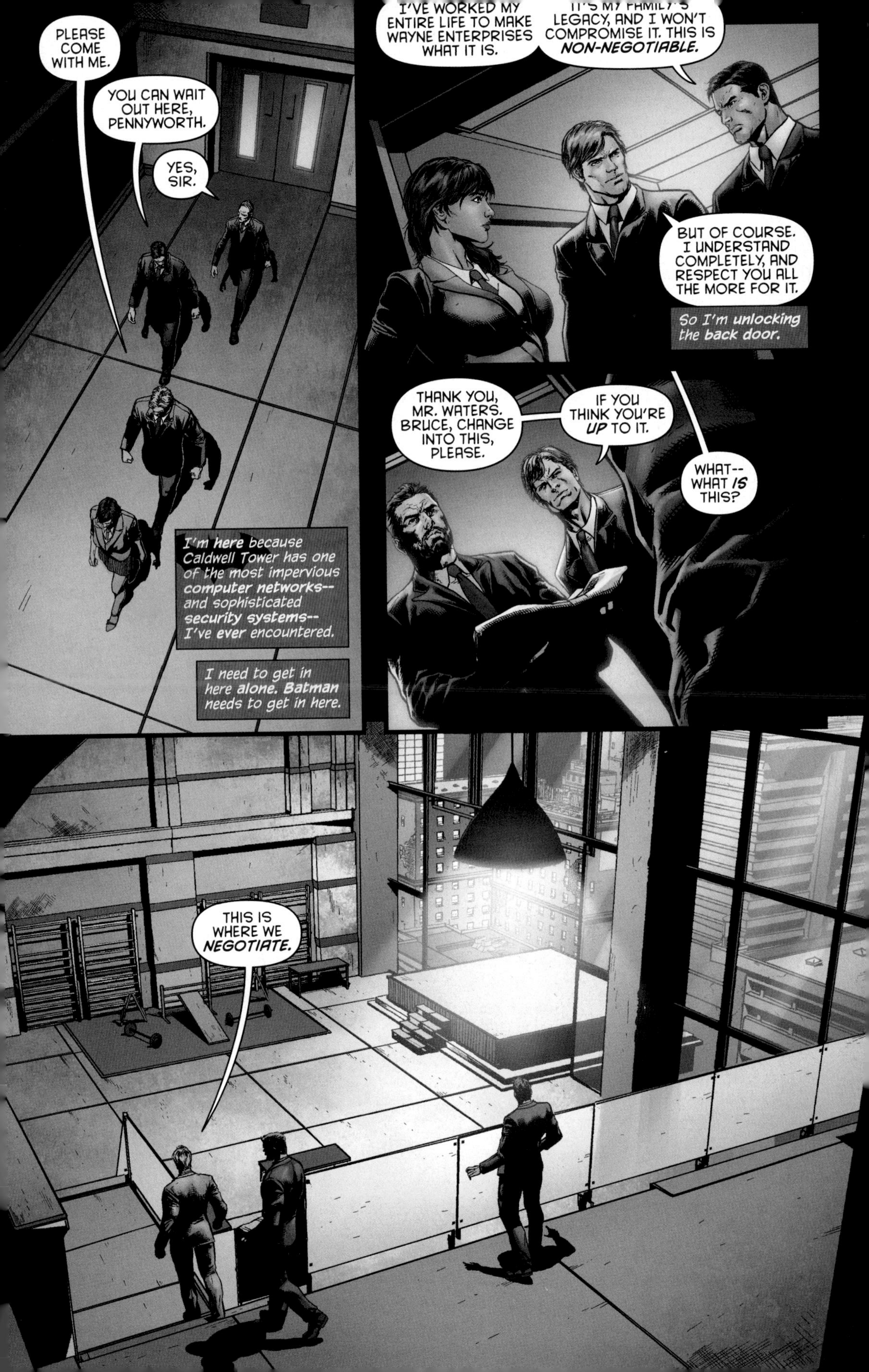
PLEASE COME WITH ME.
YOU CAN WAIT OUT HERE, PENNYWORTH.
YES, SIR.
I'm *here* because Caldwell Tower has one of the most impervious *computer networks*-- and sophisticated *security systems*-- I've *ever* encountered.
I need to get in here *alone. Batman* needs to get in here.
I'VE WORKED MY ENTIRE LIFE TO MAKE WAYNE ENTERPRISES WHAT IT IS.
IT'S MY FAMILY'S LEGACY, AND I WON'T COMPROMISE IT. THIS IS *NON-NEGOTIABLE.*
BUT OF COURSE. I UNDERSTAND COMPLETELY, AND RESPECT YOU ALL THE MORE FOR IT.
So I'm *unlocking* the *back door.*
THANK YOU, MR. WATERS. BRUCE, CHANGE INTO THIS, PLEASE.
IF YOU THINK YOU'RE *UP* TO IT.
WHAT-- WHAT *IS* THIS?
THIS IS WHERE WE *NEGOTIATE.*

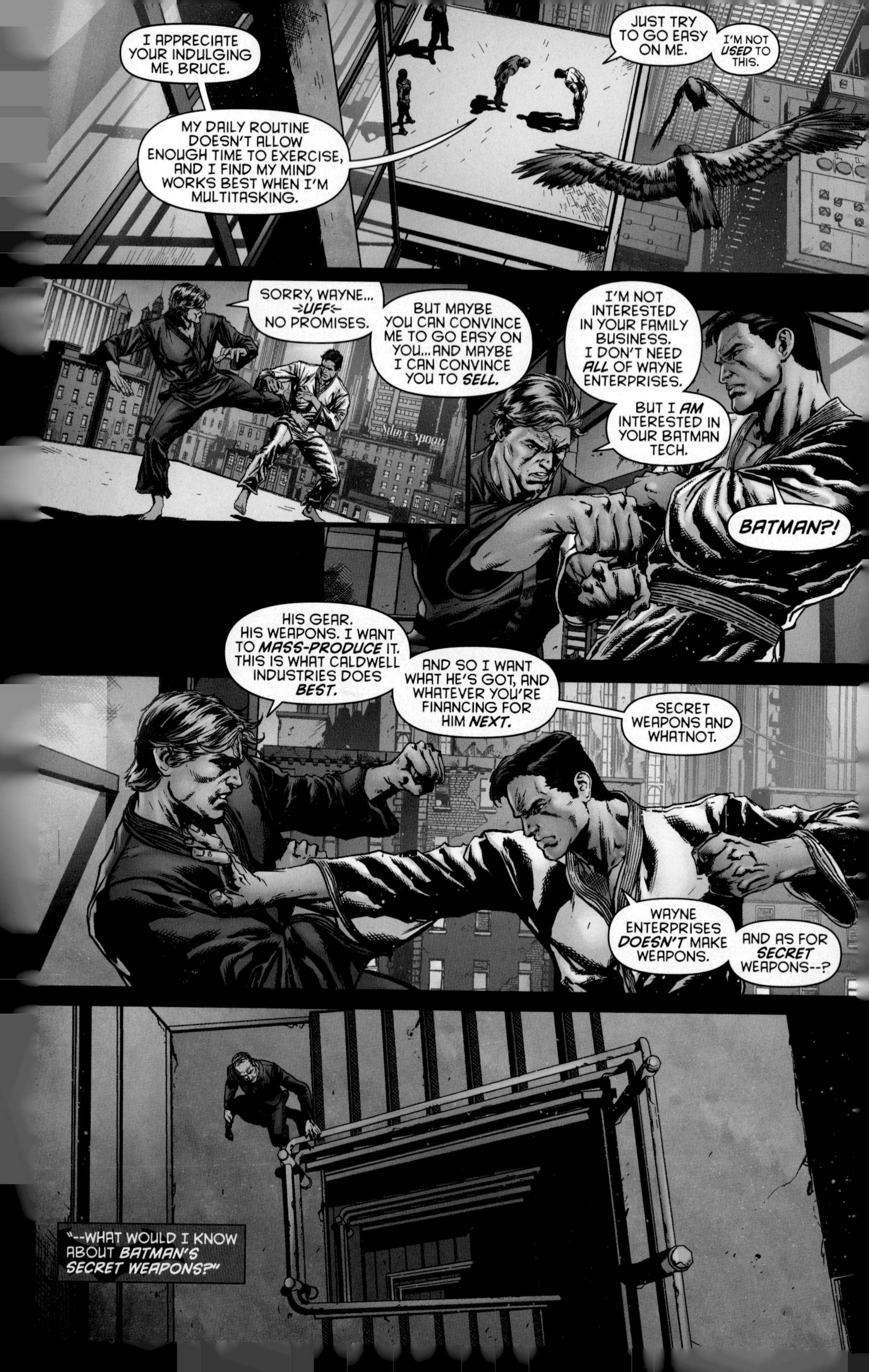
I APPRECIATE YOUR INDULGING ME, BRUCE.
MY DAILY ROUTINE DOESN'T ALLOW ENOUGH TIME TO EXERCISE, AND I FIND MY MIND WORKS BEST WHEN I'M MULTITASKING.
JUST TRY TO GO EASY ON ME.
I'M NOT *USED* TO THIS.
SORRY, WAYNE... *UFF* NO PROMISES.
BUT MAYBE YOU CAN CONVINCE ME TO GO EASY ON YOU...AND MAYBE I CAN CONVINCE YOU TO *SELL.*
Silver Spoon
I'M NOT INTERESTED IN YOUR FAMILY BUSINESS. I DON'T NEED *ALL* OF WAYNE ENTERPRISES.
BUT I *AM* INTERESTED IN YOUR BATMAN TECH.
BATMAN?!
HIS GEAR. HIS WEAPONS. I WANT TO *MASS-PRODUCE* IT. THIS IS WHAT CALDWELL INDUSTRIES DOES *BEST.*
AND SO I WANT WHAT HE'S GOT, AND WHATEVER YOU'RE FINANCING FOR HIM *NEXT.*
SECRET WEAPONS AND WHATNOT.
WAYNE ENTERPRISES *DOESN'T* MAKE WEAPONS.
AND AS FOR *SECRET* WEAPONS--?
"--WHAT WOULD I KNOW ABOUT *BATMAN'S SECRET WEAPONS?*"

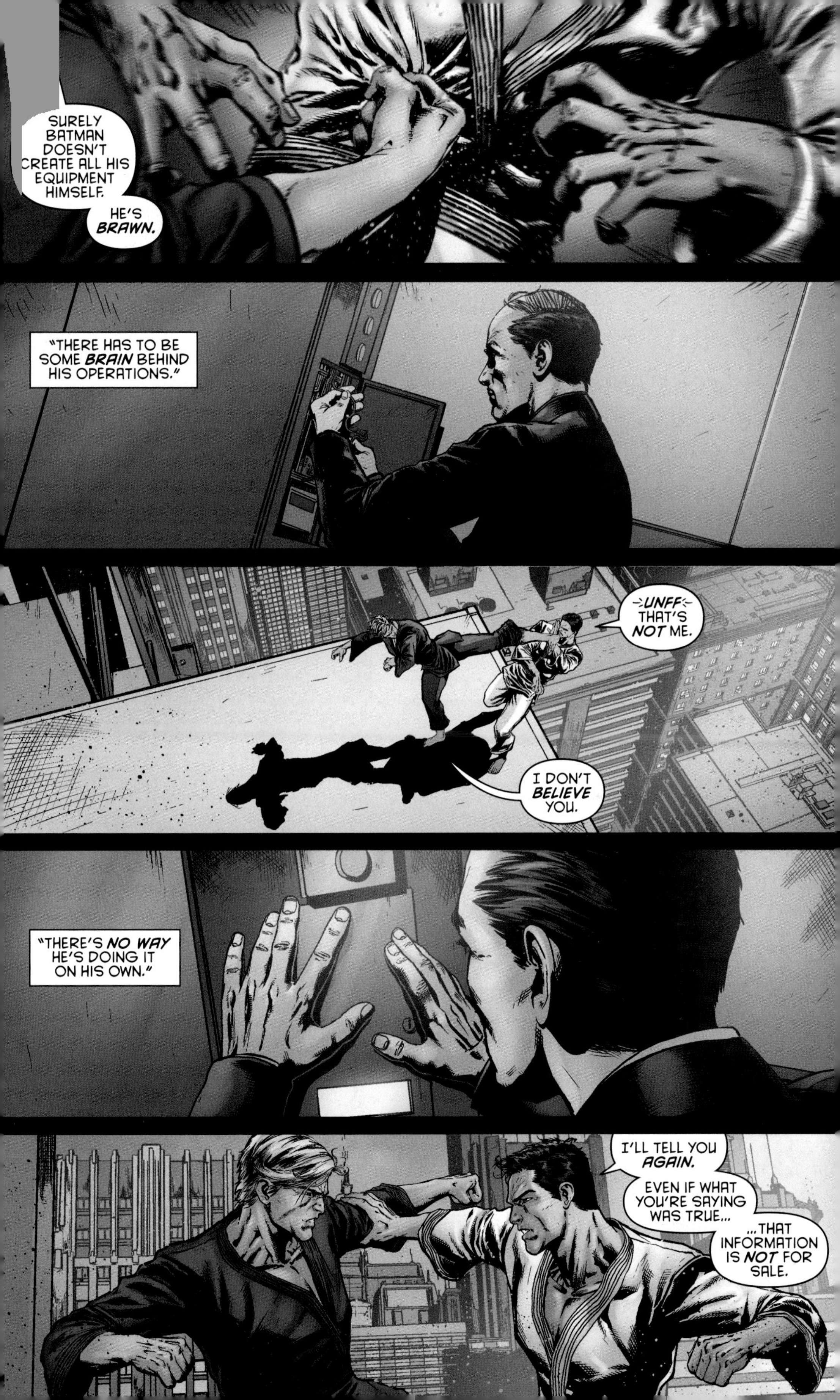
SURELY BATMAN DOESN'T CREATE ALL HIS EQUIPMENT HIMSELF.
HE'S BRAWN.
"THERE HAS TO BE SOME BRAIN BEHIND HIS OPERATIONS."
UNFF THAT'S NOT ME.
I DON'T BELIEVE YOU.
"THERE'S NO WAY HE'S DOING IT ON HIS OWN."
I'LL TELL YOU AGAIN.
EVEN IF WHAT YOU'RE SAYING WAS TRUE...
...THAT INFORMATION IS NOT FOR SALE.

AND NEITHER AM I!

If I wanted to, I could end this here.

And I *do* want to.

I want to *badly*.

But in the end, I stop.

Because this isn't the way.

NOT BAD, WAYNE. YOU GOT IN A COUPLE DECENT SHOTS THERE.

I GOT *LUCKY*.

NONSENSE. YOU'VE HAD A BIT OF TRAINING.

I THINK YOU MIGHT HAVE KNOCKED OUT ONE OF MY *CONTACTS*.

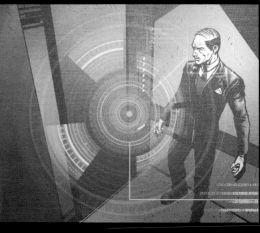

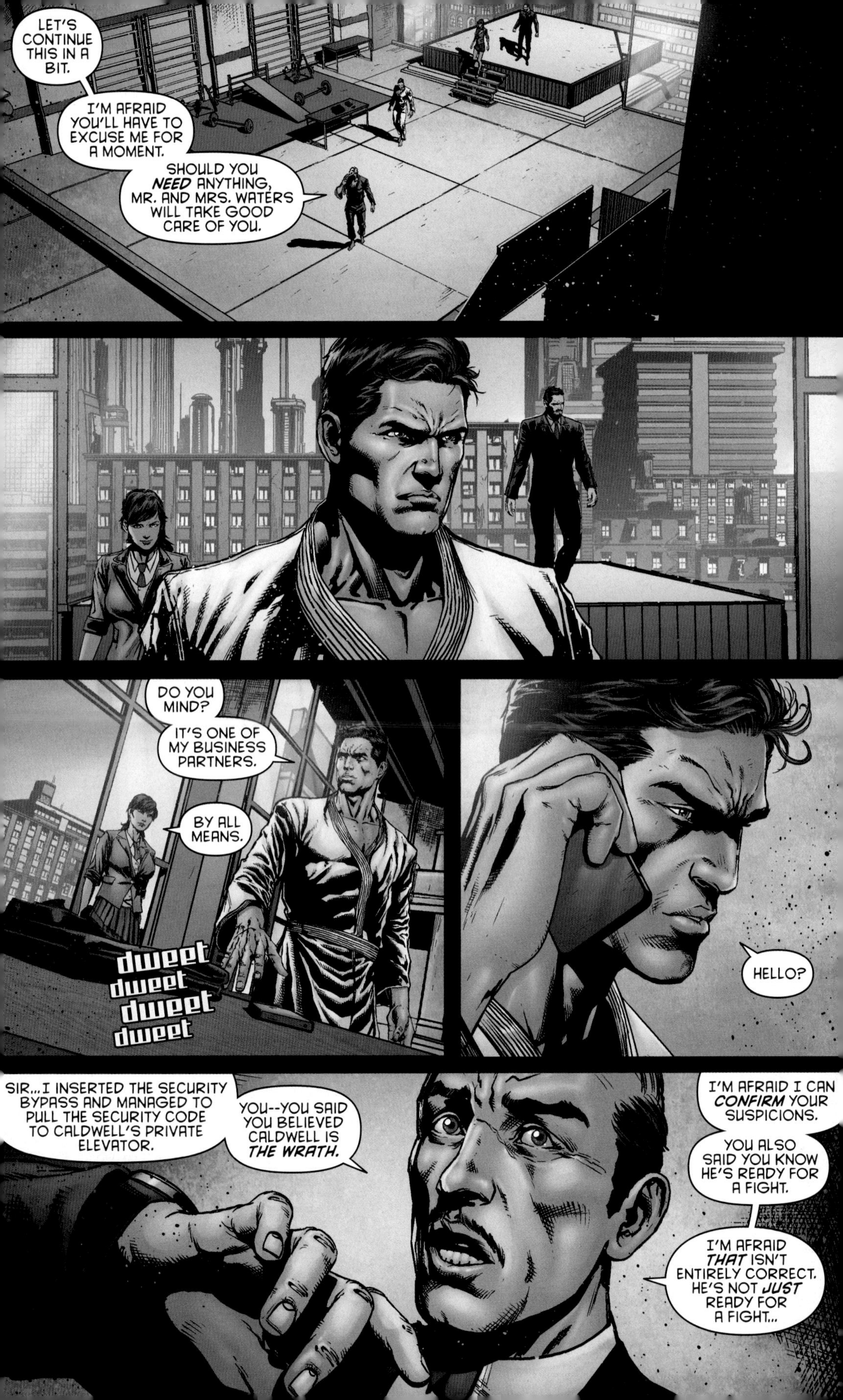
LET'S CONTINUE THIS IN A BIT.
I'M AFRAID YOU'LL HAVE TO EXCUSE ME FOR A MOMENT.
SHOULD YOU *NEED* ANYTHING, MR. AND MRS. WATERS WILL TAKE GOOD CARE OF YOU.
DO YOU MIND?
IT'S ONE OF MY BUSINESS PARTNERS.
BY ALL MEANS.
dweet dweet dweet dweet
HELLO?
SIR...I INSERTED THE SECURITY BYPASS AND MANAGED TO PULL THE SECURITY CODE TO CALDWELL'S PRIVATE ELEVATOR.
YOU--YOU SAID YOU BELIEVED CALDWELL IS *THE WRATH.*
I'M AFRAID I CAN *CONFIRM* YOUR SUSPICIONS.
YOU ALSO SAID YOU KNOW HE'S READY FOR A FIGHT.
I'M AFRAID *THAT* ISN'T ENTIRELY CORRECT. HE'S NOT *JUST* READY FOR A FIGHT...

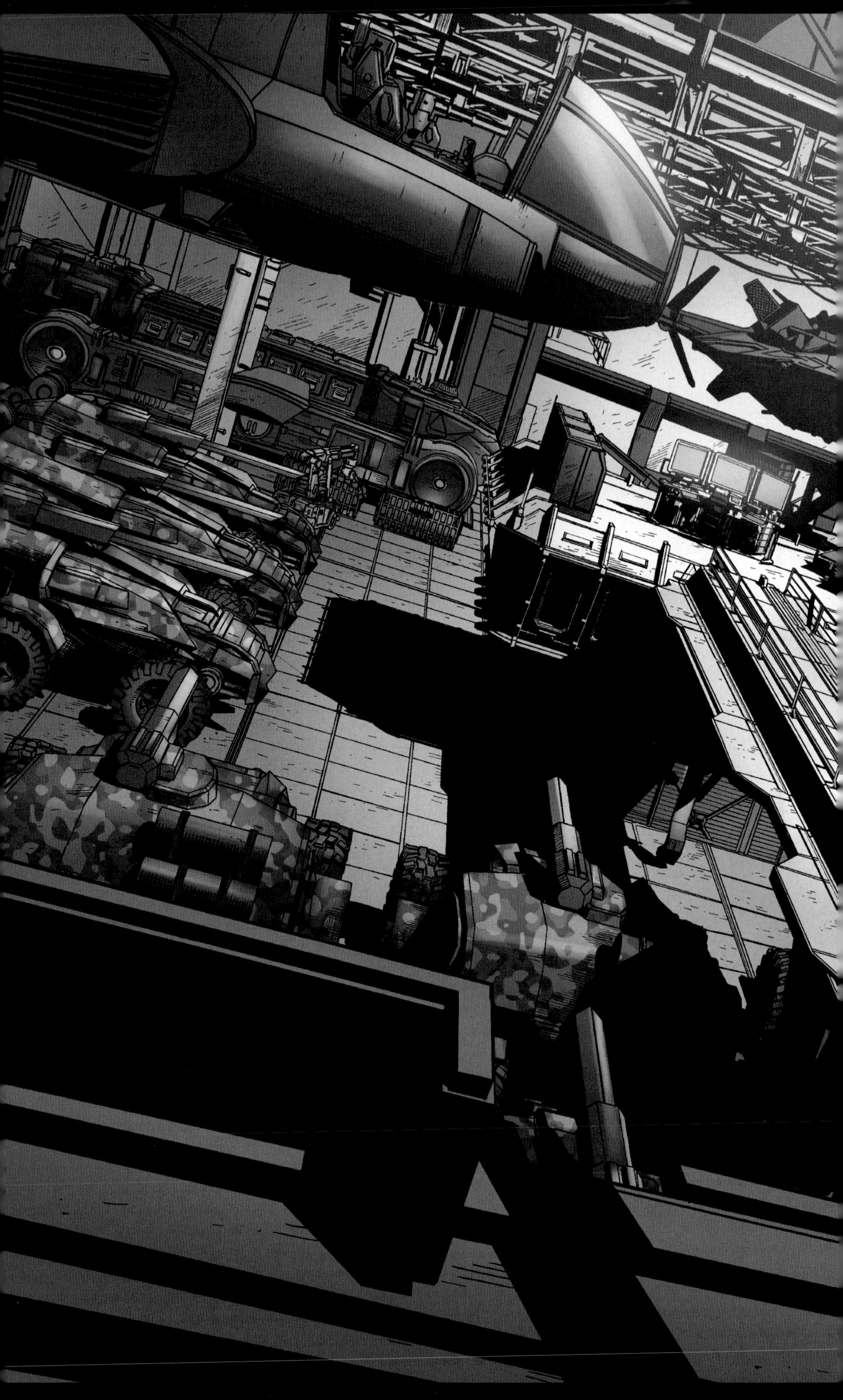

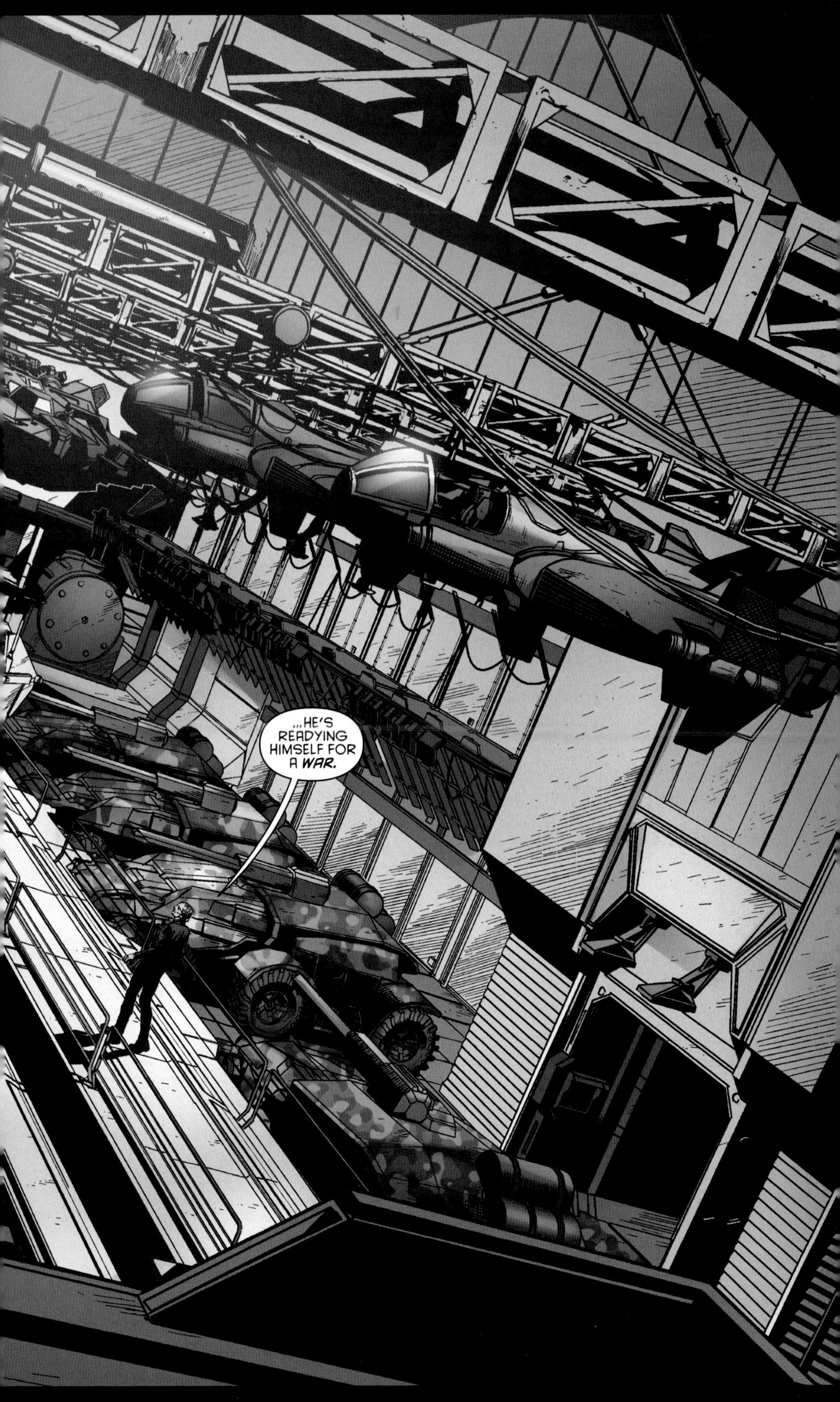
...HE'S READYING HIMSELF FOR A *WAR.*

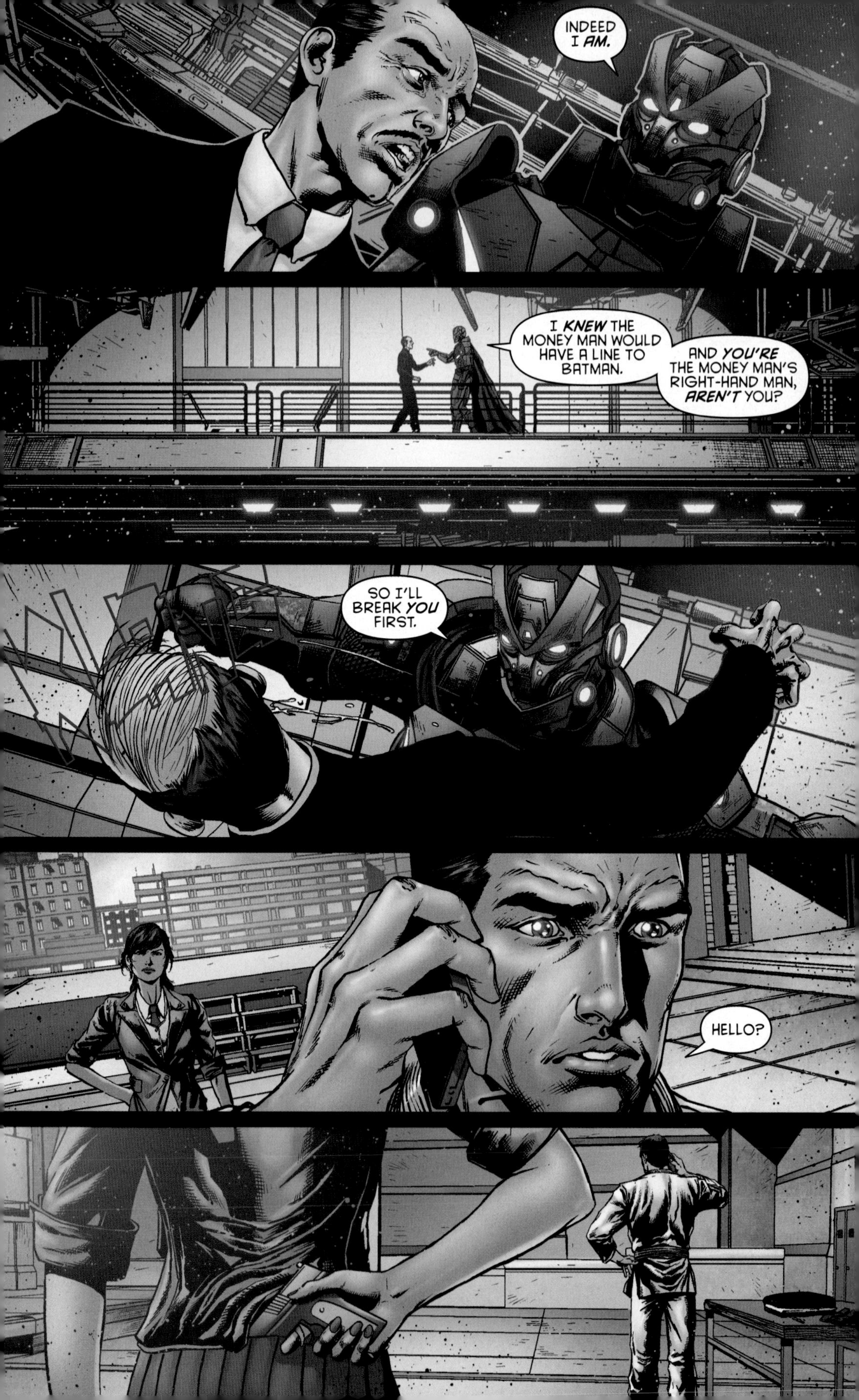
INDEED I AM.
I KNEW THE MONEY MAN WOULD HAVE A LINE TO BATMAN.
AND YOU'RE THE MONEY MAN'S RIGHT-HAND MAN, AREN'T YOU?
SO I'LL BREAK YOU FIRST.
HELLO?

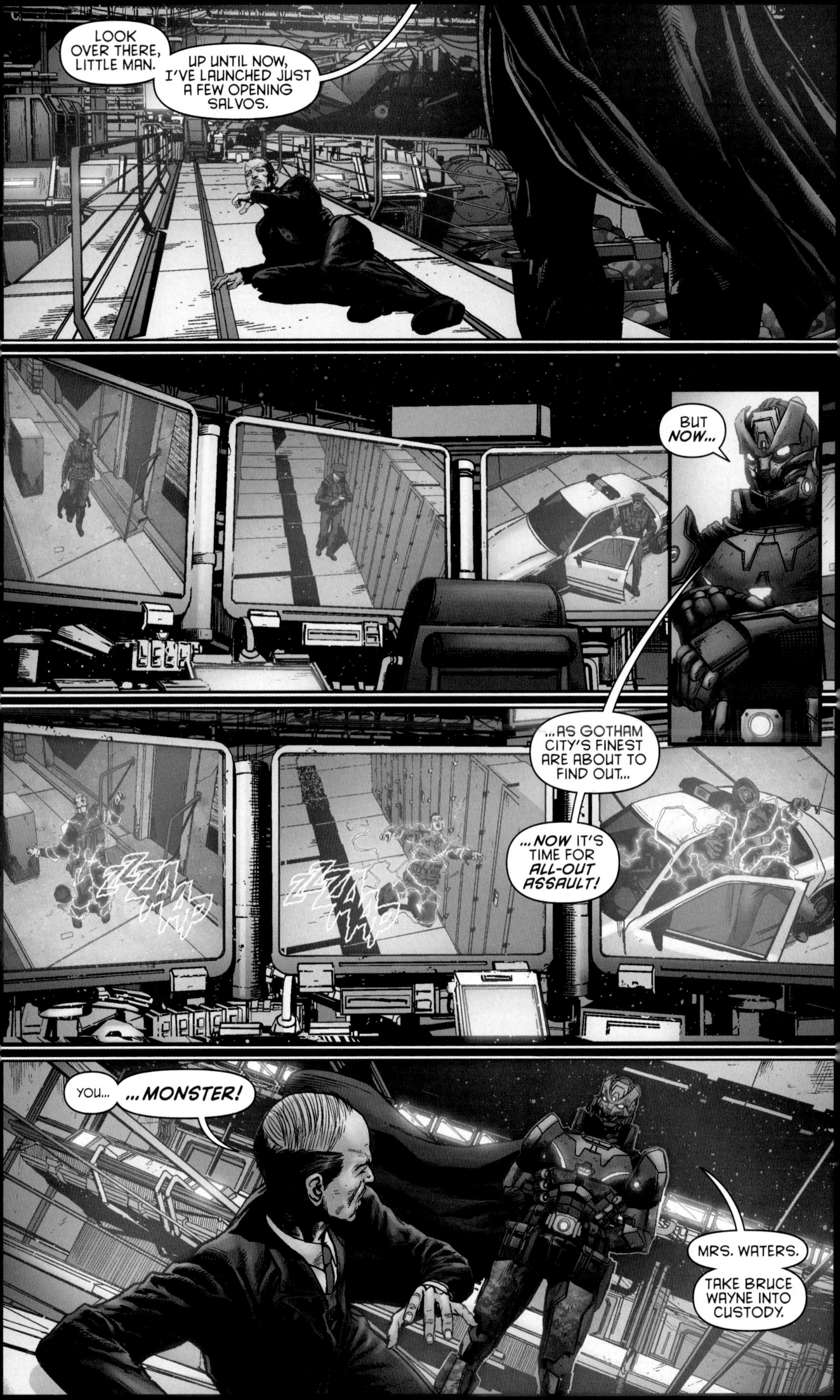
LOOK OVER THERE, LITTLE MAN.
UP UNTIL NOW, I'VE LAUNCHED JUST A FEW OPENING SALVOS.
BUT NOW...
...AS GOTHAM CITY'S FINEST ARE ABOUT TO FIND OUT...
...NOW IT'S TIME FOR ALL-OUT ASSAULT!
Z-ZAP
Z-ZAP
YOU...
...MONSTER!
MRS. WATERS.
TAKE BRUCE WAYNE INTO CUSTODY.

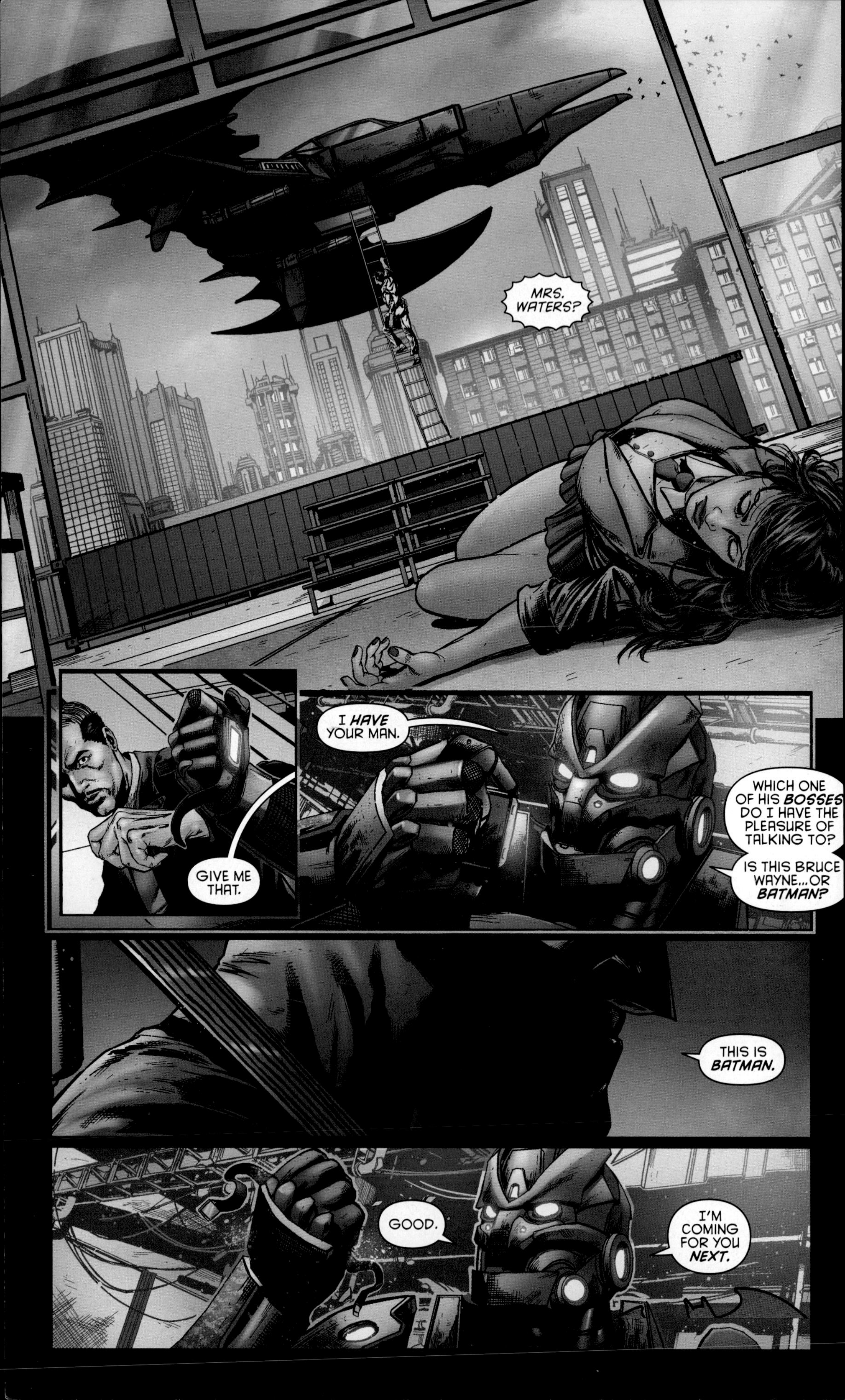
MRS. WATERS?
I HAVE YOUR MAN.
GIVE ME THAT.
WHICH ONE OF HIS BOSSES DO I HAVE THE PLEASURE OF TALKING TO?
IS THIS BRUCE WAYNE...OR BATMAN?
THIS IS BATMAN.
GOOD.
I'M COMING FOR YOU NEXT.

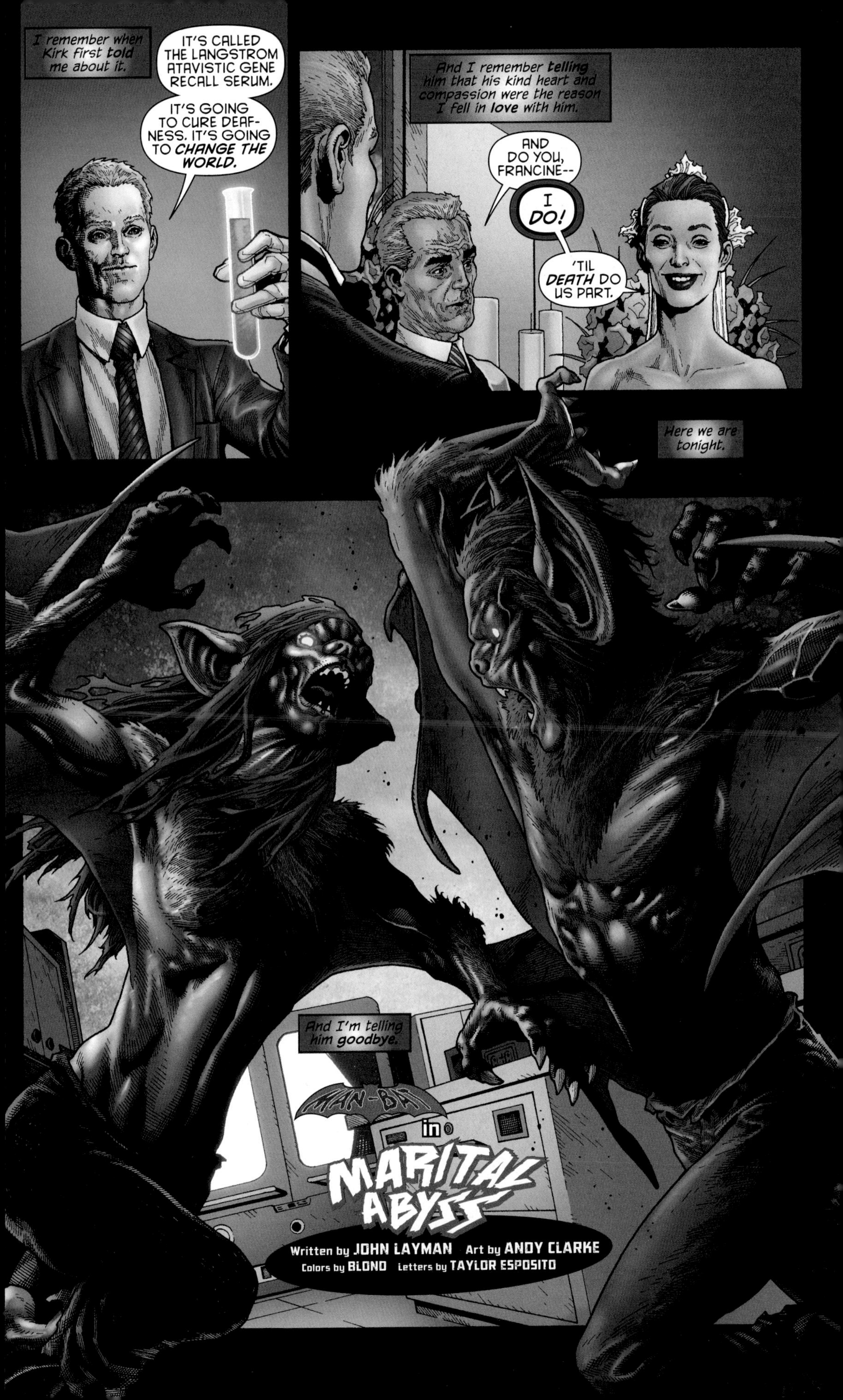
I remember when Kirk first told me about it.
IT'S CALLED THE LANGSTROM ATAVISTIC GENE RECALL SERUM.
IT'S GOING TO CURE DEAFNESS. IT'S GOING TO CHANGE THE WORLD.
And I remember telling him that his kind heart and compassion were the reason I fell in love with him.
AND DO YOU, FRANCINE--
I DO!
'TIL DEATH DO US PART.
Here we are tonight.
And I'm telling him goodbye.
MAN-BAT in MARITAL ABYSS
Written by JOHN LAYMAN Art by ANDY CLARKE
Colors by BLOND Letters by TAYLOR ESPOSITO

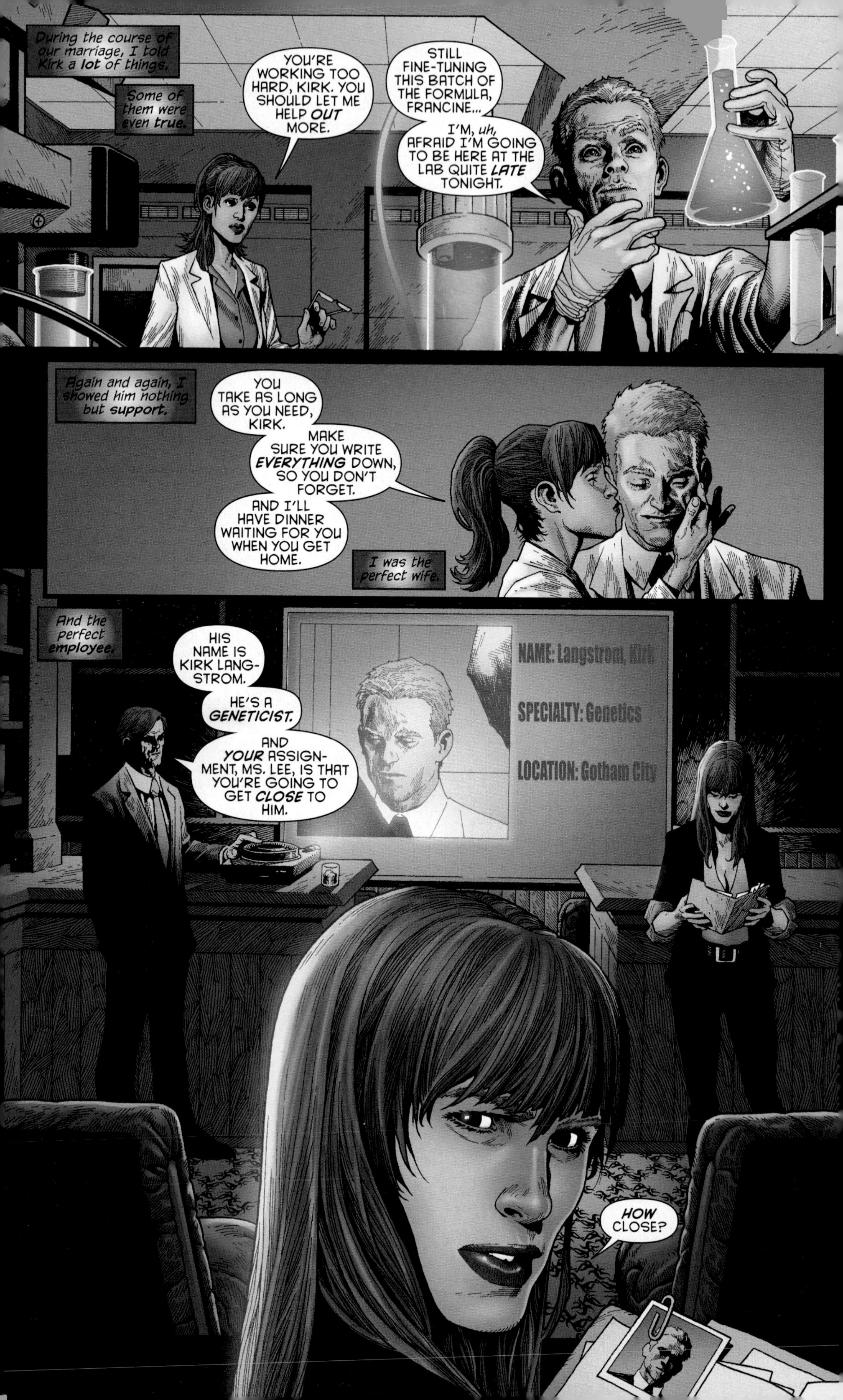

During the course of our marriage, I told Kirk a lot of things.
Some of them were even true.
YOU'RE WORKING TOO HARD, KIRK. YOU SHOULD LET ME HELP OUT MORE.
STILL FINE-TUNING THIS BATCH OF THE FORMULA, FRANCINE...
I'M, uh, AFRAID I'M GOING TO BE HERE AT THE LAB QUITE LATE TONIGHT.
Again and again, I showed him nothing but support.
YOU TAKE AS LONG AS YOU NEED, KIRK.
MAKE SURE YOU WRITE EVERYTHING DOWN, SO YOU DON'T FORGET.
AND I'LL HAVE DINNER WAITING FOR YOU WHEN YOU GET HOME.
I was the perfect wife.
And the perfect employee.
HIS NAME IS KIRK LANGSTROM.
HE'S A GENETICIST.
AND YOUR ASSIGNMENT, MS. LEE, IS THAT YOU'RE GOING TO GET CLOSE TO HIM.
NAME: Langstrom, Kirk
SPECIALTY: Genetics
LOCATION: Gotham City
HOW CLOSE?

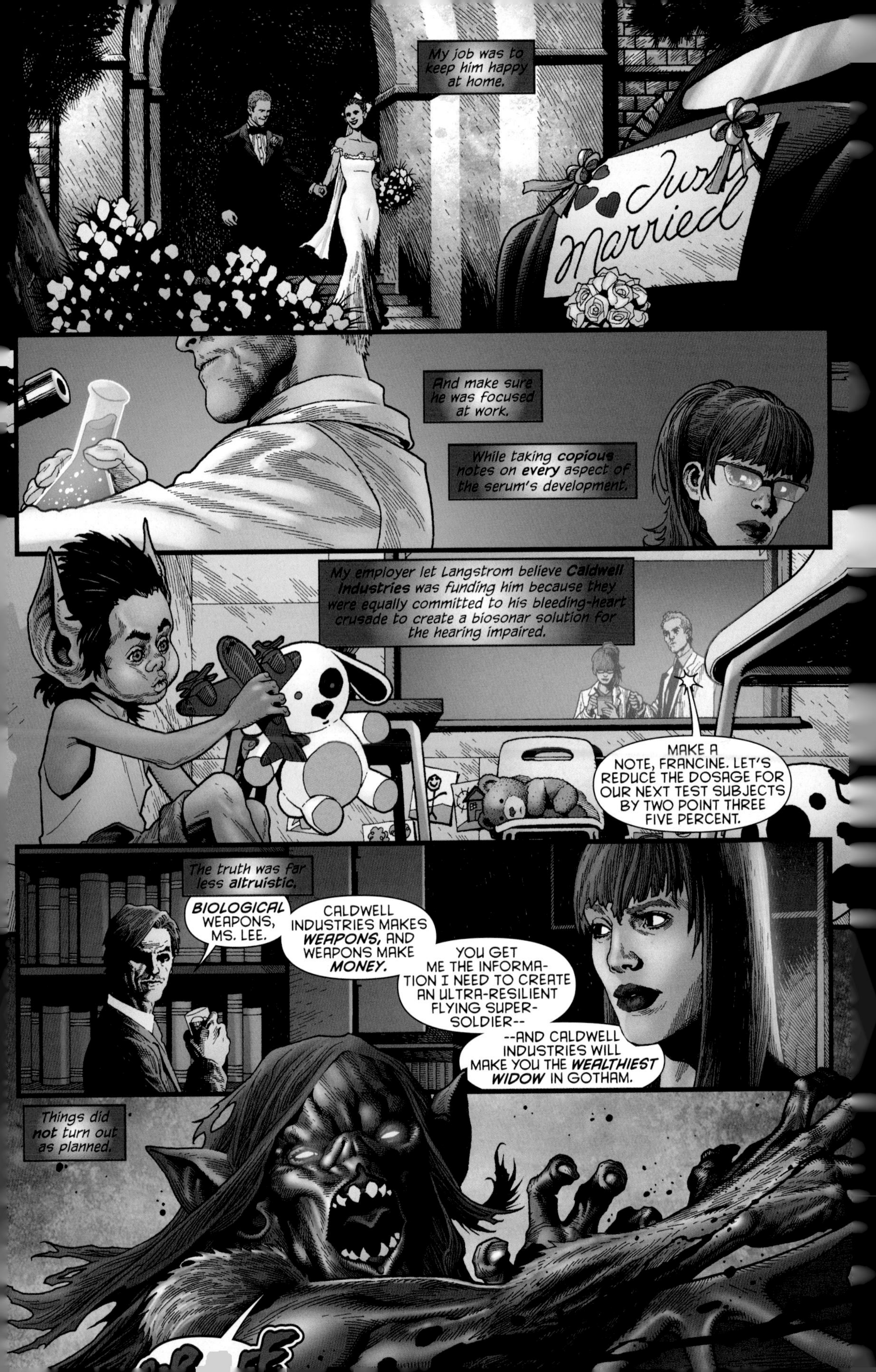

My job was to keep him happy at home.
Just Married
And make sure he was focused at work.
While taking **copious** notes on **every** aspect of the serum's development.
My employer let Langstrom believe **Caldwell Industries** was funding him because they were equally committed to his bleeding-heart crusade to create a biosonar solution for the hearing impaired.
MAKE A NOTE, FRANCINE. LET'S REDUCE THE DOSAGE FOR OUR NEXT TEST SUBJECTS BY TWO POINT THREE FIVE PERCENT.
The truth was far less **altruistic.**
BIOLOGICAL WEAPONS, MS. LEE.
CALDWELL INDUSTRIES MAKES ***WEAPONS,*** AND WEAPONS MAKE ***MONEY.***
YOU GET ME THE INFORMATION I NEED TO CREATE AN ULTRA-RESILIENT FLYING SUPER-SOLDIER--
--AND CALDWELL INDUSTRIES WILL MAKE YOU THE ***WEALTHIEST WIDOW*** IN GOTHAM.
Things did **not** turn out as planned.

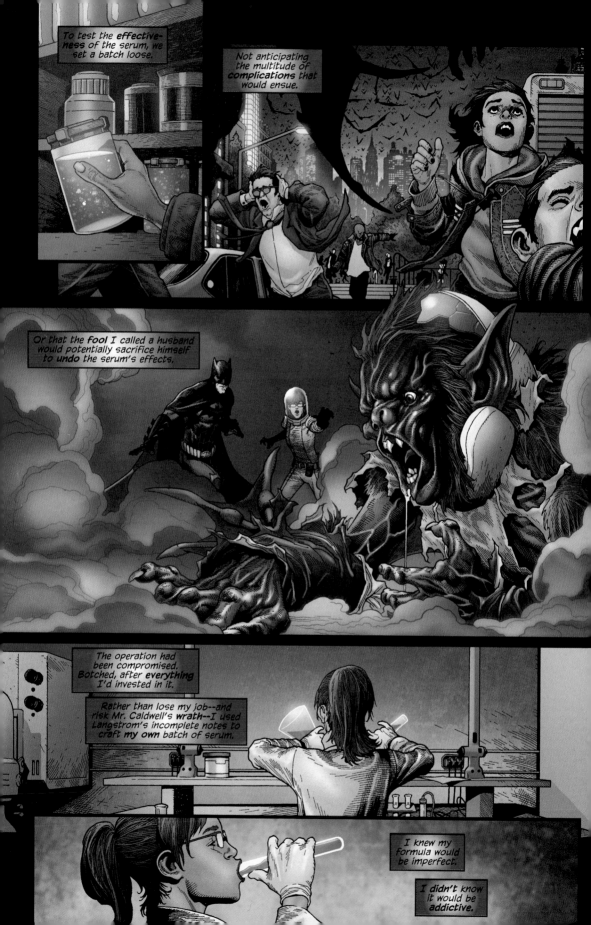

To test the **effectiveness** of the serum, we set a batch loose.

Not anticipating the multitude of **complications** that would ensue.

Or that the **fool** I called a husband would potentially sacrifice himself to **undo** the serum's effects.

The operation had been compromised. Botched, after **everything** I'd invested in it.

Rather than lose my job--and risk Mr. Caldwell's **wrath**--I used Langstrom's incomplete notes to craft my **own** batch of serum.

I knew my formula would be imperfect.

I didn't know it would be addictive.

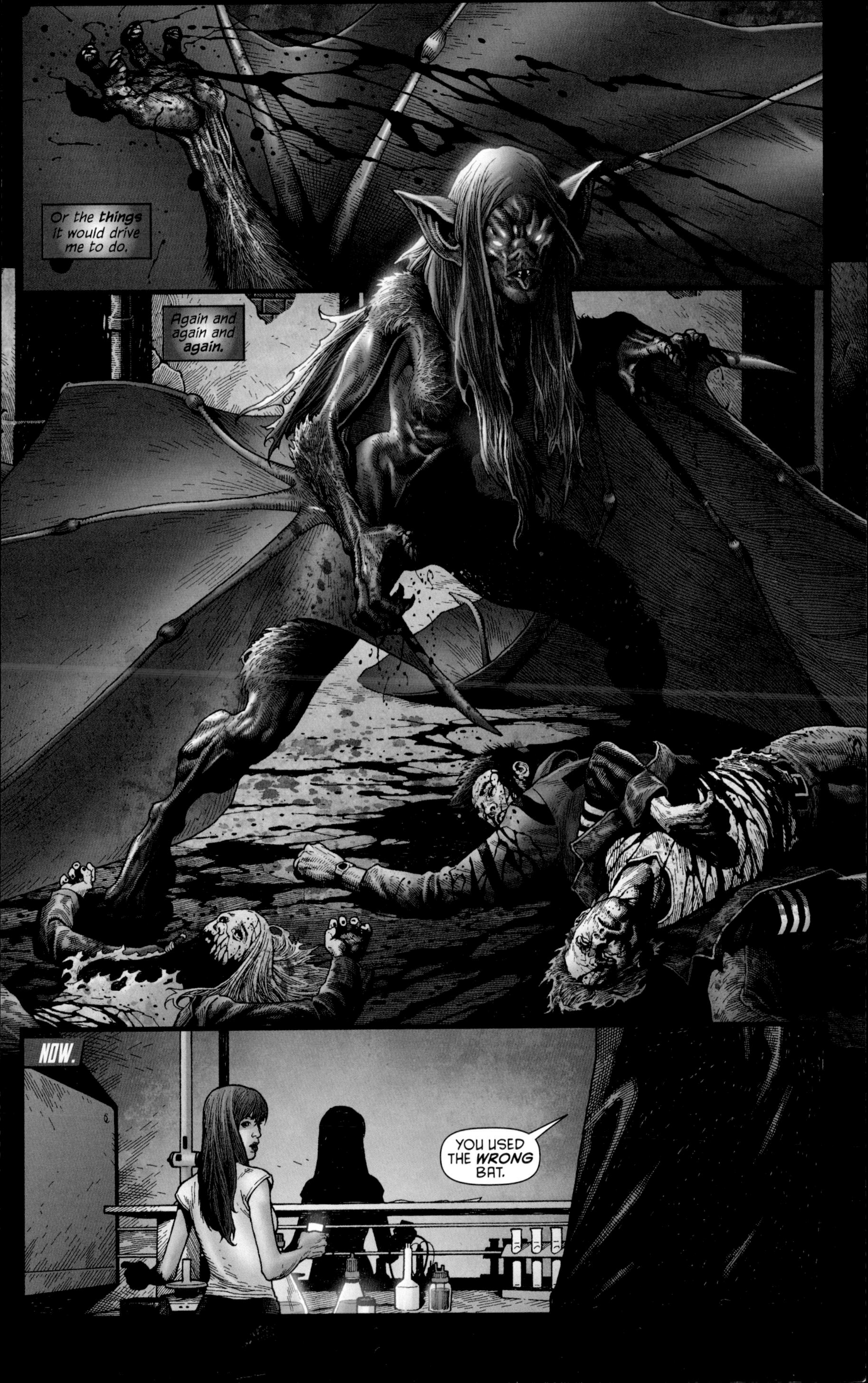

Or the **things** it would drive me to do.
Again and again and ***again.***
NOW.
YOU USED THE ***WRONG*** BAT.

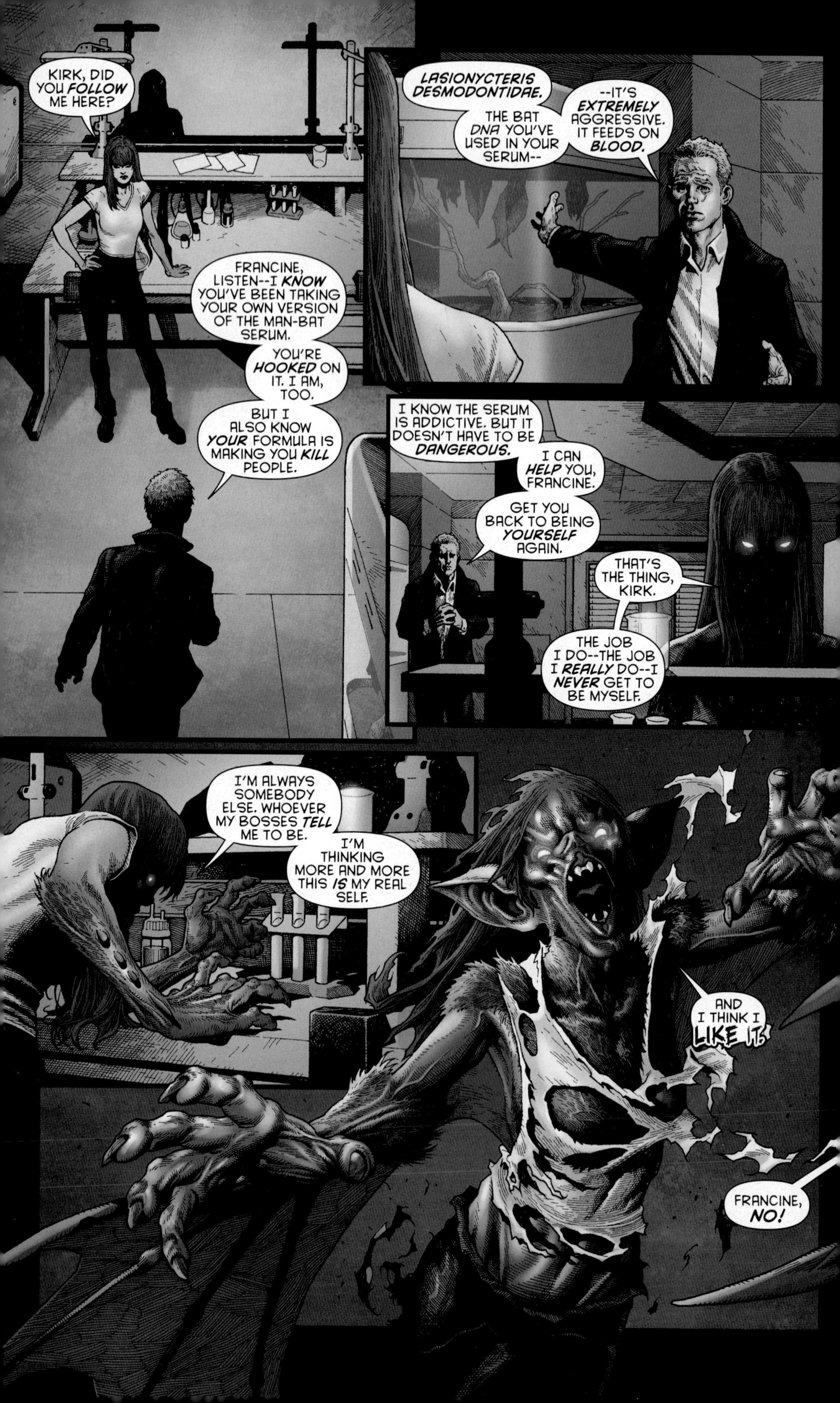
KIRK, DID YOU FOLLOW ME HERE?
LASIONYCTERIS DESMODONTIDAE.
THE BAT DNA YOU'VE USED IN YOUR SERUM--
--IT'S EXTREMELY AGGRESSIVE. IT FEEDS ON BLOOD.
FRANCINE, LISTEN--I KNOW YOU'VE BEEN TAKING YOUR OWN VERSION OF THE MAN-BAT SERUM.
YOU'RE HOOKED ON IT. I AM, TOO.
BUT I ALSO KNOW YOUR FORMULA IS MAKING YOU KILL PEOPLE.
I KNOW THE SERUM IS ADDICTIVE. BUT IT DOESN'T HAVE TO BE DANGEROUS.
I CAN HELP YOU, FRANCINE.
GET YOU BACK TO BEING YOURSELF AGAIN.
THAT'S THE THING, KIRK.
THE JOB I DO--THE JOB I REALLY DO--I NEVER GET TO BE MYSELF.
I'M ALWAYS SOMEBODY ELSE. WHOEVER MY BOSSES TELL ME TO BE.
I'M THINKING MORE AND MORE THIS IS MY REAL SELF.
AND I THINK I LIKE IT.
FRANCINE, NO!

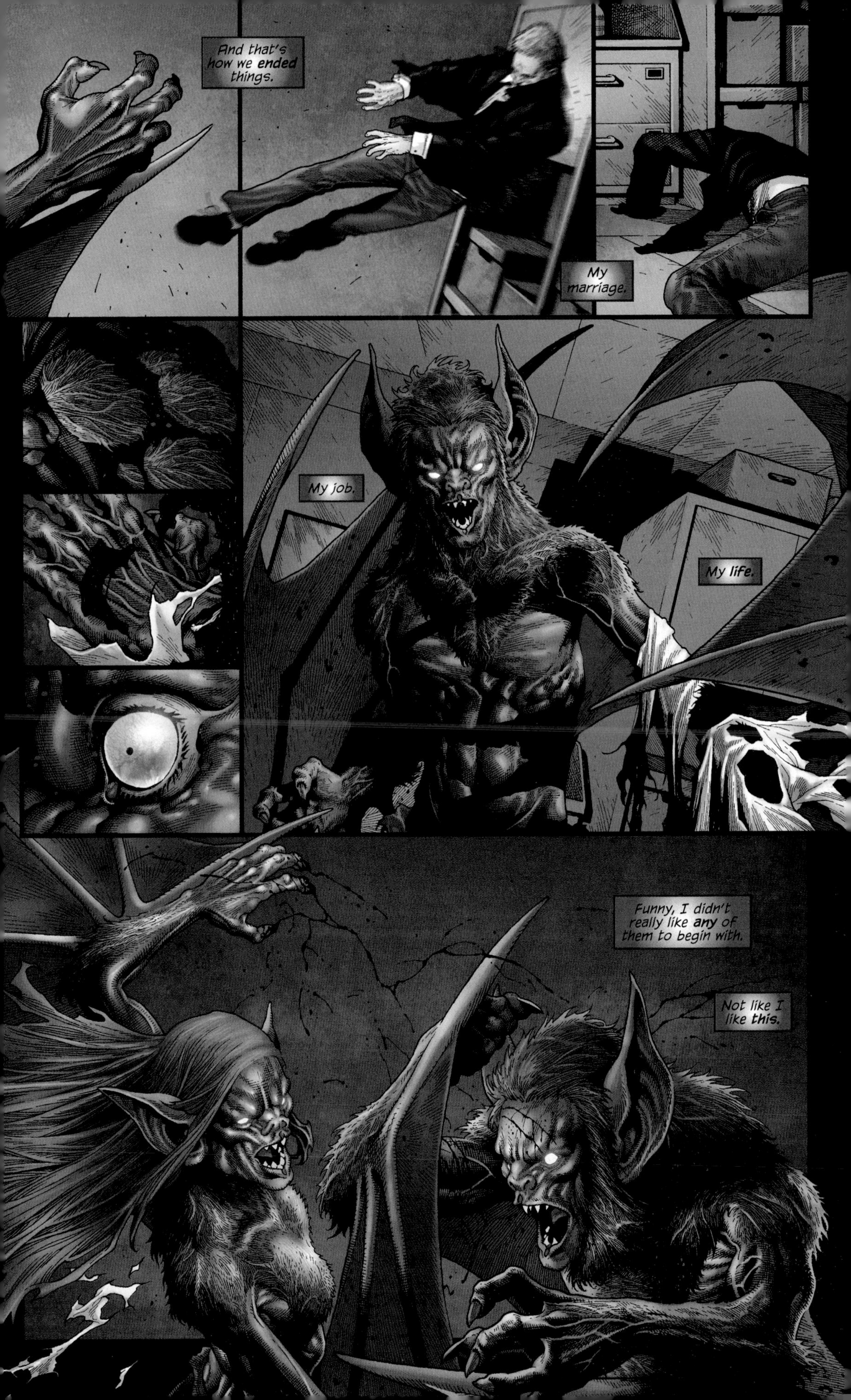
And that's how we ended things.
My marriage.
My job.
My life.
Funny, I didn't really like any of them to begin with.
Not like I like this.

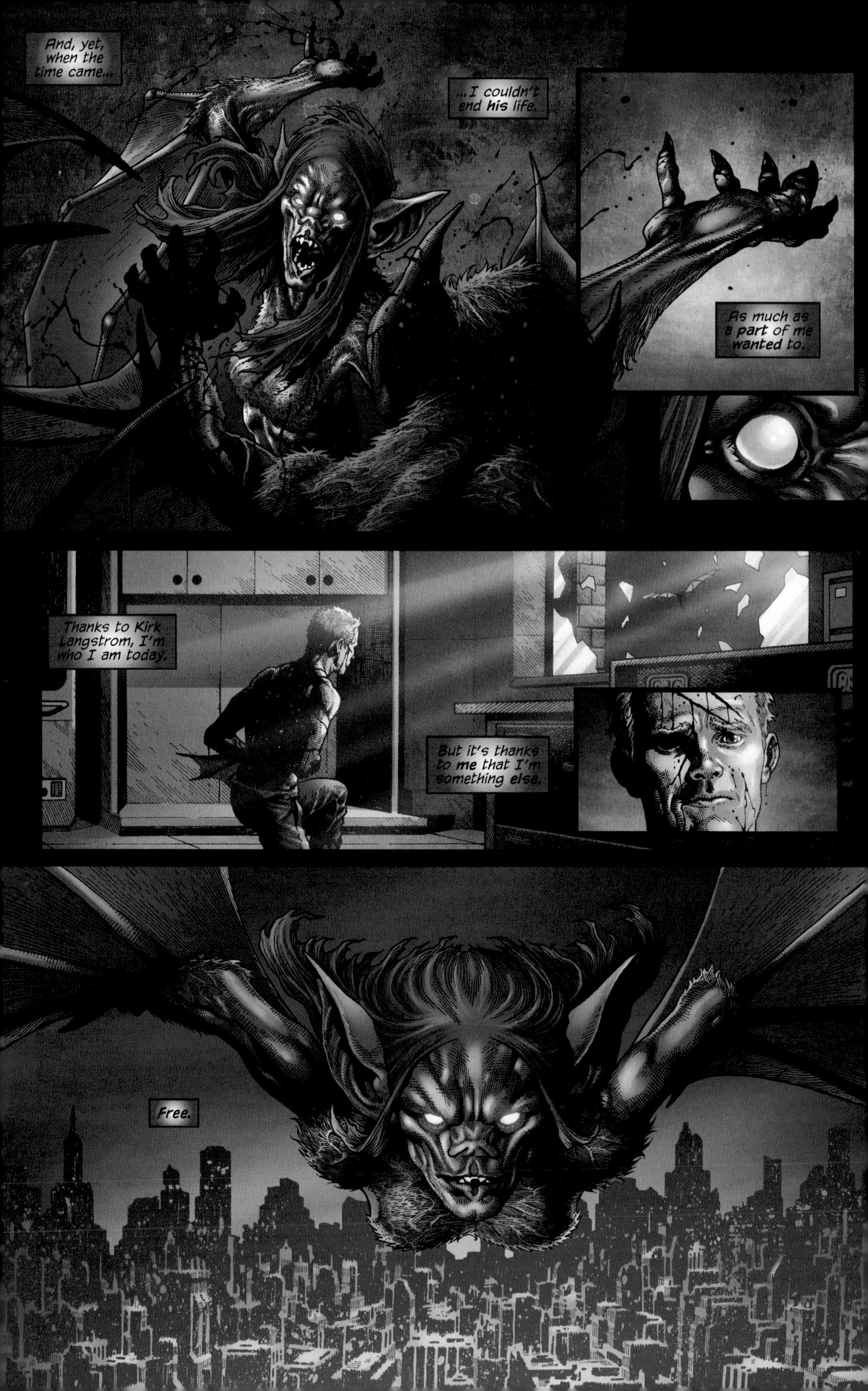
And, yet, when the time came...
...I couldn't end his life.
As much as a part of me wanted to.
Thanks to Kirk Langstrom, I'm who I am today.
But it's thanks to me that I'm something else.
Free.

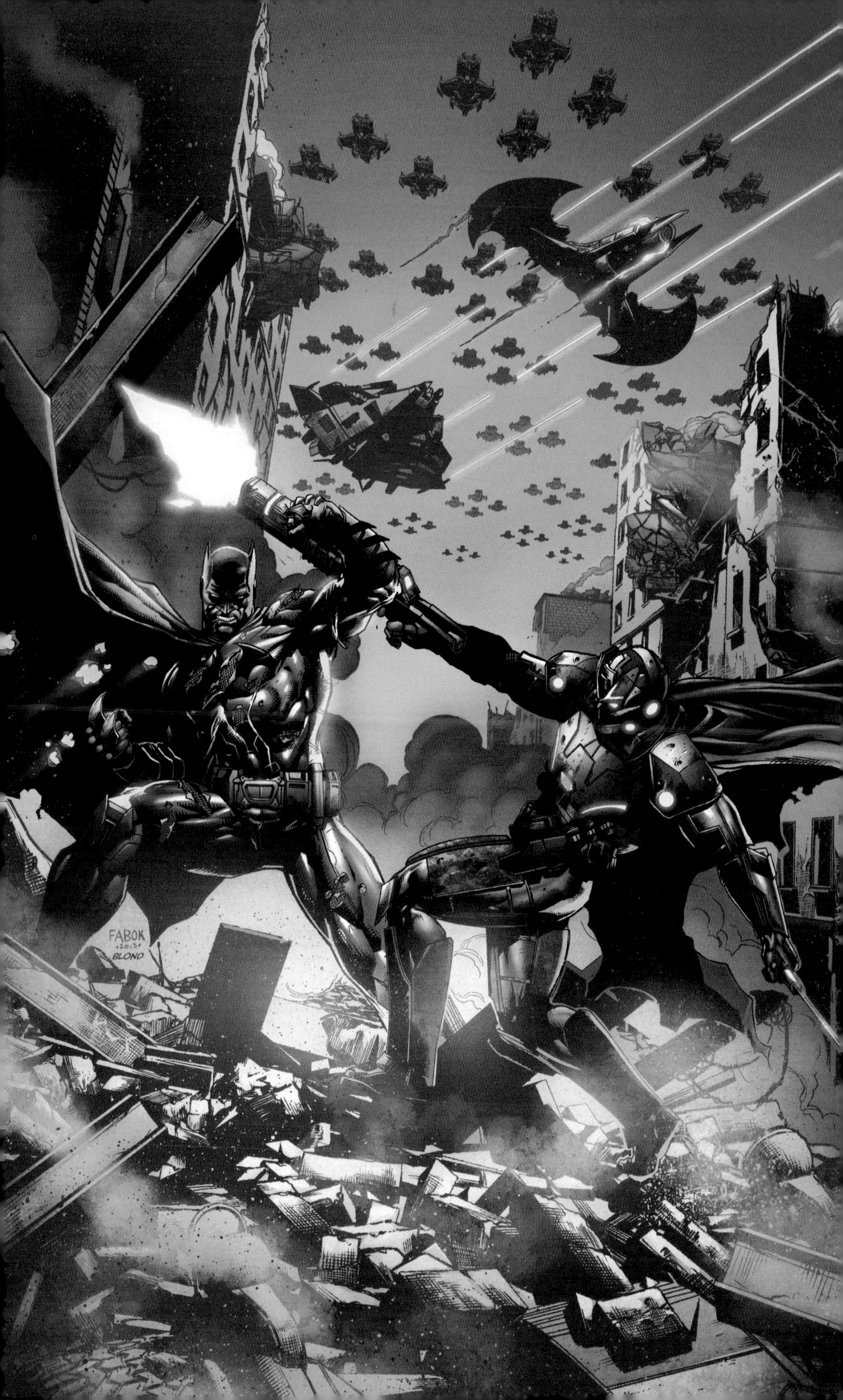
FABOK
2013
BLOND

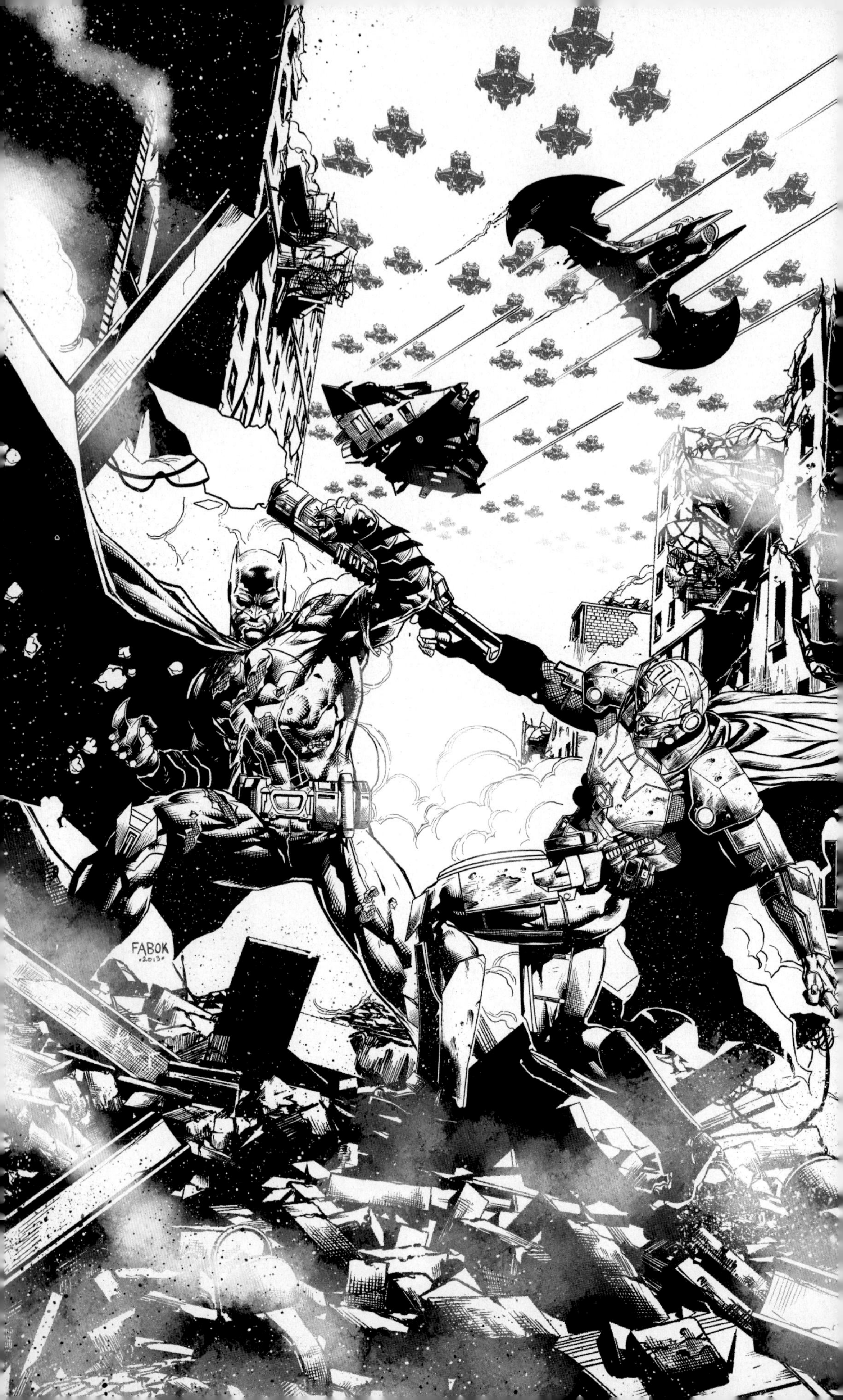
FABOK
2013

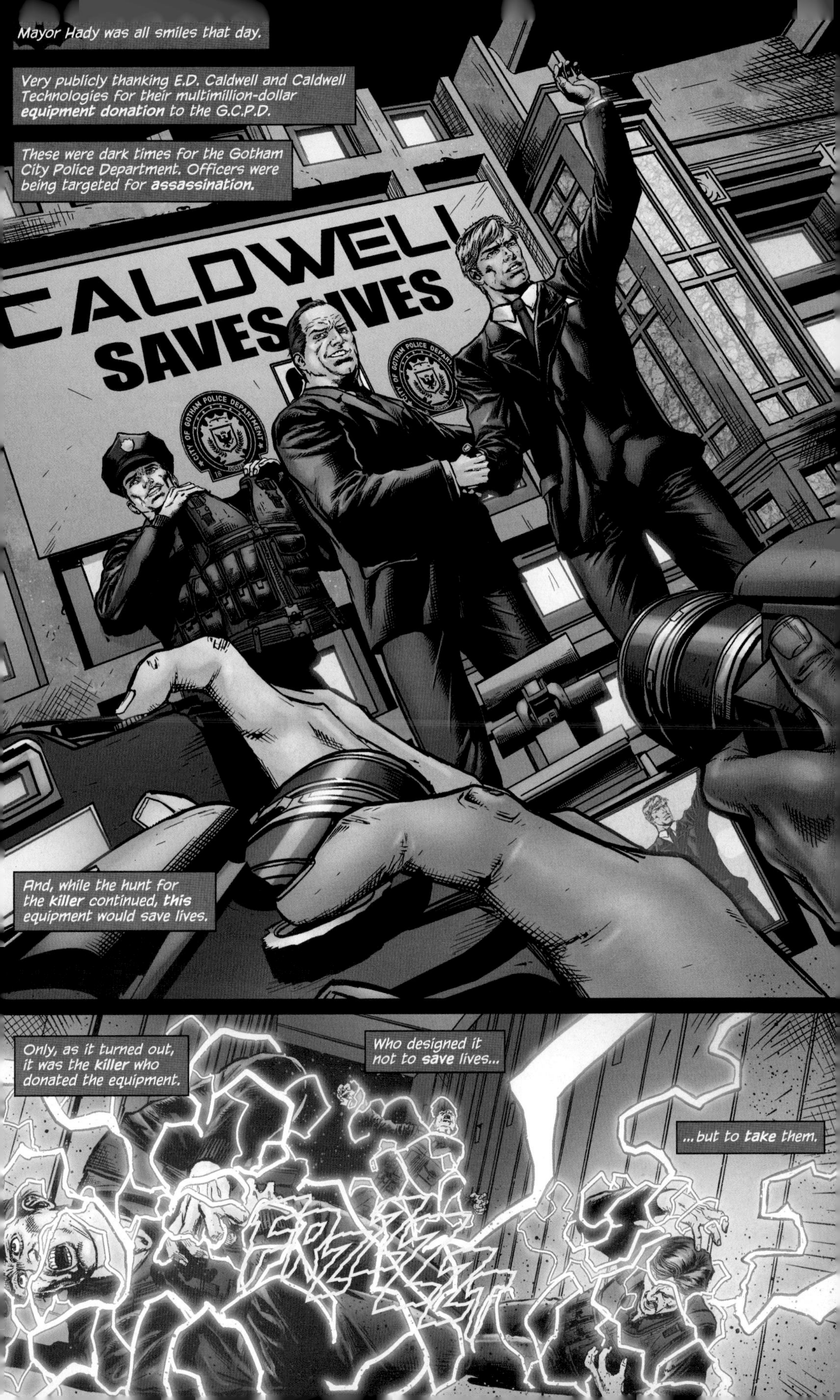
Mayor Hady was all smiles that day.
Very publicly thanking E.D. Caldwell and Caldwell Technologies for their multimillion-dollar **equipment donation** to the G.C.P.D.
These were dark times for the Gotham City Police Department. Officers were being targeted for **assassination.**
CALDWELL
SAVES LIVES
CITY OF GOTHAM POLICE DEPARTMENT
And, while the hunt for the **killer** continued, **this** equipment would save lives.
Only, as it turned out, it was the **killer** who donated the equipment.
Who designed it not to **save** lives...
...but to **take** them.

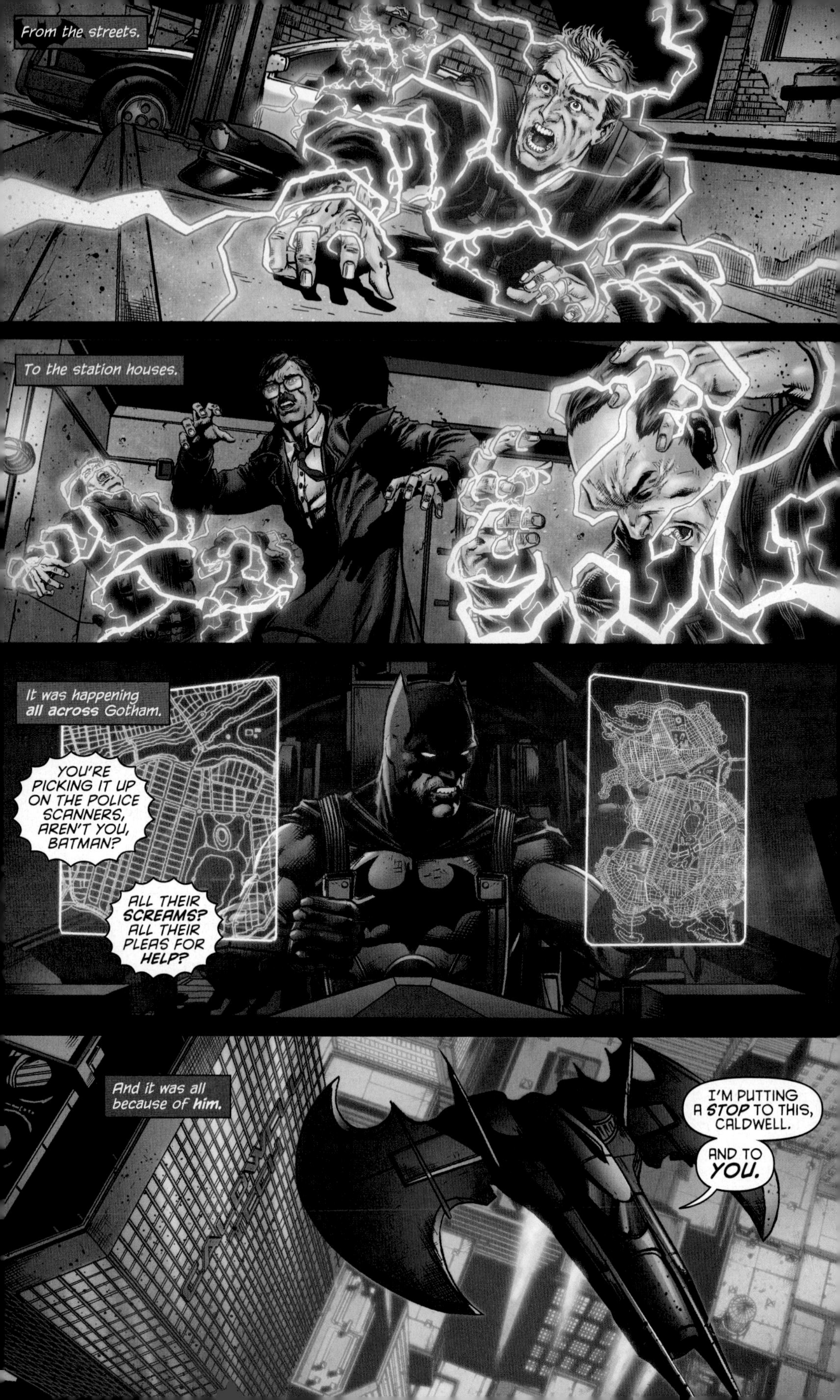
From the streets.
To the station houses.
It was happening all across Gotham.
YOU'RE PICKING IT UP ON THE POLICE SCANNERS, AREN'T YOU, BATMAN?
ALL THEIR SCREAMS? ALL THEIR PLEAS FOR HELP?
And it was all because of him.
I'M PUTTING A STOP TO THIS, CALDWELL.
AND TO YOU.

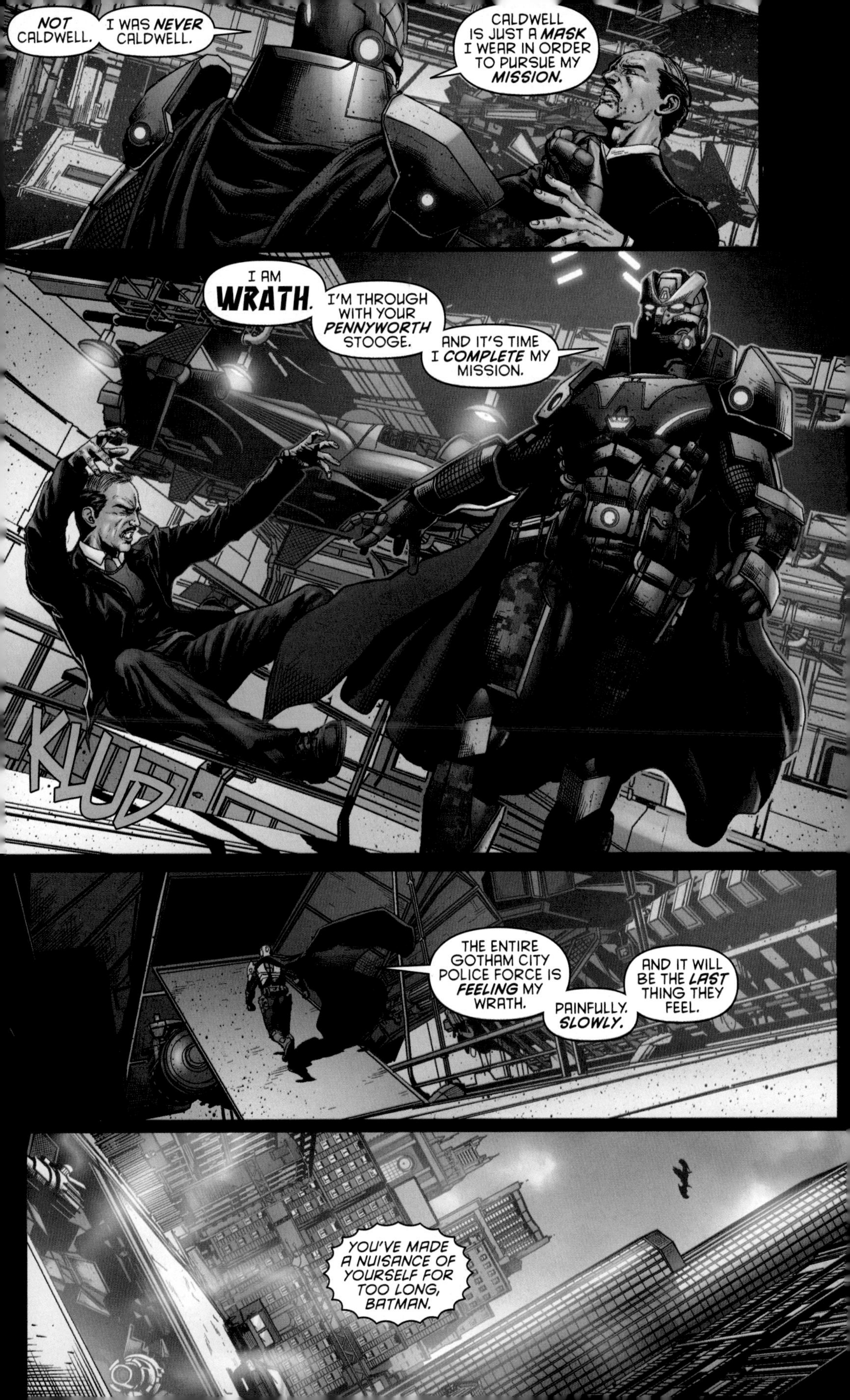
NOT CALDWELL.
I WAS NEVER CALDWELL.
CALDWELL IS JUST A MASK I WEAR IN ORDER TO PURSUE MY MISSION.
I AM WRATH.
I'M THROUGH WITH YOUR PENNYWORTH STOOGE.
AND IT'S TIME I COMPLETE MY MISSION.
KLUD
THE ENTIRE GOTHAM CITY POLICE FORCE IS FEELING MY WRATH.
PAINFULLY. SLOWLY.
AND IT WILL BE THE LAST THING THEY FEEL.
YOU'VE MADE A NUISANCE OF YOURSELF FOR TOO LONG, BATMAN.

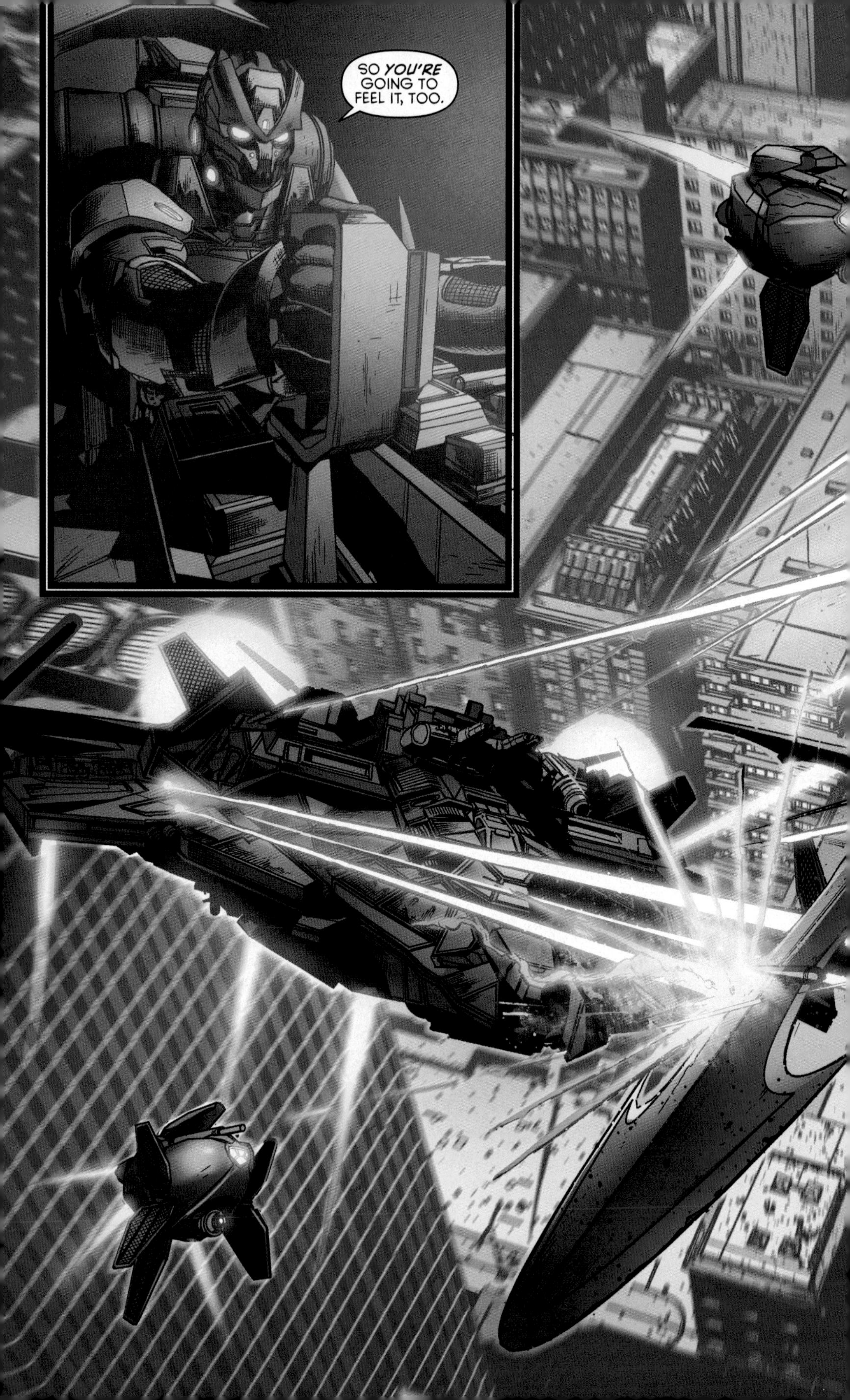
SO *YOU'RE* GOING TO FEEL IT, TOO.

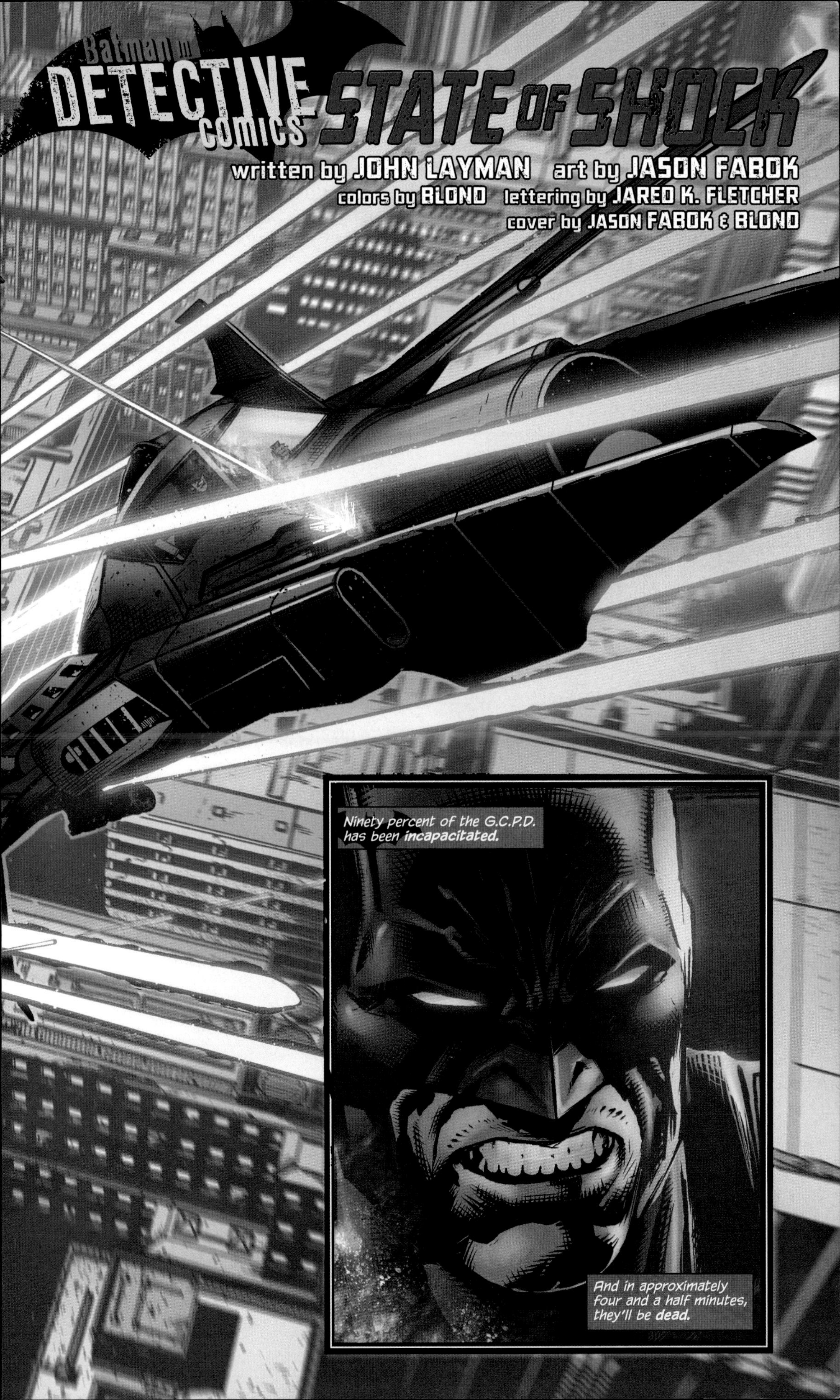
Batman in
DETECTIVE comics
STATE OF SHOCK
written by JOHN LAYMAN art by JASON FABOK
colors by BLOND lettering by JARED K. FLETCHER
cover by JASON FABOK & BLOND
Ninety percent of the G.C.P.D. has been incapacitated.
And in approximately four and a half minutes, they'll be dead.

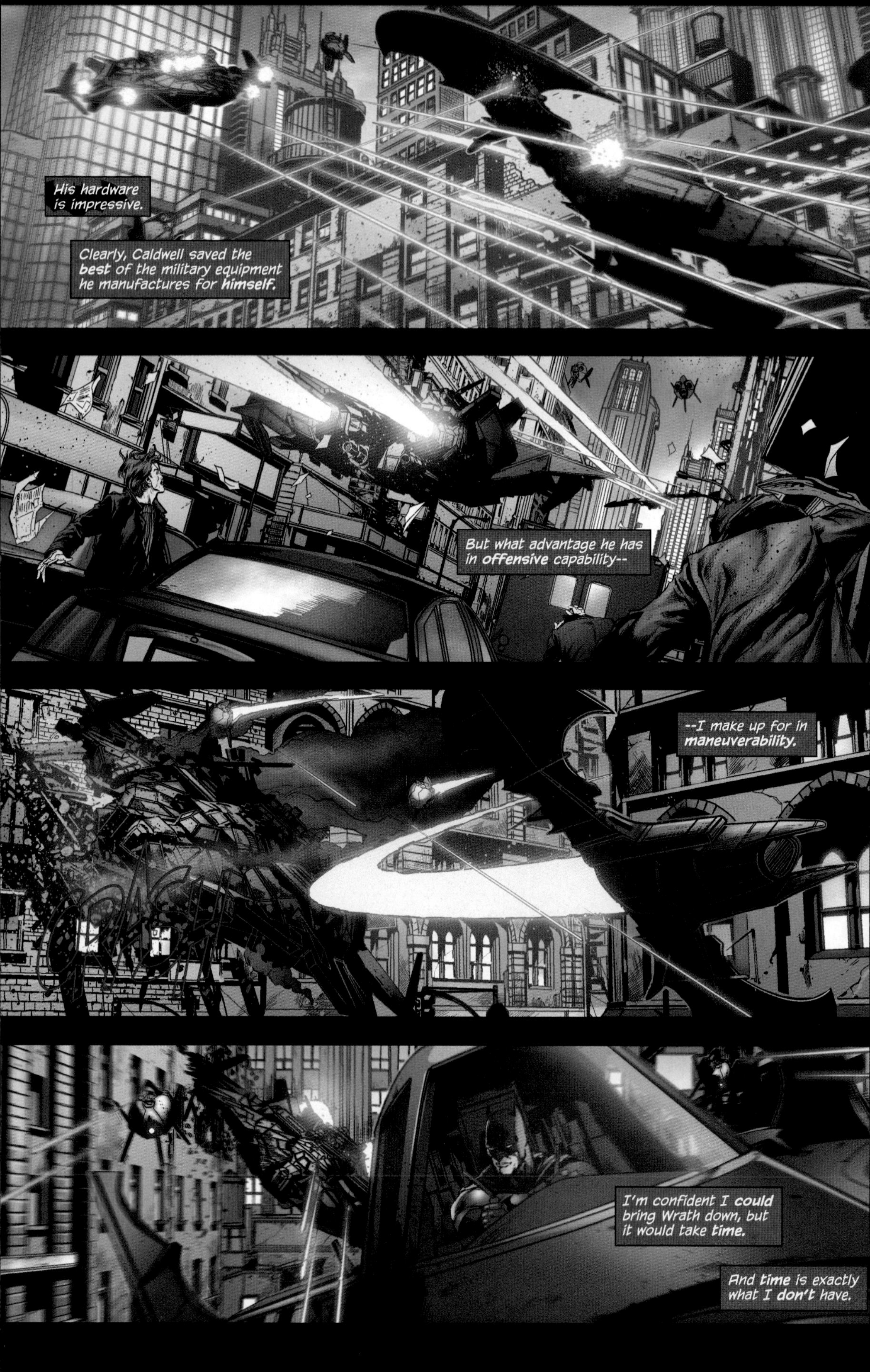
His hardware is impressive.
Clearly, Caldwell saved the best of the military equipment he manufactures for himself.
But what advantage he has in offensive capability--
--I make up for in maneuverability.
I'm confident I could bring Wrath down, but it would take time.
And time is exactly what I don't have.

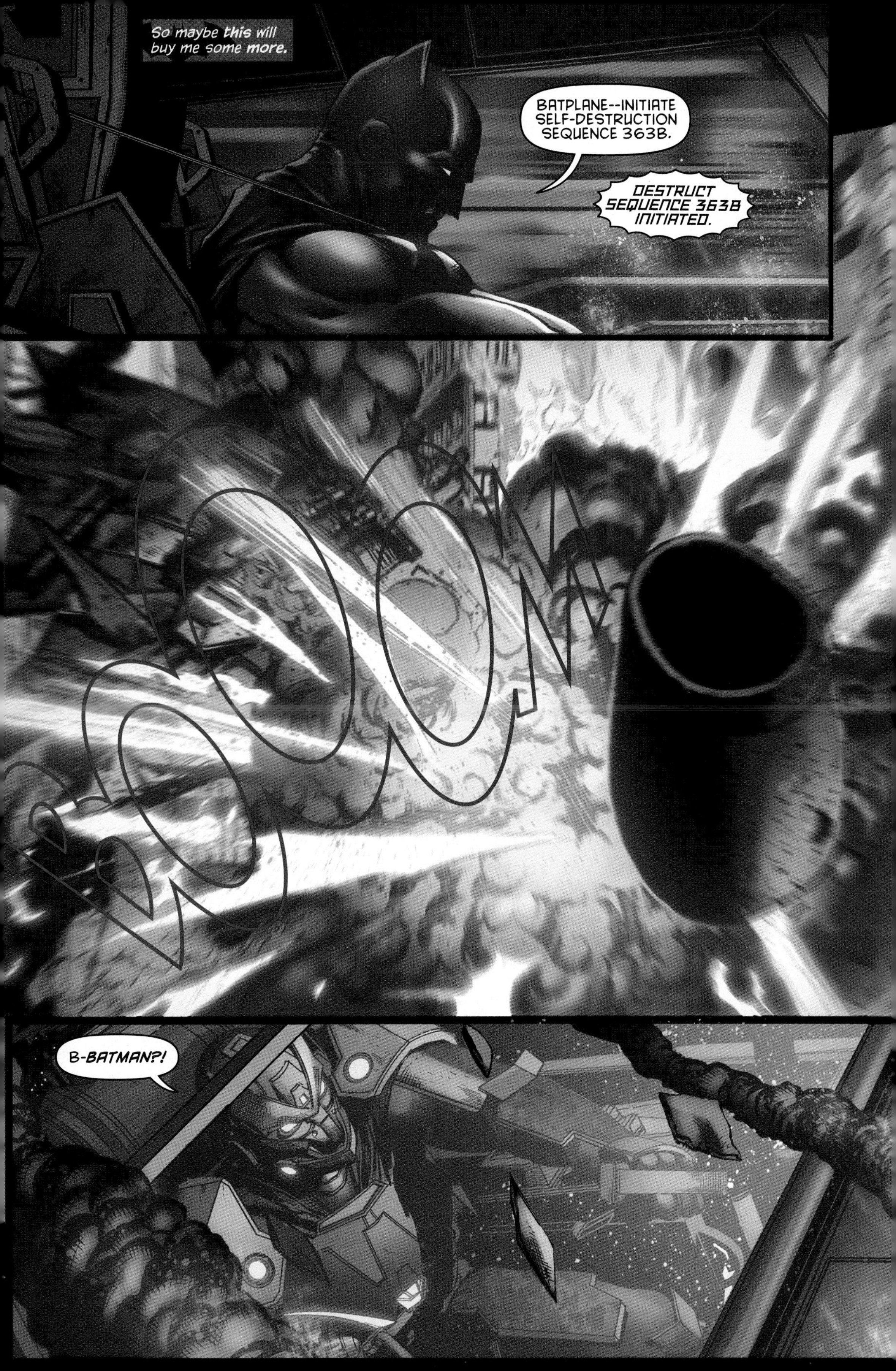

So maybe this will buy me some more.
BATPLANE--INITIATE SELF-DESTRUCTION SEQUENCE 363B.
DESTRUCT SEQUENCE 363B INITIATED.
BOOOM
B-BATMAN?!

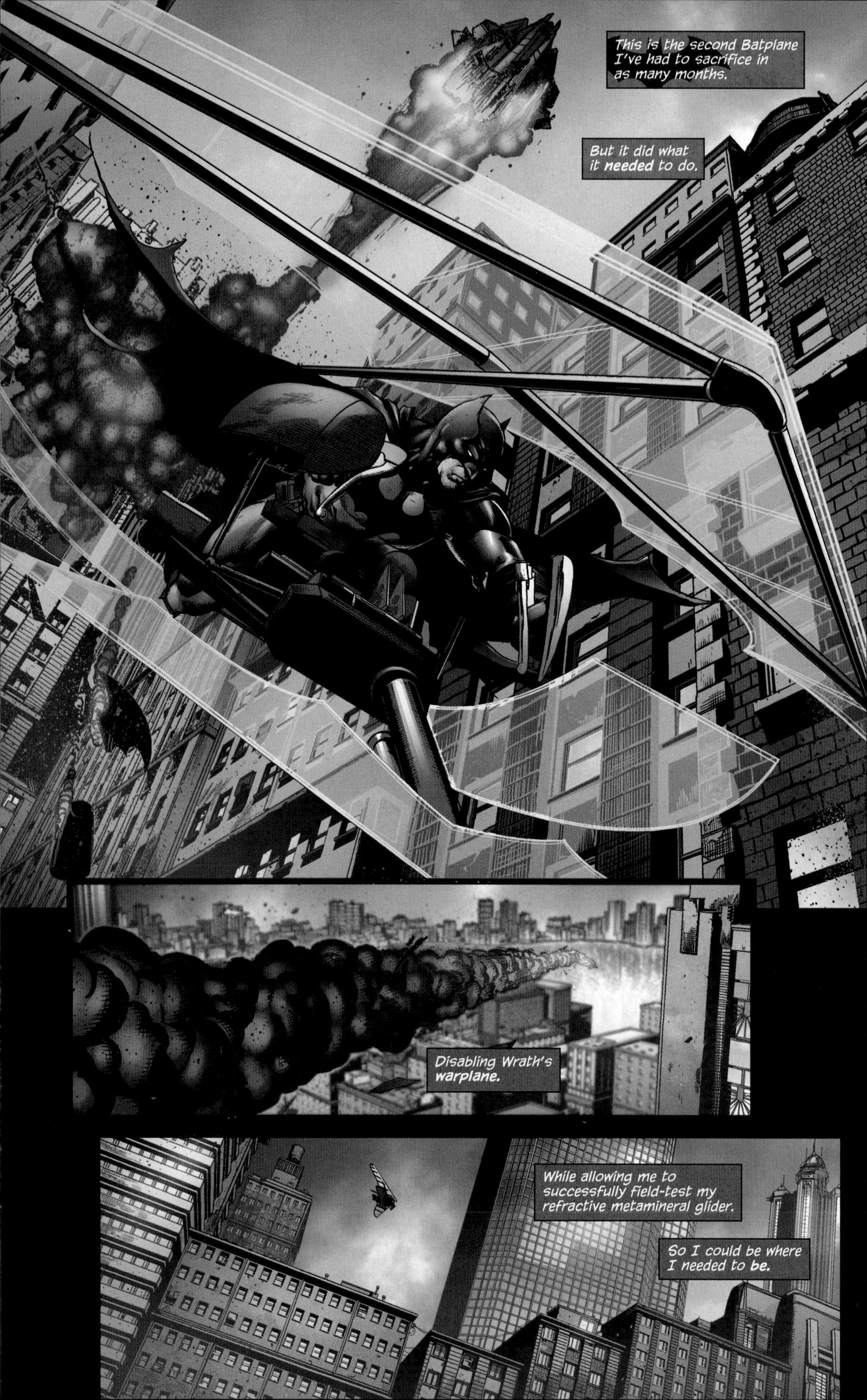
This is the second Batplane I've had to sacrifice in as many months.
But it did what it **needed** to do.
Disabling Wrath's **warplane.**
While allowing me to successfully field-test my refractive metamineral glider.
So I could be where I needed to **be.**

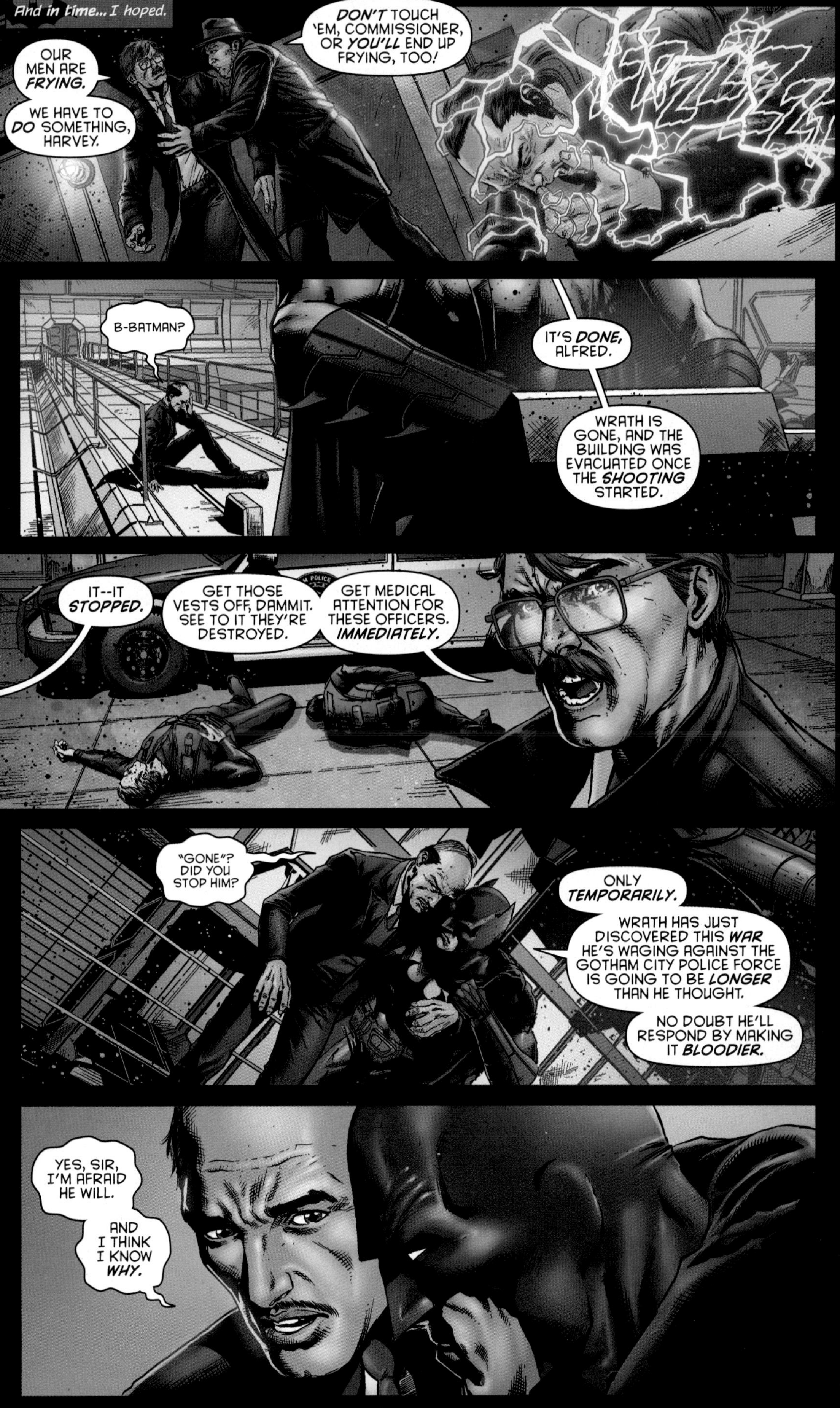
And in time... I hoped.
OUR MEN ARE FRYING.
WE HAVE TO DO SOMETHING, HARVEY.
DON'T TOUCH 'EM, COMMISSIONER, OR YOU'LL END UP FRYING, TOO!
B-BATMAN?
IT'S DONE, ALFRED.
WRATH IS GONE, AND THE BUILDING WAS EVACUATED ONCE THE SHOOTING STARTED.
IT--IT STOPPED.
GET THOSE VESTS OFF, DAMMIT. SEE TO IT THEY'RE DESTROYED.
GET MEDICAL ATTENTION FOR THESE OFFICERS. IMMEDIATELY.
"GONE"? DID YOU STOP HIM?
ONLY TEMPORARILY.
WRATH HAS JUST DISCOVERED THIS WAR HE'S WAGING AGAINST THE GOTHAM CITY POLICE FORCE IS GOING TO BE LONGER THAN HE THOUGHT.
NO DOUBT HE'LL RESPOND BY MAKING IT BLOODIER.
YES, SIR, I'M AFRAID HE WILL.
AND I THINK I KNOW WHY.

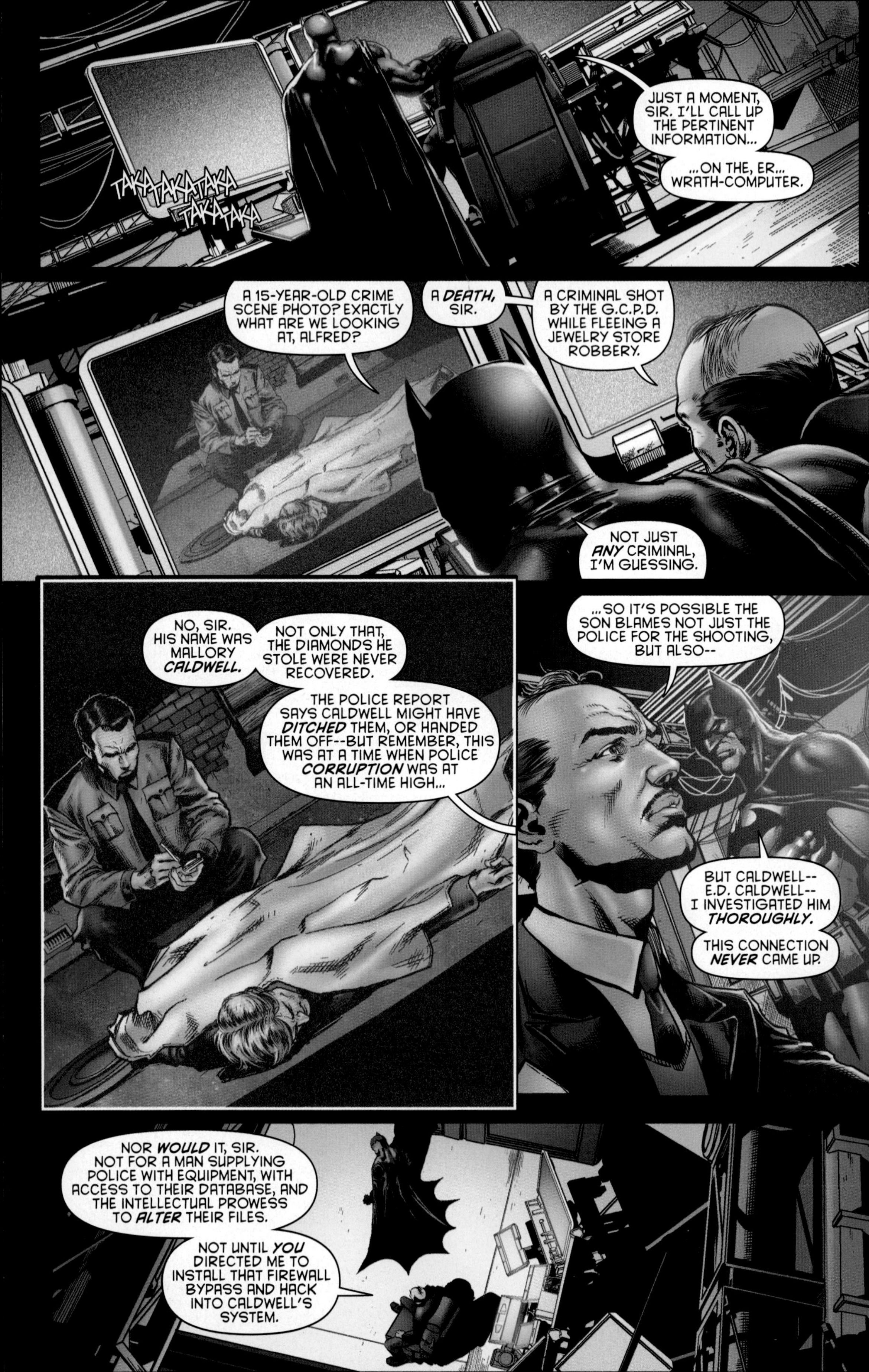
JUST A MOMENT, SIR. I'LL CALL UP THE PERTINENT INFORMATION...
...ON THE, ER... WRATH-COMPUTER.
TAKA TAKA TAKA TAKA TAKA TAKA
A 15-YEAR-OLD CRIME SCENE PHOTO? EXACTLY WHAT ARE WE LOOKING AT, ALFRED?
A DEATH, SIR.
A CRIMINAL SHOT BY THE G.C.P.D. WHILE FLEEING A JEWELRY STORE ROBBERY.
NOT JUST ANY CRIMINAL, I'M GUESSING.
NO, SIR. HIS NAME WAS MALLORY CALDWELL.
NOT ONLY THAT, THE DIAMONDS HE STOLE WERE NEVER RECOVERED.
THE POLICE REPORT SAYS CALDWELL MIGHT HAVE DITCHED THEM, OR HANDED THEM OFF--BUT REMEMBER, THIS WAS AT A TIME WHEN POLICE CORRUPTION WAS AT AN ALL-TIME HIGH...
...SO IT'S POSSIBLE THE SON BLAMES NOT JUST THE POLICE FOR THE SHOOTING, BUT ALSO--
BUT CALDWELL-- E.D. CALDWELL-- I INVESTIGATED HIM THOROUGHLY.
THIS CONNECTION NEVER CAME UP.
NOR WOULD IT, SIR. NOT FOR A MAN SUPPLYING POLICE WITH EQUIPMENT, WITH ACCESS TO THEIR DATABASE, AND THE INTELLECTUAL PROWESS TO ALTER THEIR FILES.
NOT UNTIL YOU DIRECTED ME TO INSTALL THAT FIREWALL BYPASS AND HACK INTO CALDWELL'S SYSTEM.

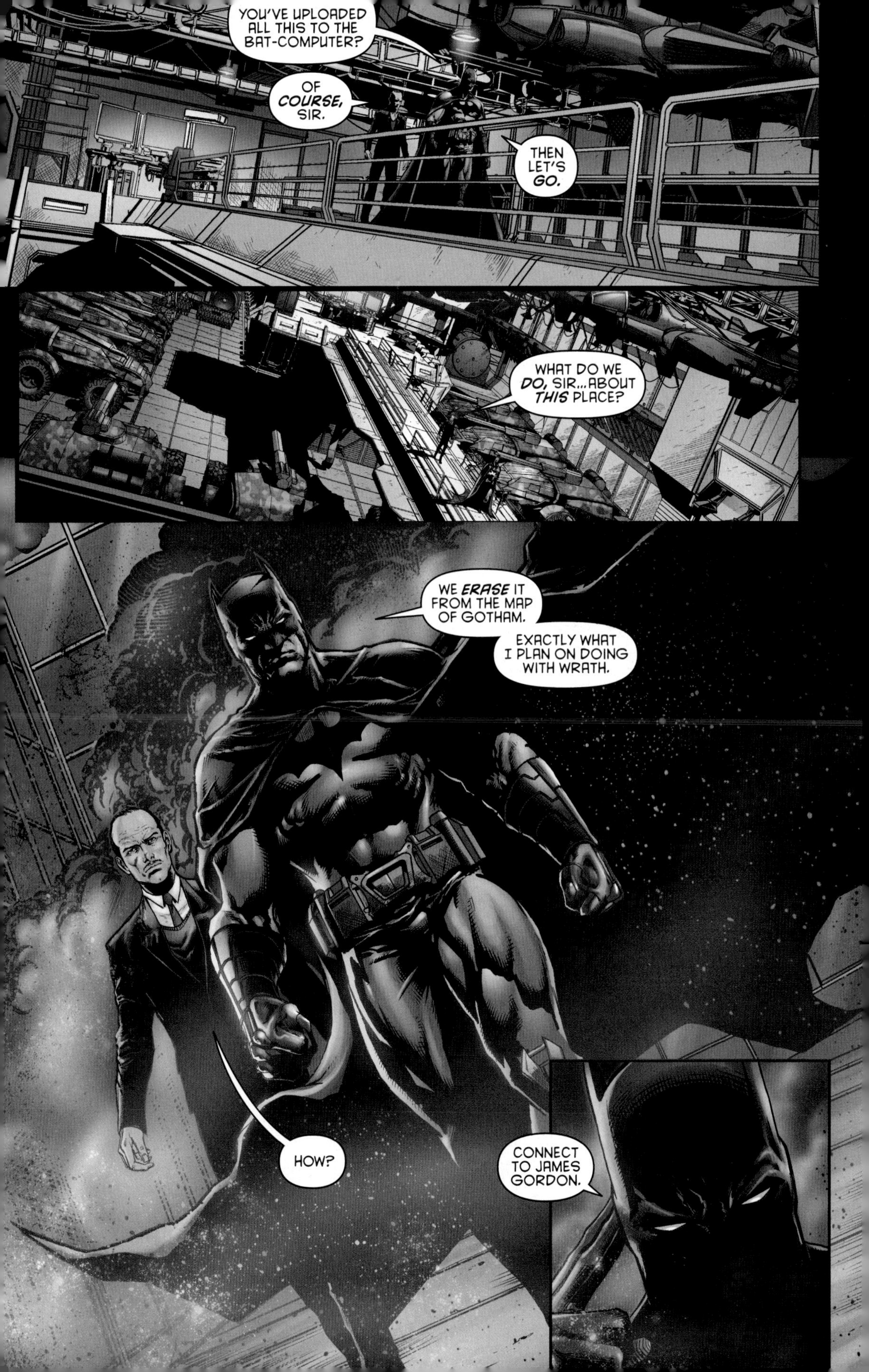
YOU'VE UPLOADED ALL THIS TO THE BAT-COMPUTER?
OF *COURSE,* SIR.
THEN LET'S *GO.*
WHAT DO WE *DO,* SIR...ABOUT *THIS* PLACE?
WE *ERASE* IT FROM THE MAP OF GOTHAM.
EXACTLY WHAT I PLAN ON DOING WITH WRATH.
HOW?
CONNECT TO JAMES GORDON.

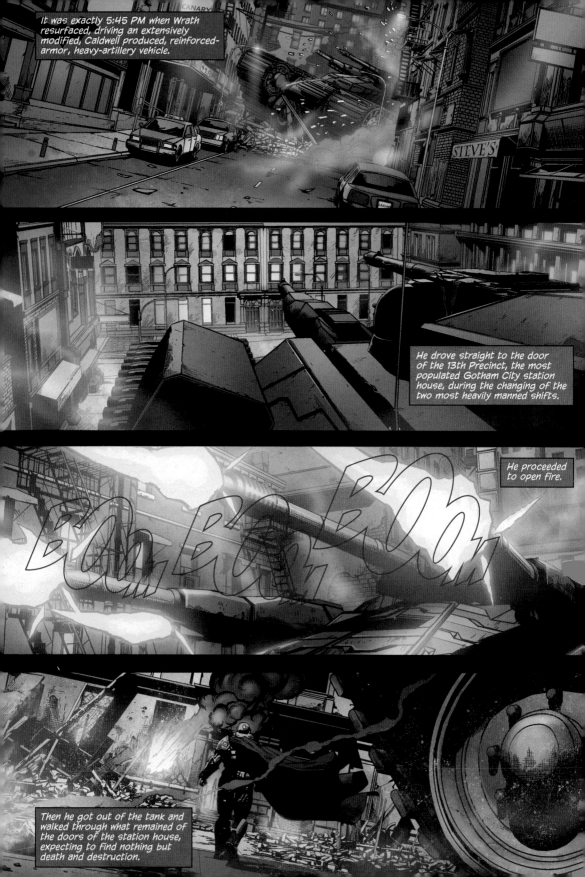

It was exactly 5:45 PM when Wrath resurfaced, driving an extensively modified, Caldwell produced, reinforced-armor, heavy-artillery vehicle.

He drove straight to the door of the 13th Precinct, the most populated Gotham City station house, during the changing of the two most heavily manned shifts.

He proceeded to open fire.

Then he got out of the tank and walked through what remained of the doors of the station house, expecting to find nothing but death and destruction.

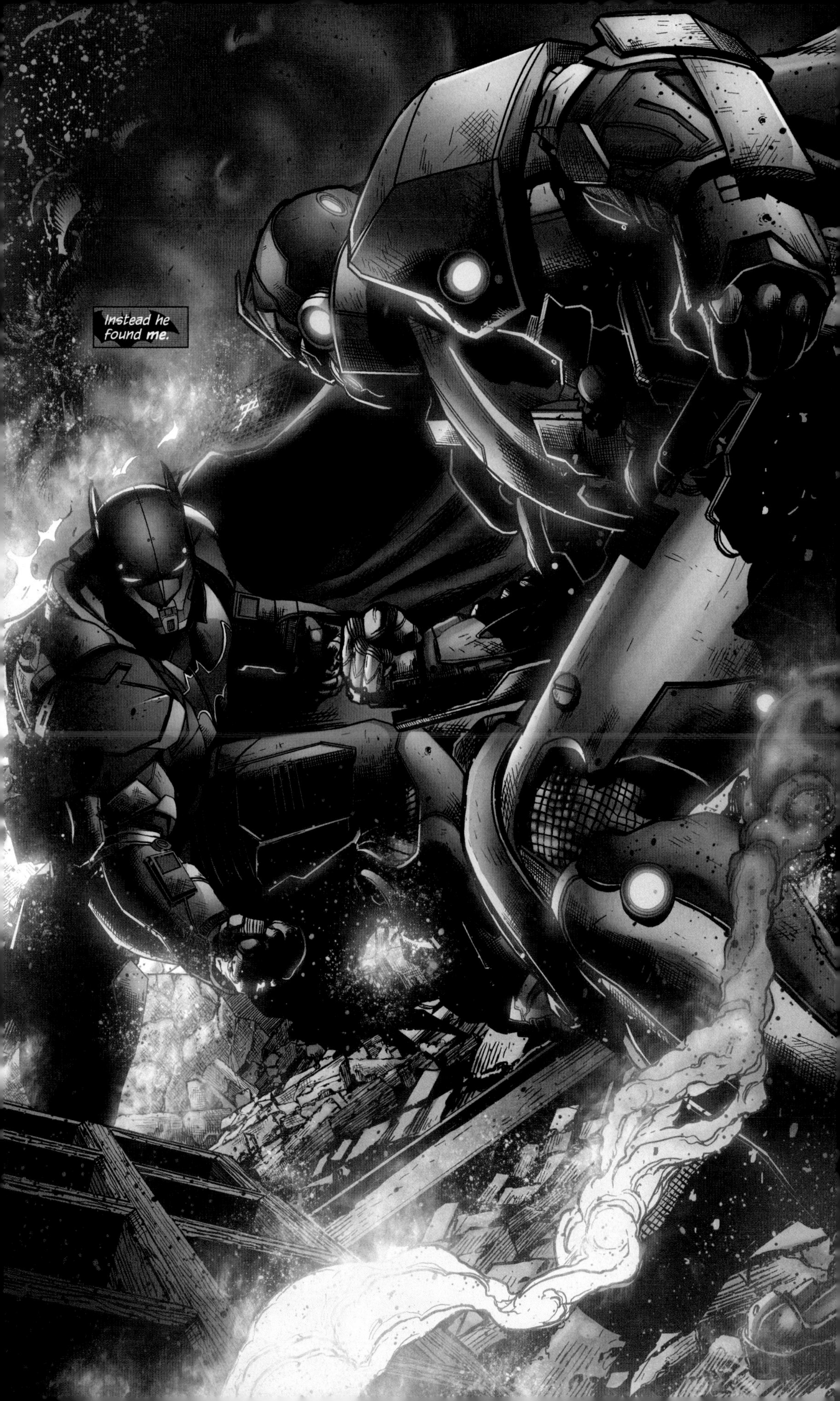
Instead he found me.

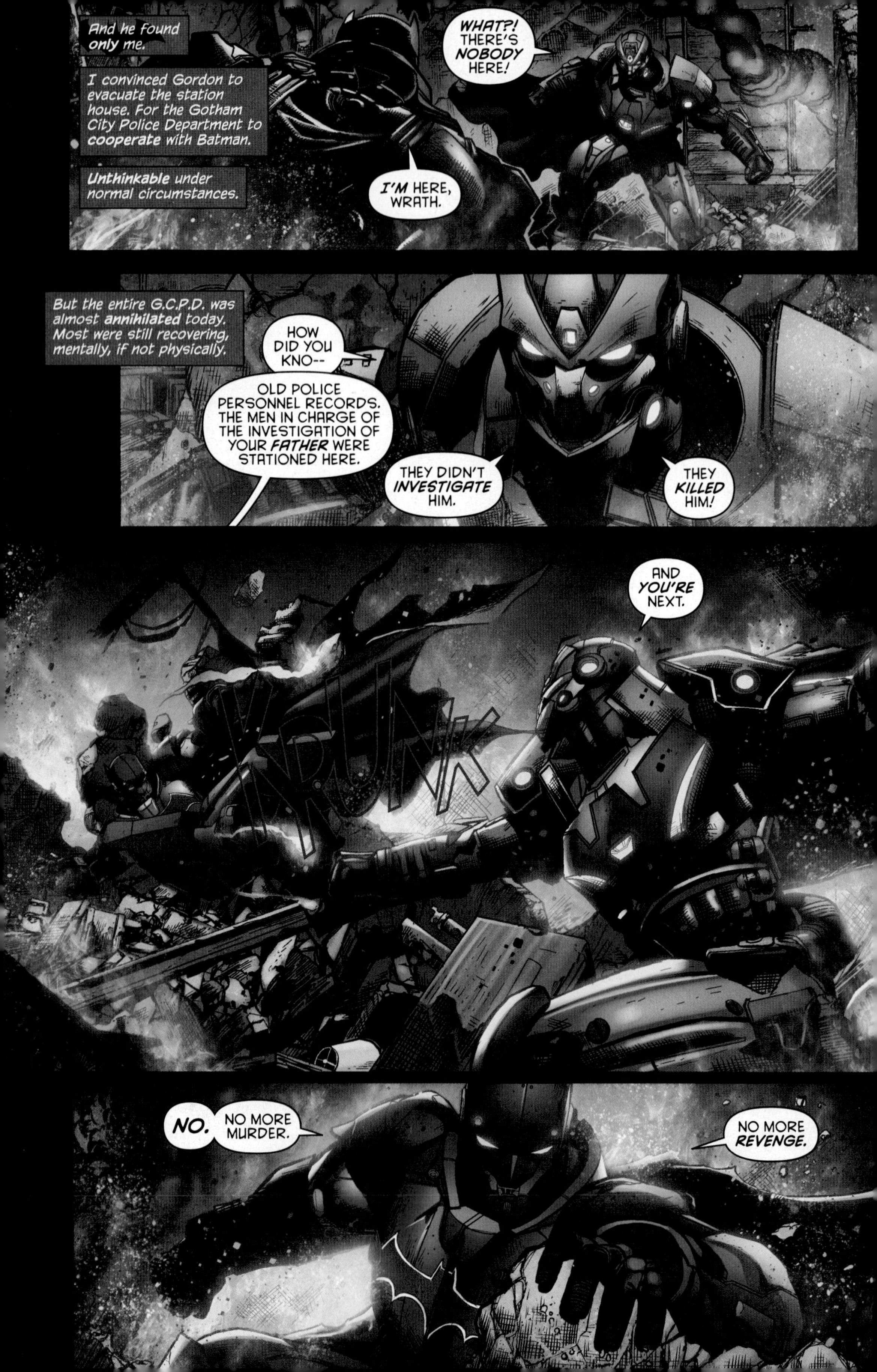
And he found only me.
I convinced Gordon to evacuate the station house. For the Gotham City Police Department to cooperate with Batman.
Unthinkable under normal circumstances.
WHAT?! THERE'S NOBODY HERE!
I'M HERE, WRATH.
But the entire G.C.P.D. was almost annihilated today. Most were still recovering, mentally, if not physically.
HOW DID YOU KNO--
OLD POLICE PERSONNEL RECORDS. THE MEN IN CHARGE OF THE INVESTIGATION OF YOUR FATHER WERE STATIONED HERE.
THEY DIDN'T INVESTIGATE HIM.
THEY KILLED HIM!
AND YOU'RE NEXT.
KRUNK
NO.
NO MORE MURDER.
NO MORE REVENGE.

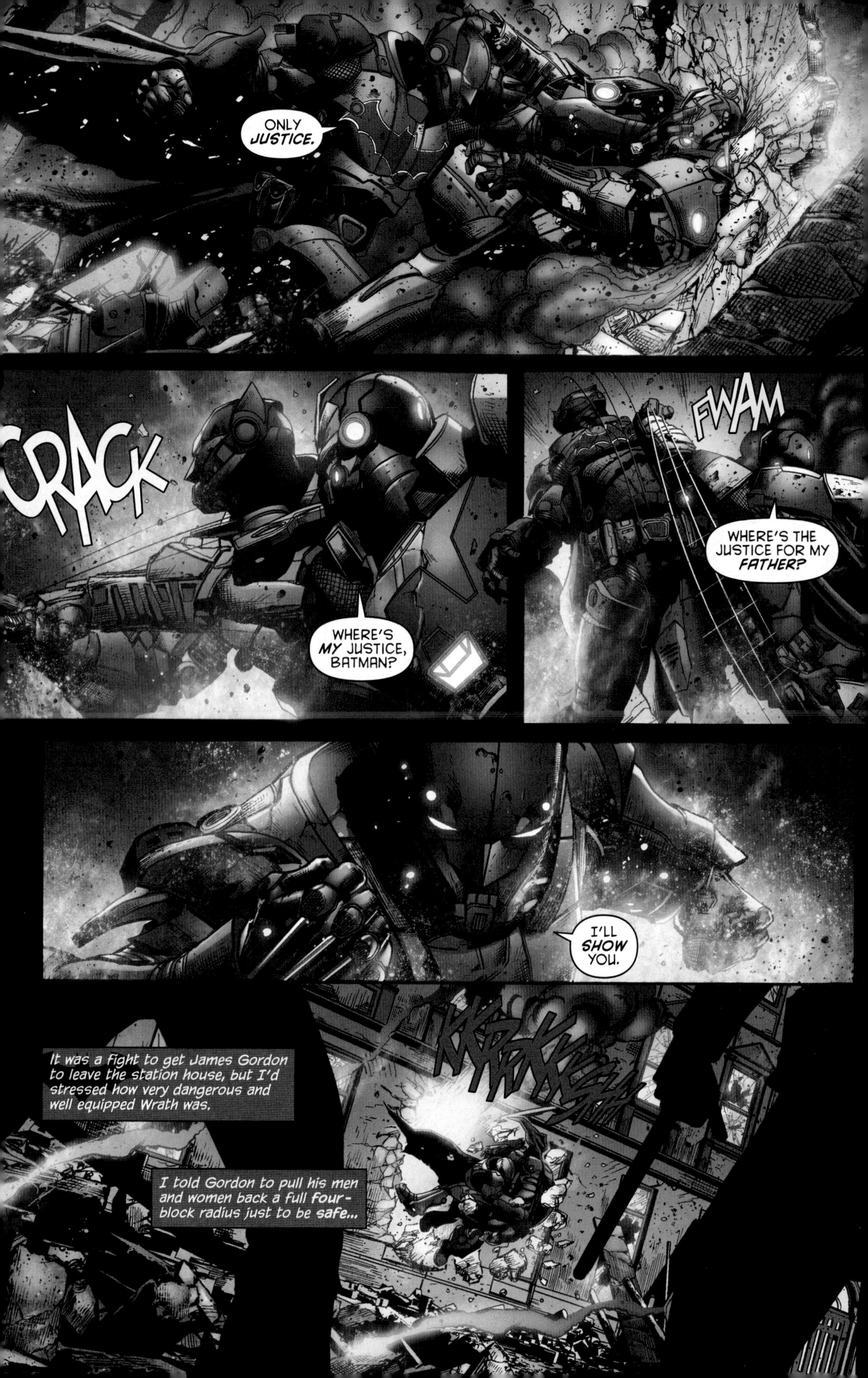
ONLY JUSTICE.
CRACK
WHERE'S MY JUSTICE, BATMAN?
FWAM
WHERE'S THE JUSTICE FOR MY FATHER?
I'LL SHOW YOU.
KKRKKSH
It was a fight to get James Gordon to leave the station house, but I'd stressed how very dangerous and well equipped Wrath was.
I told Gordon to pull his men and women back a full four-block radius just to be safe...

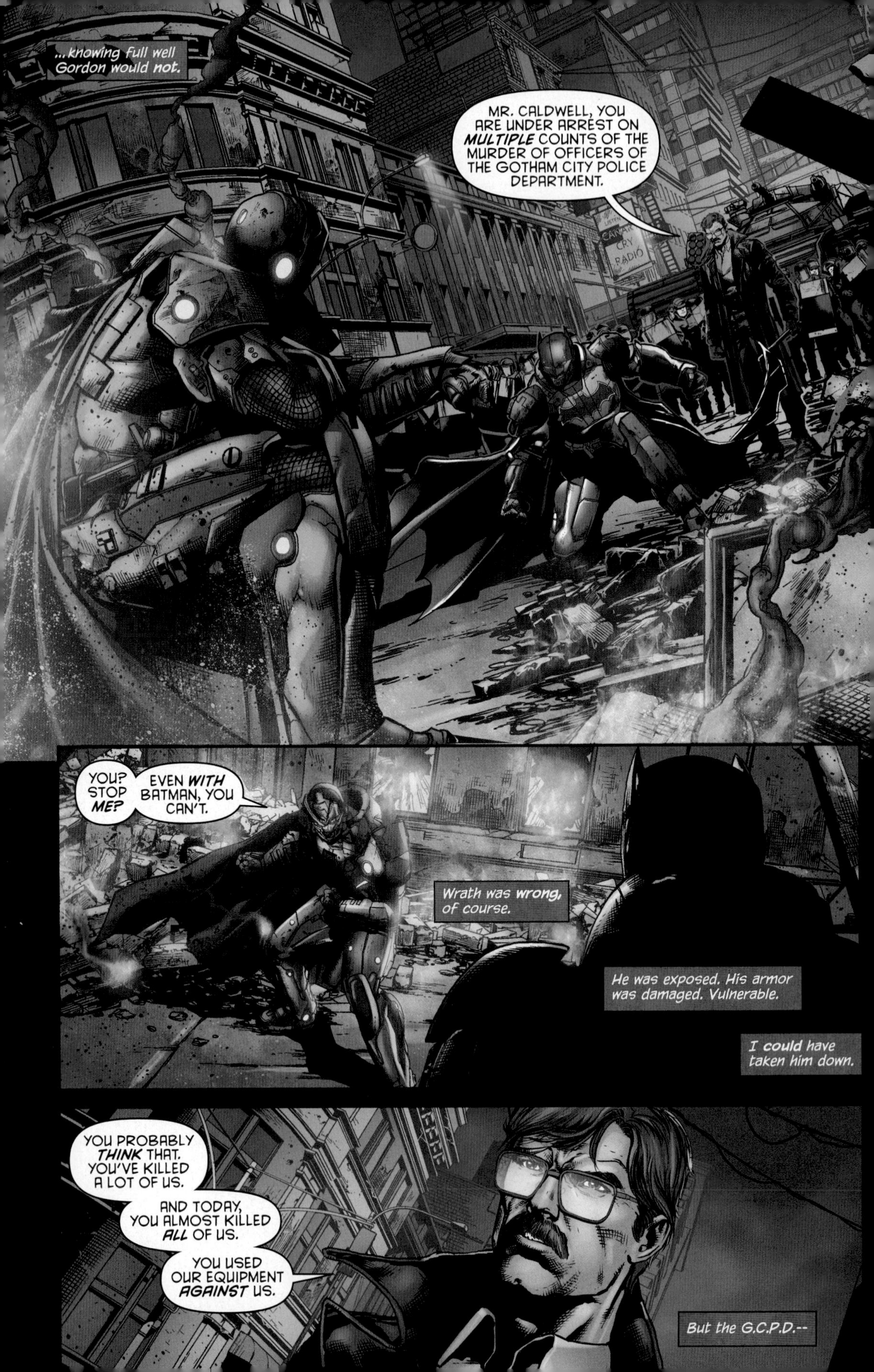
...knowing full well Gordon would **not.**
MR. CALDWELL, YOU ARE UNDER ARREST ON ***MULTIPLE*** COUNTS OF THE MURDER OF OFFICERS OF THE GOTHAM CITY POLICE DEPARTMENT.
LISTEN CANARY CRY RADIO
YOU? STOP ***ME?***
EVEN ***WITH*** BATMAN, YOU CAN'T.
*Wrath was **wrong,** of course.*
He was exposed. His armor was damaged. Vulnerable.
*I **could** have taken him down.*
YOU PROBABLY ***THINK*** THAT. YOU'VE KILLED A LOT OF US.
AND TODAY, YOU ALMOST KILLED ***ALL*** OF US.
YOU USED OUR EQUIPMENT ***AGAINST*** US.
But the G.C.P.D.--

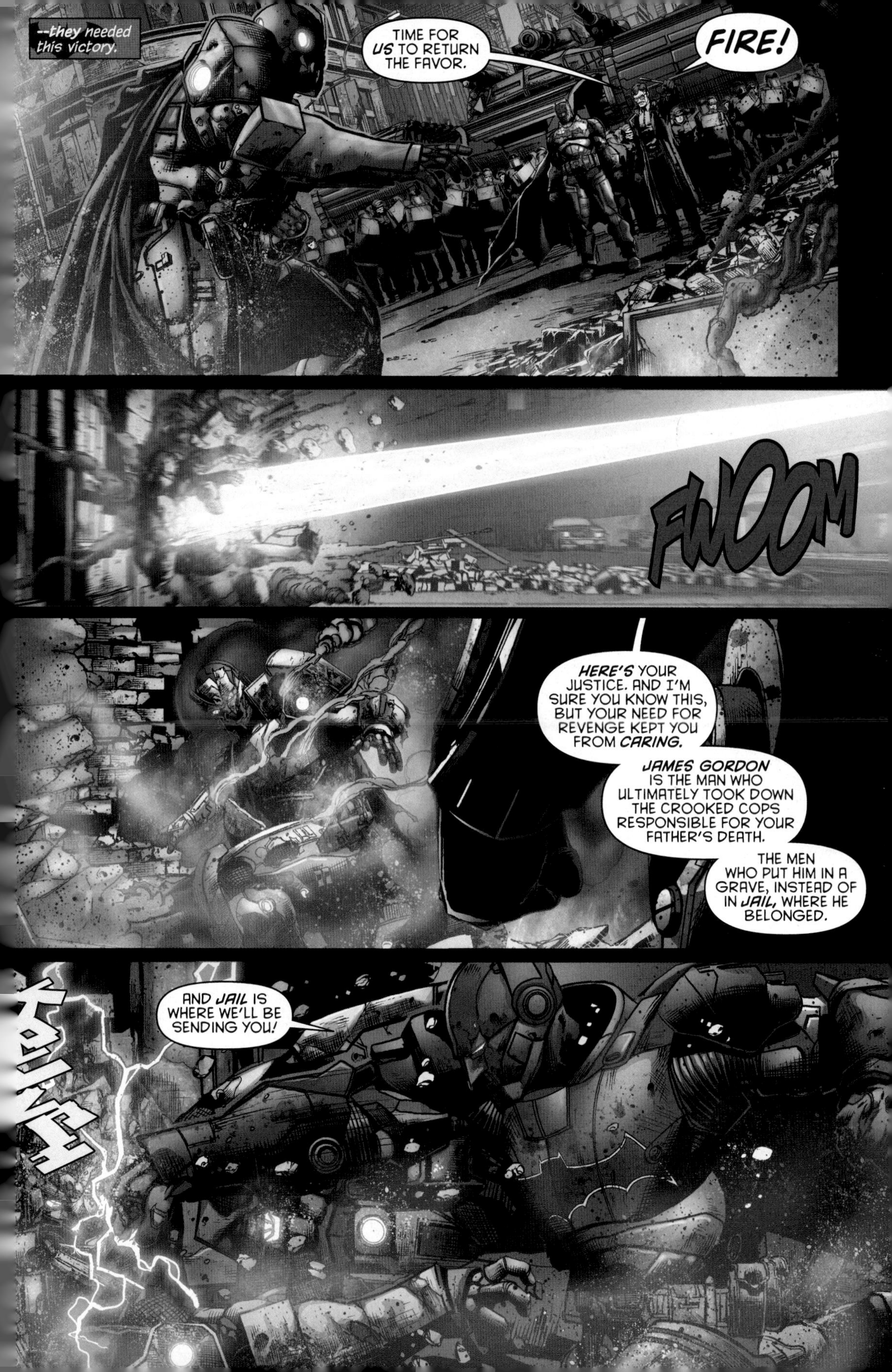
--they needed this victory.
TIME FOR US TO RETURN THE FAVOR.
FIRE!
FWOOM
HERE'S YOUR JUSTICE. AND I'M SURE YOU KNOW THIS, BUT YOUR NEED FOR REVENGE KEPT YOU FROM CARING.
JAMES GORDON IS THE MAN WHO ULTIMATELY TOOK DOWN THE CROOKED COPS RESPONSIBLE FOR YOUR FATHER'S DEATH.
THE MEN WHO PUT HIM IN A GRAVE, INSTEAD OF IN JAIL, WHERE HE BELONGED.
AND JAIL IS WHERE WE'LL BE SENDING YOU!

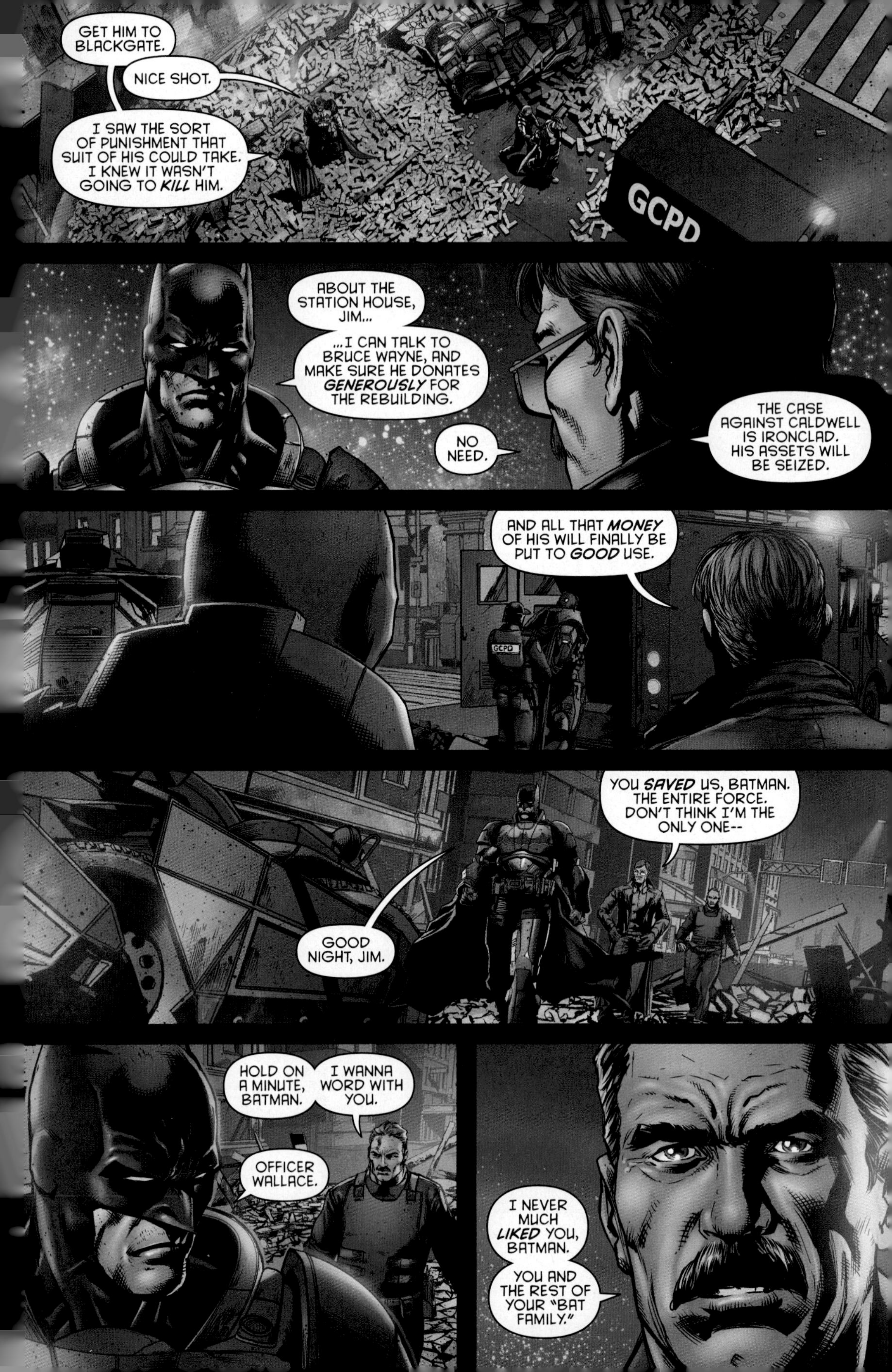
GET HIM TO BLACKGATE.
NICE SHOT.
I SAW THE SORT OF PUNISHMENT THAT SUIT OF HIS COULD TAKE. I KNEW IT WASN'T GOING TO *KILL* HIM.
GCPD
ABOUT THE STATION HOUSE, JIM...
...I CAN TALK TO BRUCE WAYNE, AND MAKE SURE HE DONATES *GENEROUSLY* FOR THE REBUILDING.
NO NEED.
THE CASE AGAINST CALDWELL IS IRONCLAD. HIS ASSETS WILL BE SEIZED.
AND ALL THAT *MONEY* OF HIS WILL FINALLY BE PUT TO *GOOD* USE.
GCPD
YOU *SAVED* US, BATMAN. THE ENTIRE FORCE. DON'T THINK I'M THE ONLY ONE--
GOOD NIGHT, JIM.
HOLD ON A MINUTE, BATMAN.
I WANNA WORD WITH YOU.
OFFICER WALLACE.
I NEVER MUCH *LIKED* YOU, BATMAN.
YOU AND THE REST OF YOUR "BAT FAMILY."

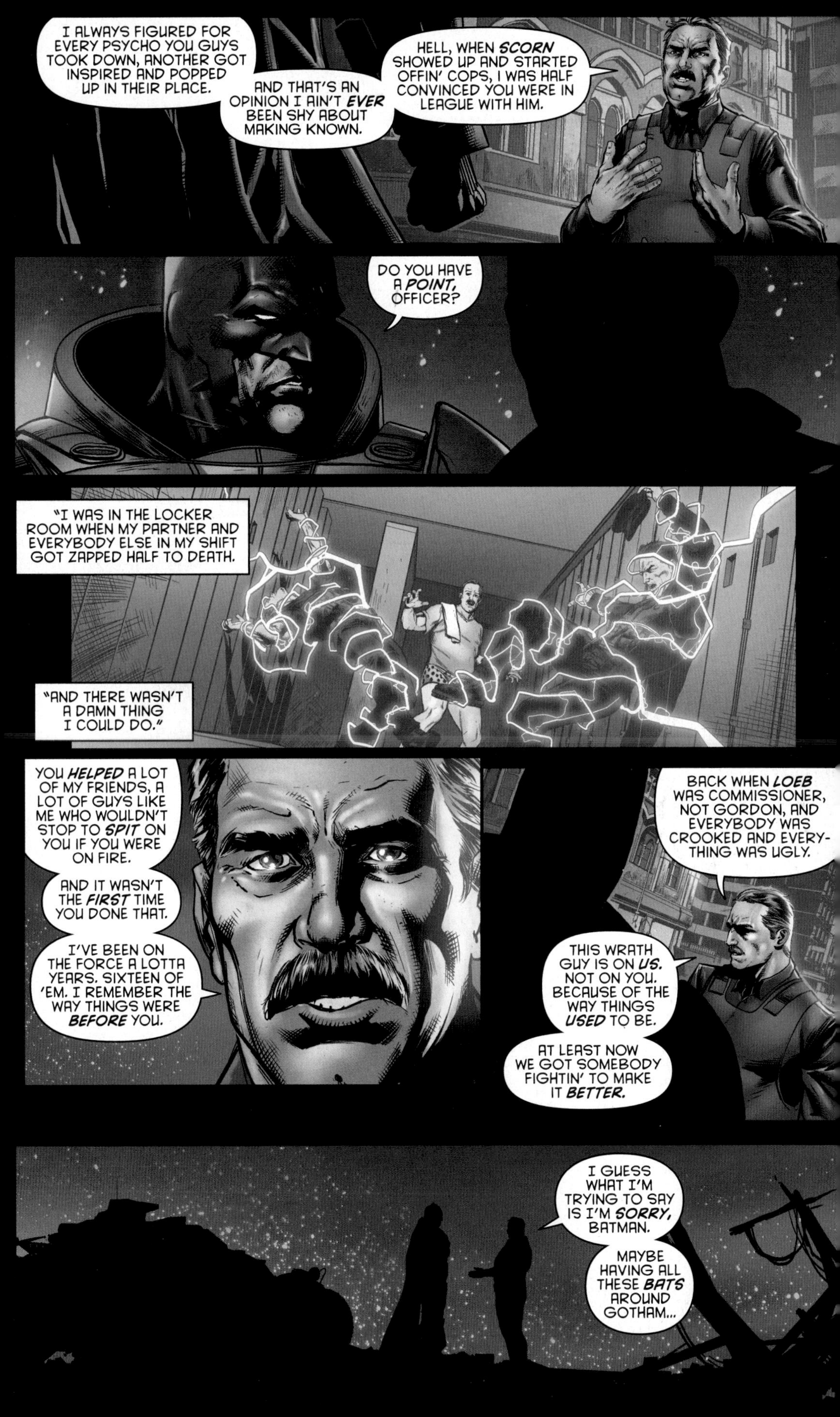

I ALWAYS FIGURED FOR EVERY PSYCHO YOU GUYS TOOK DOWN, ANOTHER GOT INSPIRED AND POPPED UP IN THEIR PLACE.
AND THAT'S AN OPINION I AIN'T EVER BEEN SHY ABOUT MAKING KNOWN.
HELL, WHEN SCORN SHOWED UP AND STARTED OFFIN' COPS, I WAS HALF CONVINCED YOU WERE IN LEAGUE WITH HIM.
DO YOU HAVE A POINT, OFFICER?
"I WAS IN THE LOCKER ROOM WHEN MY PARTNER AND EVERYBODY ELSE IN MY SHIFT GOT ZAPPED HALF TO DEATH.
"AND THERE WASN'T A DAMN THING I COULD DO."
YOU HELPED A LOT OF MY FRIENDS, A LOT OF GUYS LIKE ME WHO WOULDN'T STOP TO SPIT ON YOU IF YOU WERE ON FIRE.
AND IT WASN'T THE FIRST TIME YOU DONE THAT.
I'VE BEEN ON THE FORCE A LOTTA YEARS. SIXTEEN OF 'EM. I REMEMBER THE WAY THINGS WERE BEFORE YOU.
BACK WHEN LOEB WAS COMMISSIONER, NOT GORDON, AND EVERYBODY WAS CROOKED AND EVERY-THING WAS UGLY.
THIS WRATH GUY IS ON US. NOT ON YOU. BECAUSE OF THE WAY THINGS USED TO BE.
AT LEAST NOW WE GOT SOMEBODY FIGHTIN' TO MAKE IT BETTER.
I GUESS WHAT I'M TRYING TO SAY IS I'M SORRY, BATMAN.
MAYBE HAVING ALL THESE BATS AROUND GOTHAM...

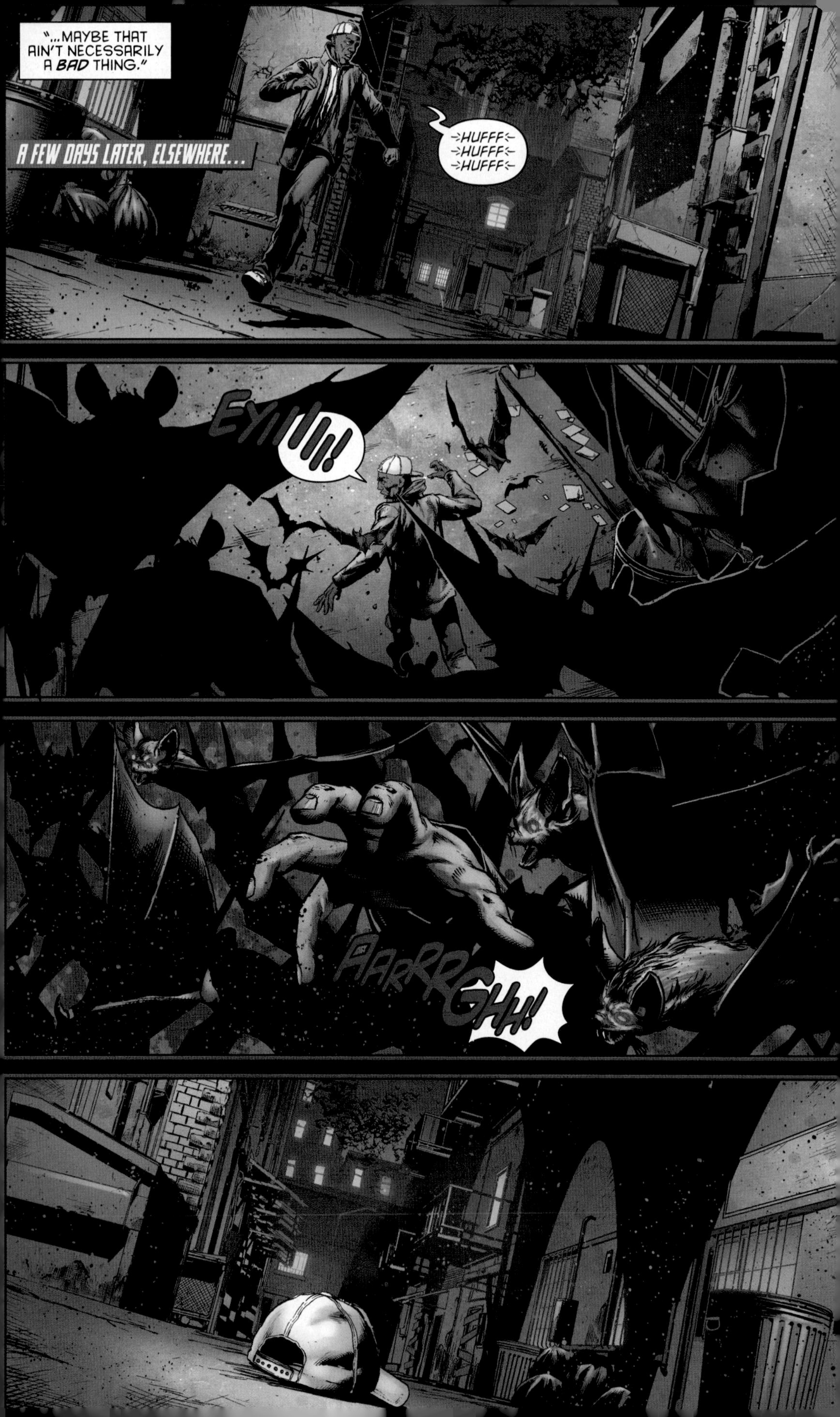
"...MAYBE THAT AIN'T NECESSARILY A BAD THING."
A FEW DAYS LATER, ELSEWHERE...
HUFFF HUFFF HUFFF
EYIIII!!
AARRRGHH!

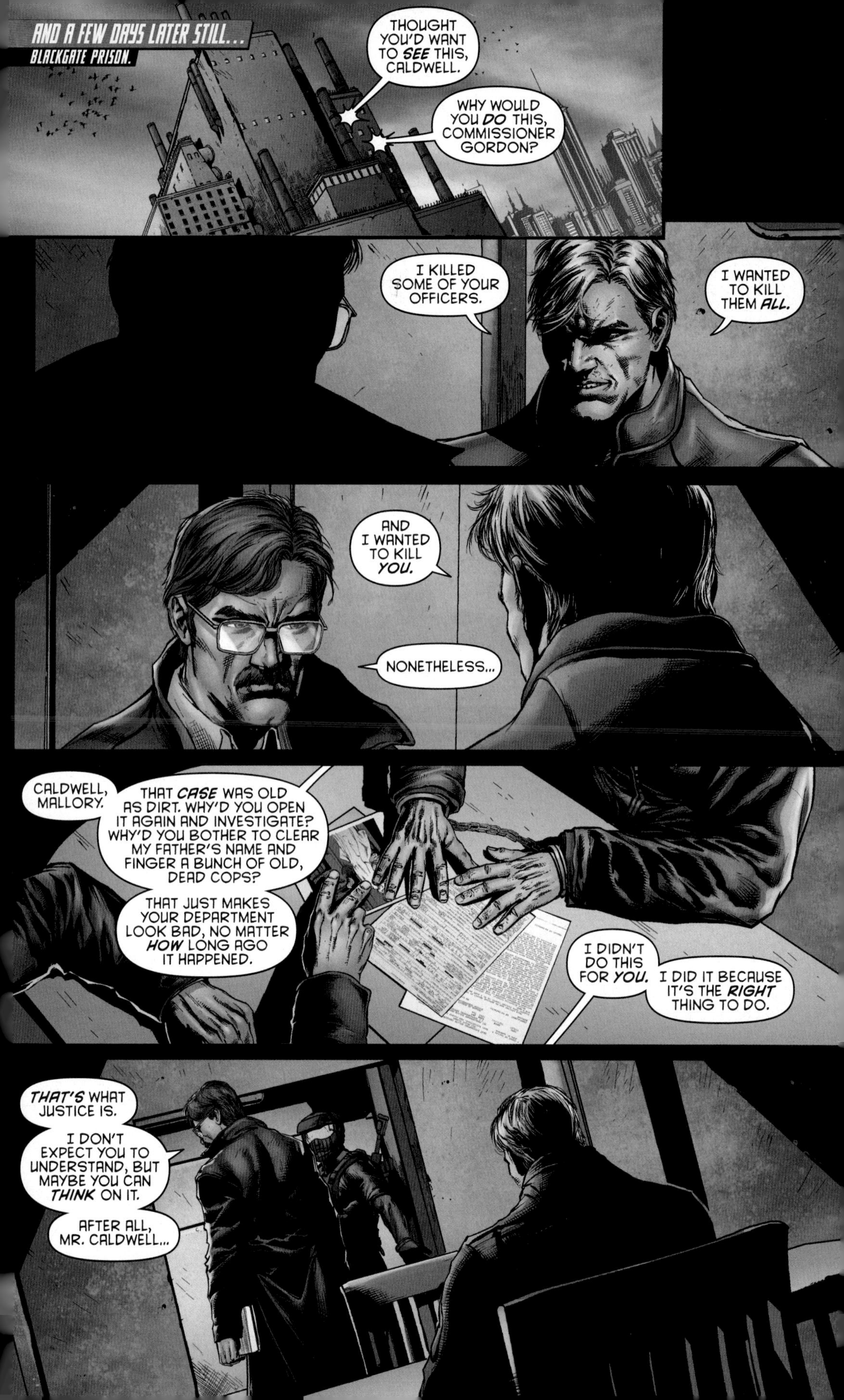
AND A FEW DAYS LATER STILL...
BLACKGATE PRISON.
THOUGHT YOU'D WANT TO SEE THIS, CALDWELL.
WHY WOULD YOU DO THIS, COMMISSIONER GORDON?
I KILLED SOME OF YOUR OFFICERS.
I WANTED TO KILL THEM ALL.
AND I WANTED TO KILL YOU.
NONETHELESS...
CALDWELL, MALLORY.
THAT CASE WAS OLD AS DIRT. WHY'D YOU OPEN IT AGAIN AND INVESTIGATE? WHY'D YOU BOTHER TO CLEAR MY FATHER'S NAME AND FINGER A BUNCH OF OLD, DEAD COPS?
THAT JUST MAKES YOUR DEPARTMENT LOOK BAD, NO MATTER HOW LONG AGO IT HAPPENED.
I DIDN'T DO THIS FOR YOU.
I DID IT BECAUSE IT'S THE RIGHT THING TO DO.
THAT'S WHAT JUSTICE IS.
I DON'T EXPECT YOU TO UNDERSTAND, BUT MAYBE YOU CAN THINK ON IT.
AFTER ALL, MR. CALDWELL...

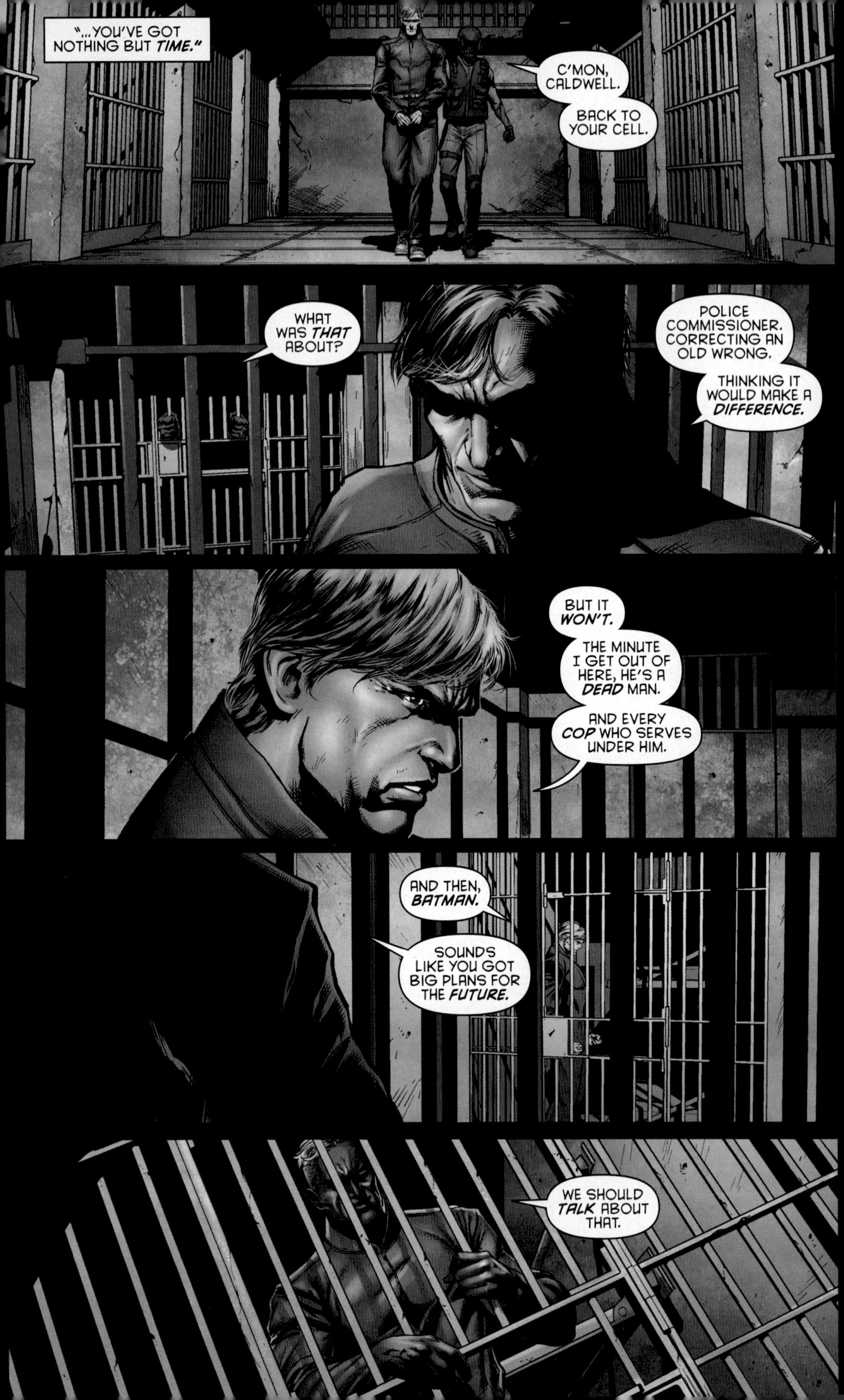
"...YOU'VE GOT NOTHING BUT *TIME.*"
C'MON, CALDWELL.
BACK TO YOUR CELL.
WHAT WAS *THAT* ABOUT?
POLICE COMMISSIONER. CORRECTING AN OLD WRONG.
THINKING IT WOULD MAKE A *DIFFERENCE.*
BUT IT *WON'T.*
THE MINUTE I GET OUT OF HERE, HE'S A *DEAD* MAN.
AND EVERY *COP* WHO SERVES UNDER HIM.
AND THEN, *BATMAN.*
SOUNDS LIKE YOU GOT BIG PLANS FOR THE *FUTURE.*
WE SHOULD *TALK* ABOUT THAT.

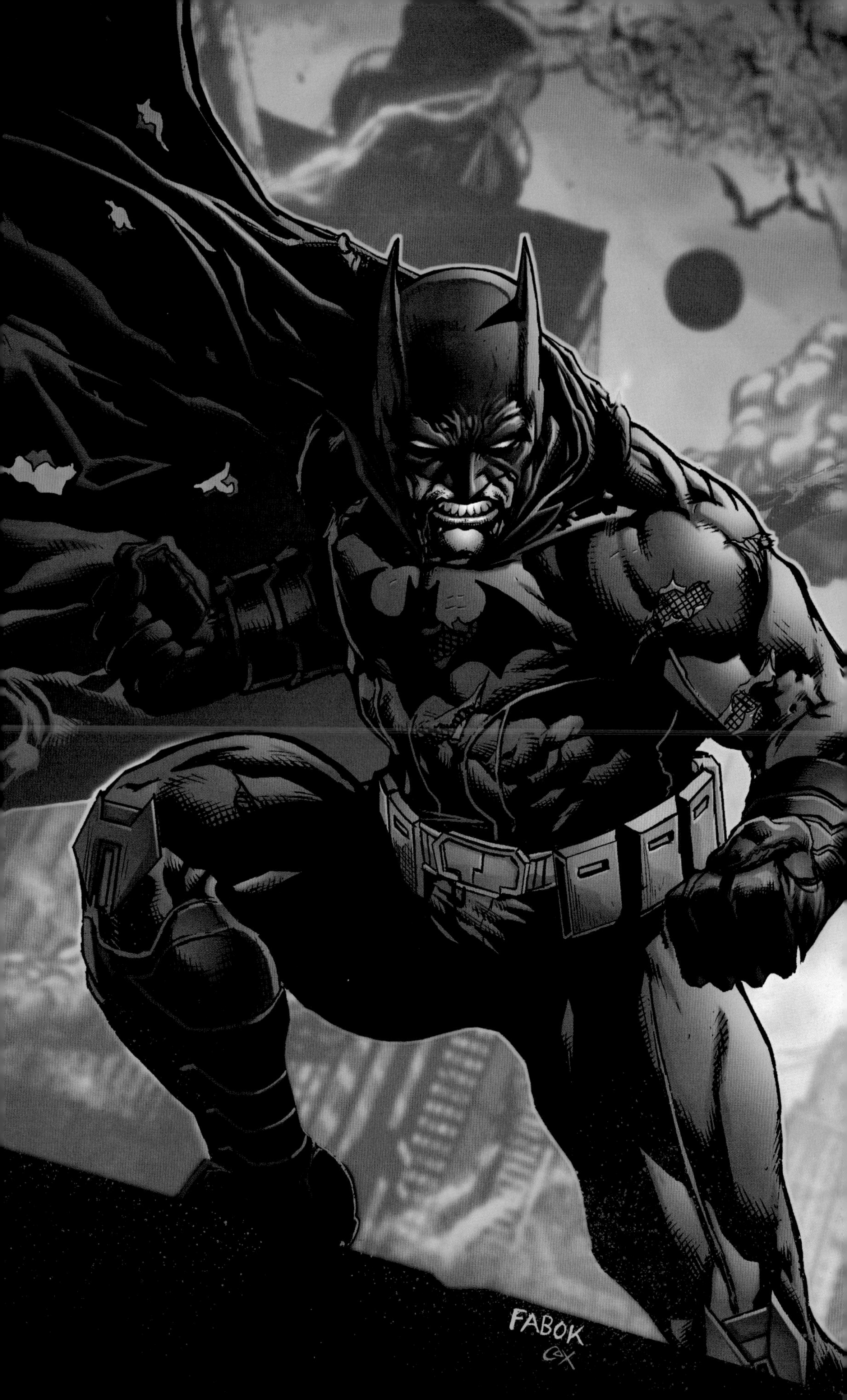
FABOK
COX

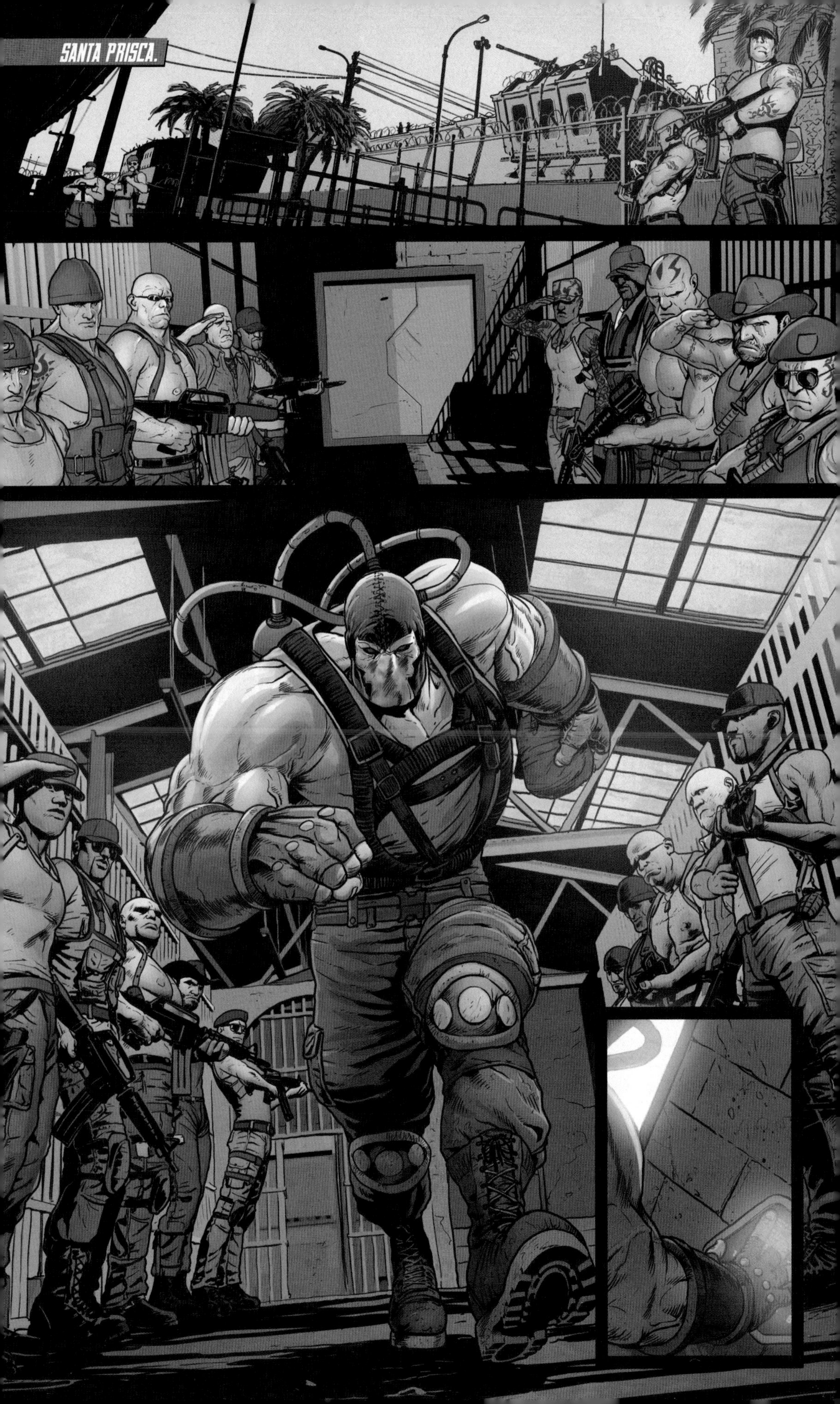
SANTA PRISCA.

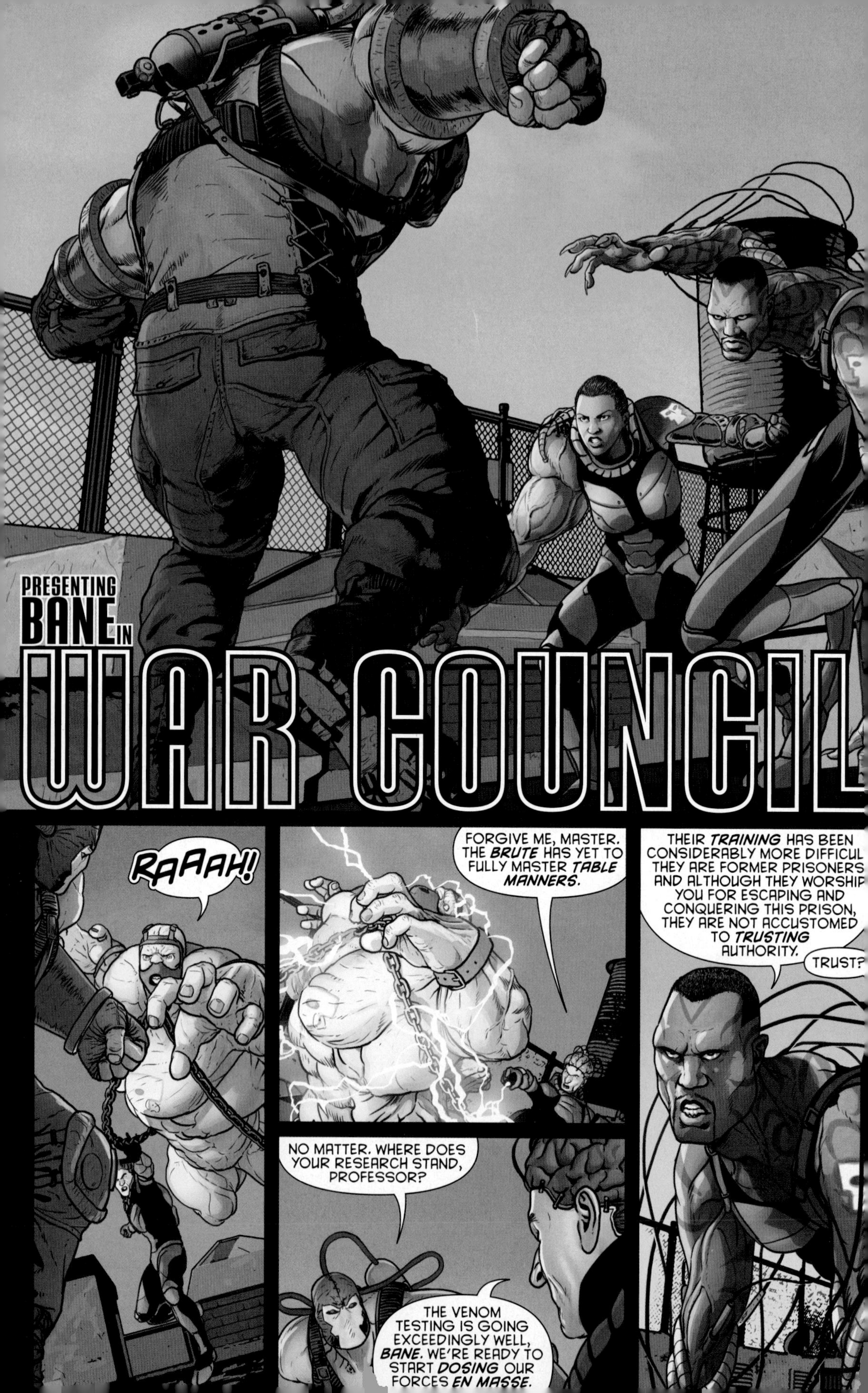
PRESENTING BANE IN
WAR COUNCIL
RAAAH!
FORGIVE ME, MASTER. THE BRUTE HAS YET TO FULLY MASTER TABLE MANNERS.
THEIR TRAINING HAS BEEN CONSIDERABLY MORE DIFFICUL THEY ARE FORMER PRISONERS AND ALTHOUGH THEY WORSHIP YOU FOR ESCAPING AND CONQUERING THIS PRISON, THEY ARE NOT ACCUSTOMED TO TRUSTING AUTHORITY.
TRUST?
NO MATTER. WHERE DOES YOUR RESEARCH STAND, PROFESSOR?
THE VENOM TESTING IS GOING EXCEEDINGLY WELL, BANE. WE'RE READY TO START DOSING OUR FORCES EN MASSE.

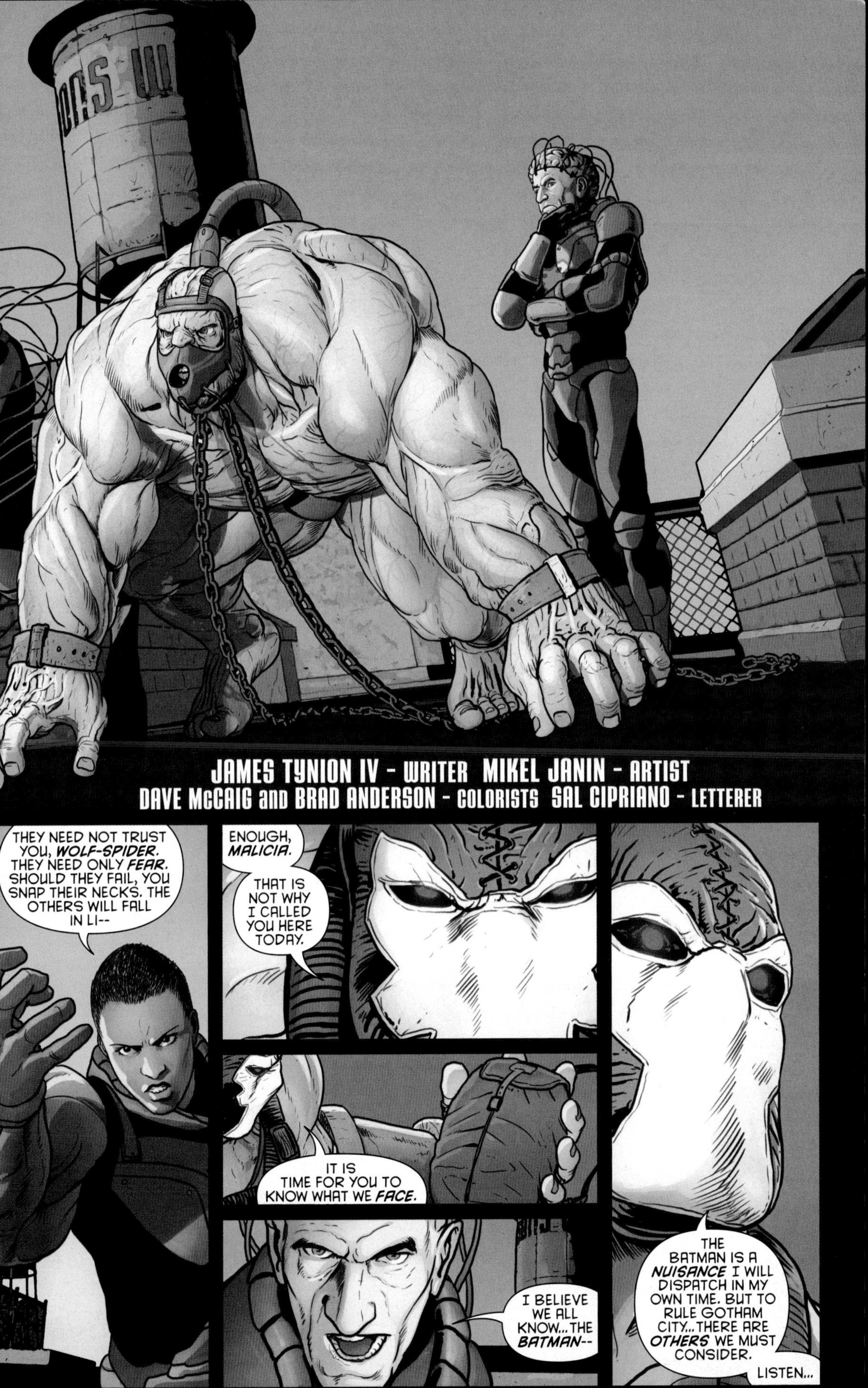
JAMES TYNION IV - WRITER MIKEL JANIN - ARTIST
DAVE McCAIG and BRAD ANDERSON - COLORISTS SAL CIPRIANO - LETTERER
THEY NEED NOT TRUST YOU, WOLF-SPIDER. THEY NEED ONLY FEAR. SHOULD THEY FAIL, YOU SNAP THEIR NECKS. THE OTHERS WILL FALL IN LI--
ENOUGH, MALICIA.
THAT IS NOT WHY I CALLED YOU HERE TODAY.
IT IS TIME FOR YOU TO KNOW WHAT WE FACE.
I BELIEVE WE ALL KNOW... THE BATMAN--
THE BATMAN IS A NUISANCE I WILL DISPATCH IN MY OWN TIME. BUT TO RULE GOTHAM CITY... THERE ARE OTHERS WE MUST CONSIDER.
LISTEN...

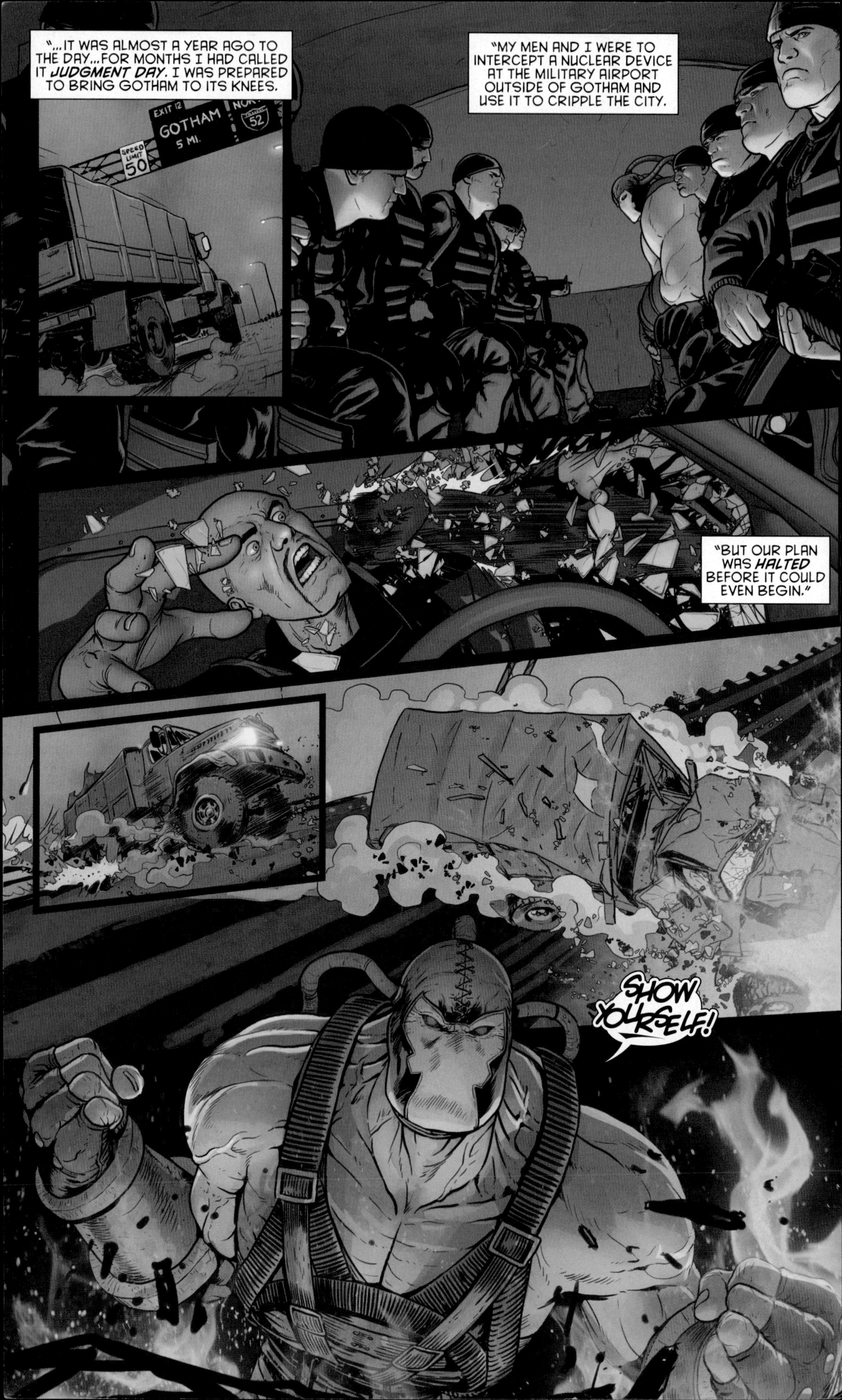
"...IT WAS ALMOST A YEAR AGO TO THE DAY...FOR MONTHS I HAD CALLED IT JUDGMENT DAY. I WAS PREPARED TO BRING GOTHAM TO ITS KNEES.
EXIT 12
GOTHAM
5 MI.
SPEED LIMIT 50
52
"MY MEN AND I WERE TO INTERCEPT A NUCLEAR DEVICE AT THE MILITARY AIRPORT OUTSIDE OF GOTHAM AND USE IT TO CRIPPLE THE CITY.
"BUT OUR PLAN WAS HALTED BEFORE IT COULD EVEN BEGIN."
SHOW YOURSELF!

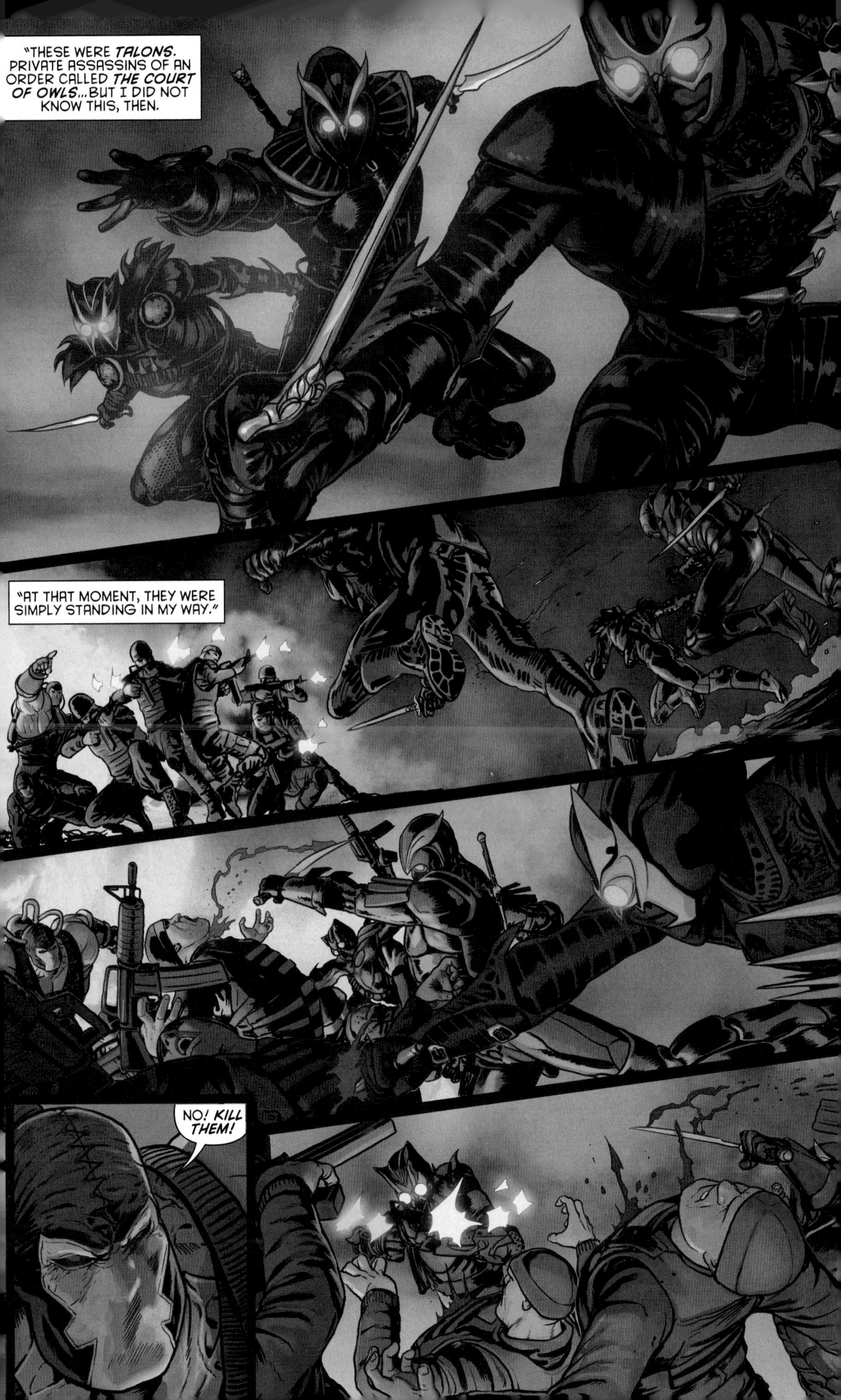
"THESE WERE *TALONS*. PRIVATE ASSASSINS OF AN ORDER CALLED *THE COURT OF OWLS*...BUT I DID NOT KNOW THIS, THEN.
"AT THAT MOMENT, THEY WERE SIMPLY STANDING IN MY WAY."
NO! *KILL THEM!*

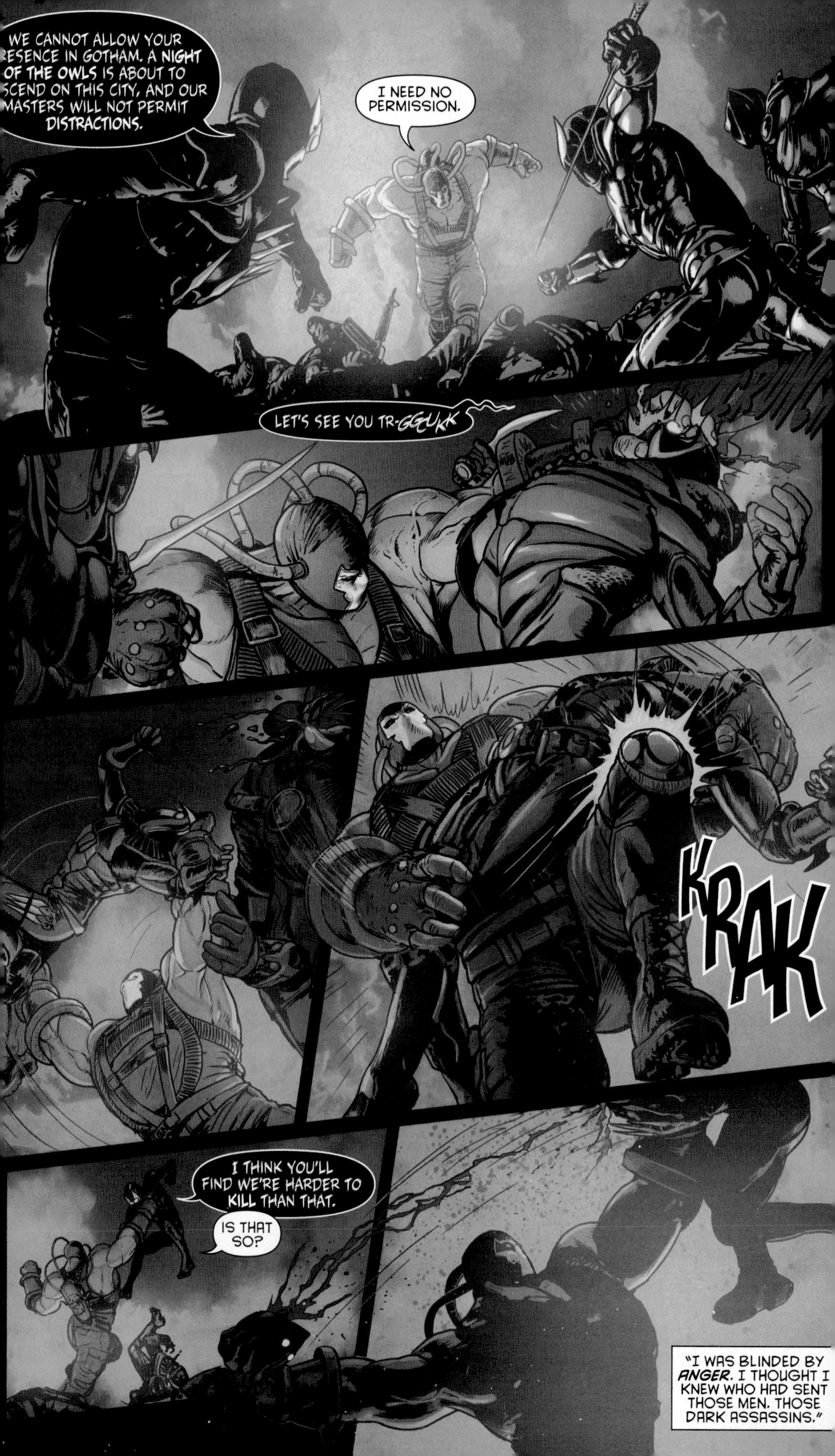

WE CANNOT ALLOW YOUR
RESENCE IN GOTHAM. A NIGHT OF THE OWLS IS ABOUT TO SCEND ON THIS CITY, AND OUR MASTERS WILL NOT PERMIT DISTRACTIONS.
I NEED NO PERMISSION.
LET'S SEE YOU TR-GGUKK
KRAK
I THINK YOU'LL FIND WE'RE HARDER TO KILL THAN THAT.
IS THAT SO?
"I WAS BLINDED BY ANGER. I THOUGHT I KNEW WHO HAD SENT THOSE MEN. THOSE DARK ASSASSINS."

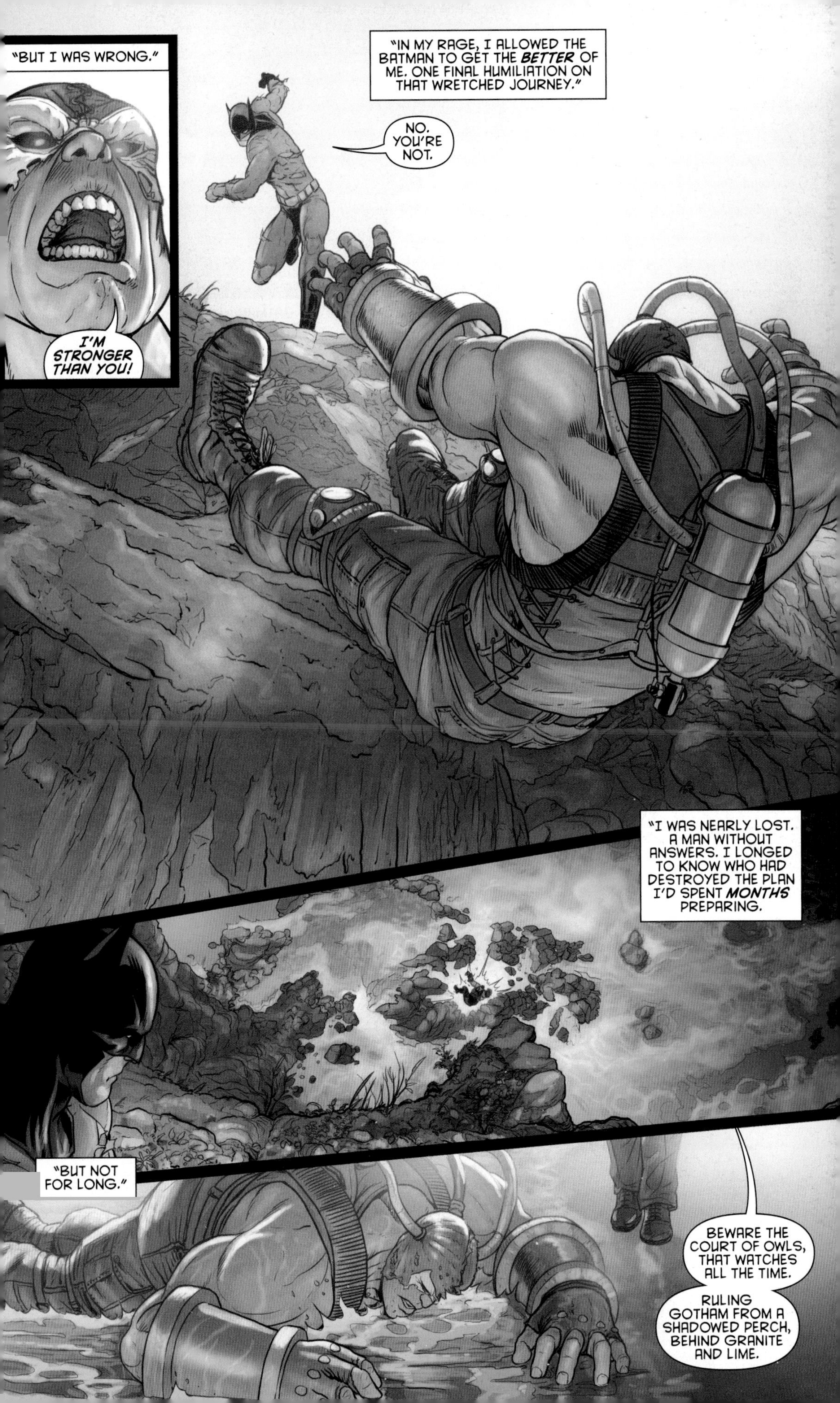
"BUT I WAS WRONG."
I'M STRONGER THAN YOU!
"IN MY RAGE, I ALLOWED THE BATMAN TO GET THE *BETTER* OF ME. ONE FINAL HUMILIATION ON THAT WRETCHED JOURNEY."
NO. YOU'RE NOT.
"I WAS NEARLY LOST. A MAN WITHOUT ANSWERS. I LONGED TO KNOW WHO HAD DESTROYED THE PLAN I'D SPENT *MONTHS* PREPARING.
"BUT NOT FOR LONG."
BEWARE THE COURT OF OWLS, THAT WATCHES ALL THE TIME.
RULING GOTHAM FROM A SHADOWED PERCH, BEHIND GRANITE AND LIME.

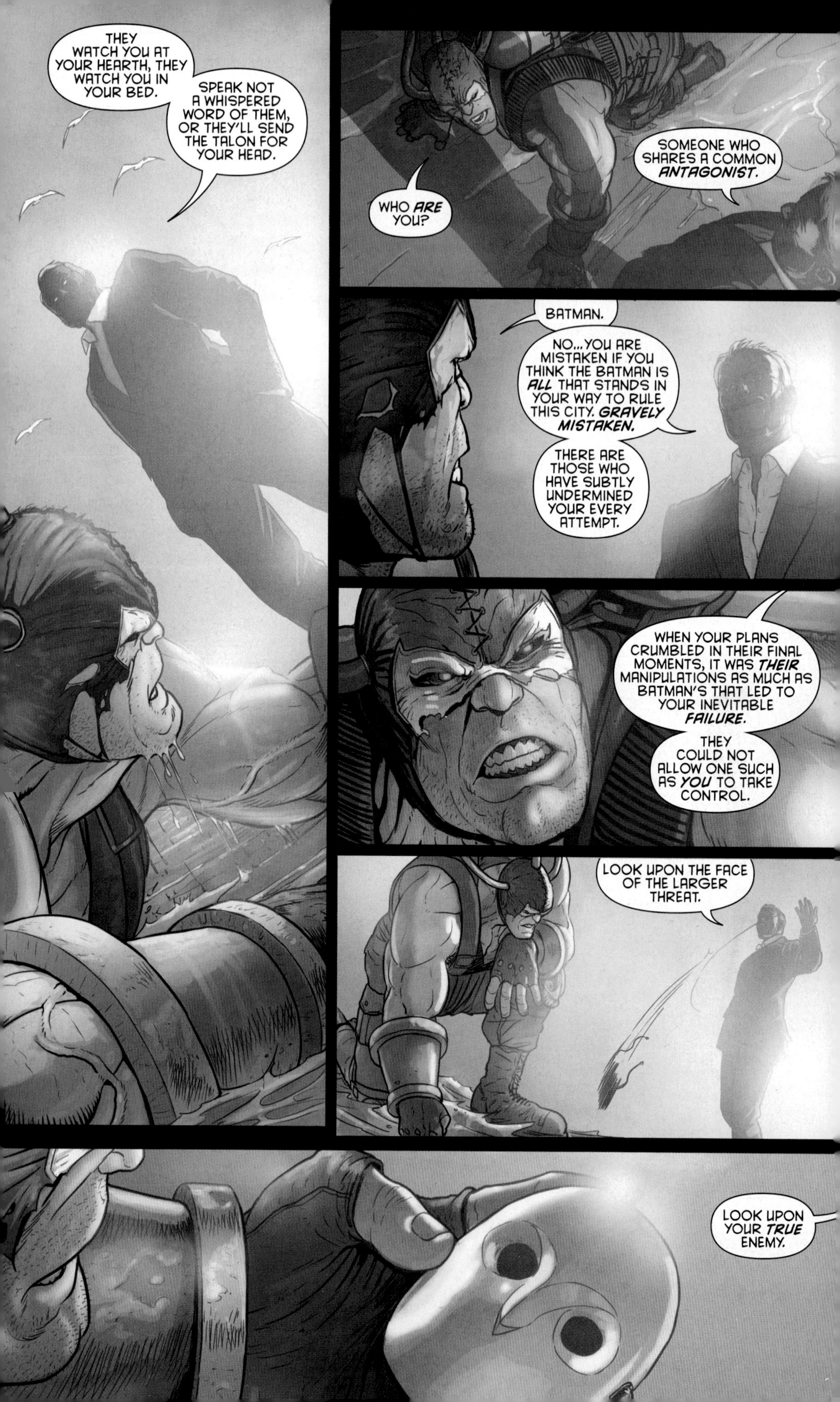

THEY WATCH YOU AT YOUR HEARTH, THEY WATCH YOU IN YOUR BED.
SPEAK NOT A WHISPERED WORD OF THEM, OR THEY'LL SEND THE TALON FOR YOUR HEAD.
WHO *ARE* YOU?
SOMEONE WHO SHARES A COMMON *ANTAGONIST*.
BATMAN.
NO... YOU ARE MISTAKEN IF YOU THINK THE BATMAN IS *ALL* THAT STANDS IN YOUR WAY TO RULE THIS CITY. *GRAVELY MISTAKEN.*
THERE ARE THOSE WHO HAVE SUBTLY UNDERMINED YOUR EVERY ATTEMPT.
WHEN YOUR PLANS CRUMBLED IN THEIR FINAL MOMENTS, IT WAS *THEIR* MANIPULATIONS AS MUCH AS BATMAN'S THAT LED TO YOUR INEVITABLE *FAILURE.*
THEY COULD NOT ALLOW ONE SUCH AS *YOU* TO TAKE CONTROL.
LOOK UPON THE FACE OF THE LARGER THREAT.
LOOK UPON YOUR *TRUE* ENEMY.

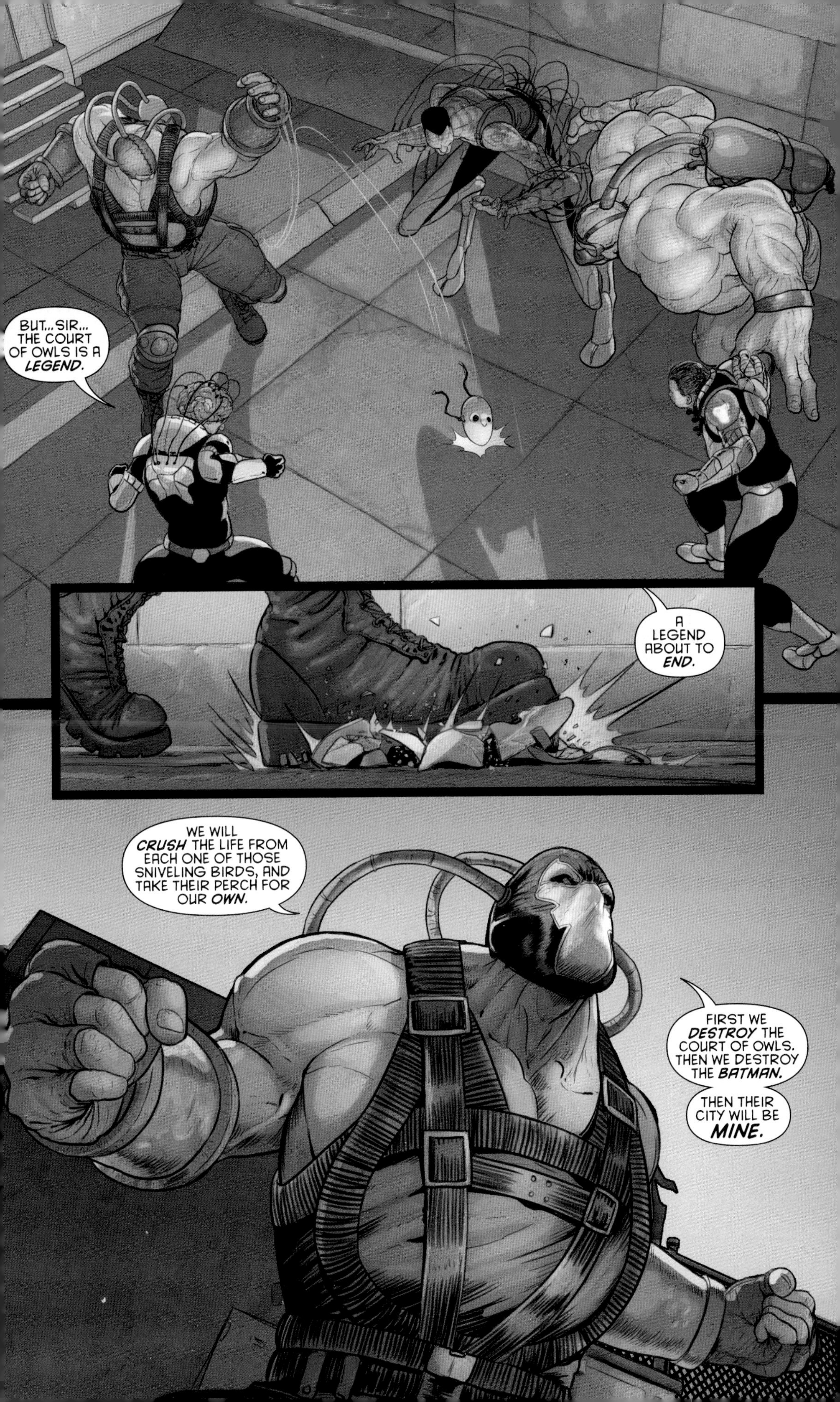

BUT... SIR... THE COURT OF OWLS IS A *LEGEND*.
A LEGEND ABOUT TO *END*.
WE WILL *CRUSH* THE LIFE FROM EACH ONE OF THOSE SNIVELING BIRDS, AND TAKE THEIR PERCH FOR OUR *OWN*.
FIRST WE *DESTROY* THE COURT OF OWLS. THEN WE DESTROY THE *BATMAN*.
THEN THEIR CITY WILL BE *MINE*.

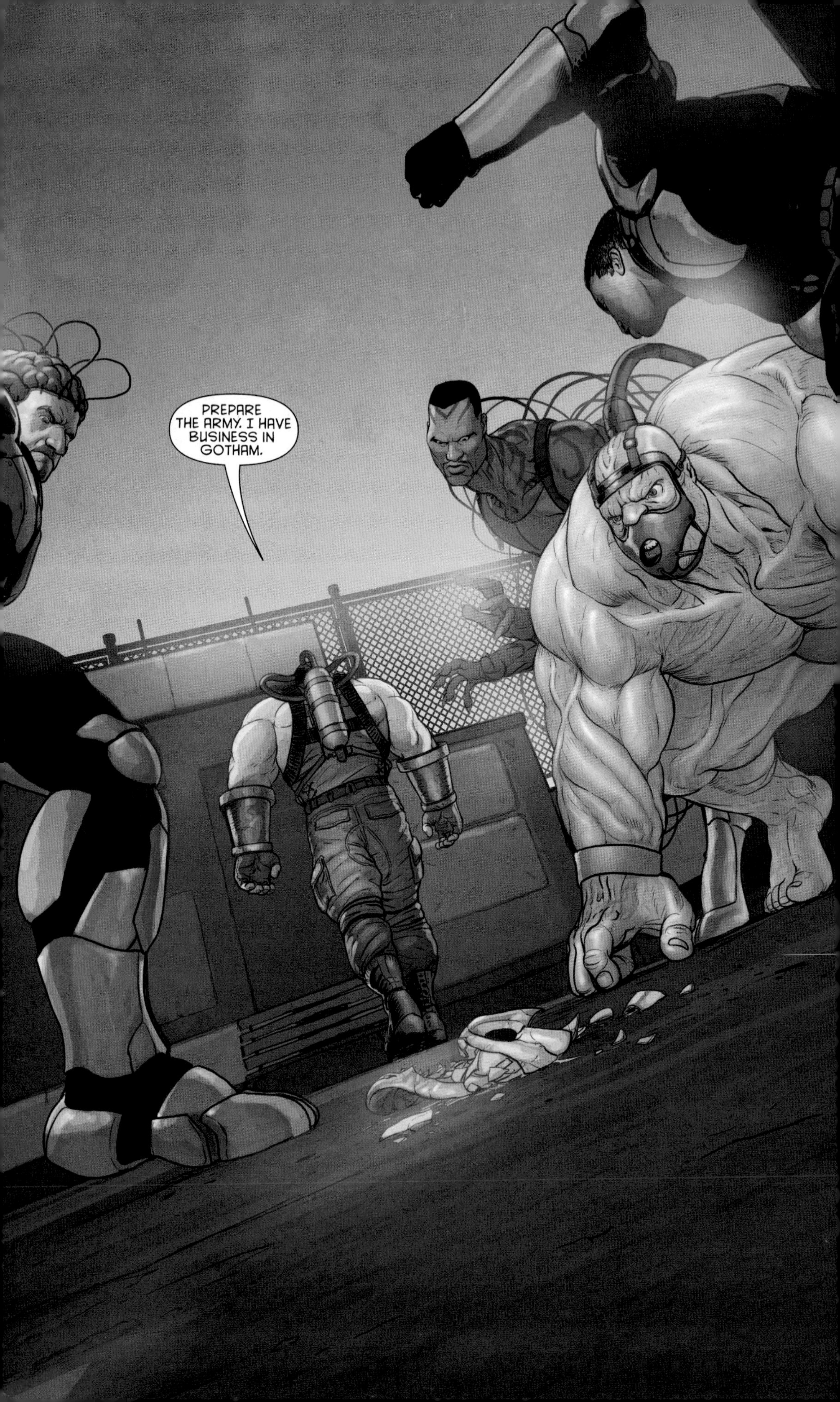
PREPARE THE ARMY. I HAVE BUSINESS IN GOTHAM.

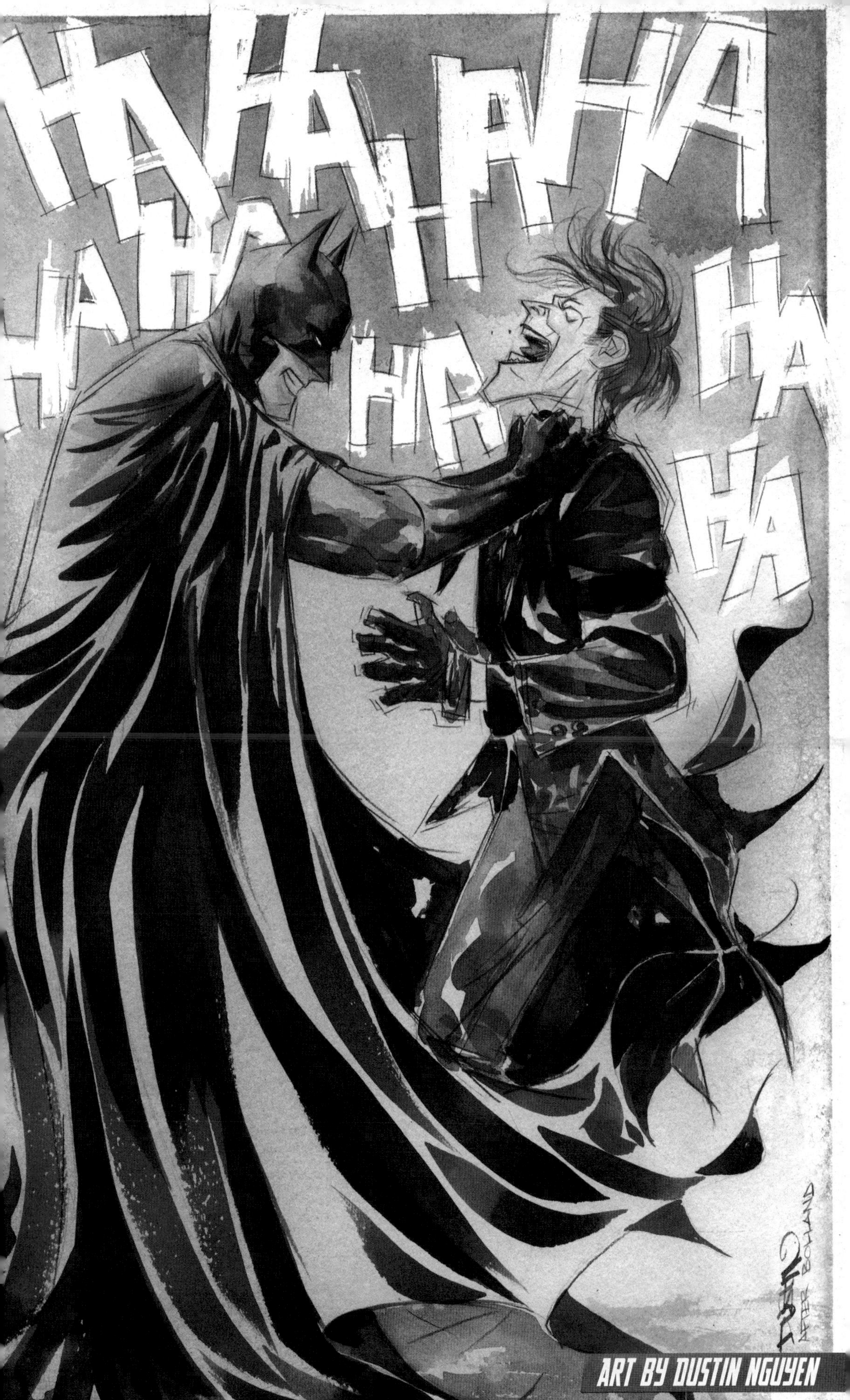
HA HA HA HA HA
HA HA HA
HA HA
HA
AFTER BOLLAND
ART BY DUSTIN NGUYEN

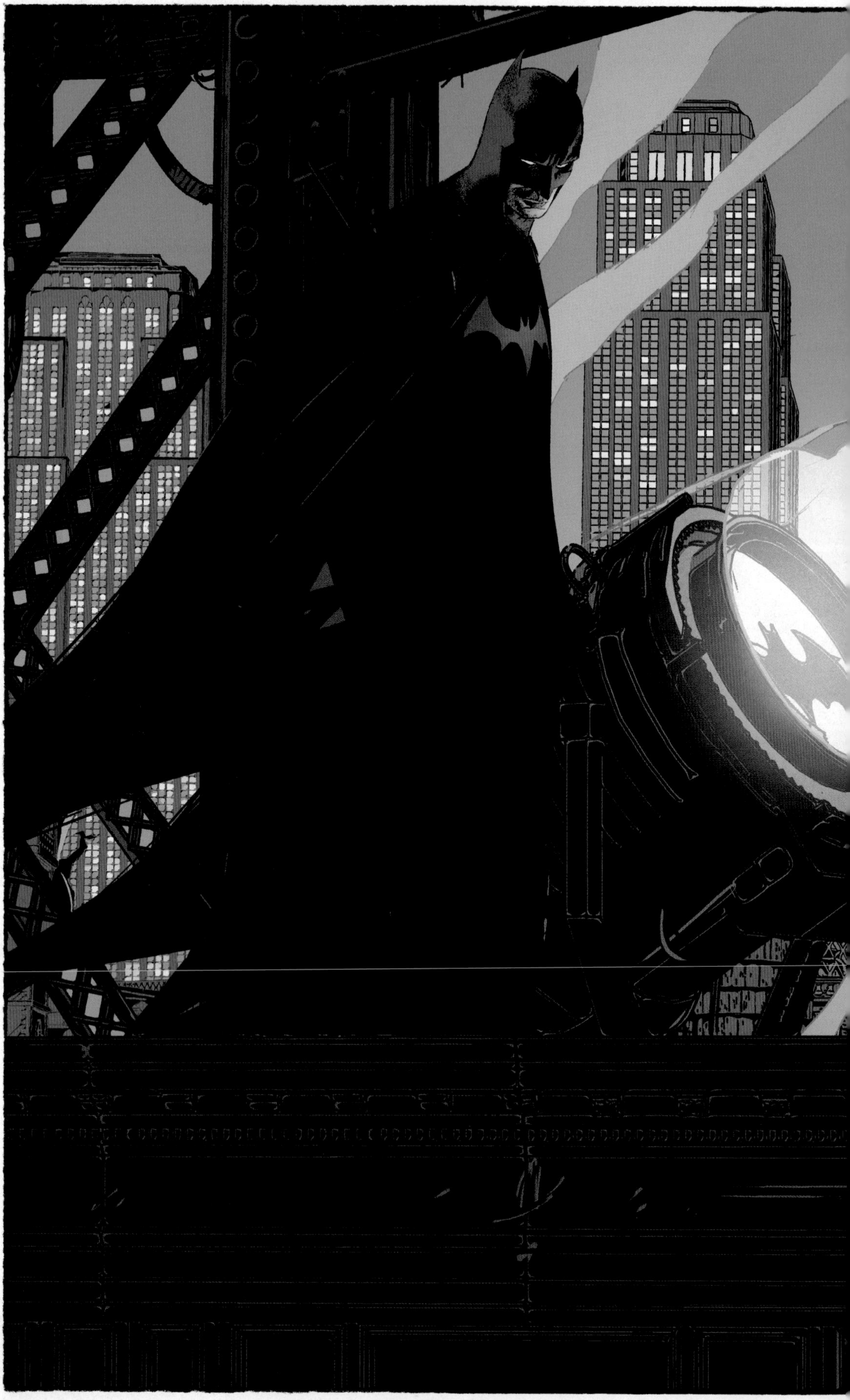

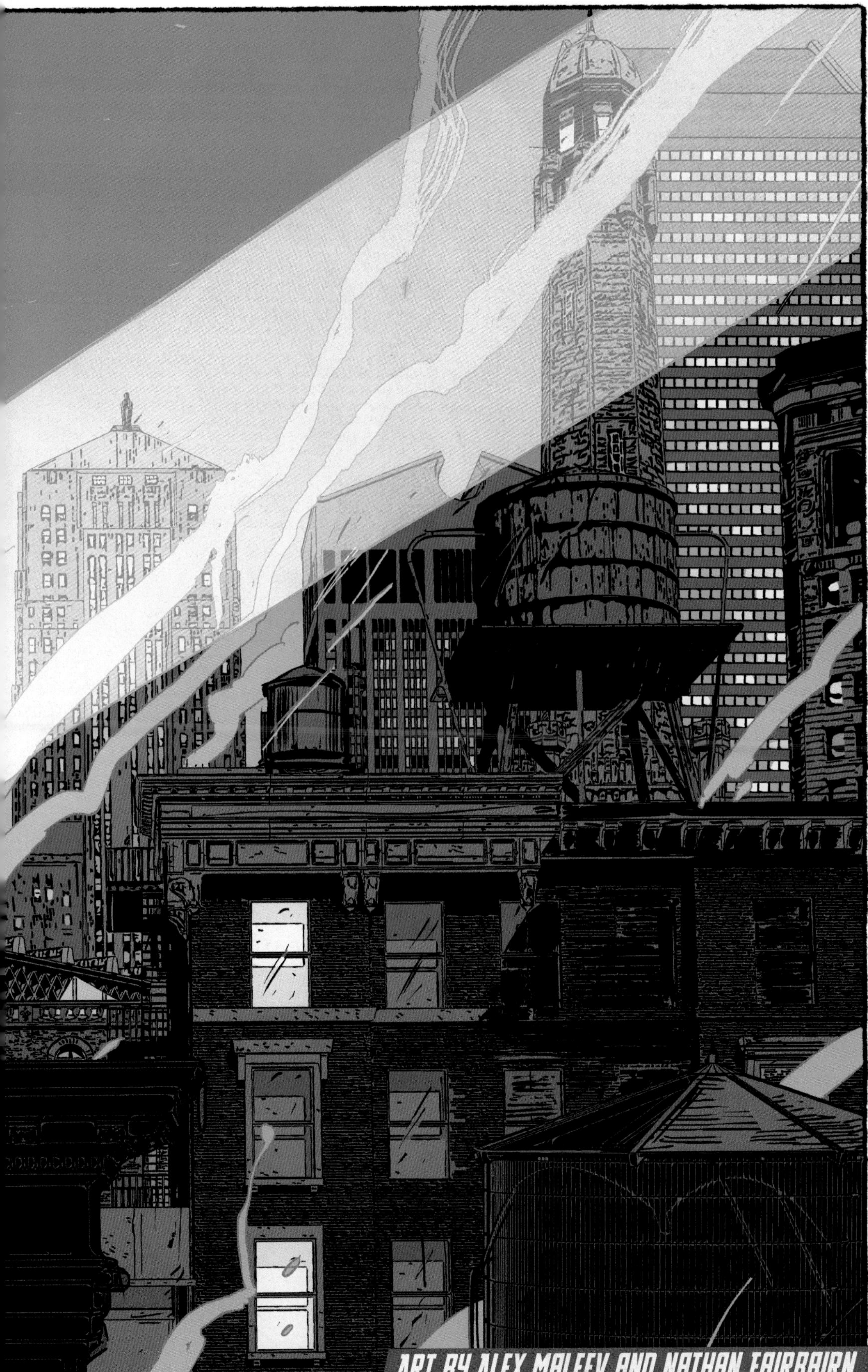
ART BY ALEX MALEEV AND NATHAN FAIRBAIRN

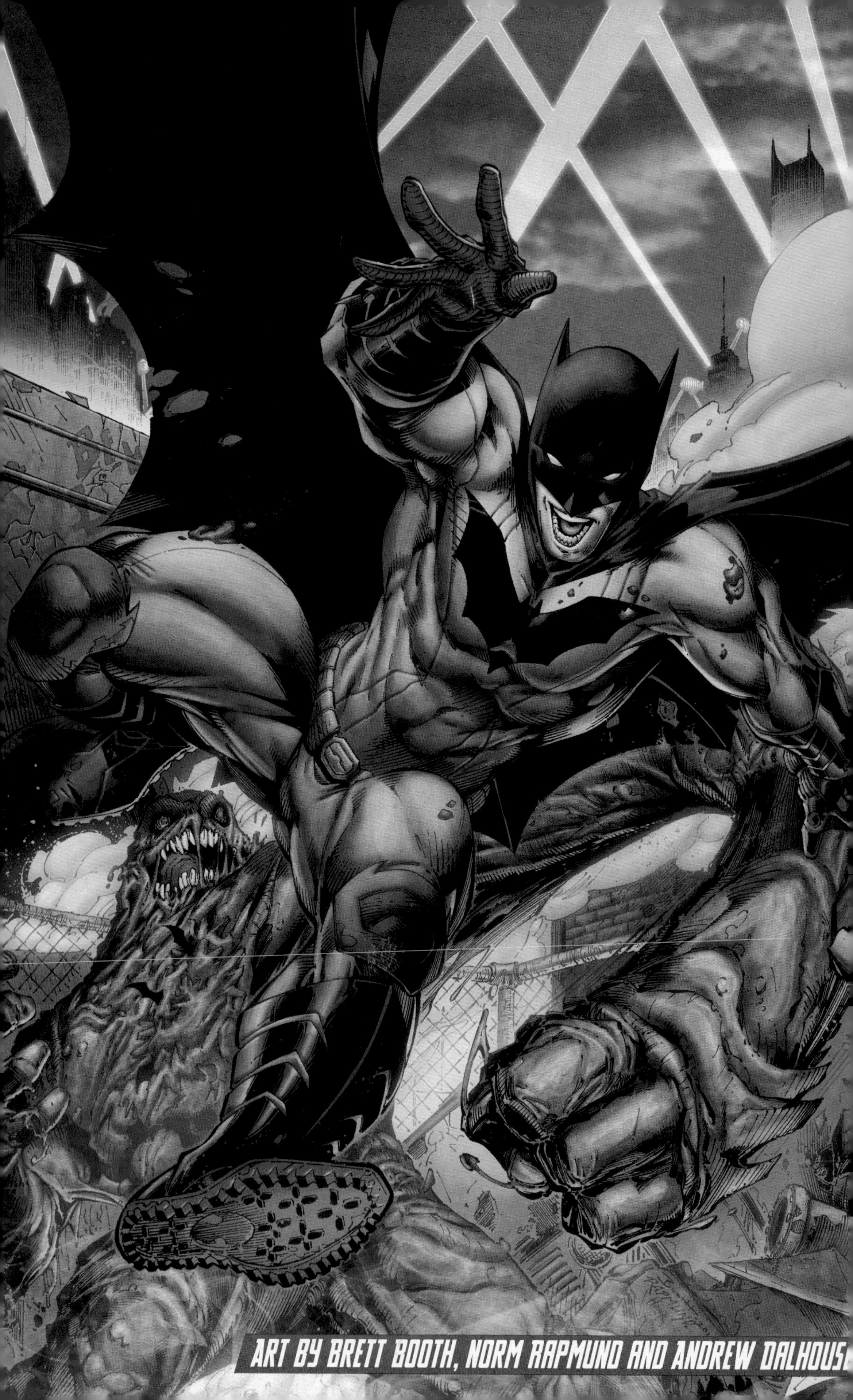

ART BY BRETT BOOTH, NORM RAPMUND AND ANDREW DALHOUS

ART BY CHRIS BURNHAM AND NATHAN FAIRBAIRN

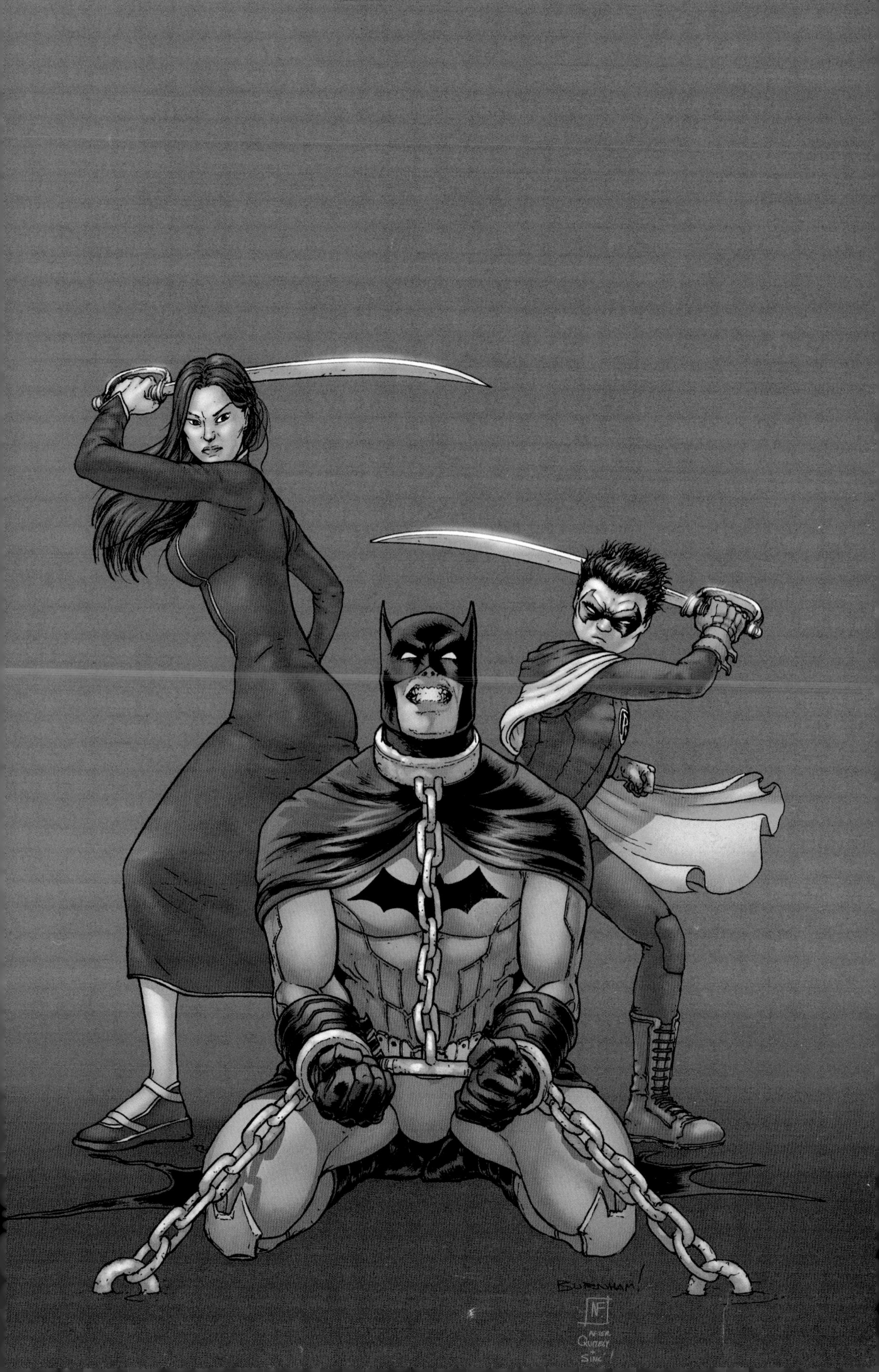
BURNHAM!

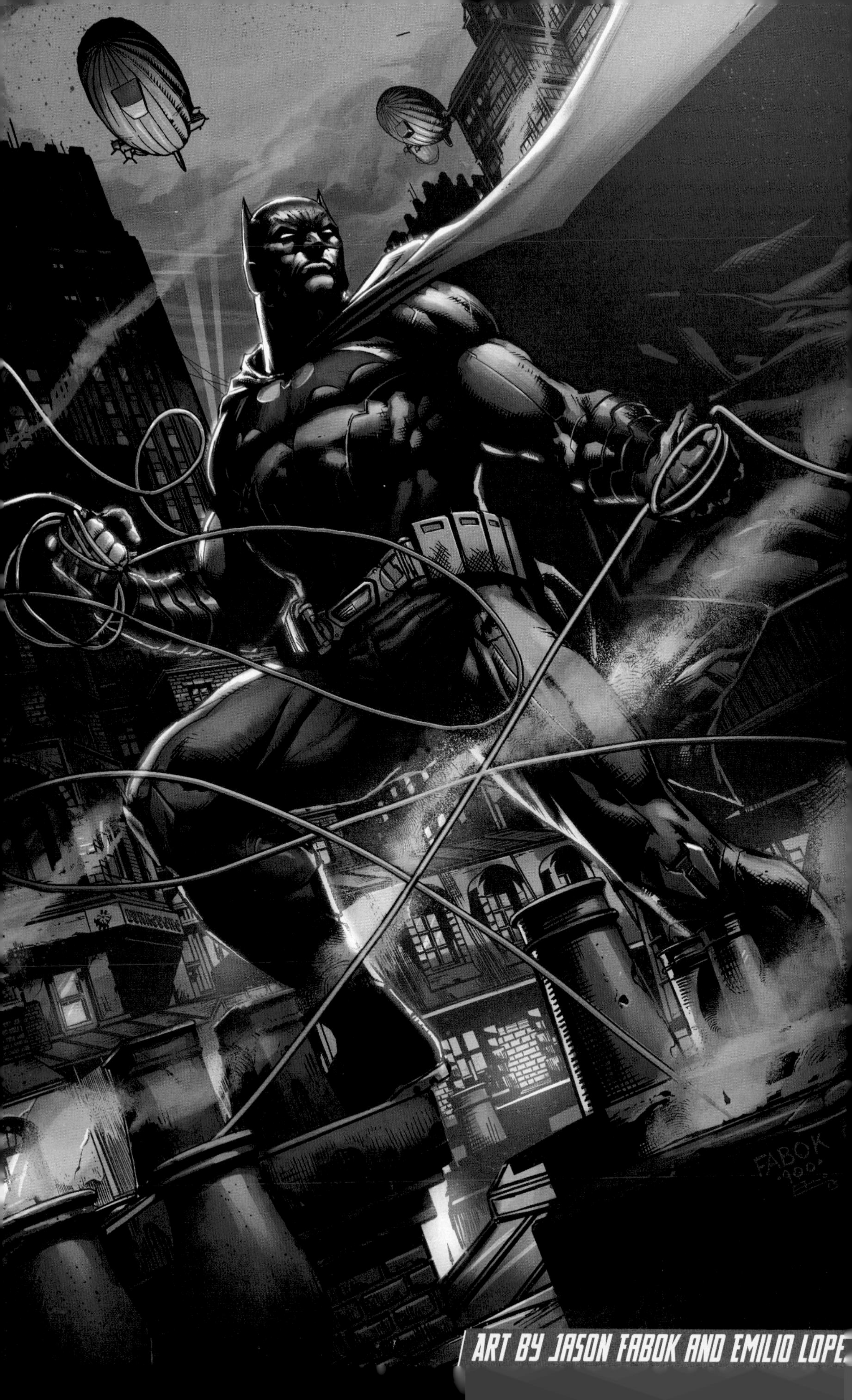
FABOK

ART BY JASON FABOK AND EMILIO LOPE

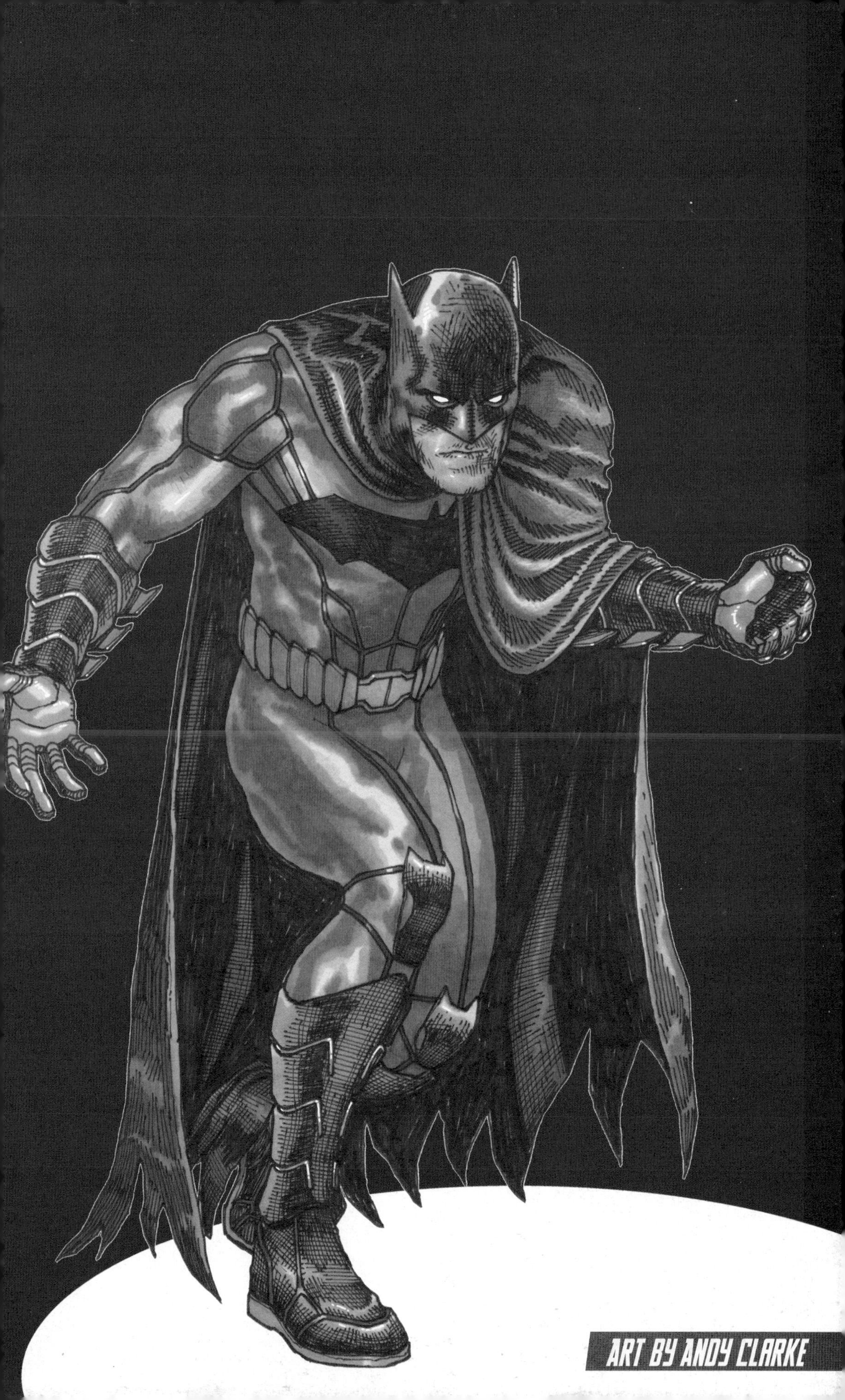

ART BY ANDY CLARKE

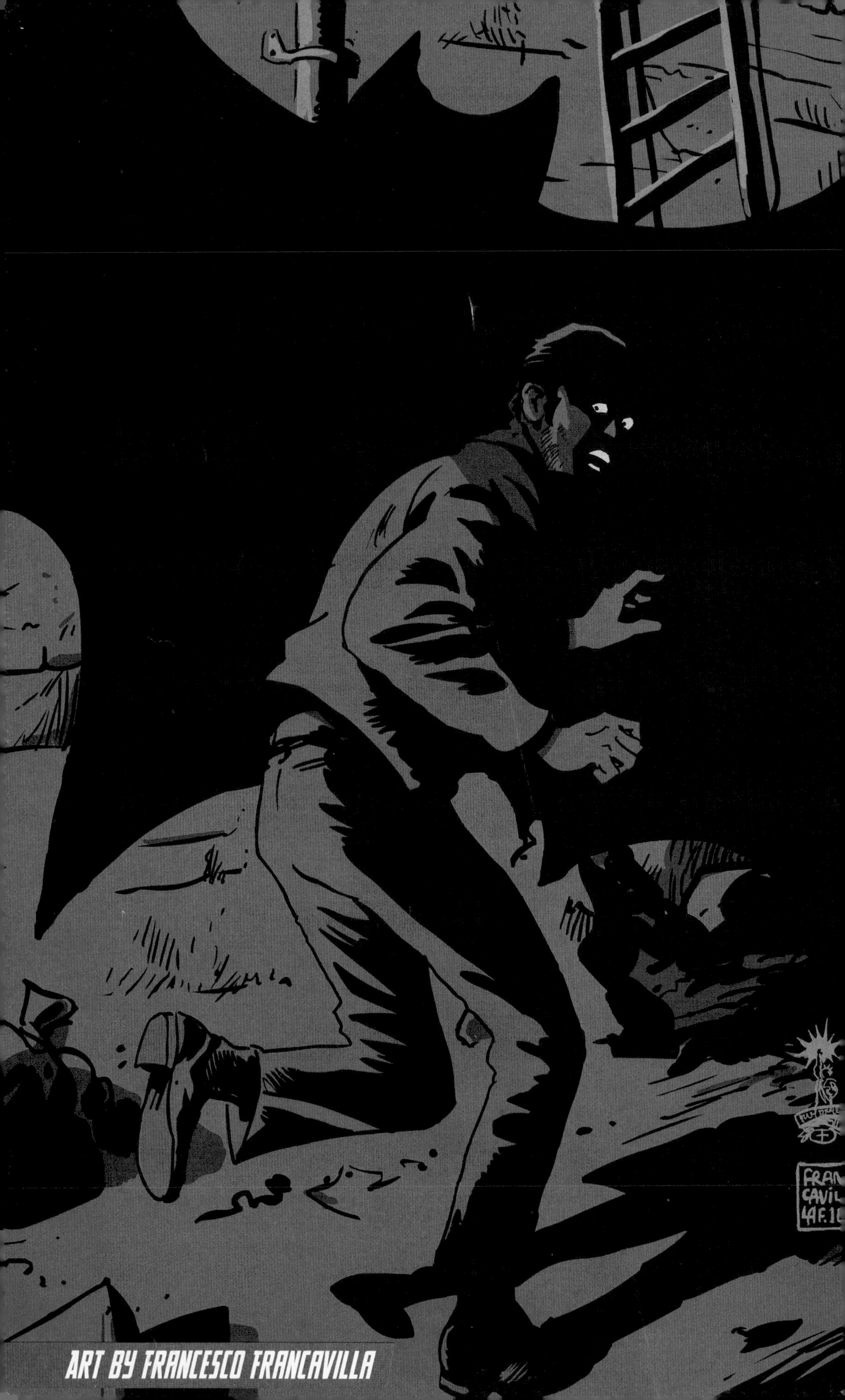

ART BY FRANCESCO FRANCAVILLA

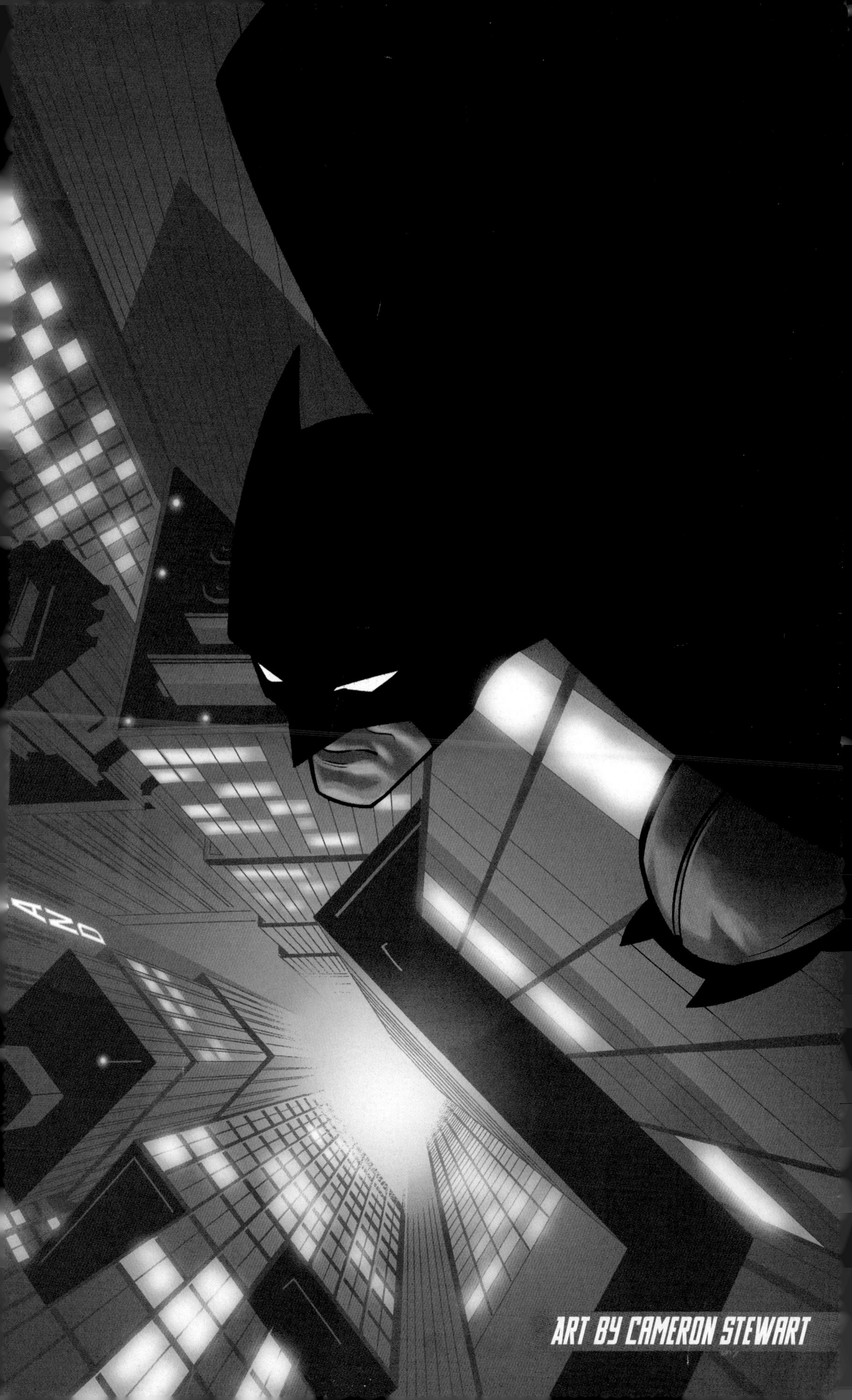

ART BY CAMERON STEWART

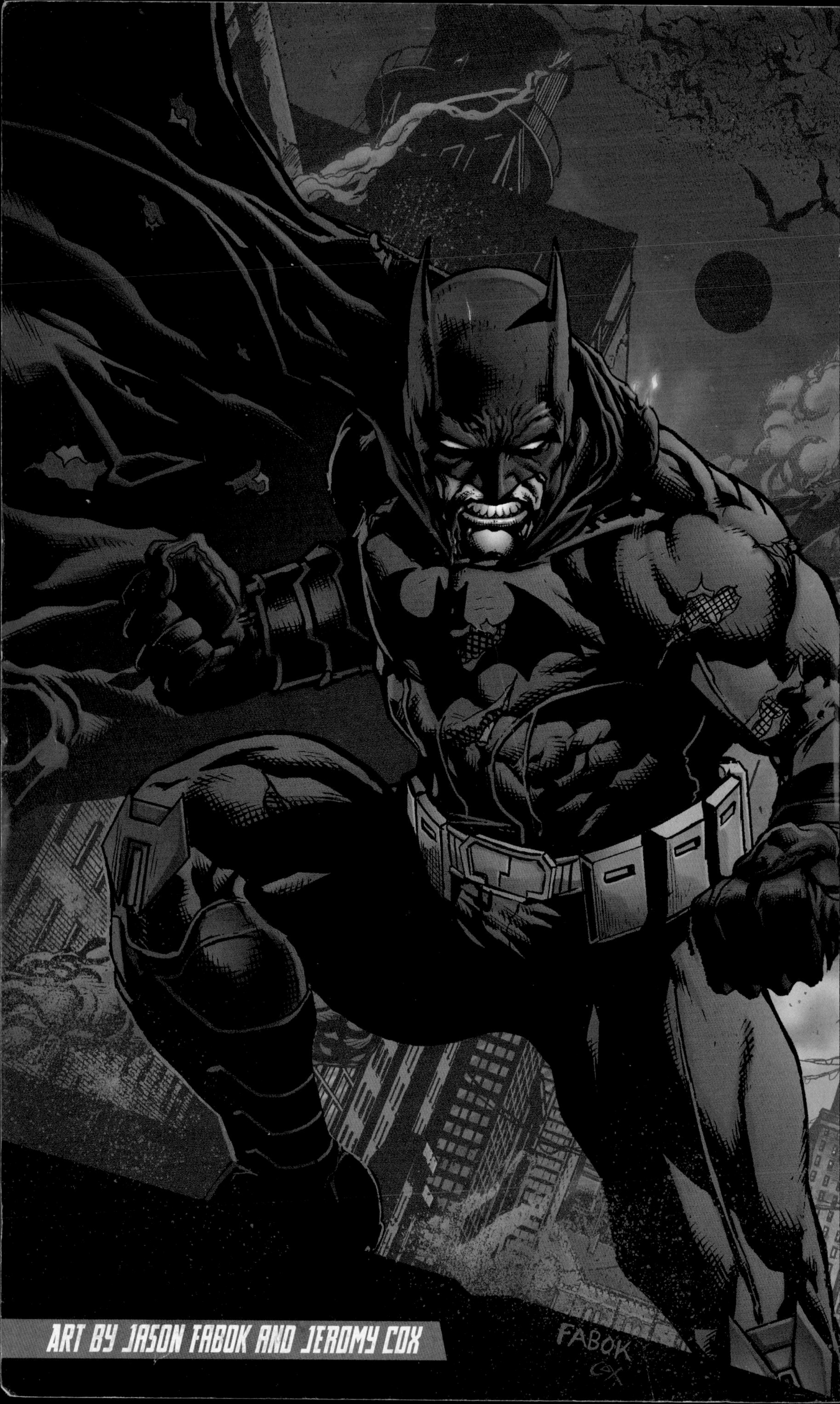
FABOK
COX

ART BY JASON FABOK AND JEROMY COX

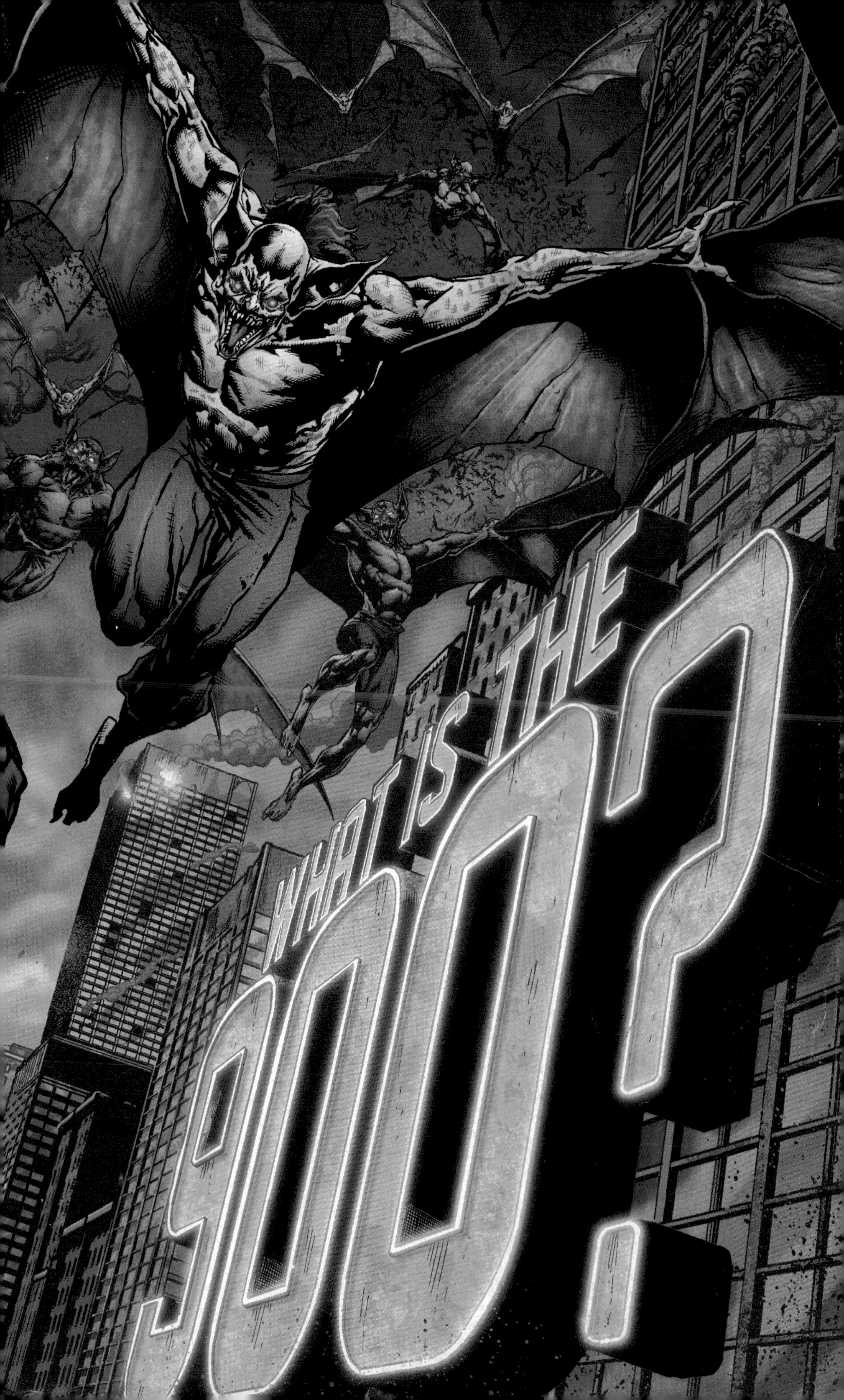
WHAT IS THE
900?

9 Variant Cover by Tom Richmond

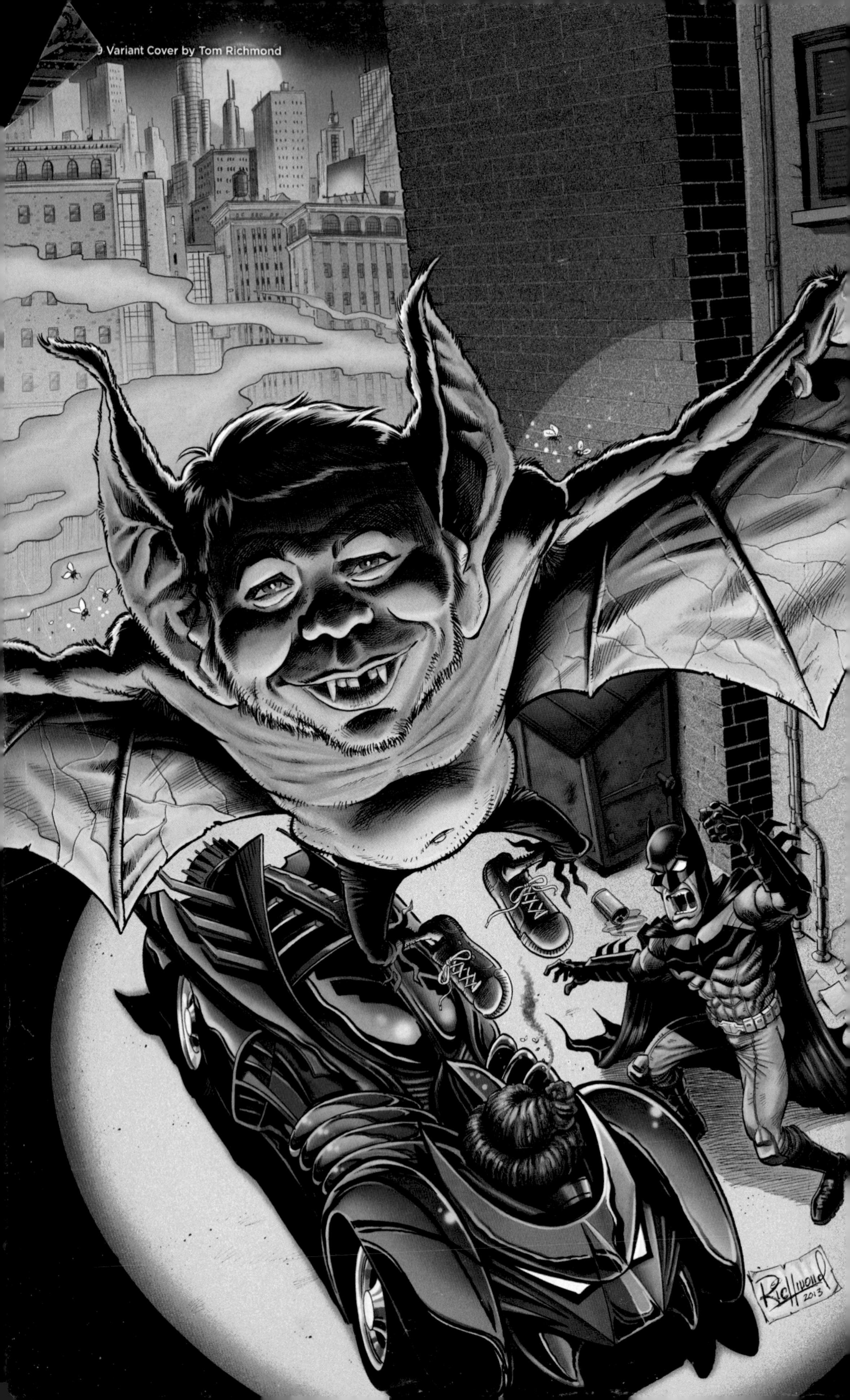